BERLIOZ

Other books by David Cairns

*

The Memoirs of Hector Berlioz, translated and edited by David Cairns
Responses: Musical Essays and Reviews
The Magic Flute and *Falstaff*, English National Opera Guides: co-author

DAVID CAIRNS

BERLIOZ
1803 – 1832
The Making of an Artist

ANDRE DEUTSCH

To Thomas, Daniel and Benjamin

First published 1989 by
André Deutsch Limited
105−106 Great Russell Street London WC1B 3LJ

British Library Cataloguing in Publication Data

Cairns, David
    Berlioz 1803−1832: the making of
    an artist.
    1. Berlioz, Hector   2. Composers − France
    − Biography
    I. Title
    780'.92'4   ML410.B5

ISBN 0 233 97994 8

Printed in Great Britain by
Ebenezer Baylis and Son Limited, Worcester

LIST OF ILLUSTRATIONS

Between pages 94–95 and 126–127

Between pages 253–255 and 286–287

CONTENTS

PREFACE

This book goes back to the winter of 1969–70, when Tom Rosenthal, then a director of Thames and Hudson, suggested that I follow up my edition of Berlioz's *Memoirs* by writing a full-scale life. Tom was to prove an untiringly patient friend and ally and a vital source of encouragement throughout the years — more of them than either of us envisaged — between the inception of the project and the completion of its first part. He would have had to wait longer but for the generosity of Kern Holoman, chairman of the music department at the University of California, Davis, one of the world's leading Berlioz scholars and himself engaged on a major life-and-works, who arranged for me to spend two terms in Davis as a visiting professor. Over a third of the book was drafted during this timely break in my career as a journalist. I also owe a profound debt of gratitude to Yvonne Reboul-Berlioz, who gave me unrestricted access to the large collection of family documents belonging to her late husband (a great-grandson of Berlioz's sister Nancy) and made me welcome at her Paris apartment in the Rue du Ranelagh. It was in the many weeks spent going through the letters, diaries and account books of the Reboul Collection that I began to get a picture of the environment from which the composer sprang, and the idea of the book I should write about him first took shape.

Despite having written his own story with a brilliance that no biographer can approach, Berlioz left a lot to be done. The *Memoirs* is a didactic work, not a confessional one. Its aim, as the author states, is to recount his career as an artist and the things in his personal life that influenced it and fed and shaped his art, to show what it is like trying to make one's way as a composer in contemporary France and to offer the young aspirant some useful hints. The book, a record and justification of his struggles, does not profess to give all the facts. There are many gaps in the tale.

This biography attempts to fill them. Nearly forty years have passed since the last large-scale work, Barzun's pioneering and monumental *Berlioz and the Romantic Century*, was published. In that time a great deal of new material has come to light. The *Correspondance générale d'Hector Berlioz*

now nearing completion in Flammarion's Nouvelle Bibliothèque Romantique includes several hundred letters previously unknown. At the same
time specialist studies have been illuminating many obscure aspects of
the composer's career. Berlioz scholarship, responding to the recent revival
and reappraisal of his music, is active as never before. All this and more I
have tried to take account of.

The limits of the book should be stated. It includes no separate
analysis of Berlioz's music (and no musical examples). The works — the
reason for writing a composer's biography — are a dominant presence,
but discussion of them is contained within the narrative of his life. It is a
life, not a life-and-works. Nor is it a psycho-biography — this not so
much from unwillingness as from want of the necessary competence.
Maybe in falling in love at the age of twelve with a goddess-like young
woman years older than himself Berlioz was projecting an image of the
good mother he had not found in his infancy; and maybe when he
dreamed he was defending his father from three kidnappers, and hacked
off the forearm of two of them with a long knife, he was really expressing,
among other things, his half-buried feelings of aggression against his
father's person and authority. But I have left such promising enquiries to
others who have the skill.

What I have set out to do is simply to tell the story of Berlioz's
apprenticeship in greater detail than it has been told before; where
possible, to visualise and explain each act and event, to show what
happened and how and why, in this formative but least well-documented
part of his life, when the son of the village doctor, brought up in a
musical wilderness, was turning himself into the composer of the Fantastic
Symphony.

If the innermost being of the man remains hidden, it can only be so.
Creative geniuses are, finally, a mystery to those who are not. We follow
them always a little way behind and rarely if ever glimpse them for an
instant full face. But there is no turning back once the quest has been
embarked on.

London, 1988

PROLOGUE

For a long time the music of Berlioz remained a sealed book to me. Each person comes to a particular composer in his own way and his own time; no rules govern the processes of musical discovery. But circumstances of cultural climate and environment may delay it. The more conditioned we are to the music we know, the more, unconsciously, we expect the unfamiliar to approximate to it. Bruckner's formal designs are usually incomprehensible, to begin with, to someone accustomed to Brahms's; and most people know Brahms's symphonies before they encounter Bruckner's. There are musicians and music-lovers who are drawn to Berlioz's music irresistibly and for whom its idiosyncrasies of style are no barrier; in their deepest being it sounds a note of instant recognition. To many others it seems alien when they first hear it and perhaps for long afterwards, as it did to me. I was brought up from the age of eight or nine in the German tradition: first Bach, then a few years later Beethoven, finally Brahms. Composers not squarely in that tradition were assimilated with difficulty if at all. (Even Mozart seemed trivial.) I remember, one day when I was in my early twenties, my sister coming home in great excitement with a recording of the Fantastic Symphony that she had just heard. She insisted on my listening to it then and there. It made absolutely no sense to me.

Nearly ten years passed before anything occurred to change this attitude. My musical tastes grew outwards from their Germanic centre but on the rare occasions when I heard any Berlioz I could make little of it. Then in 1957 Covent Garden produced *The Trojans*. I went to the dress rehearsal and the première. Unlike many others, bouleversés by the experience (the origin of the modern Berlioz revival), I was only partly persuaded. But had I not had to go abroad immediately after the first night I should certainly have returned to Covent Garden for a later performance. For by then my interest had been aroused. Not long before, a cousin had played me the old 78 recording by Jean Planel of "Le repos de la sainte famille" from *The Childhood of Christ* and had lent me the *Memoirs* (in the Everyman edition, with its racy, sympathetic translation by Katharine Boult). I was charmed by the strange sweetness and purity of the piece; and I was

11

riveted by the book: the personality of the author intrigued and attracted me. I felt I must reconsider my rejection of his music and have another shot at it.

The opportunity came a few months later. The Chelsea Opera Group performed *The Damnation of Faust*, under Meredith Davies. I played in the orchestra, in the percussion section. We had half a dozen rehearsals. Gradually, in the course of them, the barriers fell away and enlightenment dawned — until I realised with delight that the language which ten years before had been so much gibberish to my musical understanding had become familiar, and made sense, thrilling, unimagined sense after all.

I give these personal details not simply to show how I became interested in Berlioz but as a means of illustrating the general problem his music poses. In a musical culture still predominantly Teutonic his language even now can take a lot of learning. For long, there were powerful extraneous factors which obstructed the process of learning it. The "Berlioz Problem" was a nineteenth-century creation, but it lasted well into the twentieth. Musical opinion labelled him a freak; and in no area of human activity are received ideas more tenacious and myths harder to dispel. It became customary to think of him as a phenomenon uniquely eccentric and sui generis, which made his admirers a race apart.

To some extent the problem was that of all new music, dependent for its acceptance on conductors and musicians capable of mastering its technical and stylistic demands, so that the performances it receives communicate it faithfully and do not distort it beyond comprehension. But in the case of Berlioz the music remained new, never receiving regular enough performances to become familiar, and making technical and stylistic demands of a formidable kind. It was not so much that it exploited the most advanced instrumental techniques and invented a few new ones as that it did so in the service of a style which musicians necessarily found hard to understand because its most prominent features were precisely those that the nineteenth century was in the process of forgetting: extended melody and complex, irregular rhythm. In an age dominated by Wagnerian harmonic polyphony, music based on opposite methods was wide open to misunderstanding. Its composer could only appear an outsider subject to no laws, and one whose methods were at odds with his aims. The two "sides" of his art, the Romantic and the Classical, were seen as the reflection of deep unresolved tensions in his nature, poles between which his magnetic but unstable genius flickered ungovernably.

During his lifetime attempts made to place him had led only to confusion. In the conservative mind he became associated with the deeply feared new movements in Germany, which were believed to imperil the very survival of music. This strange error helps to account for the extraordinary ferocity with which his French critics attacked him. Such an idea — Berlioz as disciple of Wagnerism — could have been thought up only in

France. But there was a kind of excuse for it in the success he always seemed to be having with the Germans. In fact, if his works excited more response beyond the Rhine than in his native country, that was because there was a serious concert-going public in Germany, ready and curious to listen to new things, new styles and forms, and not because of any strong German affinities in his music. His roots were in France, in the music of French composers or composers who had been assimilated into the French tradition. But this cardinal truth was hidden, both by the novel aspects of his music and because the tradition was in rapid decline by the time he emerged as a composer to be reckoned with. Gluck, Spontini, Le Sueur, Méhul, Cherubini — they were his chief influences in the years when he was learning to speak with his own voice. A decade later they were passé.

Here is one source of the Berlioz legend. He had roots but they were concealed because the music from which they came had ceased to be familiar. People were conscious only of the strangeness of his style, combined with something disconcertingly old-fashioned. In a musical society divided by rival factions, his music satisfied no one orthodoxy. To the academic establishment, always peculiarly narrow and rule-obsessed in France, it was unacceptable by reason of its disregard of the "principles of sound composition" — principles which Beethoven himself deserved the severest censure for flouting — and by reason of its restless modernity. But the modernists, though excited by it and in particular by its enrichment of the expressive possibilities of the orchestra, could not wholly accept it either: its antecedents, its whole bent, were too opposed to theirs. Berlioz and Wagner both set out from Beethoven (the discovery of whose music marked the final and decisive stage in Berlioz's artistic formation); but they took quite different directions, and it was the Wagnerian that appeared to lead to the future. At the very moment when Wagner was writing his most advanced score, *Tristan and Isolde*, the score that was to have the greatest influence on the music of the next fifty years, Berlioz was summing up his life's work in a classical epic of the ancient world, steeped in the spirit of Gluck and Spontini, Claude Lorrain, Virgil — *The Trojans*. When Berlioz went through the manuscript of *Tristan* which Wagner presented to him he found the harmonic idiom incomprehensible. Yet this same conservative, whose *Treatise on Modern Orchestration* takes a good third of its examples from the operas of Gluck composed seventy or eighty years earlier, can introduce the *Treatise* with the late-twentieth-century watchword, "Any sound-producing body utilised by the composer is a musical instrument."

Berlioz's isolation should not be exaggerated. He had his admirers and champions, German, Russian and English but French as well, to whom his music, "paradoxes" and all, spoke directly, without impediment. And so far from leading nowhere it was to influence composers as diverse as Bizet, the Russian Five, Mahler, Busoni and Stravinsky. But, as he himself recognised, his time had yet to come: "If I could only live till I am a hundred and forty, my musical life would become decidedly interesting." If much in his works sprang from a past already fading from memory when he first presented them, much was ahead of its time and awaited an age capable of responding to it. A harmonic and orchestral texture predominantly linear, a lean, lucid sound with no trace of the all-pervasive instrument of nineteenth-century composition, the piano, a method of composing in which the main formal and expressive agent is melody, an emphasis on rhythm, a concern with timbre and space as elements of composition — such things had so to speak to be rediscovered before a style based on them could be widely understood. Above all it needed the advent of a retrospective age in which all epochs are potentially equal, all styles admissible, one thing is no longer judged by another, and the only laws a piece of music must be true to are its own. Modern culture's comprehensive awareness of the past, its revival of more and more forgotten works, and at the same time the profound upheavals in musical composition, have between them virtually abolished the old concept of a norm against which music such as Berlioz's could be measured and found wanting. The historical factors that made him seem a freak have run their course. Thanks to much more frequent performance and to recording, his works are no longer more talked of than listened to. They have become familiar.

The classic case of the Berlioz score that everyone knew about and no one knew was *The Trojans*. Its discovery, at Covent Garden in 1957, was correspondingly revelatory in its effect. At a stroke the whole picture changed. The significance of those performances was summed up at the time by Robert Collet in *The Score*:

> What seems immediately to have struck many people [...] was that this music was utterly different from the idea of Berlioz handed out to us by writers on music, and not only the stupid ones. Until very recently it was customary to hear quite knowledgeable musicians and amateurs talk of Berlioz as a wayward Byronic eccentric, with an interest in the orchestra that was unusual for his day, and an undoubted gift for musical *grotesquerie*, but otherwise a striking figure in musical history rather than a truly great composer. No one who has listened to *The Trojans* with even partial under-standing can accept such a superficial and one-sided view any longer.

He was speaking of musical opinion in Britain, a country with a tradition of interest in Berlioz going back to the composer's visits to London. But the consequences — of which the publication of the full score, more than a century after its composition, and the issue of a complete recording were only the most obvious — were to be felt far beyond Covent Garden.

The last few years have seen Berlioz the quondam bugbear of the professors become a respectable subject of academic research. Scholars have begun to examine his scores without prejudice and find out what they contain and how they are written. The study of his compositional procedures now going on in American and British university music departments is bringing to recognition a composer radically different from the wild man of myth who composed by flashes of lightning and was great, if at all, by accident. It has become normal to treat him like other composers. Even a French critic might hesitate before expressing himself in the language and tone of Emile Vuillermoz in his *Histoire de la musique*, published in 1939: "It is positively painful for a musician to have dealings with Berlioz's music, with its slapdash writing, clumsy style, and messy, chaotic methods of composition."

The distinguished French musician Henri Barraud has declared that Vuillermoz's pronouncements on music in general reveal an incompetence so profound as to render everything he wrote null and void. Yet it is not enough simply to dismiss such a passage as too extreme to bother about. Its hysteria may have something to tell us not merely about the writer but about the music that had so unpleasant an effect on him. The old received idea of Berlioz as subverter of artistic law and order continues to arouse feelings of insecurity. And not only the idea but the music itself, and notably its sense of violence: violence barely contained and sometimes bursting out with frightening force — what Berlioz's contemporary the critic Blaze de Bury called "the smell of carnage that rises from some of his scores", and Colin Davis has described as his ability to "generate terror". There is in his music, especially the music of his youth, an electrical atmosphere by which some people are unsettled as by certain kinds of weather. It is, maybe, as natural for one person to make him a scapegoat as it is for another to identify with his heroic struggles and love him for his very humiliations.

Even when one takes him for himself and not as a symbol, there remain barriers. His is not consoling music. Its nerves are exposed. With all its ardours and exaltations, it is disturbingly alive to the torments of man's existence, outside and within. Its passionate sense of beauty carries with it an acute awareness of how frail and ephemeral beauty is. It understands the tragic limitations of life, the discrepancy between imagination and fact, the chaos that waits beyond the edge of civilisation, the terror of isolation in an empty universe. There is a core of reserve at the heart of its most fiery intensities. You cannot wallow in it. It can be intoxicating, but to the spirit more than to the senses.

In this he differs from the Romantic composers who were his contemporaries. Their aims may have been similar to his; their methods are not. His art objectifies the emotions which inspire it. He stands apart, too, from most of his fellow-artists in France, the writers and painters. For all the similarities, he seems beside them a figure from an older time. He may share their postures and preoccupations, their literary enthusiasms, their beliefs, their subjects, their self-consciousness as artists, their attachments to the contrast of extremes, and their sense of the past. But his nostalgia is more deeply ingrained, more ancient. Again and again we hear in his music this note of antiquity: sometimes as a sadness "old as man's weariness", sometimes as a freshness from the youth of the world. It is this indefinable but unmistakable tone that made Heine compare him to "a colossal nightingale, a lark the size of an eagle, such as we are told existed in prehistoric ages", and that a modern writer[*] has defined as an "ache for an earlier, a kind of pre-moral beauty". The yearning for a golden age is no mere conventional pose with Berlioz; it is a condition of his existence. When, after writing his Virgilian epic *The Trojans*, he said that he had spent his life "with that race of demigods", he was stating the truth.

Such an artist, compounded of such seeming opposites, could not have been other than problematical, just as his career as a composer in mid-nineteenth-century Paris could only have been a record of frustrations and unfulfilled hopes and the isolated triumphs which win a battle but not the war. Some have sought to explain the ill luck that seems to cling to him throughout his life, and to pursue him in death, by reference to malevolent destiny: he was "born under an evil star", a "mauvaise étoile". Others have interpreted it as self-induced, the projection of inner contradictions: Berlioz was the author of his own misfortunes. But the explanation is simpler. Certainly his music would have created difficulties — of comprehension, interpretation, performance — whatever age he had lived in. Like Biblical man he was "born to trouble as the sparks fly upwards". But the problem was exacerbated by history. And, French to the marrow though he was, he chose the worst possible age and environment to live in. "What the devil was the Good Lord thinking of when he had me born in 'this pleasant land of France'?" His cri de cœur says it all. The contradictions were between an artist of his ideals and the values and organisation of musical culture in contemporary Paris: and the outcome was inevitable. It was no accident that the two chief roads to success, the Opéra and the Conservatoire, were both barred to him; no accident that the spiritual heir of eighteenth-century tragédie lyrique, who had been brought up to believe that the theatre was the natural goal of a composer, composed fewer than half a dozen operas, only one of which was commissioned by a Paris opera house; no accident that the greatest French composer between Rameau and Debussy remained outside the establishment; that the finest conductor of his time was passed over in favour of lesser talents whenever there was a post to be filled; that the Société des Concerts performed his music on only two occasions in the first thirty-five years of its prestigious existence; that he obtained no settled position in French musical life; that in consequence he had to

* Victor Gollancz.

fight every inch of the way, hardly ever enjoying the freedom he needed, forced to dissipate his energies on peripheral activities; and that in the end the struggle wore out his resilient spirit and the repression of his creative fires burned him up, silencing his eager genius at its height.

Ernest Newman, surveying the obstacles and frustrations that Berlioz had to battle against throughout his career, concluded that "the work he actually did [. . .] seems only the more wonderful". True: *The Trojans*, the Requiem, *Nuits d'été, The Damnation of Faust, The Childhood of Christ*, the Fantastic Symphony, exist; and they have never been more widely performed and more clearly understood. But when we consider what he might have done in other circumstances, and the works that were fated to remain locked in his imagination, never to receive form, how can we think of his life as other than tragic?

1

The Green and Golden Plain

The young genius from the provinces who comes to Paris with his originality unstifled by the weight of the past is a dominant theme of French nineteenth-century culture, celebrated in the writings of Stendhal, Balzac and Flaubert among others. In that respect Berlioz was one of a numerous company.

Early environment provided, in however unlikely a form, a friendly climate for the seed that had been implanted in him. Where the seed came from remains a mystery. We cannot account for the upsurge of creativity in a well-to-do provincial family after generations of solid, unremarkable men of affairs. Ancestry explains him as little as it explains most exceptional spirits, though it is not for want of trying. Various notions have been advanced. The presence of noble and knightly Berliozes in crusader rolls of the thirteenth and fourteenth centuries has been held to prefigure the man's essentially aristocratic cast of mind. There has been much speculation about the physiognomy and the termination -oz: the aquiline nose and the incidence of the name in Savoy are thought to indicate an Italian origin. (Traces of the name have also been found in Naples; nor should it be forgotten that there was a Neapolitan colony in Grenoble, not to mention the bands of Italian mercenaries that roamed the region in the sixteenth century.) On the other hand it is noted that on his mother's side he descended from a line of Austrian counts of very warlike appointment. Even the ancient world and the Greek inheritance have been pressed into service: for what does the combination of blue eyes and red hair suggest (if indeed his hair was red, about which there is doubt) if not a throwback to some ancestral Thracian colonist of the western Mediterranean? Anything rather than that a great composer should be French.

Equally, it gets us only so far if we interpret his advent in quasi-biological terms as the culmination of several vigorous and prolific generations (his father was one of eleven children, his grandfather one of nineteen, his great-grandfather one of fifteen, and the average age at death of his six previous ancestors in the male line was over seventy). Nor can we do more than register the fact that the five years of the

Consulate, 1799 to 1804, as though by an unleashing of genetic energy accumulated in the turmoil of the French Revolution and its wars, saw the birth in turn of Balzac, Delacroix, Victor Hugo, Dumas, Berlioz, Alfred de Musset and George Sand. It is a fabulous concentration of talent; but it cannot be accounted for, except in the most imprecise and metaphorical terms.

What can be said is that by the beginning of the nineteenth century the Berlioz family had evolved to a point where its environment favoured the cultivation of a certain kind of intelligence and the development of the imagination. Hector Berlioz had behind him two generations of professional men. Before that, the family had been involved for at least a century and a half in commerce. The earliest direct forebear named in the brief family history written by Dr Berlioz, Hector's father, is Claude Berlioz, merchant tanner of La Côte St André, who was born in about 1590 and who willed that his remains "be interred in the tomb of his ancestors"; he was "rich by the standards of his time, since he bequeathed his daughter Jeanne 550 [livres] over and above her marriage settlement", but "was unable to sign his will, being illiterate".

Until the middle of the eighteenth century the male offspring, when they were not priests or monks, had continued to be merchants and tradesmen. The last of them, Dr Berlioz's grandfather Joseph Berlioz (1700–1799), heralds a change. A merchant tanner himself like his forebears, it is he who "made the fortune of our house, with the six thousand francs that was his portion. His shrewdness and good management, and it must also be said his luck, enabled him to acquire bit by bit various pieces of land, vineyards, the house we live in today (which he rebuilt almost completely), the mills, the new meadow, the large garden and the barn adjacent to it, the properties at St Etienne [six miles to the south-east across the plain from La Côte], and the estate at Les Granges near Grenoble." Joseph Berlioz's social standing rises with his wealth and he is made a member of the three-man municipal council of the town. Of his two surviving sons the elder becomes a Carthusian monk. The younger becomes a lawyer. He is Louis-Joseph Berlioz, the composer's grandfather. He consolidates this new departure in family tradition by marrying the daughter of the local doctor. He practises at the High Court in Grenoble and then buys himself a post as tax official in the Court of Audit. He adds to the family estates by purchasing property in Grenoble and a country house a few miles outside on the slopes of the Isère valley at Murianette. Under the Republic, which he is totally out of sympathy with, he is imprisoned and has his property confiscated. He gets it back but retires from office and takes no further part in public affairs.

Berlioz's grandfather on his mother's side, Nicolas Marmion, another Grenoble lawyer, also gives up his legal practice when still quite young and retires to the country, to Meylan on the opposite slopes of the valley from Murianette, to cultivate his garden and write interminable letters in verse to his friends and relations. And when it is the turn of Louis Berlioz the doctor to take over the family property at La Côte and marry and have children, he will, despite a passionate interest in medicine, devote as much time to the management of his estate and the pursuit of his hobbies as to his practice.

Thus a new element, leisure, enters the reckoning — leisure, and independence. Louis-Joseph intends his eldest son Louis to take up his profession, the law. In the event it is his younger sons, Benjamin and Victor, who become lawyers. Louis resists his father's wishes. He does study law for a while, but is unable to overcome his "repugnance to glosses and commentaries, the greater importance attached to the form than the content, the endless twists of legal equivocation, and the rapacity of that breed of men who swarm about the palace of Themis". He tries mathematics, studies literature, teaches himself English and Italian, dabbles in drawing and music. Finally, after three years of uncertainty, at the age of twenty he "embraces the study of medicine with a marked sense of vocation". It takes him, briefly, to the School of Medicine in Paris. He is the first to escape over the rampart of mountains that has confined his race in their narrow corner of France for centuries, into the wider world beyond. His son will follow in his footsteps; and he will not return.

On the 1st of January 1815 Dr Louis Berlioz sat down and took stock of his possessions and fortunes. Several considerations prompted him to do so. Peace had lately returned to France after twenty-five years of violent upheaval and heroic exertions; but it was an uneasy peace: the nation was exhausted and divided. Anything could happen. He himself was thirty-eight, just past the mid-point of life. He must assure the future of his son Hector, aged eleven, who would one day, perhaps even quite soon, succeed him, and whose education he had lately taken charge of; and there were three small daughters and their interests to safeguard. He had been going through family papers and searching in the local archives. All in all it seemed the moment to consolidate the traditions of his house and, for the benefit of his children, put in writing the story of its rise to its present position, at the same time describe and explain to them the great but perilous events that he had witnessed, the Revolution, the Empire, the fall of Napoleon, the Austrian invasion, and give them some advice on how to lead their lives and what to do in the event of another revolution. He loved his life at La Côte — his family, his medical practice and research, his estate — and he felt it threatened.

The resulting "Livre de Raison of Louis-Joseph Berlioz, doctor of medicine residing at La Côte St André", a large volume, 34 centimetres by 23, bound in cardboard and doeskin, containing nearly three hundred neatly written pages and kept from 1815 to 1838, combines the functions of family chronicle and register of the estate. The first section traces his branch of the Berlioz clan, "established at La Côte or in the neighbourhood for four hundred years and more", recounts his own youth and early career, describes the political conflicts of the 1790s and the rise, triumph and eventual defeat of Napoleon, and gives a chronology of the arrivals and departures of foreign troops during the occupation of La Côte the previous year. After that it lists his property — houses, barns, mills, greenhouses, woods, fields, vineyards, with their location, dimensions and value — and makes an inventory of his surgical instruments, his silver, his extensive library, and what they cost him. Next comes the narrative of Napoleon's return, followed by an account of the second occupation of La Côte. From then on the entries are generally briefer, and the book becomes more a catalogue than a written account. Births and deaths (sometimes with clinical details) are noted as and when they occur, as well as the fluctuations in the temperature during the harvest months, the progress of new buildings, the repair or replacement of household furniture. Money borrowed from or by him is entered, and the interest. So are the lease of land or buildings to a numerous tenantry and the proceeds of the sale of corn, wine, oil and silk. Agriculture is prominent. Hedging and ditching, planting of trees, repairing of mill-wheels, construction of carts and wine-vats, the wine harvest, the weather, are transcribed in Homeric, or Virgilian, detail. In due course the annual reckoning of household expenses will include the purchase of a flute in its mahogany box and, later, of two guitars. The Livre de Raison is the record of the economy of a well-to-do country estate in the first few decades of the nineteenth century and the main documentary source for the background of Hector Berlioz's shadowy early years.

The biography of Berlioz begins with his father. He was the dominant influence in his son's early life. In a sense he remained so for long afterwards; for although the son asserted his independence in his choice of profession (as the father had done), the desire to win his father's approval for it was to the end a powerful, if partly unconscious, motive behind his actions. We know from the *Memoirs* and from his letters how important it was for him to believe in his father's love for him, how eagerly he grasped at any sign his father gave of interest in his career. Berlioz was well over forty by the time the old man died, and a composer of European renown with more than half his work complete, and he had seen his father only two or three times in the past sixteen years; yet his death left him with a sensation, beyond the immediate grief, of profound dejection and disorientation. "I feel as if my life no longer had an object," he wrote soon afterwards; "instinctively, all my efforts had always been directed towards him: I wanted him to show he approved of them, I hoped he would be proud of what I did."

Dr Berlioz's decision to undertake his son's education himself was one of the crucial events of Berlioz's early life. Learned, undogmatic, sympathetic, endlessly inquisitive, a voracious reader, a dreamer, a dedicated observer of men and things, the doctor was Rousseau's ideal of the "negative educator" to the life, leaving his pupil to his own devices for long periods, putting new discoveries in his way and then letting him make them himself. By example rather than precept the young Hector acquired, or rather developed within himself, many of his father's tastes and attitudes of mind: his appetite for literature, his feeling for the civilisation of the ancient world, his scientific curiosity and his clinical detachment even where his own sensations were concerned, his interest in geography and geology, his belief in the virtue of experiment and innovation.

As a boy, Berlioz held his father in a respect bordering on awe. At the same time, in the hours they spent together as pupil and teacher there grew between them a sense of affinity. On the father's side, as he set about bringing the boy up as his heir and successor, the consciousness of it must have gladdened his heart, just as later the hopes he had founded in him would make their dissensions the more grievous and the final disillusionment the crueller.

The opening paragraph of the Livre de Raison, placed after the family tree which introduces the book, strikes what seems in retrospect a faintly ominous note:

> Traditions preserved in families [. . .] can on occasion be of great importance. Our curiosity in any case loves to feed on information about our forefathers. We take pride in knowing where they came from and what they did; most men feel respect for the past. The young can sometimes be checked in their follies and excesses when they see how much it cost their ancestors to assure the way of life their descendants enjoy. They will hesitate more than once before deciding to sell property which bears on all sides the identifiable imprint of their kith and kin. On reading the record of merit and repute, they will strive to emulate it; the spirit of a virtuous father, remembered by his children, must keep them in the way of duty. Sustained by these hopes, I am resolved to set down the history of my family, and I counsel my posterity to carry it on likewise.

It would be wrong, however, to read into these solemn admonitions an inkling of what was to come. It was Dr Berlioz himself who, soon afterwards, gave Hector his first instruction in music, an art he was fond of and had cultivated as a young man. He was evidently pleased with his son's response and talked about it when he went to Grenoble to see a patient; for a family friend who met him there, and who wrote to Joséphine Berlioz a few days later, ended her letter with the innocently prophetic words, "Give my love to Hector the musician." But as yet the cloud was no bigger than a man's hand. It is doubtful if Louis Berlioz felt any presentiments in that direction. What lay behind his homily was a

general anxiety. The crises of 1814 had preyed on a temperament inclined
to pessimism. He worried about money. Running an estate was expensive
and had incurred him debts that would not be quickly paid; and the
Austrians, quartered on the town for six weeks, had cost him more than
1,200 francs. The family conflict over Hector's career lay still undreamed
of in the future.

True — as Louis Berlioz now recalled — he had himself in his youth
been a rebel against paternal authority. He and his father had fought for
several years before Louis had finally won his point and, abandoning the
law for good, taken up medicine. There had also been bitter disagreements over the great central questions of the day. "All the fine talk about
liberty and equality which rang in my ears, the triumphs of our armies,
the memory of Athens and Rome, went to my head, as they did to many
others', and I often taxed my father's forbearance sorely." But that was
many years ago now. Fathers never expect their sons to be as awkward as
they themselves were at the same age. It is clear that Dr Berlioz looked to
his son to be in all senses his successor and, equally, that it was not his
son's artistic career as such that shattered him but what it involved: the
abandonment of the cherished heritage, the breach in the continuity of
the race.

The instinct, all-powerful in the French bourgeoisie, for the advancement of family and the consolidation of property, was in Dr Berlioz's case
deepened and intensified by personal loyalties and predilections. His
passionate attachment to La Côte St André was something his wife's
friends in busy, bustling Grenoble could never comprehend. They pitied
her for living in such a backwater and marvelled that her husband the
doctor was content to bury himself there when his talents could have won
him fame on a much wider stage. "Dreary" ("maussade") is the word
they use to describe it; nothing interesting or important happens there.
"I don't really feel any compunction at rattling on like this," writes one
of them complacently; "I know a letter is always valued at La Côte." But
the seclusion was what Dr Berlioz liked, and the bustle what he shunned.
He loved going round his estate, on horseback or on foot, supervising the
latest planting, the repair of a boundary fence or a wall, the construction
of a new and larger wine-vat, the renovation of a mill or a hayloft, the
testing of an idea he had had for improving the yield of his vines. He
loved immersing himself in the petty diurnal round of gentleman-farming.
He loved the sense that his ancestors had lived and laboured in the same
ancient market town for centuries before him, had trod the same vine-
clad slopes and looked down across the same level plain towards the
undulating foothills to the south and the great shining peaks farther away
to the east. He was proud of what they had achieved and conscious that
those achievements had made possible the life which, with all its cares,
he so relished, above all for the precious advantage of active leisure it

gave him: time to read, to meditate, to have ideas and follow them up, opportunity to practise medicine not as a livelihood but as a pursuit.

Friends and relatives were quite right: Dr Berlioz had the talent to become a famous doctor, if only he had had the ambition. He was to a considerable extent self-taught. His decision to take up medicine, in 1796 when he was twenty, coincided with the opening of the Ecole Centrale in Grenoble (in the former Jesuit college, Rue Neuve), under the law passed the previous year by the Convention in Paris, and he enrolled for the course in natural history given by Villard and the course in chemistry given by Trousset, pupil and protégé of Stendhal's grandfather Dr Gagnon. But medical studies were still languishing under the decree of 12 August 1792 which had closed down schools of medicine as being institutions of privilege; and Louis Berlioz had had, as he said, to learn the art of healing by himself and do all his reading as well as his dissection on his own, "without the help of any lecture or demonstration". For a time he worked in the military hospital in Grenoble, which was full of wounded from the campaign in Italy. In 1801 he spent a term at the reopened School of Medicine in Paris, and towards the end of the following year success-fully sat his examinations there, sustaining his thesis on "Phenomena and disorders associated with the first onset of menstruation".

If he attended the official opening of the Ecole Centrale in Grenoble, he must have heard Dr Gagnon's inaugural address on the progress that science had made "since systems were abandoned in favour of the search for truth by the path of experience and experiment". French medicine, the most highly regarded in Europe, was going through a period of violent transition, in which medieval doctrines continued to flourish at the same time as important advances were being made by brillantly original minds; and Dr Berlioz reflected it in his beliefs and practices. The book he published in 1816, *Mémoires sur les maladies chroniques, les évacuations sanguines et l'acupuncture* — in part a revision and extension of prize essays submitted earlier to medical societies in Bordeaux, Montpellier and Paris — is a mixture of antediluvian theorising and acute observation. He cites with great deference the writings of Broussais, one of the foremost bleeders of the time, a systematist of the old school who ascribed all disease to inflammation of the intestines; but his own enthusiasm for cupping and leeches is tempered by native scepticism and steadied by a Johnsonian "bottom" of common sense. He was blessed with an in-dependent and enquiring mind, which led him naturally to untried or neglected methods. He was a pioneer in hydrotherapy and in certain techniques of surgery, though not interested in the reputation they could have brought him. He seems to have been the first person in the West actually to try acupuncture; for though it had been known about since the seventeenth century, when Ten-Rhyne described its use among the Chinese and Japanese, no European doctor before Louis Berlioz had put it into practice, or at least recorded the fact. The sixteen pages of his book devoted to acupuncture are a model of empirical science.[*]

If his medical knowledge seems primitive and often obscurantist by modern standards, that was so of medicine as a whole. The profession, too, was far less defined and regularised than it was to become. Doctors in the provinces still tended to be either poorly paid artisans of relatively low social status or well-to-do bourgeois for whom doctoring was less an end in itself than an aspect of general culture, one activity among many, though one which by serving the community could help to realise the ideal of the good life. But then as now, the best doctor was not necessarily the most technically proficient so much as the most experienced and practical, the doctor who combined flair with humility and who when he could not save his patients yet took trouble over them and showed them and their families kindness and understanding. When Louis Berlioz died the whole town followed his coffin to the cemetery. He was mourned most of all by the poor, whom he had so often helped by looking after them for little or no fee as well as by more general acts of philanthropy.

"Le bon Louis": all accounts of him agree as to his kindness, his willingness to put himself out to help people of all sorts and conditions, his sense of duty to his fellow-men. It is a true picture so far as it goes; but what it leaves out is as important.

The supporting players in the drama of a famous man's life all too easily acquire fixed, two-dimensional characters which, once given them, are theirs for good or ill. Dr Berlioz has been represented by almost every writer on the subject as a man of fundamental fair-mindedness and lucidity of judgment; balanced, meticulous, reasonable, an authentic product of the Enlightenment. This is a half-truth; but he believed it himself. "Papa thinks he is completely objective," wrote Hector to his Uncle Victor in 1825, the period of most intense conflict over his career. "This gives him, so he says, a great advantage over me in my constant state of Enthusiasm, that of seeing things in their true light." That was how Dr Berlioz saw himself — as a rational man beset with problems not of his making. But another letter of Hector's from the same period bears a revealing annotation in the doctor's hand: "Monument to folly and blind, unbridled passion." The letter, though very strongly expressed, argues Hector's case with clarity and cogency; Dr Berlioz, however, was beyond recognising it.

He had not outgrown his turbulent youth so much as he liked to think.

---

* They are the origin of modern interest in acupuncture. See the entry on the subject in *Dictionnaire encyclopédique des sciences médicales*, Paris 1864: "[...] We have to wait till 1810 to encounter the first practical application of acupuncture in Europe: it was carried out by a French doctor, Dr Berlioz [...] Dr Berlioz's example found a convinced imitator in Dr Haime of Tours. His success was witnessed by Bretonneau [...] From that moment [...] the practice spread generally."

The portrait of him, painted in late middle age and now hanging in his study at La Côte, says as much. Below the broad, rather noble forehead and above the long, fine nose, the dark eyes look warily out on the world with a suggestion of passion held in check as much by timidity as by self-control. The slight twist of the firm-set mouth hints at bitterness as well as resignation. The whole appearance intimates that much more is going on behind it than the steady gaze and air of having seen it all would have us believe. It inspires sympathy but also a certain unease. It is the face of a "good man", perhaps, but of a far from simple one.

By the time it was painted the sitter had had his share of grief and disillusionment. His daughter Nancy's diary, dating from the 1820s, shows him increasingly exhausted and depressed by the strain of dealing with his rebellious son. The entry for 21 July 1824 is typical: "We talked of my brother this afternoon. My father is dreadfully affected by it all. 'I have always been unfortunate,' he said. 'My childhood was not happy, my youth was very stormy, and now the son who was to have been my consolation is destroying the happiness I might have had.'" But the self-pity and tendency to melancholia and morbid obsessiveness that Nancy's observations suggest are already present twenty years earlier in a strange letter written to his wife during the first months of their marriage. Joséphine Berlioz, then about six weeks pregnant, was staying with her father. The letter gives an unexpected insight into Louis Berlioz's temperament.

La Côte, Friday 2 Floréal [22 April 1803]

Another time, my Joséphine, do not wait until an opportunity presents itself but write at once, either direct or by the mail. I went this morning, with all the impatience you can imagine, so as to be present when the postman's packet was opened. You cannot conceive the state I found myself in when there was only a letter from Benjamin [his brother], which admittedly reassured me as to your health, but which did not and could not suffice. In despair, I hurried back to the house; the most ghastly forebodings crowded into my imagination, my ideas were in so great a turmoil that I cannot say which of them tormented me most. My whole being seemed on the point of dissolution; I believe I actually wished that that would happen. I saw myself born to be for ever wretched, I pictured humanity in the blackest colours, I all but cursed the day I was born, and invoked the hour of my annihilation. At that moment I was resolved to write to you. But I would have had to cover the pages at a stroke — and what pages! How I congratulate myself that my pen refused to make you the witness of my frenzy! After a few seconds in this state of helplessness, I decided to set off there and then. Scarcely had I passed the Château de Grenouilles when I met your messenger. She asked me if I was going to Grenoble. How eagerly I seized the blessed letter that she handed to me! Yet I strove to contain my raptures; I rapidly scanned it, then rushed back here to read and re-read it absolutely undisturbed. I saw that my Joséphine had not forgotten me. I felt ashamed that my despair had made me so unjust; and, my joy restoring me to reason, I was as angry with myself as you must be on reading this account. But forgive me — you must realise that love never goes hand in hand with reason; the preservation of that which is most precious provokes the greatest alarm. Sensible of the worth of the treasure I possess, knowing my Joséphine's heart, could I be untroubled at the idea that she had forgotten all about me for five days — whereas for me not a minute passes, not an instant, without my thinking of her? I had gauged your heart by my own, and I was not wrong; your letter has proved to me that in the midst of Meylan's delights you still thought of La Côte. Never again for any reason, on any pretext, expose me to tortures as terrible as those I suffered this morning. Oh my dearest! I believe that another such experience would be the end of me.

The days have dragged since you left. I do not wish to cut short your enjoyment, but I beg you not to prolong my suffering more than you have to. Make up your mind how long you wish to be away, and tell me definitely when I can hope to bring you back. I can't really be away for more than a week, so decide now when you want me to come. How delightful it will be, that moment when I can clasp you in my arms! But how dearly it must be paid for! I used to laugh when I read the poets' woeful tales of absence and its ills. I could not believe their rhymes expressed true feeling. Ah! I know now too well, it is no invention.

Can Victor and Benjamin really have failed to find a carriage to take you to Meylan? Tell them that I am deeply disappointed at their lack of despatch. In your condition it is excessively imprudent to tire yourself beyond your strength. Reflect that your existence is now tripled; think that two other lives depend on yours. Promise me that you will not go on any more such expeditions; they frighten me too much.

Goodbye, my dear Finette, give my love to your father. You love him too much for me not to cherish him, even were he not so richly deserving it. Goodbye once again — though it is a cruel word to say. I shall cease loving you only on ceasing to exist.

L. Berlioz

What lay behind this outburst? Are we to imagine some dark insecurity, a tormenting jealousy and suspicion of his young wife's former haunts and the admirers she might be seeing there? Or a simple anxiety, personal and professional, about her health and the well-being of the child she was carrying, at a potential danger-point in early pregnancy? Whatever the reason, it is hardly what we should expect from the balanced, level-headed man he is supposed to have been. He may be able to analyse and rationalise his panic after the event; but at the time, in the stress of the moment, imagined terrors drive him demented.

When we examine the Livre de Raison the first impression of neat, orderly thoroughness is qualified. The entries turn out to be surprisingly — and to a biographer maddeningly — unmethodical. One year his expenditure is listed in detail; the next year the total only is given. This sort of inconsistency applies to such varied items as the yield of the vintage, the readings of the thermometer outside his study window, and the dates of Hector's departures for Paris. He gives the wrong year for his own marriage; and the date of his son's marriage to an actress — a subject of passionate concern and intense distress to him — is entered incorrectly.

The received idea of Berlioz's mother is no less misleadingly one-sided. Posterity has not been kind to Joséphine Berlioz. It has taken its cue from the *Memoirs*, where she scarcely appears except as the spokesman of extreme provincial prejudice against the arts, while Dr Berlioz is liberal and humane even when most strenuously opposed to his son's vocation. The one thing remembered about her is her cursing her son for wanting to be a musician. In nearly all biographies of Berlioz it is she, not her husband, who appears as the highly strung and hyper-emotional member of the partnership. Dr Berlioz is seen as a kind of French equivalent of Mr Bennet in *Pride and Prejudice*, ironically saluting his wife's nerves as his "old friends" and retreating into his books whenever the domestic scene becomes uncomfortably hot: a man who, like Mr Bennet, "captivated by youth and beauty and that appearance of good humour which youth and beauty generally give, had married a woman whose weak understanding and illiberal mind had very early in their marriage put an end to any real affection for her".

The records suggest a different and much less black-and-white picture. Berlioz himself, according to Ferdinand Hiller, the German composer who made friends with him in Paris in the late 1820s and to whom he talked about his childhood, "spoke of his mother with love, in which however were mixed pity and regret because of the prejudice, as he called it, that she had with regard to religion and art". This prejudice, I think, explains the way Joséphine Berlioz is treated in the *Memoirs*. The role she plays there is dictated by the book's avowedly didactic purpose, which is, in part, to give an account of the difficulties confronting the would-be composer in France, not to tell in full the story of his life. There is no doubt that in adult life Berlioz felt closer to his father; they had tastes and interests in common which he did not share with his mother. She was incapable, at a conscious level, of understanding her son. ("Quelle tête!" she exclaims in her letters as she recounts his Parisian "folies".) It was less uncongenial to cast her as the motivating force in the family struggle against his musical career. In fact, the documents show that it was his father who, though in practice irresolute and vacillating, was the more implacably opposed to it.[*] But his mother's diehard views on art

---

[*] For example, a letter of Nancy Berlioz, written just after the first performance of Hector's Mass in 1825, describes her mother as secretly proud of her son's success though not daring to admit it to herself, whereas her father is actually annoyed by it and will only say, coldly, "What of it?"

and artists were an essential part of the book's picture — a true picture — of French bourgeois bigotry and philistinism. They epitomised what his career had been dedicated to combating. What most appalled him about them, when he recalled the event, was that they could provoke a confrontation of such violence and horror "between so loving a mother as mine was" and her son.

Joséphine Berlioz's religious convictions and devotion to orthodox Catholic doctrine and observance would not at first have estranged her from her son, who went through a deeply religious phase in his teens. It was only when his vocation took shape, and he declared his wish to become a composer, that religion, or rather the clerical attitude to the artist's life, became an issue and raised a barrier between them. Until that point, there is no reason to doubt Ferdinand Hiller's testimony that Berlioz's mother was a vital part of that affectionate environment of which Hiller received so strong an impression from listening to him talk about his early years.

An anonymous tribute to the Berlioz family, written at the time of the first Berliozian celebrations at La Côte in the 1880s and evidently referring to the period 1815–25, makes a point of her tenderheartedness. "Madame Berlioz — what a kind, sympathetic friend she was! She felt everyone's misfortunes — which inspired a friend of the household to the amusing saying: 'If Madame Berlioz knew of the sorrows of the King of Morocco, she would suffer for him.' " This was how she was remembered by someone who had come to the house as a child, in the days when it was still a centre for gatherings of local friends and visitors from farther afield; for Joséphine Berlioz had a reputation for sociability and was popular in the neighbourhood as a hostess.

Berlioz himself testifies to her intuitive perceptiveness. It is she who, in the *Memoirs*, is shown as having sensed the importance of his childhood love for Estelle Dubeuf. There is no suggestion in the documents that anyone else in his family circle thought of it as more than a passing crush, to be remarked on, laughed at, and forgotten. But Joséphine Berlioz did not forget, and she showed that she still remembered fifteen years later, when chance and her sense of mischief conspired to bring him once again briefly into contact with Estelle.

By that time Joséphine Berlioz was nearly fifty, with not many years left to live. It is not until this final period that we first encounter her in her letters. The earliest letters date from 1829, when she was forty-five, past her prime and much given to seeing the dark side of life. They are loud with complaints about her eternal "gastritis", her husband's deafness and inaccessibility, Hector's mad ideas, the political situation, the silk-worm crop, the washing, and the general unsatisfactoriness of the world. Yet, with all their complaining, there is a kind of zest about these rambling unpunctuated epistles that endears her to the reader, despite their bourdon of woes. Once launched, she flows unstoppably on, never pausing for breath, sweeping spelling and syntax aside, veering without warning from topic to topic, gossiping, admonishing, chiding, throwing up her hands, yet somehow communicating not petty-mindedness or gloom but a native appetite for life that no suffering can extinguish. They are unmistakably the letters of a "character".

No portrait of Joséphine Berlioz has survived. Various accounts suggest that she was tall and slim. She was generally reckoned something of a beauty, with her fresh complexion and large candid eyes. But her nature — open, ingenuous, warm-hearted — was considered still more pleasing. That was how she appeared to more than one observer around the time of her marriage, at the age of eighteen, and so she remained, even after the griefs of motherhood (two of her six children died in childhood) had begun to take their toll.

Who, from the outside, can judge the truth of a marriage, the secret reality of the constantly shifting day-to-day relationship between two people, even when they are one's friends, let alone when one never knew them and they have long since been dust? It seems that Berlioz's parents ended by growing apart, and came to play their roles accordingly. Differences in education and outlook between the liberal, agnostic scientist and the convent-reared dévote, differences that a more straightforward and confident man might have taught both of them to overcome, gradually hardened. In the event their love, sincere and passionate though it had been, lacked the depth of mutual understanding and the fund of freely and habitually shared feelings that could have enabled it to withstand a succession of domestic tragedies and the strain of worsening health. Grief, material anxieties and incipient deafness forced Dr Berlioz increasingly into himself; and his wife became more frustrated and nervy as he became more withdrawn and uncommunicative. Disagreement over how to deal with their son was one more wedge driven between them. But all this is to look twenty years into the future. In its beginnings the marriage of Louis Berlioz and Joséphine Marmion was, on his side at least, and on hers, if not from the very first, then soon afterwards, a true love-match.

Even in an age in which marriage was above all a means of advancement and the strengthening of the two families concerned, and arranged marriages were the norm and the dowry all-important, the independent-minded young doctor was hardly the sort to marry against his inclination or with indifference. But the alliance also satisfied the social requirements. The two families had been neighbours for some time, both in Grenoble, where they lived in the same street, the Rue Pertuisière,* and at Murianette, a village a few miles to the east in the foothills of the Alps overlooking the

* The street, which no longer exists, led from the Place St Claire to the Rue du Lycée.

Isère valley. Very likely they were acquaintances of longer standing, for in the 1780s Louis-Joseph Berlioz, the bridegroom's father, had practised at the bar in Grenoble at the same time as the bride's father, Nicolas Marmion, his junior by three years. They had both, too, been widowed young and in the same year, 1791. A union between their eldest children would naturally have suggested itself. The Marmions, though not such substantial property-owners as the Berliozes, were a family of some distinction – Joseph Marmion, the bride's grandfather, had been one of the leading medical lights of Grenoble – and there were only two children to divide the inheritance between: Nicolas Marmion had not married again after the death of his beautiful young wife, Victoire. Joséphine Marmion was quite a catch: fashionably slim, pretty and spirited, a belle of the Grenoble season, which was just then in full swing – it was carnival time – and about to lose one of its brightest ornaments. On his side Nicolas Marmion must have been pleased to see her handsomely settled; he had retired early to devote himself to his garden, his neighbours and his muse, and was living on his investments. She was only eighteen, but it was never too soon to have one's daughter provided for.

Louis Berlioz and Joséphine Marmion were married in February 1803. In recording the event in his Livre de Raison Dr Berlioz ascribed it to 1802, and the mistake has been perpetuated. In fact, as the book states correctly a few pages further on, he got married after his return from a visit to Paris, made towards the end of 1802 with the purpose of sitting his final medical exams and sustaining his thesis. The marriage contract was signed in the family house at La Côte St André on the morning of Saturday 6 February 1803, in front of a numerous company of friends and relations; after which, following immemorial custom, there would have been a reception with food and drink, before everyone piled into carriages and drove the thirty miles to Grenoble. From there it was only about half an hour along the Isère to Meylan, where next morning, Sunday 7 February – the bridegroom and his party having probably spent the night in Grenoble or else at Louis-Joseph's country house at Murianette on the opposite side of the valley from Meylan – the marriage was celebrated: first under civil law at the mairie, then in the village church a couple of hundred yards down the steep hillside from the bride's father's house.

Nicolas Marmion duly signalised the event in verse, with a brief but telling "Lines to my daughter on her wedding-day", to which his cultivated son-in-law replied with some well-turned alexandrines. The gratified troubadour (as he called himself) entered both poems in the book that recorded the fruits of his muse. The next entry, two or three weeks later, is a 250-line "Epistle to my son-in-law". And a few entries further on, in November or December, we find him happily picturing the scene at La

Côte as the young couple, surrounded by friends and relations, await the arrival of the "tender token of their love" with which, as he had predicted on their wedding-day, "Heav'n soon will crown our handiwork".

In Nicolas Marmion's poetic world this token is invariably a son, whose coming will ensure the continuance of the line; it is also assumed that his parents will not waste time but will see to it that he appears as promptly as the rules of propriety permit, or very soon after. Both conventions were observed. The baby was born ten months after the wedding, and it was a boy.

In his *Memoirs* Berlioz raised an ironic eyebrow at the deplorably unheroic circumstances of his birth, heralded by none of the portents which in poetic ages foretold the coming of those predestined for fame: unlike Alexander's mother or Virgil's, his had had no vision of future greatness. With the exception of the agitated letter quoted above, the surviving documents evoke a picture of undisturbed contentment. The young wife kept up a lively correspondence with her friends, who regaled her with accounts of the balls and charade parties which somehow managed to go on without her, and scolded their beloved Finette for allowing herself to be snatched from them by that unfeeling Monsieur Berlle (as the name Berlioz was pronounced in Dauphiné). But there were regular journeys to Grenoble, and visits by friends to the big house fronting the main street of La Côte which Louis-Joseph Berlioz, now quite reconciled to his son's medical career, had made over to him as part of his marriage settlement.*

Life in the noisy, sleepy market town went busily on, not greatly affected by the news from the world outside, the renewed outbreak of war in May and the talk of the invasion of England, preparations for which were visible in troop movements in nearby Grenoble. The only recorded event of note in the district during Joséphine Berlioz's pregnancy was the formal reintroduction of Catholic worship after the ten-year cult of the Goddess Reason with which the Revolution had attempted to replace it. It was an event particularly welcome to Louis-Joseph and his pious new daughter-in-law, rather less so to his free-thinking son the doctor (though

---

* Louis-Joseph Berlioz is described in the Livre de Raison as "of medium height, well proportioned and muscular. He was methodical in all his habits, and abstemious to a fault. Scrupulously devout, he never questioned the grounds for his belief and would have thought it a sin to wish to do so. The decrees of the church in his eyes were final. He had little book-learning, but an uncommon good sense guided him in every circumstance of life. He never had any time for the revolutionaries, and held rigorously aloof from all public office. He was thrifty, and increased his wealth by shrewd management and timely acquisitions; but he was not in the least miserly and stinted nothing that was needed for our education. His conversation was jovial, but he was not fond of being contradicted. He was very strict with his children until they attained the age of twenty; after that he was never anything but a friend and affectionate father to them."

he acknowledged its civic advantages). At the same time a new curé was installed. The previous incumbent, Claude Berlioz (uncle of Louis-Joseph), who had lived in exile at Sion in Switzerland during the Terror, had recently returned to his native parish, but the diocesan authorities over-ruled local opinion, appointed Curé Berlioz to the nearby parish of Vinay and chose a younger man, Claude Durand, in his place. The town council had for some time been at work rescuing their church from the ravages of atheism; the interior and exterior of the nave were repaired; 6,000 francs was spent on new ornaments, and the thirteenth-century bell-tower was repaired. After the firing of mortars, a procession of local dignitaries accompanied by the band of the National Guard with side-drums at the head marched to the presbytery and thence to the church, where High Mass was celebrated. Mayor Buffevent's speech of welcome to the new curé gives a flavour of this undisturbed corner of a province which had interpreted the Revolution very much in the interests of the property-owning middle class:

> [. . .] You come to this commune as an angel of peace. Your pastoral guidance, at once stirring and persuasive, will bring to an end within our walls the dissensions that sprang from a revolution unprecedented in the annals of the universe. Each one of us will feel the need to sacrifice on the altar of concord all petty interests of partisanship and personal vanity. It is the desire of one and all, and especially of the general council, that all parties forget the past. Never doubt our zeal, sir, to support you in the arduous but glorious career that is opening before you. Inspired by the government's example, there is none among us but is deeply aware of the im-portance of your sacred office. The tragedies of the Revolution have all too clearly proved to us that the return of order and happiness will come about only through submission to the law, both civil and religious, and through the respect due to the priesthood. It is my prayer that the terrible lessons taught us by ten years of anarchy and disaster may never be forgotten. [5 July 1803]

The sentiments sum up cautious, canny La Côte. Alone among the towns of the district it had remained largely impervious to the patriotic republican enthusiasm which under the Revolution inspired its neighbours to change their names. St Etienne de St Geoire, just across the plain to the south, became "Marothon", St Marcellin became "Les Thermopyles", Vienne "La Patriote", St Laurent du Pont "Laurent-Libre" and Lyons "Ville-Affranchie". La Côte St André contented itself with the prosaic "La Côte Bonne-Eau" (in tribute to its liqueurs). Even so the townspeople declined to adopt it. Incoming letters addressed to the mairie or to the Society of the Friends of Liberty and Equality might use the official name: letters going out were firmly headed "La Côte St André" or at the most "La Côte André". This lack of zeal had its advantages. Unlike La

Tour du Pin, the nearest town of comparable importance on the other side of the hill to the north, La Côte never acquired a guillotine.*

Two months after the installation of the new curé, Joséphine Berlioz was at her father's house in Meylan — the first of the late-summer visits to the village on the slopes of the Isère valley that were to become a family tradition and to play so potent a part in the imaginative life of her son. If Dr Berlioz went too, the harvest and the call of his practice brought him back to La Côte ahead of her.

La Côte, Friday 29 Fructidor [16 September 1803]

Tell me, my adorable love, what I have done to deserve all the sweet things you wrote to me on Tuesday, and what has prompted the hymn of praise you lavished on me? Is there in fact so much merit in loving you, and should I be praised so much for the efforts I make to please you, heavenly woman? Love has placed his blindfold over your eyes. I don't know where you can have noticed that perfection with which you charge me, and which alarms you. Yet I found the style of your letter quite delightful, and I should like to know the extraordinary cause that obtained me so charming an epistle, for I am eager to receive more like it. The sole defect I find in it is that of being a little too short; when you are in the mood to write such agreeable things it's a crime to be so brief. Yes, my dearest Finette, your letter has given me intense pleasure; there is a warmth about it that your pen had not managed to express before. It is not that I previously doubted you loved me, you have told me so a hundred times — but never before with such force. If I were not afraid of becoming wearisome in repeating the declarations that I have already made a thousand times, I too would tell you that I am conscious of all the worth of the treasure I possess, and that I do not feel I am unworthy of it — if a heart on fire with love may deserve you. [. . .]

Soon afterwards friends and relations gathered round for the accouchement. Nicolas Marmion, from his "rustic homestead", pictured the scene at La Côte and the cheerful company assembled there: Dr Berlioz's younger brothers — Benjamin (his favourite), outwardly calm, spending much of his time painting in the studio, his reserved manner only hinting at the pleasure he feels, and Victor the young law-student, who has put himself in charge of the baby's pot and who is not nearly serious-minded enough for one who within a month will be an uncle; the good Louis himself, tears of happiness in his eyes, entertaining the others of an evening with music ("E'en so the mate of Philomel / Of motherhood

---

* A reflection of this attitude may perhaps be seen in the fact that in the Berlioz marriage contract drawn up at La Côte the bride's names — Marie-Antoinette-Joséphine — are given in full, with no concession to ideological rectitude, whereas in the comparable document at the mairie of Meylan "Marie-Antoinette" becomes "Antoinette".

beguiles the cares / With loving and voluptuous airs, / Her constancy requiting well"); Lucile Marquis, a bosom friend of Joséphine's, who is helping to get the baby's clothes ready and is likened to one of the Graces attending Venus at the birth of Cupid; and the old man, Louis-Joseph Berlioz, full of pious sentiments on the solemnity of the occasion, he too unable to hold back his tears at the thought of seeing himself renewed in his grandson.

The child was born on Sunday 11 December 1803. The following day the parish register of La Côte St André in the arrondissement of Vienne recorded the birth of

> Louis Hector Berlioz at 5 in the evening yesterday, Sunday, the nineteenth day of the month of Frimaire in the twelfth year of the French Republic, legitimate son of Citizen Louis Joseph Berlioz, officer of health domiciled at La Côte St André and of Marie Antoinette Joséphine Marmion his wife.*

On the 14th the baby was baptised in the church of St André in the presence of family and friends and the two godparents, Nicolas Marmion — the troubadour had in the meantime arrived — and Sophie Brochier, the child's great-grandmother. His given names reflected the times. Under the Revolution, saints' names had been frowned on. Napoleon's Concordat with Rome had restored them to favour, but parents were still encouraged to call their children after the great figures of antiquity. Louis was in any case a family name. But from the first the child was Hector.

The baby's progress was noted in the letters that passed between Joséphine Berlioz and her friends. One of them, Nancy Clappier, came from Grenoble on a visit and on her return wrote to congratulate Joséphine on "the little monkey's appetite. Your present plumpness is just what it should be for the moment, for it proves you're well able to feed him. I trust that when you have weaned him you will become our own Finette once again" (1 April 1804). Lucile Marquis, who had been longing to come and see them again and embrace "ce bel Hector" but had been kept at home by a last-minute change of plan, was able to report the delight of Nicolas Marmion, who was going about exclaiming, "It's *incredible* — the baby is so beautiful. It's *incredible!*" In May mother and child went to stay with Nicolas Marmion in Grenoble. Dr Berlioz remained behind to see to one or two patients and the mowing of the new meadow (his horses were short of fodder); he and his father were also busy with the reconstruction of a mill, fifty yards down the street from

---

* Louis Berlioz was still at this stage only an "officer of health"; he had qualified before the enactment of the law of 10 March 1803 (19 Ventose an XI) — the law which, in addition to restoring the medical schools to their full status, formally established the various grades of medical practitioner in France. It was not till the following March, 1804, that he exchanged the "certificate of aptitude" awarded him in December 1802 for the diploma of the Paris Medical School, which entitled him to call himself "doctor of medicine".

the family house. His letter of 19 May, as loving as the one of the previous September quoted above, but less formal in expression, speaks of his longing to be reunited with his wife and son:

What bliss it will be when I can rejoin you and once again embrace my wife and caress my little Hector! [...] Goodbye my dear, most dear Joséphine; to you I devote the few free moments that I have today, and I end as I began, by assuring you that I love you, I adore you, and shall love and adore you always [...]

Though it is nice to know that his mother had enough milk for him, one would willingly sacrifice these glimpses of Hector as a baby in arms for one clear sight of him as a boy of eight or ten. As it is, there is no direct evidence of him between the spring of 1804, when he was six months old, and the beginning of 1816, when he was twelve. These years show a general dearth of family records. Quite a lot of letters have survived for 1803—4, but after that almost nothing until 1815—16. In the sequence of Nicolas Marmion's verse-letters there is a similar hiatus. Dr Berlioz did not start his Livre de Raison till 1815. And nearly all the main incidents that Berlioz describes in the early chapters of the *Memoirs* belong to his teens. We see him briefly around the time of his birth; then the mists descend and it is another twelve years before he emerges and begins to take identifiable form. In that first obscure part of his existence, what events and forces shaped his personality? What environment?

La Côte St André, market town and agricultural centre, chief administrative seat of the district, just off the main route from Grenoble to Lyons, had at the beginning of the nineteenth century (and for most of the succeeding century and a half) about 3,500 inhabitants. The correspondence, mostly female, that has survived from that time gives the impression of a place with the small-mindedness of the Grenoble that Stendhal describes but without the amenities or the scale and the diversity of social entertainment that gave life in Grenoble the illusion of importance. If Dr Berlioz and his wife are not French equivalents of Mr and Mrs Bennet, La Côte seen through the eyes of its middle-class women is reminiscent of its contemporary, Jane Austen's Meryton. The same small-town preoccupations absorb it: the latest rumour of a regiment being quartered there for the winter, the latest ball, the latest conundrum or bouts-rimés, the latest moves in the marriage game, the latest arrivals in the district and what their manners and their complexions are like, the latest death, who has left what to whom, who has had whom to dinner and how they were dressed, who are the new eligible young men, who will be the next girl to get engaged; only, no Mr Bingley or Mr Darcy appears and confounds the realists by marrying for love.

But Louis Berlioz was happy there. His household was a world on its own, exceptional both in its culture (its library alone would have singled it out in a society in which, as Stendhal remarked, it was very rare to find a man prepared to put much capital into objects as unproductive as books) and in its social and economic importance. As the hub of an estate comprising several dwellings, numerous farm buildings and ninety acres of land, the large cool house on the south side of the narrow main street of La Côte was a humming centre of activity the whole year round. All the various crops with their different harvest times, of which the vintage, lasting the best part of a month, was only the most demanding: hay, rye, wheat, oats, barley, buck-wheat, fruit, walnuts, chestnuts, root-crops; the planting, felling, trimming of trees — lime, poplar, hawthorn, mulberry; the building of new barns, the repair and retiling of old ones; the endless work on the two water-mills; the digging of ditches; the employment and care of the hired labourers who carried out the unskilled jobs; the culture of silk-worms, a tricky, time-consuming and very messy business, the responsibility of the women of the family; the curing of ham and bacon and the making of the many by-products — sausages and pies, gelatine, lard, bristle, skin for jar-covers — of the huge pig, weighing up to 350 lbs, that was bought each year as an essential part of the domestic economy; the smoking of 50 lbs of fish; the laundry, done only twice a year (a mark of a prosperous family, with enough linen to last for six months), but for that reason an operation on a Herculean scale — this and far more, not left to bailiffs and housekeepers to look after but the direct concern of the master and mistress, kept the household busy from dawn to dusk.

The near self-sufficient farm unit, once common in rural and semi-rural economies, is now so much a thing of the past that it is hard to picture the reality. Hard, too, for the imagination to people the empty house with living inhabitants. It is now the Musée Hector Berlioz; and though structurally much the same and restored to something like its early nineteenth-century state, it seems, in its embalmed silence, never to have been anything but a museum. But it must have been a pleasant house to grow up in. The low-beamed spacious entrance hall, three steps down from the street (almost everything in La Côte St André is on a slope), culminated in two flights of wide stone stairs, one leading down to a southward-facing courtyard and garden, the other going up to french windows opening on a three-sided wooden gallery that overlooked the courtyard. On the same level as the gallery, their windows giving on to it, were, to the left, a beamed and flagged kitchen, with a curtained alcove for a bed, and opposite it the doctor's study. The stairs, doubling back, arrived after a few more steps at the full landing, from which the three chief rooms of the house were reached, the dining-room, drawing-room and main bedroom, all three with tall double windows fronting the street. Two further floors repeated the same split-level pattern, one facing south and overlooking courtyard and garden, the other facing the houses on the north side of the street and beyond them the steep hillside on the lower slopes of which La Côte St André was built. There was a large attic at the top of the house (partly used for drying the washing), with dormer windows from which the distant Alps were visible, and capacious cellars and store-rooms at the bottom.

The left-hand or easterly of the two wings at the back of the house was a barn, containing stable, woodshed and hay loft; but the western wing, except at ground level where there were store-rooms with great stone vats, was part of the living quarters. According to a tradition reported by the French historian Julien Tiersot at the end of the last century, one of its first-floor rooms, just along the gallery from the doctor's study, was the schoolroom where the young Berlioz worked at his lessons. From the window of the room you looked out on to the cobbled courtyard, with its water pump in the corner and its sundial, and on to the rectangular garden where a fountain played and above whose massive red-tiled walls, on summer days, the Plaine de Bièvre and its border of wooded hills shimmered in the heat.

Wherever you went in La Côte the country was there at your feet. From its northern to its southern limits was only a few hundred yards; the side streets that hurried down the slope, intersecting the main east-west thoroughfares, seemed to run straight into the fields, and at their top end was the sheltering hillside, more densely cultivated then than now and rich with vines, chestnut and walnut. The plain too was intensively farmed. Berlioz's first biographers, getting to know his native landscape at the time of the severe agricultural depression and depopulation of the 1870s and 1880s, accused him of exaggerating its charms when he described the plain of La Côte as "green and golden, its stillness filled with an indescribable dreamlike grandeur".* But in the early years of the century, though there might be the occasional recession, and conscription in the last desperate period of the Napoleonic Empire would briefly take its toll of the workforce, the land was prosperous and, except on marshy ground, yielded abundant crops. From the broad summit of the ridge, where honey-stoned farms stood among groves of birch and oak (remnants of the royal forest of medieval times), you could sometimes see Mont Blanc nearly seventy miles to the north-east; but from almost anywhere on the slope below, the view was splendid enough. The patchwork plain, extending for only half a dozen miles in a southerly direction before rising to the foothills of the Vercors, to the east swept in a slow upward curve

---

* E.g. Tiersot: "[...] pour qui n'y est pas né, cette large étendue, sans verdure et sans eau, apparaît vraiment triste et nue"; and Boschot: "[...] le sol est si sec, si pierreux [...] Dans le pays de Berlioz, la nature ne fait pas venir aux lèvres le mot de *beauté*, ni celui de *mystère*."

towards the granite-flecked limestone cliffs of the Chartreuse massif —
above which, a little to the right, the vision of the great snow-peaks of the
Belledonne range hung in the clear air — while to the west the level
ground seemed to stretch for ever, past the site where, it was said,
Hannibal on his way to conquer Rome encamped and reviewed his army
after subduing the Allobrogi, on and on till it merged in the far-distant
valley of the Rhone and was only ended by the faint blue rampart of the
Cévennes.

Against the green hillside the town made a contrasting glow of red tiles
and warm amber stone. The houses were of brick, or of sandstone,
sometimes dressed, more often with the large rounded stones and the
mortar exposed, giving them a rough but solid appearance. The poorer
were glorified hovels, the richer had carved wooden balconies under high
projecting eves, or substantial gateways with heavy nail-studded oak
doors, surmounted by flat-topped turrets. Everywhere was tiled in the
warm red terracotta common to the south of France: thick, curved tiles
on the gentler-sloping roofs, flat but with a rounded lower edge on the
steeper.

The town's pride was the open covered market, or "Halles", which
occupied most of the central square, a vaulted timbered structure two
hundred and fifty feet long with five wide aisles, built in the late thirteenth
century of oak from the forest which at that date extended over most of
the plain. Every Thursday was market day. In addition there were six
specialist fairs at different times of the year, two of them created under
the Revolution, four dating from time immemorial, which brought the
people of a dozen surrounding communes crowding into La Côte. The
other main centre of social activity was the Esplanade at the south-east
corner of the town, where the men played boules and the band of the
National Guard practised, and the women and children walked among
the lime trees on fine Sunday afternoons.*

Though the paving of the streets had been begun in 1791 under the
stimulus of the Revolution, some were still rough as well as badly drained;
but there were gardens everywhere and fountains, and the fields were
never far off. Many of these were owned by Hector's father. A large-scale
map of La Côte St André, prepared by the town council in 1819—21 as
part of a plan to widen the streets and extend and rename some of them,

---

* Today the Place Hector Berlioz, presided over by Lenoir's statue of the composer. The big
open space that in the modern La Côte is the Place St André, adjoining the church, did not
exist, being at that time largely occupied by the cemetery, later moved to its present position on
the western outskirts of the town.

The splendid Halles, constructed in 1274—5, was the work of Maître Jacques de St Georges.
A few years later Edward I brought Maître Jacques over to England and put him in charge of
his great programme of castle-building in North Wales.

shows Dr Berlioz to have been the biggest proprietor among the middle class after the Rocher family (makers of the liqueurs which still bear their name). The house opposite the family home in the main street — partly occupied by Hector's great-grandmother Sophie Brochier, partly leased as a shop and blacksmith's forge — belonged to him. So did two other houses, a big garden, several barns, the meadow to the east of the Esplanade, and other fields and vineyards scattered round about. And just beyond the eastern limit of the town, in the hamlet of Le Chuzeau, on a gently sloping spur of the hillside, he had acquired a large farmhouse, with adjacent barns surrounding a great yard, walled garden, orchard and fields. The Ferme du Nand, as it was called, was only half a mile away but it was secluded and quiet and a favourite resort of the family in summer especially, away from the dust and heat of the town, with a superb prospect to the south and east.

By the time he was grown up Hector would know all that landscape intimately, would have walked over the whole surrounding countryside and would think nothing of covering thirty miles in a day — an idea alarming to the more sedentary Berlioz scholars (who have seen in such "foolhardy" exploits, so sapping to the constitution, an explanation of the breakdown of his health in later years), but quite natural to an inhabitant of a mountainous region like Dauphiné. The mountains themselves would soon become familiar, from regular visits to the house of his grandfather Nicolas Marmion at Meylan above the winding Isère on the lower slopes of the Mont St Eynard, facing resplendent Taillefer and the Belledonne peaks. Les Jacques, Grandfather Marmion's farm at Murianette on the other side of the valley, perched on a shoulder of land from which the green hillside fell almost sheer to the valley floor, had an even more spectacular view, with St Eynard and the Grande Chartreuse directly opposite, the sharper peaks of the Vercors to the left, and to the right a great curving sweep of valley crowned by the far-off gleam of Mont Blanc.

On the Meylan side too there was a wonderful feeling of space. The mountains soared, and the spirit was lifted up and soared with them. In Grenoble they leaned over you and penned you in. But Grenoble seemed too intent on its own business to notice. Built at the junction of two important rivers, the Isère and the Drac, capital of the province of Dauphiné, seat of an archbishopric and a high court, boasting its own law school and, as a fortified town near the frontier, its own regiment, a centre for banking as well as commerce, swarming with lawyers, soldiers and tradesmen, liberal, acquisitive, insatiably litigious, endlessly "getting and spending", it pursued its affairs with an impervious consciousness of its own superiority. Though quite small, with a population of less than 30,000, it had nothing to learn from anybody. Paris, as Stendhal remarked, was "far from being regarded as a model". Grenoble, indeed, had shown Paris a thing or two. Only recently its native energy and common sense and its tradition of independence (going back to the Middle Ages, when Dauphiné was separate from France) had reasserted themselves decisively. In 1787 and again in 1788 — before the Revolution — the leading citizens had put matters right and taken the law into their own hands; they had set up their own assemblies, to resist royal encroachment on their rights and to vote long-overdue reforms, and in doing so had set the example which the National Assembly in Paris was to become famous by following.

Hector's sisters, like other middle-class girls of La Côte, learned to look on Grenoble with admiring eyes and were always begging to be allowed to go there, but he himself seems never to have taken to it, though it was only in adult life that it would become for him (as for Stendhal) the symbol of bourgeois philistinism and pursuit of material gain. As a child he went there fairly often. It was on the way to Meylan; by the time they had reached Grenoble — half a day's drive from La Côte — they were near their goal. Sometimes they stopped and stayed a few days in the city. The family had numerous friends there, and relatives: both Hector's grandfathers had houses in the town, and his uncles Victor and Auguste, his father's younger brothers, lived there, Victor a lawyer, Auguste a doctor like Louis (they had been at medical school in Paris together, sharing lodgings in the Latin Quarter). In 1811, when Hector was seven, both Auguste and Victor got married, so there were expeditions to Grenoble to attend the weddings.

Relatives and friends often made the six-hour journey in the opposite direction to stay with the Berlioz family, bringing news of the great world: uncles and aunts; Grandfather Berlioz, who spent quite a lot of his time there, helping his son the doctor with endless building projects; Grandfather Marmion, when he could tear himself away from his garden; old curé Berlioz from Vinay on the other side of the plain; the occasional army officer or official of the National Guard, billeted at the house for a night or two on his way to or from Grenoble or Vienne or Lyons; and a regular flow of Joséphine Berlioz's female friends. The unmarried ones came to help her with her confinements. Two years after Hector's birth a daughter was born, christened Anne-Marguerite but known as Nancy (after her godmother, Joséphine Berlioz's great friend Nancy Clappier), and a year and a half later another girl, Louise.

Why seven years then elapsed before Joséphine Berlioz had another child, whether she suffered poor health or miscarried, is not known. Nancy, when two days old, all but died of infantile asphyxia. Death was a not infrequent visitor during Hector's childhood; it would later remove a brother and a sister. Often, of course, it took the old. One winter evening when he was six his great-grandmother Sophie's clothes caught fire as she stood in front of her fireplace, and though Dr Berlioz ran across the street and put out the flames by enveloping her in a blanket she died twenty-four hours later of multiple burns. A cousin, the notary Joseph Berlioz who had drawn up Louis Berlioz's marriage contract, fell into a bog one night the worse for drink and was found next morning face downwards in the mud, choked to death. (He may not have been greatly mourned in the Berlioz household, having been on bad terms with them ever since his brother, the old curé, had left everything to his cousin Louis-Joseph, the doctor's father, instead of to him.) The really bitter blow was the death from pleurisy of Louis Berlioz's favourite brother, Benjamin, in 1807 at the age of twenty-seven — a disaster, he wrote, that left him "with a sense of loss that I will carry with me to my grave". Medical science, even in the hands of the "bon Louis", was often powerless against disease.

From time to time news came that some Côtois serving in the Grande Armée had been killed or badly wounded. In 1806, according to the records, 176 from La Côte and the surrounding communes were on active service. But, for the population as a whole, the cost of glory in those brief years of the Empire's heyday was not onerous. The army did not require expensive supplying; it lived off the country it was fighting in (one of the reasons for its amazing mobility), and half of it was made up of foreign troops. Looking back on this period during the early months of the Bourbon Restoration, Dr Berlioz judiciously observed that though Frenchmen might now execrate "the very name of Buonaparte, accusing him of the most monstrous crimes. and the most disgusting vices and at the same time denying him not only military genius!!! but even courage", it was with their tacit consent that he had got where he had. "Throughout the years of his prosperity taxation was not excessively heavy; there was a semblance of liberty; even conscription took no more than a section of the nation's youth, and agriculture was never left short of labour. [It was] the conquered territories, in Germany especially, [that suffered], exposed to the arbitrary extortions of the Emperor, the generals' depredations and the remorseless rapacity of the troops."

La Côte St André, like everywhere else, applauded the great series of victories that Providence seemed to have ordained for French arms — Ulm, Austerlitz, Jena, Wagram. With the rest of the nation it repeated in church that God had "made the Emperor his minister and representative on earth", and "to honour and serve the Emperor is to honour and serve the Lord God Himself"; and every 15 August it marked the Emperor's birthday, which was also the feast of the Blessed Virgin, by a fête, with a fireworks display at the corner of the Esplanade, as it did his marriage in 1810 to Princess Marie-Louise of Austria and the birth of the longed-for son, the King of Rome, the following year — an event which inspired Nicolas Marmion to send the Emperor a complimentary ode.

Most of the time the great business of the realm impinged little. There had been a flurry of excitement in January 1802 when Citizen Bonaparte passed a few miles away in the plain on his way to Italy. Mayor Pascal, doyen of the mayors in the département, was there to greet him, having marched at the head of a goodly detachment of La Côte's National

Guard in full uniform the previous night and waited since dawn in pouring rain. After that the town returned to its daily concerns.

The Berlioz family were usually in Meylan in mid-August, so would miss La Côte's celebration of the Emperor's birthday. But they were no doubt present on 29 April 1810 at the "fête des époux", a picturesque ceremony stimulated by Napoleon's marriage to the Austrian princess earlier the same month. The town gave a sumptuous civic wedding to a young veteran, a carpenter called Claude Néty, lately invalided out of the army because of wounds received in Spain. His bride was furnished with a dowry by the municipality and a wedding dress costing 100 francs. Local dignitaries, including all the mayors of the canton and the drum major of the National Guard, were treated to a banquet, and there were illuminations and fireworks and an ascent by a hot-air balloon. The event had a special link with the Berlioz family in that the bridegroom's sister Monique Néty was, as maidservant and later as housekeeper, an important and much-loved member of their household for most of her life.

The Spanish campaign had a closer, more personal interest for them. Joséphine Berlioz's brother Félix Marmion was involved in it. He was a cavalry officer, a second-lieutenant in the First Dragoons. The previous year, aged twenty-two, after a couple of years with his regiment in Prussia and Poland, he had twice distinguished himself for bravery in Spain: once at the Battle of Uclès when his squadron captured seven banners and, the official citation stated, a "prodigious number" of the enemy, the second time in a reconnaissance outside Santa Cruz de la Mudela when, sabre in hand, Félix led his troop at full gallop in a dawn attack on a Spanish strongpoint and personally took seven prisoners, one of whom, the best mounted, he had to pursue to the gates of the town.

His advent was always an occasion for his nephew Hector. When on leave at his father's house at Meylan, Félix would sometimes ride the thirty-odd miles over to La Côte; or he would appear at Meylan while they were staying there, arriving

> still hot from the breath of the cannon's mouth, decorated with the marks of a lance-thrust, a grape-shot wound in the foot or a magnificent sabre-slash across the face. He was then only an adjutant in the Lancers; young, enamoured of Fame, ready to give his life for a glance from her, believing Napoleon's throne as unshakeable as Mont Blanc; gallant, high-spirited, an enthusiastic amateur violinist and an excellent singer of *opéra-comique*.

So his nephew, years later, recalled him in the days when he "followed the glittering trail of the great Emperor".*

---

* Félix Marmion was not in the Lancers at the time of which Berlioz was writing, but in the First Dragoons. His regiment only became the First Lancers when it was re-formed under the Bourbon Restoration of 1814.

Félix Marmion brought into Hector's consciousness an air not only of danger and glory but of urbanity, sociability, hedonism, insouciance, style — a worldliness far removed from that of the Dauphiné bourgeoisie. Nicolas Marmion was forever urging his son, in prose and verse, to settle down and make a profitable marriage, but he had no inclination to do so. He was dedicated to the roving life. Its pleasures — women, drink, fine horses, hunting, gaming, the theatre — were already in his blood. The army gave him them. Above all the Napoleonic army. There had never been one like it. Its speed of movement (based on the new techniques of mobility which Napoleon was the first to exploit on a grand scale) bewildered its enemies and exhilarated its own men. Nothing was impossible with such a leader. The great surgeon Larrey spoke for thousands of them when he described himself as "one of those joined by unbreakable chains to the chariot of the modern Alexander. So long as he pleases to lead, all who are bound to him must follow."

The Grande Armée in the years of its pride seemed to epitomise the new age that the Revolution had brought into existence, the swifter tempo of life it had unleashed. It was different from anything seen since the days of Ancient Greece. Its discipline and martial vigour were assured by something at once more binding and more becoming to free men than the repressive hierarchy and brutal floggings abolished by the Revolution but still practised by their enemies: a combination of esprit de corps, personal devotion to the Emperor, and the prospect of rapid advancement. Men became generals before they were thirty. Every soldier truly carried a marshal's baton in his knapsack; it was no empty boast. Promotion was there for anyone with the talent and the will to win it. Even those who lacked them were upheld and fired not only by hope but by the whole joyful chivalry of the army, the sense of belonging to a fighting force unique in modern history.

Félix Marmion remained a second-lieutenant for six years, finally being promoted to lieutenant during the occupation of Moscow and to adjutant a year later. This was not, as some biographers have stated, because his brother-in-law's father Louis-Joseph Berlioz had been in trouble as a monarchist sympathiser during the Terror but because, as official reports noted, he was, though a fine soldier, too easy-going; his character lacked the necessary steel to make him a consistently good leader of men.*

Tall, dashing, sociable, a born raconteur, he none the less incarnated to his young nephew the glamour of the Grande Armée; and the boy,

---

* E.g. (from the reports in his dossier): "plenty of ability but little sense of purpose"; "would be a first-rate officer if he would apply himself a little more to his work". The same cheerfully improvident nature led him to pile up gambling debts, in the belief that something would always turn up to extricate him. Later, when his father finally dug his toes in, he would borrow increasingly large sums from his brother-in-law Dr Berlioz.

listening to the grown-ups arguing with him about Bonaparte, and drinking in his stories of the great campaigns — the bloody victories of Eylau and Friedland, the intoxicating war of movement over the arid plateaux of Spain, the unbelievable horrors of the Russian winter, the masterly tactics of the final doomed but brilliant rearguard action of 1814 — was filled with a fascination with Napoleon that he was not to forget for the rest of his life. The spell he came under then, as with so many of his contemporaries, was so strong that nothing subsequently, not all his adult aversion to war and conquest and all forms of human aggressiveness, could break it or reason it away. Every reminder of it — the reminiscences of his passionately Bonapartist teacher Le Sueur, the sight of the famous Napoleonic battlefields in Italy, the return of the Emperor's ashes from St Helena to the Invalides — would serve to stir profound feelings, which found a reflection in his music: for the visionary grandeur of the Requiem, the Te Deum and *The Trojans* is partly Napoleonic in origin.

But in the young Berlioz's growing imagination Napoleon was part of something wider, or rather stood for a larger idea, of fundamental importance: the idea of a new world, an unprecedented adventure of emotion and spirit, a revolutionary conception of life lived more fully, more intensely, more consciously than before; a world where the old barriers to eager youth were down, where there was nothing that was not waiting to be achieved, and knowledge, experience, beauty, truth were there to be discovered and possessed by him who could get them. It was a belief, an intimation, common to that whole "pale, nervous, fiery generation" (in Alfred de Musset's phrase), "conceived between battles, educated in seminaries to the roll of drums"; and Berlioz in his remote corner of France, educated only briefly at the local seminary but reliving his uncle's fabulous tales, was subject to it too and would base his life on it.

The scars that his uncle showed on his return from the front were part of the mystique, though shrugged off with a laugh. Berlioz remembered them correctly. Félix Marmion had his nose and both lips cut by a sabre stroke when fighting the English at Chiclana outside Cadiz in March 1811, and a year and a half later he was shot through the left foot by a round of canister at the Battle of Borodino.

By that time the war had gone wrong. The Empire was degenerating inexorably. After the retreat from Moscow, in which the army of 700,000 that had invaded Russia six months before was all but annihilated (and in which Félix Marmion needed all his sanguine temperament and animal spirits to survive), conscription was for the first time ruthlessly enforced and the minimum age lowered from twenty to eighteen. The departure of recruits for Grenoble, led by the rapporteur of the National Guard, became a commonplace event at La Côte St André. France was feeling the cost of war with a vengeance now. The system was breaking down: agriculture was seriously undermanned, conscription openly resisted even by the peasants, taxes increasingly burdensome, trade in decline, and a corrupt administration scrambling to safeguard its position under the next régime. And by January 1814 the Grande Armée was fighting on French soil, bringing to its homeland the habit, too deeply ingrained to be given up, of feeding itself by plundering local resources.

As Dr Berlioz later noted in his Livre de Raison, "the result of all this confusion was the collapse of public morale and an intense hatred of the Emperor. The advent of the enemy was regarded as a blessing by a large number of Frenchmen. Means of defence were neglected. The generals themselves betrayed their trust to satisfy their grievances or to secure their fortune." Bonaparte, travelling south through France on his way to exile on Elba, was obliged to pass through Lyons at night, and eventually to go in the disguise of an Austrian officer.

News of his fall and the recall of the Bourbons reached La Côte early in April 1814. The town had been under occupation for a week by 20,000 Austrians, cavalry and infantry. The nervous citizens had hastened to comply with the order to hand over all weapons of any kind within twenty-four hours on pain of death — too precipitately, Dr Berlioz considered, since "no house-to-house search was made, and in any case it would have been easy to dismantle them and hide the pieces". As it was, "the enemy took the best for their own use and burned the rest". Altogether the occupation, which lasted ten weeks, cost the town fifty thousand francs. As a member of the council the doctor took his turn to serve as mayor on a rota which involved twenty-four hours' duty round the clock, and was also in charge of supplying a particular commodity — he does not say which — to the invading forces.

His anxieties did not end with the final departure of the Austrians on 5 June 1814. Joséphine Berlioz had been pregnant throughout the final chaotic months of the Empire, and had given birth to a daughter, Adèle, during the occupation. Under considerable stress, with foreign officers billeted on the house on top of other worries, she could not produce enough milk. The child was sickly, and there were fears for its life.

It was thus in an apprehensive mood that Louis Berlioz, on the first day of 1815, reviewed the state of his fortunes and of the nation's. True, not all was discouraging. There were signs that trade was beginning to pick up. In his own life he had some cause for satisfaction. Teaching his son Hector was proving a rewarding experience. And the monograph on blood-letting which he had entered for the Paris Medical Society's prize essay on the subject (and which in an earlier less developed form had won the Bordeaux Medical Society's prize some years before) had been commended and had resulted in the society's making him an associate member. But the future as a whole was dark with uncertainties. His children were constantly falling ill, so that he hardly dared go to Grenoble even for a few days. And the country was slow to recover from its recent traumas.

Tranquillity reigns in France; but it seems as though we no longer know how to enjoy it; the native liveliness of the French has yet to be reborn. The army continues to regret its leader. The people fear the clerical tithe and the restitution of émigré property [...] The great majority of Frenchmen are filled with devotion and respect for the King. They wish him a long reign, and all realise that he alone can consolidate our new political structure. On the other hand, they are afraid he may place too much confidence in the companions of his exile, and that all public positions will be overrun by the old nobility.

Encouraged — to the disgust of all sensible people — by the "absurd Duc de Berry and the arrogant Duchesse d'Angoulème", the old nobility were seizing every opportunity to humiliate the new.

In his biography of Berlioz, Adolphe Boschot insists on calling the doctor an "Ultra", or pure royalist, and makes much of the fact that Hector was brought up as "the son of an Ultra". Yet the words just quoted, and many similar expressions of opinion in the Livre de Raison, are the language not of an extremist but of a non-political conservative with a deep emotional commitment to law and order and a confirmed revulsion from violent controversy. In political crises "above all eschew Enthusiasm", he advises his children. The Ultra party was nothing if not violent in its opinions; and so far from pinning its faith on the King, it nicknamed him "the white Jacobin"* and regarded him and his ignoble Charter as having compromised criminally with the Left. Dr Berlioz had ultra friends among the gentry of Grenoble, like the Faure family (Roland Faure, one of those to whom he gave his medical services free, was a member of the reactionary parliament of 1816, the notorious "chambre introuvable"). But he was totally out of sympathy with the party's dream of putting the clock back to the ancien régime. He disliked it for the same reasons that he hated the Bonaparte of the later Empire and the Hundred Days: it made for social instability and interfered with freedom of thought.

As a young man he had been attracted to Republicanism. His first ardour had cooled (though, unlike the great majority of private individuals, he continued to date his letters by the official Republican calendar right up to its abolition by Napoleon), and it had been replaced by profound scepticism as to the likely benefits of drastic political action — in which progression of ideas his son would follow him. "The best government, generally speaking, is the government one has," he writes in the Livre de Raison; "it is very rarely that the people gain from changing it." As happens in middle life to most one-time reformists, his interest in a new order of society gave way before his interest in his property and his growing family, and his humanitarianism found its outlet in numerous acts of personal philanthropy. Society could be improved in small ways only. The King was the best hope for all classes. Neither the tiny

---

* "White", from the Bourbon flag, which had once more replaced the Tricolour.

revolutionary minority nor the émigrés and the priests, tiresome though they were, posed a serious threat. "One man alone was to be feared; and he came."

On 1 March 1815 Bonaparte landed in the Gulf of Juan with a thousand men and, avoiding hostile Provence, marched unopposed through the mountains to Grenoble, where he was received with acclamation. Opposition melted away; the troops sent to bar his route threw down their arms. He stayed a couple of days in Grenoble; then, while government newspapers continued to represent him as a fugitive bandit hounded from pillar to post by an enraged populace, resumed his triumphant progress. On the 9th he passed through the village of La Frette, two miles to the east of La Côte St André, travelling in an open barouche at a walking pace because of the crowds that came to see him riding by. From Lyons his march was "an eagle's flight". News of his arrival in Paris on the 20th reached the mairie of La Côte on the 22nd, but at first was not believed, and dismissed as a propaganda lie, so swift had been his coming.

The Berlioz household was in a turmoil of apprehension and excitement, like everyone else. Félix Marmion, since the previous October a captain, was once again on active service and fighting for his adored Emperor. Dr Berlioz was "torn between hope and despair, constantly bewailing the fate of my country and of my children, and cursing Buonaparte", but he fortified his resolution with a stoical quotation from Horace ("impavidum ferient ruinae") and vowed to "work calmly and coolly for the preservation of my family and fortune". He turned down the offer of a professorship in the new medical faculty that Napoleon had promised to set up in Grenoble as a reward for its loyalty: "in such circumstances a man of honour cannot accept any position of the kind".

In June came Waterloo, Napoleon's exile to St Helena, and the second Bourbon Restoration. This time the reaction was far more violent, and the atmosphere of reconciliation precariously established was shattered. In the département of Isère more than two hundred mayors were removed from office. Prefects encouraged "loyal subjects of the King" to denounce all troublemakers. Informing was rife. The "White Terror", worst in the far south but quite energetic in Dauphiné, persecuted those who had too openly sided with Bonaparte during the Hundred Days. Its excesses in turn drove into opposition and sometimes into conspiracy men who had been royalist in 1814. The département of Isère was disturbed by constant rumours of uprisings, a few of them genuine. In 1816 a disastrously bad spring and summer led to severe shortages and misery on a wide scale, itself provoking social unrest.

The burden of foreign invasion was also greater than the first time. La Côte St André suffered an occupation harsher than in 1814 and nearly twice as long. For four months, from early July till the end of October, the camp fires of the enemy were visible just outside the town to the west, and the nights were noisy with their songs. On top of an official requisition which obliged the citizens to do everything for their visitors, even repair their boots, looting was common. The Piedmontese behaved well (though they cut down many of Dr Berlioz's young mulberry trees for stakes and completely stripped the osiers and willows in the meadow to construct hutments), but the Hungarian hussars and the Cossacks were much less disciplined, and there were ugly incidents.[*] Feeding the conquerors was made more difficult by an epidemic of cattle disease, and a special commission, including the doctor, was set up to deal with the problem. A regular succession of officers were quartered on private houses throughout the town. Two young Piedmontese officers of the Acqui regiment stayed for a fortnight with Louis and Joséphine Berlioz, who were almost sorry to see them go, they had been such easy and interesting guests and had provided them with sorely needed distraction.

For the family had been stricken by a terrible loss. In April their beloved daughter Louise, aged seven, had caught a mild throat infection that was going round. At first it had seemed nothing to be alarmed at. When Dr Berlioz realised it was serious, he fought desperately to save her, but to no avail. Louise died, of a pharyngeal abscess, at 8 o'clock on the morning of 16 April.

Not long afterwards his father Louis-Joseph Berlioz fell ill. He declined steadily throughout May, June and July, his sons Louis and Auguste sharing the medical care of him. None of the many different remedies they tried was successful, and he died in Grenoble on 17 August.[†] Louis' family were then at Meylan, and he joined them there.

The double blow cast a pall of grief over Louis Berlioz. At the end of 1815, as he recorded the events of that dreadful year, he still wept uncontrollably. There were times when he felt ready to follow his dear ones. His little daughter Adèle, aged less than two, was ill with a very worrying cough and had been discovered to be asthmatic. And now to add to his anxieties there were fresh rumours of Napoleon's return (so persistent that Mayor Buffevent had to post a proclamation refuting them). He had, too, spent far more than he could afford. "The annual taxes have been virtually tripled. Moreover I spent two thousand four hundred francs on the repair and redecoration of the house. Without doubt the time was badly chosen; but my wife and I wanted distraction from the sadness of our thoughts. Alas, for me it was not very successful. My daughter, my father — tears prevent me from writing more."

---

[*] Perhaps it was after these Hungarians that the Berliozes named a new puppy Pandour (a Hungarian marauding soldier). We know of him from a letter to Louis Berlioz from Félix Marmion, reporting the eccentric behaviour of the wife of the general in command in Grenoble which earned her a public rebuke from her husband, whereupon "she went slinking abashed from the dance floor rather like Pandour the day we chased him out of your bedroom."

[†] Seemingly of kidney failure originating from gout.

How had these cruel events affected Hector, just turned twelve? What tears did they cost him? We cannot say. We know that for many years he would be close to his eldest sister, Nancy, and that he doted all his life on the youngest, Adèle, ten years his junior; but there is no record how much Louise had meant to him, or what his relationship had been with his paternal grandfather. In any case his childhood was on the point of ending; his existence was about to move into a new phase and, for us, from obscurity towards the light.

2

Episodes in the Early Life of an Artist

It is a move towards the light, not yet fully into it. A great deal remains shadowy. We see him in flashes. The discoverable facts of his boyhood are like the landmarks of a country only roughly mapped, or like fragments of an incomplete score; we have the main themes, but don't know how the piece goes. What follows is not an ordered, chronological narrative but a series of episodes.

The first comes from the latter end of childhood. In the spring of 1815, when he was eleven years old, Berlioz took his first communion, at the convent of the Visitation where his sister Nancy was a boarder. More than thirty years later he recalled the event as though it were yesterday. He had got up at dawn. At six o'clock the almoner of the convent, Monsieur Petit, came for him, and they walked westward along the empty street and out of the town.

> It was spring; the sun was smiling, a breeze played among the whispering poplars; some delicious fragrance filled the air. Trembling with emotion I crossed the sacred threshold and was admitted to the chapel. There, in the midst of my sister's young companions all dressed in white, I prayed with them and awaited the solemn moment. The priest came forward, Mass began; I belonged to God. I received a shock when the priest, with that boorish bias in favour of his own sex that certain men retain even at the Lord's table, beckoned me to come up to the altar first, ahead of those charming girls who, I felt, should go before me. However, I went up, blushing at the undeserved honour. As I took the sacrament a chorus of virginal voices broke into the eucharistic hymn, and I was filled with a mystic yet passionate unrest which I was powerless to hide from the congregation. I thought I saw Heaven open, a Heaven of love and chaste delight, a thousand times purer and more beautiful than the one I had so often been told about.

The music that precipitated this moment of ecstasy — he was amused and pleased to discover some years later — was "Quand le bien-aimé reviendra", "When my sweetheart comes back", an artless lilting air from Dalayrac's opera *Nina, or The Woman Crazed with Love*, adapted to the words of the liturgy (a common practice in the church at the time); he recognised the tune when he heard it at the Paris Opéra. But its simplicity and freshness went straight to his heart as he knelt in the chapel, already moved by the solemnity of the occasion, the young girls in their white dresses and the beauty of the spring morning outside, agitated by the unexpected action of the priest, and in that light-headed and highly responsive nervous state brought on in young adolescents by getting up very early and going to communion on an empty stomach.

It was, he says, his first musical experience; and he acknowledged the symbolic aptness of the fact when he chose it to begin his autobiography. Learning to play the flute and read at sight comes later. From the outset music, to him, means drama; it means a ceremonial art, with power to give expression and form to the central moments of life.

With the first communion belong two episodes from later in his boyhood which give us a further glimpse of the future artist in embryo. The catalyst, again, is music experienced in a context of religious ritual. The earlier of the two, dating from several years after the event just described, also took place in church. He recalled it forty years later, at the time of the composition of *The Trojans*, in a letter in which he speaks of his long familiarity with the *Æneid* and its characters, of having "spent his life with that race of demi-gods"; to show how they "fascinated him from the first", he recounts an incident of his boyhood:

It was during the time in my classical education when, under my father's direction, I was construing the marvellous twelfth book of the *Æneid*; my imagination was possessed by the splendour of its characters: Lavinia, Turnus, Æneas, Mezentius, Lausus, Pallas, Evander, Amata, Latinus, Camilla and the rest. I became like a sleepwalker, "living within my dream's bright kingdom" (to borrow a line from Victor Hugo). One Sunday I was taken to Vespers. The sad persistent chant of the psalm *In exitu Israel* produced the magnetic effect on me that it still produces today, and plunged me into the most lifelike daydreams of the past. I recognised my Virgilian heroes, I heard the clash of their arms, I saw Camilla the beautiful Amazon running, I watched Lavinia, flushed with shame, weeping, and poor Turnus, and his father Daunus and his sister Juturna, I heard the great palaces of Laurentium ring with lamentation — and an immense feeling of grief came over me, my chest tightened, I left the church in floods of tears, and cried the rest of the day, unable to contain my epic affliction; no one could ever get me to confess the reason for it, my parents never knew, had no inkling, what sorrows had seized my childish heart that day.

The other incident takes place out of doors; but the context is again that of religious ritual, and again a liturgical chant brings on the crisis. Here, he is describing the first time he was attacked by the classic malaise of the Romantics — "the cruel malady — psychological, nervous, imaginary, what you will — that I will call the disease of isolation ['mal d'isolement']":

> One fine May morning when I was sixteen, I was sitting in a field at La Côte St André, in the shade of a group of large oak-trees, reading a novel by Montjoye called *Manuscript Found at Mount Posilippo*. Absorbed though I was in my reading, my attention was distracted by the faint plaintive sounds of singing coming across the plain at regular intervals. The Rogation procession was passing nearby; the voices I heard were the peasants', chanting the litany of the saints. This time-honoured visitation of the hillsides and the plains in springtime, to ask for heaven's blessing on the fruits of the earth, has something poetic and touching about it that moves me inexpressibly. The procession halted at the foot of a wooden cross decorated with leaves; I saw the people kneel while the priest blessed the land. Then it moved slowly off and the melancholy chanting resumed.
>
> From time to time our old curé's quavering voice was clearly audible, with snatches of phrase:
>
> > Conservari digneris
> > (*The peasants*) Te rogamus, audi nos!
>
> And the pious throng passed on, further and further into the distance.
> > (*Decrescendo*)
> > Sancte Barnaba,
> > Ora pro nobis!
> > (*Perdendo*)
> > Sancta Magdalena,
> > Ora pro ...
> > Sancta Maria,
> > Ora ...
> > Sancta ...
> > ... nobis.
> > ......
>
> Silence ... rustle of young wheat swaying in the light morning wind ... cry of amorous quail calling to their mates ... a bunting, full of joy, singing from the top of a poplar tree ... an intense peacefulness ... a dead leaf falling slowly from one of the oaks ... the dull beat of my own heart ... Life, surely, was outside me, far away, very far ... On the horizon the Alpine glaciers reflected the rays of the mounting sun in great flashes of light ... Over there lay Meylan ... beyond the Alps Italy, Naples, Posilippo ... the characters in my book ... burning passions ... some secret unfathomable happiness ... Away, away! Oh for wings, to devour distance! I must see, admire, I must know love, rapture, the flame of an embrace, I must live life to its limits! ... but I am but an earthbound clod. These characters are imaginary, or exist no longer ... What love? ... What fame? ... What heart? ... Where is my star, my *Stella montis*? Vanished no doubt for ever ... When shall I see Italy?
>
> And the fit burst forth in all its fury; I suffered agonies, and lay on the

ground groaning, convulsively tearing up handfuls of grass and wide-eyed innocent daisies, struggling against the sensation of *absence*, against an appalling *isolation*.

How clearly these two passages speak of Berlioz's music, or rather what echoes of it they arouse! How much of it, we can say with hindsight, is already present, both generally and specifically, style and content, particular works and the climate and atmosphere of his art!

In the second passage it is as if he were describing one of his own compositions. The shimmer of the wheatfield, the crying quail and the spacious shining landscape recall the slow movement of the Fantastic Symphony, with its viola tremolo and piping woodwind calls and sense of wide horizons: a movement which in its musical idiom powerfully reflects the influence of Beethoven, especially of the Pastoral Symphony, but which undoubtedly draws on recollections of that first attack of spiritual isolation that fell upon him out of a clear sky in a field at La Côte St André, ten years earlier. The emotional storm that breaks forth in the middle of the movement — the melody struggling to free itself and take wing, the trembling fortissimo chords and convulsive syncopations rising to a violent climax, then subsiding into sobs as the paroxysm ebbs — is an unmistakable rendering in musical terms of the state described in the autobiographical account. A comparison that Berlioz once made between this Adagio and the Adagio in *Romeo and Juliet* is pertinent here. They evoked, he said, two different states of love: the *Romeo* Adagio the warm expansive love of the south, the Fantastic the desolate unhappy love of the north. "In the one it is love in the *presence* of the beloved object; in the other, love in the *absence* of the creature whom he asks for from all Nature."

The chanting of the peasants in the Rogation procession recalls another Berlioz score, *The Damnation of Faust*. "Sancta Magdalena, ora pro nobis. Sancta Maria, ora pro nobis": the words strike a bell. They are the litany of the peasants kneeling at a wayside cross, whose chant ironically punctuates the last stage of Faust's road to hell — that progress of an ardent, baffled soul towards total isolation that is the subject of the work. The chant itself, as Berlioz himself indirectly tells us, was one that he used to hear in his boyhood. In the chapter of the *Memoirs* on Italian musical life he quotes it as an example of a litany from a different, non-Italian culture, that of his native Dauphiné, and heads it "tune from La Côte St André". We can thus, as it were, find the music for one of the crucial episodes in his early life, and establish another link between his boyhood and the art of his maturity.

In other ways too the Rogation procession — a rite that originated not far from La Côte, in the fifth century — left deep impressions on his consciousness. Not only is it an ancestor of several movements in which religious processions approach and then move away: the Pilgrims' March in *Harold in Italy*, the Prayer in Act 3 of *Benvenuto Cellini*, the entry of the Wooden Horse in *The Trojans*. More generally, it anticipates two typical features of his musical idiom: the protracted diminuendo ending and the unvaried chant or "monotone".

Berlioz often ends a movement or a work "perdendo", the notes growing fainter and fainter, sometimes separated by longer and longer silences. Think of the Pilgrims' March; the ebbing clarinet melody that floats above the shuddering strings in the epilogue to *The Death of Orpheus*; Hylas the homesick sailor in the fifth act of *The Trojans* falling asleep before his song is complete; the dwindling voices of the reapers as they pass on their way home from the fields in *Sara la baigneuse*; the barely audible rocking of the cellos at the end of the fourth *Nuits d'été* song, "Sur les lagunes", as the boat moves onwards into the night, leaving the widening ripples of its wake on the empty sea.

In particular he loves the long musical vista, as a body of sound passes gradually out of earshot — but nearly always, however quiet the music, charged with a feeling of momentousness and fatality. The effect may be mysterious, as in the Roman sentinels' march in *The Childhood of Christ*. Or it may be vividly dramatic: for example, the finale of Act 3 of *The Trojans*, where the rapid diminuendo suggests a great throng of people pouring forth to war, or the Prix de Rome cantata *Herminie*, where the melody of Erminia's prayer for Tancred's safety hangs on the air while the hoofbeats of her galloping horse recede, or the chorus of students and soldiers which closes Part 2 of *The Damnation of Faust*, where the long column winds from sight, leaving, for all its rowdy high spirits, an atmosphere of desolation. In the Pilgrims' March the diminuendo conveys the sense of a solitary observer left behind in the midst of a wide landscape, listening as the procession moves away into the deepening dusk.

Equally characteristic is the construction of a movement around a short phrase of unvarying pitch. Berlioz's music is full of such monotones. They spring to mind at the mention of his name: the single-note chant repeated with the insistence of a bell throughout the Funeral Procession in *Romeo and Juliet*; the cicada-like pulsation of woodwind and horn in the Septet in Act 4 of *The Trojans*; the dark lament of violins and horns sending waves of pain over the smooth surface of the harbour in "Sur les lagunes"; the monastery bells that sound at intervals across the Pilgrims' March, summoning the music back to the home key; the immemorial cry, fragmentary, unchanging, of the souls in purgatory in the Offertorium of the Grande Messe des Morts.

Such movements testify to the lasting impact of ancient liturgical chant on Berlioz's mind. And to it too may be traced one more characteristic of his music: the addiction to the minor or flattened sixth, that note beloved of the Romantics but so particularly personal to Berlioz as to be a sort of trademark or fingerprint. Four of the five monotones just cited exemplify it. The minor sixth – often given special emphasis by being introduced as an alien note, "like a worm i' the bud", into a major key – is found right through his work. It is present in the last piece he composed, the Distant Chorus in *Beatrice and Benedict*, and in his earliest surviving manuscripts, his accompaniments to popular romances and his own hesitant attempts at song-writing. Its source was the modal chants of the church. The melodic sigh of a rising and falling semitone – the fifth followed by the sixth, then the fifth again – is the salient feature not only of the Rogation litany but of the "tonus peregrinus", the plainchant – old as Charlemagne – to which the Vespers psalm "In exitu Israel" was sung. For evidence of the direct influence of this chant and its plaintive sixth on the young Berlioz we need only look at the song he wrote as a boy to some verses in Florian's pastoral *Estelle et Némorin*: "Je vais donc quitter pour jamais / Mon doux pays, ma douce amie" – the theme familiar from the opening of the Fantastic Symphony.

As to the connection in Berlioz's mind between the tonus peregrinus and the *Æneid*, it needs no divining, as we have seen. This was the "sad persistent chant" that called up, that Sunday at Vespers, the dazzling vision of Virgilian heroes which overwhelmed his "childish heart". The remembered chant was still "producing the same magnetic effect" on him forty years later while he composed *The Trojans*. Its effect is manifest in the opera. In no music does the minor sixth carry so intense an expression of grief, above all in the scene of Dido's despair, "Je vais mourir dans ma douleur submergée". We know that experiences such as the one in the church at La Côte were the springs from which the opera flowed; the work, in his own words, was written to "satisfy a passion that flamed up in my childhood". "Is it not a strange and marvellous manifestation of the force of genius?" he goes on, in the letter (already quoted) that describes the power of Virgil over his youthful imagination and the vision he had at Vespers; "a poet dead thousands of years shakes an ignorant, artless boy to the depths of his soul [. . .] with scenes whose radiance devouring time is powerless to weaken." Ignorant and artless he may have been; but the sympathy with suffering that is the mark of so much of his finest music, the sense of the tragic, the response to the past, were already alive in him. His imagination had contact with the unending generations of human life distilled in an old modal chant, a landscape shaped by human hands, a line of verse.

One further episode in which the destiny of the future artist is shaped again concerns the *Æneid*:

[Virgil] was the first to find the way to my heart and fire my nascent imagination. How often as I construed the fourth book of the *Æneid* for my father did I feel my heart swell and my voice falter and break! One day, already disturbed from the very beginning of my oral translation by the line "At regina gravi jamdudum saucia cura" ["For some time now the queen, restless with love's cares"], I arrived after a fashion at the turning-point of the drama. But when I came to the scene where Dido dies on her pyre, surrounded by the gifts and the weapons of the false-hearted Æneas, and pours forth on the bed — "that bed with all its memories" — the angry stream of her life-blood; when I had to speak the despairing utterances of the dying queen, "thrice raising herself upon her elbow, thrice falling back", to describe her wound and the fatal love that convulsed her to the depths of her being, the cries of her sister, her nurse, her distracted women, and that agony so terrible that the gods themselves are moved and send Iris to end it, my lips trembled and the mumbled words would scarcely come. At last, at the line "Quæsivit cœlo lucem ingemuitque reperta" — at that sublime image of Dido "looking for light to the sky and moaning when she found it" — I was seized with a nervous shuddering and, in the impossibility of going on, stopped dead.

It was one of the occasions when I was most grateful for my father's unutterable kindness. Seeing how embarrassed and confused I was by such an emotion, he pretended not to have noticed it, and getting up abruptly he shut the book. "That's enough, my boy", he said; "I'm tired." And I ran off, out of sight of all, to give myself up to my Virgilian grief.

3

Dream Kingdoms

Exactly why, and when, Dr Berlioz became his son's teacher is not certain. Perhaps the realisation of Hector's unusual intelligence made him want to have a hand in developing and shaping it. (Later he would undertake part at least of the education of his daughters Nancy and Adèle and his youngest son Prosper.) But he may have turned teacher to begin with in response to circumstances. La Côte St André seems to have been without public education for a time. The local school, run by the church and housed in the former monastery of the Franciscan Order of the Recollection on the eastern outskirts of the town, closed in the summer of 1814. By an Imperial decree of November 1811 schooling throughout France was supposed to have been taken over by state-subsidised lycées, but the petit-séminaire at La Côte remained in ecclesiastical hands for another two and a half years. It was to this school, two hundred yards down the main street from his father's house, that Hector was sent: by his own account when he was ten — that is, some time in 1814 — and in order to learn Latin. According to the same account he had not been there long when his father removed him, "having decided to undertake my education himself". That would tally with the temporary closure of the school in July 1814; and it would be quite natural that Berlioz in later years should remember the fact of his leaving the school and having his lessons at home, but not the cause of it. By the time the school reopened Dr Berlioz was too deeply involved to send him back.

This chronology was challenged by one of Berlioz's first biographers, Edmond Hippeau. In about 1880 Hippeau talked to two of his former schoolfellows, Charles Bert, who became a doctor, and Joseph Favre, son of the clog-maker of La Côte. They both maintained that Hector went to the petit-séminaire much later than he said, and that he remained there for several years. They remembered him as having been a vigorous drummer, leading his class when the school marched in procession or paraded on the nearby Esplanade, and also a dedicated practical-joker, given among other pranks to setting off fire-crackers, and on one occasion being accused of trying to blow the place up. (Perhaps his father was asked to take him away.) The practical joking sounds more like a teenager

59

than a boy of ten. But Favre was over eighty and Bert in his late seventies by the time they talked to Hippeau; they were recalling events of more than sixty years earlier. Against their testimony must be set the clear recollection of the man himself: he learned his Virgil, his Horace, his La Fontaine, his geography, as well as his first anatomy, from his father.

That Hector's Latin and French lessons took place at home is also implicit in a letter of the 1820s from his sister Nancy (written in verse, in the manner of their grandfather), in which she reminds him of their childhood together in the paternal home — halcyon, already far-off days when the only cloud in their sky was having to "memorise our *Fables* and translate Horace and Virgil". The certificate of Berlioz's baccalauréat, which he took in Grenoble in 1821, clearly states that he studied his Philosophy and Rhetoric "dans la maison de son père". This is in contrast to nearly two thirds of the surviving contemporary certificates, in which the two subjects are listed as having been studied in one of the local schools. (Where the candidate has done so privately, the words "with a tutor" are often added — a not uncommon practice among the well-to-do — but they are absent from Berlioz's diploma. Private tutors were employed in the Berlioz household from time to time. Even the learned and resourceful Dr Berlioz couldn't teach his children everything; thus the Livre de Raison's list of expenses for the year 1819 includes the items "Maître de mathématique" and "Maître de danse".) In sum, whenever it was that Hector attended the petit-séminaire, there is no doubt that a large part of his schooling was carried on at home.

Louis Berlioz's decision to be his son's teacher had profound consequences. Looking back on his upbringing Berlioz concluded that not being educated at school was a handicap: one led too sheltered an existence, instead of getting inured early to the realities of life. This undoubtedly made it difficult for him when (in his own words) still "an awkward, unworldly child", he first tried to make his way in Paris. But the advantages were greater. By being taught at home, by a teacher of catholic interests and undulled curiosity, he developed young a wide-ranging mind and a habit of independent thought; and he avoided the moulding processes of orthodox education which, in France especially, can be fatal to the growth of imagination and to what Stendhal called "the *horde of felt emotions* that schooling not only does not form but prevents from being formed".

The education Berlioz received helped to foster in him at an early age an intensely active imaginative life. His father was not a hard taskmaster. He preferred to suggest, not impose. In the words of Ferdinand Hiller, to whom Berlioz often talked about his childhood, Hector was "intellectually stimulated without being overtaxed [...] The boy was left to himself a great deal, and could give rein to his inclination for daydreaming in the presence of Nature."

"More perhaps than was good for him," the prudent Hiller adds.

Certainly the force, the tenacity of his imagination would play havoc with his personal happiness and ensure that fulfilment in love, contentment, peace would for ever elude him. "My whole life", he told Pauline Viardot in 1859,

> has been one long, ardent pursuit of an ideal that I created for myself. My heart, eager for love, declared itself instantly whenever it found one of the qualities, one of the charms belonging to that ideal. Alas, disillusionment quickly followed and showed me that I had been mistaken.

"Accursed faculty that makes our life a perpetual mirage!" he exclaims in self-mockery on discovering the Feast of Corpus Christi in Rome to be a mean and shoddy affair, grotesquely unlike the modern equivalent of the grand musical rites in Ancient Egypt or the Temple of Solomon that he had imagined. "You are a man dominated by the imagination," he writes to a friend, "therefore you are an infinitely unhappy man." Yet for the creative artist this faculty, this capacity for conceiving extreme states of love, grief, ecstasy, alienation, and experiencing them within himself, was the source of his being: to it he owed not only the intensity of his music but also the protean variety it embraces. The works of no composer are more different one from another. Each one has a feel, a colour and dramatic atmosphere, unique to itself; each inhabits its own poetic world. In creating each he was absorbed into it, he became it, and "lived within his dream's bright kingdom". This power of empathy was learned in childhood, in the uninhibited cultivation of a hyper-vivid imagination, and in the books he read and re-read and brooded on during the long hours of "day-dreaming alone in the presence of Nature". Most adolescents have daydreams. Few pursue them, or are able to separate their dream figures from their own ego and personify them, so that they take on a life of their own and the dreamer can actually "hear the clash of their arms and the palaces of Laurentium ringing with lamentation, and see Camilla the beautiful Amazon running", see the dying Dido struggling to raise herself, and feel her agony of spirit in his spirit.

The sense of the tragic and the heroic, which we can only say was an instinct that he was born with, was fed by his reading: the *Æneid* above all, but also Plutarch's prosaic tales of the great figures of antiquity, Rollin's Roman history, Lhomond's *De viris illustribus urbis Romæ*, and the passages in *Génie du Christianisme* where Chateaubriand discusses the tragic passions of the ancient world.

Berlioz's literary education may be charted in some detail. He himself, directly or indirectly, tells us a good deal about it. There is also the inventory of the books in his father's library given at the beginning of the Livre de Raison, supplemented by a further list from the time of the sale of the library after the doctor's death, since lost but cited by Hippeau. And there is the baccalauréat certificate of 1821.

The sources tend to corroborate each other. Virgil and Horace are the Latin authors the *Memoirs* say his father made him study and learn lines from by heart for his daily lessons; and it is a passage from Horace's *Poetics* and two from the *Æneid*, together with a paragraph of Cicero's *Pro Archia*, that he is asked to translate for his bac. One of the Virgil excerpts is from Book VI: Æneas, guided down to Hades by the Sybil, approaching the Styx and seeing the multitude of the dead press forward, "their hands stretched out in longing for the further shore". The other comes from the capture of Troy in Book II; it is the scene where Cassandra is dragged from Minerva's sanctuary, "her brilliant eyes uplifted to heaven — her eyes alone, for her hands were chained", and Corebus leads a desperate attempt to rescue her.

Again, we read in the *Memoirs* that in his fascination for Asia and the South Seas — a lifelong passion conceived from the great atlas he found in his father's library — he neglected to study the geography of his native country: "My father used to say of me, rightly, that I 'knew the name of every one of the Sandwich Islands, the Moluccas, the Philippines, and was thoroughly familiar with the Torres Strait, with Timor, Java and Borneo, yet could not so much as tell you how many départements there are in France.'" And in the bac certificate, under "Geography", he is awarded a "médiocre" for "Rivers of France, course of the Loire and the Rhone".

The books he mentions having got to know in his youth duly figure in the inventory of the library: La Fontaine's *Fables*, Florian's *Estelle et Némorin*, the works of Cervantes, Plutarch's *Lives*, Montjoye's *Manuscrit trouvé au Mont Pausilype*, D'Alembert's *Elémens de musique théorique et pratique*, Bernardin de St Pierre's *Paul et Virginie*, Volney's *Voyage en Syrie et en Egypte* and Humboldt's *Tableaux de la Nature* among others.

To read them over his shoulder, and in the light of what we know of his subsequent ideas and sensibilities, is to be confronted with countless correspondences. Some are superficial, and spotting them no more than a game, amusing to play but hardly instructive (easy though it may be, for instance, to imagine young Hector's indignation at reading in Plutarch of the disdain in which superior Athenians like Alcibiades and Antisthenes held his own instrument, the flute). At other times it is as if we were watching the impression forming in the wax of his consciousness; we can as it were draw the map of his imaginative world as it came into being. For with Berlioz the impression persisted; it did not become overlaid in adult life or "fade into the light of common day". The intimate interaction between life and books characteristic of him as an adult was established in his youth. It was not simply that he imitated what he read. He was himself René, calling on Nature to give him the beloved that his whole being craved; he was Némorin, prone and clutching the earth in the convulsions of grief; he was Rousseau's Saint-Preux, forgetting his agitations, breathing more serenely, in the grandeur and pure cool air of the mountains.

Even Montjoye's cloak-and-dagger novel of love, honour and revenge in mid-eighteenth-century Spain has its "Berliozian" texts: Paris as a city that swarms with musicians, yet whose natives are of all peoples the most bereft of natural musical feeling; the violence and susceptibility of the mob, eternal dupe of impostors, never pausing to consider until it has already destroyed the object of its momentary fury; the dedication of Western man to passionate, total, incurable love. In sharing the hero's deep and aching melancholy over the sudden loss of his dearest friend, he would have thought of himself and his close companion Imbert, his music teacher's son, whose loss he mourned. And when he read, of one of the characters, that his face bore the honourable scar of a sabre-cut received at Cadiz, it was his Uncle Félix to the life — the same wound exactly, the same town. I say "even" Montjoye's novel, because the one comment ever made about it is that it is a "mauvais roman". In fact *Manuscrit trouvé au Mont Pausilype* is a perfect example of the "good bad" novel. With its skilfully sustained atmosphere of mystery and intrigue, its saturnine, sharply drawn villains (notably the Mephistophelean soldier of fortune Ratziouski) opposed by recklessly chivalrous heroes, and its swift action and frequent changes of scene (emphasised by the narrative's letter form), it is a book to rivet any right-minded teenager.

It was one of several books with Spanish settings which fostered in Berlioz his imaginative extremism, his "espagnolisme", to borrow Stendhal's word for the cult of heroism, beauty, unheeding generosity of heart, regardless of calculations of personal advantage: a cult common enough among adolescents, but which in Berlioz, as in Stendhal, was never outgrown, making both of them pass in the eyes of solid men of the world for hopelessly naïve, inexperienced children.

The supreme expression of the cult was *Don Quixote*, that "triumphant yet tragic apology for heroic illusion" which, against every expectation that we have of it when we first begin to read the tales of the old lunatic's fatuous adventures, ends by establishing their profound meaningfulness and showing us that "nothing in the external world — whatever power of giving buffets it may have — is as real as the passion, or the mania, or the illusion, that we each of us carry in our own head" (John Cowper Powys).

Like every sympathetic reader before or since, but with particular intensity, Hector identified with the Don, "born by Heaven's will in this Age of Iron to revive the Golden Age, he for whom are reserved the perils, the great exploits, the valiant deeds". His heart beat in time with many pertinent scenes and sentiments: Don Quixote picturing the first encounter between the knight-errant and his lady-love — gazing into one another's eyes until, without knowing how or why, they find themselves enmeshed in love's inextricable net, yet with a deep pain in their hearts, unable to express in words their desires and longings — or their first separation, or the passage, as memorable for its robust common sense as for its enthusiasm, in which Cervantes defended "men renowned for their genius, great poets, famous historians", against the envy of "those who take a delight in finding fault":

> I could wish these censors [...] would pay a little less attention to the spots on the bright sun of the works they are criticising. For if *aliquando bonus dormitat Homerus*, let them reflect how much of the time he spent awake, shedding the light of his genius with the least possible shadow. It may well be that what seem flaws to them are like the moles which sometimes enhance the beauty of a face.

There was the scene where Don Quixote stays at an inn in a room decorated with painted hangings depicting the abduction of Helen and the tragic tale of Dido and Æneas, the sight of which prompts him to observe that had he but lived then, Troy would not have burned nor Carthage have been destroyed, for he would have slain Paris and all those calamities would have been avoided.

The young Hector also noted with interest the Don's admonition to the Man in the Green Greatcoat whose son, in defiance of his father, wants to give up his scholastic studies and devote himself to poetry: "You should let your son go where his star calls him." And in the *Life of Cervantes* that prefaces Florian's adaptation of *Galatea* he read of Cervantes' having become a writer against the wishes of his parents, who intended him for medicine or the priesthood.

Florian was a special favourite of his early adolescence. His pastoral idylls of shepherds and shepherdesses making gentle, sexless love beside purling flower-fringed brooks, or expiring of unrequited passion in obscure grots far from the haunts of men, have not worn well, and the adult Berlioz duly came to recognise their feebleness. But in his early teens the fork of his imagination vibrated to their touch. They represented his first and persistent idea of love, of constancy carried to the tomb, of feelings so intense that without the tears they precipitated one's being could not survive them. Their lovelorn shepherds wandered through landscapes he could identify with his own, playing the flute and dreaming of the absent fair.

Most of all Florian to him meant the pastoral novel *Estelle et Némorin*. He had discovered it in his father's library and "read and re-read it secretly a hundred times". Before he ever set eyes on Estelle Dubeuf, his "morning star", the presiding deity of his life, he was Némorin, adoring in imagination his dark-eyed, black-haired shepherdess but parted from her, to be reunited at last after a long and harrowing separation; he was the unhappy shepherd, seated in the shade of a sycamore, his head in his hands, his flute left unregarded at his feet, while his dog crouched beside him, gazing at him with anxious, tender eyes; he was the blessed lover walking with his beloved beside the river's winding course, through groves of young fig-trees and acacias, across turf dotted with iris and narcissus, while pomegranate blossom scented the spring air and beyond the valley's wooded slopes snow-covered peaks closed the far horizon. He learned that "the flame which consumes and gives life kindles but once" (and, Florian is careful to add, "pure souls sacrifice it to virtue"); "this irresistible attraction, this swift impulse of every thought and feeling towards a single object, these mortal fears, fierce hopes, bottomless griefs, belong to first love alone."

Later he tasted the much stronger meat of Rousseau's *Julie, ou la nouvelle Héloïse*. In the Preface to his own *Memoirs* Berlioz made fun of the Rousseau of the *Confessions*, "appearing 'before God, book in hand' and declaring himself 'the best of men'". But what chords the novel's long, palpitating narrative struck in his youthful fancy and how eagerly he absorbed its wealth of observations on nature and art. The resonant descriptions of Alpine landscapes were easily assimilated to his expeditions above Meylan and Murianette, and the account of the sublime effect of mountains on the spirit seemed an echo of his experience. Then, there was this telling passage on the power of dramatic music, to quicken his lately awakened instincts:

> But when, after a series of pleasant airs, they came to those grand expressive pieces which depict the tumult of passionate emotion, I forgot singing, imitation, music itself: I was listening to the very voice of grief, of rapture, of despair; I could see the weeping mothers, the betrayed lovers, the raging tyrants; and in the agitation of my feelings was scarce able to remain still in my place. I realised then why this same music which before had bored me now roused me to exaltation. It was because I had begun to understand it; and the moment it was able to act on me it did so with all its force. No, Julie, one does not experience such sensations by halves. They are extreme or they are nothing — never moderate or merely lukewarm. One has either to remain impervious, or let oneself be moved immeasurably. Either it is the empty babble of a language of which one understands not one word, or it is an overwhelming sensation which sweeps one away and which one's soul is powerless to resist.

Such sensations were not open to all; they were the patrimony of those who had been granted "the fatal gift of a soul that feels".

> He that has received it must expect naught but pain and sorrow on this earth [...] He will be the victim of prejudice. Absurd conventions will stand in the way of the just aspirations of his heart [...] But he will also be capable of creating his own misery, by his reckless attachment to the truthful and the beautiful while the heavy chains of necessity drag him back

to earth. He will look for supreme happiness, without recollecting that he is a man. His heart and his reason will be constantly at odds, and the boundlessness of his desires will store up for him frustrations without end.

It could be a summary of Berlioz's life.

Of all the texts of his upbringing the most specifically prophetic is the *Æneid*. We have seen how the recital of Dido's woes moved him, and how a mental evocation of Book XII, prompted by an ancient psalm-chant, was enough to precipitate an emotional crisis, one Sunday afternoon at Vespers in the church at La Côte St André. Much more, of course, was involved in the genesis of *The Trojans* than a childhood fascination recalled in middle age. The intimate knowledge of all twelve books that he drew on to write the opera came from a lifetime's reading; the *Æneid* remained to him a companion, and Virgil himself a friend whom not to have known in the flesh was a real and keen regret. But the sense of personal affinity with poet and poem was already active in these years. Though Berlioz's later references to his childhood mention only Books IV and XII, the baccalauréat certificate cites II and VI; and it is likely that the whole epic became familiar territory to him. It was a world of mystery and beauty, passion, high deeds and fabulous adventures. Once the barrier of language had been crossed, a young reader need never tire of exploring it: for its action – the death of Laocoön, Troy's fall, the Trojan Games in Sicily, Turnus in mortal combat with Æneas; for its marvellous descriptive passages – the numinous bay enclosed by wooded crags where the shipwrecked fleet makes landfall on the North African coast, Dido's radiant progress through Carthage to the temple of Juno, the boats gliding up the sylvan Tiber to the Arcadian kingdom of Evander, the wan shingly wastes of the great Stygian mere; for its unforgettably evocative visual images – Æneas, from the roof of his house, seeing the flames of burning Troy reflected right across the straits of Sigeum, the God of Sleep "parting the darkness" and slipping down to the doomed Palinurus while the ship sails serenely on through the starry night, Dido in Hades turning away from Æneas into the glimmer of the forest without a word, the shades of dead Greek warriors, roused by the gleam of Æneas' breastplate, opening their mouths to give their war-cries but producing only a faint whimper; for its shafts of compassion, when the perspective of the epic alters to show the fate of the survivors – the forlorn huddle of captive women and children in the courtyard of Priam's palace, Andromache in Epirus weeping over the rites of her long-dead husband, Dido writhing in the terrible protracted agony of her sleepless nights. And beyond the griefs of individuals and the graphic violence of their deaths, the vision of a golden age – as yet he formulated it in boyish terms — "when the heroes, sons of the gods, wore splendid armour and cast finely wrought javelins, their glittering points set in a ring of gold".

There were also Chateaubriand's evocations of Virgil to pore over — Virgil "the friend of the solitary, companion in life's secret hours", creator of an incomparably sad music. The section of *Génie du Christianisme* devoted to "Passionate Love" contained a series of chapters in which Dido's state of mind as portrayed in the *Æneid* was analysed and compared with that of Héloïse, Rousseau's Julie and Racine's Phèdre, among other tragic heroines of the Christian era. Later in the same book, under "The Poetics of Christianity", a chapter on "The Marvellous, or Poetry and Its Treatment of Supernatural Beings" compared Æneas' dream in Book II with Athalie's in Racine's play. Though Chateaubriand's purpose here was to demonstrate the deepening and intensification that the coming of Christianity had brought to man's consciousness and imaginative perception, he did not stint his admiration for the pagan poet. Hector read that the dream was

a sort of epitome of Virgil's genius, comprising within a narrow span all the different kinds of beauty that are peculiar to him. Note, to begin with, the contrast between this fearful vision and the tranquil hour at which the gods send it to Æneas. (No one establishes time and place more touchingly than the poet of Mantua.) [. . .] From this melancholy contrast comes the truth that Nature accomplishes her laws untroubled by man's puny revolutions.

Thence we pass to the depiction of Hector's shade. The phantom contemplating Æneas in silence, its "great tears", its "swollen feet", are the details that a master painter selects to make his subject take life before our eyes. Æneas' cry: *quantum mutatus ab illo!* is a hero's exclamation, enhancing the grandeur of Hector. *Squalentem barbam et concretos sanguine crines* ["matted beard, hair clotted with blood"]: behold the ghost. But Virgil makes a sudden and characteristic change: *Vulnera . . . circum plurima muros accepit patrios.* Everything is in that: eulogy of Hector, remembrance of his woes and those of his country for which he received "so many wounds" [. . .] Then the silence of Hector, his deep sigh, followed by *fuge, eripe flammis*, make our hair stand on end. The final touch of the picture combines dream and vision in a doubly poetic image: it is as if, in bearing in its arms the statue of Vesta and the sacred flame, the ghost were bearing away Troy from the face of the earth.

In Chateaubriand's *Génie du Christianisme, ou Beautés de la religion chrétienne* appear, combined and emphasised, most of the leading themes of the adolescent Berlioz's imaginative life: religion, love, literature, the poetry of Nature, the romance of distant lands, nostalgia for the ancient world, Romantic melancholy.

Beyond its specific purpose, *Génie du Christianisme* set a current of sympathy flowing between the author and a whole generation of young

French men and women, kindling their imaginations over a wide range of feelings and ideas: the power of the great epic writers, Nature in its immense diversity and grandeur, the poetry of ruins, the spell of the distant past, the beauty of immemorial popular rituals and the haunting melancholy of the music accompanying them, the pangs of awakening consciousness and the ardours and perils of the solitary adolescent soul. More than any other work, it was the primer of early French Romanticism.

Berlioz, like hundreds of others, steeped himself in it. He enjoyed the celebratory accounts of writers he admired, especially Virgil and Bernardin de St Pierre. And from a footnote to a discussion of the latter he copied out a passage about the death of the young poet André Chénier, guillotined in 1792, who on the scaffold, it was said, exclaimed — striking his forehead: "To die, when I had something here!"

No less, he revelled in the long, sonorous passages of natural description, inserted by Chateaubriand as illustrations of the immanence of God in all things ("one does not return an unbeliever from the kingdoms of wild Nature"). The accounts of the author's voyage in America were meat and drink to him, feeding the curiosity about remote countries that had first been aroused before the atlas in his father's library and then intensified by the many travel books that the library contained. The southern hemisphere — especially South-East Asia and the islands of the Pacific Ocean — was his chief delight; but he loved too to visit in imagination the great forests and rivers and cataracts that Chateaubriand evoked. He visualised the herds of bison on their tumultuous yet orderly migration over the plains of Louisiana; the little fleets of black squirrels crossing a lake with their tails hoisted for sails; a rattlesnake charmed into gentleness by the sound of a flute played by a Canadian Indian, during a journey among the Onondaga tribe; the splendour of the American night and its sense of illimitable space, such as the most beautiful nights in Europe could give no conception of; nights spent standing on the bridge of his ship on the calm Atlantic, listening to the hiss of the prow as it moved through the water sending a trail of phosphorescent sparks along the ship's side, while the watch smoked their pipes in silence and the deep-blue dome shone with a myriad stars: "Never hast Thou troubled me more with Thy greatness than on those nights when I was suspended between sky and ocean, immensity above my head, immensity beneath my feet."

The book's religious musings chimed with the boy's experiences and set solemn, joyful echoes ringing. It praised the hymns and prayers of the Catholic Church, the ceremonies and processions — Rogations, Corpus Christi, Epiphany, Holy Week — and dismissed those "gloomy sects which affect an evangelical austerity and seek a 'religion without ceremonial'" (and of which Berlioz would remark, in the opening chapter of his *Memoirs*, that had he had the misfortune to be born into one of them he would have abjured it and embraced Catholicism "at the first prompting of poetic instinct"). On the sacrament of Communion he read:

> It is at the age of 12, in the springtime of the year, that the adolescent is united with his Creator [...] To quote Voltaire (who will hardly be considered a biased authority), "Man receives God into himself, in the midst of an awesome ceremony lit by a hundred candles, after music has enchanted his senses, at the foot of a golden, gleaming altar. The imagination is captivated, the soul seized and filled with emotion; scarcely breathing, freed from all worldly attachment, one becomes one with God; He is part of our flesh, of our blood."

And on the central mystery of the Christian belief there were these resounding words:

> The Incarnation shows us the Lord of the Heavens in a sheepfold – "He who commands the thunder wrapped in swaddling clothes, He whom the universe doth not contain confined in the womb of a woman". Antiquity would have known how to respond to this miracle. What pictures would Homer and Virgil not have left us of the nativity of God in a manger, shepherds hastening to the crib, wise men led by a star, angels coming down into the wilderness, a virgin mother worshipping her new-born son, and all that mingling of grandeur, innocence and enchantment!

This – with hindsight – is like the scenario of a dramatic work, a challenge. It brings *The Childhood of Christ* to mind irresistibly. When Berlioz wrote the work, thirty years later, he had recourse – consciously or not – to the idiom of the ancient psalm-tunes and noëls on which he was brought up and which Chateaubriand praised for their grave, sweet simplicity.

Génie du Christianisme contributed directly to another Berlioz score, the work which both marks his coming-of-age as a composer and sums up an aspect of the spiritual autobiography of his youth and early manhood: the Fantastic Symphony. "I conceive an artist gifted with a lively imagination, in that state of soul which Chateaubriand so admirably depicted in *René*" (a semi-autobiographical story that originally figured, as a parable, in the *Génie*). Thus the earliest reference to the completed symphony, in a letter to a friend. A few weeks later, in the first published version of the symphony's programme, this is defined as "a young musician affected by the mental malady that a famous writer has called the 'intimations of passion' ('vague des passions')." In the section of *Génie du Christianisme* which discussed Dido, Julie and Bernardin de St Pierre's *Paul et Virginie*, Chateaubriand explained what he meant by it:

> It remains to speak of a state of soul which, we believe, has not been studied hitherto: that state which precedes the development of the passions, when

our faculties, young, active, fully formed but confined, are exercised only on themselves, without aim or object. Unhappily, the more civilised people become, the more this state of *vague des passions* increases. The multitude of examples before our eyes, the numerous books which treat of man and his feelings, make us knowing without the experience of it [...] Imagination is rich, abundant, full of marvels, existence poor, dry, disenchanted. One inhabits, with a full heart, an empty world.

A few lines further on Chateaubriand spoke of the "birth of that culpable melancholy which generates itself in the midst of the passions, when those passions, having no object, burn themselves out in a solitary heart". And in the preface to the separate edition of *René*, he named "rêverie", the "exaggerated love of solitude", as the new vice peculiar to the young men of this century, which Jean-Jacques Rousseau and Goethe (in his *Werther*) had infected them with. Here is the first formulation of the famous "mal du siècle", the spleen, ennui, nostalgia, alienation, felt in different forms and degrees and expressed by so many of the great spirits of the nineteenth century besides Berlioz.

Chateaubriand identified it as a disease of consciousness and therefore of Christian societies, to some extent inborn in man but intensified by civilisation, which fanned "his impossible desires, his impulsion towards unknown beauty". The reveries went beyond human fulfilment; the imagination was too abundant, too rich in marvels to be realised in the prosaic world. But Chateaubriand diagnosed better than he cured. His moral tale, whose source was the still-remembered passions of his own adolescence, only enhanced their charms and made more potent the poison he set out to correct. The music of his style was a siren song which drew his young readers to it, even while it warned of despair.

At night, when the north wind shook the house and the rain drummed on the roof, or when through my window I watched the moon plough the cloud-banks like a phantom ship toiling over the sea, it seemed to me as if deep in my heart life were quadrupled, as if I had the power to create worlds. Ah! could I but have made another being share the ecstasies I felt! [...] Alas, I was alone on the face of the earth. A secret lassitude crept over my body. The disgust with life that I had known since childhood returned with renewed force. Soon my heart gave no more nourishment to my mind. A profound sensation of ennui was all that told me I was alive [...]

I was overwhelmed by a superabundance of life. Sometimes I would flush suddenly and feel as though streams of burning lava were pouring through my being. Sometimes I cried out involuntarily [...] I lacked something—something that would fill the void of my existence. I went down into the valley, I climbed high up on the mountain, summoning with all the force of my desires the ideal object of my waiting passions. I embraced it in the

winds, I heard it in the river's roar. All things were this imagined phantom
— the stars in their courses, the very life-force of the universe.*

"My whole life has been one long, ardent pursuit of an ideal that I
created for myself." It could be René speaking, or François-René
Chateaubriand himself, who in his youth "created for myself a woman
composed of all the women I had seen". But it is Hector, looking back
over all his days and identifying the master-principle of his existence. His
description of the "mal d'isolement" is once again an echo of René's: "at
such moments [...] one has no wish to die, on the contrary one wants to
live, one wants it utterly, one longs to give oneself to life with a thousand
times greater energy. It is an immense capacity for happiness, which
grows frantic at remaining unused and which can only be satisfied by
delights proportionate to the superabundance of feeling that one is
endowed with."

Was it Chateaubriand the enchanter, the seductive stylist, as Adolphe
Boschot suggests, who gave Berlioz his fatal "initiation" into the "mal du
siècle", into the cult of the unreal and the deliberate melancholy it fostered
— a drug "alien to the robustness of his race"? At least one can say that
the seed fell on fertile ground. The descriptions struck deep into his
consciousness and took root in his imagination because they described
familiar experiences. He recognised the states that Chateaubriand-René
spoke of: they were his own. He had seen his ideal object. Némorin had
found his Estelle; and she was unattainable.

* Cf. Berlioz on the Adagio of the Fantastic Symphony (quoted above): "love in the *absence* of
the creature whom he asks for from all Nature".

4

Estelle

Estelle Dubeuf was the younger daughter of a Grenoble tax official. Her grandmother on her mother's side, Madame Gautier du Replat, had a villa in Meylan, and Estelle and her elder sister Ninon spent part of every summer there. The white house stood on its own, amid trees and vines, above the main part of the village where Nicolas Marmion lived, high on the green hillside under the great granite bastion of St Eynard which, though lower in altitude than its neighbours in the Grande Chartreuse, dominates this part of the Grésivaudan by its fortress-like bulk. Behind the house, a little higher up the slope, was a patch of woodland and a ruined tower. Below, the ground plunged down to the valley hundreds of feet beneath.

Berlioz might well have come across Estelle earlier than he did. Not only were Nicolas Marmion and Anne Gautier neighbours, but the two families had personal links. Joséphine Berlioz's close friend Nancy Clappier was Madame Gautier's niece. Félix Marmion's letters, too, speak of visits to the Dubeuf household in Grenoble. As it was, by the time Hector first became aware of Estelle she was in her late teens, tall, upright, with a splendid head of dark hair, large eyes and a dazzling smile, and he was twelve, steeped in *Estelle et Némorin*, already awake to the idea of romantic love, a willing victim. The first sight of her was an electric shock to his whole being. During the days that followed he went about in a dream, gripped by a sadness that was like a physical pain. The pain sharpened into tormenting jealousy at the sight of any man addressing his divinity. In the long drawing-room that occupied the first floor of his grandfather's house he stood on the fringes of the company, eyes lowered, staring fascinated at her pink satin dancing shoes as she floated by. Once, his Uncle Félix, riding over from Grenoble, came straight in, confident and joyous as always, and went on to the dance floor still wearing his spurs; the sound of their triumphant jingling as he danced with Estelle was a fresh twist of the knife that Hector never forgot. At night in his grandfather's house he lay awake in a trance of unhappiness, by day he hid in the tall fields of maize or in the secret corners of the orchard, away from the knowing smiles of the grown-ups. He said nothing to anyone, but they all knew, though none of them really understood, not even his mother, nor even Estelle herself, the first to guess — else surely she would not have teased him about it as she did! One evening, at a party in Madame Gautier's garden, someone suggested prisoner's base. This is a game of catch between two equal sides, each with its own base or "home", which begins with the men choosing in turn a female partner. It was agreed, with many nods and winks, that the youngest should choose first. But he could not: he stood mute, with pounding heart, unable to say a word. The laughter was getting louder, when Estelle seized his hand and cried, "All right, I'll choose. I pick Monsieur Hector." And they laughed even louder. The pain of it! She too was laughing, looking down at him from the heights of her cruel beauty.

So he remembered Estelle, and remembered her always.

In the *Memoirs* Berlioz implies that he saw Estelle in the course of one summer holiday only, that of 1815. This can hardly be so; and it is contradicted elsewhere in the book. In any case, in 1815 Félix Marmion was not at Meylan to dance with Estelle, but at Agen on the Garonne with the First Lancers in the chaotic aftermath of Waterloo. He was not back till the winter, when he danced with both the Dubeuf sisters, teaching them the Kalamaik, a peasant courting dance he had picked up in Eastern Europe during the Napoleonic campaigns. The following summer he was still in the district, waiting to be posted to a regiment. The two families, in fact, were on friendly terms. Berlioz certainly rekindled his devotion on more than one late-summer visit to Meylan. In 1818 he was still experiencing "the delight of seeing his radiant *stella montis* again".

By then he was fourteen and she twenty-one. The first tense self-conscious contacts had given way on her side to the easy tolerance and slightly bossy affection of a young woman for her boy admirer, and he had lost his tongue-tied shyness in her presence. She walked with him over the sacred mountainside, where the trees stood motionless while the summer hung suspended and the heavy grape-clusters ripened in the glow of the sun. It became her kingdom. Estelle was the genius of the place. Every corner was linked with her indissociably. Like the hero of *Estelle et Némorin* he invested each object with her numinous presence. All his life he would remember it — everything: the bend in the path where she stopped to pick some flowers from a clump of sweet-scented pink vetch, lovely and fragrant as herself; the cherry tree on whose trunk she lightly rested her hand; the bramble bush where she reached across to gather blackberries; the delicious moment when, as he was crossing a very steep piece of ground (for such things held no terrors for him), she cried out in sudden alarm, "Take care, don't go near the edge!"; the day she took him to the window of one of the front rooms of her grandmother's house and with a proud gesture of her arm and a smile of pleasure showed him the sweep of the valley floor far below.

Most vivid of all, the image of her standing above him on a rock, serene, majestic, gazing across the valley eastwards to the high mountains, while he looked up at her, adoring her beauty, dreaming of the time when, grown up and a great composer, he would write an opera on Florian's *Estelle* and bring the score to the rock as an offering, and she would find it there one morning when she came to watch the sunrise. That was how his imagination represented her: as the goddess, seen always from below, her eyes turned away towards the infinite, or if turned to him, looking down at him with a remote smile. Her step and bearing, the carriage of her head, are to him those of a divinity; and when he sees her again, nearly fifty years later, he will recognise them instantly, like Æneas recognising Venus by the same transcendent signs.

He seems to have accepted her inaccessibility, and his rôle as humble worshipper, without question. Such docility is quite untypical of the adult Berlioz. He pursued Harriet Smithson with tenacious stubbornness; once persuaded that she embodied his ideal, he would not let go. But Estelle was from the first and forever beyond him; and the titles he gave her, the variants of her name, are an acknowledgment of her constant and destined remoteness. She is the wood-nymph of the St Eynard; she is Stella, his "étoile", his "stella montis", "stella del monte", "stella matutina" — the star whose dazzling light irradiated the morning of his life and who reappeared at its close, still bright, steadfast, and "seeming to smile on him from afar". His world in the meantime had spun away into other orbits; but, after passing close to her again in 1848, it returned finally and came to rest where it began, facing her. Yet in a real sense she had been with him all the time. On his way back from Italy in 1832, coming down the valley past Meylan, he looked up and saw as in a vision the white house and the old tower high above him in bright sunshine but seen through a veil of tears. Five years later, during the composition of the Requiem (a work haunted by the absence of God), he twice dreamt that he was sitting under a tree in Madame Gautier's garden, alone; Estelle was not there, and he kept calling out, "Where is she? Where is she?" It was she, he told her in old age, who had all unknowingly "dictated" to him his most intimate music, the love theme in *Romeo and Juliet* and much else.

There is more here than the desire to lend a semblance of unity and purpose to the turmoil of his life. Certainly Estelle in the *Memoirs* plays a mythic rôle. She is the central symphonic "theme" of the work: fully stated at the outset, thereafter seeming to fade from sight but still glimpsed at intervals, and returning, outwardly altered yet unchangeable, to preside over the end. How otherwise? That had been, he realised, her rôle in his existence. What she had done was to implant in his imagination an ideal, for which he must forever seek an equivalent, an embodiment, in life and in art. She gave him his task; she showed him what his quest would be. That is one reason why he sought her out again at the end, when the last of his loves lay buried in the cemetery and when his career was over and he had set down the last note of music he would ever write. It was an act of recognition, a return to the springs of his creative being. His art began with her. Not only love but Nature, poetry too, had for him their origin in her. The three things were from the first deeply interfused; they became — in a way that shows the creative impulse active in him at an early age — part of a rich complex of related ideas and feelings, in which his religious instinct also mingled, associating the cult of his virgin goddess with that of the "stella matutina" to whom he prayed in church. At the same time that he fell in love with Estelle his senses awoke to the magic power of Nature, from whose beauty her beauty drew added glamour and mystery. In the same way, love and poetry intensified each other's power. If Virgil was able to "find the way to his heart and fire his nascent imagination", if Dido's heartbreak could prostrate him with vicarious sorrow, it was because of Estelle. Through her he discovered grief and the sadness of life, Virgil's "lacrimæ rerum", and the realisation of his solitariness, the conviction that love as he experienced it was doomed never to find an equal response in another being. She revealed beauty to him as something visionary, distant, godlike, rarely if ever attained, yet to be striven for constantly. In doing so she set him on a path of exaltation and suffering that would colour the whole character of his music.

For the moment, he was a boy in his early teens, only beginning to dream of becoming a composer, half admitting his ambition to himself but not yet daring to voice it to those in charge of him. He composed music — songs mostly — inspired by his passion for Estelle. Almost none of it has survived. But one authentically Berliozian melody has come down to us from childhood, a direct reflection of the Meylan experience, dictated by Estelle. We know it as the theme for muted strings which begins the Fantastic Symphony; but it was originally a song set to some verses from *Estelle et Némorin* that expressed the despair of the lover forced to leave the woods and streams of his homeland and the presence of the beloved. The similarity between the tune and the chant of the litany to the Virgin, "Stella matutina", has already been noted. Berlioz seems to have destroyed all his adolescent efforts at composition when he began to study music in earnest in Paris. But he remembered this tune half a dozen years later as he was starting to work on the symphony, and recognised in it "the overpowering sadness of a young heart first tortured by a hopeless love". It is his earliest characteristic composition, springing fully formed out of the unpromising environment of his upbringing, pointing the way to what he is to become.

5
Hector the Musician

Ferdinand Hiller, surveying Berlioz's upbringing, concluded that "there has probably never been a famous composer whose childhood was wasted in circumstances less favourable to musical development". It depends what kind of childhood one believes is the best preparation for a composer. Berlioz did receive preparation, but of another sort. Hiller was looking at it, quite reasonably, from the conventional idea of a composer's training. From that point of view, Berlioz had not been through the proper channels. (The same sort of thing was said of Wagner.) By eighteen, the age at which he first came into contact with serious music, most of his contemporaries were in the thick of it, as well as having acquired a grounding in their craft. He certainly had a lot of catching up to do when he went to Paris.

Certainly, too, the lack of a piano in his upbringing, which Hiller particularly deplored, had very important consequences. In orthodox eyes the piano was indispensable; musical training was not to be thought of without it. The development of the instrument and its sustaining pedal, with the rich blending of timbres and the progressively more complex harmonic language they fostered, was a crucial influence on orchestral music in the nineteenth century; and it was partly because Berlioz, in never learning to play it, was not subjected to that influence, that his music — linear in style and conceived directly in orchestral terms — seemed so disconcertingly different.[*]

In one sense Hiller's diagnosis was correct. The absence of a keyboard instrument — a natural focus of domestic music-making — is symptomatic of the primitive musical environment that Berlioz was born into. Music was part of the background of life, but largely in popular, unsophisticated forms: church litanies, the horns of the hunt, the shepherds' pipes, the

---

[*] A comparable "lack" can be seen in the musical education of the young Stravinsky, the twentieth-century composer who "took the pedal" out of orchestral music. Although, unlike Berlioz, he was taught the piano (and always made use of it in composing), his teacher made him play without the pedal.

76

fife-and-drum music to which the schoolchildren marched at the seminary down the road, the folk-tunes sung by the labourers in the fields and the women at their household chores. Berlioz remembered his mother singing "Que je voudrais avoir une chaumière", and no doubt other pastoral airs of the kind. The contemporary French romance — that amiable, senti-mental genre, traces of whose popular origins survived in its gently lilting dance-rhythms — marked the limit of sophistication in the everyday musical culture of La Côte. Songs extracted from the opéras-comiques of Grétry, Dalayrac, Boieldieu and lesser practitioners were purchased or copied for the entertainment of the salon or adapted for the ballroom (and, as we have seen, for the church). Félix Marmion, whose voice was much in demand at parties, never tired of singing them. This was the music that the young Berlioz knew best, and it left its mark on many of his melodies.

Félix Marmion was a keen violinist as well, and at dances, when not footing it himself, was more than ready to play. One or two people in the town were also string players of a sort. When, in 1817, La Côte acquired a resident music teacher they formed themselves into a quartet. A string quartet by Ignaz Pleyel, a pupil of Haydn's, seems to have been the most advanced music that Berlioz heard during his entire childhood and early youth. That, and a couple of pieces from Gluck's *Orphée* with guitar accompaniment that he discovered in his father's library, constituted the summit of his musical experience until he was nearly eighteen. It is not surprising that the sound of the full orchestra and chorus of the Paris Opéra electrified him.

Formal public music-making at La Côte St André was in the enthusiastic but inexpert hands of the band of the National Guard, the citizens' militia founded in 1789. Military bands were an integral part of the process whereby, under the Revolution, music was used to educate the populace in civic consciousness and a martial spirit. The idea of the community united in celebration and worship found its ultimate expression in the large-scale ceremonial odes, cantatas and marches of Le Sueur, Méhul, Gossec and Cherubini (a tradition later to be revived in Berlioz's symphony for wind instruments, the Symphonie funèbre et triomphale, and to some extent also in his Requiem and Te Deum); but it permeated all levels of national life. Everyone was taught to sing secular hymns extolling the fatherland and, from 1805 onwards, the Emperor, and to march in step to the sound of brass, woodwind and percussion on all public occasions; and the vogue of the military band survived the collapse of the Empire.

La Côte St André did its zealous best to follow the national example, but resources and skill were limited. An inventory of November 1820 lists twenty-one players: 1 piccolo, 10 clarinets, 3 horns, 1 bassoon, 1 trumpet, 1 serpent, 1 tambourine, 1 bass-drum, 1 cymbal-player and 1 player of the pavillon chinois or "Jingling Johnny" (a wooden pole with metal

crescents projecting on either side, from which small bells are suspended).
To these should presumably be added a number of side-drums. Four
months later the serpent-player has retired, and one of the clarinettists is
apparently learning it in his place (he is not found among the clarinets
any more, and is named as player of the serpent the following year);
another clarinettist has changed to piccolo; and a trombone is listed, but
without anyone to play it.

A letter addressed by members of the band to the Commander of the
National Guard a year or two later gives a far from reassuring picture of
the band's standard of performance:

> [. . .] In the two months since you delegated Monsieur Deléon to play first
> clarinet, an almost unanimous complaint has been heard among us, and this
> because we have realised that we are supposed to play with him on all
> occasions, i.e. on parade as well as at rehearsals. We should like it if possible
> for Monsieur Allard to play the first part whenever we play in public [. . .]
> Monsieur Deléon plays well on his own or with Monsieur Montsenis, who is
> able to follow him; but as he is not used to leading a band and plays without
> a sense of the beat, going much faster at some times than at others, it is
> quite impossible to play properly with him. It is quite the opposite with
> Monsieur Allard, who was taught to accommodate himself to us by Monsieur
> Dorant [master of music at La Côte, c. 1818–22] and has played regularly
> with us. At least when we are on parade we should like to play with him, so
> that we avoid public humiliation. We were going to speak to you about it
> when the new regulations were drawn up, but Monsieur Deléon was there
> and, for fear of hurting his feelings, no one said anything. Another thing we
> must tell you is that he has pieces of music that he makes us play once or
> twice at rehearsal – we pick our way through them once with some difficulty
> and then he makes us play them in public. On one particular day when this
> happened, connoisseurs were obliged to leave the church before the end of
> Mass [. . .] [c. 1823]

In her diary, at about the same date, Nancy Berlioz describes standing at
a corner of the street with her girl friend Elise Rocher as the band went
past, and the two of them stuffing handkerchiefs into their mouths to stop
themselves bursting out laughing at the excruciating din.

This was arguably a low point in the band's fortunes, following the
departure of Maître Dorant the previous year and the apparent failure to
appoint another professional musician in his place. But the surviving
documents suggest that the level of musical activity fluctuated frequently
during these years and that it was difficult to sustain it for long.

The first recorded signs of life coincide with the last months of the
Consulate and the beginning of the Empire (1805–6). Mayor Buffevent
entered into correspondence with an instrument-maker in Lyons called
Bernard about the purchase of instruments needed to bring the band up
to a respectable strength. An E-flat clarinet was bought, "made entirely

of ivory", and a bassoon together with a dozen reeds, and a serpent was ordered but unfortunately could not be supplied in time for the Feast of Corpus Christi as it was on loan to another band. The pavillon chinois that had been ordered duly arrived but was found to be too small and was sent back; a larger replacement was discussed but turned down as being too expensive. Money was in short supply. The funds of the National Guard evidently would not run to much expenditure on music, bills were slow to be settled, and Bernard suggested payment in kind: "I will let you have the serpent in exchange for 16 bottles, i.e. half-litres, of the finest quality Eau de Canel from the DuRocher [Rocher] brothers of La Côte [...] It must be good Eau de Canel, superfine, of your oldest distillation" (11 July 1805). Protracted negotiations for a pair of Turkish cymbals — "the genuine Smyrna article", which Bernard was prepared to let them have reduced, at 300 francs — ended in the purchase of a pair from a dealer in Vienne for nearly half the price, despite Bernard's warning that he "knew the Vienne pair and wouldn't give 36 francs for them".

A year later Mayor Buffevent was again writing to Bernard, this time for a music master. Bernard replied that he had just the man, and he was coming right away, as the bearer of the letter, a Monsieur Bouchmann from Condrieu (on the Rhone, below Lyons), "professor of music, who has been head of music for various corps, a thoroughly honest and well-respected man, perfectly versed in his profession, plays the clarinet, can teach the horn, plays flute, bassoon and violin. He is just the person to get your band going and put life into it. I have informed him of your terms, 100 francs a month, and have persuaded him to set out at once." He came, and liked what he found. A few weeks later he wrote from Condrieu, where he had gone back to complete some unfinished business; the letter, signed "Bouchmann artiste" and addressed to the Mayor, apologises for his being detained till the following week ("la saimaine prochenne") and assures "Monsieur le Mere" how happy he is in his new post: "Je suis Charmai de lai abithe Permis vos Amateur" (May 1807). The spelling recalls the justice of the peace mentioned in *Guy Mannering* who, on being appointed, wrote for a copy of the official statutes: "Please send the ax relating to a gustus pease." But La Côte was evidently satisfied with the artistic services of its music master. A year later the threat of losing him caused the Mayor to appeal to the forty leading citizens to contribute to a subscription so that Bouchmann could stay and carry on his good work — for there was "no need to remind them" of the social advantages music brought to their town. "We have among us a master of music who is a man of talent; the fine pupils he has produced since he came to live in this commune leave no doubt on that score. It is essential to get him to stay here some time longer so that they may make still further progress."

How much longer Bouchmann stayed in La Côte is not known. The next document, a letter to the Mayor signed by eight officers of the National Guard, dates from nearly nine years later and shows the band on the point of collapse, instruments lacking or in disrepair and morale at a low ebb: "Our National Guard is in danger of losing its band, the soul of the organisation." The officers appeal to the Mayor to let the town have a music master; they are prepared to contribute financially to making such an arrangement possible (March 1817).

Two months later a contract was drawn up "between the Mayor of the town of La Côte St André and Monsieur Imbert, Master of Music", in which it was agreed

1° that M. Imbert undertake to give lessons in vocal and instrumental music to twelve pupils of the town for the price of eight francs a month

2° he will instruct the band of the National Guard, conducting it and seeing that it holds two rehearsals a week

3° if some less well-off musicians of the aforementioned Guard wish to have private lessons, he will give them to them for the price of five francs a month

4° the commune will, on these conditions, supply him with lodgings in the town hall, and will guarantee him the sum of a hundred francs a month in the event of the twelve pupils not sufficing to make up the sum

5° the agreement will have effect for one year from this date 20th May 1817

Imbert, a second violinist from one of the theatres in Lyons who also played the clarinet, stayed for over a year — his contract was renewed in May 1818 — and the fortunes of the band took an upward turn. A code of rules was drawn up: strict obedience to their captain; nothing to be said or done to disturb the peace or provoke a fellow-member; neat and orderly turn-out for public parades; monthly inspection of instruments to see that they are being kept in good condition; rehearsals every Thursday and Sunday, attendance at which is obligatory, with a fine of one franc exacted for absence except on legitimate grounds — however, the cymbals, bass-drum and tambourine players are excused Thursday rehearsals, being piece-workers (which shows that the National Guard was not the exclusive preserve of the bourgeoisie).

Imbert set about having existing instruments repaired and acquiring new ones — a horn and a trumpet — and a fresh selection of pieces for the band to play. How to pay for all this was, as always, a problem, and permission to draw money from the annual fund had to be sought from the Sub-Prefect of the département, Alphonse Anglès (a former schoolmate of Stendhal), the correspondence dragging on for several months. In the end half the cost of the new horn seems to have been met by the player concerned, and Imbert paid for the music himself. "Time is passing and we are not taking sufficient advantage of M. Imbert's sojourn among us," wrote the Captain of Music to the Commander of the National Guard. Happily, his contract was renewed for another year. The Mayor was fully aware of the "advantages that accrue to this commune from the presence of a master of music who will continue to conduct and instruct the military band, and to maintain a taste for wholesome recreation among the young while furnishing them with agreeable accomplishments".

The engagement of a master of music seems on the face of it a purely municipal initiative. But the version given in Berlioz's *Memoirs* — that the impulse came from his father who, impressed by his son's musical aptitude, persuaded a few well-to-do families of La Côte to join him in getting a professional musician from Lyons (among whose duties would be to direct the band) — could well be at least partly true. The first clause in the agreement is not directly related to the National Guard: it concerns the provision of music lessons, vocal and instrumental, to certain inhabitants of the town. And it is noteworthy that when renewing the contract the following year the Mayor, in default of sufficient funds from the communal purse, enlisted the aid of several private citizens for the guarantee of Maître Imbert's salary. One of them was Louis Berlioz; and one of Imbert's most assiduous pupils was his son Hector.

We know virtually nothing of the part that music played in Berlioz's very earliest years. His journalistic writings contain many personal allusions, but few to the first period of his life, and those are generally facetious. Thus in one article he mentions the blacksmith whose forge was on the other side of the street just opposite his father's house (in fact the blacksmith, Claude Ferlet, was a tenant of Dr Berlioz): "Every morning at four o'clock, from my infancy, he would wake me with the measured clang of his anvil, thus contributing significantly to the development in me of a sense of rhythm, which my enemies claim that I lack." In another article, entitled "Le chant des coqs et les coqs du chant", a discussion with his neighbour at the opera about the effect of the intrusive vocal trill in dramatic music, provoked by a triumphant prima donna who has just drilled a hole in his eardrum, reminds him how as a child he found the crowing of cocks equally painful to his nervous system; so much so that he used, he says, to wait in ambush for the unsuspecting birds and, just as they flapped their wings and prepared to crow in that exasperatingly unmusical way of theirs, leap out and cut short their song, occasionally laying one dead with a well-aimed stone.

In the *Treatise on Modern Orchestration*, speaking of the timbre of the clarinet, which has for him "something both feminine and heroic, redolent of the great women of antiquity", he remarks that the unison of massed clarinets in a military band, heard in the distance, has always moved him deeply and in the same way as the reading of the classical epics, filling his mind with images of the ancient world. But such experiences seem less likely to refer to the band of the La Côte National Guard and its gallant but uncertain performances than to the bands that he heard later in Paris.

What music he first responded to and how it affected him — what shepherds' airs, what hunting calls, what songs sung to him by his mother (other than "Que je voudrais avoir une chaumière"), what tunes coming from the camps of the Spanish prisoners-of-war in Grenoble — he does not tell us.

When an identifiable piece of music can be associated with him (apart, that is, from the Dalayrac air sung at his first communion), he is twelve, and it is a folk-tune. At about the beginning of 1816 he found an old flageolet (a kind of recorder) at the back of a drawer he was rummaging in, and immediately tried to pick out the popular song "Malbrook s'en va t'en guerre".[*] His father came out of his study and begged him to stop, promising to teach him as soon as he had time. "In fact he taught me without much trouble; by the end of two days I was master of 'Malbrook' and able to regale the family with it." Berlioz's mocking account of the incident dares us to take it seriously. ("What biographer worth his salt could fail to detect here the germ of my aptitude for large-scale effects of wind instruments?") Yet there is a certain poetic aptness in the choice of tune, with its 6/8 metre and the "Berliozian" shape of its recurring opening phrase. The incident has at least a symbolic significance. Six-eight time, a fondness for monody (so untypical of the nineteenth century as a whole) and for melodic lines which move stepwise rather than in large intervals: all three features of Berlioz's music (to which may be added a fondness for rhythmic alteration) are also those of folk-music, and attest to what is after all not surprising, given his early environment — the important part played by folk-song in the formation of his style.

Thanks to the family correspondence we can date the episode of the flageolet fairly precisely. In a letter to Dr Berlioz which, from references to Shrove Tuesday and the Carnival, belongs to February 1816, Félix Marmion, then in Grenoble awaiting a posting in the newly constituted Bourbon army, renders account of various family commissions: "The flageolets that I am sending Hector are nothing special, but they are even in tone and accurate in intonation. Remind him not to blow too hard, as it makes them go out of tune. I haven't yet got any music to send him; no one here has any for the instrument."

His uncle's present only whetted his appetite for something better. A few weeks later he was making arrangements to get some from Paris. A friend of Dr Berlioz, the Grenoble notary Joseph Faure, had been elected one of the deputies for Isère and was in Paris for the session of Parliament (the so-called Chambre Introuvable of 1816), and his eldest son Amédée was with him. The twelve-year-old Hector commissioned the younger

---

[*] "Malbrook" apparently goes back long before the Duke of Marlborough and the French wars, but only became widely known in France in the 1780s, after the nurse of one of Marie-Antoinette's children had introduced it to the royal household. The flageolet differs from the recorder partly in having six holes, not eight, and in two of them being at the back of the instrument. It remained popular longer in France than in England, where it began to be ousted by the recorder in the second half of the seventeenth century. Pepys, however, was a keen player of the flageolet.

son, Eugène (aged nineteen), to ask his brother to buy him some flageolets. A letter from Dr Berlioz to Joseph Faure, written on 4 April 1816, ends: "Hector says will Monsieur Amédée please not forget the two flageolets that Monsieur Eugène asked for on his behalf."

To the same period belongs the letter quoted in Chapter 1 from a Grenoble friend of Joséphine Berlioz, in which the phrase "Give my love to Hector the musician" occurs. The letter is dated 24 March, with no year or postmark; but references to Félix Marmion and his attempts to resume his military career (interrupted between December 1815 and June 1816 by the upheavals in the French army following the collapse of the Napoleonic régime) show the year to be 1816. Dr Berlioz was in Grenoble and had been talking about his son's musical leanings; they, and indeed the boy's general intelligence and his lively imagination, were a solace to him, still grief-stricken by the death of his beloved daughter Louise the previous year and now full of fresh anxiety over the health of the baby, Adèle: at times she was so poorly that he hardly dared go away. But he was in Grenoble again at the beginning of May to see a patient. Perhaps on the same visit he bought the flute that he gave Hector about this time. More likely the flute was his own and he had played it himself in his younger days, for he was able to explain the mechanism to Hector and show him how to play it. He had already — inspired by the episode of the flageolet — shown him how musical notation works and taught him to read music. Now, together with the flute, he gave him a copy of Devienne's manual, *Méthode de flute théorique et pratique*. This was the standard work of the period; it had been published in 1795, just at the time when the young Louis Berlioz had become actively interested in music.

Devienne's *Méthode* included, along with the standard exercises in agility, tone, phrasing, breath control and rhythm, tunes from opéras-comiques and vaudevilles current at the end of the eighteenth century (more Dalayrac, and Grétry) as well as popular songs like "Ah, vous dirai-je, maman" (our "Twinkle, twinkle little star") and "Je suis Lindor", and little sonatinas in the style of Pleyel and Clementi. Hector worked diligently at it; at Meylan that autumn he proudly played the Musette from Dalayrac's *Nina* to his father as the two of them sat on the hillside above Estelle's grandmother's house, at the foot of the old tower, with the valley and the shining Isère far below them. Perhaps it is not fanciful to see in the "ideal" character and sense of illimitable space of so many passages for solo flute in Berlioz's works a memory of childhood happiness in the freedom of mountain scenery. One thinks of the Sanctus in the Requiem, where the flute's long, exalted phrases hang serene and weightless in the upper air, or the melody in the final section of the Serenade in *Harold in Italy*, sounding as though from hundreds of feet above us, or the descant — a single span of sixteen bars — to Faust's passionately nostalgic "Te reverrai-je encor, heure trop fugitive, où mon âme au bonheur allait enfin s'ouvrir?"

By the beginning of 1817, when he was thirteen, he had developed into quite a passable flautist; and under Imbert, who arrived in the spring, he continued to progress until he could get his fingers round the virtuoso concertos of Drouet, court flautist to the Emperor Napoleon, whose music makes a feature of rapid scale passages, arpeggios and double-tonguing.*

Imbert, who came to the house every day, also gave the boy singing lessons and developed his still-unbroken voice and his sight-reading ability, so that Hector was doubly in demand at family gatherings.

Exactly how long Imbert stayed in La Côte is not known. Some time in the autumn or winter of 1818 he returned to Lyons. According to the *Memoirs* he did so following the suicide of his son. Berlioz says that Imbert fils, who was slightly older than him, was a good horn-player, and that they became friends. In the summer of 1818, just before the Berlioz family went on their annual visit to Grandfather Marmion's at Meylan – which was usually in August – young Imbert came to the house and took a strangely solemn farewell of his friend: "Let's embrace – perhaps I shan't see you again." It transpired that the young man hanged himself on the day Hector left for Meylan.

There is no trace of his death in the local registers. Yet it is certain that Imbert père did give up his post and was replaced by another, and that he had a son who played the horn. A letter from the Captain of Music to the Commander of the National Guard, written on 27 January 1818 with the purpose of asking for some new instruments, including a horn, mentions him: "M. Imbert reckons that in March his son will be able to take the horn part. We should also consider having a little uniform made for him, as he plays the clarinet well enough to parade with us." And just over a month later, on 1 March, the signature "Imbert fils" appears under that of his father on a document listing the regulations that govern the members of the band.

Young Imbert's death or disappearance remains a mystery. We can only guess at its effect on Berlioz's feelings. But the sudden removal of his precocious friend, in tragic circumstances, is unlikely to have silenced, in the imagination of so tenacious a dreamer, the musical ambitions already beginning to make themselves heard. He did not yet dare voice them to his father, but he had become aware of them within himself.

A great deal of this period is obscure. The written record is far more detailed than it is for the early years, but it is sketchy all the same, and to fit the different pieces of evidence together into anything like a clear pattern and set up a chronology of events requires a good deal of

---

* For some reason Berlioz is often described as having never learned to play an instrument. He kept up the flute during his student days, and was a good enough player to consider joining a professional orchestra in 1826. He also became a competent guitarist.

guesswork. Municipal archives are one source of information. The entries in Dr Berlioz's Livre de Raison are another. There are the various musical manuscripts that have survived, most if not all of which seem to belong to the time of Imbert's successor Dorant. There are letters, in particular the two (possibly three) that Berlioz wrote to Paris music publishers in 1819, when he was fifteen. And there are the early chapters of the *Memoirs*. Like any other reminiscences of childhood these should be used with caution. Written thirty years later, in 1848, they are not an exact chronological account — they do not presume to be — and on matters of detail and emphasis they sometimes contradict the much earlier (though not necessarily more accurate) autobiographical sketch that Berlioz supplied to a journalist friend in 1832. None the less they are indispensable, and the fact that their detailed statements, where they can be checked against documentary sources, are generally found to be correct entitles them to be treated with respect.

Used together, the different kinds of evidence may help us to approximate to the truth. For example, when did Dorant, Imbert's successor, arrive? The date has a bearing on the history of Berlioz's first years as a composer. According to the *Memoirs* Imbert left La Côte when his son died (i.e. *c*. August or September 1818) and was succeeded by François-Xavier Dorant, a musician from Colmar in Alsace, "almost immediately". The accounts for 1818 in the Livre de Raison include the sum of 86 francs for "Maître de musique". Since their respective contracts show that Imbert received 8 francs a month and Dorant 10, the 86 francs could have been made up of 56 for Imbert (seven months, January to July) and 30 francs for Dorant, which would mean that Dorant began teaching in October. It is true that the only surviving contract with Dorant dates from the next summer, July 1819. But it does not follow that it was not preceded by an earlier agreement, since lost. The contract differs from those of Imbert in being made not with the municipality but with four private citizens, Louis Berlioz, Antoine and Louis Rocher, and François Bert, and in being concerned only with the lessons that Dorant is to give their children. Dorant's duties as conductor of the band of the National Guard must have been dealt with in a separate agreement. None has survived; but his signature appears on a set of band regulations dating from June 1819, which shows that he was already working in La Côte before the private contract of 24 July was drawn up. Furthermore, the item 220 francs for "Maître de musique" in the Livre de Raison under 1819 suggests that Dorant taught in the Berlioz household for the full year. The *Memoirs* state that Dorant began by giving Nancy (aged twelve or thirteen) guitar lessons and that Hector, after sitting in on them, determined to have some himself. If true, this could account for the 220 francs — twelve months and ten months, at 10 francs a month: Nancy was taught for the whole year and Hector from March onwards. That in turn would mean that Dorant to begin with was engaged to teach Nancy only, with the implication that Dr Berlioz, while not wishing to stifle his son's musical talent, felt that it had had enough external encouragement: the important thing now was to get him started on his medical studies, his repugnance to which Dr Berlioz could not bring himself to take seriously. The new flute, which Hector had long wanted his father to get for him, and which the Livre de Raison records as having been purchased on 26 January 1819 from Simiot the younger, instrument-maker, Place du Plâtre, Lyons — "made of red ebony, with 8 keys of silver, slide ditto, and a foot-joint in C" — was intended as the carrot. But if the above interpretation of the evidence is correct, the inconsistency and vacillation that mark Dr Berlioz's handling of his son would seem to be reflected in his giving in, a month or two later, to his desire to have guitar lessons. It is noteworthy that in this same month of March 1819, while on a fortnight's visit to Grenoble, Dr Berlioz bought a new guitar.[*]

From this same month of March 1819 comes the first documentary evidence of Berlioz as a composer. On about the 21st he wrote to the Paris firm of Janet et Cotelle, offering to send certain works of his with a view to publication. If, as seems likely, Dorant was already at La Côte, the boy may have sought his encouragement and practical advice. Dorant, a more experienced and resourceful musician than Imbert, was a man of the world but also an original who would not automatically pooh-pooh the attempt of a fifteen-year-old self-taught provincial to get his music published.

La Côte, 25 March 1819[†]

Sirs,

Having the intention of getting various musical works engraved, I am writing to you in the hope that you can answer my purpose. I should like you to undertake their publication on your account, in return for a certain number of copies that you will let me have. Be so kind as to reply as soon as possible whether you will do it. I shall then send you a medley for flute,

---

[*] 16 March. Other items of expenditure on this journey include a lamp, a pair of braces, eight orange trees and eight pots to put them in, the binding of nine books, and a white straw-bonnet for his wife. The Livre de Raison's entries for the spring of 1819 give a picture of the varied activity on the estate: "29 March finished layering the vines, 46 women-days and 131 men-days. [Women received 0.60 a day, men 1.25 and a jar of wine.] 12 April repaid Victor [his brother] 800 francs for the second-hand gig he bought me. 15 April paid M. Bardousse for 9 ells of canvas for seat-covers for the gig. 25 April paid Favre the carpenter for a double-doored deal cupboard that he put in the ground-floor parlour. 8 May my wife hatched one and a half ounces of silk-worm seed. 11 May four carts brought a load of sandstone from Voreppe. 18 May paid Duc for replacing the grill on the bath cylinder. 19 May paid Moleyin the saddler for repairing the 4-wheeled carriage damaged in an accident."

[†] The figure at the top of the letter is unmistakably "25", but the actual date must have been about the 21st; the letter arrived in Paris on the 25th, when it was stamped with the Paris postmark. Mail took three to four days to get from La Côte to the capital. Janet et Cotelle replied on the 27th.

horn, two violins, viola and cello. During the time that you are engraving this work I can send you some songs with piano accompaniment and various other things, subject to the same conditions.

I am yours truly,
Hector Berlioz

On receiving a reply from Janet et Cotelle — presumably a refusal — he tried again and wrote to the firm of Pleyel, polishing the style a little. This time the songs with piano accompaniment are not mentioned, and the medley is "composed from selected airs". "Please let me know at your earliest convenience how long you will need to engrave it, and whether it is necessary to prepay the package. I am your humble and obedient servant Hector Berlioz" (6 April 1819). Once again the response, sent on the 10th, seems to have been negative.

The medley ("potpourri concertant") is also mentioned in the *Memoirs*, where — as in the letters — it is described as being written for sextet; and the selected airs are identified as Italian. The context of the narrative suggests that its composition belongs to the period of Imbert's residence at La Côte (the horn part presumably being written with Imbert fils in mind). If that is so, the date cannot be later than the early summer of 1818, since the work was followed by two quintets for flute and string quartet, both of which were apparently tried out before the departure of Imbert in the late summer or autumn.*

No doubt both the potpourri concertant and the quintets were worked over subsequently and the score that was offered for publication in the spring of 1819 was an improvement on the one that was played the previous summer; the potpourri may have been chosen in preference to the quintets as being the kind of piece more likely to be accepted from an unknown composer (who was careful not to reveal his age). No doubt, too, even in its revised form the work would have been rejected at a glance if it had ever been seen by a publisher. At this stage Berlioz had had no lessons in composition, even the most rudimentary, from anyone. In so far as he had found out anything about its mysteries, he had found it out for himself. Rameau's *Elémens de musique théorique et pratique*, discovered in his father's library and seized on with enthusiasm, had succeeded only in baffling him; he sat up late puzzling over it, but to no purpose. Even as "simplified by M. Dalembert", its learned disquisitions presupposed some knowledge on the part of the reader; and without a piano or even a guitar to experiment with, he could not make head or tail of it. None the less, determined to learn how to write music, he laboriously arranged some duets for three and four parts as an exercise and persuaded the

---

* The performers of the quintets were Berlioz (flute), Imbert (first violin), Alphonse Robert — Berlioz's cousin and, later, fellow medical student — (second violin), and two unnamed local amateurs (viola and cello).

local musicians to try them. It was a fiasco: after a few bars the players collapsed in helpless laughter and the experiment was abandoned. But though humiliated he was not going to give up. He realised that he had not got the first idea how to form chords, let alone how to move from one to another; but he could listen, and learn that way. The string quartet of which Imbert and Alphonse Robert were the two violins met on Sundays after Mass; and a quartet by Pleyel that they performed one Sunday gave him his first inkling of how a musical work was constructed. He borrowed the parts and wrote them out as a score, which he pored over in conjunction with Catel's *Treatise on Harmony*, a far less abstruse and ambitious manual than Rameau's that he had managed to get hold of, and the first glimmerings of light began to dawn.[*] The result was the potpourri concertant and the two flute quintets. This time no one laughed. The second quintet proved too difficult for the anonymous viola and cello, but the first was a success.

Some time at about the end of the same year, 1818, or early the next, the conviction that had been forming dimly in his mind began to take clearer shape, and he knew what he was going to be. Where had it come from, this certainty that he would be a composer? Once it took root in him, what gave it the force to survive and grow? His family naturally saw it as adolescent fantasy, not to be regarded seriously for a moment: quite apart from the insuperable social objections, it was against all the rules. Indeed, compared with the other great self-taught composers who have had to contend with the hostility of relatives or circumstances — and there have been plenty of them — Berlioz had far more against him. Handel, Wagner, Elgar, whatever the initial obstacles they had to overcome, were in touch with a vital musical tradition and drew strength from it. The experience that convinced the fourteen-year-old Wagner that he must be a composer was hearing Beethoven's Seventh Symphony.

Berlioz's conviction had absolutely nothing like that to nourish it. It was an act of faith, sustained by the imagination. There was no great orchestral work for him to hear — there was no orchestra. The nearest he got to it was a blank piece of manuscript paper that he came upon one day — he does not say where or how — with twenty-four staves on it. Until that moment a full score was something unknown to him. He had read about symphonies and operas in the lives of the great composers that he found in Michaud's *Biographie universelle* but the fact had no reality for him. The only scores he was familiar with were flute solos, solfèges with figured bass, or operatic extracts with piano or guitar accompaniment. It had never occurred to him to think in any real sense of music written on such a scale. In a flash he had a glimpse of a whole new, mysterious world, far off but clear, till then utterly unguessed at.

---

[*] At the same age Wagner was trying to teach himself composition by working through Logier's *Method of General-Bass*, borrowed from the library unbeknown to his family.

The idea of the multitude of different instrumental and vocal per-mutations that all those lines could give rise to dazzled him. That was his revelation. The "creator of the modern orchestra" was introduced to his métier by a sheet of music paper.

The incident illustrates the powerful visualising character of Berlioz's imagination. It had a decisive effect, giving his musical ambitions a new impetus. His mind had already been feeding on the idea of the composer's career and identifying with the great musicians whose lives were recounted in Michaud's biographical dictionary, which had begun appearing a few years earlier, in 1811, and to which Dr Berlioz subscribed. Volume 17, including Gluck, came out in 1816, volumes 18 (Grétry) and 19 (Haydn) the year after. They made, he says, a profound impression on him; and the truth of that assertion is borne out by the persistence in his adult writings not only of ideas first encountered there but sometimes of actual phrases: an article on Gluck's *Alceste* written in 1859 echoes words that he had read in Michaud more than forty years earlier.

In the article on Haydn (which he turned to in the belief that the Pleyel quartet he had studied was by Haydn — such misattribution was common at the time), he learned of the great man's beginnings in the obscure village on the Austro-Hungarian frontier where he was born and where like Hector himself he played the drum on feast-days, and of his long struggle and years of poverty before his talents were recognised and undying fame rewarded them. The entry on Dalayrac (volume 10) des-cribed how his father, a government official in the south of France, intended him for the bar and only very reluctantly let him have a violin teacher; how as a result his legal studies were neglected, the teacher was sent away, and the boy took to practising in the attic, out of earshot of his parents, but was overheard by the local nuns, who betrayed his secret; and how in the end his father, won over by his persistence, gave in and allowed him to follow his vocation.

Above all, he read and re-read the long and eulogistic entry on the great Gluck, "the greatest composer of whom the lyric stage can boast". It told of his heroic efforts to emancipate himself from the vain and frivolous conventions of Italian opera (of which the Abbé Arnaud "most truly remarked" that it is but a concert in costume and the drama merely a pretext); his abandonment of "the beaten track of prejudice and routine" to pioneer a new, more austere and grander, unified art based on the principle of fidelity of dramatic expression; and the glorious works, noble in tone and rich in pathos, with which he conquered Paris. The article emphasised the originality and eloquence of Gluck's use of the orchestra (an admiration that would be reflected in Berlioz's *Treatise on Orchestration* twenty-five years later):

Who has made the instruments speak as powerfully as Gluck? [...] It is in his orchestra that you will find the solemn rites of sacrifice, the horrors of war, the force of the winds, the howl of the storm, the thunder's roar; the cry that recalls the love-sick Renaud to glory, the awesome depiction of hell, the

lamenting dead, the baying Cerberus, and the eternal peace of the Elysian
Fields.

There were those who found fault with Gluck's vocal melodies; but
"what can one say to people who see melody only in our trivial *ariettes*,
who would restrict music to a mere combination of pleasing sounds and
ask only for their ears to be satisfied — whether they are moved or not
being a matter of indifference to them?" Gluck made no concessions.
Dramatic truth was the sole rule that must never be flouted. Several
anecdotes (the writer continued) could be cited in illustration of it. When
someone complained about the repetition of a single note in the aria
"Caron t'appelle" (in *Alceste*), the composer replied, "My friend, in
Hades passion dies down and the voice loses its inflections"; and the
article told how at a rehearsal of this passage, in search of the unearthly
sound he wanted, he made the two horns play with their bells joined one
to the other. There was, too, the scene in *Iphigénie en Tauride* where
Orestes says, "Peace returns to my heart", while the orchestra seems to
contradict the words. "Gluck was asked, 'Why, then, these muttering
cellos, these snapping violins [violas]?' 'He's lying,' the great man answered;
'he murdered his mother!'"

The origins of Berlioz's musical aesthetic are in the Michaud article on
Gluck. But it would be several years before he encountered Gluck's works
face to face. For the moment Gluck was an idea. He represented what
the fifteen-year-old Berlioz knew within himself that he was going to
be.

The proof of the depth and tenacity of this inner certainty, the test of
its validity, is that he did become a composer, against probability, against
his family's disbelief, against — one could say — almost all the evidence.
The secret fantasy was translated into fact; the elaborate daydreams, for
most adolescents an escape from reality, were for him a preparation for
reality. His imagination — to his family it was "imagination" and nothing
more — was ignited by the tiny spark he sensed within himself. But there
was precious little objective sign of it at this stage, and by the same token
almost nothing for him to go on himself. He knew, but had no reason for
knowing. As for his parents, they had only his word for it; and every
motive — of prudence, self-interest, affection — was against their taking
it.

With hindsight we can see faint premonitions of his musical personality
in the guitar accompaniments to a collection of twenty-five romances by
Dalayrac, Boieldieu, Martini and others that exists in his hand.* The

---

* The appearance and layout of this "Recueil de romances" — the most substantial manuscript
from Berlioz's childhood — suggest that it was intended for publication, though never published.
The name of the arranger has been scratched out subsequently with a knife. Apparently Berlioz,
on one of his visits to La Côte from Paris, was about to destroy the manuscript, when his friend
Joseph Favre begged him to give it to him instead, which he did, but only after removing his
name from the title page and table of contents.

accompaniments frequently depart from conventional figurations and harmonies in an attempt to colour the music in response to the words. A romance of his own composition to a text by Florian, "L'arabe jaloux", also shows a feeling for dramatic expression. Though the harmony is full of mistakes, the melody is not without interest: it mirrors the "jealous rage" and "cruel fears" that the subject of the poem experiences in the midst of his bliss, with sighing, broken phrases and fluctuations between major and minor which momentarily take the song out of its genre. And in one childhood song — as we have seen — the force and intensity of his feelings draw from him an authentic utterance: the Florian setting "Je vais donc quitter pour jamais / Mon doux pays, ma douce amie", which later became the opening theme of the Fantastic Symphony. The original has not survived, and there is no knowing what the harmony was like; but, as has been pointed out, Florian's lines fit the melody played by the violins at the beginning of the symphony. Tiersot remarks, not without justice, that the song "tells us that [Berlioz] had only to follow his natural course for his genius to develop to the full". Suddenly he is himself — so much so that a decade later the melody can be incorporated unchanged in the work that marks his coming of age after a long and laborious apprenticeship.[*]

We do not know whether he wrote other things, since lost, that were equally prophetic. If he did, they were not likely to have convinced his parents that his talent was exceptional and should be treated as a vocation. It was not in their outlook to be so convinced or to concede that music was a possible vocation for their son and heir. Dr Berlioz took an interest in his son's first compositions and, though critical of them, was impressed by a theme in one of the quintets when Hector, at his request, played the flute part through to him. "Ah, now that is what I call music!" he exclaimed on hearing what was to become the second subject of the *Francs-juges* overture. But it didn't alter his fundamental opinion. Music was simply not an admissible career for the heir to a property built up painstakingly over the generations. Hector's place was there, in the ancestral home. Later, in all their protracted struggles, it would be less the artistic career itself that Dr Berlioz objected to than what it involved: the apostasy.

To many bourgeois, of course, an artistic career was bad in itself. Berlioz did not exaggerate when he described the rigidly disapproving attitude of many provincials, his mother included, to all arts connected with the theatre: in becoming a composer ("which to the French means the theatre") he was indeed, in their eyes, "treading the broad road that

---

[*] Berlioz acknowledged the tune's significance in his life when, not long before his death, he inscribed it on the frontispiece of the *Memoirs*. Perhaps its very meaningfulness to him as an adolescent was the reason why he did not include it with the other romances that he published not long after his arrival in Paris, but kept it to himself.

leads to disgrace in this world and damnation in the next". The self-examination manuals of the time — pamphlets designed to jog the memory of the faithful before they went to confession — state unequivocally that it is a sin to go to the theatre. We can see a reflection of this belief in an exchange of letters between Nancy Berlioz, Hector's sister, and her friend Elise Rocher, recently married and living in nearby Valence. Elise had allowed herself to be lured by her husband's parents — devout though both of them are, she hastens to add — into seeing Ducis' *Othello*, and had enjoyed it so much that although she knew she shouldn't she had gone again, to see *Hamlet* (which made her cry till her head ached). Nancy (aged seventeen) was shocked and told Elise's aunt, who sent her niece a sharp reprimand and absolutely forbade her to attend another show. The chastened girl went to confession to be absolved; she chose a confessional said to be occupied by an indulgent priest, but was given a terrible dressing down. Although she blames Nancy for betraying her secret, she doesn't question that what she did was sinful.

This was admittedly the extreme view. The young Dumas, at about the same time, was having a much more relaxed encounter on the subject with his spiritual director (who was looking for someone to partner his niece at the Whitsuntide ball). "You can dance, can't you?" — "What makes you think that, Monsieur l'Abbé?" — "Oh come — don't you remember, at your last confession you accused yourself of having gone to the theatre and the opera and of having been dancing?" Women were expected to be more virtuous than men. They were also more prone to bigotry, being more subject to the influence of priests, especially during the Bourbon Restoration when religious revivalism and church militancy were at their height and the priesthood was striving to recapture its pre-Revolutionary power and influence. Even so, the high moral rectitude of Joséphine Berlioz and her daughter does not seem to have been shared by all their female friends. The letters of some of them suggest a more worldly approach: the acting world is a hotbed of atheism and licentiousness, no doubt; one lowers one's voice when talking about it; but one goes to the theatre all the same. Bourgeois society was ambivalent on the subject, and double standards operated.

On the whole the environment in which Berlioz grew up was not unsympathetic to the performing arts. Joséphine Berlioz may have acquired at her convent school a pious horror of the professional stage (which she passed on to her eldest daughter); she did not get it from her father. Nostalgia for Paris and its theatres is a frequent refrain in Nicolas Marmion's verse-letters. He and his circle at Meylan were forever dressing up and were dedicated to amateur theatricals — not only charades but quite elaborate productions of plays. Like many people's, his attitude was inconsistent and contradictory. He disowned his grandson and godson Hector when he married an actress, and appears to have had nothing more to do with him in the remaining two and a half years of his life. Yet a little earlier, when Hector seemed on the threshold of fame with the success of his quasi-dramatic "Episode in the Life of an Artist" (1832), far from being scandalised the old man was delighted at the thought that "Polyhymnia's boards" (i.e. the opera house) would soon echo to the sound of his triumph. When that happened, even Hector's mother would "fly / To join the joyful-hearted throng / Upon the margin of the Seine, / E'en as Camillus' mother, fain / To follow with attentive eye / Her son's triumphal car along".* Félix Marmion, Joséphine Berlioz's brother, was a keen theatre-goer. He was also very fond of music. Opéra-comique was his favourite art, and several letters in the family archives mention his fame as a singer in the drawing-rooms of Grenoble and Meylan; but he could respond to more serious things: another letter speaks of the deep impression made on him by a performance of a Cherubini mass that he heard when he was garrisoned at Valenciennes. Yet he too saw music as an adornment of a man's existence, not its main business.

Such an outlook was (and is) not confined to the French provinces. Even in Germany — even in a profoundly musical family and in the case of a precocious and dazzling talent — music was not generally considered a respectable profession. Mendelssohn's uncle Jacob Bartholdy was quite clear in his mind that his nephew should not take it up, and said so to the boy's father (who as it happened didn't agree with him): "The idea of a professional musician will not go down with me. It is no career, no life, no goal [...] Let the boy go through a regular course of schooling and then prepare for a career in the civil service by studying law at university. His art will remain his friend and companion [...] Or should you design him for a merchant, let him enter a counting-house early." This, essentially, was Dr Berlioz's attitude, sharpened and deepened by his passionate desire that the son to whose education he was devoting so much care should succeed him and carry on the family tradition — for, besides Louis Berlioz himself and his brother Auguste, their grandfather on their mother's side, François Robert, had practised medicine at La Côte, and the boy's maternal grandfather, Joseph Marmion, had been a distinguished surgeon. Medicine was in his blood. It was the right and natural career for him, and his father's dearest wish — surely a potent additional reason!

Perhaps in order to support his contention that it was the noblest of all professions, he sent to Paris for a framed engraving of Girodet's painting "Hippocrates Rejecting the Gifts of Artaxerxes". It was joined soon after by two Greuze engravings, bought in Paris and framed in Lyons, "The Paralytic Waited on by his Children" and the dramatic "A Parent's Curse" (a warning?), in which a son who has defied his father by

---

* On the other hand there is no doubt that it was the success of a sacred work, the Requiem, that gave the family the most gratification.

enlisting as a soldier is cursed by him. Not that Hector's childish objection to a medical career should be taken to heart. It was perfectly explicable as a sensitive and imaginative boy's shrinking from the idea of blood and sickness; time, habit and patient argument would overcome it. Dr Berlioz was encouraged to believe that he would come round to a reasonable and positive attitude by his evident bent towards science. Hector was keenly interested in the natural world and soaked up information about it. They talked geology and physics as well as literature on their walks together. The boy was a good learner. And now that he had begun working at his anatomy, getting accustomed to the sight and handling of a skeleton and studying the human bone structure from the life-size coloured illustrations in Monroe's *Treatise on Osteology* (which Dr Berlioz had used when he was teaching himself medicine), he was on the right road. True, his cousin and fellow-pupil Alphonse Robert was making more rapid progress, and Hector had sometimes to be chided quite severely for coming to their joint lessons inadequately prepared. But Alphonse, one must remember, was two years older. Hector had given his solemn promise. Once this adolescent craze for music found its natural level, all would yet be well. There was everything to be said for music as a hobby; here again Alphonse, a talented violinist, was a model. Dr Berlioz persisted in believing that it could be kept like that, and he emphasised his belief by the gift of the new flute at the moment when Hector was starting on his anatomy studies. Two years later, on Hector's passing his baccalauréat, his father presented him with a new guitar.

By that time, however, he had stopped paying for him to have guitar lessons. The list of expenses for 1821 in the Livre de Raison makes no mention of a "maître de musique" (whether or not the same was true of 1820 we cannot tell, since no itemised list is given for that year). Exactly when Maître Dorant left La Côte is uncertain. By early 1822 the town was looking for a new music master; but Dorant was still there in the spring of 1821, six months before Berlioz left for Paris to study medicine: his signature is on a National Guard document dated 21 April. There is abundant evidence in the shape of manuscript notebooks in his hand to show that he was active throughout his time at La Côte both as teacher and as arranger of music for the dances held in the local drawing-rooms as well as for the band of the National Guard. Some of this material, including the notebooks which contain items in the hands of both Hector and Nancy, may belong to 1819 or 1820; but on the last page of one, a book of waltzes for violin and two horns "appartenant au Sieur Dorant", there is a note dated 18 February 1821 — the draft of a love letter to an unnamed Côtoise with whom Dorant was in clandestine correspondence.

It is possible to see the non-employment of Dorant by Dr Berlioz in 1821 (and in 1820?) as a measure of prudence on the doctor's part. But the true explanation could be the purely pragmatic one given in the *Memoirs*: that the initiative came from Dorant himself, who announced

Dr Louis Berlioz: portrait by an unknown artist. Hector was the first of his six children, three of whom survived into adult life.

A page from Dr Berlioz's Livre de Raison, *the family chronicle and register of his estate which he kept from 1815 to 1838. The extract records the births of his children.*

Berlioz's sisters — Above: *Adèle: portrait by an unknown artist.*
Below: *Nancy: portrait by V.D. Cassien. Nancy, the nearest to him in age, was his
chief confidant in the family until her marriage in 1832, but Adèle became closer to him,
despite the ten-year gap between them.*

La Côte St André, le 6 Avril 1819
Répondu le 10 —

Monsieur,

Ayant le projet de faire graver plusieurs œuvres de musique de ma Composition je me suis adressé a vous esperant que vous pourriez remplir mon But; Je désirerois que vous prissiez a votre Compte l'Edition d'un pot-pourri Concertant composé de morceaux choisis, et concertant pour flutte Cor, deux violons, alto et Basse; Voyez si vous pouvez le faire et combien d'exemplaires vous me donnerez, Répondez moi au plus-tôt je vous prie si cela peut vous convenir combien de temps il vous faudra pour le graver et s'il est necessaire affranchir le Paquet; J'ai l'honneur d'être avec la plus parfaite Consideration votre Obeissant Serviteur

Hector Berlioz.

Mon adresse est : à Mr Hector Berlioz. a la Côte St André Dept de l'Isère

Berlioz, aged fifteen, writes to the Paris firm of Pleyel, offering for publication a "medley composed from selected airs" for flute, horn and string quartet.

candidly that he had nothing more to teach his pupil, as he was now as good a guitar-player as his master. If that is true, the fact that Nancy too stopped having lessons could be explained simply as a sensible act of economy (given that she showed no obvious aptitude for music) and not as an attempt to guard Hector from temptation by keeping Dorant out of the way. A third possibility is suggested by the baccalauréat records in the university archives in Grenoble, which appear to reveal that Berlioz's successful examination for his bac in March 1821 was a second attempt, and that he had presented himself the previous December, at the same time as Alphonse Robert, and failed. (The second time round, though adjudged weak in History and Geography, he passed "à l'unanimité" — most candidates got "à la majorité" — and with the comment, "The candidate has been taught thoroughly, and displayed intelligence.") What lay behind the initial failure, whether it represents a major crisis or a minor stumble, there is no means of telling; but it prompts the thought that the guitar lessons may have been brought to an end simply so that he could concentrate on passing the exam. This is an example of the ambiguity of the evidence (where there is any) from the first period of Berlioz's life.

No document shows us the seventeen-year-old Hector's state of mind, torn between filial piety and an equally deep but vague inner presentiment that his life was not going to be "spent at the bedside of the sick, in hospitals and in dissecting-rooms" but was destined for something quite different. The conflict must have been intense. But it was largely a silent conflict. My impression is that the central question of medicine versus music went underground during these years, or rather that not until he reached Paris and went to the Opéra and came directly under the influence of Gluck did it burst out into the open and become a fully acknowledged issue between him and his parents. Till then it had never been stated in those terms. "Children reason little," he wrote to his father, years later, recalling their disagreements over his career. "Yet they feel instinctively the inopportuneness of certain things." From the first he felt certain he would not be a doctor, and had tried to say so; but he lacked the means to convince his father. Outwardly, the matter had been settled at the beginning of 1819 when his father had called him into his room and told him that it was time for him to begin his preliminary medical studies. Using as a bribe the offer of the new flute he knew Hector longed for, he had exacted a promise from his son. The earnestness of his manner and the awe that for all his gentleness he inspired, together with the lure of the coveted flute, had proved too much for the boy. Powerless to refuse, he had stammered out a faint "Yes" and gone back to his room and flung himself on the bed in utter dejection.

For the next two and a half years osteology was part of his curriculum — along with Latin, Philosophy, Rhetoric and the rest — as he struggled to overcome his aversion and acquire a grounding in it, preparatory to his becoming a full-time medical student. Given his natural curiosity and incipient interest in science, it is unlikely the subject struck no sparks in him. But the study-periods with his violinist cousin Alphonse were sometimes spent more on musical talk than on the demonstrations they were supposed to be preparing for their next lesson; and more than once his father lost his temper with him.

Yet up to and including his departure for Paris in 1821 the issue remained unspoken: it was not something that was discussed, with his father or his mother. He continued to write songs, and accompaniments to popular romances, and to play the guitar and the flute; but his thoughts he kept for the most part to himself. The attempt, in 1819, to get some of his music published in Paris — successful in the case of one song, "Le dépit de la bergère" — would thus have been a tacit declaration of intent, made in the vague hope of impressing his parents. He confided his half-formed ambitions to his sister Nancy (Hector was known as a "composer" among her girl friends and rather looked up to on account of it); but she was only thirteen, and of limited use as an ally. It may have been Félix Marmion — always ready to have a foot in both camps — who put up the money for the publication of "Le dépit de la bergère". Félix Marmion certainly had a pretty good idea what was in his nephew's mind. He talked about it to a certain Madame Husson, friend, benefactor and former mistress of his who lived in the town of Toul, in Lorraine, where his regiment, the First Dragoons, was garrisoned. In February 1821, when he was in Dauphiné on leave, engaged in a delicate mission to persuade his father to pay off his gambling debts, she wrote to him to ask what success he was having, and then added: "Tell me also about your other relatives. I think you must be finding it difficult to prevent yourself from sympathising with your nephew in his enthusiasm for music. Indeed, although I say it to you alone, I would rather be Mozard [sic] or Grétry or Baillot, etc. (and others too whom I do not know and who are perhaps greater) than an inspector of domains or forests." Félix Marmion would very probably have spoken of his nephew's aspirations to his sister and brother-in-law on one of his frequent visits to La Côte St André, only to have them brushed aside: it was a totally absurd idea, not even worthy of consideration. And no doubt the worldly-wise Captain of Dragoons did not disagree with them.

There is no sign that Dr Berlioz had begun to grasp the problem. In so far as he was aware of it, his mind shied away. There were other worries to attend to. Politics had continued to make highly unwelcome intrusions on his peace of mind. These were unsettled years in Dauphiné, and in Lyonnais, in the aftermath of the Hundred Days and the second Bourbon Restoration. The province was alive with rumours of plots, by leftists reacting against the "White Terror", by Ultras dissatisfied with Louis XVIII's moderation and dreaming of replacing him with his brother the

Comte d'Artois (the later Charles X). Very often such rumours (some-times fabricated by the Right to arouse fears of incipient revolution) came to nothing; but not always. The Didier Conspiracy of May 1816 was a genuine, though bungled, attempt by a loose coalition of Bonapartists and a few officers on half pay to take over Grenoble by force. It had been easily foiled and bloodily put down, but it had disturbed the whole département and revived fears of renewed civil strife. Félix Marmion, characteristically, enjoyed himself and contrived to turn the affair to his advantage. In Meylan at the time, still awaiting a commission in the reorganised French Army, he was put in command of the local National Guard and immediately posted a detachment half a mile down the road to Grenoble; nothing untoward occurring, he sent his "brave men back to their ploughshares". A few weeks later the *Gazette* commended Captain Marmion for "assembling the peasants of his canton during the recent troubles and inspiring them to march against the rebels".

For Dr Berlioz the affair had tiresome long-term consequences. Against his will he found himself drawn into public life. In June 1817 an Ultra conspiracy set nearby Lyons briefly in uproar. At the same time the Mayor of La Côte, Buffevent, died after fifteen years in office. A group of influential citizens urged Dr Berlioz to agree to be nominated in his place. As a man of the centre, loyal to the King and the Charter and associated with neither extreme, yet a firm believer in law and order, a property-owner of proven integrity and active benevolence, respected by all classes, he was felt to be the ideal choice at a time not only of political but also of social unrest, caused by acute shortages and high prices consequent on the occupation and the disastrously wet summer of 1816. With intense reluctance, and after several weeks of pleading and badgering, he gave in and was installed as mayor at the beginning of September 1817. (He was then forty-one years old.) In the event he was in office for only three months. On going through the files he discovered a grave irregularity: his predecessor had apparently appropriated to his own use nearly 8,000 francs from the resale of the petit-séminaire to the church eight years earlier. There was no record of the money having been spent on municipal business; it had simply disappeared. As a peacemaking mayor Dr Berlioz had no intention of setting the town by the ears by making the scandal generally known; but as a man of probity he could not condone the offence and go on as if nothing was wrong. He resigned, pleading poor health and pressure of work. To the consternation of the La Côte establishment the Prefect nominated as his successor the grocer Joseph Charbonnel. A known radical, outsider, eccentric (and womaniser), Charbonnel was unlikely, to say the least, to produce harmony in the town; and he was quite certain to let the cat out of the bag about the accounts. At a crisis meeting held in the doctor's house it was decided to seek a breathing-space, so that the accounts could be put "in order" and an item of expenditure concocted for the missing money. A deputation went to Grenoble, and a postponement of Charbonnel's installation was obtained. When it expired, Dr Berlioz was persuaded to refuse to swear him in as his successor. Tension and tempers rose. The second time the mayor-designate presented himself at the mairie, accompanied by the commander of the National Guard, there was no one there to admit him. Eventually a solution was found: Charbonnel was installed, but only as a stand-in, and a few months later he was replaced by a safe compromise candidate, a wealthy La Côte proprietor called Adolphe de Monts. (It is his signature that is on Imbert's contract of May 1818.)

The whole affair was exceedingly distasteful to poor Louis Berlioz; it confirmed his low opinion of politics (and no doubt contributed to his son's), making him resolve to keep well clear of them in future. At any rate he was free again to concentrate his worries on his estate, his family and his own incipient deafness, and to devote himself to the everyday preoccupations of farming and doctoring. At the beginning of 1818 the medical societies of both Bordeaux and Lyons responded to his book on chronic diseases by electing him an associate member (Lyons also asking him to contribute to a forthcoming volume of monographs), and the prestigious Paris society did the same the following year. It was a relief, instead of poring over dubious administrative documents, to sign a straightforward agreement with the son of one of his tenants for daily handiwork, including curry-combing the mare, sweeping the road outside the house, watering the gardens, digging and weeding the garden at Le Chuzeau (his country house just outside the town), feeding the cows and leading them to the bull. He was putting in hand a number of improvements at Le Chuzeau, and spent a large part of the autumn out of doors there, supervising the work and, once, saving the lives of two of his workmen who were nearly buried in a landslip. The wine harvest, after the bad years of 1815, 1816 and 1817, was looking up. There was a good crop in 1818, and again in 1819; and in 1820 he made a handsome profit on the sale of wine, which went some way towards offsetting the previous losses. Prices, too, had steadied.

Political events remained something of an anxiety. There was an outcry on the Right when Abbé Grégoire, notorious "Jacobin", member of the regicide Convention of 1792, won a seat as a deputy for Grenoble in the elections of September 1819. Six months later the Duc de Berry, son of the Comte d'Artois and hope of the Bourbon dynasty, was stabbed to death in the foyer of the Paris Opéra; the murder polarised opinion between the two extremes and dealt a blow to the politics of reconciliation. The assassin, Louvel, who at his trial protested that he had had "the sound of the cannon of Waterloo in his head ever since 18 June 1815", became a hero of the Left, "a figure out of Plutarch". Angry crowds mobbed the Duc d'Angoulême when he visited Grenoble soon afterwards. Louis XVIII, with an eye on European chancelleries alert for fresh tremors of revolution in France, was obliged to appoint a right-of-centre government; and the dream of a centre party uniting royalism and liberalism, which Louis Berlioz shared, receded still further. Education, too, was disturbed by becoming a political battleground: the medical school at Montpellier, a hundred miles to the south-west, closed as a result of student agitation against the encroachments of the priesthood.

At least he was not directly involved any more, and could observe these gloomy signs of the times from a distance. Napoleon's death on St Helena, on 5 May 1821, removed one potential source of national discord. In any case there were troubles nearer home, present tragedies to be endured. The health of the little girl, Adèle, though still far from good, improved; but four years after the death of their daughter Louise, Louis and Joséphine Berlioz buried another child. Their second son, Jules, born in December 1816, died one evening in May 1819, "probably of an extravasation in the fourth ventricle of the brain, after 21 hours' illness and having been in perfect health just before". This brief note in the Livre de Raison and the entries of his birth and death in the Actes Civiles of La Côte are the solitary records of the little boy's existence. Of the effect of his death on his brother and sisters, of the grief of his parents and whether it brought them closer together and halted, temporarily, their drifting apart, we know nothing. But a few months later Joséphine Berlioz became pregnant again, and the following June her last child, Prosper, was born. Within a few years he would be being seen as a compensation not only for little Jules' death but for the "loss" of the eldest son; Nicolas Marmion would actually describe him as having replaced Hector as the son of the house.

For the moment, however, that recreant was treading the path of virtue. He passed his bac in March 1821; and as an unsettled June and July and a hot dry August gave way to an unusually cool autumn, plans were made for him and Alphonse Robert to go to Paris in time to enrol at the School of Medicine for the start of the academic year. On 26 October the mairie of La Côte issued him with the passport required for travel outside the département. A few days later he said goodbye to his father (deep in the wine harvest), his mother, sisters and brother, and set out on the five-day, 350-mile journey to the capital, taking with him their anxious hopes and the secret turmoil of his own divided thoughts.

In retrospect, the main themes of Berlioz's existence are laid down in these first seventeen sheltered, momentous years. The very name his parents choose for him is heavy with destiny. Never have boyhood experiences played a more vital part, not only in providing a well of recollected emotion for the artist to draw on all his life but in deciding the character of his art.

Educated at home, he is allowed to preserve unblunted an abnormal capacity for feeling and to develop by wide and voracious reading a superabundant imagination. He shares the dreams of his generation − a fascination with Napoleon and his brilliant headlong career, a passionate curiosity about far-off lands − and also its nightmares, a chilling sense of isolation, of total estrangement from beauty and love and companionship, attacking without warning and turning all to dust. His response to nature is awakened in the valleys and mountains and plains of Dauphiné, a landscape whose mixture of grandeur and lucidity, movement and stillness, gleaming peaks, vast blue distances, sinuous contours and swift and violent climatic changes will find a mirror in his music; and from the first this awareness is associated with the onset of romantic passion, expressing itself in hopeless love for a girl six years older than himself, image of the unattainable ideal of which he is to be a willing victim all his life. In this hyper-active state his imagination seizes on Virgil, feeding on the tragic passions of the *Æneid* and creating from its heroic narrative a familiar country to which his soul "can in a moment travel". He falls under the spell of religion. Though his beliefs will not survive into adult life, the impression of the Catholic ritual is never effaced; the very loss of faith will leave a powerful imprint on his many sacred works.

Religion, nature, romantic love, adventure, fame, travel, the distant past, a paralysing loneliness − any or all of these are common obsessions of sensitive adolescence. What is uncommon in Berlioz is their tenacity − almost, their purposefulness. It is as though in everything that happens to him he is carrying out a programme. By the time he leaves home and goes to Paris the nature of the artist he is to be is determined in all essentials.

What was he like? How should we picture Berlioz, six weeks before his eighteenth birthday? The information on his passport provides the earliest extant portrait: "height 1 metre 63 centimetres [just over 5 ft 4 ins], hair fair, forehead normal, eyebrows fair, eyes grey, nose good ['bien'], mouth average, beard incipient, chin round, face oval, complexion high, distinguishing marks none"; but in the manner of such documents it tells us practically nothing beyond the fact that he still had an inch or two to grow. Indeed, less than nothing: for many descriptions testify to his eyes being not grey but blue and his hair an unusual fiery blond; and "nez bien", whatever that means, hardly does justice to the great beak which will figure so prominently in written accounts as well as in caricatures.*
The young Hector springs more palpably if unexpectedly to life in the testimony of a contemporary of his, who reported that he had a passion for dancing, and that he possessed a pair of green leather boots of which he was inordinately proud.

---

* "Talking of noses, no news from Hector," writes Adèle Berlioz to her sister Nancy in May 1832, when the family is awaiting his return from Italy.

In concentrating on the future artist and on what was prophetic and extraordinary about his adolescence we are in danger of overlooking another Berlioz: the boy who did ordinary boyish things, who lived from one day to the next, was no hothouse plant and did not spend all his time alone cultivating a tragic sensibility, was lively and active and could even on occasion be high-spirited, played with his friends, enjoyed family expeditions, and got into trouble not for wanting to be a composer but for being naughty. He tends to be forgotten because he has been overshadowed by the image of the Romantic artist; but he was a real person, and he left some evidence of himself. This Hector was an energetic walker and explored the whole countryside on foot. He played boules with the boys of the town under the lime trees on the Esplanade on Sundays. He was known as a prankster, was given to setting off firecrackers, liked hoaxes: there was a summer evening, long afterwards talked of, when he and Antoine Charbonnel (son of the controversial figure who succeeded Dr Berlioz briefly as mayor) disguised themselves as itinerant musicians and successfully passed the hat round up and down the main street of La Côte for quite a while before they were recognised.

Three other traits: he was a natural leader, he was on easy terms with boys older than himself — Robert two years older, Joseph Favre four, Amédée Faure seven, Imbert fils two — and he made friends without regard to class: with the members of the prosperous Rocher clan, with Charbonnel the grocer's son, with Joseph Favre who like his father was a clog-maker.*

There is a further qualification to be made to the image of the budding Romantic and the dreamer "living within his dream's bright kingdom". This account of his early education has emphasised the development of poetic imagination and dwelt on the extreme impressionability of the young Berlioz, electrified by emotions too strong for him, identifying with the characters of his favourite books and acting out their griefs and exaltations in his own being, because that was the beginning of his formation as an artist. But there is another aspect, complementary to it, hardly less essential to the creative process, and that is the ability to detach himself from his deepest experiences and observe and note and retain them, so that his brain remains active while his emotions are in tumult, and during a shattering attack of spleen he analyses his sensations like a scientist recording an experiment, or on the point of shipwreck, while crossing to Italy, he can examine the scene with the eye of a

---

* All three characteristics — leadership, friendship with older boys, indifference to social distinctions — are exemplified by a letter (no longer extant) from Berlioz to Favre inviting his friend, who plays clarinet, to join a group of musicians he is getting together to accompany the Corpus Christi procession. The contents of the letter were reported to Tiersot by Favre's son Henri, who had come across it among his father's papers and kept it for a while but had eventually thrown it away, not thinking it worth preserving.

bystander — the ability (as he said during the composition of *The Trojans*) to be most cool when the feelings to be expressed are at flame heat.

His early education fostered this analytical side of his artistic make-up no less than the imaginative side. From his father he acquired an interest in science, developed in formal lessons, conversations and his own reading. It survived his renouncing medicine and embracing the career of composer. The scientifc habit of mind, besides acting as a corrective to his exalted temperament, influenced his approach to the problems of composition.[*] The persistence of this early interest is shown by the frequent occurrence in writings and letters, throughout his life, of scientific terms and imagery — including, under "scientific", geology and natural history.

To evoke the mal d'isolement which first attacked him as he listened to the distant Rogation procession, he has recourse quite naturally to a metaphor drawn from physics.[†] He uses an analogy from engineering when, in speaking of his work as a critic, he admits that sometimes he forces himself for diplomatic reasons to praise a work he dislikes, yet in spite of his efforts his real opinion comes out between the lines "just as in the action of a hydraulic press the water seeps through the pores of the metal". A harp chord, played at the correct pitch after the singer has sung the preceding phrase flat, "hisses like a spoonful of molten lead in cold water". During his journey to Italy in 1831, in the midst of the violence and confusion of the storm which seems on the point of drowning him along with everyone on board, the sight of the huge waves foaming over the deck reminds him of Humboldt's description of the South American boa constrictor covering its victim with a mucous slaver before devouring it.[†]

In his literary education Romantic influences are balanced by Classical. His father, as was natural in a man of his time and background, nurtured him on the poets, dramatists, philosophers and moralists of the Grand Siècle and the Enlightenment. If Berlioz did not read them at first as avidly as he read Chateaubriand, Rousseau or Virgil, he learned a taste for them, and it lasted. In his adult writings Molière's comedies, Boileau's verse, La Fontaine's fables are cited so often that it ceases to be a matter of quotation: they are part of the furniture of his mind. Our preoccupation

---

[*] See for example the way he set about teaching himself the craft of writing for orchestra, systematically comparing what he heard with what was written in all the major scores of the repertory and also getting his musician friends to experiment with new ideas and techniques.

[†] A passage from the great explorer's *Tableaux de la Nature*, a copy of which was in his father's library. From Humboldt also comes the image of the "mighty bird of Chimborazo's snowy summits" invoked by Berlioz as metaphor for Beethoven's spirit, in the adagio of one of the late quartets, soaring into the remote ether. Humboldt describes watching a condor wheeling above him in the Andes at an altitude of over 23,000 feet.

with the arch-Romantic is apt to make us forget what strong roots he had in the preceding culture and how deeply his art was influenced by the neo-classical inheritance. There is a close analogy, if not a causal connection, with his constant search for clarity of musical style and refinement of orchestral texture. Berlioz's orchestra, for all its expansion of the means and range of expression, aspires to the classical ideal of separation of timbres. The rich blendings of Wagner and Schumann represent a quite different, piano-based aesthetic. Berlioz writes nineteenth-century music with an eighteenth-century sound. His sense of intellectual affinity with La Fontaine, Molière and Boileau is paralleled by his lifelong devotion to Gluck, the composer whose operas formed the basis of his musical education during his first years in Paris, before the advent of Weber and Beethoven. Even after his discovery of Beethoven — the decisive event of his musical development — he remains faithful. Beethoven does not exclude Gluck, any more than Shakespeare banishes Molière.*

Any discussion of Berlioz's boyhood is drawn inevitably into anticipating the future: the main themes of his adult life are so clearly prefigured in these first introductory years, the child is so unmistakably father to the man, the voice of destiny speaks out so loud and bold. "I am driven involuntarily towards a magnificent career," he writes to his father from Paris. That was two or three years later, after many months of family strife; but the temptation is to see the issue as already clear-cut and to all intents settled in his mind by the time he left his native town at the end of October 1821, in effect never to return. Just because his inner conviction was vindicated and he did against rational likelihood become a great composer, it is hard to imagine him hesitating. Quite apart from genius, the degree of certainty and the force of will required to turn oneself in eight years from a callow provincial who has never had a lesson in composition or heard an orchestra into the composer of the Fantastic Symphony seems hardly to admit the possibility of doubt. Overpersuadability was surely one weakness that Berlioz never suffered from. Nor timidity either: a boy of fifteen who writes to the leading Paris publisher, demanding that he publish his music, may be naïve but does not lack determination or audacity. How can he have been still uncertain two and a half years later — he above all for whom music was not a choice but a necessity, the indispensable outlet of his passionate, electric nature, the condition of his existence?

Yet such inconsistencies ought not really to surprise us. We should remember how young he was — not yet eighteen and though in some

---

* Cf. Byron, who remained faithful to his classical forbears Dryden and Pope, championing them against the aspersions of the Lakeland poets. Even if Berlioz had been a writer, not a musician, one could not imagine him, like Dumas (as reported by Delacroix in his *Journal*) inveighing against "the feebleness of Racine, the emptiness of Boileau, the total absence of melancholy in the writers of the so-called Grand Siècle".

ways precocious in other ways young for his age — and how strongly he was still bound to his parents, how much under the sway of his father. In his Autobiographical Sketch of 1832 he puts it quite succinctly: "Prevailed upon and captivated by the loving affection that his father showed constantly towards him, for two years he followed under his guidance the path [medicine] on which he had entered so unwillingly." So strong is the bond that nearly four years later, and just after the successful public performance of his Mass, he will dutifully return home, to be subjected to fresh pressure. Not till 1826 will he finally assert his independence to the extent of going his own way regardless of what his parents think — and even so a sense of close family ties will remain with him all his life, surviving periods of estrangement.

Add too that the extreme fluctuations of mood that he was prey to all his life, between elation and apathy, were particularly difficult to cope with in such a situation, and would have made an attitude of defiance all the more impossible for him to sustain at this stage. A part of his mind must, too, have recognised the force of the arguments against a musical career. He was conscious of how abysmally little he knew. Once the die was cast all his energy and determination, all his intelligence and methodical application would be concentrated on making up for lost time. For the present, an inner core of conviction, buried deep within him, was surrounded by conflict, bewilderment, doubt.

Another factor may be worth mentioning. This hesitation of his may reveal not only his youth and immaturity and dependence on his parents but also an obedience to the deep instincts of the race, the Dauphinois, which his fellow-countryman Stendhal defined as a combination of passion and caution, timidity and will-power, peculiar to the inhabitants of that region of France. "I must tell you that sometimes you do things too precipitately. I believe one should reflect a great deal about what one intends to do and then, when every measure has been taken, strike a decisive blow so that all the barriers are thrown down. Prudence and force — they're the only way of getting where you want to in this world." That is not Stendhal but Berlioz, writing to his friend Ferdinand Hiller. It conforms exactly to Stendhal's identification of the "type dauphinois": the ability to think level-headedly before taking a decision and, once it is taken, to stick to it, the mixture of intensity of feeling — found already in boys of fourteen, though quite unknown in Parisians of the same age — with a shrewd refusal to act on one's initial impulse.*

Thus, as he and Alphonse Robert travel northwards in the cramped, rattling diligence, we should think of him as poised in suspension between two looming prospects each as ill-defined as the other. On one side — his

* Where the Provençal will give vent to violent abuse, the Dauphinois stores up the insult within himself. The readiness to conceive lasting animosities from quite minor wrongs, a Dauphinois trait which Stendhal recognised in himself, was also characteristic of Berlioz.

heart beats faster at the thought — a new world of music and theatre. On the other, equally unimaginable, the School of Medicine. That is why his father is sending him to Paris. Hector has given him his promise, and means to keep it. But in Paris he will be going to the Opéra. He will be able to see the great Gluck in all his glory and hear the works he has been longing to hear ever since he first read about them in Michaud. For the moment, there is no need to think beyond that. It is enough, and it makes the thought of medical school almost bearable. It has been his dream for the last three years, and it is about to come true.

6

To Paris

———◆◆———

The public stagecoach of those days averaged no more than three or four miles an hour over the heavy, rutted surfaces. It took eight hours to get from La Frette, the staging-post two miles east of La Côte, to Lyons — a distance of only thirty miles. From Lyons there was a direct service to Paris, a journey of four days and nights of almost incessant bumpy, noisy motion, with a mere forty-five-minute stop twice during the day for a meal at a wayside inn, and otherwise only the briefest halt every few hours to change the horses. The early nineteenth-century traveller expected nothing better; but, for a provincial arriving in the capital for the first time, the fatigue of the journey intensified the impression of strangeness, vastness and turmoil. The Lyons coach entered Paris from the south-east and after crossing the Place de la Bastille turned north and then west along the boulevards, to the terminus in the courtyard of the Messageries, Rue Notre-Dame des Victoires, near the Bourse. From there to 104 Rue St Jacques, where Berlioz and Robert had rooms booked, was a cab-drive through the heart of the city, along narrow crowded streets of towering tenement buildings, past great churches and museums and palaces and over the river to the Latin Quarter.

A present-day traveller, if he or she could see the Paris of a century and a half ago, would naturally be astonished at how small it seemed. To this day the centre remains so compact that you can conveniently get about in it on foot. In 1821 there was very little beyond that. Napoleon's unfinished Arc de Triomphe (renamed the Arc d'Angoulème) marked the extreme north-west point of the city; Montparnasse was on the edge of open country, Montmartre a separate village; the triangle of land whose apex is today formed by the Rue Lecourbe and the Boulevards Garibaldi and de Grenelle was a cultivated plain dotted with farms.[*]

---

[*] Hazlitt, visiting the city three years later, remarked that "Paris differs from London in this respect, that it has no suburbs. The moment you are beyond the barriers, you are in the country to all intents and purposes. You have not to wade through ten miles of straggling houses to get a breath of fresh air or a peep at nature [...] not a hundred yards from the barrier of Neuilly, you see an old shepherd tending his flock, with his dog and his crook and sheep-skin cloak, just as if it were a hundred miles off, or a hundred years ago."

These much narrower limits, however, contained well over half a million inhabitants, and a large number of them were crammed into a few square miles north and south of the Ile de la Cité. The first sight must have been bewildering to the two new arrivals from La Côte St André. Their fellow-Dauphinois Stendhal, arriving in Paris on his own twenty years earlier, had noted as his immediate impressions the sorry sight of lopped trees in the public gardens, the depressing lack of mountains, the clangour of the innumerable clocks striking the hour, and the profound solitariness of city life. But Berlioz and Robert had little leisure to feel lonely. The academic year was beginning; and, having installed themselves in their furnished rooms a few minutes' walk from the School of Medicine, they bought linen coats, surgical instruments, textbooks, pens and note-books and, along with a couple of hundred other students embarking on the four-year course required for qualifying as doctors, signed the first of their sixteen termly inscriptions in the school register. Monsieur Drouault, proprietor of their hôtel meublé at 104 Rue St Jacques, acted as their surety.

The broad thoroughfares that bisect the modern Latin Quarter, the Boulevards St Michel and St Germain, did not then exist. They and the Rue des Ecoles were the creation of Haussmann, who imposed them in the 1860s on a street plan not greatly changed since the Middle Ages. In doing so he obliterated the top half of the Rue de la Harpe and reduced the Rue St Jacques — since Roman times the city's main southern artery and so named because it was the start of one of the ancient European pilgrim routes to the shrine of St James at Santiago de Compostela — to a minor road. Yet this district, the modern fifth and sixth arrondissements, for seven centuries the home of the University of Paris, remains one of those where the sense of the remote past is strongest. Behind the boulevards, in the labyrinth of grey twisting side-streets, some still unpaved, with their doorways opening on a warren of further entrances and their ill-lit stone staircases smelling of cats, or in the old covered markets of St Germain and Maubert, you can almost fancy yourself in the Paris of Gargantua and Pantagruel, and it is not difficult to imagine the university community that the seventeen-year-old Berlioz found himself pitchforked into. The cafés then as now swarmed with students disposing of the universe or announcing a masterpiece or a definitive new system of society. Many of the buildings were the same. The exterior of the School of Medicine fronting the Rue de l'Ecole de Médecine is substantially as it was then: the long colonnaded façade, with railings between the columns, the handsome portico surmounted by an allegorical frieze depicting the Spirit of Benevolence (before the Revolution it had been Louis XV) giving orders for the construction of the Schools of Surgery. The steeply raked lecture theatre where Professor Amussat taught anatomy still exists, though the courtyard was not yet presided over by the statue of Bichat, the brilliant scientist who had died in 1802 at the age of thirty, having inaugurated the modern science of clinical pathology, and whose *Anatomie générale* Berlioz kept on the dissecting-room table beside him as he and Robert investigated their "subject" muscle by muscle, bone by bone and organ by organ.

We can also imagine what a shock this vibrant, restless new physical and mental environment gave to the nervous system of one so highly strung and so callow and inexperienced, untaught even in the lessons in human life that are learned in the hurly-burly of the local high school. The most obvious shock came from his first encounter with humanity in its extreme form, in the dissecting-room of the Hospice de la Pitié (in south-east Paris, near the Jardin des Plantes). He himself later described the scene, with a ghoulish realism that needed no touching-up:

> The sight of that appalling charnel-house — the disconnected limbs, the grinning visages and gaping skulls, the bloody quagmire underfoot and the disgusting smell it gave off, the swarms of sparrows squabbling over their scraps of lung, the rats in the corner gnawing the bleeding vertebrae — filled me with such terror that I jumped through the dissecting-room window and ran all the way back to my lodgings as though Death and his hideous train were at my heels.

His immediate reaction was that medicine was a total impossibility, and he cast round desperately for some way of escape. Within twenty-four hours, however, he had got the better of his feelings and, urged on by his cousin, was able to return to the Pitié and cover his revulsion under the medical student's time-honoured macabre jesting. Robert and he quoted Racine to each other while they dissected their corpse and threw the unwanted bits to the sparrows:

> "Thou giv'st the little birds their daily bread." — "And o'er all Nature's realm my bounty spread," I retorted, tossing a shoulder-blade to a large rat which was looking at me with hungry eyes.

The other great shock to his sensibilities — not recoiled from but passionately desired — was the Opéra. He went there soon after reaching Paris, and received the longed-for revelation. It was as though (he said later) a young man born with the instincts of a sailor but knowing only the lakes of his native mountains were suddenly to find himself on board a three-decker ship on the open sea: a young man, we may add, who had been thinking of the sea day and night and only waiting for the moment when he would encounter it. To Berlioz's disappointment no work of Gluck's was on the playbills; he had just missed *Iphigénie en Tauride*, which had been performed on 2 November. But Salieri's *The Danaids* was on, and he went to hear it on the 14th. He knew the name well, from the Gluck article in Michaud's *Biographie*, where it was actually treated as an unfinished work of Gluck, "completed by Salieri in the happiest manner".

It was all he had dreamed of:

The pomp and brilliance of the spectacle, the massive sonority of orchestra and chorus, the inspired pathos of Mme Branchu and her extraordinary voice, the rugged grandeur of Dérivis, Hypermnestre's aria, in which I discerned, imitated by Salieri, all the characteristics of Gluck's style as I had conceived it from the pieces from his *Orphée* in my father's library, and finaliy the tremendous bacchanal and the sad voluptuous ballet music that Spontini added to his old compatriot's score, disturbed and exalted me to an extent that I will not attempt to describe [. . .] I hardly slept that night, and the next day's anatomy lesson suffered accordingly. I sang Danaus' aria "The kindly strokes of destiny" as I sawed my "subject's" skull; and when Robert, impatient at my humming "Descend into the sea-nymph's breast" when I should have been consulting Bichat's chapter on nerve-tissue, exclaimed, "Oh come on, we're not getting anywhere, in three days our subject will have gone bad — eighteen francs down the drain; you really must be sensible!", I replied with the hymn to Nemesis, "Goddess insatiable for blood", and the scalpel fell from his hand.

No doubt the dialogue is embellished (though he certainly did enliven the dissecting-room with extracts from newly heard operas); but the account does not exaggerate the explosive effect of the experience. Salieri's score would strike us as thin and stiff, Gluck without the genius. To the seventeen-year-old Berlioz it was the real thing. Remember that until that moment the most considerable body of sound he had heard was the band of the local National Guard — a dozen and a half wind instruments played out of tune — struggling through arrangements of popular marches and romances. The Opéra orchestra contained more than seventy musicians, many of them among the finest in Paris,[*] and the chorus was nearly as big. Ferdinand Hiller expressed it exactly when he said, "I doubt if it is possible for those of us who have grown up with music and the theatre to have any conception of the impact that such an experience, musical and dramatic, must have had on someone who had never heard anything remotely like it but whose whole being was primed to feel everything to do with music and poetry to the uttermost. It was a spark in a powder-keg."

There were six further performances of *The Danaids* before the end of 1821, and though we have no record of Berlioz's going to hear it again it is certain he did, and that from the first he spent many of his evenings in the splendid new theatre in the Rue le Peletier just north of the Boulevard des Nations (the modern Boulevard des Italiens) which was to be his spiritual home for the next six years. Built to replace the one in which the

---

[*] The Conservatoire Concert Society, formed in 1828 from the élite of Paris musicians, drew a third of its eighty-six members from the Opéra orchestra.

Duc de Berry had been assassinated, and opened only three months before, the Opéra had excellent acoustics and a capacity of 1,937. There were three performances a week, on Monday, Wednesday and Friday (and in addition an occasional Sunday benefit evening and a weekly masked ball during the Carnival season). Except on gala nights or for spectacular new productions it was not difficult to get a ticket, and a bench seat in the pit cost only 3 fr. 60 — about a dollar in modern terms.

Within a few days of his first visit to *The Danaids* he was back at the Opéra, this time for a benefit performance for the actor Dufresne (Sunday 18 November), at which the main item was another work of the Gluckist school, Méhul's *Stratonice*. The programme ended with *Nina*, the ballet composed by Persuis after Dalayrac's opera, in one number of which, a touching scene for the mad heroine danced by Mlle Bigottini to a cor anglais solo, he was surprised and moved to hear the tune of the hymn sung six or seven years before at his first communion; on asking a neighbour of his whom he had noticed mouthing the words, he learned that it was by Dalayrac.

A few days after that, to his joy, *Iphigénie en Tauride* was announced, and on 26 November, after what had seemed an age though it was no more than three weeks since his arrival, he was able to fulfil the ambition implanted several years earlier by Michaud's account of Gluck's "sombre and tragic" masterpiece, the drama of "two friends who, each striving to save the other's life, dedicate themselves to death for one another's sake, and whose executioner is the sister of one of the victims".[*] He tried to give his sister Nancy an idea of how wonderful it was:

Imagine, to begin with, an orchestra of eighty musicians who perform with such precision that you'd think it was a single instrument. The opera begins: you see far off a great plain (oh, the illusion is complete) and farther still a glimpse of the sea. A storm is heralded in the orchestra, dark clouds descend slowly and cover the plain; the stage is lit only by flickers of lightning piercing the clouds — but with a truthfulness and a perfection that have to be seen to be believed. There is silence for a moment, no actor on stage, the orchestra muttering, it's as if you can hear the wind sighing — you know, as you do when you're alone in winter and you hear the north wind moaning. Well, it's just like that. Then little by little the tension mounts and the storm bursts. Orestes and Pylades appear, in chains, brought by the barbarians of

---

[*] "No extraneous ornament, no vain display, no frivolous dance, weakens or deflects the work's severe simplicity. There is one solitary ballet, and that ballet makes one shudder. The chorus, participating in the action in the manner of the Greeks, far from diluting the plot strengthens it [...] There is no overture: the drama begins with the very first down-bow" (*Biographie universelle*, vol. 17, p. 519). The work had just been revived at the Opéra. Adolphe Nourrit fils, making his Opéra début, was Pylade, Dabadie was Oreste, and Mlle Leroux (later Mme Dabadie) Iphigénie.

Tauris, who sing the fearsome chorus "We must have blood to expiate our crimes". It's more than one can stand. I defy the most insensitive person to be unmoved at the sight of those two unhappy creatures disputing which is to have the good fortune to die, and when at last the choice falls on Orestes – well, it's Iphigenia the priestess of Diana, you see, it's his sister who has to slaughter her brother. It's frightful. I can't even begin to describe to you the feeling of horror one experiences when Orestes, overcome, sinks to the ground and says, "Peace returns to my breast". He dozes, and then you see the ghost of his mother, whom he killed, gliding round him, with various spirits holding an infernal torch in each hand and brandishing them about him. And the orchestra! It's all in the orchestra. If you could only hear how every situation is depicted in it, above all when Orestes appears to have grown calm – well, the violins hold a long note, very soft, which suggests tranquillity; but below it you hear the cellos murmuring, like the remorse which despite his apparent calm still sounds in the depths of the parricide's heart. [13 December 1821]

It was under the influence of a performance of *Iphigénie en Tauride* at the Opéra that Berlioz finally decided that he was going to be a composer, whatever the obstacles, and summoned up the courage to write to his father and tell him so. But that was later, towards the end of the following summer, after months of brooding and inner struggle, and long hours of study during which he pored over the score and copied it out until he knew it by heart. The account just quoted is very much that of a naïve enthusiast, his head full of Michaud, who has just encountered the work for the first time and remembers it very imperfectly. It is also the letter of a boy, just turned eighteen, who had not yet found his feet in the big city and was not yet ready to defy his parents or even to contemplate doing so. His sister had written to ask him to tell her about the "pleasures and pains" of his new life. "For the latter", he replied, "I answer with La Fontaine: 'Absence is the greatest of all afflictions.' But there are others as well, caused partly by studying a subject that repels me, partly by the discouragement I so often feel when, after working really hard, I reflect that I know nothing, that I have everything to learn, that perhaps Father will not be pleased with me, that perhaps – who knows? I would never finish once I began to describe to you all the gloomy thoughts that depress me." That was written after he had been in Paris for about five weeks. He grew gradually less unreconciled to his medical studies; but the attitude of submissiveness to his father persisted for a long time.

In terms of the issue of medicine versus music this period is a development of the last two years at La Côte St André, a kind of "phoney war". In March 1822, a few months after his arrival in Paris, he had a couple of romances published at his own expense by a minor firm (one of them, "Le maure jaloux", a revised version of a song that appears in one of the La Côte manuscript books, the other a new composition, "Pleure pauvre

Colette"). But on the surface nothing was changed; the conflict remained within him, not yet avowed to his parents.

The diary which Nancy Berlioz kept from February to June 1822 gives only a hint of the troubles to come.

> 14 April   I wrote to Hector. Mama unsealed my letter to read it, which vexed me exceedingly.

> 7 May   Wrote to Hector [. . .] Mama again read it, greatly to my annoyance.

Had there been more going on, Nancy — only sixteen but sharp-eyed and inquisitive — would undoubtedly have divined it. To judge by her brief account of them, none of Hector's letters contained anything more overtly subversive than laments of the kind just quoted (e.g. "24 April I got a very sad letter from Hector, it made me feel sorry for him; truly, one is much to be pitied with the imagination one has at eighteen"). The one letter of his that has survived from 1822 (written to Nancy) is a cheerful one. It breathes no word of discontent except with the musical standards and uncomfortable crush at a private ball that he and Alphonse attended at the home of the Teisseyres, a Grenoble family of their acquaintance. The Teisseyres had a house in the Rue Chanoinesse, just behind Notre-Dame, and had befriended the two young men, inviting them twice during the Carnival:

> Perhaps you think balls in Paris are quite different from ours. If so, you're wrong. The only difference is that there are many more people — sixty dancers instead of our sixteen — and despite the size of the drawing-rooms they're so thick on the ground that the men have to stand behind the women for lack of space, and pay constant attention where they put their feet so as not to tread on someone. Dress is just a uniform white for the women and black for the men. Perhaps you'll think the orchestra is superb. Well, it's not even as good as ours. Just think of it — two violins and a flageolet. Isn't it pathetic! I couldn't get over it. And for nearly the whole evening those poor fellows played contredances taken from ballets that I'd heard at the Opéra — you can imagine what a delightful contrast. Eventually we couldn't bear it any more, and left at 1 o'clock, wondering how we were going to get out of Sunday's engagement.

Luckily his uncle Félix Marmion was in town on leave, spending his evenings doing the shows, seeing Talma and Mlle Mars act and Baillot the famous violinist play and visiting his beloved Opéra-Comique at the Feydeau before moving on to the gambling tables, and his presence provided an excuse:

> We went to see my uncle, who said we absolutely must dine with him next day; so we wrote to M. Teisseyre, giving him the impression that my uncle was merely passing through Paris and wanted to spend the evening with us,

which got us out of it very neatly. We had a delightful dinner with him and cousin Raymond, and afterwards went to the Feydeau to hear Martin.* They were performing *Azémia* and the *Voitures versées*. Ah, that made up for it! I drank in the music. I thought of you, sister, and how you would have enjoyed it. The Opéra perhaps would give you less pleasure. It's too serious for you; whereas Dalayrac's touching, enchanting music, the gaiety of Boieldieu's, the incredible tours de force of the actresses and the perfection of Martin and Ponchard — oh! you know, I should have fallen on Dalayrac's neck if I'd been next to his statue when I heard the aria — for which no word is adequate — "Ton amour, ô fille chérie". It was more or less the same feeling as I had at the Opéra when I heard the aria "Versez tous vos chagrins dans le sein paternel" in *Stratonice*. But I can't begin to describe that music to you. [20 February 1822]

The letter breaks off at this point; the rest is lost. But it does not seem to have contained anything to displease or alarm his family; Nancy at any rate noted in her diary that the whole letter "gave me great pleasure".

Of the six other letters from Hector referred to in the diary, all spoke of troubles of various kinds, but mostly other people's, not his. Two, written in early March 1822, were filled with the disturbances caused in reaction to aggressive propaganda on the part of the right-wing religious party known as the Congregation, whose flamboyant and politically slanted services in St Eustache and other churches brought the students out in force. Berlioz and Robert became involved in one of the demonstrations — whether as spectators or participants is not clear. Hector's account of the wounding of a young man, apparently during a police charge, roused Nancy to "very special feelings" of sympathy.

A month later, on 8 April: "A gloomy letter from Hector: M. Alphonse has no hope of being able to make himself mend his ways" ("se faire réformer"). For curiously enough the medical student with serious problems at that moment was not Hector but Alphonse. What they were we do not know; but a week later, to the astonishment of the family, Alphonse himself suddenly walked in. He spent some time closeted with Dr Berlioz, who succeeded in persuading him to return to Paris. However, he stayed on in La Côte for another three weeks, and during that time visited the Berlioz household frequently. "M. Alphonse came to see us and told us a lot about their way of life, Hector's especially" (18 April). Alas, she fails to specify what he told them, and instead lapses into pious moralising: "the conversation interested me very much, for I experience great pleasure

---

* Reigning baritone and star of the Opéra-Comique for thirty-five years. He was by then over fifty, but his voice — famous for its exceptional compass as well as for its beauty and elegance — was still greatly admired.

The Feydeau was Félix Marmion's Mecca. In a letter of a few weeks earlier, commenting on Hector's enthusiastic reports of the Opéra, he expresses surprise at his preferring it to the Opéra-Comique, whose superiority — acknowledged by all true "children of Apollo" — he will surely come to recognise, "for the honour of his good judgment".

from hearing those I love being talked of." On another occasion (24 April), "M. Alphonse spoke to me a great deal about the theatre."

"Le spectacle" — above all the opera — was playing an increasingly large part in Berlioz's life. A few days after Alphonse left for La Côte, Gluck's *Iphigénie en Aulide*, with Mme Grassari as Iphigénie, Mme Branchu as Clytemnestre and Dérivis as Agamemnon, was revived at the Opéra. By this time he was a regular frequenter of the pit; he had been back to see *Iphigénie en Tauride* and *The Danaids*, and had fallen under the spell of the two Spontini operas, *La Vestale* and *Fernand Cortez*, that were to have so important a role in the forming of his own musical style. But he went as an aspirant to medicine, not to music. The statement in the *Memoirs* that he was "on the way to becoming a student like countless others" when one evening he went to the Opéra has been generally treated with amused incredulity; and certainly it foreshortens the conflict in the interests of dramatic presentation. As we have seen, there was nothing fortuitous about his first visit to the Opéra. It had been his lodestar before he came to Paris, and once arrived he wasted no time in going there. Where the *Memoirs* are correct is in their emphasis on how long the subsequent struggle lasted. For the best part of a year — the last two months of 1821 and a good part of 1822 — he lived "like countless other students", working — however half-heartedly — at his studies during the day and in the evening going to the opera or the theatre. As he himself put it in the Autobiographical Sketch of 1832, "Placed thus [. . .] between the music of Gluck and the prose of Bichat, he nevertheless kept for a whole year, aided and guided by his friend and fellow-student Robert [. . .], the promise he had given his father to work hard at his courses." The register of inscriptions at the Ecole de Médecine for 1822 bears this out. "Berlioz, Louis Hector" in his hand appears under all four terms.

This is in itself an indication that he did indeed work hard — at any rate, hard enough to make respectable progress. Attendance at courses was obligatory; as few as two absences from any one course could result in a student's failing to obtain the "certificat d'assiduité" which he was required to present when signing on again at the start of a new term. A poor performance in the end-of-term exams, too, could lead to suspension from medical school. The records of these exams have not been preserved; but Berlioz must have satisfied the examiners, to have been permitted to continue studying at the school.

That he pursued his studies well into 1822 is also shown by his having attended Gay-Lussac's physics lectures, given at the Jardin des Plantes. Physics, unlike chemistry, did not appear in the syllabus of the first-year medical student until the second semester of the academic year, which ran from April to July.

To us, looking with hindsight and with all the facts of Berlioz's career before us, the period of unwilling medical studies appears a mere interlude, a brief and unimportant aberration from his destined path. But to him at the time it must indeed have sometimes seemed that he was turning willy-nilly into a medical student without hope of escape, pulled into the hectic absorbing world of the Parisian university community, from time to time discreetly unburdening himself to his sister, but going on with it, in his own words "stoically resigned", and already a hardened joker of the dissecting-room. Despite himself he was drawn to the anatomy course by the personality of his teacher, Amussat, in whom he recognised an artist and felt a kindred spirit. Amussat was barely twenty-four, only six years his senior, but he seemed to have lived twice as long and achieved amazing things. Largely self-taught, he had joined the Grande Armée as an assistant surgeon at the age Hector was now, had taken part in Napoleon's masterly rearguard actions of 1814 and the last defiant fling of Waterloo, and been decorated for bravery. Since then he had rapidly made a name as an innovator in surgical techniques and a bold and imaginative researcher. Amussat was a vivid illustration of the Napoleonic doctrine of careers being open to talent, and an inspiring model.

This was altogether an exciting time to be taking up medicine. Paris had more hospital beds and therefore provided a greater opportunity for clinical observation than any other city; and it was free from the moral and legal restrictions on dissection that retarded progress in Britain and America. French medicine had begun at last to match the previous century's advances in physical science and to discard the old semi-mystical systems of thought in favour of a disciplined empirical approach. The new spirit and methods were making Paris the medical centre of the Western world, to which students from other countries gravitated.[*]

Without at all abandoning his objections to a medical career, Berlioz could not help responding to the invigorating intellectual climate of the university. He also sampled some of the courses available outside his own subject — Lacretelle's lectures on French history at the Sorbonne, Andrieux's on literature at the Collège de France, both just round the corner from his lodgings in the Rue St Jacques; and though he soon dropped the former for lack of time, he never missed Andrieux's if he could help it. Andrieux, humorous, cunning defender of the ancien régime in art (but not in politics), was a famous lecturer. The old man held court every Wednesday at noon, playing to a packed house, talking about anything and everything, hopping from subject to subject — Aristotle, natural history, his cat, the puling self-pity of the new "Romantic" poets — in a seemingly whimsical sequence of anecdote, exhortation and mockery, but always ending — to show how poetry should be written — with a passage from La Fontaine or Boileau, read in a cracked apology for a

---

[*] One of them, who signed his first inscription at the Ecole de Médecine (for the grade of "officier de santé") the same term as Berlioz, was Thomas Hodgkin (the discoverer of Hodgkin's disease). At Guy's Hospital in London he was to continue Bichat's pioneering work on tissues.

voice but with a mastery of timing and ironic inflection that had the hall spellbound.

Within Hector's own field not all was disagreeable by any means. He found Thénard's chemistry lectures at the Jardin des Plantes fascinating, and even more so Gay-Lussac's physics lectures: no penance to have to work at such a subject. Just how attracted he was to physics is emphasised by the passage in the *Memoirs* which describes his finally giving way to his impulse towards music and throwing himself body and soul into his musical studies: so absorbing were they, he says, that not all his admiration for Gay-Lussac or the powerful appeal of the subject could compete with them, and he "even neglected" the course in experimental electricity that he had started with him.

The moment of truth, when it came, was not a sudden flash of illumination. It was the result of a slow accumulation of pressure, growing to the point where the floodgates could hold no longer and his pent-up ambitions poured out with uncontrollable force. At the end of July 1822 he had passed his exams, which qualified him for the second year of medical studies. But by then a crucial event had taken place. He had discovered the Conservatoire Library. The library was open daily till three in the afternoon to any member of the public who wanted to go there. Among its contents were the full scores of the works that he had been listening to at the Opéra. How he found out about it we do not know: very probably at the Opéra, in conversation with some fellow-habitué of the pit who turned out to be studying music at the Conservatoire. The discovery brought about a transformation in him. It was the first vital step in the long process of teaching himself to be a composer, turning him from an amateur into a serious student of music. Before, his attitude had been that of many another fanatic, intensified maybe but not essentially different. He had absorbed dramatic music like a sponge, learning his favourite works by ear, reliving them in his head, vibrating to them, possessed by the splendour and beauty of their sounds. Now, he could put notes to these sounds; he could bring them down out of the air and lay them out in front of him, dissect and analyse and classify them, use them for knowledge as well as delight, make them serve his purpose and show him how it was done.

It was a decisive experience. "Once admitted to the sanctuary, I never left it." That is not quite accurate: as we have seen, he kept sufficiently in touch with his medical studies to complete the first-year course. But every moment he could snatch from it, during the swelteringly hot summer term of 1822, was spent at the round table in the reading-room in the Rue du Faubourg Poissonnière. Every morning or early afternoon that was free from lectures he hurried there. In his excitement he forgot to eat, and would continue working obliviously through the lunch hour. He made his own copies of the scores he studied, as practice, as an aid to memory, and so as to be able to take them back to his room and go on studying them after the library closed. A 120-page manuscript folder of pieces from the two *Iphigénies* in his hand has survived, written in a fine calligraphy; the first page of each set of extracts (beginning, respectively, with Agamemnon's "Brillant auteur de la lumière" and Iphigénie's "O toi qui prolongeas mes jours") is inscribed: "Copied from the score in the Conservatoire in 1822". By the time either work was performed again he knew them both inside out. They had been taken into his bloodstream and become woven into the fabric of his waking and sleeping thoughts. In growing impatience he watched the billboards for one of them to reappear. By a fortunate accident Berlioz's first Gluck studies in the Conservatoire Library coincided with a lull in Gluck performances at the Opéra; for three months, from late May to late August 1822, both *Iphigénies* — the two Gluck works in the current repertoire — were absent from the programme. This very deprivation sharpened his desire; and when, on 21 August, he at last heard *Iphigénie en Tauride* again it was the consummation of a passion that had grown through interminable weeks of waiting.* As he listened, luxuriating in the nobility and sadness, the sheer beauty of the music, the last of his defences gave way. He came out of the theatre with his mind made up. He must be a musician. For that career and that alone he was meant. There lay his destiny, whatever the obstacles his family might put in its way.

Buoyed up by his decision he wrote to his father immediately, giving voice to the thoughts which he had kept to himself for so long. Music was his vocation, there was no longer any possibility of hiding the fact, he knew it, it was stronger than him; and he pleaded with his father not to oppose it. Dr Berlioz's reply was affectionate but firm, and perfectly uncomprehending. He had no doubt that this was merely a temporary delusion on the part of his son, who would soon recognise it and return to the ways of reason and good sense.

It was the first exchange in a "war of words" which was to "last nearly four years and serve only to make the whole family wretched, each sticking obstinately to his own point of view" (Autobiographical Sketch). "Everything was tried — entreaties, threats, loss of allowance, caresses, promises for the future, curses even — to bring him back to what they called the right path."

For the moment the field of battle shifted to La Côte St André. It was the summer vacation, and Berlioz went home for part of it. He was there

---

* In an article in the *Gazette musicale* twelve years later Berlioz recalled the three months of dearth, and how one morning, glancing mechanically at the billboards in the Place Cambrai (today the Place Marcellin Berthelot), he was seized by a sudden nervous trembling and could hardly manage the few yards back to his lodgings. "'What is it?' said R[obert], seeing me wild and distraught, with a handkerchief to my nose. 'Did you fall? You're bleeding — what happened?' — 'At the Opéra — tonight — they're doing — *Iphi* — *Iphigénie en Tauride*.' 'God!' And we stood there, struck dumb at the thought that we were going to see Gluck's great masterpiece that very evening."

for a month or six weeks, during part of September and the first three weeks of October. We know nothing about this first return visit, except that the weather was fine and that by the middle of September Dr Berlioz was involved in the wine harvest, which was early that year following an exceptionally mild winter. Of what passed between him and his son, what sort of reception the rebellious medical student got from his family, there is no record. Nancy Berlioz had given up her diary (and would not resume it for another two years); and only one family letter survives from this time, a peremptory note to Joséphine Berlioz from her father Nicolas Marmion telling her to stop sending him begging letters on behalf of her brother Félix, since he absolutely refuses to pay any more of his debts. But the great issue was certainly discussed, and resolved in a way that for the moment perhaps lightened Dr Berlioz's anxieties; for on 21 October Hector took the coach back to Paris, where he signed on at the Ecole de Médecine for the start of the second year. At the same time he changed his lodgings. The address named in his inscription is no longer 104 Rue St Jacques but 71, further down the hill on the other side of the street. (The house still stands, having survived the creation of the Rue des Ecoles, which cuts across the Rue St Jacques just above it.) Whatever the reason for the move, it was not because no. 104 was no longer in business as an hôtel meublé: two other medical students in the register for November 1822 give it as their address. The register also shows Alphonse Robert as having moved, not to 71 with Hector but to 79, the Hôtel de Nantes. After a year together the two cousins had separated — whether because of a quarrel or because Alphonse no longer felt equal to the responsibility of watching over his volatile junior there is no means of knowing. But the hand of Dr Berlioz may well be detectable in Hector's going to live at 71 Rue St Jacques. This was the address of the Chevalier Broussais, the eminent surgeon and medical theorist, one-time pupil of Bichat, whom Dr Berlioz admired and with whom he had corresponded occasionally since the publication of Broussais' *Traité des phlegmasies chroniques* in 1808, a work cited many times in Louis Berlioz's *Mémoires sur les maladies chroniques*. It is not unlikely that Dr Berlioz himself arranged for Hector to rent a room in the same house as the great man, who would keep an eye on the poor deluded boy and whose proximity, and that of his son Casimir Broussais, a medical student a year ahead of Hector, could in any case be expected to exert a beneficent influence.

If that was his hope, it was doomed by an event outside his control. On 21 November 1822 the Faculty of Medicine was closed down. At intervals during that year the university district had been the scene of political disturbances, in protest at the growing censorship of the press, the wretched condition of the rapidly swelling urban proletariat of Paris and what was considered by many the excessive influence of the priesthood in secular affairs and especially in the educational system. Louis XVIII's government, in one of its most illiberal phases, reacted with a series of purges in which many academics lost their jobs. Not all the riots were of great significance. (One ended in good-humoured laughter when an old peer of the realm, whose carriage had been stopped by a crowd of young men insisting on his crying "Long live liberty!", replied "I will willingly do so, provided that you give me liberty to proceed.") But the network of police informers reported a large increase in the number of left-wing secret societies after the model of the Italian Carbonari, most of them with their offices in the Latin Quarter. Medical students, with law students, were particularly given to political agitation. Several were suspended after the demonstrations against the Mission de la France in February—March 1822 (in which, as we have seen, Berlioz and Robert found themselves involved). In August and September the intensely unpopular trial of the four sergeants of La Rochelle for conspiracy — a conspiracy which expressed, however clumsily, the widespread and deep discontent among the non-commissioned officers of the Bourbon army — aroused passionate feeling in the university. Turbulent crowds gathered daily outside the Palais de Justice, on the Ile de la Cité, where the trial was being held. Two medical students were arrested and imprisoned for an alleged plot to rescue the condemned men. A couple of months later, at the ceremony held by the Faculty of Medicine on 18 November for the opening of the new academic year, the Rector of the University, Abbé Nicole, presiding in place of the Dean of the Faculty, was booed; the service ended in confusion and shouts of "Down with the clergy!" and the Rector was jostled as he left the hall. A petition of loyalty was hastily assembled, signed by more than a thousand students. But the government had already decided on drastic measures. The Ecole de Médecine was shut by royal decree.

It remained shut for five months. By the time it reopened, on 25 April 1823, without eleven of its less reliable professors, Berlioz was no longer a medical student. His name appears in none of the subsequent registers. Nor is it to be found on the petition of loyalty drawn up five months before by those intent on getting on with their studies. Alphonse Robert signed it. But Berlioz was already committed elsewhere. He had become a pupil of the composer Jean-François Le Sueur.

7

Apprentice Composer

Some time in the latter part of 1822 Berlioz had got to know a music student called Hyacinthe Gerono, who was in Le Sueur's composition class at the Conservatoire. They had first met in the library, and a common enthusiasm for Gluck led to their becoming friendly. Gerono was six years older. He had already been at the Conservatoire nearly nine years, studying solfège to begin with, then flute — Berlioz's own instrument — and cello, then harmony followed by counterpoint, and finally composition under Le Sueur, and had published a Theme and Variations for cello with piano accompaniment. Berlioz confided to him that he was trying to learn to be a composer himself — he was working on a cantata for voice and orchestra on a poem by Millevoye, "The Arab at the Tomb of his Steed" — but had to admit that he had no teacher. The enthusiasm with which Gerono spoke of Le Sueur aroused his interest. Egged on by Berlioz's questions, Gerono waxed lyrical about him and hinted that he might find a way of arranging for his young friend to join the Master's composition class. Soon afterwards, to Berlioz's joy, Gerono brought the news that Le Sueur would see him.

The interview was a success. Berlioz had come armed with the score of his cantata and, in reserve, a three-part canon. While he waited, Le Sueur gave the cantata a thorough scrutiny, then, handing it back, said, "There is a great deal of warmth and dramatic movement here, but you do not know yet how to write, and your harmonies are so spattered with mistakes that it would be pointless to indicate them to you. Gerono will be so kind as to make you conversant with our harmonic principles, and as soon as you know them sufficiently to understand me I shall be happy to have you as one of my pupils."

The prentice musician, only too well aware how little he knew, must have been profoundly encouraged by the praise and not at all downcast by the criticism. For the next few weeks he sat at the feet of the faithful Gerono and learned Le Sueur's system of chord formation and progression, derived from Rameau, whose treatise he had wrestled with vainly five or six years before. At first, with his naturally sceptical intelligence, he felt inclined to challenge some of the rules which his friend was expounding with such religious fervour; but he sensed that that would not do. Clearly, in the school of Le Sueur they had the force of law. Before long, received into the friendly warmth of Le Sueur's circle and charmed by the old man's personality, he himself had come to accept them unquestioningly.

The arrival of Le Sueur in Berlioz's life, coinciding with the closure of the medical school, was of crucial importance. Looking back on it years later, though he acknowledged a deep debt of gratitude to his teacher for countless kindnesses and vital encouragement, he regretted the time spent learning antediluvian theories — only to have to unlearn them subsequently — when there was already so much lost time to make up. There may be a certain justice in that. It is probably true that in terms of the acquisition of a personal style and the technique to make it effective Le Sueur taught him less than he taught himself, by trial and error and the exercise of patient self-criticism, by his private course in orchestration at the Opéra and by his own analysis of the works of Gluck, Spontini, Weber and Beethoven — the last-named of whom represented a kind of music undreamed of in Le Sueur's narrow world and quite bewildering to him. Le Sueur, once a pioneering force in French musical life, a feared and envied innovator, had become in late middle age (he was sixty-two when Berlioz met him) something of a reactionary, out of touch with the new trends and as a theatre composer an almost forgotten figure. Yet the gains outweighed the losses, and the influence was more pervasive than Berlioz imagined.

Le Sueur's theories may have been antediluvian, and embodied in interminable, mostly unpublished pamphlets of medieval longwindedness and wayward erudition; and the young pupil, in the first flush of uncritical admiration, spent long hours listening to his master expound them and discussing them with him. But if Berlioz's mature works owe little to Le Sueur's, they incorporate a remarkable number of Le Sueur's practical aesthetic ideas: to mention only one, the necessity, in the composition of religious music, of cultivating a special style for large and resonant buildings, a style in which space virtually becomes a musical element like melody and harmony. This idea (not confined to Revolutionary France, of course, and exemplified in the early Baroque period and the late twentieth century among others) was a feature of the music composed under the Republic; but Le Sueur took it further than his colleagues. His "Chant du 1er Vendémiaire", written to celebrate the eighth anniversary of the Republic, was performed by four orchestral and choral groups placed at different points in the Invalides, the same church in which thirty-six years later Berlioz's Requiem had its first performance. It was directly from Le Sueur that he received the Revolutionary tradition of large-scale ceremonial music which found renewed expression in the Requiem, the Te Deum and the Symphonie funèbre et triomphale.

Again, although Le Sueur's protracted speculations about rhythm in the music of the Ancient Greeks and its relatively greater complexity and significance than in modern Western music were necessarily somewhat vague, given the dearth of direct evidence, and reliant on the collation of a mass of abstruse and arcane texts, and although these speculations bore little fruit in his own music, they dropped a fertile grain of suggestion into the mind of his pupil, whose music would achieve the emancipation of rhythm to which Le Sueur aspired.

Here, as in the whole emphasis that he placed on the essentially dramatic nature of music and the obligation of the composer to be faithful at every moment to the expressive demands of the situation, Le Sueur's rôle was not so much to guide his pupil in new directions as to vindicate those in which his instincts were pointing him. From his boyhood Berlioz had responded to music as a dramatist. His experiences at the Opéra only confirmed what he felt intuitively. The feeling for rhythm, too, must have been an innate sense. What Le Sueur did was to provide a justification, a systematisation of Berlioz's instincts.

Le Sueur's advent was altogether providential. Simply having a teacher at last from whom one could learn how to compose was a boon. But Le Sueur was not just any teacher. He was one of the most celebrated in Paris: Director, with Cherubini, of the Chapel Royal (where his masses and oratorios and motets were regularly performed before the King) Member of the Institute, Professor of Composition at the Conservatoire, composer of operas which though not at present in the repertoire had won popular acclaim not long since and the accolade of Napoleon himself, and last but not least a master who knew how to inspire a rare devotion and dedication in his pupils. To be one of them and to be able to put "pupil of the Chevalier Lesueur"[*] after your name on the title page of your compositions was a marvellous boost to your confidence. Whatever Berlioz subsequently learned from Le Sueur in the seven or eight years of their close relationship, the immediate benefit was moral. We cannot exaggerate what it meant to him that a figure of such eminence endorsed his secret ambitions and gave him fatherly encouragement just at the moment when, having finally taken the plunge, he was struggling to become a composer, if possible with his family's approval but without it if it had to be. The knowledge that Le Sueur believed in him and was sure he would one day be a distinguished composer was a priceless strength which would serve him well in the battles to come.

Early in March 1823, or at the end of February, Dr Berlioz summoned him home. No letter survives, but it is likely that he threatened to cut off his allowance unless he came back. The date of his return can be inferred to within a few weeks, first from an entry in the Livre de Raison: "20 March [1823] sent Alphonse Robert a money order for two hundred and twenty francs [...] to settle the debts left by Hector in Paris, amounting to a hundred and sixty francs", and secondly from the fact that Hector

---

[*] This was how Berlioz and most others wrote the name.

was still in Paris on 26 February, on which day he went to the Direction générale de l'imprimerie et de la librairie at the Bibliothèque Royale in the Rue de Richelieu and entered his name in the register as depositor of the obligatory six copies of three songs that he had recently had published. No doubt they and a fourth song, deposited a few days earlier by the publisher, Boieldieu jeune of 92 Rue de Richelieu, had been engraved at the composer's expense, and that fact explains the debt which he confessed to his father he had left behind him in Paris.

This time there is less uncertainty about what passed between father and son. The great issue was out in the open with a vengeance. It had been the subject of an increasingly heated exchange of letters during the previous three months. Dr Berlioz, while continuing to pooh-pooh a musical career as sheer folly, but half accepting, with bitterness in his heart, that medicine was a lost cause, had suggested law instead. Law — the profession of two of Hector's uncles and both his grandfathers — was as much a family tradition as medicine. Félix Marmion, who had been in Paris for a few weeks in January (in pursuit of a wealthy married woman from his former garrison town), added his voice in support of it. He seems to have felt not unsanguine about the results of his diplomacy: though his nephew was like a brick wall whenever the question of music was raised, he had not actually rejected law out of hand.

The idea did not long survive Hector's return to La Côte. His father argued and pleaded (though perhaps without great conviction, as someone who in his own youth had found his brief legal studies highly antipathetic). But, fortified by the confidence given him by his proud new status as pupil of Le Sueur, his son stood his ground. He did not want anything to do with law. It was music or it was nothing.

The two principals in the dispute left no direct record of those fraught, unhappy two months. The *Memoirs* do not explicitly mention the visit; and Dr Berlioz's temporary defeat was concealed in a laconic note in the Livre de Raison: "11 May [1823] handed over to Hector on his departure for Paris, 400." The course of events, however, is reflected in the comments of that interested observer and arch-trimmer Félix Marmion, who was kept informed by letters, mostly from his niece Nancy. His replies show, in their fluctuating tone and emphasis, how the wind was blowing.

Valenciennes, 25 March [1823]

It was not till yesterday, my dear Nancy, that I learned of Hector's departure [from Paris]. Alphonse, whom I had begged to let me know, wrote to tell me of this important and, I hope, decisive step in my nephew's reformation. Yes, I hope that he will not have been rescued in vain from the temptations that Paris offered him for the indulgence of his folly. I hope that the sight of his father, consumed by the grief he has caused him so long, will have a salutary effect on him. Otherwise, there is nothing left to hope for. If the pain, the dreadful pain, he has caused you all does not prey on his mind and move him to the point where he makes a firm resolve to start a new life from now onwards, if he doesn't open his heart to his father's counsel, then he is a lost child and for my part I think I would rather not set eyes on him again. The grief his stubbornness has brought you, I have sincerely shared with you; I cannot suppose it was lessened even by the joy you must have felt when he arrived home. For you to take pleasure in his return he must have a change of heart, and give a firm guarantee that he means seriously to study law [. . .]

Valenciennes, 19 April [1823]

Your letter, my good little Nancy, distressed but hardly surprised me. From the letter I had earlier from Alphonse, in which he gave me a detailed account of his separation from Hector and the latter's departure, I can guess all the grief that you are going through. Is it true, then, that there is no hope left, that we are doomed to blush with shame over one who was to have been our pride and joy? His imperviousness to his mother's tears and his father's gnawing sorrow pains me more than his wilful passion. Is the wretch blind to the future he is storing up for himself? Is he determined to poison his family's existence? Will he make no effort to cure himself? As you point out to him, and as I myself have told him a hundred times, it is not necessarily impossible. At least the attempt would earn him our gratitude, and even if he did not succeed (which is difficult to believe), at least we should consider him more to be pitied than blamed. But I can visualise from here his sullen resistance, his rejection of the sort of generous resolve that honour, reason and above all his father's life should absolutely require him to make, whatever the price. You rightly say and I agree with you that the ties of nature and friendship impose a duty on him. How have I deserved it that since I left Paris he has written to me only once, and a couple of trivial lines at that? But I regard him as no longer himself, as being sick. May he be cured, may he only desire to be cured, and we will recognise him again as he was, responsive, kind, loving! [. . .]

In the second week of May the conflict was temporarily resolved. Louis Berlioz gave in, and Hector returned to Paris. A tearful Joséphine Berlioz wrote to her brother Félix, to report the unexpected turn of events.[*]

Félix Marmion, naturally pragmatic and disinclined to look on the tragic side of things for long, promptly changed tack and wrote in warm support of his brother-in-law's decision, adding some practical advice:

---

[*] It was very probably then that the dramatic scenes recounted in the *Memoirs* took place: Dr Berlioz waking his son early, before the household was up, to tell him his secret decision; Nancy, struck by the change in her brother, worming the truth out of him; Joséphine Berlioz confronting her son and kneeling before him, clasping his knees and imploring him to stay, and when he refused, cursing him and fleeing the house; the family searching for her and finding her in the orchard, reading, only to see her run away and hide from them; Hector and his sisters weeping, Dr Berlioz calling to her and getting no answer; Hector leaving for Paris without seeing his mother again.

Valenciennes, 2 June [1823]

So you have had to yield, my dear Louis, to your son's irresistible bent. I can imagine very well what it must have cost you, and how cruel for you to have to give up the high hopes that this child had aroused in you. I entirely approve what you have done, for I have no doubt that you had convinced yourself, since his return to La Côte, that he would have nothing to do with either medicine or law. In fact it's a crisis that has to be given time to pass. Knowing Hector's character and his amour-propre as I do, I believe that either he will succeed completely or he will get fed up with it. In the latter case, he will still have somewhere to turn; with the education he has had he will still be good for many things. I have said this to you a hundred times and I repeat it. That being so, the alternatives are not so appalling; but you will need a great deal of patience. In the event of failure, he must be allowed to see reason by his own reflections and not by renewed advice from you, which could irritate him and make him persist, from a mixture of pigheaded- ness and embarrassment. We have all had to strive against his strange inclination and thank God we tried with all our strength; but for the present we should let him be and not speak about it to him except when he does so to us. I have heard nothing from him since he arrived in Paris, where he must be now, according to my sister's letter [. . .] I have felt for her in her distress at the decision which you had to take in the end, and which she was not expecting. I wish she would realise that there are certain things that one has sometimes to allow to take their course, and that there is a limit to resistance. I pray fervently that Hector's disenchantment will come soon, if he does not have the stamp of genuine talent. In that case he will have many errors and much lost time to make up for; but we should not despair of either. I urge you to cheer up and above all to be patient. You and Joséphine should console one another; what has happened was beyond the reach of rational argument and of the most loving persuasion [. . .]

Hector, however, had not got his way entirely, certain though he might be in his own mind about his future. Stronger and more single-minded than his father, knowing what he wanted, he had won himself a breathing space, no more. His father let him return to Paris and agreed to continue supporting him there, but under certain conditions. He could go on with his musical studies if he insisted — that was an inestimable point gained — provided he did not burn his boats. Clearly the idea was that by being given his head he would find out before long that he had been mistaken about his much-vaunted vocation, and be "cured". When that happened he would be able to turn to something else, having in the meantime not severed his connection with more conventional studies.

What that something else was is a bit of a mystery. Six or seven months after returning to Paris with his father's permission to go on studying music (at any rate for a limited period), Berlioz was awarded the diploma of bachelier ès-sciences physiques.* On 12 January 1824 he

---

* By this time he had left 71 Rue St Jacques and rejoined his cousin Alphonse Robert a few doors further up the hill at no. 79 (Hôtel de Nantes).

took the oral examination at the Faculty of Sciences at the Institute and passed, by a majority of two examiners to one. Both the formal report of the exam and the certificate of aptitude state that the candidate "intends to take up medicine". Certainly, if that had been Berlioz's intention, he would have had to pass the exam. Under a new regulation, would-be medical students who had not signed on by 9 May 1823 at the reopened Ecole de Médecine were required to obtain the baccalauréat ès-sciences physiques. Berlioz did not sign on (he was in La Côte St André at the time), which notwithstanding his previous four terms of study automatically made him liable to the regulation if he wished to continue with the course. The subjects on which candidates were examined were Mathematics, Physics, Chemistry, Zoology, Botany and Mineralogy, but the knowledge required was fairly rudimentary, and he had already studied some of them. It would have been perfectly feasible for him to prepare for the exam on his own, in his lodgings, without attending any college — Sainte-Beuve, another distinguished medical drop-out, did so a few months later — and presumably that is what he did. But, having passed the exam and got his diploma as a student "destiné à l'étude de la médecine", he did nothing further. There is no trace of his name in the register of inscriptions at the Ecole de Médecine for 1824 or for any subsequent year.

One is tempted to interpret the whole episode as one more twist in the family drama, with the vacillating Dr Berlioz, goaded by his wife's tears and reproaches, changing his mind yet again and, going back on the agreement reached before Hector left for Paris, once more using the threat of an end to his allowance in an attempt to make him resume his medical studies, and Hector yielding so far as to take the exam but then digging his toes in. But a likelier theory is that taking the exam was part of the bargain struck with his father before he left, and the declaration of intent about medicine was simply a formality. The idea behind taking the exam was thus — in his parents' eyes — that it should lead to his pursuing some kind of scientific, non-medical career: after all, he had always shown a keen interest in science, and only recently had followed Gay-Lussac's course with the greatest enthusiasm.

A letter from Nicolas Marmion to his daughter Joséphine, written soon after her son's abrupt departure, lends support to this interpretation.

Meylan, 18 May [1823]

Your letter, my dear Joséphine, caused me much distress, and I sympathise with your pain at the unexpected parting. Yet I cannot blame your husband's action. His affection for his son is far from blind. He wishes to deliver him from a life of idleness [*sc.* at La Côte] and turn his youth to good account before it is too late. I believe [Hector's] tastes and inclinations promise well. He will not devote himself exclusively to music: his liking for the higher sciences will lead him to cultivate them, in the only place [Paris] where one

Above: *Notre-Dame and the Quai des Orfèvres, on the Ile de la Cité. Berlioz rented a room in the Rue de Harlay (just off the picture to the left) in the mid 1820s.*
Below: *The interior of the Paris Opéra, during a performance of Auber's hugely successful* La muette de Portici. *Berlioz was a regular of the pit throughout his student years.*
Both engravings are from Paris and its Environs *(1831) by Pugin and Heath.*

Above: *Bust of Gluck by Jean-Antoine Houdon (c. 1775).*
Below: *"D'une image, hélas, trop chérie" from Gluck's* Iphigénie en Tauride, *in Berlioz's hand: part of a selection of pieces from both Gluck's* Iphigénie *operas which he copied in the Conservatoire Library in 1822.*

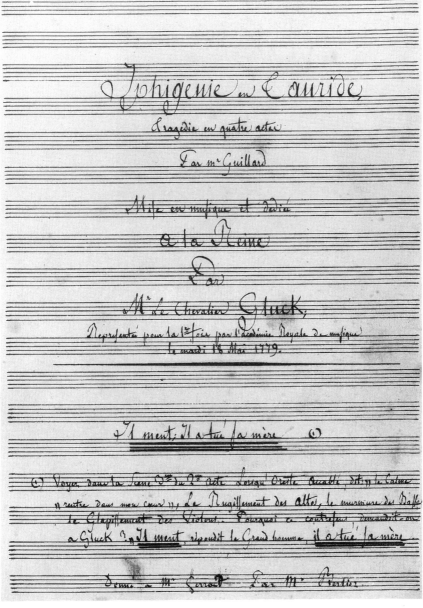

Berlioz copied the entire full score of Iphigénie en Tauride *in the spring of 1824. On the title page he quotes Gluck's retort to the objection that Orestes' words are inconsistent with the agitation in the orchestra: "He's lying. He murdered his mother!"*

Dessiné au Physionotrace et Gravé par Quenedey rue neuve des petits-champs n° 15 à Paris 1818.

J. F. Le Sueur

Membre de l'Institut, Surintendant de la Musique du Roi.

Se vend chez Quenedey Rue Neuve des Petits-Champs N° 15 à Paris.

Dép. à la Dir. Gén.^{le}

Jean-François Le Sueur, Berlioz's first teacher, and staunch supporter and friend during
his apprenticeship. The portrait is by Quenedey and dates from 1818.

can find the right conditions and teachers. He will return at least once a year to show you the progress he has made, and in a few years' time you will have the pleasure of seeing him enjoying an agreeable existence. You love your child too much to see him vegetating beside you in a village and devoting himself to idleness. We can hope that the knowledge he acquires will put him in the way of filling a reputable position. So, my dear, look at things in a more favourable light and do not make a catastrophe out of a separation that is not for ever. He will make it less painful for the family by writing home regularly, and the friends you have in the capital will keep you informed of his conduct. He has a strong interest in leading an irreproachable life, so as not to be summoned home again. I am sorry I cannot be with you just now to dry your maternal tears, but I will do everything in my power to give you two or three days after your silk-worms are over. I have just completed the culture of my hemp. God grant it succeeds! [...]*

Hector's family clung to the belief that reason and common sense would yet prevail, and music find its natural place as a hobby, the adornment of a proper and worthwhile career. The mirage was still floating before Nicolas Marmion several months later as he wrote a letter (in verse) to his granddaughter Nancy shortly after receiving the news that Félix had been mentioned in despatches for bravery during the war in Spain. He must (he said) set his muse to penning a hymn of praise to his valiant son. Hector will write the music for it and Nancy sing it in honour of the hero's return.

But the dream was fading fast. Hector was committed to music. It was no longer a hobby but the centre and object of his existence, and he worked for his bac in the moments that he could spare from it, not the other way round as his family hoped. His serious musical studies date from this time. Before, though he had thought and dreamed music day and night, in a practical sense he had been merely dabbling in it. Now, with a much clearer appreciation of what was required and how far he had to go, he set himself to learn the craft of composition.

Almost nothing is known of Le Sueur's methods of teaching. Given his nature, they are unlikely to have been rigorous. To judge by Berlioz's failure in the Institute exam in 1826, they did not make a feature of fugue. Yet their efficacy is attested by the extraordinarily large number of pupils of his who were successful in the Prix de Rome, the Institute's annual competition for the best student composer. In the sixteen years between 1822 and Le Sueur's death the prize was won eleven times by one of his pupils.

Even more significant is the fact that of the very small handful of French composers who achieved more than passing distinction in the

---

* There is perhaps an echo of this idea of a career in science, as alternative to doctoring, in Le Sueur's remark to Berlioz after the performance of his Mass two years later: "You're not going to be a doctor or an apothecary, you're going to be a great composer".

middle years of the nineteenth century, as many as three — Berlioz, Gounod and Ambroise Thomas — were students of his. This in turn suggests that he possessed the still more necessary virtue of letting his pupils discover their identity for themselves.

In his *Life of Richard Wagner* Ernest Newman makes the valid point that Wagner and Berlioz (both of whom, according to many of their academic critics, were not "properly taught") learned far more about the art of composition by their own dogged private study, carried on in ways peculiar to themselves and adapted to their particular musical constitutions, than conventional instruction could possibly have taught them. True; but Le Sueur played a vital rôle in that process. He supplied the conditions in which Berlioz by his own efforts could find himself. That the pupil's compositions in the first two or three years should have closely imitated the master's (as was only natural); that Le Sueur could teach him nothing about instrumental music, being interested exclusively in vocal; and that Berlioz should have had finally to emancipate himself from Le Sueur's influence in order to submit fully and fruitfully to Beethoven's — none of this diminishes the importance of what the old man gave him. It might be argued that his association with Le Sueur delayed his development by intensifying the "old-fashioned" elements in his artistic personality. But that would be to take no account either of his background or of contemporary musical life. His cultural upbringing already disposed him irresistibly towards tragédie-lyrique; and in the musical climate of the time there was nothing that, for him, could have challenged its supremacy. Weber's music was unknown in Paris, and the advent of Beethoven's, at the Conservatoire concerts, nearly five years off. The only new music of consequence that was available — in large quantities — was Rossini's, against which the young Berlioz was fortified by temperament and conviction. If he had never met Le Sueur he would still have been a dedicated Gluckist, and his early musical development would have followed the lines laid down by Gluck and his successors, of whom Le Sueur was one of several. Le Sueur provided a focus for an enthusiasm which he shared but did not create.

The admiration Berlioz felt for his teacher was not one-sided. Le Sueur was attracted and intrigued by the personality of the young man — in many ways still only a boy — whom fate in the improbable person of Gerono had cast in his way: he was naïve and ingenuous yet so quick to understand, passionate yet clear-headed and sharp-witted, so open to music, so inventive — so wonderfully full of promise. Perhaps Le Sueur, who had lost his two sons young, saw in him a surrogate son. Perhaps too, as Adolphe Jullien suggests, he sensed that he had found an artistic heir who would continue his master's work and give renewed life to his ideas in the next generation. It is more than likely that, knowing his difficulties with his family and the periodic reductions he suffered in his allowance, Le Sueur charged him only modest fees for his lessons.

Such generosity, admittedly, was not unusual with him. The young German violinist Chrétien Urhan lived free in the household for five years. As Berlioz himself remarked, in an obituary tribute to Le Sueur in 1837, "He cherished his pupils; he was lavish with his teaching and with his affectionate advice to them, helping them in every way he could and reckoning neither money nor time."*

As a private pupil, not a member of Le Sueur's composition class at the Conservatoire, Berlioz went regularly to his house, 18 Rue Ste Anne near the Bibliothèque Nationale, a few streets from the Tuileries, where Le Sueur shared the direction of the king's music with Cherubini. But gradually over the next few years a closer relationship developed between them. Berlioz became almost one of the family. He dined with them and acted as escort to Mme Le Sueur and the two elder daughters at dances; and on Sundays when his master was on duty at the Chapel Royal he would join him in the orchestra and listen while he explained to him the intentions behind the work — often one of Le Sueur's gentle Biblical oratorios, *Rachel*, *Naomi*, *Ruth and Boaz* — that was about to be performed. He was introduced to many of the distinguished musicians who served in the Chapel orchestra and choir. Sometimes when the service was over Le Sueur would invite Berlioz to join him in his afternoon walk, and they would pace together beside the Seine or up and down the smooth gravel walks and among the classical statuary and the ornate fountains of Le Nôtre's magnificent Tuileries Garden, deep in conversation.

The talk might be of one of their common enthusiasms — Virgil, Ossian, the Old Testament, the Middle East and its vast deserts and ruined civilisations (at that time a passion of Berlioz's), Napoleon, Gluck. Le Sueur recalled that, when he was still director of music at the Church of the Holy Innocents in Paris, dreaming of writing an opera but held back by the admonishments of his curé, he had once seen Gluck, one evening in this very garden, had been within a few feet of him without realising who it was — a tall, powerfully built man with severe features and a look at once dreamy and passionate, wrapped in an immense fur pelisse and grasping a great bamboo cane, more like a club than a stick: the passers-by stopped to stare at him and the crowd grew so thick that the stranger was obliged to leave the garden, making his escape through the throng. "Who was it?" Le Sueur had asked. "Gluck," they said. "That was Gluck." And from that moment he knew that he must compose for the theatre.

To encourage his young friend, Le Sueur confided in him many intimate

* Le Sueur also tried to help Berlioz by pleading his cause with his father, writing to assure him that his son, who "oozed music at every pore", was certain to succeed as a composer, and arguing that Dr Berlioz had a sacred duty not to oppose so obviously God-given a vocation. Unfortunately this line of reasoning was unacceptable to the free-thinking doctor, who in his reply, which began, "Sir, I am an unbeliever", rejected it out of hand.

details of his embattled career. He told him at length of his early struggles, the difficulties he had had to contend with, and the triumphs he had won despite all the obstacles put in his path; the innovations he introduced at Notre-Dame in the way of expressive, dramatic religious music, including the use of a full orchestra — unheard of till then and in scandalous disregard of the sacrosanct distinction between church and theatre — and the violent controversy they aroused; his feud with the academic establishment which led to his being excluded from the Conservatoire for fifteen years; his long-nurtured operatic ambitions, which Sacchini encouraged but the archbishop opposed, and his first opera, *La caverne*, finally composed in the liberating early years of the Revolution. Oh, it had had everything against it, cabals, malicious gossip, the singers themselves quite certain before they had heard a note of it that an opera by a church composer couldn't be any good; right up to the last moment the whole thing was in doubt (how generous Cherubini had been, taking some of the rehearsals and conducting the première when the composer was too nervous to do it adequately); but it was a triumph — and then, so insatiable is the human spirit, immediately this victory he had fought for so anxiously and tenaciously was won he fell into a strange depression: with nothing left to fear or to hope for, everything seemed to go out of him and he felt only a great emptiness.

La caverne, a melodrama of kidnapping and brigandage derived from Lesage's *Gil Blas*, first performed at the Feydeau in 1793, was the operatic hit of the Republic. But it was surpassed under the Empire by *Les Bardes*, the opera based on his beloved Ossian. That was the proudest moment of Le Sueur's life — when Napoleon summoned him to his box after the third act, made him sit down next to him and showered him with praise on the splendour of his music, the like of which he had never heard, ending with the much-quoted and curious compliment, "The second act in particular is inaccessible" (the newspapers, reporting the incident, discreetly modified the Imperial barbarism to "incomparable"). Next day the composer received a gold casket, with "The Emperor Napoleon to the author of *Les Bardes*" engraved on the inside, and the cross of chevalier of the Légion d'honneur.[*] He adored Napoleon and never tired of discussing him. But the Republic too — what potent memories it evoked, those heady days when the whole nation sang and the leading composers of the day held public rehearsals in the streets of Paris and taught the populace the tunes of the hymns they had written for the great musical festivities that filled the Champ de Mars. Such tales found in Berlioz a willing listener; mixed with exalted notions of the ceremonies of

---

[*] Twenty years later when Charles X, at his coronation (at which music by Le Sueur was performed), awarded him the superior rank of officer of the Légion d'honneur, he turned it down.

the ancient world, they fed a vision of the musician as mentor of the people that remained with him all his life.

Le Sueur was also a sympathetic listener and a wise counsellor, advising his pupil how to deal with the pressure from his family, encouraging him to be patient and diplomatic while standing firm. Charmed by his company, he let him argue freely and challenge the philosophical and religious propositions he put forward, and even dispute his cherished musical theories. In doing so he gave him what R. W. Southern has called "the most magnanimous gift a tutor can make his pupils — to provide them with material for disagreement".

More often than not the pupil's opinions reflected his master's. Le Sueur's practical preoccupations — his concern with questions of acoustics, the placing of instruments, concert pitch — as well as his general values lie behind the letter which appeared in the *Corsaire* above the signature Hector B___ on 12 August 1823.*

Monsieur le Corsaire,

Is it possible you have become a true-blue dilettante? It seems it must be so, for in your issue of the 10th of this month you print a dialogue between a partisan of the Italians and a patron of the Opéra whom you name "Bawler" [Crifort], which seeks to prove that *La Vestale* would be better located at the Théâtre-Italien than at the Opéra.

How, sir, can you suffer such a proposition to be put forward? Granted, the title rôle is inadequately performed; granted, the triumphal march is invariably disturbed by the wretched bass-drum player, who plays out of time because he is placed too far from the orchestra to be able to hear it properly; granted, at several points in the work the orchestra accompanies too loudly. But why is the great central rôle badly taken? Because it is no longer taken by Mme Branchu. It is to be doubted whether Mme Pasta, with all her talent, would come near our lyric tragedienne in this kind of music. Why do they bawl at the Opéra in certain passages? Because the Opéra's pitch is a tone higher than it should be. Is M. Levasseur — who admittedly does not bawl — really capable of replacing Dérivis? Would he sing the tremendous finale of the second act without embellishing it? Why does the orchestra make so much noise? Because Spontini's works are scored too heavily. The Italian orchestra would play them quietly only by virtue of the fact that it is half the size, or by suppressing three quarters of the orchestral parts in order to lend greater prominence to Garcia's ornaments and portamentos.

---

* The *Corsaire* was an arts daily which had started publication a month before, on 11 July. One of its occasional features was a "Polémique musicale" on topics of the moment. On 10 August an anonymous dialogue appeared which took the side of the Théâtre-Italien, where Rossini reigned supreme, against the Opéra, the home of the French school. Berlioz was stung to reply, and his riposte appeared two days later.

One should go into the matter a little more deeply before judging; one should read the score to discover if it is the orchestra's fault when the music is too loud or the composer's. That is just what our dilettante fanatics are not prepared to do. Yes, fanatics; and to prove it I will repeat what I heard from their own mouths at the most recent performance of *The Marriage of Figaro*. On the way in, one of them remarked to his friend, "I've only come today to kill time, it's Mozart." A moment later he got into conversation with a Mozartian. The subject of Gluck came up. "Oh Gluck," he said with an air of disdain, "I wasn't talking about him — he didn't write music, he wrote plain-chant." There's judging for you! It's the same with their pronouncements on other composers. The Rossinian mentioned *Virginie*, in which he claimed to have discovered an aria that he considered not at all bad. How fortunate! M. Berton would be charmed to hear his music praised by an amateur of his discrimination.

Come on! Who would seriously deny that all Rossini's operas put together could not stand comparison with a single line of recitative by Gluck, three bars of melody by Mozart or Spontini, the least chorus by Lesueur! That at any rate is my opinion, and I am no fanatic of French music.

Yours etc.

Hector B

The idea of planting a mine under the Théâtre-Italien and blowing it up one evening with its entire congregation of dilettanti might have to be abandoned as impractical, for all its attractions; but he could at least carry on the battle in print. A second contribution to the *Corsaire*'s "Polémique musicale", which appeared several months later, returned to the subject of the dilettanti and to the question why it was that, whereas they almost choked with emotion at the "pathos" of *La gazza ladra*, works like the two *Iphigénie*s or Salieri's *The Danaids* left them unmoved. In answer, Berlioz resorted to heavy sarcasm:

The reason, of course, is that at the Opéra they sing so badly. They are merely dramatic (frequently sublime), confining themselves to realising the composer's intentions. What could be more ludicrous than Mme Branchu in the rôle of Clytemnestre in *Iphigénie en Aulide*? She adds not one note to her rôle, not even in the aria "Jove, hurl thy thunderbolt", where it would be so appropriate: for a roulade of a dozen notes on the first line would depict admirably the flash of lightning piercing the clouds; on the second, "may the Greeks be ground to powder, crushed beneath thy blows", a little *martellato* would do nicely for the crushing of the Greeks; while the last, "within their blazing vessels", would be rendered in a superior manner by a chromatic scale of trills, in imitation of the flames leaping from the burning ships. Such are the accomplishments these gentlemen require of all singers; and so long as Mme Branchu is content to harrow her listeners and make them weep, so long as she persists in not singing the rôle of Hypermnestre in *The Danaids* as she sings "What calm my spirit breathes" in *The Mysteries of Isis* or "How delightful are these flatt'ring tributes" in *Iphigénie en Aulide*, the *dilettanti* will say she bawls [...] [11 January 1824]

Berlioz's youthful antipathy to Rossini and all his works blinded him — as he later acknowledged — to his genius and even to the charm of a score like *The Barber of Seville*, which in a less partial state of mind he would not have failed to respond to. But impartiality was out of the question. The Parisian musical scene was divided between the partisans of the new Italian school and those who remained loyal to the old French school (which included naturalised Italians such as Salieri, Sacchini and Spontini), and it was the Italian school that was in the ascendant. In its survey of the year 1823 the *Almanach des spectacles* declared that the Italian Opera "is all the rage. The title 'dilettante' is à la mode. He who is not a dilettante is beneath consideration. The advent of the great composer Rossini has almost revived the famous war of the Gluckists and the Piccinnists." Sober-minded judges likened him to a kind of combination of Titian and Michelangelo. "Since the death of Napoleon", began Stendhal's preface to his life of Rossini (published in 1824), "another man has arisen who is talked of day in and day out in Moscow as in Naples, in London as in Vienna, in Calcutta as in Paris. The fame of this man knows no bounds but those of the civilised world, and he is not thirty-two years old." A dozen of his works were in the repertory of the Théâtre-Italien, and fashionable Paris deserted the Opéra and flocked to hear them. In November 1823 the conqueror came to Paris and was fêted by the artistic establishment at a great banquet given in his honour by the Conservatoire. Le Sueur himself, representing the Conservatoire in the absence of Cherubini, was obliged to propose the toast to "him whose fiery genius has blazed a new trail in the theatrical profession and signalised a new era in the art of music".

Against the extreme claims of the cult and its blasphemous rejection of his adored Gluck, and against a style so opposed to his idea of opera, Berlioz could only react with equal violence. He had his own exclusive cult. Gluck and Spontini were the ideal. The study of high dramatic music, tragédie-lyrique and its successor, Spontinian grand opera, was a religion which commanded his entire devotion, body and soul. Later, his attitude would relax considerably. Though still deriding what he regarded as the anti-dramatic nonsenses of Rossinian opera in its cynical and perfunctory moods — the repetition of a single stereotyped cadence formula (parodied by Berlioz in the ophicleide solo in *Benvenuto Cellini*), the inevitable crescendos, the brutalising din of cymbals and bass-drum used in invariable tandem as a routine means of whipping up physical excitement, the mania for vocal display, the relentless vivacity of manner, the tendency for even the most expressive passages to give way suddenly to triviality and empty decoration — he could recognise the greatness of the *Barber* and delight in *Le comte Ory*, and admire with reservations the grandeur of *William Tell*, Rossini's final bow to the French tradition. But in 1823, in the intransigence of his teenage enthusiasms, it was all or nothing. Gluck and Spontini represented the ne plus ultra of dramatic music. They were the true gods. The new pagan deity was anathema.

It has been said that Berlioz's professed abhorrence for the contemporary Italian style is contradicted by the clear signs of its influence to be found in his own music. Thus Rossini left his mark on such things as the *Waverley* overture and the brilliant 6/8 ensemble "Ah maintenant de sa folle impudence" in Act 2 of *Benvenuto Cellini*, as well as on certain general stylistic tendencies (a fondness for accents on the off-beat, for example); the tenor solo "Te ergo quæsumus" in the Te Deum is decidedly Italianate in character; and so on. But the inconsistency is more apparent than real. For one thing, what sounds like Rossini can sometimes be attributed to an earlier source, common to both Rossini and Berlioz — Spontini. For another, it was not so much modern Italian music per se that he rejected as its abuses, the anti-dramatic conventions which in his view were constantly dragging it down, and its corrupting influence which led singers to disfigure the vocal line in French operas with ornaments in the Italian mode. Besides, composers, whatever their principles, are in Practice much less bothered about where they get their ideas than are the historians who write books classifying them. Berlioz is no exception. Equally, he was capable of appraising his gods in a dispassionate spirit and of concluding (as we saw in the first *Corsaire* article) that Spontini was inclined to over-score his operas, or that Gluck's horn parts were sometimes unimaginative or even inept and the dénouement of *Alceste* a very trumpery affair — "a case of Homer not so much nodding as losing his head".

Music history, curiously, has tended to present Berlioz as someone who was not influenced by anybody but sprang from nowhere. In fact, as with any other young composer, his style was formed from a multitude of influences, and he was open to all, ready to try anything. Even at the extreme point of his anti-Italian bias he frequented the Théâtre-Italien, listened to what it had to offer, and noted what he heard. Its performances were on Tuesdays, Thursdays and Saturdays, and thus alternated with the Opéra's. He got to know *La gazza ladra*, *Otello*, *Tancredi*, *Mosè in Egitto*, as well as the works by other composers that Rossini-fever left room for, such as *Matrimonio segreto*, *Figaro* and *Don Giovanni*.

We know, from the casual reference in his first letter to the *Corsaire*, that he was at the performance of *Figaro* on 24 July 1823. Putting together many such references in his correspondence and criticism and making deductions from others, we are able to confirm what we should guess anyway, that he lived in the theatre. The lyric theatre predominantly, but not solely: he went to plays and followed the great actors and actresses of the day, Talma, Mlle Mars, Mlle Duchesnois, Frédérick Lemaître, as well as the singers. Two plays he saw which formed the basis of compositions written or begun soon afterwards were Lamartelière's *Les francs-juges, ou les tems de barbarie* at the Ambigu-Comique in 1823, and at the Odéon the same year (along with much Molière and Racine) Saurin's *Beverley, ou le joueur*. But there were certainly others.

Then there was the Opéra-Comique. Though it was not what it had been — the works of Cherubini and Méhul that twenty years before had made French opera famous in Austro-Germany (inspiring Beethoven to write *Fidelio*) had largely vanished from the repertoire, and Berlioz got to know them from the scores in the Conservatoire Library — he frequented it none the less and heard Grétry, Boieldieu and Auber and the occasional piece by Dalayrac.

The Opéra, above all, was his haunt. When Berlioz arrived in Paris at the end of 1821 Gluck's long reign was drawing to a close; but he was just in time to catch its last few years. In the second half of the 1820s almost the whole of the Gluckist school went into eclipse. Only Spontini's *La vestale* and *Fernand Cortez* — works that bridged the gap between tragédie-lyrique and grand opera — held their own in the new era dominated by Rossini's French creations or adaptations — *Guillaume Tell*, *Le comte Ory*, *Moïse*, *Le siège de Corinthe* — and by Auber's prodigiously successful *La muette de Portici*.[*] Up to the middle of the decade, however, the works of Gluck and his successors, though less and less popular with the general public, still figured in the Opéra's programmes. In the four years from 1822 to 1825 Salieri's *The Danaids* was performed 26 times, Sacchini's *Œdipe à Colone* 33. *Orphée*, revived in 1824, achieved 28 performances in the first eighteen months (but only 21 more in the five years after that). Then as now, *Orphée* was the most popular Gluck opera; even the dilettanti thought it tolerable. The beautiful *Armide* was in the repertory for only two seasons, 1825 and 1826, when it was heard fifteen times in all. The two *Iphigénie*s appeared only sporadically on the bills; and *Alceste*, revived in 1825, was given a mere handful of performances. But to a young man of Berlioz's temperament the sense that the tradition was threatened and the old gods under attack aroused a yet more passionate loyalty.

Often, of course, even in the first years of his discipleship, the temple was given over to frivolities, feeble and spurious creations old and new such as Rousseau's *Le devin du village*, Lebrun's *Rossignol* or Hérold's *Lasthénie*. He had tried them and found them wanting. A fairy-opera called *Aladdin, or the marvellous lamp*, occupied the theatre for over a hundred evenings. Whatever the opera, it was almost invariably followed by a ballet; to begin with, at least, he would stay to hear it.[†] Worst of all was when a work by one of the masters was replaced at the last minute,

---

[*] The statistics for the total number of performances of all Gluckist operas in two successive four-year periods — that is, excepting *La Vestale* and *Cortez* but including new or revised works like Berton's *Virginie* and Kreutzer's *Abel* — tell their own story: 1822—25, 184; 1827—30, 31. Compare these with the following figures for the latter period (1827—30): *La muette de Portici* 122; *Guillaume Tell* 52; *Le comte Ory* 86; *Le siège de Corinthe* 76; *Moïse* 51.

[†] Cf. above, p. 112, where at the ball at M. Teisseyre's the band plays tunes he recognises from ballets he has heard at the Opéra.

and he would only discover the fact when the orchestral attendant went round putting out the music of some quite different and inferior piece. When that happened Berlioz and his fellow-worshippers would rise in a body and leave the theatre, "swearing like marauding soldiers who discover water in what they had taken to be brandy-casks", and loudly consigning to perdition the composer of the offending work, the manager who inflicted it on an innocent public, and the government which allowed it to be performed at all.*

Such disappointments only made more sacred the occasions when they were able to worship the true gods. During these years Berlioz gathered round him a group of like-minded enthusiasts. Some, like his fellow-pupil Gerono, were already regulars of the pit. Others were friends from La Côte St André studying in Paris, who were accustomed to following his lead: the cousins Edouard and Marc Rocher (chemistry and medicine respectively), Marc's elder brother Hippolyte (law), Alphonse Robert and Charles Bert (medicine), Laurent Pion (law). And there was a whole new circle of friends that he had made in Paris. Some were medical students, whom he kept up with after his own defection: Ferdinand Laforest, Georges Dubouchet (fellow-lodgers at 79 Rue St Jacques), and Auguste Berlioz (no relation) from Lyons. Others were law students, including two of the most important, Albert Du Boys and Humbert Ferrand, both of them from his part of France: Du Boys from Grenoble, son of an appeals judge, Ferrand from Bellay (thirty miles east of Lyons), son of the local chief justice. Du Boys held weekly reunions for fellow-Dauphinois who found themselves in the capital. Berlioz had met him before, but got to know him well only after his arrival in Paris. He wrote poetry and was interested in music; two of the songs that Berlioz published in the winter of 1822 – 23, "Le montagnard exilé" and "Toi qui l'aimas, verse des pleurs", are settings of verses by Du Boys. At one of Du Boys' gatherings Berlioz met Humbert Ferrand and felt drawn to him instantly: a short young man with squeaky voice and nutcracker physiognomy but with a warmth of manner and a vehemence of opinion that contradicted his unprepossessing appearance and won Berlioz's heart. Ferrand and Du Boys were staunch Gluckists. So was Augustin de Pons, an aristocrat from the Faubourg St Germain, a man of impulsive nature and vigorous enthusiasms and antipathies, as uncompromising in his passion for his favourite works as Berlioz himself.

Other more occasional members of the club sometimes fell short of the proper zeal and had to be kept up to the mark. When they wavered he harangued them with missionary fervour and dragged them off to the

---

* Berlioz's dislike of works in which he found only "a mixture of platitude and falseness of expression," was as intense and as physical as the delight he experienced from the music he loved. At its worst, he said, it was as though he had swallowed some nauseating liquid which his stomach insisted on rejecting. "I vomit it from every pore."

Opéra, if necessary giving them tickets bought out of his own pocket while pretending that they came from a friend in the management. Though younger than many of them he was their leader, and once they had all forgathered in the pit he would take charge, stationing them at the particular point where the work they had come to hear would sound best, according to how it was scored for orchestra, chorus and solo voice and whether the scenery was enclosed or open — he had tried every part of the pit, so knew from experience which was the right place. They would get there early, to be able to sit where they wanted; and if there were any among them who didn't know the work in question he would go through the text while they waited, singing the more important passages, explaining how the most striking orchestral effects were obtained, and generally talking them into a suitable state of advance enthusiasm. Then, as the orchestra began to assemble, he would comment on the players:

> That's Baillot. Unlike some solo violinists he doesn't save himself for the ballet; he doesn't consider it beneath him to accompany an opera by Gluck. In a moment you'll hear him play a passage on the G string which sounds right through the orchestra.
>
> That big red-faced old boy there, Chénié, the leader of the double basses, is as good as four ordinary players, and you can be sure his part will be played exactly as the composer wrote it — he's not one of your simplifiers.
>
> The conductor should keep an eye on Guillou, the first flute, who's coming in now. He takes extraordinary liberties with Gluck — he transposes the sacred march in *Alceste*, written for the bottom register of the flute, up an octave so that it will sound more prominent, which completely destroys the composer's intention.*

Once the overture had begun, nothing was suffered to disturb their religious concentration on the performance. Occupants of neighbouring benches were actively discouraged from humming, beating time or, especially, talking, which they would silence by resorting to the famous mot invented by a music-lover: "Those damned musicians are depriving me of the pleasure of hearing what this chap's saying". The only disturbance permitted — indeed required — was a loud protest whenever the performers themselves tampered with the text. Ernest Legouvé has left a vivid picture of one such incident, at a performance of *Der Freischütz*, when in the introduction to Caspar's drinking song one of his neighbours (Legouvé had not yet met Berlioz) rose suddenly from his seat and shouted out, "Not two flutes, you fools — two piccolos!"

> In the midst of the ensuing hubbub I looked round and saw a young man literally shaking with rage, his fists clenched, his eyes blazing, and a head of

* *Memoirs*, chapter 15.

hair — how can I describe it? An immense umbrella or movable canopy, overhanging the beak of a bird of prey!

Unfortunately for the veracity of this tale, no performances of *Freischütz* were given in Paris during the period Legouvé is recalling. But as a general impression it is undoubtedly true to life. Berlioz had studied his favourite works so thoroughly that he knew them by heart; and any deviation from the text was a shock to his nervous system as well as an affront to his cherished beliefs. The addition of cymbals to the first Scythian dance in *Iphigénie en Tauride* or the removal of the trombones from Orestes' recitative "Quoi! je ne vaincrai pas ta constance funeste" in the same work was like a knife wound. The sanctity of the composer's work was fundamental to his artistic creed.

To have conceived an idea at once so idealistic and so logical is typical of the young Berlioz's originality. His provincial simplicity of mind led him unaided to a conclusion which we take for granted but which was then almost unheard of. Fidelity to the score is very much a late twentieth-century preoccupation, foreign to the nineteenth. It is one of the many points on which Berlioz was out of tune with his time. Altering the orchestration even of the most eminent composers (not to mention cutting their works wholesale) was accepted practice; people thought nothing of it. Wagner touched up Beethoven's symphonies (regarding the Ninth as particularly in need of his attention) and rescored *Iphigénie en Aulide* and *Don Giovanni*. Weber was unusual in protesting so indignantly at the version of *Freischütz* that was given in Paris in 1824—25; the arranger was genuinely unable to see that he had done anything wrong — on the contrary: he had helped to make the work "go".

If Berlioz's account of it is to be believed, the on-the-spot criticism practised by him and his friends was effective: next time *Iphigénie en Tauride* was given, the trombones played and the cymbals were silent; and thanks to the same method the new ballet music substituted for Sacchini's in *Œdipe à Colone*, which Augustin de Pons had taken violent exception to, disappeared forthwith. The ordinary members of the public found all the fuss somewhat mystifying: presumably, that knot of ostentatious young enthusiasts represented some kind of claque, they applauded so vigorously and in places where nothing of any great moment was happening — a line of recitative, a change of key, an isolated note on the oboe. The leader of the real claque, Levasseur, only too well aware that such unrehearsed applause could upset his carefully calculated manoeuvres, looked askance at it and regarded Berlioz and his friends as very dubious allies.*

---

* Appropriately for a leading member of a profession which traced its origin to Roman times, to the corps de claqueurs employed by the Emperor Nero to applaud his theatrical performances, his first name was Augustus.

When their favourite singers were on form there was no need of a claque. Dérivis, a vehement, rather unpolished artist and the bête noire of the dilettanti but a powerful dramatic bass capable of great eloquence, was very popular with them and sang in most of the Opéra's repertory.* But their idol was Mme Branchu. She was over fifty and her career was nearing its end when Berlioz first heard her; she no longer sang Julia, the vestal heroine of Spontini's opera (the part she had created fifteen years earlier), and though there was talk of her resuming the title rôle in *Iphigénie en Tauride* she refused to so long as the pitch adopted at the Opéra remained so high. The only Gluck rôles he heard her sing were Clytemnestre in *Iphigénie en Aulide* and Alceste. But, with Hypermnestre in *The Danaids* and Statira in Spontini's *Olympie*, and with Méhul's *Stratonice*, Berton's *Virginie* and Kreutzer's *La mort d'Abel*, it was enough. Those last four years of Mme Branchu's career left a permanent impression on him. For Berlioz she was simply "tragédie lyrique incarnate"; her interpretations remained the ideal, combining "minutely studied effect and sudden unpremeditated genius". She taught him the grand style just at the moment when the tradition of classical opera was on the point of disappearing. The voice, though no longer in its prime, was still large and lustrous, with a particularly rich and easy middle register and a wide range of dynamics and colour. She was accused by the dilettanti of forcing it. But what he remembered, as much as the orchestra-engulfing power of her fortissimo, was the way she could fill the Opéra with her softest tones, making the subtlest nuances of feeling audible all over the theatre. The fine aria in *The Danaids* in which Hypermnestre pleads with her father not to condemn his family to certain death became something quite extraordinary, he recalled, through her mastery of vivid and varied expression: the stifled sound she imparted to the opening lines, "Par les larmes dont votre fille/Arrose en tremblant votre sein" — sung as though the singer were choked by sobs, in an extreme pianissimo which yet allowed every note and every syllable to be heard — suddenly swept aside, at "Craignez des dieux la justice suprême", by the fury of her voice in full spate. Clear, eloquent diction was an essential element in such inspired re-creations. It was a lesson in dramatic singing that he never forgot. If *The Trojans* expressed his lifelong devotion to Gluck and

---

* Hazlitt, who heard him as Iarbas in Piccinni's *Didon* in 1824, shared the dilettante view: "Dérivis [was] a perfect Stentor. He spoke or sung [*sic*] all through with an unmitigated ferocity of purpose and manner, with lungs that seemed to have been forged expressly for the occasion. Ten bulls could not bellow louder, nor a whole street-full of frozen-out gardeners at Christmas." Hazlitt's opinion is echoed by the anonymous author of the Dérivis entry in *Petite biographie des acteurs et actrices des théâtres de Paris* (1826): "M. Dérivis is quite a good actor, I grant, especially in *Œdipe à Colone* and *La Vestale*: but let us not profane the title of singer by according it to a man better fitted to vie with the foremost bawlers of our public squares than to occupy a leading place on our lyric stage." The *Journal de Paris*, on the other hand, praises his "deep voice and noble gestures" in the rôle of Agamemnon in *Iphigénie en Aulide* (17 April 1823).

to the "resurrections of the ancient world" which struck so deep a note of recognition, Mme Branchu and her superb declamation were surely in his mind when he conceived the tragic utterances of Cassandra and Dido, "Malheureux roi, dans l'éternelle nuit", "Je vais mourir dans ma douleur immense submergée", "Dieux immortels, il part", "Pluton semble m'être propice".

That the culminating work of his career should mark a return to the faith of his youth shows not merely the stubbornness of his loyalties but also how powerful was the influence of that early formative period. During his first three years in Paris, until the production of *Der Freischütz* at the Odéon in the winter of 1824–25, he was a single-minded disciple of the French neo-Classical school. A further three years would pass before the discovery of Beethoven in the spring of 1828, the event which completed the formation of his musical personality and led to the composition of his first wholly characteristic works, the *Eight Scenes from Faust* and the Fantastic Symphony. Even then, even after the revelation of a music of incomparably greater emotional range, formal scope and complexity, richness of texture and physical impact, Gluck and Spontini remained active mentors. The Fantastic Symphony itself, for all its novel elements, exemplifies this: its great arching melodic lines are descendants of the long-breathed melodies of the two *Iphigénie* operas, *Alceste, Fernand Cortez* and *La vestale*.

Of course, music is in reality a much more fluid substance than the generalisations of historians would suggest, and constantly escapes their categories. There are passages in Gluck's *Armide* which already seem to breathe the air of a freer, less circumscribed age, and still more so in Spontini's French operas – daringly expressive harmonies and effects of colour that look forward to Verdi and Wagner. The young Berlioz also heard *Don Giovanni*, the quintessential "demonic" Mozart opera which the nineteenth century was to find a source of obsessive fascination. Yet the more we study this first period of Berlioz's apprenticeship the more, I think, we must be struck by the almost exclusively French and Classical character of the musical outlook that the future Romantic acquired from it. One consequence was his equivocal attitude to Mozart. Le Sueur adored Mozart, and Berlioz came to love him almost unreservedly. But Mozart, at this stage, was largely the preserve of the despised Théâtre-Italien, whose performances were hardly calculated to break down his prejudice. The orchestra was notoriously bad (a worse handicap to Mozart than to Rossini) and the singing does not appear to have been very idiomatic (not till he heard Sontag as Susanna in London in 1851, he said, did he experience "Deh vieni" other than crudely sung). And in the intolerance of his religion, in which only Gluck and Spontini were allowed to be sublime, he was duly shocked to find Mozart descending to the level of Rossini and making Donna Anna burst into a flourish of coloratura at a moment of high solemnity in the drama (the second half of the aria

"Non mi dir"); it was as fatuously undramatic as Desdemona's outbreak of incongruous scales and roulades in the second act of Rossini's *Otello*, in the midst of that poignant appeal "Se il padre m'abbandonà". How could one trust, how could one truly admire a composer who so betrayed his dramatic genius?*

Les mystères d'Isis, the version of *The Magic Flute* revived at the Opéra in 1823, was another matter. But here what appealed to him was the noble dignity of the religious scenes — Mozart's most Gluck-like music, apart from *Idomeneo* (which was not performed in Paris at that time). Berlioz's final conversion to Mozart, which came about through his discovery of the quartets and quintets, took place some years later. Instrumental music ranked low in Le Sueur's hierarchy of values. Dramatic, vocal music, whether sacred or secular, was what counted; and his pupil reflected his beliefs. Only when he had achieved his emancipation, under the influence of Beethoven, would he compose a large-scale work for orchestra alone — a full seven years after the beginning of his studies with Le Sueur. Until then he wrote as a matter of course for voices.

His main diplomatic efforts during this period were directed to securing an opera libretto and getting his Mass performed. The major works of the mid-1820s, apart from the Mass, are the opera *Les francs-juges*, the Scène héroïque — a dramatic cantata for soloists and chorus on the Greek war of independence — and an oratorio with Latin text, *The Crossing of the Red Sea*, which has not survived but which we can assume was modelled on the Old Testament Latin oratorios of Le Sueur.

We may also note that when he decided to try his hand at writing an opera the first person he turned to was that eminently classical figure and pillar of the literary ancien régime François Andrieux, whose lectures at the Collège de France he still sometimes attended. He wrote to him not long after his return from La Côte St André in the second half of May 1823. The letter has not survived; but Andrieux's courteous refusal is quoted in the *Memoirs*:

17 June 1823

Sir,
    Your letter interested me keenly. The zeal you demonstrate for the noble art of your choice will assuredly bring you success. I wish it for you with all my heart, and I should be only too glad to be able to help you obtain it. But the business you propose to me is not for a man of my age; my ideas and my studies lie in other directions. I should strike you as a barbarian were I to

---

* Legouvé describes attending a performance of Rossini's *Otello* with Berlioz. "I found [Desdemona's scales and roulades] very stirring, but they infuriated him. At the end of the act, he leant over and murmured in my ear, in a voice as expressive as the melody itself, 'If my father renounces me, if my father renounces me —'. Then, with a sudden burst of sardonic laughter, and faithfully reproducing all the coloratura of the score, 'I don't give a damn, I don't give a damn, I don't give a damn!' "

tell you how many years it is since I set foot in the Opéra or in the Feydeau. I am sixty-four. To aspire to write love-lyrics would ill become me; and as for music, I ought to be thinking only of Requiems. I regret that you weren't born thirty or forty years earlier, or I later: we could have worked together. Please accept my excuses, which are only too real, and my sincere and affectionate greetings.

Andrieux

Andrieux brought his reply in person to Berlioz's lodgings in the Rue St Jacques, climbing several floors to a small door through the cracks of which came the smell of onions. It was opened by a thin, startled young man holding a frying-pan. "Oh, M. Andrieux — if I'd only known. You've surprised me in the middle of ... " — "Please, no apologies. Your rabbit smells delicious and I should have loved to share it with you, but my stomach is no good any more. Carry on, my friend, don't burn your dinner just because an academician who's written a few stories has called on you." Andrieux stayed for some time, leaning forward grasping his stick and chatting to his young friend about music. When he mentioned that he was an admirer of Gluck, Berlioz gave a convulsive bound, upsetting some of the contents of the frying-pan — only to replace it disappointedly on the stove when Andrieux added, half to himself, "I'm fond of Piccinni too."[*]

Berlioz had no doubt heard that in his youth Andrieux had written one or two librettos; and it seems likely, from the tone of Andrieux's letter and from his coming to call on him, that in the course of attending his lectures Berlioz had contrived to have himself introduced to the old man.[†]

---

[*] The incident, reported briefly in the *Memoirs*, is recounted at greater length by Daniel Bernard, editor of the first collection of Berlioz's letters.

Though the famous Gluck—Piccinni controversy had long ceased to be an issue, it was natural that Berlioz should feel cool towards the composer whom at that stage he knew only from the history books, as the rival of Gluck. Piccinni's *Didon* was not revived at the Opéra till the following year. Berlioz found some of it very impressive, as he reported to his friend Edouard Rocher: though the recitatives were poor — absolutely unvarying, like Italian recitatives, without any distinctive character or any dramatic expression in the orchestra — the set numbers were superb. The "sublime duet 'C'est donc toi que Didon couronne' [for Iarbas and Æneas] had a tremendous effect on me — about three quarters of the effect that Cain's aria 'Abel seul est aimable' [in Kreutzer's *La mort d'Abel*] produced on us: that will give you an idea of it." Unfortunately Dido was sung by a newcomer, Mlle Noël, with a splendid voice but no notion how to use it, no sense of style or acting ability, and no idea of musical declamation. "The little sensibility she appeared to show is attributable to Piccinni's warm and expressive melodies, which there's no resisting. She sang the aria 'Ah, que je fus bien inspirée' well; but the scene of Dido's fury — God, I'm still trembling with rage. Her delivery of 'Tyriens, accourez! Embrasez les vaisseaux! Que dis-je, malheureuse!' — oh Madame Branchu, where are you!" Thirty years later this Virgilian scene found echoes in the libretto of Berlioz's *Troyens*: "Armez-vous, Tyriens! Carthaginois, courez [...] brûlez leurs vaisseaux! [...] Que dis-je? [...] O malheureuse!"

[†] That they remained on friendly terms is suggested by Andrieux's presence at the Institute prize-giving the year Berlioz won the Prix de Rome (1830) — the only occasion the Institute records show him as having attended.

The notion of suggesting to a person of his eminence that they should collaborate on an opera was none the less, as he later remarked, an odd one. But it was characteristic of the nineteen-year-old Berlioz that he had no qualms about it. It was not in his nature to feel abashed. At the age of fifteen he had felt able to write to a leading music publisher suggesting that he publish his compositions. And in his simplicity he regarded it as perfectly natural to be on easy terms with one's gods. Hero-worship did not exclude familiarity. The fact that he idolised Mme Branchu was no reason for not making friends with her, and accordingly he did so. Not that it was always so simple. Kreutzer, composer of the sublime *Mort d'Abel*, bit his head off when he asked him to perform his Scène héroïque at one of the concerts spirituels; and Berlioz was quite unprepared for it, having imagined that, because he admired Kreutzer and had expressed his admiration in a rapturous letter to him, the great man would be as accessible and affable as Le Sueur.

Side by side with his naïve egoism went a growing realisation that to get on in Paris a young composer had to have contacts — with the musical world, with the academic establishment, with politics, the civil service, the press — all of which he must be prepared to exploit in order to get his music performed. It was wonderful to be on friendly terms with Mme Branchu; it could also be useful. There is a temptation to see his letter to Kreutzer as a less than disinterested move on the young Berlioz's part, and to detect an element of calculation in its rhapsodies. But the probability is that the letter belongs to the summer of 1823, two years before the démarche on behalf of the Scène héroïque. Kreutzer's *La mort d'Abel*, which inspired the letter, was revived at the Opéra on 17 March 1823, with Nourrit as Abel and Mme Branchu as his mother Eve. Berlioz was at La Côte at the time, but he could have seen it any time from 23 May onwards, and had certainly done so by 13 October, the last performance before the appearance of his second article in the *Corsaire* (11 January 1824), which refers to the work. The letter is couched in the swooning, adolescent style of the worst contemporary novelettes, which also argues for an earlier rather than a later date:

> Oh genius! I faint — I die! Tears choke me. God! *The Death of Abel*.
> How vile the public is. It feels nothing. What on earth does it require in order to be moved? Oh genius! And what am I to do, I, if one day my music depicts passion? I will not be understood either — since they fail to crown, fail to bear in triumph, fail to prostrate themselves before the creator of all that is beautiful. Poignant, harrowing, sublime! Oh! I can restrain myself no longer. I must write — but to whom? To the genius? No, that I dare not do.
> To the man, then — to Kreutzer. He will laugh at me. No matter. I should die ... if I held my tongue. Ah, if only I could see him, could speak to him. He would understand me, he would perceive what is passing in my harrowed soul.
> Perhaps he would restore to me the courage I lost when I witnessed the

insensibility of those contemptible riff-raff, who are scarcely worthy to listen to that clown Rossini's pitiable puppetries.

I should never finish, but that the pen falls from my hand.

Ah! Genius!

                                        H. Berlioz (pupil of Lesueur)

In due course he would discover that Kreutzer the man was equally unapproachable.

"Si un jour ma musique peint les passions ... " To depict passion: from the first that was his aim.

Very little of what Berlioz composed in these years has survived. One consequence of his becoming a student of Le Sueur's was that publication of his music ceased — for one thing, because to engrave the kind of music he was now writing, for full orchestra with voices, was prohibitively expensive, but also because he was all too clearly aware of being a mere beginner, with everything to learn. Except for a set of variations for guitar on "Là ci darem la mano" — a potboiler issued in 1828, of which no copy has survived — no work of his appeared between the group of romances published in the winter of 1822–23 and the *Eight Scenes from Faust* of 1829, the first major work of his that he considered good enough to be printed. The earliest complete composition that survives in its original form is the Scène héroïque, or the Greek Revolution, which belongs to the latter part of 1825. Otherwise all that exists from the first four and a half years of his Parisian apprenticeship (1822 to 1826) are a single movement from the Mass and fragments of *Les francs-juges*. The rest has vanished. Nevertheless we have a fairly clear idea of what he was composing during this period; and, despite gaps certainly due to compositions that have left no trace, we can draw up a rough chronological table:

1822 (second half)	*Le cheval arabe* (cantata)
1823	*Estelle et Némorin* (opera)
	The Crossing of the Red Sea (oratorio)
1824	*Beverley* (dramatic scena)
1824–25	Mass
1824(?)–26	*Les francs-juges* (opera)
1825	Scène héroïque (cantata, on the Greek war of independence)
1826	*Richard en Palestine* (projected opera)

The choice of subjects, with the possible exception of *Estelle et Némorin*, shows the bent of Berlioz's imagination. He is not interested in light music, music that merely entertains. It has got to be music in "the grand style, dramatic or sacred". And quite often, as befits a child of the Revolution, it is a theme of popular resistance to tyranny and oppression.

Le cheval arabe, his first work on a sizeable scale, was the score which Berlioz took with him to the interview with Le Sueur, and which led to his being accepted as a pupil. Le Sueur thought that, with all its mistakes, it contained "a great deal of warmth and dramatic movement". The work has disappeared. But one can see why the subject, quite apart from the appeal of its topical "Eastern" setting, should have attracted a budding dramatic composer. "The Arab at the Tomb of his Steed" is a lament whose five stanzas are begun and ended and linked by a refrain-like couplet: "This noble friend who trod the winds / Sleeps 'neath the desert's shifting sands." Though the verse is weakly conventional, its form and its wide range of picturesque scenes and sentiments suggest a musical setting. 1) The warrior calls on the passer-by to share his grief, and recounts how the "prince of chargers", transfixed by an arrow at the height of his prowess, fell, clouding the limpid source with his life's blood. 2) He describes the revenge he took on the murderer, striking off his head with one blow; then how, turning to his stricken horse, he found him lifeless, and raised his burial mound on the desert plain. 3) Since then nothing has had any meaning for him — life, fame, pleasure, the perfumed airs of his beloved Arabia. 4) For the horse was his constant companion, his brother-in-arms against the Moor, bearing him swift as an arrow to every encounter of war or love. 5) Yes, you were her friend too — the lovely Azéïde, she who was softer than the gentle gazelle, sweeter than the palm-tree's shade. Her hand caressed your quivering neck. But, faithless, she abandoned me — while you stayed true!

The author was Charles Millevoye, a young poet who had died six years earlier in somewhat romantic circumstances and whose collected works had been issued posthumously only a few months before the composition of the cantata. Berlioz may have known the poem for some time — it figured in the slim volume of *Elégies* that Millevoye published in 1812. Or perhaps one of his new literary friends, Humbert Ferrand or Albert Du Boys, introduced him to the collected poems. Both of them knew about his musical projects and were involved in some of them. Du Boys was the author of the text of two of the songs which Berlioz published about this time, and Ferrand would later collaborate with him on *Les francs-juges* and the Scène héroïque.

It was a friend who supplied the text for the next work of which we have any record, the opera *Estelle et Némorin*. Discouraged by the failure of his attempt to secure a literary celebrity (Andrieux), he lowered his sights and settled for Gerono instead. Gerono got to work and produced an adaptation of Florian's story, which Berlioz set to music in the late summer of 1823. According to the composer himself the whole thing — Gerono's dramatisation and verses and his own music — was of the utmost feebleness. He describes it as "milk-and-water" ("rose-tendre") and adds: "Fortunately no one ever heard a note of this composition, prompted — futile prompting! — by my memories of Meylan." On the face of it the work falls outside the category of "music in the grand style" that he had set himself to achieve; it seems to indicate a reversion to adolescence, recalling his juvenile daydreams about composing an opera on *Estelle* and laying the score as an offering at the altar of his goddess on the sacred slopes of St Eynard. The episodic character of the pastoral tale and the frequent songs interpolated into the narrative would suggest that the work took the form of a ballad opera in the manner of Dalayrac's *Nina*, perhaps incorporating some of the *Estelle* settings he had written as a boy, including "Je vais donc quitter pour jamais / Mon doux pays, ma douce amie". But it would be rash to make assumptions about a score that has totally disappeared. Florian's story, with all its "fadeur", provided him with "the motive and the cue for passion"; the "memories of Meylan" were of only too recent date. The feebleness, then, would have been in the execution, not in the intention; and what made it futile and impotent ("impuissant") was simply his inability at that stage of his apprenticeship to write music that began to match the strength of his feelings.

Practically nothing, either, is known about the next two compositions, the Latin oratorio *The Crossing of the Red Sea* and the scena for bass and orchestra from *Beverley*. The text of the oratorio was presumably adapted from the Vulgate.* Berlioz showed Le Sueur the score in November or December 1823. Seven or eight months later he took it up again, finding it "terribly messy in certain passages" but nevertheless hoping that, having revised it, he would be able to get it performed. This is a double preoccupation of these years, familiar to aspirant composers: desire to have his compositions heard, dissatisfaction with them. As he progresses

---

* Behind the choice of genre and subject lay the example of Le Sueur's Biblical oratorios, and also perhaps of an earlier *Crossing of the Red Sea* by Le Sueur's former colleague François Giroust which figures in the catalogue of music performed in the Tuileries chapel between 1802 and 1830. But it is indicative of Berlioz's general romantic interest in the Middle East (an interest he shared with his master) that three of his compositions in this early period — the oratorio, the cantata *Le cheval arabe* and the projected opera *Richard en Palestine* — have Middle Eastern settings. French consciousness had been made actively aware of the region by Napoleon's Egyptian expedition and the many scientific, literary and architectural studies issued in the wake of it. It also became a favourite with painters.

he is aware of the imperfections of what he has just written. The awareness is a measure of the progress. Yet it is vital to get one's music played: how else learn from one's mistakes and advance in one's craft, not to mention one's career? As he remarks in the *Memoirs*, "Every composer knows the importance of getting your foot in the stirrup — and the difficulty of doing so in Paris."

With *Beverley*, however, he felt he had made a step forward. The piece was taken from *Beverley, ou le joueur*, a translation by Bernard-Joseph Saurin — dating from the 1750s but still popular — of one of Garrick's hits, *The Gamester*, a middle-class tragedy of a compulsive gambler and his road to ruin, down which he is impelled by his own weakness but also by the machinations of a false friend, the villainous Stukeley, who has designs on his wife. Berlioz saw the play at the Odéon, where it was in the repertory in 1823 with Perrier in the title rôle. The likeliest passage to choose for a dramatic scena is the final scene of the play, in which Beverley, in prison for debt, and suspected (wrongly) of murder, gives way to passionate self-recrimination on his misspent life before expiring in the arms of his wife. Berlioz describes the work as sombre and vehement, and was pleased with it. In composing the music he had Dérivis' powerful bass and strenuous style in mind; and, clearly, the ideal thing would be to get him to sing it. Thanks to his friendly relations with Mme Branchu that was unlikely to present much difficulty. But when? And where? A special event like a benefit performance, with its mixed programme into which a piece like this could easily be fitted, was the obvious occasion. At just such an event not long before — a miscellaneous entertainment given at the Odéon in the presence of members of the royal family — Dérivis had sung a new cantata by Schneitzhoeffer. When, soon afterwards, the Théâtre-Français announced a benefit for the great actor Talma on 1 April 1824, at which in addition to Lemercier's *Jane Shore* there was to be an act of the ballet *Clari* and therefore an orchestra, it seemed the answer to prayer. All he had to do was to go and see the great man and persuade him to add his score to the programme. Berlioz actually set off over the river to the Rue de la Tour des Dames; but the nearer he approached and the more he imagined the reality of confronting Talma, face to face, the more alarmed he became. He was shaking all over by the time he reached the door, and could not bring himself to pull the bell, but turned away, defeated.

Such acute shyness is not inconsistent with what was said earlier about his precocious use of contacts. It was one thing to write to Kreutzer, Le Sueur's colleague, or to cultivate the friendship of Mme Branchu, having found a means of being introduced to her. But, for a "semi-civilised young enthusiast" (his own words) to call unannounced on Talma — the greatest name in the contemporary theatre and a figure of magical power and authority — was bound to seem increasingly ill-advised, as the first impulse began to cool during the forty-five or fifty minutes it takes to walk from the Rue St Jacques to the Rue de la Tour des Dames.*

Berlioz's bright idea having come to nothing, he could find no way of getting *Beverley* performed. But shortly afterwards, in the spring of 1824, his luck turned. He got to know Masson the choirmaster of the church of St Roch in the Rue St Honoré, just round the corner from Le Sueur's house in the Rue Ste Anne. Perhaps Le Sueur had a word with Masson and introduced his young pupil to him. At any rate, the possibility of performing *The Crossing of the Red Sea* at St Roch was discussed. And then in May 1824 Masson came up with a firm proposal. He asked him to compose a Mass for the Feast of the Holy Innocents, the choirboys' saint's-day, at the end of December. It was what Berlioz had been waiting for. He had got a performance at last.

---

* Cf. the awestruck sensations of the young would-be playwright Alexandre Dumas on being introduced to Talma on the day when he was due to see him act for the first time, in the rôle of the Emperor Sulla in Jouy's play. "At eleven o'clock we rang the bell of the house in the Rue de la Tour des Dames where Mlle Mars, Mlle Duchesnois and Talma all three lived, door to door. Talma was getting dressed; but Adolphe [Dumas' friend Adolphe de Leuwen] was a regular visitor and was admitted [...] [Talma] held out his hand to me. I had an impulse to kiss it. With the ideas I had about the theatre, Talma was to me a god — an unknown god, it's true, unknown as Jupiter was to Semele, but a god who, appearing to me in the morning, was going to reveal himself fully that same evening. Our hands touched. Oh Talma! If only you had been twenty years younger, or I twenty years older!" At the door of Talma's dressing-room, after the performance, he felt his heart beat as fast as "the humblest petitioner who ever waited in fear and trembling to see the real Sulla".

8

A Time of Trial

In the same month as Masson's commission, Gluck's *Orphée* was revived at the Opéra for the first time since Berlioz's arrival in Paris two and a half years before. He had spent part of April in the Conservatoire Library copying, as an exercise, the whole of his beloved *Iphigénie en Tauride*, absent from the Opéra since the previous November. Now he could steep himself in the work which, in the shape of the two extracts he had discovered in his father's library several years earlier, had given him his first vague, thrilling idea of Gluck's music. By the end of May *Orphée* had had six performances, and without doubt he was at them all. There were five more in June and July. But he did not hear them. At the beginning of June he took the coach to La Côte St André.

Though we cannot be sure, it seems Dr Berlioz summoned him home. The period following his return to Paris the previous May, with his father's qualified assent to further musical studies, coincides with a dearth of family correspondence. No letters between Hector and his parents or sisters have survived, and there is nothing from Félix Marmion; nor did Nancy keep a diary during this period. As to the Livre de Raison, it is not conclusive. The sums it records as having been sent to Hector during his student years are not necessarily to be taken at face value, since we know that they often included money to pay for items, books especially, that his father commissioned him to buy on his behalf and post to La Côte. However, even with some deductions allowed for purchases, the figures suggest that throughout the second half of 1823 and the first five months of 1824 Hector continued to receive his monthly allowance of 120 francs, if not with absolute regularity. An additional item of 100 francs sent on 20 January 1824 looks like a present — Dr Berlioz's response to the news, which reached him a day or two before, that Hector had passed his baccalauréat ès-sciences physiques on the 12th. As we have seen, Hector apparently did not follow up his bac with any further studies, medical or scientific. But we should remember that his father had decided on a policy of patience: since the boy would not listen to reasoned argument from his elders and betters the only way he would be brought to see the futility of this musical chimera was by being left to discover it for himself by painful experience.

Despite this, the evidence of the Livre de Raison points to the fact that Hector's journey to La Côte at the beginning of June 1824 was the result of a sudden summons; for, only a fortnight before, his father had sent him a banker's order for 240 francs, a sum corresponding exactly to two months' allowance. If that is so, it was very likely the news of Masson's commission for a Mass that made Dr Berlioz send for his son. The very news that Hector imagined would please his father, as a sign of solid progress on his part, alarmed and irritated him. It was the last thing he wished to hear. In any case it was high time Hector came back. More than a year had passed since he was last home.

This time the atmosphere — to begin with — was quite different. The summons must have been friendly and tactfully phrased, for Hector travelled to La Côte in buoyant mood. He felt much more confident; he was coming home on holiday, not as a prodigal but as the eldest son who was making his way and proud of it, and sure he could persuade his parents of the fact. An incident during the latter stages of the journey, at Tarare a little north of Lyons, seemed a good omen and confirmed his optimistic humour. During a halt he was drawn into conversation with two art students, pupils of Gros and Guérin on their way to Mont St Bernard for some landscape-painting. He had avoided them at first (as he reported to Humbert Ferrand) because they looked like dilettanti. Suddenly, one of them began humming a chorus from *The Danaids*.

"*The Danaids*!" I exclaimed. "Then you're not one of the dilettanti?"

"Me — dilettante? I've seen Dérivis and Mme Branchu thirty-four times in the rôles of Danaüs and Hypermnestre."

"Oh ..." And without further preamble we fell on each others' necks.

"Ah, sir — Mme Branchu ... ah sir — Dérivis ... what talent! what fire!"

"I know Dérivis well," said the other one.

"And I — I likewise have the pleasure of knowing the sublime lyric tragedienne."

"Ah, my dear sir, how lucky you are. They say that quite apart from her prodigious talent she's remarkable for her intelligence and her qualities of mind and character."

"That's absolutely right. But, gentlemen," I said, "why, if you're not musicians, haven't you caught the dilettante virus? How is it that Rossini hasn't caused you to turn your backs on nature and common sense?"

"Because, being accustomed to seek grandeur and beauty and above all nature in painting, we could not fail to recognise them in the sublime scores of Gluck and Salieri, nor in the singing — at once gentle, heart-rending and awe-inspiring — of Mme Branchu and her worthy colleague. As a result, the kind of music that's in fashion at the moment attracts us as little as would mere arabesques or the flim-flam of the Flemish school."

Well, Ferrand, what do you think of that! *There* are men of feeling, there are connoisseurs who are worthy to go to the Opéra, to hear *Iphigénie en Tauride* and understand it! We exchanged addresses, and will meet again when we get back to Paris.

Twenty-four hours later he was in La Côte. His family received him (he wrote to Le Sueur) "as I had expected, that is to say with great warmth". His mother's tearful scenes which had darkened his visit the previous year seemed a thing of the past. "Hector arrived this morning [Whit Sunday, 6 June]," wrote Nancy in her diary, which she had taken up again a fortnight before. "Mama is lavishing loving attention on him. I was sure her extreme goodness would not fail her with her son. He is somewhat changed for the better," added the eighteen-year-old girl judiciously; "his manners are a little more polite, and his conversation is quite witty."

The first weeks were taken up with sociabilities, supper parties, visits to or from friends and relations. For the children — Nancy, Adèle (ten), Prosper (four) — it was an exciting change to have their big brother home from Paris, with his caustic tongue and his funny stories. Hector enlivened the family circle and when he was in the mood his animated talk would revive their spirits, exhausted after a day spent in the silk-worm nursery.

Hector came back from dinner with M. Deplagne in a gay humour. After supper he described some very amusing comedies and farces he had seen. He gave a brilliant account of his adventure at Auxerre [on the coach route from Paris to Lyons], where they passed themselves off as actors arrived from Paris. We laughed till we ached — Mama too: it did us good to see her. [Nancy's diary, 21 June 1824]

In the joy of his homecoming the great unresolved question was pushed to one side.

His father's unconcealed pleasure in his company, his mother's "loving attentions", the courteous message Dr Berlioz charged him to give Le Sueur, expressing gratitude for the care he had lavished on his son — all this led Hector to imagine that the issue was as good as settled. "My father is entirely on my side," he wrote to Ferrand; and even his mother seemed to be taking it in her stride: she was already talking calmly of his return to Paris. "I have had to endure none of those unhappy and useless reproaches which succeeded only in making us both wretched," he told Le Sueur in a letter written a few weeks later. For safety's sake his father advised him not to talk music in his mother's presence; but father and son did so frequently. "I've passed on to him those curious discoveries that you were good enough to show me from your work on music in the ancient world. I couldn't persuade him that the ancients knew harmony — he is full of the ideas of Rousseau and the other writers who cling to the opposite opinion. But when I quoted that passage from a Latin author, I think it's Pliny the Elder, which gives details of how the voice is accompanied and how the orchestra can depict feeling by means of rhythms different from that of the voice part, he was quite staggered, and admitted that there was no answer to such evidence. 'Only', he said, 'to be convinced, I would wish to have the work in front of me.'"

Berlioz might have to keep off the subject of music when his mother was in the room; but when he was free to he talked of nothing else. "Impossible to have a conversation of any length with him on anything but his art," complained Nancy in her diary. "He goes on and on about his opera — but as to anything else ... "*

His letter of 22 June to his fellow-Côtois Edouard Rocher, one of the band of Gluckists, who was still in Paris (the summer term not having yet ended), is taken up almost entirely with questions and exhortations about the Opéra, from which he is temporarily banished.

> La Côte St André, Tuesday
>
> So you're incapable of writing to me, you bugger, by all that's sacred — when they put on *Iphigénie en Aulide* and me not there to hear it! I presume you went. You will have understood it better this time and been more moved by it. Who played Achille — and Iphigénie? Was it by any chance Mlle Grassari? Was Lafond adequate? Let me know quickly — the moment you get this letter. I'm in such a state, the devil take me, I feel as if I'll be finished and done for in another month. My head is full of *Iphigénie en Tauride*; the other day while singing some pieces from it I was completely overcome, and was seized by such a trembling that I wept and broke out in a great sweat; my heart beat so violently that, having gone up to my room so as not to be discovered in this state, I virtually fainted on to a chair the moment I entered the room. And I can't go and see it! And Mme Branchu will never play Iphigénie! ... Oh, by the way, I didn't tell you, the last time I called on her she said there was talk of lowering the pitch, and if they did she would resume the rôles of Alceste, Armide etc.
>
> Ah! *Alceste Armide There* are two operas — and with the added advantage over *Orphée*, that they will be disliked by the dilettanti swine, whereas *Orphée* made the mistake of being approved by them.
>
> Yesterday Deplagne the younger took me to dinner at Pion's, with Victor Robert. We drank white wine — ah, white wine! — and a capital leg of lamb. It was bucketing with rain, we went and came back under good umbrellas. The sound of the water coming down made my flesh creep and I said, "Grands Dieux! soyez-nous secourables! détournez vos foudres vengeurs!"†

The weather in mid-June was wet and blustery, after a glorious start to the month. Dr Berlioz, in the Livre de Raison, recorded almost continuous

---

* The opera may be *Les francs-juges*. In a passage omitted from the published text of the letter of 10 June Berlioz asks Ferrand whether he is "still working just as hard on our project". Ferrand was the librettist of *Les francs-juges*.

† "Great gods! lend us your aid! turn away your avenging thunderbolts!" — Iphigénie's invocation during the storm which opens the work. The excessively high pitch, which had risen nearly a tone in half a century, was frequently discussed in the papers (e.g. *Journal de Paris*, 17 April 1823). In 1825 the Opéra lowered it a semitone, and Mme Branchu sang Alceste, though not Armide.

rain from the 12th to the 26th. He was busy most of June with various repairs, indoor and outdoor, to his property. The women of the house toiled at the silk-worm crop, which was a disappointingly poor one. Laure Berlioz, Victor's wife, and their daughter Odile (aged eleven) came to stay. In the evening the household forgathered at the supper table and afterwards in the drawing-room, where sometimes there was company or cards or they played some kind of poetry game or just chatted and argued. When he was in good spirits Hector kept them amused with his conversation. Nancy noted her brother's fluctuating moods in her diary. On 22 June (the same day as his letter to Edouard Rocher) she wrote:

> Hector is not at all talkative this evening. With him everything is spontaneous; he is always quite transparent — never the slightest effort to regulate the vagaries of his humour. If he is gay, so much the better; if he is gloomy, it can't be helped: it's as if he weren't there, and whatever is being talked about he takes no part. When I think at all seriously of his position, it saddens me.

Outwardly, however, his visit continued to pass off well enough. In the last few days of June the weather turned fine and hot again. His Uncle Victor drove over from his country house at nearby St Etienne to join his wife and daughter and tipped him and Nancy a 20-franc piece each when no one was looking. Two days later Victor and Laure Berlioz took Hector back with them to Grenoble.

He stayed there ten days. It was probably there that (as he reported in his letter to Le Sueur) he tried to work on the Mass commissioned for St Roch in December; but, finding that the liturgy struck no sparks in him at the moment, he took out the score of his oratorio *The Crossing of the Red Sea* and began revising it with a possible autumn performance at St Roch in mind. It was easier to find time to himself there than it had been at La Côte. The perennial issue of a musical career was certainly broached by his uncle and aunt. They were affectionate but unquestioningly opposed to it — Victor from a worldly point of view, Laure (like her sister-in-law Joséphine Berlioz) because music, being involved with the theatre, was not a profession for respectable right-thinking people. When Hector remarked teasingly that to hear her talk you would suppose she would be seriously put out if Racine had been a member of her family, she floored him by replying, "Well, my dear, you know, a good name matters more than anything."*

---

* "Lesueur nearly choked with laughter when, back in Paris, I reported to him this typical mot; and whenever he was in high spirits he never failed to ask me for news of Racine's enemy, my 'old aunt', though she was then young and pretty as a picture: he naturally attributed such an outlook to extreme old age" (*Memoirs*, chapter 10).

Hector went back to La Côte on 8 July. The air was full of the delicious scent of freshly mown hay, but it was very hot, and he arrived home to find the household in a state of agitation over the maid Julie, ill with a high fever: she had been bled several times, recorded Nancy; "Mama cried, Papa is quite worn out." Hector too, it seemed, had come back not in the most responsive of humours. "To a mass of questions he replied only yes, no, I don't know, I haven't thought, etc. After supper I took Mme Pion for a walk on the Esplanade in the moonlight, it was cool after the fierce heat of the day."

The emotional as well as the atmospheric pressure was building up. "9 July. Dreadfully hot. After supper we went to the Esplanade [. . .] My brother made me sweat with embarrassment, he is so uncivil, so lacking in graciousness."

If a confrontation was looming, the threat receded a few days later and the immediate pressure relaxed: Mme Berlioz went off with Nancy to stay with friends in St Geoire en Valdaine, twenty-five miles away in the hills to the north-west.

They were away five days. During their absence Hector and his father argued out the whole question of his future once again and came to some kind of interim agreement, the main point of which was that Dr Berlioz granted him a further period of trial in which to prove himself. If a year from now he had failed to provide evidence of substantial progress, he must acknowledge that he had been mistaken and give up the whole idea once and for all. The date of his return to Paris was fixed for ten days hence.

On the 19th his mother and Nancy came back. From then until his departure a week later the household was in continuous crisis. It was a period of trial of another sort, and he found himself far less equipped to cope with it. Nancy, though tending to echo her parents, and more often disapproving than sympathetic in her attitude to her brother, gives glimpses of the intense strain he was under. Only twenty, young for his years and still emotionally tied to his family, at times he could scarcely bear it.

19 July. We were hardly back before Mama realised that Hector had sent his trunk off and would soon be following. On discovering it she broke down and wept a lot, and upbraided him quite harshly, but justifiably. He took it with a most distressing air of unconcern. He can't wait to go. He is forcing us to wish for it as much as he does. I am indignant to see him so hard-hearted [. . .] If I could only see a touch of sensitivity in him, if he would at least make a gesture of affection by staying a little longer — but no, he is as inflexible as a rock.

20 July. A very boring day. Mama still crying, my brother as unmoved as ever. God knows what my poor father is going through. Today he gave me a look so touching that I could hardly keep back my tears. In the evening, walk with the children to Le Chuzeau — a horrid walk. Mama lamenting

the disasters caused by the hail [a freak hailstorm two days before had injured several people, killed a sheep and damaged property]. Nothing but lamentations; there's no end to them.

21 July. We talked of my brother this afternoon. My father is dreadfully affected by it all. "I have always been unfortunate," he said. "My childhood was not happy, my youth was very stormy, and now the son who was to have been my consolation is destroying the happiness I might have had."

22 July. I had a brief conversation with my brother, which confirmed what my father said about him, that in the end he will achieve nothing. He wants to prove to me, by absurd reasoning, that he is doing the right thing by following his tastes and inclinations. In the meantime he is very unhappy, and we as well. The whole household is in deep gloom.

23 July. This evening Papa has just exhausted his remaining eloquence and affection in an attempt to move my brother and bring him back to a more reasonable line of conduct. He replies with the absurd argument that he was "born like this". He curses his existence — instead of seeking to make it happy and useful.

24 July. What ghastly emotions! My brother is still unshakeable in his false principles and unhappy determination. M. Alphonse [Robert] arrived at midday and surprised us by making an urgent plea for Hector to stay a few days longer. But the present situation makes such a delay out of the question.

25 July. He has gone! — not without causing us to shed many tears, Mama especially.

What went wrong to precipitate the desperate scenes which ended a visit that had seemed to begin so well? For one thing, he had misunderstood the warmth of his parents' welcome, in his naïve and wish-fulfilling eagerness interpreting it as acceptance of his point of view. He imagined, because his father was happy to talk music to him, that he had finally won him over to his vocation.

On the face of it, it was his mother and her overwrought emotions that set everyone by the ears, disturbing the accord established between father and son and forcing the reluctant Dr Berlioz into angry confrontation. But a more perceptive assessment is given in Félix Marmion's letter, written the previous year and already quoted, in which he spoke of Hector refusing to be swayed by "his mother's tears and his father's gnawing sorrow".* Joséphine Berlioz's attitude was quite straightforward. Her convent upbringing had given her a vague but strong conviction that an artistic career was sinful; and for a son of hers to go in for it was

---

* See above, p. 124

grievous and bewildering. She considered that her husband was wrong to give way to him. Having a tendency to obsessiveness, she let herself brood on it; and being a nervous and excitable person she did not keep her feelings to herself but, when roused, made a scene about it. Yet the success of Hector's Mass, the following year, gratified her in spite of herself. A Mass was a sacred work; and how could that be wrong?

Louis Berlioz's attitude was altogether more complex and contradictory. Loving his son intensely, feeling a deep affinity between them and drawn by the magnetic pull of his personality, he wavered and half gave in, wishing the issue away, putting off the evil hour, then swung back violently. Given his own personality and principles and the force of Hector's will, he could not simply forbid him to study music and cut off at a stroke the means of his doing so: it was not in his nature to act like that. He could only vacillate, reason, argue, and finally rage helplessly, nurturing within himself the "gnawing sorrow" that his wife vented in tears. The success of the Mass angered him because it brought nearer to reality the thing that for ten years he would fight, with inadequate weapons, to suppress: the deeply unpalatable fact that his eldest son was going to be not the dreamed-of heir to his practice and property but a musician. His wife's scenes reacted on his own fiercer tensions, releasing a hostility that went deeper than hers.

Of what it had cost Hector, his uncle Félix Marmion, writing to Nancy a fortnight later, showed a keener understanding than the boy's parents:

> I had indeed guessed part of the painful circumstances of Hector's departure, and he himself gave me the gist in a letter which I received on the same day as yours [. . .] As to this so-called insensibility of his, I do not believe in it at all. His letter, written spontaneously and unaffectedly, persuaded me quite to the contrary. I believe in his grief and can absolutely imagine the terrible effect his father's heartrending plea must have had on him. "It is a moment that will stay in my memory for ever," he says. And I expect a happy result from the feelings with which he said goodbye to you and which nothing is going to make him forget [. . .] [But] since your father has decided to allow him more time, it is essential that he resign himself and wait for a favourable crisis.

Despite Dr Berlioz's decision, hostilities continued. Veering again, he sent his son an angry letter in which, it seems, he poured scorn once more on his vocation and prophesied disaster. He also expressed his annoyance at the contents of a note that Hector had left for his cousin Alphonse Robert. Berlioz waited till his feelings had calmed down, then sent the following patient but determined declaration:

Paris, 31 August 1824

My dear Papa,

　　I need not tell you how much your letter surprised and hurt me; you yourself can be in no doubt of it, and I dare to hope your heart disavows the wounding remarks it contained. I do not understand either how the letter I left for Alphonse can have roused you to such a point; it contained nothing, I think, that I haven't said or communicated to you a hundred times, nor do I believe that in speaking of my parents I let fall any expression inconsistent with the feelings of a loving and respectful son.

I am driven involuntarily towards a magnificent career — no other adjective can be applied to the career of artist — and not towards my doom. For I believe I shall succeed; yes, I believe it. There is no point in being modest about it. To prove to you that I am not simply trusting to luck, I think, I am convinced that I shall achieve distinction in music. All outward signs encourage me to believe so, and the voice of nature within me speaks louder than the most rigorous dictates of reason. I have every imaginable chance in my favour, if you will only back me. I'm starting young, and wouldn't have to give lessons to support myself, as so many have to. I have a good knowledge of some things and have acquired the rudiments of others in such a way as to be able, in time, to master them, and I know I have experienced passions strong enough not to be mistaken about them, when the time comes to depict them or give them utterance.

If I was condemned without reprieve to die of starvation in the event of not succeeding (in fact I would persist none the less), your reasons at least, and your worries, would be better founded. But that is not the case. Putting it at the lowest estimate, I can count on having in due course a private income of two thousand francs; make it only fifteen hundred, I could live all right on that amount, or even twelve hundred: I should be content with that, even if music were to bring me in nothing at all. You see, I wish to make a name for myself, I wish to leave some trace of my existence on this earth; and so strong is the feeling — which is an entirely honourable one — that I would rather be Gluck or Méhul dead than what I am in the flower of my age. The celebrated Marcello had the same ambition, and he had to conquer prejudices far greater than there normally are against artists, as he was son of the Doge of Venice, and his father would rather his son had been at the bottom of the sea than in a career which in his eyes disgraced him and his whole family. Well, who now would know there was once a Doge of Venice called Marcello if his son had not immortalised the name by sublime religious music that is still performed in all the principal churches of Italy and Germany?

You have often pointed out the enormous difference there is between me and M. Lesueur in the matter of subsidiary knowledge — he knows the ancient languages and mathematics. But, as he was telling me only yesterday, this is knowledge that he acquired, like everyone else, at college and then went much more deeply into later, when he perceived the links that exist between certain sciences and music. He became a great musician before he was a learned musician; and if learning Greek and Hebrew and mathematics has not figured in my preliminary plan of studies, I can assure you that that will neither increase nor lessen the chances I am taking in devoting myself to music.

That is the way I think, the way I am, and nothing in the world will change me. You could withdraw all support from me and force me to

leave Paris; but I do not believe it, you would not wish to make me lose
the best years of my life — to break the magnetic needle because you
can't stop it obeying the attraction of the poles.

Farewell, dear Papa; read my letter again, and do not attribute it to
momentary excitement. I have perhaps never been calmer.

I embrace you tenderly, as well as Mama and my sisters.

Your respectful and loving son,
H. Berlioz

P.S. Charles [Bert] is well.

Dr Berlioz did not withdraw all support. He continued to pay Hector
his allowance. He also continued to hope against hope for a miraculous
conversion, and to lament the trick that fate had played on him ("My
father tired and sad all day; he keeps himself to himself and, I think,
takes pleasure in his gloomy ideas. His health and his son — there are
the two great obstacles to his happiness" — Nancy's diary, 22 October
1824). Hostilities grew gradually less intense; and Berlioz took a deep
breath and resumed the interrupted course of his life: lessons with
Le Sueur, composition, study in the Conservatoire Library, friendships,
evenings at the opera, the quest for a performance.

9

First Performance

A few days after writing to his father, Berlioz sent his friend Edouard
Rocher — back at La Côte for the summer vacation — a long report on
the revival of Piccinni's *Didon*. The letter's most important news came at
the end. His family's persecutions, he wrote, were only spurring him on
the more to the composition of his Mass. He was working hard at it. "I
am promised great things for the performance."

For the next four months (September to December 1824) the Mass and
the arrangements for its performance, planned for 28 December, dominated
his thoughts and actions — to the exclusion of other events of far-reaching
influence in his life, the most important being his introduction to German
musical Romanticism in the shape of Weber's *Der Freischütz*, performed
for the first time in Paris at the Odéon in December.

Three months earlier the King, Louis XVIII, had died, after a short
illness. His death, as well as causing the temporary closure of all theatres,
resulted in the accession of his charming, debonair and irredeemably
reactionary brother and the chain of events which would lead within five
years to the July Revolution and the end of the Bourbon monarchy.
Charles X's reign began with promises of less restrictive laws and all the
rest of it, but the régime was quick to show its true colours. It was noted
that the new king refused to see a delegation of deputies, playwrights and
managers which came to request formal Christian burial for the actor
Philippe after the coffin had been turned away from the dead man's
parish church. As Dumas later remarked, "Authority won the day, as the
saying is; only, it is with such triumphs that Authority commits
suicide [...] From that time the liberal statements made by Charles X
on coming to the throne were judged at their real worth."

A week later, on 25 October, Louis XVIII's funeral mass was celebrated
at the church of St Denis on the northern outskirts of Paris, where the
body had lain in state for the past month. Cherubini's great Requiem
Mass in C minor was performed. Berlioz went to hear it, and observed

with interest and indignation that the heavy black drapes covering every inch of the huge wooden construction erected for the performers absorbed the sonority to such an extent that the music, disappointingly, made little effect.

But that observation would be for a later time (as would his assimilation of the strange, enchanting new idiom of Weber's opera). Immediate practical matters claimed his attention. His own Mass was nearing completion. Le Sueur had looked at it and approved what he saw. The performance was only two months off, and an orchestra and additional choristers had to be found. Masson the choirmaster of St Roch was all optimism: there was no problem, they would collect the players and singers required; however, as neither he nor the composer was used to conducting such large forces, they must get someone who was. And they must get the best. A plan was hatched with Le Sueur to persuade Henri Valentino, one of the two chief conductors at the Opéra, to take it on. Valentino had put in for the post of conductor at the Chapel Royal (where he was one of the violinists), and since Le Sueur was co-director of the Chapel there were grounds for hope. Berlioz went to see him, bearing a letter of recommendation from Le Sueur and a copy of the score. After studying the work Valentino agreed to conduct it, despite some misgivings about the means he would have at his disposal. By the use of various personal contacts a fine enough orchestra and chorus had been put together — on paper. The only question was how many of them would turn up.

On 11 December the composer celebrated his twenty-first birthday. Meanwhile the Mass had been completed and the St Roch choirboys were busy copying the parts. As the great day drew near, invitations were printed and sent to newspapers, friends and admirers, and likely patrons.

> You are requested to attend the MASS FOR FULL ORCHESTRA composed by M. H. Berlios [*sic*], pupil of M. Lesueur, which will be held in the parish church of St Roch at 9.30 precisely on Tuesday 28 December 1824, the feast of the Holy Innocents, patron saints of the honoured choirboys of the said parish.
>
> > Yours very truly
> > S.P.E. on behalf of all the choirboys
> > Fleury
>
> The choirboys venture to hope that you will be so kind as to support them with your patronage.

The general rehearsal was scheduled for 12.30 p.m. on the previous day, Monday the 27th. We know this because the one surviving copy of the invitation, addressed in Berlioz's hand to a certain Devivier, contains an annotation (in another hand) to that effect. Well before the appointed hour Berlioz was in the church, with a band of friends and supporters (including the redoubtable de Pons). So were Masson and Lefebvre, the organist of St Roch, and no doubt Le Sueur as well. The desks were all in place, with the newly copied music set out on them. Valentino duly arrived. But the musicians were slower to appear. 12.30 came and went, and still there were important gaps. Masson's "large forces" had resolved themselves into a skeleton orchestra and chorus.

The totally inexperienced composer struggled against a rising panic, mixed with shame at presenting the conductor of the Opéra with such a motley collection of performers. Masson tried to calm him down; he kept telling him that it would be all right on the day, there was no need to worry, everyone would turn up tomorrow. Meanwhile they must get started. Valentino raised his bow resignedly and the rehearsal began. But at once a fresh calamity was revealed. The honoured choirboys of the parish had been more willing than expert, and the orchestral parts were riddled with mistakes – not only the odd key-signature or accidental missing or a wrong note here and there but whole sections omitted. Conductor and composer attempted to repair the damage, and the rehearsal proceeded after a fashion. But the players grew increasingly disheartened and began to get up and leave, thinning the depleted ranks still further.

A council of war was held. There could be only one conclusion. The rehearsal was brought to an abrupt end and a notice cancelling tomorrow's performance was posted on the door of the church.

"Thus ended my long cherished dream of hearing my music played by full orchestra." But only for the time being. After the first moments of despair he rallied and, encouraged by his friends, took stock. He must simply try again. Masson, Lefebvre, Valentino were all quite emphatic that to give up now was unthinkable. But the experience had taught him some useful lessons and he must apply them. The first thing to do was to revise his score: he had heard enough of it to realise that there were things in it that badly needed altering. Secondly, they would have to be sure of their "forces" next time, and that meant paying the orchestra and chorus. But what on earth with? The only practical idea anyone could think of was Ferrand's audacious suggestion that he should approach Chateaubriand, explain the whole situation to him, and ask him for a loan so that the Mass could be performed. He if anybody would understand and respond. It was a long shot; but nothing would be lost by making it. In the event nothing was gained either, except a prompt but courteous refusal, which Berlioz received on New Year's Day, 1825.

Paris, 31 December 1824

You ask me, sir, for twelve hundred francs. I have not got them. If I had they would be yours. I have no means, either, of being useful to you with the government. I sympathise keenly with your difficulties. I love art and honour artists; but sometimes the trials that talent is put to are the cause of its succeeding, and the hour of triumph compensates for all that one has suffered.

My dear sir, please accept my regrets; they are very real.

Chateaubriand

There for the moment the matter rested. Some other source of money would have to be found. In the meantime there was the score to be gone over. After that all the parts must be written out afresh; and he would have to do it himself — a labour of many weeks.

The new year brought other, less sympathetic, letters. He had had no choice but to write to his family and admit that his hopes of the decisive success they had been led to expect had been disappointed, or rather deferred. Nancy reported it in her diary on 3 January 1825:

> My brother has written a letter which has had the usual effect, that of reducing Papa and Mama to despair [...] This fatal letter announced the contretemps he suffered over the performance of his Mass, which could not be given because, he said, of the ill will of the musicians who decamped in the middle of the rehearsal. This reverse, so far from putting him off, merely inflames his genius. He will tell himself that he is not the first person it has happened to: were not the early plays of Crébillon unanimously rejected by the actors? etc.

Nancy was showing signs of ceasing to be the uncritical echo of her parents' views. "There is something terribly exaggerated in the way they regard my brother's failings. If he were to cover us with shame and infamy their reaction could not be any stronger." In this she was perhaps influenced by her godmother, the sensible Nancy Clappier, who refused to see Hector's "vocation" as the end of the world. "I am quite of your opinion about Hector, and while sympathising with his parents' distress I cannot help, as I look about me and make comparisons, preferring their son with his faults to the vast majority of our young men [...] It is a fault, not a vice. I beg them to keep this reflection in mind and to consider how much more fortunate they are than an infinite number of fathers and mothers."

At about the same time, however, Nicolas Marmion, a more accurate barometer of family sentiment, was writing a verse letter largely devoted to saluting the four-year-old Prosper as the white hope and future glory of the Berliozes; nothing further was to be expected of his brother.

Now began the most violent phase in the conflict over Hector's career. The St Roch débâcle had naturally been seized on as a fresh argument for ridiculing his hopes; but Dr Berlioz's passionate objections lay beyond questions of success or failure, as a remark in one of his letters to his son made abundantly clear: Hector was quite mistaken if he supposed that success would ever persuade his father to change his mind.

Their correspondence grew increasingly bitter. It was made more so on the parents' side by the protracted illness of little Prosper. For two months the household at La Côte was in an agony of anxiety. The boy's temperature went rocketing up and down. One day he seemed better, the next he coughed without stopping for several hours. It was feared he might go blind; at times his life seemed to hang by a thread. Louis and Joséphine Berlioz and Nancy took turns to sit with him through the night (Nancy keeping herself awake with Scott's *Waverley*). In their anguish and physical and mental exhaustion the parents wrangled over the invalid's treatment. To add to their nightmare, Adèle (aged ten) developed measles.

Under the strain of these events relations between father and eldest son deteriorated still further. On 25 January Dr Berlioz sent Hector 200 francs, noting in the Livre de Raison: "This sum will have to suffice him till 10 April." For the next three months a sustained though futile attempt was made to order him home. But Dr Berlioz, at the end of his strength, delegated the task to Nancy. The nineteen-year-old girl was forced to act as her parents' mouthpiece; and it was to her that Hector replied in an angry letter which is undated but which probably belongs to the second half of March 1825.

My dear sister,
I implore you to write to me at once and tell me what reasons have induced Papa and Mama to maintain this forbidding silence since I replied to your letter. If you read my reply you will certainly not have found in it anything but the expressions of a dutiful and respectful son, for I told my father that if he insisted I would, despite my objections and the futility of my returning to La Côte, sacrifice a whole year's work, and my future for several years ahead, to his wishes. Let me know as soon as possible whether they have no intention of sending me any money either for setting off or for staying here, and what is supposed to become of me. I confess I cannot contemplate my stay at La Côte without alarm, since even you are so prejudiced against me that you have no compunction in writing me a letter in which you claim that I have to prove

1) that in being a musician I do not cease to be a son, a brother and a friend
2) that the profession of composer is not incompatible with social life
3) that I am capable of reasoned thought
4) that I am not ruled by instinct
5) that I am able to observe time, place, custom, decency
6) that I am not hostile to all order, moral and physical
7) that I can combine the qualities of an honest man with those of a composer
8) that I can merit esteem while striving to win admiration.

It follows from this that if I possess all the defects that you tell me I must correct, I am a *bad son*, a *bad brother* and a *bad friend*, a *social outcast*, an *idiot* and a *fool*, a *dishonest man*, a vile and despicable creature, in a word a brute beast, a dangerous animal. In consequence I advise you strongly, in case I return to La Côte, to have a kennel built for me in the farm-yard where I can be kept chained up, for fear of accidents. You see, sister, what extremes of absurdity such irrational emotions and prejudices lead you to.

I am not the less your brother and your friend

H.B.

Hector's sarcastic logic was lost on his family. Dr Berlioz, having read the letter through, wrote at the bottom, "monument to folly and blind, unbridled passion" ("délire des passions"); and Nancy, in her shocked reply, faithfully echoed her father's vocabulary.

By the middle of April direct communications had been resumed, to the extent of his mother's consenting to write to him, though only to echo his father's uncomprehending attitude and accuse Hector of lying when he said that a letter he had written in the first half of March must have got lost in the post. In his reply, addressed to his father, he made a further vain attempt to plead with him, putting forward, with all the calm he could muster, arguments showing that he was under no illusions as to the difficulties of becoming a composer, that he knew he had the will and the patience and the ability to overcome them, that it grieved him immeasurably to hurt his father but the one thing beyond his power was to stifle his natural bent towards music: "I am capable of extraordinary effort, nay of an astonishing perseverance, in order to reach an objective that my heart is set on;* but to struggle continually against myself [. . .] at every moment to resist my deepest impulses, which would rise up again as fast as I suppressed them, is totally impossible for me." All such reasoning left his father's rooted, bitter opposition untouched.

The letter ended, with some temerity, with a request for money:

The 200 francs which you kindly sent me at the beginning of the month [April] won't last beyond the 3rd or 4th of May, as I was obliged to give 50 fr. which were overdue for manuscript paper and copying that I had to pay for. Then I bought a hat which cost me 20 fr. I had my boots repaired for 14 fr. And I had two pairs of shoes made, 14 fr. I am also going to make a request, my dear Papa, which may strike you as tactless. I have an intense desire to acquire the complete works of Volney, made up, as you know, of the *Ruins*, *Travels in Syria*, the *Description of the United States*, the *Letters on Greece*, and the *Researches into Ancient History*. This superb edition, the only one that exists, is on the point of going out of print, the Government has forbidden a reprinting, and the price is rising all the time. Three months ago it was selling for 40 fr., at the moment it can't be had for less than 64, and in spite of this there are only twenty copies left.

Farewell, dear Papa, please believe that I am not so far from being what

---

* A little later in the same letter Berlioz mentions the great explorer Levaillant (who had recently died), citing the pertinacity of his genius and his uncomplaining willingness to face any hardship in pursuit of his goal.

you wish me to be, and that one day I will make you amends for the pain I have caused you.

Your respectful and loving son,
H. Berlioz

The clearest and most comprehensive statement of his position and aims comes in a letter to his uncle Victor Berlioz, written two months earlier in the hope of getting him to intercede on his behalf.

Paris, 18 February 1825

Dear Uncle,

You will no doubt be surprised by the purpose of this letter. It is to beg you to act as mediator between my father and me. The deep affection he has for you leads me to hope that he will pay attention to your advice; and the fact that your opinions generally accord with his is bound to make him see that if you plead my cause you believe it is right.

This is what I can say in my favour. To begin with, Papa thinks he is completely objective; this gives him, so he says, a great advantage over me in my constant state of Enthusiasm, that of seeing things in their true light. In his last letter he began by telling me that I am "mistaken when I hope that my persistence will wear him down or that success will change his mind". That is as much as to admit that even if I should become a Gluck or a Mozart he would never consent to my being a musician. Is one being objective when one thinks like that? Consider the consequences of such a view. I said to him one day that if every father had acted like him there would have been no poets in Europe, no painters, architects, sculptors, composers. His answer was: "What a calamity!" Was that objective? [. . .]

My father also says that a state of Enthusiasm destroys all good qualities and causes men who are possessed by it to be weak, immoral, egoistical and despicable. As an example he cites La Fontaine, who abandoned his wife and children. But, without going into all the reasons which led the renowned fabulist to act in this way, and which everybody knows, I can retaliate by citing Boileau, the great Corneille, Racine, Gluck, Grétry, Lesueur and countless others. All their contemporaries agree on the qualities that made them men of good repute quite independently of their genius. And for sure, if the creators of the *Horaces, Athalie, Iphigénie en Tauride, Silvain* and *Les Bardes* were not possessed by the demon of Enthusiasm, I do not know what one should call the fire that animated them.

No doubt you will ask me, dear Uncle, what I base my hopes of success on.

I believe the time for me to make a big name for myself in the theatre is a long way off; but I have great hopes of a solemn mass, which will definitely be performed four or five months from now. Recently, as you may have heard, I had intended to have it performed, but the impossibility of collecting the large number of performers it requires without paying them, and its difficulty, excessive for a work which is not going to be given very often [i.e. because of the disproportionately high cost of rehearsals], were insurmountable obstacles. I have just revised my score and removed the most difficult things. I showed it once again to M. Lesueur who, after studying it closely for four days, said as he gave it back to me: "It's heartbreaking that your parents are set on stopping you. I have not the slightest doubt you will succeed in music. It is quite clear that you will do great things. There is a staggering imagination in this work; the sheer quantity of its ideas astonishes me. Its defect is that there are too many. Restrain yourself, restrain yourself, and try to be simple." Here is what he said about my Mass to someone who reported it to me: "That young man has the dickens of an imagination. His Mass is astonishing; there are so many ideas in it that with his score I could write ten of my own. But it's stronger than him, he has got to fire all his guns at once, he's determined to dumbfound everybody." More or less the same things were said to me by the conductor of the Opéra [Valentino], who after spending a week going through my score undertook to direct the performance. And I had a letter of compliments and advice from M. Lefebvre the organist of St Roch, who was present at the rehearsal which we began but which I wouldn't allow to be completed, the day before I was due to give my Mass in the church. A man of my acquaintance talked to him about me, and among other things M. Lefebvre said: "In a few years' time he may be our greatest composer."

All this is very encouraging; but what I chiefly count on is a certain driving force that I sense within me, a fire, an energy that I cannot describe exactly, which impels me so singlemindedly towards one objective — music in the grand style, dramatic or sacred — that I do not feel the same thing at all for light music, and I would not cross the road to hear an opéra-comique.

To sum up: it seems that Papa, so far from being objective, has become so overwrought that he now writes me things that he was far from believing a year ago; it is evident to me that I shall succeed; it is certain that nothing can make me change course, but that as my father considers me mad, I am not the one who can make him give up his prejudices.

That is why I implore you, dear Uncle, to reflect carefully on my position, setting aside all preconceptions, and plead my cause, less for me myself than to restore peace of mind to the most loving of fathers. If you take my part I do not despair of regaining the happiness which his affliction has made us lose.

Your affectionate nephew,
H. Berlioz
79 Rue St Jacques.*

How to get his Mass performed was still the great question. At one point, it seems, there was hope of its taking place at Ste Geneviève (the Panthéon). Why Ste Geneviève was chosen instead of St Roch or what special circumstances prompted it is not known. In any case, the plan had apparently been dropped by the time he wrote to Victor Berlioz. We

* The letter achieved its object. A week later Nancy noted in her diary: "My uncle, who had always criticised my father for being weak with Hector and had been all for harsh measures, has written a letter calculated to undermine a father's resolve. This eloquent and moving plea for the defence had been solicited by a long epistle from Hector" (26 February 1825).

know about it only because of a reference in a letter of four weeks earlier (21 January 1825) to an engineer called Letexier whom he had met two evenings before at the Opéra: "If, sir, you are still in Paris on 19 March, it is probable that I shall have a solemn mass of mine performed at Ste Geneviève. Dérivis, I hope, will sing the solos, and if your occupations allow you to come and hear it I shall be most gratified [...]"

Berlioz's encounter with Letexier took place during a performance of Sacchini's *Œdipe à Colone*, with Dérivis in the title role. His subsequent account of it gives a vivid idea of the atmosphere at those ritual Evenings at the Opéra, which the letter corroborates:

I had taken along with me a friend, a student whose knowledge of art was confined to billiards but whom I was determined to convert to music. The sorrows of Antigone and her father made little impression on him, and after the first act I gave him up and moved to a bench in the row in front, so as to be out of reach of his distracting sang-froid. But chance, as if to preserve the contrast, had placed on his right another enthusiast, as deeply moved as he was impervious. I soon became aware of it. Dérivis had just had a splendid burst of eloquence in his famous recitative "Mon fils! tu ne l'es plus! Va! ma haine est trop forte!" Engrossed though I was in the poetry and antique power of this fine passage, I could not help overhearing the dialogue which was going on behind me between my man, who was peeling an orange, and his unknown neighbour, who was in the grip of an intense emotion.

"My God, sir, be calm."

"No, it's too much! It's overwhelming, it knocks you out!"

"Really, sir, you shouldn't be so affected. You'll make yourself ill."

"Leave me alone ... Ah!"

"Come on, sir, cheer up. It's only a play ... May I offer you a piece of this orange?"

"Oh, it's sublime!"

"It's from Malta."

"Divine art!"

"Do have some."

"Ah, sir, what music!"

"Yes, it's very jolly."

While this incongruous exchange was proceeding, the opera had reached the lovely trio "O doux moments" which follows the reconciliation. The insidious sweetness of the simple melody was too much for me, in my turn. I hid my face in my hands and started to weep, like a man in the depths of misery. As the trio ended, two powerful arms lifted me bodily off my bench, nearly crushing my ribs. It was the unknown enthusiast. Unable to contain his emotion any longer, and noticing that among all the audience around him I alone seemed to share it, he embraced me frantically, blurting out, "B-b-b-by Heaven, sir, it's beautiful!" Not the least taken aback, my face disfigured with crying, I answered by asking him, "Are you a musician?"

"No, but I feel music as deeply as any man."

"By jove, it's the same thing. Give me your hand, sir. You're a splendid fellow!"

Thereupon, regardless of the sniggers of our neighbours and the blank astonishment of my orange-eating neophyte, we exchanged a few whispered words; I gave him my name, he told me his [...] *

Despite the new attractions of the Odéon, where *Freischütz* remained top of the bill all that winter, the Opéra was still the favourite haunt. February saw the reappearance of Mme Branchu, after six months' break, in *The Danaids*; and in the spring Gluck's *Alceste*, a work she had promised to appear in whenever the Opéra lowered its pitch, was revived for her, with Nourrit fils as Admète and Dérivis as the High Priest. It was Berlioz's first chance to hear a work that he had long learned to love and venerate during happy hours in the Conservatoire Library. There were six performances between late April and early June, and he was at all of them. Though the general standard was pretty rough and ready, these were evenings of high delight, prepared for by thorough study of the score.†

By this time, however, he was getting desperate. Soon the year of trial set by his father would have expired and he would have nothing tangible, no incontrovertible achievement, to show for it. The curé of St Roch had fixed a date for the performance of the Mass — Sunday 10 July, the feast of the Sacred Heart — but there were still no performers. A nucleus of musicians from the Chapel Royal had been persuaded to give their services and form the basis of an orchestra and chorus — and now after all they would not be available: the King was going to his country residence at St Cloud on the day in question and they were needed there. Thanks to some influential contacts supplied by his friend Albert Du Boys he managed to arrange an interview with the Vicomte Sosthène de La Rochefoucauld, the great landowner and horse-breeder who had been put in charge of the newly created Department of the Arts, and actually saw him twice. Not surprisingly, nothing came of it. All that he was given (as he reported to Du Boys) was permission to have the Opéra orchestra provided he could pay for it. "The dear man — he 'authorised' me to spend a thousand francs if I had them, and granted the musicians full and perfect liberty to pocket them."

He was back where he had started. The curé, nevertheless, was extremely reluctant to cancel the performance a second time. But how could reliable

---

* The incident forms the climax of chapter 15 of the *Memoirs*: "Evenings at the Opéra — missionary work — scandals exposed — a display of enthusiasm — deep feelings of a mathematician".

† It was while deep in *Alceste* that he was rudely interrupted one day by Cherubini and the Conservatoire porter Hottin, having incurred the director's wrath by ignoring the new rule about segregation of the sexes and using the entrance reserved for women. The encounter, which led to an angry exchange followed by a chase round the table, is described in *Memoirs*, chapter 9.

forces be assembled without being paid for, and where was the money to be found for that?

Four weeks from the appointed day he went to the Opéra to see Piccinni's *Didon* — the first opportunity since the previous December — and ran into Augustin de Pons in the foyer. De Pons had been at the abortive rehearsal of the Mass, but it was some time since their paths had crossed. On catching sight of Berlioz he called out across the foyer in his booming voice: "What about the Mass? Is it rewritten? When are we really going to perform it?" — "Good God, yes — it's rewritten, and recopied. But how am I supposed to get it performed?" — "How? Damn it all, by paying the performers. What do you need? Let's see — twelve hundred francs? fifteen hundred? two thousand? I'll lend it to you." — "Please, not so loud! If you really mean it, I'm delighted to accept your offer. Twelve hundred will do." — "Then that's settled. Come and see me tomorrow morning, I'll have the money for you. We'll engage the Opéra chorus and a powerful orchestra. Valentino has got to be satisfied, we have got to be satisfied, and by God it's going to work."

Next day Berlioz went round to de Pons' house in the Faubourg St Germain and it was all arranged. There need be no half measures now. (Alphonse Robert chipped in with a loan of 80 francs to cover the hire of extra instruments.) It would be a powerful orchestra all right, formed from the Opéra and the pick of the Théâtre-Italien. To make doubly sure he went to see Duplantys, the Opéra's director, and secured his blessing on the enterprise.

He was now heavily in debt, a condition that always irked him (all his life he would have a fastidious dislike of owing money); and at once he set himself to the laborious business of repaying it. Some pupils he had managed to find paid him one franc an hour for lessons in flute, guitar and solfège. To live more economically he left his hôtel meublé and fellow-lodgers at 79 Rue St Jacques and, moving down the hill to the Ile de la Cité, rented a small fifth-floor room at 27 Rue de Harlay on the corner of the Quai des Orfèvres, a few hundred yards west of Notre Dame. He also gave up eating in restaurants and established a régime of bread with raisins, prunes or dates, bought for a few sous at the local grocer's shop and eaten in the afternoon sun on the nearby terrace of the Pont Neuf, at the foot of Henri IV's equestrian statue.*

A few days before the performance he and Ferrand took a cab and toured the offices of newspapers and periodicals, inviting them to send a critic and to put in a preliminary announcement. Ferrand had friends on the *Gazette de France*, the *Diable boiteux* and the *Globe*, and Berlioz was on good terms with the *Corsaire* staff. At the same time they pulled every

---

* "while I tried to keep my mind off the poule au pot which the good king imagined his peasants having for their Sunday dinner."

string they could think of to get influential people in society and the arts to come and hear the work.

The performance took place, and was all that the composer had hoped. He had had a work of his performed at last, by an orchestra and chorus of 150, and it had had a vivid impact on the audience. The dramatic movements, as he reported to Albert Du Boys, made the biggest impression: the Kyrie, the Crucifixus, the Et iterum venturus, the Domine salvum and the Sanctus. "When I heard the crescendo at the end of the Kyrie my chest swelled with the orchestra and my heart pounded in time with the strokes of the timpanist. I don't know what I was saying, but at the end of the piece Valentino said to me, 'My friend, try to keep calm, if you don't want to have me lose my head.'" Berlioz himself played the tam-tam in the Et iterum venturus — the movement in which, according to the critic of the *Quotidienne*, "M. Berlioz has given untrammelled scope to his imagination" — and struck the instrument with such force that the whole church reverberated. But the less resounding or gentler numbers were also admired. The *Corsaire* declared that the Gloria in excelsis, with its "pure, simple and utterly original theme", had "enchanted the large audience", and the *Journal des débats* also singled it out as one of the two movements (the other was the Et iterum venturus) that had been "particularly remarked by connoisseurs". And the O salutaris — music "of the noblest and most religious effect" (*Corsaire*) — drew a spontaneous tribute from the formidable Mme Lebrun, singer at the Opéra and celebrated character, who leant over, her witchlike features creased in a glittering smile, and grasping his hand exclaimed: "B — me, my dear child, that's a Salutaris with no flies on it; I bet none of the little f — rs in the Conservatoire counterpoint classes could write a piece so neat and so damn religious."*

The moment the performance was over he was surrounded by musicians — his own performers and the many who had come to hear the work; they were shaking him by the hand, tugging his coat, showering him with compliments, till he felt dizzy. Next it was the ordinary music-lovers, forcing their way into the orchestra, asking which was the composer. "One of the more eager rushed up, knocking over chairs and desks, till he got to me. 'Sir, which is the maître de chapelle — can you tell me?' — 'Who — M. Lesueur?' — 'No.' — 'You mean the conductor, M. Valentino?' — 'No, no — the author of the music.' — 'That's me.' —

---

* "F and B were her two preferred consonants", Berlioz recalled, also remembering how splendid she looked and sounded when, as Diana, she descended in her celestial car at the dénouement of *lphigénie en Tauride*, uttering her lines "with majestic breadth and in slightly masculine tones [...] Her one defect, especially in the last years of her life, was a rather too close resemblance to the weird sisters in *Macbeth*."

'Ah ... ah ... ah ...' I left him at the first letter of his alphabet."
Other strangers came up and congratulated him, asked him if his favourite
movement wasn't the Sanctus or whatever, assured him that he knew
how to write music that conveyed the dramatic situation. When Mme Le
Sueur and her daughters appeared and told him his master was waiting
for him at home, he made his excuses and prepared to leave, only to be
summoned to the sacristy to listen to fresh congratulations by the curé of
St Roch, followed by a long harangue to the effect that he was destined to
lead the public taste — perverted by Jean-Jacques Rousseau in music as
in literature — back to the true way, for he wrote from the heart, not
from the head: "*Ex pectore*, sir, *ex pectore*, as the great St Augustine
expressed it." At last he was free, and he hurried round the corner to the
Rue Ste Anne. Le Sueur's eldest daughter answered the bell. "Papa, he's
here!" And the next moment: "Let me embrace you! By jove, you're not
going to be a doctor or an apothecary, you're going to be a great
composer. You have genius — I say it because it is true. There are too
many notes in your Mass, you have let yourself be carried away, but in
all this ebullience of ideas not a single intention misfires, all your pictures
are true. The effect is extraordinary. And I want you to know that
everybody felt it. I had chosen a seat by myself, in a corner, on purpose
to observe the audience, and you may take my word for it that if it hadn't
been in a church you would have received three or four right royal
rounds of applause."

The emperor of the claque, the great Augustus, put the same point
slightly differently when Berlioz saw him at the Opéra a few nights later.
"I hear you made your début at St Roch. Why didn't you let me know?
We'd have all come along." — "I didn't know you liked religious music." — "Good heavens, what an idea! But we'd have really warmed
things up for you." — "How? You can't applaud in a church." — "You
can't applaud; but you can cough, blow your nose, shift your chair,
scrape your feet, say 'Hm, hm', lift your eyes to heaven — the whole box
of tricks. We'd have done you a nice job and made it a hundred per cent
success, just like a fashionable preacher."

The day after the performance, at the wedding of Mme Branchu's
daughter Paméla (celebrated in the church of St Vincent de Paul in north
Paris, where Dérivis, Dabadie and Adolphe Nourrit sang Gossec's unaccompanied O Salutaris), he basked again in the glow of renown and
met a number of people who were glad to shake the hand of a new
celebrity. Three days later in its review of the concert the *Journal des débats*
announced that the Mass did "the greatest credit to this young pupil of
M. Lesueur. This first success augurs well and suggests that he will
succeed in the genre of dramatic music." True, the long and impassioned
article in praise of the Mass that Ferrand had written for the *Gazette de
France* had not appeared after all; and several journals, like the *Globe*, the
Diable boiteux and *Pandore*, which had promised to send a critic had not

done so. But, in addition to the papers already referred to, there were favourable notices in the *Moniteur universel*, the *Drapeau blanc* ("a début of this brilliance entitles us to expect great things"), the *Journal de Paris* and the *Aristarque français* — journals representing every shade of opinion.

All this was heady stuff. Fame, however temporary, was a help. But the experience counted more. Even more valuable than getting other people to hear your music was hearing it yourself. It was the first opportunity he had had to put his ideas to the test and find out how his compositions sounded. *The Arab and his Steed*, *The Crossing of the Red Sea*, *Beverley*, his previous attempts at large-scale music, had remained on the desk, untried. Now, in the midst of his excitement, he listened. Thrilling though it was to hear what he had written take form as he had imagined it, there were places, he saw at once, where he had failed to realise his intentions, and others that were just badly written. "The first step has been taken successfully," he wrote to his mother a few days after the performance, "but I have not the less been made aware how much work I have to do. Numerous defects, which escaped the audience as a whole, carried along by the force of my ideas, were brought home to me, I recognised them, and another time will strive to avoid them."

The letter home, this time, was no penance to write. Knowing that several of his Côtois friends who had returned on vacation immediately after the performance would give the family news of it, he had waited until he could report that his "success had been sanctioned by the papers", and not, he said, because he doubted that the news would please them. "Despite your wish, and Papa's, to see me follow other studies, your affection for me is too great for you to be upset by something that has given me such joy." Half a dozen newspapers already had spoken of him in terms of praise and encouragement. Unfortunately none of them was available at La Côte, but he was collecting them to bring back with him. "I want to arrive among you armed with my documentary evidence [mes pièces justificatives]."

The letter, superficially at least, is full of a proud confidence. But if Berlioz, elated though he was, was under no illusion as to the ultimate value of his Mass, his hope that it would bring about a change of heart in the family was sadly mistaken. Instinct, perhaps, had made him address the letter to his mother. She, as Nancy observed, could not help feeling pleased in spite of herself. Dr Berlioz was visibly annoyed, and merely remarked, coldly, "What of it?" To his exasperation, Hector's companions kept talking about the Mass and the prodigious effect it had made. He even had to endure a letter of congratulation from his old friend the Grenoble appeals judge Joseph Faure, who had read the account of the Mass in the *Moniteur* and, having heard that Louis Berlioz's relations with his son were so strained that they were possibly no longer in communication with each other, and also knowing that the newspaper in question was not sold in La Côte, had transcribed the review for him, adding an irritating little homily on the necessity of accepting his son's vocation. Nancy, writing to a friend, reported that her brother's belief that his success would finally overcome his parents' resistance was a delusion. "Papa has never been less favourably disposed towards his art." She felt it her duty to write and warn her brother. "I should like, dear friend, to add to your joy by telling you that it is shared by our parents, but you would soon find out the deception [...] I prefer to speak frankly and tell you that Papa will not suffer anyone to congratulate him on the subject."

A fortnight after receiving his sister's letter Hector set out for La Côte St André. In some ways this is the most obscure of all the four annual visits that he paid to his family during the period of their most active opposition to his career. We know only from a letter of Nancy's (her diary was once more in abeyance) that he reached home on 16 August, and from an entry in the Livre de Raison that he left again on 7 November. What happened during the twelve weeks he was there — the longest of the four visits — there is very little means of knowing. The account in the *Memoirs*, though ostensibly concerned with this particular visit, reads more like a conflation of several (the other three, in fact, are not mentioned in the book), a compression of confrontations and arguments that were spread over a number of years. Some details seem to refer to an earlier stage, before the success of the Mass had marked him out as a composer with a future. It is more likely that the traumatic scene with his mother (already referred to), which ended with her disowning and cursing him, took place not on this occasion but two years earlier, in 1823. Her objection to the career of musician — a more narrow-minded but also less irrational objection than her husband's — was that it involved contact with the sinful world of the theatre. The success of Hector's Mass did not come into that category, and was in itself a matter for pride; and though she was reluctant to admit it, it pleased her, whereas it only made Louis Berlioz more incensed.

That there was no question of Hector's having been ordered home against his will is clear from the letters he wrote after the St Roch performance to his mother and to Albert Du Boys. It was part of the bargain struck the previous summer, when his father had once more set a trial period of a year, after which he was to abandon the study of music once and for all unless he could show good reason why not. On the other hand, the "glacial reception" and the barrier of silence that the *Memoirs* speak of in connection with this visit are corroborated by the letter that Nancy wrote to her bosom friend Elise Julhiet (née Rocher) the day after Hector's return. Whatever hopes he may still have had of a metamorphosis in his father's attitude had been quickly dashed: "My brother arrived yesterday. The joy I felt at seeing him again was so soon poisoned, and mixed with so much bitterness, that it is more like pain than pleasure. He is of course the same as ever, or rather, madder than ever! My father too hasn't changed his attitude to him, with the result that this creates a wall of separation between them."

The twelve weeks that followed are almost a blank. The Livre de Raison tells us that the weather remained very hot and dry throughout the rest of August and the first ten days of September, and that at the beginning of October it turned cold and gloomy. The annual family visit to Meylan took place as usual, in August or September, and Hector was one of the party (later he would recall the eleven-year-old Adèle striding determinedly ahead of the rest of them on an expedition up the Mont St Eynard). While in the region he no doubt saw Albert Du Boys as he had planned. Throughout October Dr Berlioz busied himself with the wine harvest. Whatever occurred between Hector and his father, the wall of separation was breached sufficiently for him to put his case and win further concessions. "Hector left for Paris 7 November. I gave him 550 francs."

The sum included 80 francs for Hector to hand over, on his return, to Alphonse Robert in repayment of his loan for the hire of instruments at St Roch. In writing to thank Dr Berlioz Alphonse must have hinted that there were other more sizeable debts unpaid, for Nancy, still the go-between, wrote to her brother and demanded an explanation. Hector was forced into a partial admission of the truth (12 December 1825): he owed 300 francs to one of his friends, a young Parisian who had come to his rescue when it looked as if he would be forced to cancel the performance a second time, just when victory was in his grasp.

> "Here," he said, "I have three hundred francs which you may make use of [...] you won't mention it to your parents, and you'll pay me back when you can — I'm not in need of it." The possibility that I could pay him back myself, and the urgency of the case, were too much for me [...] I bet every other young man in my position would have done the same. I had every intention of never speaking of it, and the question of the 80 francs which Alphonse lent me for the hire of instruments, and which Papa kindly gave me to repay him with, would not have come up either if Alphonse could have waited till I had accumulated enough through my work and my economies [...] I venture to hope that Papa will not regard as a fault an action that was simply the natural consequence of the situation which I was in and which I shall not find myself in again.

Whatever Papa thought of this special pleading, a day or two after Hector's reply to Nancy arrived he paid up and sent him 300 francs. In due course Dr Berlioz would discover that the loan had been rather more substantial and that 600 francs were still outstanding. The St Roch debt, the full extent of which was only gradually and reluctantly acknowledged, would be a further cause of discord for many months to come, and would be used as a weapon in the continuing struggle and at times as a pretext for drastically reducing the parental allowance. Yet Berlioz's return to

Paris in November 1825 marks a decisive stage in his emancipation, his progress towards psychological if not financial independence. From now on, with the experience of the Mass behind him, his attitude is markedly less compliant. The conflict with his parents is not over by any means; but this time it will be three years before he comes back to La Côte. Meanwhile he will resist all attempts to make him do so. When he next visits his family it will be as a Conservatoire student of two years' standing and with the accolade of runner-up for the Prix de Rome.

10

"They manage as they can"

———◀◆▶———

On 14 December 1825, six weeks after his return to Paris, Berlioz wrote to his close friend Edouard Rocher to commiserate with him on the death of his father, Louis Rocher, after a long illness. The letter is affectionate and practical, urging him to throw himself into his work and by that means to try to find some respite from his grief. Rocher, he says, loves the study of chemistry as much as he loves the study of his art, so it can be for him the same resource as Berlioz finds in music. "I speak from experience. I have just overcome a violent passion which was tearing me in two, and which would have done for me but for music." Proof, he adds, that his father was mistaken when he said that he would be defenceless against the first passion that came along.

And that is all we know about it. What sort of relationship it was, physical or platonic, requited or unrequited, consummated or not, with whom, with what kind of person, why it had to be overcome — of all this there is absolutely no indication. Berlioz's love life during his first half-dozen years in Paris — that is, between his teenage adoration of Estelle Dubeuf and his infatuation with the Shakespearean actress Harriet Smithson which began in the autumn of 1827 — is a blank.*

Unlike Rousseau and Chateaubriand, whose autobiographies recount their sexual experiences from adolescence on with some frankness, Berlioz in his *Memoirs* is extremely reticent on the subject. He warns the reader at the outset not to expect "confessions"; and the first experience of physical love that he acknowledges is his love affair with the young pianist Camille Moke, which took place in 1830 when he was twenty-six. All things considered, it seems unlikely that it was the first, however backward he may have been when he arrived in Paris eight years earlier. But of

---

* I have found only one other reference, in a letter written to Joséphine Berlioz in July 1825 by her cousin Raymond Roger de la Londe, who had read of Hector's Mass in the newspapers: "I must admit to you that for my part I should very much like to hear some of his music. It must be tuneful and [illegible word], for I recollect Félix having told me that he had already been in love."

that, too, we have no evidence one way or the other. It is conceivable that Berlioz is referring obliquely and ironically to his having been totally chaste in adolescence, when he describes how his regular visits to the confessional invariably took the form of his saying "Father, I have done nothing" and the priest replying "Well, carry on, my child" — an exhortation which, he adds, "I followed all too faithfully for a number of years". On the other hand, there is no activity about which human beings are less truthful, more prone to self-deception and moral evasiveness and more adept at keeping principle and practice separate than sex. Some of the books that Berlioz devoured in his teens were of the sort calculated to excite auto-erotic fantasies: not least his favourite Florian with his demure, pseudo-innocent tales of teasingly sundered lovers, or Rousseau's *La nouvelle Héloïse* or the protracted coitus prolatus of Chateaubriand's crypto-pornographic forest idyll *Atala*. Yet for all we know his erotic impulses were entirely sublimated at this stage of his development, to be awakened only when he had matured physically, and to be given outlet under the stimulus of the sexually emancipated student society of Paris.

Equally, for all his idealisation of romantic love it is hard to believe that in those early Parisian years, living in the Latin Quarter, with its permissive atmosphere and easy opportunities, he had no experience of a less immaterial and more transient kind of relationship, and unlike his fellow-lodger Charbonnel was never "out chasing grisettes" and sometimes catching them. But of the "violent passion" that in November or December 1825 would have "done for him" without the resource of music and hard work, there are, regrettably, no details.

Only the hard work has left evidence, in the composition, apparently in the space of a few weeks, of the Scène héroïque, to a poem by Ferrand on the topical theme of the Greek war of independence — a stirring call to arms for two bass soloists, chorus and full orchestra, written in a vigorously warlike style that, in Berlioz's words, "bore on every page the stamp of Spontini's powerful influence".

Such rapidity of composition suggests a new-found confidence. And indeed a note of authority not heard before can be detected in the music and in the letters written in the ten months between his return to Paris and the beginning of his formal studies as a fully enrolled member of the Conservatoire of Music in the autumn of 1826, an authority that reflects the success of his first public appearance as a composer with the St Roch Mass in July 1825. During these months, in addition to the Scène héroïque, he wrote the bulk of his three-act opera *Les francs-juges*. Whatever their faults, their crudities and miscalculations, and with all their stylistic dependence on Spontini and the French Revolutionary school, these scores have uncommon energy and show signs of an original and individual voice. The promise that observers had noted in the Mass, and the predictions of a bright future in dramatic music, seem well on the way to fulfilment.

Yet these same works served to bring home to him the frustrating obstacles that blocked the path of the young composer in Paris. Attempts to get them performed were fruitless — not for want of strenuous efforts and not because either of them was rejected as inadequate but because of the general lack of provision for the performance of new works. Kreutzer, to whom Berlioz (with influential backing) applied to have the Scène héroïque included in one of the Lenten concerts spirituels at the Opéra, turned him down flat on principle, without even looking at the score. The failure of *Les francs-juges* to secure a production at the Odéon was due not to the obscurity of Ferrand's libretto (which might have been a reason for rejection) but to the mundane fact that the theatre was refused permission to put on new French operas. The long weeks Berlioz spent copying orchestral and vocal parts for a projected run-through of his opera went for nothing. Consequently, between the performance of the Mass in July 1825 and the concert that he gave, on his own initiative and in the teeth of a good deal of opposition, in May 1828, he could find no opportunity to try out anything he had written, and this at a time when he was developing fast as a composer. The music existed on paper, but its sounds reverberated in his mind only. In the summer of 1826 he received another brusque reminder of how far he had to go. He entered for the Prix de Rome, the competition held annually at the Institute for the best dramatic cantata by a young composer, and was turned down in the preliminary exam.

These setbacks, he was forced to acknowledge, were part of his education. He had assumed naïvely that Kreutzer would be sympathetic to his approach: surely his own deep admiration for Kreutzer's *Mort d'Abel* had created a secret bond of sympathy between them and, besides, hadn't Le Sueur himself warmly recommended his Scène héroïque to the great man? But all he got was a flea in his ear. The boorish Kreutzer did not conceal his impatience at the young student's request. He kept his back turned, did not even deign to address his visitor face to face. No, it was out of the question, they could not possibly perform new works at the Opéra's concerts spirituels, he should know perfectly well that the Opéra did not exist to give a hearing to the young. Berlioz retired in confusion and mortification. A few days later Mme Le Sueur tackled Kreutzer at the Chapel Royal (where he played violin in the orchestra) and asked him straight out what he thought was supposed to become of young composers if they were denied a chance to get themselves known. They manage as they can, was the cross reply. "What would become of us if we pushed them forward like that?" It was a prime example, Berlioz reported to Edouard Rocher, of the spirit of selfishness which made people at the top try to prevent others getting there. "They don't want to share the cake with anyone else. But I should never have thought Kreutzer was one of them."[*]

It was not in Berlioz's temperament, however, to leave matters there. Kreutzer might still be outfaced, or outflanked. Influential contacts who had proved useful when the performance of the Mass was in doubt might be used again. (Had not the *Aristarque français* declared, in its review of the Mass, that "nowadays, when our young composers have such difficulty getting themselves known, to obtain recompense for one's work it is not enough to have talent: one also requires influence"?) Through his friend Albert Du Boys, who now worked in the Department of Arts, he managed to get an interview with one of the sub-inspectors, Le Normant, and went to see him one Sunday morning at his home in the Marais. The interview went well; and the possibility of a new regulation helpful to young composers was raised. Whether or not the idea came in the first place from Berlioz, he seems to have found Le Normant very much in favour of it. Nevertheless he judged it diplomatic to follow up the interview with a letter reaffirming his position in writing. He took it round to Le Normant's address the same day. The letter shows Berlioz attempting to have Kreutzer's hand forced at ministerial level and at the same time to guard against other possible weaknesses in his position.

Dear Sir,
  Since this morning, when I had the honour to see you, I have been having a few thoughts on the subject of our conversation, and take the liberty of communicating them to you.
  You expressed to me your intention of speaking to M. le Vicomte de La Rochefoucauld [Director of Arts] of a new regulation which would have the effect of giving young composers the opportunity to have works performed at the concerts spirituels. I venture to ask you if you would be so obliging as to wait a few days before you tell him what you think of the project. I believe that if the regulation were effected before I obtained a definite and favourable answer from Kreutzer, I should risk becoming subject to a general law and therefore, for this year's concerts, losing precedence and the advantage of the recommendation which I owe to your kindness.
  For this reason I would be most grateful if, when you see M. de La Rochefoucauld, you mention only the scant hope that Kreutzer gave me — without actually having got to know my score — and the ridiculous objection he made that "the performance of my score would necessitate fresh study such as one does not have to give to the music of Haydn, Beethoven etc., etc. which is performed every year".

---

[*] A realisation that he and his sort of music were on the way out may have contributed to Kreutzer's unsympathetic attitude. *La mort d'Abel*, his one opera still in the repertoire, had totalled only five performances in 1824 and 1825. After one more, in March 1826, it disappeared altogether.

He knows perfectly well — and everyone agreed with me about it at the Opéra just now — that a work which does not last more than fifteen or twenty minutes, which no one is required to learn by heart but which will be sung copy in hand by a chorus capable of performing at sight, and which has only a few difficulties of ensemble, would not necessitate more than two rehearsals and would not involve the artists in much loss of time.

I doubt if Kreutzer will persist for long in his stubborn opposition, given the powerful support that I have.* In addition, M. Dubois the manager [of the Opéra], Mme Branchu, M. Valentino, and not least Lesueur, who has examined my work with the closest attention, are all on my side.

Once again, sir, I should like to apologise for troubling you, and to tell you how grateful I am for all that you have done for me.

Your obedient servant,
Hector Berlioz

Paris, 15 January 1826
Rue de Harlay no. 27

But Kreutzer did persist, ignoring the solicitations of the above-named allies (to whom Berlioz added Gardel, the Opéra's chief choreographer, and the singer Ferdinand Prévost) and unpersuaded even by a letter from la Rochefoucauld himself instructing him to be so good as to examine the score that had been submitted to him; and the campaign came to nothing.

In March Ferrand published, anonymously, the text of his poem: "Scène Héroïque à Grands Chœurs ET A GRAND ORCHESTRE [...] Musique de M. Hector Berlioz". And for a moment a fresh hope presented itself. One of Berlioz's acquaintances in the Opéra orchestra, none other than Tulou the eminent flautist, offered to include the work in a concert he was planning to give. In the event the concert did not take place. For the time being Berlioz had to give up any idea of getting his score performed. To put on a concert himself was hopelessly impractical. He was still in debt for the last one.

Even before his disappointments over the Scène héroïque he had voiced his sense of frustration in a letter to his sister Nancy. "I am sure that if I were known my existence would be quite different; but my reason tells me that time alone can produce the desired effect, and that those whose lot I envy have been through the same trials as I am going through now and have experienced the same sensations. But that being so, my state is as painful and tantalising as would be a slave's who saw his comrades released one after another and who knew that his own deliverance was coming but not when it would come" (12 December 1825).

---

* Including perhaps, as Pierre Citron suggests, the Comte de Montesquiou, whose help had been sought over the performance of the Mass, and the Comte de Chabrillant and the Isère deputy Chenevaz, both of whom would use their influence to enable Berlioz to give his concert in the Conservatoire Hall in May 1828.

The profound unsatisfactoriness of the musical scene and his own obscure and powerless position in it were emphasised by the event that occurred at the end of February 1826. Weber spent four days in Paris, on his way from Dresden to London for the première of *Oberon* at Covent Garden; but Berlioz did not succeed in meeting him. Just before the visit there had been an exchange of fire in the press between the protesting composer and Castil-Blaze, author of *Robin des bois*, the arrangement of *Der Freischütz* which had been playing to full houses at the Odéon throughout the previous year, to the enrichment of Castil-Blaze but not of Weber. Encouraged by the profits of his enterprise, Castil-Blaze concocted a second Weberish entertainment, *La forêt de Sénart*, a pasticcio whose plot derived from an old comedy, *La partie de chasse de Henri IV*. It opened at the Odéon on 14 January 1826. This time other composers were pressed into service (among them Mozart, Beethoven and Rossini), but Weber was the principal donor with six pieces, two from *Der Freischütz*, one of which had not figured in *Robin des bois* (the B-major Andante in 6/8 from the finale of Act 3), and four from *Euryanthe*, orchestrated by Castil-Blaze himself from the vocal score. Weber's publisher in Paris, Maurice Schlesinger, tried to stop him, but there was no clear copyright law giving him unequivocal power to do so; and Castil-Blaze suffered no worse inconvenience than the two open letters from Weber which appeared in the *Corsaire*, a week after *La forêt de Sénart* opened.

Weber had written to him privately, more in sorrow than in anger, five weeks earlier. Not getting a reply (Castil-Blaze later claimed he never received the letter, though according to Weber it was delivered to his address by the Saxon ambassador in person), Weber followed it up with a more vehement protest. In the meantime he had got wind of the *Forêt de Sénart* project. He sent copies of both letters to Schlesinger with instructions to distribute them to the Paris press. By the time they appeared, in the *Corsaire* only (on 22 January 1826), *La forêt de Sénart* was already playing.

The affair provides an instructive glimpse of practice and principle in the musical world of the time. In the first letter Weber expresses bewilderment that so distinguished a figure, author of the admirable *Opera in France* and a man whom he had long looked forward to meeting on some future visit to Paris, could behave with such apparent lack of justice and consideration: could get hold of the full score by totally illegal means (*Der Freischütz* being unpublished) and put it on the stage, and then continue to behave as if the composer did not exist, by appropriating his commercial rights, to the extent of actually publishing the score himself. He, Weber, could not believe that a man who had written so nobly on art and the responsibilities towards it could consciously choose to ignore what one artist owed another, and he was appealing, confidently, to Castil-Blaze's better nature.

The second letter attempted to take a firmer line.

Dresden, 4 January 1826

Sir,

You have not considered it necessary to honour me with a reply to my letter of 15 December. Reluctantly, I must write to you a second time.

I have been informed that a work containing pieces from *Euryanthe* is to be put on at the Odéon Theatre. I intend to put on this opera in Paris myself; I have not sold the score and no one in France owns it — you have presumably taken from an engraved vocal score the numbers you wish to make use of. You have no right to mutilate my music by introducing pieces whose accompaniments are your own. It was quite enough to include in *Der Freischütz* a duet from *Euryanthe*, the accompaniment of which is not by me.

You force me, sir, to have recourse to popular opinion and to state publicly in the French press that I am being robbed, not only of music that belongs to me and to no one else, but also of my reputation, by the performance of mutilated pieces with my name on them. To avoid public controversy, which is never of any benefit to art or to artists, I beg you with great insistence to remove at once from the work that you have arranged every piece which belongs to me.

I prefer to forget the wrong that has already been done to me; I shall not mention *Der Freischütz* again. But let the matter stop there, Sir, and allow me still to hope that we may meet in a spirit worthy of your talents and your intelligence. I beg to remain, etc.

Ch.-M. de Weber

Three days later (*Débats*, 25 January 1826) Castil-Blaze replied. Quite unabashed, he argued that he was fully within his rights. That an author's domain stopped at the frontier was generally accepted — witness the fact that French works (including his own *Opera in France* and *Dictionary of Modern Music*) were exploited in Germany, in German versions, without their authors being a cent the richer for the transaction. This was a perfectly natural quid pro quo, and he had quite legitimately profited from it when he was last in Germany, when he had bought 40 kilograms of scores at Mainz, from which he had extracted whatever he found worth performing. Furthermore, it was common knowledge that foreign operas were successful in France only if rearranged according to French dramatic methods. Before a work could be staged the music must of necessity be cut and adjusted. Indeed, was this not precisely the experience they had had with *Der Freischütz*? Out of respect for M. Weber's genius they had presented it, on the first night, in its pristine integrity [this was totally untrue], and the audience had booed. It was only in its adapted form, on the second night, that the show had become a hit. Castil-Blaze concluded, with consummate effrontery, in tones of injured innocence: "I am upset that a person of the distinguished talent of M. Weber should feel offended by the alterations which we have introduced into his opera in order to ensure its prodigious success [...] My enterprise has had as

its object to make his splendid masterpiece known in France, and to add
to the laurels which Germany, Prussia, Holland and England have already
laid on the score of *Der Freischütz*."*

This in turn drew a scathing rejoinder from Schlesinger in the *Corsaire*
(1 February). Schlesinger accused Castil-Blaze of hypocrisy, quoting a
conversation they had had in front of witnesses, in which he had revealed
an attitude of complete cynicism, and also challenging his statement that
French authors received the same treatment in Germany. On the contrary,
unlike Castil-Blaze, German translators of foreign works got no author's
royalties, for the simple reason that they were content to translate and
not to alter. Castil-Blaze might, technically, be acting within French law,
but public opinion would pillory him.

Castil-Blaze, however, gauged matters more realistically. Public opinion,
if it raised an eyebrow momentarily, refused to get very agitated and soon
forgot, and *Robin* and *La forêt* continued to figure on the bills.

Berlioz followed the correspondence with indignant sympathy. He had
himself had a tilt at Castil-Blaze over his *Débats* review of Gluck's *Armide*
only a month before, pitching into him at the end of another "Polémique
musicale" which he contributed to the *Corsaire*.

[...] Who could restrain an impulse of indignation on reading the reviews
of *Armide* written by several journalists, among others M. *** of the *Débats*?
What! The finale of the first act "produces no effect"? "Notre général vous
rappelle" "causes no emotion"? The music for Renaud and Armide "lacks
development and invariably sounds truncated"? The whole work is composed "on a fallacious method of declamation which we have since rejected"?
What do you want then, you wretch? You can have no blood in your veins if
the tremendous war-cry that summons the love-lorn Renaud back to glory
fails to make you shudder. But what does this "we" stand for? M. ***. Who
is it that has rejected Gluck's method? M. ***. Who finds half the music of
Armide absurd? M. ***. Who finds the poem bad, the principal rôle anti-
musical, the embellishments paltry, the ballets dull? M. *** again. But
who, you will ask, is this implacable critic, this righter of wrongs, this
universal improver? No doubt some great composer, some lyric poet, at the
least a member of the Academy. No: he is more than all these. He is
M. Castil-Blaze.

It had not taken Berlioz long to rumble Castil-Blaze's ignoble role in
Robin des bois. In accordance with his normal practice he compared what

* Castil-Blaze's claim that *Der Freischütz* was given on the opening night as Weber wrote it
was a barefaced lie. The performance was indeed a failure; but the opera was given from the
first in a mutilated version. Immediately after the opening night Castil-Blaze had the ingenious
idea of announcing that the work was being radically revised. The not very perceptive Odéon
public swallowed the bait, and at the second "première" a week later the work was applauded.
To that extent he had "ensured its success" in France.

he heard with the score, and was shocked to discover large discrepancies. Though less extreme than the Lachnitz version of *The Magic Flute*, it was bad enough. As he grew into the work, he could measure the damage done to it. He had found Weber's music strange at first when he encountered it the previous winter — it was so different from what he was accustomed to (and quite apart from Castil-Blaze's meddling, the feeble cast did not help) — but had felt increasingly drawn to it the more he heard and studied it. Here was a new style, richly, disturbingly new, with profound implications for music and for himself. Here was another god to add to his Pantheon, what was more a god blasphemed.* His admiration and his sense of injustice were equally aroused. Weber's protest, so brazenly, so insolently answered by Castil-Blaze, chimed with his own beliefs about the sanctity of the score and the inviolability of the composer's intentions. How he longed to see him and lay his tribute at his feet! But in vain: during Weber's brief stay no opportunity presented itself, the historic encounter failed to take place, and the two men never met.

This may seem odd, given Weber's itinerary during these four days: visits to the Feydeau (Opéra-Comique) to see Auber's *Emma* and Boieldieu's *La dame blanche* (the new hit that winter); Spontini's *Olympie* at the Opéra; a session at the Conservatoire, sitting in on Fétis' composition class; calling at the church of Ste Geneviève and being hoisted up a hundred feet to the platform just under the dome where Antoine Gros was working on his allegorical painting "The Assumption of the Virgin"; calls paid on Cherubini, Auber, Catel, Berton, Paër, and on Le Sueur himself. But it is less surprising if we recall that, in contrast to Rossini, whose appearance a year or so earlier was made in the glare of triumphant publicity, Weber arrived in Paris incognito. He had preferred not to have his presence trumpeted in advance. His health, he knew, was too frail to stand up to the public confrontation with the egregious Castil-Blaze that would be likely to follow; he must conserve his strength for London. So he slipped into Paris without prior announcement. Only one paper noted his arrival, in a brief news item.

Weber's visit to Le Sueur two mornings later could thus have taken the old man by surprise. Le Sueur, not expecting it, would not have forewarned his pupil. As it was, going round to see Le Sueur later the same

---

* At one of the performances (Berlioz later recalled), he and his friend and ex-fellow medical student Dubouchet were involved in an altercation with the man next to them in the pit, a "great carrot-headed lout who took it upon himself to hiss Agathe's second-act aria, claiming that it was 'baroque' and that there was nothing good in the opera except the Waltz and the Huntsmen's Chorus. Our music-loving neighbour was duly removed from the theatre; and Dubouchet, as he adjusted his slightly rumpled cravate, called out, 'What do you expect? I know the fellow — he's a grocer's assistant from the Rue St Jacques'. And the whole pit applauded''.

morning, Berlioz found his master in a state of pleased wonderment: "I have just this moment had a visit from Weber! If you had come five minutes sooner you would have heard him playing whole scenes from our French scores: he knows them all."

Thereafter it seemed a matter of fatality that he should go on missing him. A few hours later, in a music shop, he was greeted with: "You'll never guess who was sitting here a moment ago — Weber!" And that evening at the Opéra, where there was a revival of Spontini's *Olympie* with Mme Branchu and Mlle Cinti, he arrived in the foyer just after Weber had gone in, and could find no one able to point him out. As he subsequently remarked, Weber that day was "like a Shakespearean apparition in reverse — visible to all save one". A couple of days afterwards Weber continued his journey to London. And two months later came the news that he was dead. He had insisted on taking up the lucrative Covent Garden offer in order that his family would have something to live on if and when his health broke down completely and he could no longer work. But the heroic effort had killed him. Meanwhile Castil-Blaze went on fattening himself at Weber's expense. "And a sailor gets fifty lashes for a minor act of insubordination," as Berlioz justly observed.

There were other injustices to inveigh against. The great Mme Branchu's appearance in *Olympie*, on 27 February, had been an occasion of rare grandeur and éclat, an example of the Opéra at its most magnificent, attended by the whole of theatrical Paris; but it had been her last: all attempts to persuade the management to renew her contract were unavailing. Berlioz reported to Edouard Rocher that she had been "if anything more sublime than she usually is. At the end, when Talma and Dérivis crowned her with a wreath I thought the theatre would collapse. After the performance the chorus came to her dressing-room and presented her with a farewell gift, a crown of diamonds of great price. She assured me that this totally disinterested tribute was the one that gave her the most pleasure of all. A deputation of members of the Institute went to see M. Sosthène [de La Rochefoucauld] to ask him to engage her for another year; but the entire complement of our leading composers was unable to get this concession from him." Spontini had begged that she be allowed to give just three more performances. But Sosthène refused, whereupon the great composer lost control, shouted at him and stormed out, slamming the door with such force that it split from top to bottom. "He went straight off to Berlin, and his opera was left in the hands of Mlle Quiney, who with Sosthène's assistance soon sank it without trace.* It's a sublime work, fully worthy of the composer of *La Vestale* — only, there are

---

* The inadequate Quiney was promoted by her father, a rich financier. It was said of her: "Take away from Mme Branchu her warmth, her expressiveness, her soul, and her acting, and you will have an accurate notion of Mlle Quiney's talent."

places where it's overloaded with brass." *Olympie* had only four further performances.

Berlioz was at the third of them, as we can deduce from a note to his friend Thomas Gounet (a civil servant in the Ministry of Education, with ambitions as a poet): "If you will be at the Café Durand on the corner of the boulevard and Richelieu at 6.30 tomorrow Friday, we can go together to the Opéra. I have a ticket for you." In fact, he was there more often than not on performance nights (Mondays, Wednesdays, Fridays). *La Vestale* and *Fernand Cortez* were regularly performed; *Œdipe* or *Didon* would occasionally reappear on the bills, and with luck there was still an opera by Gluck once or twice a month — though *Armide*, with the unfortunate Mlle Grassari "quite crushed by the title rôle", had had disappointingly few performances.

On nights when a work of proven vacuity was on but there was nothing to tempt him at one of the other houses, he would sometimes go to the Opéra none the less, to see one of his friends in the orchestra and discuss some technical matter with him or just to spend the evening warming himself before the big fire that was kept burning in the foyer: it saved him fuel in his attic room in the Rue de Harlay. The weather was cold and damp and he was having to economise and lead a generally straitened existence; a large part of the debt to de Pons had still to be settled.

As spring warmed into summer he put the disappointment of the Scène héroïque behind him and threw himself into his various operatic projects. The grand-opera libretto on the death of Hercules which Du Boys had written for him with the Opéra in mind had been rejected (the good Sosthène, it seemed, had set his face against tragic dénouements); but a friend of Ferrand's, Léon Compaignon, a trainee barrister with literary pretensions who lived in Chartres, had been recruited to adapt *The Talisman*, Scott's novel about Richard Cœur-de-Lion and the Third Crusade, for the Opéra-Comique. That summer and autumn letters went to and fro between Paris and Chartres, as they struggled to fashion a *Richard en Palestine* worthy of the original, which would catch and exploit the growing vogue for Scott.

Above all, there was *Les francs-juges*, Ferrand's splendid drama of intrigue, tyranny and heroism set in the Black Forest at the end of the Middle Ages. It was intended for the Odéon, of which Berlioz had been a habitué for the past eighteen months (since the advent of *Freischütz*) and where he was on friendly terms with the violinist-conductor Nathan Bloc. The management was interested in the work, had as good as accepted the libretto, merely stipulating a few changes, which had been made. Permission to put on new operas by native French composers — a right at present confined to the Opéra and the Opéra-Comique — had been applied for and there was reason to hope it would be granted. Berlioz, aware that he might be asked quite soon to present his score, worked at it with concentrated energy and enthusiasm during the torrid summer months of 1826. He finished the second act at the end of June, in a heat-wave so intense that his room "sous les toits" in the Rue de Harlay was like a furnace and he had to cool off at intervals in the nearby Seine. When Le Sueur read through the two completed acts he was full of praise; and his delighted pupil, conscious himself that it was the best thing he had yet done, could hardly wait to go on to the third and final act. First, however, there was the Prix de Rome competition to deal with; that would take up most of July. On the 11th he presented himself at the Institute — Le Vau's handsome domed edifice by the Seine, Mazarin's bequest to Paris — and with five other candidates sat the preliminary exam, which consisted of a fugue. The following morning the music section of the Institute — Cherubini, Catel, Berton, Boieldieu, Gossec, Le Sueur — met, considered the fugues, and decided that two of the six candidates should not go through to the competition proper, the compo-sition of a cantata. One was Berton's pupil Alphonse Gilbert. The other was Berlioz.

The moment the result of the concours d'essai was declared, pupil and master met to decide what should be done. The conclusion was obvious: Berlioz must enrol at the Conservatoire for the academic year beginning in twelve weeks' time.

It may be wondered why Le Sueur had not made him do so before. The reason is a practical one: Berlioz could not have enrolled any sooner. During his first three years in Paris his whole status was in doubt; there was not the slightest question of his father's consenting to his becoming a full-time student of music. The stir caused by his Mass aroused the interest of the Director of the Conservatoire, Cherubini, who asked Le Sueur to send his clearly very talented pupil to see him. It may well have been settled between them then that Berlioz should enrol at the Con-servatoire, on the assumption that now he had proved his point by having a large-scale work performed in public, his father could be expected to agree. In the event, as we have seen, Berlioz spent the next two and a half months in further protracted debate with his father which resulted only in another temporary, compromise solution. By the time he returned to Paris in November 1825 the Conservatoire term was already six weeks old. Accordingly he continued as Le Sueur's private pupil, and devoted himself to composing the Scène héroïque and Les francs-juges.

We do not know whether his father stipulated that he go in for the Prix de Rome, Dr Berlioz having made success in it a condition of further support, or whether Le Sueur encouraged him to enter. The very modest level of Berlioz's fugue does not suggest that he had been prepared for the competition by much training in fugal technique. But Le Sueur, or Berlioz, may have reasoned that that need not be a serious handicap, given his manifest talent for the composition of a dramatic cantata, the main matter of the Prix de Rome. A poor fugue did not necessarily debar a candidate from getting through the preliminary round — according to the official report of 1825 "only one" of the fugues was "treated satisfactorily" — or even from winning a prize. The report on the 1821 competition states that the fugue of the prizewinner, Rifaut, was less accomplished than his cantata but that in the opinion of the jury this should not stop him being adjudged the winner. And in 1825 Claude-Joseph Paris, a pupil of Le Sueur, was awarded second prize despite his fugue having been "very weak". There may have been some truth in Berlioz's contention that what most disqualified a candidate was being outside the system: unless you went through the proper channels they would not consider you. Although the regulations stated that candidates did not have to be Conservatoire students, in practice those admitted to the main competition always were.

But if so, it was all the more necessary to conform. Parents or no, he would have to sign on for the coming academic year and take the official course in counterpoint and fugue. Le Sueur packed him off to see Cherubini. Berlioz reported the fact a couple of days later to Edouard Rocher, while remaining silent on the subject of his recent failure:

> Lesueur is determined that I should go in for the Institute competition next year, and to that end, to assure me the protection of Cherubini, wants me to take a course in counterpoint and fugue at the Conservatoire. I have been to see Cherubini. When I offered to show him something of mine, so that he knew what I could do, he answered: "No, no, there's no need, I know you. Just bring me a copy of your birth certificate."
>
> Till now I was only on the Conservatoire's books as a private pupil of Lesueur's. It was because of that that Cherubini himself, after the performance of my Mass, asked Lesueur to send me to see him. There you have another example of the professors' amour-propre: as soon as they spot any aptitude in a student they want to grab hold of him. When people can say that I have had lessons in counterpoint at the Conservatoire, Cherubini will give me his full support. If not, he won't!
>
> As a consequence of all this, as Cherubini asked me the other day why I hadn't brought him the copy of my birth certificate, would you please [get it from the mairie and] send it to me as soon as possible.

Whatever the setback to his hopes of academic success and the blow to his own amour-propre, one good result was that he did not have to lock himself up at the Institute for three weeks and write a cantata to a prescribed text but was free to get on with the third act of his opera. There is an irony in the juxtaposition. The young musician who was not considered good enough to be admitted for the Prix de Rome, the authorised test of the budding dramatic composer, was already capable of the vehemence and formidable rhythmic drive of the final section of the duet in Act 1 of *Les francs-juges* and the freshness and felicity of the Shepherds' Chorus, with its confidently handled echo effects, and within three months would have composed the overture, the first of his works to establish and maintain a place in the repertoire.

No doubt the irony was not lost on Berlioz. But he was careful, in his letter to Rocher, to refrain from telling him that he had in fact already "gone in for the Institute competition" and had failed. The longer the news was kept from La Côte the better. There was trouble enough from that quarter. His father had discovered the full extent of the St Roch debt. De Pons, concerned at the privations his friend was being driven to to pay the money, and also realising that at this rate it could be years before he got it all back, decided on drastic measures. Without consulting him he wrote to Dr Berlioz and told him his son owed him 600 francs.

It was, as Berlioz acknowledged, a grievous blow to his father, and it rebounded heavily. Dr Berlioz was already in a state of irritated concern over the large sums that his brother-in-law Félix Marmion had recently borrowed from him. That spring he had had to withdraw a total of 9,000 francs from the bank in Grenoble to settle Félix's gambling debts with various fellow-officers in the Third Dragoons and other regiments. He was in no state to take kindly to news of more debts. On the day of his rejection by the music section of the Academy Hector received a letter enclosing a money order for 600 francs and informing him that next year his allowance would be cut to 50 francs a month.

A month later, on 14 August, came a second and worse bombshell. Dr Berlioz had found out about the Prix de Rome débâcle. How, we do not know, nor what language he used his "tardy son to chide"; but the money he now sent Hector — 150 francs — was, he said, all that he was able to give him for the remainder of the year. "He wants to reduce me to submission by gradually cutting it down to nothing," wrote Berlioz to Edouard Rocher. But there could be no question of submission now. The mere idea of capitulating and crawling back to La Côte incensed him. He would do anything rather than that. Sooner than give in he would emigrate. For a week or two it was on the cards that he would go to South America. He had always dreamed of travelling, of crossing the ocean to the New World in the footsteps of Chateaubriand; here was an opportunity. It was a desperate remedy but it might be the only course. Through an acquaintance who was also interested in going there he made enquiries at the Brazilian consulate about a possible post as first or second flute in an orchestra. The answer was encouraging: though there could be no prior guarantee, a foreign artist could earn a large salary.

By the time he wrote to Edouard Rocher, in the second week of September, calmer counsels had prevailed.

The Brazilian consul said he would pay my passage and that of the young man who spoke to him and who would have gone with me, but he wouldn't give a definite undertaking nor pay anything in advance. It was partly this that decided me. In addition, I had no money to get to Le Havre, and I don't know Portuguese, and it takes a good four months to learn it. Charles [Bert] and Charbonnel put all these arguments to me; but the strongest, to me, were the shock my going would have been to my parents and the enormous setback to my career. For one thing, I would have had to forgo the Prix de Rome, for which I am favourite now that Paris and Simon are no longer on the scene. At least, M. Lesueur is on record as stating that I should win first prize not more than two years from now, if justice is done. I'll have only dunces against me, apart from this year's second prize, who is bound to be given preference, in accordance with the admirable practice of the Institute's so-called "competition".[*] Furthermore, if I went to Buenos Aires[†] the opera I have written and those I am to write would run the risk of never being performed in Europe, damn it. So I'm staying.

For the moment he could survive on the money he had put aside for repaying de Pons, which was no longer necessary: to that extent he could be thankful for his father's draconian scrupulousness. For the future, if he was to remain in Paris and not go off and make his fortune in South America, something dramatic was required. Some time in late August or early September a bizarre solution presented itself. An important new vaudeville theatre, the Théâtre des Nouveautés, was announced. The theatre, which would have 1,250 seats, was being built on a site in the Rue Vivienne opposite the Bourse, a block or two from the Conservatoire. There might be a vacancy for flute in the orchestra.[§] By the time Berlioz applied at the manager's office, it had gone. What about the chorus? Nothing there either; however, there was a possibility they might need an extra bass, and if he liked he could leave his name and address. A few days later a note from the management informed him that auditions for the vacant position were being held at the Freemasons' Hall in the Rue Grenelle, off the Rue St Honoré.

The account in the *Memoirs* was based on the Autobiographical Sketch of 1832 and, though fuller, differs from it only in minor details.

When I arrived, five or six poor devils like myself were there already, awaiting their inquisitors in nervous silence. They included a weaver, a blacksmith, an actor sacked from one of the minor boulevard theatres, and a lay clerk from St Eustache. A bass was wanted. I was at best a second-rate

---

[*] J.-B. Guiraud, the second prizewinner, duly won first prize the following year. The winner in 1826, C.-J. Paris, had come second the year before.

[†] Presumably this is an example of French haziness about foreign parts, and for Buenos Aires one should read Rio de Janeiro. Berlioz was evidently less strong on South America than he was on the East Indies. It may be said, in his defence, that he was not himself directly involved in the approach to the Brazilian consul.

[§] All this suggests that he had kept up his flute playing. According to an account of his life published in the *Gazette musicale* at his death, he played a flute concerto at a public concert in 1826 or 1827.

baritone; but perhaps our examiner would not go into that too closely.

He proved to be the manager in person. He appeared with a musician called Michel [...] whose violin was to do for our accompaniment.

The session commenced. My rivals sang in turn, after their fashion, the various pieces that each had prepared. Then it was my turn. The huge manager (rather pleasingly called St Léger) asked me what I had brought.

"I? Why − nothing."

"What do you mean, nothing? Then what do you propose to sing?"

"Whatever you want me to sing. Isn't there some score here, a solfège, a book of exercises?"

"No, we haven't anything like that. Besides", he added with a touch of scorn, "I don't imagine you can sing at sight."

"Excuse me, I'll sing at sight anything that's put in front of me."

"Ah! that is different. Well, then − but as we've no music, is there some well-known piece that you can sing by heart?"

"Yes, there's *The Danaids, Stratonice, La Vestale, Cortez, Œdipe,* the two *Iphigénies, Orphée, Armide* − "

"All right, all right! Deuce take it − what a memory! Well, since you're so ominiscient, give us 'Elle m'a prodigué' from Sacchini's *Œdipe.*"

"With pleasure."

"Can you accompany him, Michel?"

"Of course I can. Only, I've forgotten what key it's in."

"E flat. Shall I sing the recitative?"

"Yes, let's hear the recitative."

The accompanist gave me a chord of E flat and I began:

> Antigone me reste, Antigone est ma fille,
> Elle est tout pour mon cœur, seule elle est ma famille.
> Elle m'a prodigué sa tendresse et ses soins,
> Son zèle dans mes maux m'a fait trouver des charmes, etc.

As the grand melody rolled forth, the other candidates cast gloomy glances at each other, recognising that in comparison with me (who was no Pischek or Lablache) they had sung not so much like cow-hands as like cows. Indeed, I saw by a sign from the big manager that they had "got the bird". Next day I was notified officially of my appointment [...] I had beaten the weaver, the blacksmith, the actor, and even the lay clerk from St Eustache [...] So here I was, while waiting to become a damned dramatic composer, turned chorister in a minor theatre − discredited and excommunicated cap-à-pie! Observe the success of my parents' efforts to snatch me from the bottomless pit.

Apparently Berlioz was at first undecided whether to accept the offer. He told Edouard Rocher in early September that when he saw what would be involved in singing in the Nouveautés chorus − the repertoire and the standard of performance − he could not bring himself to "slum it" to that degree, and was trying instead to join the chorus of the Opéra, but it was difficult to get into, and Le Sueur was opposed to it, both on musical grounds and because he said it would be likely to harm his reputation as a serious composer to be a member of the Opéra chorus. "He's offered me money several times, but I cannot accept without having the least idea when I could pay it back, and I don't want to be in debt to anyone, even him. In the meantime, while I wait to make up my mind definitely, I'm getting fat on pears and plums and copious draughts of water." He had moved house, too, back to the Latin Quarter. "I'm living at 58 Rue de la Harpe, in the Hôtel de Bourges. Charbonnel is my neighbour; we have adjoining doors. I'm learning Italian. I absolutely need a piano, to learn to accompany my singers [for *Les francs-juges*], but I can't afford to buy or hire one, damn it! But of course all this is 'for my own good'."

The decision could not be put off, however; it had to be taken willy-nilly. Berlioz signed on at the Nouveautés. Work was not due to start till the beginning of November, but the chorus were getting paid their salary (50 francs) for the month of October. In due course, as rehearsals proceeded in preparation for the opening, planned for 1 January, he found his worst forebodings realised. *The Straw Man, The Little Beggar Girl* and the other blown-up vaudevilles which formed the company's repertoire were every bit as appalling as he had feared.

However awful, the job meant regular money. He added to it by earning a few more francs correcting music publishers' proofs, by picking up some more pupils when the holiday season ended, and by continuing to eat very frugally, and was even able after all to afford a cheap piano which, together with some pictures of his musical heroes, gave the poky room in the Rue de la Harpe a more civilised air. In the middle of September his mother had unexpectedly sent him 100 francs, part of which he spent on a set of kitchen utensils. He and his fellow-Côtois Antoine Charbonnel (who was in Paris to study chemistry) had agreed to pool resources and establish a common cuisine. At first it caused a little friction: there was a scene between them about Berlioz's habit of carrying their purchases back from the market quite openly, which Charbonnel, less emancipated from provincial ideas of respectability, found very embarrassing. On the whole, however, the joint ménage worked satis-factorily and suited them both. Each left the other free to lead his own life (with the result that Berlioz, who also had his provincial pride, was able to keep his theatrical career hidden from Charbonnel and give the impression, when the Nouveautés opened, that he was spending his evenings teaching when he was actually "treading the boards"); but together they lived a slightly less spartan existence than each would have done separately. For Berlioz the diet of prunes was enriched by cheese, leeks, and cutlets fried in lard (entered by Charbonnel in the housekeeping book under the pharmaceutical term "axonge"). On special occasions they might even lash out on a capon. Charbonnel would also go off on hunting excursions to the wooded Plaine de Montrouge, to the south-west beyond Montparnasse, and come back with a few quail for lunch, which he trapped by means of the net and the decoy birds that he had himself constructed. Charbonnel was a great handyman. He carved them each a pair of very passable clogs out of pieces of firewood, and was forever knocking together useful gadgets for the household. "We lived like princes (in exile)," was Berlioz's later comment. It reflected the sense of relief he experienced. For the moment, the tension relaxed. He could breathe again. He was finally free of the debts which had been hanging over him since the performance of his Mass, obliging him to dissemble to his father. It was at the price, admittedly, of the drastic curtailment of his allowance; but he was in a position to ride that blow, thanks to the Nouveautés job. For the first time he had a measure of financial independence, of immunity from family pressure. He need depend on no one's charity and no one's grudging and changeable acquiescence.

With all its alarms and frustrations this was a contented and productive period in Berlioz's life. He was working hard and well. Whatever his sceptical family thought, whatever the Academy mandarins decreed, he believed in himself. He was making progress, he was sure of it. Each work took him a little nearer the goal which, though it was still a long way off, he could see clearly before him. Like Keats at the same age he could say that what he was writing was as good as he had the power to make it, and that he was his own best judge. "When I want to know if a thing of mine is good," he told Nancy, "I put it on one side once it's finished and give myself time to recover from the excitement which composition always produces in my system. Then when I am absolutely calm again I read my work as if it were not by me." He could have echoed Keats' conviction that "Praise or blame has but a momentary effect on the man whose love of beauty in the abstract makes him a severe critic of his own Work. My own domestic criticism has given me pain without comparison beyond what *Blackwood* or the *Quarterly* could possibly inflict, and also when I feel I am right, no external praise can give me such a glow as my own solitary reperception and ratification of what is fine."

The third act of *Les francs-juges*, written in July and August, was, he felt, up to the first two. In September he completed the opera, and sanctioned his resolution, by writing the overture — his first orchestral work, and the first composition by which he would be known to posterity. Though the published version, which did not appear till 1835, is scored for bigger forces than the 46-man Odéon orchestra for which the overture was conceived, and undoubtedly incorporates other changes and revisions as well, the composition of September 1826 marks a vital stage in his development as a composer[*].

---

[*] The theme in D-flat major for trombones in the introduction was an imaginative leap in the dark. As he admitted later, at the time he had only a vague notion of the technique of the instrument. Having written the passage, he took it with a good deal of trepidation to show to one of the trombonists in the Opéra orchestra. The man told him that the passage should make a splendid effect, and that D flat was a key which suited the trombone admirably. This reassurance so delighted Berlioz that he went back to the Rue de la Harpe with his head in the clouds and, not looking where he was going, tripped and twisted his ankle.

He could feel the power growing in him. His opera, he told Edouard Rocher, was the best thing he had yet done. Only, he feared it might not be to the taste of the Odéon public, which Rossini's *Dame du lac* and Meyerbeer's *Marguerite d'Anjou* (the latest offerings) had hardly prepared for something so devilishly sombre and dramatic. But the libretto was as good as accepted, and they must proceed on the assumption that the Odéon would get its licence to perform new French operas. He had helped to organise a petition to the Arts Secretary, La Rochefoucauld, signed by all the young composers. They had not yet had a reply, but when it came it might be favourable, and he must be ready for that eventuality. During the autumn and early winter he continued to work at his score, revising it here and there and then getting down to the laborious job of copying out the orchestral parts for the possible run-through of some of the numbers which Bloc, the assistant conductor at the Odéon, had offered him in the event of official permission being granted.

At the end of 1826 Berlioz fell ill — perhaps with the throat infection which is a recurrent feature of his medical history; at any rate the illness was severe enough to make him spend several weeks in bed and interrupt work on the parts of *Les francs-juges*, and to worry his mother, who bombarded him with alarmed reproaches. When he had recovered he patiently tried to explain, in a letter to Nancy, why he had not got his cousin Alphonse Robert to attend him, instead of calling in doctors of unknown capabilities:[*] "Alphonse was busy at the time with new and lucrative appointments, on top of his work at the Hôtel-Dieu [the main general hospital of Paris]. He had two anatomy demonstrations a day, attended by quite a number of students. In addition he had several sick people in various parts of Paris to see to (one of whom needed regular visits), which was bringing him in a good deal. Thirdly, I didn't need him. So why make him waste his time when it was being so usefully employed?" He went on to give an edited description of his daily life:

> Now let me answer Papa's questions about what I'm doing. I have so much to do that every minute is taken up from seven in the morning, and only in the evening can I snatch a few moments' respite. The Odéon is on the point of getting authorisation to perform new operas, and I want to take advantage of this opening and be ready to be one of the first to submit my score. My opera was finished two months ago, and I'm working at copying out the parts of the numbers that I want to produce for the audition when the time comes. It's an immense labour which, combined with my harmony pupils, takes up the whole day. I've bought an alarm clock and get up every

---

[*] Who were probably invented to stop his mother fussing.

morning at 7, sometimes at 6. I'm finding it hard to accustom myself, and if it weren't for the uproar my clock makes I should never be able to get out of bed and set to work by the light of the lamp. I tell you this with the greatest reluctance; for I am perfectly well aware of the difficulties I have to overcome, and I would much rather not expose myself to the inevitable homily: "You see — you're killing yourself, and all for nothing, you will never make it, etc., etc." But I am also well aware that they're the normal difficulties of the first step, that all young men in every career have to face them and it has always been so, at least for those who don't wish to remain at the foot of the mountain.

Papa should have received, a few days ago, the fourth volume of Andras [clinical reports from the Charité Hospital] and *Le bon jardinier* [agricultural almanach]. Poor Crouillebois [bookseller, publisher of Dr Berlioz's *Mémoires sur les maladies chroniques*] has just lost his second wife.

Farewell, dear sister, try when you write to tone down your reprimands a little.

20 January 1827

The letter shows the ambiguous state of Hector's relations with his family, and his father's constantly vacillating tactics. Dr Berlioz continued to rely on him to purchase things he needed in the capital and pay for them out of the money he sent him, and this was duly done. The threat to give him nothing further in 1826 after the 150 francs sent in August had not been carried out. On the other hand Dr Berlioz was sticking to his declared intention of reducing his monthly allowance to 50 francs, and was sending it as irregularly as ever. His far more single-minded and determined son, on his side, was bent on bringing his father round to his way of thinking and convincing him of the reality of his vocation. He could not see — it was fortunate for him he could not — that it was not a question of convincing him, and that the more he proved himself as a composer the unhappier his beloved father became.

The next eight months — from January 1827 to the momentous arrival of the Shakespeare company from England in September — are particularly meagre in correspondence and in documentary evidence generally. It is as if the records themselves were marking time until the great event which set his land-locked existence on course for the open sea. Apart from a brief note to Léon Compaignon (librettist of the abortive operatic project *Richard en Palestine*), the next letter, also to Nancy, dates from June. In between we have merely two letters from Nancy to Hector (one of them an unfinished draft — Nancy, a diligent stylist, usually drafted her letters), in the first of which she acknowledges receipt of a large parcel apparently containing a human skull, and in the second of which she asks him to buy her a complete Racine like the one her father gave her the previous summer, in one volume, with gilt-edged pages, for a friend who is shortly to be married, with a morocco tag inside the binding inscribed "In token of a friendship as deathless as these immortal masterpieces". Otherwise there is only a note to Mme Berlioz from a young student, Alexandre Figuet, from the village next to La Côte, Beaurepaire, informing her that he is about to leave for Paris, carrying with him commissions for various Côtois in the capital, and wondering whether Madame has any for Monsieur her son, whose friend he has the pleasure of being: evidence, along with one or two other references, that Berlioz was still actively in touch with his childhood friends in Paris, even though their regular meetings in the pit at the Opéra had had to be suspended owing to his enforced attendance in the chorus at the Nouveautés.

Hector's letter of 4 June, like the January one, is partly taken up with a report of errands performed. But the tone is more relaxed and confident.

[...] I have to give Papa an account of his commissions. M. Baillière [medical bookseller] has given me the January bulletin, which, to avoid another error, Antoine Charbonnel is bringing with him. I've told Crouillebois that there is nothing more for us to sort out; he claims that by now Papa will have had the two volumes of Michaud [*History of the Crusades*]. As it's not impossible that he has, I thought it best not to send two more. I've not yet paid him what is owing to him, because my finances would not have stretched that far. Of the 200 francs which Papa sent me on 15 April and which I should have had on the 1st, I spent 28 francs for the subscription to the medical journal, 11 on your Racine, 11.50 which were due to Alphonse for Papa's commissions, 1.80 for the life of Béclard [anatomy professor at Angers], total 52 francs and a few cents. That left me 150 francs for April, May, and for June which has just begun and which I would not be able to get through if I paid Crouillebois.

Enough about finance. You never tell me about your reading. I think well enough of you to believe that you know your Walter Scott inside out — that giant of English literature; but Cooper — do you know Cooper, the American Scott? Although he doesn't equal or approach his model in characterisation and dialogue, one has to admit his pictures of untamed nature are admirable, and the main characters are full of interest. Among them is one who appears in three different books — the famous hunter Natty Bummpo, a unique figure, a European who from a taste for solitude has become virtually a savage, a philosopher of the wilderness. He appears first in *The Last of the Mohicans*, then in *The Pioneers* and finally in *The Prairie*. That's the order in which one should read the three novels. As you proceed you get more and more attached to the hunter, and though you know his death is coming — he's 90 — I can't describe how moving it is. *The Prairie* came out only a month ago, I devoured it straight off. I reached the end at 7 in the evening, and was still at the foot of one of the columns of the Panthéon in tears at 11 o'clock. I urge you to read all three of them [...]*

* James Fenimore Cooper was living in Paris at the time, in the Rue St Maur, Faubourg St

The letter to Nancy is silent on the subject of his meagre diet. His parents must have wondered anxiously how he managed to survive. They were not attempting precisely to starve him into submission; but they imagined he would grow increasingly disenchanted with the spartan existence he was forced to lead, and abandon his folly the sooner in consequence. They did not know of the 50 francs a month he was earning as a member of the chorus at the Nouveautés. He had, naturally, refrained from mentioning it.

The theatre opened finally, after more than one postponement, on 1 March. Every evening he betook himself wearily across the river to the Rue Vivienne and got dressed and made up for the show. From prudence as well as pride he let his fellow-lodger believe that he was giving lessons: if Charbonnel discovered what he was really doing, it would become known at La Côte and his family would find out. His close friends had been sworn to secrecy; but to minimise the risk of being recognised he made himself up as an old man. Sometimes the characteristic profile was disguised by a false nose. So at least the tradition handed down by his friends maintains; and though it has a slightly mythological ring there is nothing inherently improbable in it.

Despite general approval for the splendid and elegant design of the new theatre (the work of Debret, architect of the Opéra) and the presence of the Duchesse de Berry in one of the stage-boxes on the opening night, the Nouveautés' inaugural season did not start well, the public reaction being less than rapturous, according to the report on the season given in the *Almanach des spectacles*:

Germain, and his novels were issued almost simultaneously in French translation as they appeared. Berlioz remained attached to them in later life (his overture *Le corsair*, begun in the late 1840s, was at one point called *Le corsair rouge*, the French title of Cooper's *The Red Rover*). The image of the noble savage in communion with unspoilt nature, which Chateaubriand had made fashionable, had a powerful nostalgic appeal for Berlioz's generation. He invoked it in a letter to a friend in 1848, at a time when the Revolution appeared to have destroyed all hope of his making a living in France: "Like a savage I hold on to my freedom, I keep moving so long as the earth bears me and there are deer and moose in the woods; and if I suffer often from cold and hunger, exhaustion, sleepless nights and the ravages of the paleface, at least I can daydream in my own time beside the waterfalls and in the silent forests, and worship great Nature and thank God I still possess a feeling for its beauties." See also the Preface to the *Memoirs* (written in the same period as the letter), with its metaphor of the stoical Indian singing as the current sweeps him and his canoe over the cataract, and the note to Mendelssohn in the style of *The Last of the Mohicans*, on the occasion of their swapping batons in Leipzig in 1843: "To Chief Mendelssohn – Great chief! We are pledged to exchange tomahawks. Here is mine. It is rough-hewn. Yours too is plain. Only squaws and palefaces love ornate weapons. Be my brother; and when the Great Spirit sends us to the happy hunting-grounds, may our warriors hang our tomahawks side by side at the door of the council chamber."

1 March   *Fifteen and Twenty and Women*   Act 1 applauded, Act 2 booed.
          The Man with a Taste for Widows   [...] The authors were
          named despite the protests which broke out at the end.
2 March   *The Blacksmiths*   Qualified success.
3 March   *The Yellow Room*   A jealous husband stays the night with his
          wife at the inn of the Two Horns, in Room 13, which is
          done up in yellow. His suspicions aroused, he becomes
          incensed. The audience, which became even more so, would
          not allow the piece to finish.

Happily things took a turn for the better with *The Straw Man* ("success");
and *Experimental Husband*, *Grandma's Young Man*, *Paris and London* and *Mr
Jolly, the Singing Bailiff* continued the good work. By 10 March the *Journal
de Paris* was reckoning that three out of the first six novelties were
successes, which made quite a respectable beginning for the new company.

Occasionally some real music found its way into the repertory. A *Faust*
pasticcio which was in rehearsal during Berlioz's time at the Nouveautés
contained, along with pieces by the theatre's musical director Béancourt,
a chorus from Méhul's *Joseph*, part of a trio from Boieldieu's *Chapeau
rouge*, the prayer from *Robin des bois* and Spontini's bacchanal from *The
Danaids*; and the overture was nothing less than Weber's overture to
Euryanthe. But that was almost more of a penance than unmitigatedly bad
music: the context, not to mention the performance, degraded it. The
synopsis of the plot in the *Almanach des spectacles* gives a flavour of the
show: "Faust, whom deep knowledge has not brought corresponding
fortune, makes a pact with the devil (Mephistopheles) so as to get rich
and obtain the hand of the fair Marguerite, with whom he is in love; but
his secret becoming known, she shuns him. Anon Mephistopheles, overcome
by a power superior to his own, is forced to beg the aid of Faust, who
alone can deliver him. Faust insists on their pact being annulled.
Mephistopheles behaves like a decent devil, and the lovers are united."
From Fétis' account in the *Revue musicale* we get an idea of the impression
the Nouveautés made on a serious musician:

The performance of the music is very imperfect. The orchestra is incapable
of making the smallest effect, the cellos and the violins being especially
weak. In consequence the overture [*Euryanthe*], which is in any case a poor
piece [!], is painful to listen to. There are some talented players in the
orchestra; but nothing can be done without the necessary numbers. As to
the actors, they sing in the most curious manner, not excepting Mme Albert,
the Pasta of the place. She has warmth, and even a voice; but it does not
begin to be properly placed. The notes, though not exactly out of tune, are
not in tune either [...] and she lacks the first notion of vocalisation or of
phrasing. Mlle Miller [...] is excessively fond of pedal points. I will
willingly share her predilection when she has learnt how to manage them. It
would be unkind to discuss the singing of Casaneuve and Arnaud, and I

shall refrain. Bouffé appeared to be opening his mouth during the ensembles, but I cannot vouch that it was for the purpose of singing. In short, the whole thing reminded me of certain minor provincial theatres in which I have sometimes found myself, for my sins. The house, however, is full of people applauding vigorously.

The reluctant chorister stuck it for several months, though he later declared that the dreadfulness of most of the music he was obliged to sing would have sent him off his head if he had gone on much longer. What made the servitude worse — like the vision of unattainable paradise vouchsafed the souls of the damned in medieval theology — was that while he was chained to his oar at the Nouveautés normal musical life was going on only a few streets away, in the real opera houses. And it underlined the cruel facts of life that had driven him to such a grisly expedient. The same musical system which perpetrated the dismal offerings of the vaudeville theatre was denying *Les francs-juges* a hearing: the Odéon had still not been granted the hoped-for licence to perform new French operas.

We catch a reflection of this morose humour in an anonymous description of Berlioz the chorister which appeared ten years later in the *Musical World*, quoted by the English musician John Ella. Though the account was no doubt garbled and touched up in the retelling, it purports to come from a contemporary eyewitness. Berlioz (Ella writes)

was first known to my informant as a chorister in a minor theatre; his reserved manners made him unsocial and unpopular with his comrades; by the musicians of the band he was remarked as eccentric in appearance, always proficient in his duties, and yet anxious to elude particular notice. My informant from motives of curiosity sought the acquaintance of this recluse, and one day [they] adjourned to a neighbouring *estaminet* to discuss divers matters on music and sip the beverage of a "Demie tasse". The humble chorister produced from his pocket a bundle of MS. scores of descriptive overtures and dramatic scenes, and amidst the fumes of tobacco, the rattle of billiards and dominoes, endeavoured by singing the *motivi* of the various movements to interest his companion. When he arrived at a particular passage, the sedate and sullen chorister, having waxed warm and earnest in his gesticulations, exclaimed "Voilà! le climax! [*sic*]" and down went his fist, smashing all the crockery upon the table.

Ella's informant may well have been quite correct in referring to "descriptive overtures" in the plural, for the *Waverley* overture, which Berlioz wrote "soon after the overture to *Les francs-juges*" (*Memoirs*), most probably dates from the first half of this year (1827). By this time he "knew his Scott inside out"; but he must have identified particularly closely with the eponymous hero of *Waverley*, whose imagination in adolescence, like his own, had been so strong that "he would exercise for hours that internal sorcery by which past or imaginary events are presented in action, as it were, to the eye of the muser", and for whom "living in this ideal world became daily more delectable". The title page of the autograph manuscript of the overture bears as an epigraph, in English, two lines from the chivalric romantic poem by the young Waverley cited in chapter 5: "Dreams of love and lady's charms / Give place to honour and to arms". This is followed by a series of extracts, in Berlioz's hand, from the French translation of the novel, dealing successively with the hero's adolescent love of solitude and melancholy reverie, his embracing the family profession of soldier, his dancing with Flora McIvor to the music of the bagpipe in the Highland stronghold of her brother Fergus, his sense of intoxication, half fear, half ardour, on the field of Prestonpans at the moment of Bonnie Prince Charlie's attack, and the victorious charge of the Highlanders.

11

Frustrations of a Dramatist

―◆◆―

Berlioz had been a member of Antoine Reicha's counterpoint class at the Conservatoire for several months when he wrote the *Waverley* overture; but the work bears no particular evidence, profound or superficial, of Reicha's influence. It does not contain any greater amount of contrapuntal activity than the *Francs-juges* overture, composed the previous autumn. The most striking features of the music — the piquancy and energetic play of the rhythms, which makes it seem at times like a rehearsal for *Harold in Italy*, the panache and general air of high spirits (here and there oddly reminiscent of Rossini), the already characteristic linear scoring, and the awkward brusqueness of some of the harmonic progressions — are attributable to his own native individuality and the schooling it had had from Le Sueur, from which it was beginning to emancipate itself. Expressively as well as technically it is still the work of a prentice composer who has yet to achieve a fully assured personal style. The long, ardent cantilena for the cellos which is the subject of the slow opening section ("Dreams of love and lady's charms") is a fine early example of Berliozian extended melody, yet curiously elusive, in the last resort unmemorable, reminding us that the melodist of the *Eight Scenes from Faust* and the Fantastic Symphony will be the product of another year or two of self-criticism and private hard work. But so far as the Conservatoire is concerned *Waverley* would have been the same, you feel, if the composer had never set foot inside it except to immerse himself in the contents of its library.

Yet it would be a fundamental mistake to regard his enrolment in the Conservatoire as an irrelevance, a pure formality undertaken for the sake of playing the game and winning the prestigious and financially indispensable but artistically insignificant Prix de Rome — to see it, in fact, as a move strictly incidental to the development of the "maverick genius" who for better or worse was constitutionally incapable of learning anything from the official system of education and rejected it as vehemently as it rejected him. Berlioz the outsider, the musical dissenter, the autodidact — that is the traditional view. But it is a misconception. It confuses his trenchant criticism of the Conservatoire with what he actually did while he was there. He thought Cherubini's pedagogy narrow and hidebound, and disagreed radically with its canonisation of fugue as the "foundation of all true composition", as well as with its general insistence on the sanctity of the "rules". At the same time he was not going to pass up the chance to profit from it. To have done so would have gone flatly against his character and his acknowledged intention of making up for lost time and learning all he could, from whatever source. Because the most important artistic lessons of his apprenticeship — Gluck, Spontini, Shakespeare, Weber, Beethoven — lay mostly outside the scope and ken of the Conservatoire, it does not follow that the Conservatoire gave him nothing. His subsequent attacks on the blinkered, reactionary ethos of the place are so amusing, and also have so strong a ring of truth, that they have distracted attention from the other side of the picture. If he was cynical about the regulations of the Prix de Rome, that perfect reflection of the spirit of Conservatoire academicism, he had the sense — once his initial scepticism had worn off — to realise that Reicha's course in counterpoint and fugue offered him something he needed. He says as much. "I learnt a lot from him in a short time"; Reicha was "an admirable teacher of counterpoint". He was extremely clear (Berlioz goes on); and "unlike most teachers, he hardly ever failed to give his pupils the reason for the rules he recommended to them, wherever that was possible". His "respect for tradition stopped well short of idolatry".

This was Berlioz looking back on his experience of Reicha's class after an interval of twenty years. But earlier, too, in an article written in 1835 on the occasion of Reicha's election to the Institute ("an act of belated justice", as he called it), he paid tribute to the depth and clarity of his instruction, and above all to the progressive spirit that animated his teaching, "although he is a professor at the Conservatoire".*

The proof of Berlioz's indebtedness is in his music. Reicha's influence is evident not merely in those fugal or quasi-fugal passages where the theme is so devised that it ends a step higher or lower than it began (the "Judex crederis" in the Te Deum and the octet "Châtiment effroyable" in *The Trojans* are Reicha-inspired), but generally in the basically polyphonic character of his music. Berlioz's formal fugues, except for the burlesque "Amen" in *The Damnation of Faust*, tend to be monolithic and rather stiff (though apt for their dramatic purpose); but he is a master of free fugato, and his works are full of it: Faust's monologue "Sans regrets", the Convoi funèbre in *Romeo*, the first forty bars of *Harold in Italy*, the opening of the Royal Hunt and Storm, the Offertorium in the Grande Messe des Morts — the list could be multiplied. Reicha did not change anything in his pupil; but, like Le Sueur, he reinforced, made more articulate, a

---

* Reicha in his quirky, cerebral way was something of a pioneer, writing whole movements in 5/4 time and predicting the coming of microtones.

natural predisposition. His advent, like Le Sueur's, was providential and the pupil came to realise the fact and to benefit richly from it.

At first the tolerant teacher found his new student something of a trial. Berlioz started the course in an uppish mood. Unlike most of the other students, who were taking the course in the normal prescribed way as a preliminary to studying composition proper, he had been doing that for over four years, had written the overture to *Les francs-juges*, had had a Mass publicly performed and praised by the newspapers two years before. Relations with Le Sueur had accustomed him to free discussion and the latitude of disagreement. The old man, too, had encouraged him to have a by no means negligible idea of his own worth; or rather, he himself knew he still had a long way to go, and did not need telling so by some dusty pedagogue. Adjustment to the more formal discipline of an institutional class was difficult at first, and he annoyed Reicha with his endless challenging questions. Gradually, however, he relaxed and settled down, and came to see that his teacher was a man of sterling sense and independence of mind, whose lessons were models of lucidity and thoroughness and whose published manuals and treatises on composition, which Berlioz consulted in the library, were marked by a rare intelligence.

Berlioz's greatest progress under Reicha's tuition probably came in the latter part of the period of about twenty months — autumn 1826 to summer 1828 — that he spent in his class. Cherubini's laconic reports on his showing in the half-yearly counterpoint exams graduate from the "undistinguished" of July 1827 to "his fugue is passable" in January 1828. But the immediate benefits of Reicha's teaching were apparent — notwithstanding Cherubini's lack of enthusiasm — by July 1827, when Berlioz passed the preliminary concours d'essai for the Prix de Rome. Indeed, as he told Nancy in a letter written just before he left his lodgings to incarcerate himself in the Institute for the statutory three weeks of the competition, his fugue had been the only one out of the four submitted fugues to get the "answer" right. Even Guiraud, last year's second-prize winner and tipped to win, had got it wrong, though he had partially redeemed himself by other qualities. "So by rights only two of us should have got through.* In fact we are four. The other two, both pupils of Berton, were admitted despite vigorous opposition from Cherubini and Lesueur. There you have a sample of how judgment works at the Institute. I'm resigned to it. They say I shall get second prize. If I do, I shall accept it, but there will be no great glory in my having vanquished my two opponents, they have not got the remotest suspicion what dramatic music is."

At 3.30 that afternoon, 28 July 1827, the music section of the Académie

---

* This would not have been unprecedented. In 1821 only two of the candidates who presented themselves passed the preliminary stage.

des Beaux-Arts met again at the Institute to choose by vote the text of the cantata. Choice fell on "The Death of Orpheus". The four candidates were brought in to the committee room and the poem was dictated to them by the venerable Permanent Secretary of the Academy, Quatremère de Quincy. They were then conducted to their respective loges, the tiny attic room, equipped with bed, table, chair, piano and commode, which would be their home and prison cell for the next three weeks.*

Life at the Institute was not all work and no play. Every evening at six the old porter Pingard unlocked them and let them out, and they descended to the main courtyard, where for the next two hours, under Pingard's supervision, they were allowed to receive visitors. In Pingard himself Berlioz discovered a rich character, an original with a sharp eye for the foibles and misprisions of his fellow-creatures, who in his rôle as Institute usher had many opportunities to observe what went on behind the scenes at the green baize table where the various academies held their deliberations, and who did not need much prompting to be gratifyingly indiscreet about it. In his youth Pingard had been a sailor and, to Berlioz's delight, turned out to have been all over the Indian Archipelago and the East Indies − Java, Sumatra, the Philippines, Timor, the very region that had fascinated the young Hector as he pored over his father's atlas − and was more than ready to talk about them and about the native girls, on whom he was an authority. They had many long, absorbing conversations together, which relieved the monastic concentration of the competitor's existence.

Candidates could also let off steam with games in the courtyard, and by holding convivial dinners to which friends from the outside world could come without let or hindrance. On the other hand it was laid down − with characteristic incongruity − that every letter, newspaper, book or article of clothing addressed to the candidates which came though the postern gate of the Institute must be scrutinised for anything it contained that might possibly be useful to them in the composition of their cantatas, as though the packages were so many game pies, with file or rope-ladder concealed under the crust to aid in the immured competitor's escape.

In his subsequent articles on the subject Berlioz had such satirical fun at the expense of the Prix de Rome that one is tempted to assume that his picture of it is a caricature. But there was no need to exaggerate. The organisation of the competition and the thinking behind it were quite as muddled and fuddy-duddyish as he claimed. Even his assertion that the cantata's poem usually began "E'en now doth rosy-fingered dawn appear" or "E'en now doth Nature greet returning day", etc. is founded

---

* Three of these loges survive to this day, under the rafters above the Institute Library. In one of them can still be seen the pencilled graffiti of several generations of candidates, including one signed by Massenet.

on fact. The openings of the 1822, 1823 and 1825 cantatas were all sunrises: "Le jour a pénétré sous cet épaix ombrage" (*Geneviève de Brabant*, 1822); "L'aube a doré les monts d'une clarté nouvelle" (*Thisbe*, 1823); "La fraîcheur du matin ranime la nature / Et l'aurore naissante, éclairant mon réveil" (*Ariane à Naxos*, 1825). Only 1821, among recent years, had offered a sunset instead.

The declared purpose of the competition was to identify the most promising student in order to award him a grant which would enable him to devote himself exclusively to composition for the next five years; the means was a large-scale work for voice and orchestra. Logically, it is difficult to quarrel with Berlioz's claim that a four-part fugue was not the best way of finding out which of the candidates were the likeliest to make a good attempt at it. The concours d'essai tested your ability to write a fugue; it did not test your ability to compose a dramatic cantata.

Whatever Berlioz's opinion of it, he had played the game sufficiently to write an adequate fugue. This time he had cleared the first obstacle and was through. Now that that was over he could get down to the serious business of the competition. He would let himself go and give the Academy what it asked for − a dramatic cantata.

He miscalculated disastrously. In his naïvety he quite failed to appreciate the true nature of the game. It was not a question of "what dramatic music is". A real dramatic cantata was not what the Academy wanted. The rules demanded rather that the aspirant composer suppress his instincts, not give full vent to them. This was a lesson that Berlioz finally learned only after three unsuccessful attempts. In 1828, with *Herminie*, he kept himself on a tighter rein and won second prize, only to throw away his advantage the following year with *Cléopâtre*, a composition of perilous originality which threw the "grave and reverend signors" of the jury into a flutter of bewildered alarm. Only in 1830, with the blameless *Sardanapale*, did he observe both the spirit and the letter of the law and win first prize.

Orphée, though less unconventional than *Cléopâtre* (as well as revealing a composer less technically assured than Berlioz had become by 1829), went much too far. The key to the Prix de Rome, the clue to the way to approach the composition of the cantata, lay not in the nature of the action represented, which was invariably tragic and usually ended in violent death, but in the vapid and conventional language in which it was enshrined. Cleopatra might clasp the asp to her bosom, Sardanapalus might set fire to his palace and perish in the flames, Herminia might gallop desperately off, clad in warrior's armour, to the rescue of her lover, and Orpheus meet a gory end at the hands of the priestesses of Bacchus: the poet saw to it that they did so with decorum.

Right from the start, however, Berlioz misread the signs. He set about his delicate task with fatal enthusiasm, behaving not like an examination candidate but like an established dramatist with full authority over the text and the right to adapt it to his own conception. In his cantata the poem's opening eight-line recitative was cut in half, the second group of four lines becoming Orpheus' first aria. The prescribed first aria disappeared, along with the ensuing recitative and the second aria (in which Orpheus was supposed to pay further tribute to the universal power of his lute). As for the third and final aria, the dramatic potential of the situation — Orpheus' vain plea to Apollo, his piteous appeal for mercy, his last dying cries of "Eurydice" — was realised by the addition of a four-part chorus of Bacchantes, singing a text supplied by the composer. The stylised, formal expression of distress gave way to an ensemble of considerable force and fury, in which the music was driven forward by a remorseless rhythmic ostinato (associated from the beginning of the cantata with the Bacchantes) and Orpheus' despairing voice was gradually overwhelmed by the weight of the chorus and orchestra (reinforced by cornets, trombones and cymbals). At the end a vivid diminuendo depicted the murderous rout sweeping into the distance. Not content with this display of "what dramatic music is", Berlioz added a highly imaginative poetic epilogue, inspired by Virgil's account of the death of Orpheus in the *Georgics* — an addition which, as he later remarked in a classic understatement, was "not required". While the sighing wind touched the strings of the abandoned lute and the "swift Hebrus" flowed on between its deserted banks, a shepherd of the Thracian mountains recalled the melody of Orpheus' song on his pipe.[*] The end of the work was thus made to balance the pastoral evocation of its opening pages. By reshaping the text and pruning its worst redundancies Berlioz had extracted a viable, self-contained scene, formed of two contrasting but complementary halves, to which he proceeded to add the subtitle "Monologue and Bacchanal".

This was magnificent, but it was not the Prix de Rome. How the jury viewed these liberties is not recorded (though it is notable that the following year Berlioz set the given text virtually unaltered). Quite apart from that, there was more than enough to sink him when the moment came for the cantatas to be performed at the Institute on 25 August 1827. It was not merely that the score's more daring tone-colours (including muted trombones for the echo of the eerie chords which suggest the Bacchantes drawing near, and the first use of cornets in a classical orchestra) necessarily came to nothing when reproduced by the makeshift piano accompaniment which the Academy[†] deemed sufficient for the

---

[*] This epilogue was incorporated four years later in *Lélio*, while the Orpheus theme became the basis for another movement in the same work, the Chant de bonheur.

[†] The Académie des Beaux-Arts was one of the five academies which made up the Institute.

purpose. Unlike its rivals, the whole score was conceived directly in orchestral terms, as well as being written with a rhythmic verve and metrical freedom which could not but floor the official accompanist. From the evocative introduction for orchestra — an enchanted grove echoing with bird song yet disturbed by an undercurrent of menace — to the concluding epilogue, it needed much more careful and sensitive adaptation to the keyboard than was practicable in such conditions.

No doubt during the week that intervened between the end of the competition and the first meeting of the jury Berlioz did what he could to instil an understanding of the music's style into the accompanist, Rifaut, as well as to coach his chosen tenor, Alexis Dupont. In the event, it was not really a question of style. Rifaut broke down completely in the Bacchanal and the performance fell apart. The jury, in embarrassment and consternation, consulted among themselves; whereupon Berton declared that the piece was simply unperformable; not even an orchestra would be able to make sense of it. And there the matter rested. Guiraud was awarded first prize and commended (the written record states) for his cantata's "sound declamation, correct style, which excludes neither freedom of imagination nor charm, a voice part well adapted to the situations indicated by the words", and in general, "in both voice and orchestra, very satisfying dramatic expression". Berton's pupils Gilbert and Despréaux — Berlioz's negligible rivals for second place — came second and third respectively. The judges decided to exercise their discretion and award an extra second prize to Despréaux, for the "elegance of his voice part" and the general "soundness of his composition, which is not lacking in originality". Of the fourth cantata there is no mention.

In theory, there was still a chance to save the situation. The music section of the Academy delivered only the so-called "jugement préparatif" or preliminary judgment which, though usually confirmed, could be reversed at the joint meeting of all the different sections of the Academy — architects, sculptors, painters and engravers as well as musicians — held a week later, at which the competing cantatas were performed for the second time. Three years before, in 1824, the music section had decided not to award the first prize, only for the Academy in full session to award it to a candidate who had not been placed at all the first time round. Berlioz would have this system to thank for his second prize the following year (1828), when he won it after failing in the preliminary judgment. But for there to be any chance of that happening now with *Orphée*, he would have had to have an orchestra at his disposal, or at least a gifted and willing accompanist who could make his score really sound at the piano.

The reality was only too different. Rifaut was quite incapable of doing anything with it. It would almost certainly be another massacre. What was the point of going through the whole humiliating business again? So, when the Academy met in full session on 1 September and listened to the cantatas, though it modified the judgment of the music section, preferring Despréaux to Gilbert in second place, there was no major reversal. In fact, only three of the four cantatas were performed. The irregularity was explained in the written record of the proceedings: "The fourth cantata not being susceptible of performance with piano accompaniment, with the consent of the Academy it was withdrawn from the competition by the author."

Berton rubbed in the lesson with patronising candour when he met Berlioz a few weeks later: he was entirely mistaken if he thought he could do something new in music. "My dear man, there is no such thing." Berlioz bowed respectfully, ground his teeth, and vowed that next time he would write for "a little bourgeois orchestra in two or three parts" which could lose nothing when reduced for the keyboard; the piano, for the orchestral composer, was a guillotine which chopped off the aristocrat's head and from which only the poor had nothing to fear.

It had been simple-minded of Berlioz to expect the Academy to react otherwise; but his resentment was not the less bitter. He felt oppressed by failure. Nothing was going right. He had gone back to the Nouveautés — he had had to the moment the three weeks of the competition were over and he was released from the Institute — but the drudgery of it now seemed worse than ever.

In the final week of August, in this mood of anger and disillusionment, he went down with an acute quinsy. The condition — a concentration of pus around one of the tonsils — is peculiarly painful and debilitating. When the abscess seeps into the surrounding tissues the whole throat together with the chewing and swallowing muscles becomes inflamed to an excruciating degree. The body's temperature may rise to 104, the pain spread to the ear on the side affected, and the jaw clamp shut. As the quinsy swells, the already sore tissues are stretched intolerably; it becomes impossible to swallow, and the saliva is left to dribble down one's chin. In extreme cases breathing itself becomes difficult, and the only remedy is to have the abscess lanced by a doctor. One evening, alone in his room in the Rue de la Harpe, maddened by the pain, scarcely able to breathe and weakened by lack of food and drink to the point where he imagined he might die, he stuck a penknife down his throat and operated on himself. The relief was instantaneous. He began to get better.

Shortly afterwards came another shift in his fortunes, from an unexpected quarter. His father got to hear of his illness. If the news of the Prix de Rome débâcle had hardened his attitude and made him resolve on sterner measures, he now changed his mind. Alarmed, he hastened to restore Hector's allowance to its former level. Berlioz promptly resigned from the Nouveautés. The quinsy had not been without its blessings.

His illness was the culmination of a summer of disappointments. An even more serious setback than the Prix de Rome débâcle was the frustration of his ambitions for *Les francs-juges* at the Odéon. The theatre had finally failed to get government authorisation to perform new French operas; a year's intensive effort, all the lobbying of the previous summer, autumn and winter, had come to nothing. In the meantime some sort of audition — the eventuality for which he had spent so many weeks copying the parts — may possibly have taken place under the auspices of the friendly Bloc; or perhaps the overture only was tried out. Though it is far from certain, it may be this that Berlioz referred to in his letter of 4 June 1827 to Nancy, when he spoke of "a success that I had recently with an instrumental composition" — clearly not a public performance, which would have earned more than this passing mention. Shortly afterwards the Odéon closed for repairs and redecoration. By the time it re-opened in the middle of August, all hopes of a production for his opera were at an end.

However disheartening, the ministerial No was in line with the principle of rigid demarcation — a legacy of Napoleon — which controlled the Parisian theatre. New French operas were the province of the Opéra and the Opéra-Comique. The Odéon's licence entitled it to perform foreign works (duly Frenchified, like *Robin des bois*) or pasticcios — musical compilations adapted to dramas in the public domain — of which Castil-Blaze's *La forêt de Sénart* was a typical example. The privileges of the major theatres were protected vigilantly. Strict rules laid down not only what kind of music the others were allowed to perform but also how much. Minor theatres which stepped outside their bounds were disciplined. The vaudeville version of *Faust* which (as mentioned above) was in rehearsal at the Nouveautés during Berlioz's choristership was postponed and subjected to revision as the result of a complaint from the director of the Opéra-Comique that it contained more music than the regulations permitted; and within a week of the Nouveautés' opening, one show, *The Man with a Taste for Widows*, had been banned from the repertory on the grounds that it was not a vaudeville but an opera. Despite periodic attempts to break it the system continued, and survived the July Revolution.* As it was, opera accounted for only about a third of the Odéon's performances; and so far from being able to widen its scope the company suffered a gradual diminution of its musical activities. Within two years, after a series of financial and administrative crises, its orchestra would be reduced to wind instruments only, opera would disappear from the repertory, and the conductor Bloc, Berlioz's friend and champion, would

---

* In 1835 a production of *Othello* at the Porte St Martin, with Frédérick Lemaître as the Moor, was stopped on the first night shortly before the curtain was due to go up, when the police served a writ on the manager, enjoining him not to contravene his licence by staging a work which "belonged" to the Théâtre-Français.

leave the company. There were no further prospects for a young composer there.

This was what Mme Branchu had meant when she warned him of the fearsome difficulties of the composer's career in France and declared that no son of hers would ever take it up if she could help it. But there was no turning back now. And whatever the obstacles, the opera house remained the goal. The Prix de Rome, in comparison, was a matter of tactics. If in order to win the prize it was necessary to compose a cantata devoid of individuality, of anything as subversive as an idea, so be it. He would do so. But the theatre was what counted. It was not only a young composer's route to success — it was the natural ambition that Berlioz's outlook and training had taught him to strive for. Hence a major theme of these years: the quest for an acceptable libretto.

We catch repeated glimpses of this preoccupation in the scanty correspondence that has survived. Subjects referred to at various times include *Atala, Robin Hood, The Death of Hercules* and *Hamlet*. There were undoubtedly others too that have left no trace. Since most of the littérateurs and would-be authors he was in contact with lived in Paris, discussions were conducted face to face and there was no need to write letters.

The one among these projects that we know about in any detail, because work on it had to be carried on by correspondence, is *Richard en Palestine*, the opéra-comique based on Scott's *The Talisman*. The librettist, Léon Compaignon, was working at the Assize Court in Chartres. Berlioz and Compaignon presumably talked over the plan of the opera when the latter was in Paris, and agreed on a scenario and a general method of treatment, which Compaignon took back to Chartres. Two versions of the resultant libretto have been preserved — Compaignon's first effort and the revision he produced after three months of painstaking correspondence. They do not say a lot for his literary and dramatic abilities. Berlioz struggled gamely, but in the end his enthusiasm for the subject, and his anxiety lest others should get in ahead of them and use it first, had to yield to his recognition that this particular treatment of it was a dead duck.

The letters are of interest, however, as showing Berlioz at grips with practical problems of dramaturgy, prosody and diction.

30 May 1826 [...] King of France's song: "bouclier"/"imposant"/ "voyant" — three successive masculine endings: impossible to set well to music [...] Richard's romance: the last two lines of each couplet are suitable neither for Richard nor for music. He has no need to speak of his childhood, having other more recent memories to recall [...] "Puisse-t-il tomber sous ses coups/Et succomber sous son épée": that is saying the same thing twice. Also, in music you should never conclude an energetic piece with a feminine ending. Try to end the last line with "coups" instead of "épée". [...]

3 June [...] Richard should not be made to speak continually of death [...] The two lines, "Oui, la vengeance etc./Vengeons-nous etc." are not necessary — remove them. You know La Fontaine's fable: "... it went a little better,/Then well, till all was perfect to the letter". So — patience!

29 June [...] I agree with you about the last verse of the invocation. Change it for me — keep the idea, but make it even more menacing if you can: the juxtaposition will bring out the gentleness of the prayer admirably. I also think you should not begin the chorus with "*Que* la gloire etc." You have already made use of that construction too much in several other numbers. Don't be afraid of going to the opposite extreme from the opéra-comique genre. If you think about it, ours is very much a grand-opera subject; moreover, Pixérécourt [director of the Opéra-Comique] far prefers the grand style, I'm reliably informed [...] Don't on any account write me a ballad or romance or anything light for Blondel. It's a vitally important piece. Give him something inspired in the wild, dreamy Ossianic vein of the old bards.

5 July [...] As for the Bard's song, it needs redoing. It's more or less the right style. But don't make him address his harp or sing the praises of the King. Those are clichés. There should be no mention of hunting either. If you can get hold of Marchangy's *La gaule poétique* you will find bardic songs in prose that are what we want; you'll only have to put them into verse [...]

24 July [...] The quartet is good, I'm very pleased with it as a whole — only I must point out that since all the characters in it are Christian they must not refer to "the gods" [...] The Bard's piece won't do as it is: it's too long and bombastic. You must steer a middle course. And it's not the right verse form for such a piece. For the situation, here is what I think would be good. Blondel must know that the knight called Kenneth is the Prince of Scotland in disguise [...] It would be a good thing to have him sing an allegorical ballad on Kenneth's situation — his disguise, his valour — in the style of the old ballads, which are simply narratives of old feats. Blondel thus recounts Kenneth's history under the guise of the tale of an antique knight, from his departure incognito from Scotland to his marriage to his beloved. The truth will be perceived only when the King learns from the despatches which Blondel has brought how things really are. You see that by underlining the knight's story a little, without making it obvious what is going to happen to Kenneth, one could do something rather striking [...]

13 September We must not present [the libretto] as it is now. It would be rejected without any doubt. There are a mass of things that need improving [...]

3 February 1827 I took your manuscript to M. Saint Ange. But as it wasn't possible for me to call on him at the time you suggested, I simply had it delivered to him. If, as you say, he is accustomed to this kind of literature he will see for himself what is wrong with your work. I should like him in particular to carry out a general revision of your verse. None of the main numbers are suitable for music, and they are not poetic enough. It is obvious that the scene where Richard fells the assassin with a footstool must

be removed. It's all right in the novel. "But there are things which in its wisdom Art/Offers the ear but keeps from sight apart."[*] The reason why the fanatic wants to murder the King would have to be explained more clearly. I must stop, I'm terribly busy. I'll write to you at greater length another time.

There are no further letters from Berlioz to Compaignon. No music has survived; even if some was sketched, probably none was composed: the libretto never got to the stage of being ready for it. Not long afterwards a pasticcio "imitated" from *Ivanhoe* was performed at the Odéon, with a score compiled from assorted works of Rossini; but the opera that was to be "worthy of Walter Scott" was still-born.

---

[*] Bossuet, *Art poétique.*

12

Les francs-juges

Given the confidence with which Berlioz handles literary questions in the letters to Compaignon, and given his natural ability, it may seem curious that it did not occur to him to try his hand at writing his librettos himself. Another twenty years would elapse before he did so, with *The Damnation of Faust*, and then only under the pressure of necessity. In the meantime, though he took an active part in devising the texts of *Benvenuto Cellini* and *Romeo and Juliet*, he left the writing of them to bona fide men of letters, as though the fabrication of verses for music were by definition something beyond his scope and capacity. *The Damnation of Faust* itself was entrusted, in the first instance, to a journalist of no very obvious talent; it was only when the composition of the music acquired a momentum of its own and began to outrun its text that Berlioz, then on tour in Central Europe and therefore inaccessible, was forced to become his own librettist — with the result that, having found it well within his powers, he wrote his remaining dramatic texts himself. But until then he seems to have assumed as a matter of course that writing the poem was outside his province. He remarks in the *Memoirs* (apropos of his initial hesitations about writing musical criticism) that he never felt much confidence that he could do something until he had actually tried his strength at it. In this case there was the weight of custom to reinforce a natural diffidence. The musician had always gone to the poet for his text. Each had his rôle to play. It was part of the order of things. Composers generally were not men of wide education and culture but specialists and to some extent artisans. Berlioz, though highly cultivated, well-read and articulate, accepted the traditional division of powers unquestioningly. In Germany, where Romanticism was active a whole generation before the movement took hold in France, it was less unheard of for a composer to combine the functions of musician and poet. E.T.A. Hoffmann wrote the texts for several of his stage works. Hoffmann, however, was at least as much a writer by profession as a musician. Wagner, who wrote all his own texts (and whose ideal of the Gesamtkunstwerk, the comprehensive work uniting many different art-forms, presupposed a single author), thought of himself to begin with as a budding poet and playwright before deciding

definitely to take up music. Even in Germany a composer with as unmistakable a literary talent as Weber could enter into a long and ultimately
frustrating partnership with the hapless Helmina von Chezy, who was a
shadow of the writer he was, and never think to relieve her of the task
and write the libretto of *Euryanthe* himself. And though it took Berlioz a
long time to reach the point, he was actually one of the first French
composers to follow Hoffmann's and Wagner's example and break with
the tradition.

The uncertainty of the young Berlioz's literary judgment is revealed
when we turn from *Richard en Palestine* to *Les francs-juges*: his incisive
criticism of Compaignon contrasts strangely with the attitude of deference
he assumes before Humbert Ferrand's superior ability. Berlioz was delighted with his friend's libretto and seems not to have doubted that it
was a very fine piece of work. Yet it is difficult to disagree with the
opinion pronounced by the Opéra jury when a revised version was read
to them in 1829, that it is long-winded and obscure. Ferrand's cloudy,
convoluted language repeatedly befogs the purpose of the words. Even
when reading them one is far from sure what they mean.

The action too, though in fact quite simple, is hard to decipher.
Important elements in the plot are introduced in offhand asides and then
apparently forgotten until they pop up several scenes later. The characters'
motives, why they are where they are, or even where they actually are, and
what they are up to when they are not there, are often inscrutable. Is
Arnold, nephew of the splendidly named usurper Olmerik and son of the
rightful but murdered ruler of Brisgaw, indeed being held prisoner in
Olmerik's dungeons, as Olmerik says he is and as Amélie, Arnold's childhood friend and destined bride (vaguely described as "a princess"), firmly
and fearfully believes? We discover almost casually that there is not a word
of truth in it when the man himself turns up safe and sound among a troupe
of gipsies, but not before the credulous Amélie has agreed to marry
Olmerik as the price of her lover's freedom. Yet here is Amélie, apparently
on the day of her wedding to the tyrant, able with complete impunity to
leave the castle, accompanied only by a duenna, and wander through the
forest, where she duly runs into Arnold. Their ensuing encounter is
remarkable for obscurity of idea and expression, though Arnold's bemused
condition may be explicable by his having just been summoned to a
midnight tryst by a cloaked and hooded figure in black — an emissary of
the Francs-juges, the members of the dreaded secret tribunal (a fact
which, however, we are left to divine for ourselves). In the end Arnold
with unexplained docility turns up in the sinister moonlit cavern which is
the Francs-juges' meeting place, escorted by his "false(?)" friend
Conrad — a pivotal but characteristically shadowy figure who is confusingly
both a Franc-juge and on the side of justice and mercy. Arnold is
condemned to be crushed to death in the arms of a huge bronze statue
which, worked by hidden springs, is employed by the Francs-juges to

dispose of their victims. But the ritual of condemnation is so protracted that before Arnold can meet his fate the soldiers of the Holy Roman Empire, whom we heard of briefly in the opening scene of the opera as an apparent threat to Olmerik's rule but who have not been mentioned since, burst into the cavern and overpower the Francs-juges, and it is Olmerik that the statue devours, before itself going up in flames.

One can imagine Berlioz the music critic having some fun with this kind of thing in his later years. Yet, turgid though it is, the libretto has some points in its favour: a certain farouche energy, much contrast of colour, and an atmosphere of a vaguely medieval sort in tune with the reawakened interest in those remote "barbaric" centuries that marks emergent Romanticism. The secret Vehmic tribunals of late medieval Germany, first described by Goethe in his novel *Götz von Berlichingen*, were one of a number of related subjects that appealed to the fashionable appetite for Gothic gloom. Scott himself paid ironic tribute to it in the introductory opening chapter of his first novel, *Waverley* (1814): "[...] had my title borne 'Waverley, a Romance from the German', what head so obtuse as not to image forth a profligate abbot, an oppressive duke, a secret and mysterious association of Rosycrucians and Illuminati, with all their properties of black cowls, caverns, daggers, electrical machines, trapdoors, and dark lanterns?" The list is almost a prescription for *Les francs-juges*.

Berlioz and Ferrand may have got the idea for their opera from seeing Lamartelière's *Les francs-juges, ou les tems de la barbarie*. The play, which contained incidental music, was revived at the Ambigu-Comique in 1823, and published the following year in a series called *Chefs-d'œuvre du répertoire des mélodrames*. It included a meeting of a tribunal the details of which are similar to those of Ferrand's final scene. A footnote in the published text cites the *Histoire du tribunal secret* by the Baron de Bock (1801) as the source of the procedures dramatised in the play. And in the same year as the publication of the play, 1824, a book by François Loève-Veimars appeared under the title *Précis de l'histoire des tribunaux secrets dans le nord d'Allemagne*.

Quite apart from the specific theme of the sinister secret court – which, though it overshadows the opera, occupies only a small part of the action – the plot conformed to conventional Romantic models of the kind lately made popular by Scott's medieval romances. All in all it was thoroughly topical. Unfortunately Ferrand, lacking first-hand theatrical experience and any sense of communication in the theatre, any judgment of timing, was unable to put it into clear and cogent dramatic form. You can see why the libretto, though apparently acceptable to the Odéon, was turned down by the Opéra. But you can also see why it appealed so strongly to the youthful Berlioz.

Of the five complete numbers that are all that survive of the 1826 opéra-comique version of *Les francs-juges*, none is at once so assured and so characteristic as the overture; there is no one piece that sounds from beginning to end like Berlioz and like no one else, as does every one of the *Eight Scenes from Faust*, composed a couple of years later. The influence of French opera of the Revolution and Empire – Méhul, Cherubini, Spontini among others – is not yet absorbed into a fully personal style (not surprisingly, considering how short a time he had been a serious student of composition). Consequently the melodic writing is rather anonymous. There is also a certain amount of harmonic gaucheness, though mostly of the kind we encounter in the works of Berlioz's models. What is remarkable about the surviving numbers of *Les francs-juges* is, first, the thoroughly assured and resourceful handling of an orchestra of modest size (smaller than the forces for which the Mass was scored) and, second and even more striking, the powerful sense of movement. The first section of the duet (modelled on the duet "Gardez-vous de la jalousie" in Méhul's *Euphrosine et Coradin*), in which Olmerik and his henchman Christiern resolve to have Arnold murdered, has the stiffness of gait, vehemence of manner and irregularity of phraselength found in much French Revolutionary opera. As the tempo quickens, however, the music begins to loosen up, to vary its constant dotted rhythm and move more supply and athletically; and the final part, long on paper (170 bars) but swift and exhilarating in performance, is a feat of sustained violence remarkable in a composer of such limited experience. The skill with which variations in the stress and the rhythmic pulsation, abrupt contrasts of dynamics, alterations in the vocal line between long legato and short, panting staccato phrases, syncopations of instrumental colour as well as beat, and brief, carefully placed explosions of the full orchestra are used separately or together to propel the duet forward in an ever more furious momentum, is masterly. Berlioz was understandably pleased with his "Fanaticism Duet". He described it as "foaming with rage" ("écumant de rage"), and the claim is not exaggerated. It is a vivid depiction of two people driven by a consuming hatred and fear. The characters may be shadowy, but their feelings leap out and grab us by the throat.*

Even at its most impersonal the music of *Les francs-juges* knows what it is doing and where it is going. It believes in itself, in its ability to convey the scene and create the required dramatic effect; it moves purposefully from point to point; each piece, however different in character, mood and pace, has a clearly perceived and projected shape. This is as true of the lilting, airy Shepherds' Chorus with its cheerful Alpine tunes and its picturesque effects of space and sudden shafts of bright colour – evocative of the broad mountain valley of the music's setting – as it is of the baleful hymn in which the hooded Francs-juges assembled in their underground cavern invoke the tribunal's ominous rites.

---

* At one point, in the second bar of a sustained unison, the singers are directed to draw their daggers and advance to the footlights.

On the face of it the score might be thought to show Berlioz emerging from his Classical tutelage and coming into the orbit of Romanticism. The historical subject, the Gothic setting, the contrast between the oppressive world of superstition represented by the secret court and its subterranean forest lair and the happy, untroubled outdoor existence of the gipsies and shepherds which Arnold shares but cannot fully enjoy, and one or two Weberish touches of orchestral colour and rhythm — all this would seem to suggest that *Der Freischütz*, the modern Romantic opera par excellence, was having its due effect, aided by *Preciosa*, the dramatisation of a Cervantes short story with incidental music by Weber, a version of which was put on by Castil-Blaze at the Odéon at the end of 1825 under the title of *Les bohémiens* (*The Gipsies*). Throughout 1825 Berlioz was immersing himself in *Freischütz*, or as much of it as was available (and though Castil-Blaze had taken gross liberties with it, a certain amount had survived unscathed and was well played by the enthusiastic young Odéon orchestra). What more natural than that it should leave its imprint on the score he composed the following year with the same theatre in mind?

Yet the striking thing about *Les francs-juges*, when we examine it, is how little the score reveals of the influence of Weber and of Romanticism generally, how comfortably, with all its touches of originality, it fits the mould of the French school. Berlioz was deeply affected by Weber — that is indisputable — but the fruits were slow to appear. His "Polémique musicale" in the *Corsaire* of 19 December 1825 still shows a mind preoccupied with classical tragédie-lyrique.

> Sir, If Gluck were to come back and witness the puerile arguments that have been exercising the literary journals for the past few days on the subject of one of his masterpieces, he would smile pityingly. "What!" he would doubtless say, "all they can find to talk about in my *Armide* are engraver's mistakes and supposed echoes of popular tunes? Is there not one person that combines a certain degree of literary ability with sufficient understanding of dramatic music to analyse my work, to give an idea of the spirit in which I wrote it, and to reveal the strokes of genius it contains, which escape the notice of a public blinded by the prejudices of the moment?"
>
> I certainly do not possess all the qualities required to fulfil the task, but though my knowledge of literature is not great my knowledge of music may be useful in such a controversy. I know all Gluck by heart, I have even memorised most of the orchestral parts, I have copied several of his scores for the purpose of study, in short I think I know him as well as he can be known.

He goes on to discuss the score in detail, and ends with a caustic attack (already quoted) on the critic of the *Journal des débats*, Castil-Blaze, who in his review of *Armide* had declared Gluck's "method" old-fashioned and of no further interest.

This was written a whole year after his first encounter with *Der Freischütz*; yet it breathes the same spirit as the letter that he wrote at the beginning of the year to Letexier, the fellow-enthusiast he had met at the Opéra during a performance of Sacchini's *Œdipe*: "To witness the public's cold indifference at performances of the masterpieces of our tradition, to hear people constantly blaspheming Gluck, Sacchini, Méhul, Lesueur, Dérivis, the sublime Mme Branchu — this is calculated to inflame sensitive natures to the very height of passion." For all the "wild sweetness" of *Freischütz* and the "intoxicating sensations" it produced in him, he is still a disciple of the French school.

The time-lag is characteristic; the process by which his creative imagination absorbed the impact of an unfamiliar style and digested the lessons to be learnt from it was, habitually, long and slow. His earliest scores — *The Arab Horse, Beverley, The Crossing of the Red Sea*, the Mass — have not survived, so we cannot say whether or not it is significant that the strongly Spontinian Scène héroïque of 1825 postdates the experience of hearing Spontini's operas by nearly four years. But it is notable that his first composition that is at all like Beethoven, the slow movement of the Fantastic Symphony, was not written till two or three years after his discovery of Beethoven's music. The principle of harmonic variation which is one of Weber's legacies to Berlioz will not appear as an important compositional practice in his music for several years, while the most Weberish sound in Berlioz, the low flutes and clarinet in the garden scene of *Romeo and Juliet* (directly inspired by Agathe's scena in *Freischütz*), dates from more than a decade later.

By contrast, the composer of *Les francs-juges* has yet to feel the full liberating effect of Weber's music. The *Freischütz* influences — the ominous sound of clarinets in the bottom register, the throbbing rhythm of Max's haunted imaginings — do not alter the work's fundamental allegiance to "our tradition". They are mostly confined to the overture, a score which does not survive in its original form and which Berlioz certainly revised, perhaps quite extensively, in addition to rescoring it for larger orchestra.*
Even the opera's experiments in instrumental sonority — for example, the innovatory use of trombones in the overture (already a feature of the original version) or the instructions to the clarinettist to play with a small leather sack placed over the instrument's bell and to the timpanist to lay a cloth on the drums so as to obtain a muffled, menacing sound in the cavern scene — are not evidence of Romantic influences. They are the result of a natural curiosity of mind allied to an exceptionally acute musical ear, and of a study of the use of the orchestra in the mainly classical repertoire of the Opéra. (The clarinet-in-a-bag came from *Fernand Cortez*.)

---

* The bass drum solo in the overture's long, mysterious central section was added in 1829. Whether this whole passage — a combined development of the Allegro's main theme and the opening phrase of the Adagio, and one of the most impressive things in early Berlioz — was part of the first version (1826), or dates from 1828, is not known.

If we judge by the sound of the score we must conclude that, despite novel touches, the handling of the orchestra in the surviving scenes of *Les francs-juges* is what we would expect from a young composer who has been taught by Le Sueur and who has studied assiduously in the school of Méhul and Spontini. It is thoroughly competent, professional, resourceful and apt; it is not particularly original. There is no sign of the Romantic Orchestra.

13

"Gluck was a Romantic"

———————◄•►———————

The "Romantic Orchestra": what exactly do we mean by the term? It is usually taken to apply to Weber's mature operas, Berlioz from the Fantastic Symphony onwards and Wagner, or at the earliest Schubert. But the rapid development in the technology of instrument manufacture already taking place in the first years of the nineteenth century was arguably one element in the complex of intellectual and artistic movements known collectively as Romanticism, in which case the innovations of the composers of the French school who were Berlioz's mentors should properly be regarded as Romantic.

Romantic ideas were stirring in the bosom of French Classicism. To consider only Le Sueur — the source of certain stylistic features which in our ignorance of his work we think of as originating with Berlioz — his grand operas *Les Bardes* and *La mort d'Adam* are proto-Romantic, particularly the latter with its ambitious uniting of different performing arts, its recurring motifs and its epic scope: nothing less than the whole of history, natural and supernatural, up to the death of Adam, and a cast in which the human race as then constituted is augmented by all the legions of heaven and hell. As Winton Dean points out, "the elaboration of the scheme, combined with Le Sueur's compulsive urge to embrace all things visible and invisible in a mammoth compound of drama, symbol, vocal and instrumental music, dancing, mime, painting and scenic spectacle", looks forward to Wagner and *The Ring*. Such a union of the arts (he goes on) was the logical conclusion of French grand opera, which itself expressed the spirit of the French Revolution. What then is "Romantic"? How far back should its beginnings, in music, be pushed? To 1792, when a review of a new work by "Citizen Méhul" described him as a Romantic? Or further — to 1780–81, the year of Mozart's *Idomeneo*, a work whose use of orchestral colour for structural and psychological purposes anticipates nineteenth-century Romantic opera?

The difficulty, in short, is as always to formulate a definition of Romanticism that does not immediately have to be qualified. For another thing, all generalisations tend to break down before the category-transcending reality of the particular musical work. Music is by its nature more resistant to classification than literature; it acts on the listener with a directness of utterance independent of period. (*Idomeneo, The Magic Flute, The Creation* transcend their time more thoroughly than the great representative literary expressions of the Enlightenment.) In the late twentieth century especially, the distinctions between the music of the eighteenth and the music of the nineteenth lose their former sharpness; Classical music may be as "Romantic" in its effect as Romantic is. When you find as deep a pleasure in Haydn as in Wagner, when you are as excited by Handel as by Mahler and as likely to be moved to tears by Mozart as by Berlioz, the old dichotomy ceases to be meaningful. You no longer experience them as separate types of music, and therefore can see no essential difference between them.

Besides, the history of Western music in the early decades of the nineteenth century does not show a disturbance on the scale and of the violence that convulsed poetry and drama. There was no comparable break with the past — there was no need of one. That is rarely how music proceeds. It proceeds from what is there, not by radical rejection of it. For all Beethoven's enormous expansion of symphonic form and expression (and if one event could be said to mark the beginning of Romanticism in music, it would be the composition of the Eroica), he did not regard Mozart as an obstacle in his path, an antagonist who had to be dethroned, and he revered Handel deeply — as deeply as Berlioz revered Gluck. Likewise Berlioz, for all the innovations he consciously introduced, thought of himself as continuing and extending the work of his immediate forebears. The acknowledged ancestors of his Requiem and Te Deum were the vast musical rites of the French Revolution; his *Romeo and Juliet* developed the dramatic symphony along lines first suggested to him by Beethoven's Ninth; *The Childhood of Christ* was, in part, a gesture of recognition to his teacher Le Sueur; and in composing *The Trojans* he felt himself to be — in his own words — Gluck's "son". We are much more aware than we used to be of the ancestry of his music and (for want of a more precise word) of the Classical elements that were active in his artistic make-up, continually refining and objectifying the Romantic. The fruitful coexistence of two strains in Berlioz recalls his contemporary Delacroix, who could, without contradiction, say in one breath that if by Romanticism was meant the free manifestation of one's individual impressions, he was a Romantic and had been all his life, and in the next breath (in answer to someone who greeted him as "the Victor Hugo of painting"), "Sir, I am a Classical artist."

Berlioz himself did not see the development of music in terms of an inherent struggle between the generations. This is illustrated by an article that he wrote in 1830 under the title "A Survey of Classical Music and Romantic Music". The distinction made is between what is dead and what is alive and vital; but the interesting thing about the article is that it does not side with the new against the old: the quarrel is not with the past itself but with its self-appointed guardians and inert beneficiaries. Berlioz's conception of musical history is admittedly somewhat restricted, simplified as it is by his belief that serious music began with Gluck and by his ignorant dismissal of the entire Baroque era; but within these limitations the article takes an essentially non-historical view of the question. Although a new world and a new form, quite unknown before, have (he says) been created recently by the orchestral works of Beethoven, the fundamental difference between the two kinds of music is one of attitude, not of period. Romantic music is music which is true to itself, not being hampered by preconceived rules imposed from without; it enjoys the freedom of what Hugo calls "the great garden of poetry wherein there is no forbidden fruit". Classical music, on the contrary, is music which is so hampered. In this light, he argues, Gluck was a Romantic — the first composer to break the chains of academicism and throw off the still more burdensome yoke of routine. So were the composers most influenced by him: Mozart (in his operas), Salieri, Vogel, Méhul and Spontini. The touchstone, in short, is truth of expression, in whatever age, and its necessary condition, the liberty of the artist — Delacroix's "free manifestation of one's individual impressions".

That was the struggle, the great issue in the second half of the 1820s, and it united the diverse, brilliant talents of the children of the Revolution on the common ground of war against the tyranny of convention. The desire to "break the chains of academicism" was no mere histrionic pose, any more than it was a plea for licence and artistic disorder, as its opponents claimed. To an extent unimaginable in England the Paris artistic establishment decreed what was and was not permissible and sought to enforce a set of rules aimed at preserving the status quo against the subversive influence of the new heresy. Ridicule and moral anathema alike were heaped on the Romantics. Andrieux was discovered by a friend striding up and down his room in a rage, with a copy of Lamartine's *Méditations* in his hand, jeering and shouting, "Cry-baby! — You're sorry for yourself, are you? — You're consumptive? — What interest is that to me? 'The dying poet! the dying poet!' All right then, die — worm! You won't be the first." Delécluze, commenting on the vogue for *Robin des bois*, deplored the "ugly" notions from the north that were daily gaining ground in France. The *Corsaire* defined Romanticism as "dreaming of lakes, mists, bats, daggers and fountains [. . .] having greasy hair growing over the coat-collar, staring fixedly at the heavens when you walk in the street, without regard to vehicles, passers-by or mud, sighing at least three times a minute [. . .] ", while the *Quotidienne* and the *Oriflamme* thundered against the corrupting effects of the new "Satanic" school of literature, and judges attributed the increase in serious crime to its perverted influence. There were eloquent appeals to the healthy doctrines which had made

French literature what it was and which it was all the more necessary to adhere to in a time of unrest and incipient anarchy. The Academy, which had reached the letter R in its revision of the dictionary, pronounced Romanticism a schism from the true faith and its productions barbaric.

The creative ferment was, however, too strong to be confined within ancient formulas. As Hugo remarked in the preface to the third edition of his *Odes* (1824), profound and far-reaching changes were at work within the literature of the new century; it was inevitable that it should be so, after a political revolution which had disturbed society from top to bottom. But the conflict was made more bitter by the old guard's sense that their days were numbered (this had already happened at the Opéra, where the public deserted Kreutzer and Berton for Rossini and Auber): an art whose values went against everything they had been taught to believe in was threatening to sweep them aside. They fought to preserve their authority and their royalties and to keep the new men out: for example, to prevent Victor Hugo's *Hernani* from being accepted by the Théâtre-Français, and then, when it was accepted, to arrange for it to be hissed off the stage, and when that failed, at least to block the poet's election to the Academy.

The Théâtre-Français (Comédie-Française) was the crucial, most fiercely contested battle-ground. It was the citadel and symbol of the rules, where language was embalmed against the corrupting air of change, and the sacred Unities still reigned: the time-span of the action could not exceed twenty-four hours, and to have moved your characters further than from one room to another would have been the height of impropriety. Not only dramaturgy and poetry but also staging, deportment and decor were hidebound by strict and vigilant convention. Talma caused a frisson of horror by coming on in the fifth act of Legouvé père's *Epicharis et Néron* in bare feet; it was acknowledged that only an actor of his supreme charisma could have carried off such an audacity. There was a similar sense of shocked decorum when in Casimir Delavigne's *L'école des vieillards* a young man was shown entering a woman's bedroom at midnight. The opening line of Hugo's *Cromwell* — "Demain, vingt-cinq juin mil six cent cinquante-sept" — was taken as a mortal affront, an impertinent gauntlet flung down at the hallowed principle of non-specificity fundamental to French verse drama. Racine had established for all time that French poetic diction abhorred detail: the naming of objects such as axes or saws, let alone the date, was incompatible with the lofty discussions that were drama's concern. This was one of the reasons why it had been so vital to keep the French stage free of the infection of the barbarian Shakespeare, and admit his plays only in doctored form, in the versions by the eighteenth-century playwright Jean-François Ducis. Ducis rewrote them in the image of classical drama, retaining merely the outlines of the plot and the names of most of the leading characters, civilising the action and adhering strictly to the Racinian principles enunciated by Voltaire in his criticism of the sentry's reply in the opening scene of *Hamlet*, "Not a mouse stirring": "a soldier, though he make such an answer in the guardroom, must not do so on the stage, before the distinguished persons of the land, who express themselves in an elevated manner and have every right to expect others to do likewise in their presence". In 1822, when an English company had presumed to perform the uncouth originals at the Porte St Martin, they had been rejected in the name of Corneille, Racine, Molière and Voltaire. Shakespeare was treated as an "aide-de-camp of Wellington" and pelted off the stage.[*]

The same disapproving, restrictive spirit was active in the musical world. (As Kreutzer said to Mme Le Sueur, "What would become of us if we helped the young?") Despite the tolerant Le Sueur and the pragmatic Reicha, it set the tone of the Conservatoire — even a comparatively enlightened professor like Fétis picked holes in the harmony of Beethoven's last quartets — and it dominated the Institute's Académie des Beaux-Arts, whose music section affected the futures of young composers in the most practical way through the award of the Prix de Rome. The Academy's attitude was summed up in Berton's remark to Berlioz: "Why try to do better than the great masters?"; if the great masters could submit to well-tested musical forms, so could he. "My great crime in the eyes of that frigid old classicist is to want to do something new."[†]

To combat this reactionary spirit, common battle lines were being drawn up; the struggles against artistic and political censorship were finally beginning to be seen as one. Increasingly, the illiberal acts of Charles X's government were identified with the life-denying restrictions of the "frigid old classicists" who clung to power and obstructed new ideas. By 1830, in the preface to *Hernani*, Hugo could lump together "ultras of every sort, classicist and monarchist", whose attempt to restore the ancien régime, in society and art, must inevitably crumble before the onward march of the united forces of liberty.

Yet the alliance of Romanticism and bourgeois liberalism which brought down the Bourbon régime (aided and abetted by the acts of the régime itself) had been slow to form. In the early 1820s political and artistic impulses and doctrines cut across each other more than they ran parallel.

---

[*] The audiences were so rowdy that there were clashes with the police, and the company moved to a semi-private theatre and played most of its ten-week season to a small public of subscribers.

[†] Cf. Antoine Elwart's report of a conversation with Berton after he had just missed winning the Prix de Rome in 1833: "He told me my style was Teutonic, and that the Romantics may say what they will, but the Institute likes Rococo music, the good old Rococo of the days of Sacchini, Paisiello and the rest. Really, it makes a young composer despair to have those ancient names constantly held up for him to admire, while all mention of Rossini or Weber and the sublime Beethoven is studiously avoided."

Liberals in politics tended to be reactionaries in art and vice versa. Andrieux, Berlioz's old acquaintance, passionately opposed both the poetry of Lamartine and the politics of the Restoration, whereas the young Hugo of that period was a dedicated supporter of Catholic monarchy. It was only gradually that Romanticism moved in a leftwards, republican direction, partly through natural development, partly in response to circumstances.* Intellectual ideas are nearly always less clear-cut, more fluid and contradictory, than the histories of them would have us suppose. (We would not, for instance, expect to find Scott — the darling of the Romantics and the creator of the Romantic conception of the past — preferring Dryden's version of *Antony and Cleopatra* to the Shakespearean original, on the strict classicist grounds that it observes the Unities; but he did.) It took the French Romantic movement a number of years to find itself and identify its enemies, sharpening its ideas on the obstacles they placed in its path.

The prefaces to the successive editions of Hugo's *Odes* illustrate this evolution clearly. The first two (June and December 1822) take their stand squarely on religious and monarchical principles; the poems, Hugo claims, aspire to that austere, consoling language that is necessary for an ancient society still pale and shaken after the orgy of atheism and anarchy from which it has so lately emerged. Just over a year later (February 1824), it remains the duty of literature to be the voice of a God-fearing and monarchical society, to lead the people back to morality and stability from the decadent experiments of the last century, and to presage the great social order founded on religion and monarchism which is to come — just as the aforesaid decadence was presaged by the dissolute and sophistical writings of Voltaire and his kind (if only the poets of the Grand Siècle had invoked Christianity instead of paganism, such disasters might have been avoided!). But now, Hugo continues, a new spirit is stirring in the literature of the nineteenth century, and it demands freedom from academicism ("le genre scolastique") in order to fulfil its mission. The rules in art set the limit beyond which one must not go; they do not prescribe the path which one must follow.

Two and a half years later, in the preface to what is now entitled *Odes et ballades* (October 1826), he carries the war into the enemy camp. There is no more talk of Catholic monarchy. Instead, there is a sustained and vehement attack on academic art. Academic art seeks to impose fixed models on artists and to set rules as to what is and is not permitted, as though the productions of the imagination could be parcelled out neatly and predictably like the rows of well-behaved blooms separated by impeccably raked gravel paths in a formal garden by Le Nôtre. The

---

* One of these was the government's alienation of Chateaubriand, which drove this eminent Romantic royalist into opposition.

imagination must be free. Freedom is not the same thing as licence. On the contrary, freedom means order as opposed to artificial regularity; it means — to pursue the analogy of the formal garden — the grand, harmonious order of a primeval forest of the New World, where instead of being transplanted from their native soil and distorted out of their pristine forms, the trees — teeming with brilliantly coloured birds — grow tall and luxuriant, and in the broad avenues between them the light and the shadow play only on natural vegetation; where, instead of being forced into a narrow, sterile round, the waters flow fruitfully and of their own free will and the rainbow hangs poised above mighty cataracts. The creative mind cannot be bound by the limitation of genres — that constricting orthodoxy which decrees that what is permitted to the Novel is forbidden to Tragedy, that what the chanson admits the ode rejects.* The sole valid distinction in works of art is between what is good and what is bad. Yet to listen to certain writers who style themselves Classicists, Hugo asserted, you would suppose that anyone who did not follow slavishly in the footsteps of his predecessors was necessarily lost to truth and beauty. That is to confound art with routine. The spirit of imitation taught in our academies is the scourge of art. It produces the same effect as certain kinds of water which cover everything placed in them, flower, fruit, bird, with a crust of stone. The original form remains visible, but petrified. Let us admire the great masters; let us not imitate them but do something different. The Classicist imitates, the Romantic originates. There is only one model for the poet — nature; only one guide — truth.

---

* "La limitation des genres" was a constant bugbear of Delacroix's as well as of Hugo's.

14

Epiphany at the Odéon

---·◆·---

In the late summer of 1827 the diverse energies of French Romanticism found what they had been waiting for: a focal point, a standard to rally to, a Bible. A theatre company from London, led by Charles Kemble, came to Paris and performed *Hamlet*, *Romeo and Juliet*, *Othello*, *Richard III*, *Macbeth* and *King Lear*. This time the English actors found a climate totally different from that of 1822. Shakespeare came most carefully upon his hour. For several years he had been increasingly and vibrantly in the air. Stendhal had recently reissued his pamphlet *Racine et Shakespeare* in expanded form, Nodier was preaching Shakespeare to the young writers who attended his Sunday gatherings at the Arsenal, the *Globe* had published a weekly series of *Etudes sur Shakespeare*, Villemain lectured on him at the Collège de France; and — a small but significant sign of the times — James Fenimore Cooper's latest novel, *The Prairie*, published in Paris that spring, carried a quotation from Shakespeare as epigraph to nearly every chapter. In 1822 the audience had rejected with outrage and derision a drama in which a man was shown strangling his wife on the public stage, and they threw vegetables and rotten eggs at the actors. Five years later they took Shakespeare to their hearts.

The fact that most of them, to begin with at least, understood English little if at all and could only, in Berlioz's words, "see Shakespeare darkly, through the mists of translation", does not invalidate the experience: it shows Shakespeare's power to o'erleap the language barrier. Beyond that, it demonstrates his importance as a symbol to the young artists of the time. In the struggle to liberate French art from the shackles of Classicism his plays were puissant weapons and potent battle-cries — "an instrument of war [against] the absolutist literary establishment", as Sainte-Beuve said of *Romeo and Juliet*. They were living proofs of the heterodox truths proclaimed by Stendhal and Hugo. Shakespeare confirmed and gave sovereign authority to their conviction that, the subject of art being life and the limits of art those of existence itself, drama and poetry could not be confined to prescribed patterns but must be free to follow their own impulse and in each instance find the form proper to them. To the Romantics, chafing under the prohibitions of academic art, he came as a saviour, bringing the new wine of a long-awaited revelation.

"It's an invasion!" wrote Delacroix to Victor Hugo in jubilant mock-horror. "Hamlet raises his hideous skull on high, Othello draws his unambiguously lethal dagger, to the undermining of all dramatic law and order. Next thing, King Lear will be plucking out his eyes in front of a French audience. It behoves the Academy to declare all imports of the kind absolutely incompatible with public decency. Farewell for ever, good taste!" No matter that he confused things a little in his enthusiasm. The effect of Shakespeare was intoxicating. It was an earthquake that burst the prison gates and set them all free.

"I saw — I felt — I understood — that I was alive and that I must arise and walk." Berlioz was not the only one to call on the language of scripture to describe so momentous an experience. The whole movement interpreted the coming of Shakespeare in religious terms, as something miraculous that changed everything. "Imagine a man", wrote Dumas, "blind from birth, receiving the gift of sight and discovering a world of which he had had no inkling. Imagine Adam waking after his creation and seeing the flower-carpeted earth before him, the glorious sky over-head, around him trees laden with golden fruit, in the distance a great shining river, at his side a naked, pure young woman — and you will have some idea of the enchanted Eden which that performance [of *Hamlet*] disclosed to me."

Such language was an attempt to do justice to the sheer life-giving abundance and diversity of Shakespeare's invention. His plays depicted existence as they felt and imagined it. Hundreds could have echoed Berlioz when he called the author of *Hamlet* "the interpreter of my life". Above all they identified with Hamlet, whose yearnings and doubts seemed to hold the mirror up to their very souls. But everything about Shakespeare was an answer to prayer: the vast range of feeling and mood, the total flexibility of poetic style, the truthfulness to life and the uninhibitedness with which it was expressed, the mixing of genres which French theory held to be eternally separate (an audacity epitomised by the scene between Hamlet and the gravedigger, which needless to say had no place in the Ducis version), the majestic repudiation of set rules and the liberating freedom of form. All this was manna to their souls, it was the voice out of the burning bush. They were enchanted, too, by his habit of intruding specific, homely details or colloquialisms and popular forms into a grand and tragic context, as in Ophelia's songs or the "Not a mouse stirring" deplored by Voltaire, or the passage — singled out for praise by Stendhal — in which Banquo observes a martin nesting above the gateway of Macbeth's castle where the king will shortly be murdered. Such poetry of contrast was entirely alien to Racinian Classical drama. To the Romantics it was the breath of life. Conservative critics might continue to huff and carp, the *Corsaire* questioning how far it was really the province of art to portray the detailed physical agonies of a dying man, *Pandore* publishing on the day of the first performance of *Hamlet* a eulogistic notice of the complete works of Ducis, the great dramatist who had curbed and disciplined Shakespeare's immoderate, disorderly creations. But Victor Hugo spoke for all Jeune-France when, in the manifesto-preface to *Cromwell*, set down after the revelation of the Odéon, he proclaimed that "Shakespeare is drama — drama that mingles in one and the same breath the grotesque and the sublime, the awe-inspiring and the clownish, Tragedy and Comedy" — and hailed him as "*poeta soverano*, the king of poets".

On the evening of Tuesday 11 September 1827 the English company performed *Hamlet*, and fashionable and intellectual Paris converged on the Place de l'Odéon, jamming the narrow streets of the onzième arrondissement (today the sixième) with the unaccustomed press of car-riages and the long queues for the cheaper seats. The Odéon, on the Left Bank near the Luxembourg Gardens, was not a fashionable theatre (it had been a late choice by Laurent, the impresario responsible for the company's visit, when negotiations to hire the Théâtre-Italien fell through). But things English were à la mode. Paris was going through one of its bouts of Anglomania, which the improvement in diplomatic relations between the two countries earlier in the year had finally made good form. One washed with Windsor soap and used lavender water; one even pretended to like English beer. English-language writers were in vogue — Scott, Byron, Moore, Fenimore Cooper of course, but also Maria Edgworth and Mrs Radcliffe — and English-language classes heavily subscribed. Stendhal, who contributed reports from Paris to various London journals, predicted that "all the upper ranks of French society who learn the English language will attend the English theatre in Paris, for the sake of acquiring correct pronunciation.*

Not surprisingly the large English colony, headed by the ambassador Lord Granville and his wife, turned out in force for the first appearance by a native company since the disastrous visit of 1822. The opening night, on the 6th, had been very much an Anglo-French occasion, with the orchestra playing "Vive Henri IV" and "God Save the King" and the actor-manager William Abbott addressing the audience in French in a speech which, while acknowledging that English dramatic poets did not conform to the canons of the Classical masters of France, expressed confidence that the more tolerant spirit of modern times and the proverbial hospitality of the French would win them a sympathetic hearing.

---

* Two months later *Pandore* reported that the arrival of the company had "greatly stimulated the study of English" and that as a result those who had been moved only in a general way by the dramatic situation were now able to follow the plays in detail.

Because the company's leading actor Charles Kemble was delayed in England, the impatience of the French to see Shakespeare could not immediately be satisfied. But the opening performance, Sheridan's *The Rivals* and, as an afterpiece, Allingham's *Fortune's Frolic*, was well received by the large audience, with takings of 5,000 francs, and the second, *She Stoops to Conquer*, two nights later, though less crowded, did more than respectable business.

They were far surpassed by *Hamlet*. The theatre, which held 1,770, was crammed to capacity. Many of the young Romantics had kept away till then, waiting for this moment: Dumas, for example, who wished to present himself virgin to the Shakespearean impact and who now, to make sure of a seat, arranged to leave his office in the Palais Royal early and was in the queue by half past four. They came in battalions. One — the "bataillon sacré des claqueurs de Shakespeare", as the critic Armand de Pontmartin later christened it — included Victor Hugo, de Vigny, Gautier, Emile Deschamps, Sainte-Beuve and the artists Delacroix, Chenavard, Paul Huet and Achille Devéria; Pontmartin watched them forgather like a troop armed for battle at the symbolically named Café Voltaire, 1 Place de l'Odéon, opposite the stage door.

Inside the packed theatre excitement — and temperature — were at fever pitch; but at the rise of the curtain there was an instant hush, and the play was followed with that rapt and concentrated attentiveness which always struck English visitors by its contrast with the noisiness of Drury Lane and Covent Garden.

Their hopes were not disappointed. Dumas, who already knew his *Hamlet* so well in translation that he had not bothered to buy the edition with facing French and English texts on sale in the foyer, found the performance a revelation, "far surpassing all my expectations". For those unfamiliar with the play the energy and vividness of the acting seemed to speak directly to their understanding. The Classicists, in the entr'actes and afterwards, might inveigh against Shakespeare's barbarities and dispute the propriety of his taste and methods: his pollution of tragedy by the vulgar and the vernacular, the scandalous mixing of poetry and prose in one play, the distastefully physical nature of the action. To most of the audience the shock was exhilarating. For some years French tragic theatre, as represented by the Comédie-Française, had been in a state of decay only concealed by the genius of Talma. Since his untimely death the previous autumn a feeling of change had been in the air. The intelligent Parisian public was ready for a new, freer dramatic style. It had tasted something like it only twelve weeks before when Prosper Goubaux's *Trente ans, ou la vie d'un joueur*, a play which ignored the classical unities, opened at the Porte St Martin. The acting of the two main performers, Frédérick Lemaître and Marie Dorval (in whom, in Dumas' words, boulevard tragedy discovered its Talma and its Mlle Mars), was unprecedented in its simplicity and naturalness, its combination of restraint and intensity, and the audiences drank it in. It prepared theatre-goers for a style of acting which, in the context of French experience of poetic drama, was far more revolutionary.

Not everything in *Hamlet*, in the performance or the work, was thought effective or was understood. The acting of most of the supporting players was acknowledged to be weak. The final piling-up of corpses — always a knife-edge moment — provoked some laughter. But Hamlet's encounter with the ghost, the play-within-the-play (the Mousetrap), the scene between Hamlet and his mother, Ophelia's madness and the cemetery scene, struck home with overwhelming force. The Mousetrap astonished and electrified them. Delécluze, in his journal, analysed in fascinated detail the action and lay-out of the scene — Hamlet sprawled most unclassically on the ground, supported on his elbow as he leant against Ophelia, and holding her fan with which he marked the effect the players' words produced on the countenances of Claudius and Gertrude — and the gradual build-up of tension in Kemble's performance to the moment when, on the inner stage, the poison was poured into the ear of the sleeping king, at which point "Hamlet crawled rapidly over to them and somehow riveting them to their chairs cried out in a brilliant torrent of words such as only the English language is capable of, 'He poisons him in the garden for his estate. His name's Gonzago; the story is extant and written in very choice Italian; you shall see anon, how the murderer gets the love of Gonzago's wife.' " The King rose, called for lights and swept from the stage; Kemble exclaimed " 'Ah! Ah!' with all the ecstasy of the trick's achievement and the joy of the first stage in the act of vengeance accomplished", and the audience burst into prolonged, impassioned applause.

Such a scene was unheard of, both in the manner of its presentation and in its fusing of genres which in France were distinct and separate. But the English had enlarged, had transformed the whole notion of dramatic art. *Pandore* voiced the general reaction when it spoke of "that English candour which allows everything to be expressed and everything depicted, and for which nothing in nature is unworthy of imitation by the drama". It was precisely this all-embracing conception of the theatre that the Romantics clasped to their hearts and minds. The theatre was not something apart from life: it was life. In life a sentry or even a gravedigger might address a prince. "Not a mouse stirring" was not exclusively of the guardroom, as Voltaire had protested; it was apt to the stage, wonderfully apt, for the stage at that moment was such a place, and no longer a stage; the actors were the characters they played, and the imaginations of the spectators went out to meet them and become one with them. The ability of the English players to identify seemingly quite naturally with their rôles was something new to the French in tragic drama. To the Romantics it was at once magical and right. It was the vindication and bodying forth of their most sacred beliefs. Dumas recognised that he was watching, for the first time in the theatre, flesh-and-blood men and women animated by real feelings; the experience, he realised, gave him "what I was searching for, what I lacked, what I had had to find — actors forgetting they were on the stage [...] actual speech and gesture such as made actors creatures of God, with their own virtues, passions and weaknesses, not wooden, impossible heroes booming sonorous platitudes".

It was this sense of utter veracity that gave Harriet Smithson's performance as Ophelia — a rôle she had last played as a young girl during her apprenticeship in Ireland — the quality of a revelation to her startled observers. In Jules Janin's characteristic but accurate epigram, "that evening she taught us English tragedy, and we made her a tragic actress". The story of her sudden blossoming to stardom has been often told.* In England Miss Smithson was generally regarded as a competent supporting player — an admired Lady Anne in *Richard III*, a promising Desdemona the only time she had been allowed to appear in the part, seven years before — and a spirited but not especially remarkable comic heroine. That was her proper level; and the English critics with a few honourable exceptions took her Parisian triumphs with a very ill grace, explaining them away condescendingly as the aberration of an audience used to nothing better and only dimly aware of what it was all about, and — as the French always were — susceptible to a pretty face. Even the English who saw her in Paris felt obliged to apologise for being so moved: the ambassador's wife, Lady Granville, reported that the Parisians "roar over Miss Smithson's Ophelia, and strange to say so did I".

On the opening night of the Odéon season she had played Lydia Languish in *The Rivals* and been favourably remarked for her beauty and charm; two nights later, as Kate Hardcastle in *She Stoops to Conquer*, she was again singled out. But nothing prepared the audience, nor her fellow-actors, nor the actress herself, for the power of her Ophelia. In Ducis' *Hamlet* the female rôle always taken by the leading actress was Gertrude; Ophelia (not Polonius' daughter but Claudius' by a previous marriage) was in any case a conventional figure, quite different from her Shakespearean homonym. Even in England the rôle was secondary, and often given to a minor actress with a good voice who could make something of the songs. Kemble felt it could be safely left to Smithson.

No precise description has been left of how she played the earlier scenes. If we can believe the anonymous account that appeared eight years later in the *Gazette musicale* (almost certainly written by Berlioz and based on what she told him), her interpretation from the very beginning of the evening gave the rôle greater weight. One gathers also that her

---

* Most recently, and best of all, by Peter Raby in his biography *Fair Ophelia*, to which this account is greatly indebted.

poise, the serenity of her beauty, was one of the things that made the intensity of her subsequent madness so devastating.

There is no power to recall an actor's performance from the distant past — to imagine what it must have been like, at that particular instant in the theatre. But the chief elements, it is clear, were first the clarity and musicality of her diction (which for Janin had something of Italian melody in it) and secondly the variety and originality of her mime. The unusual emphasis on mime was partly studied — perhaps a compensation for the lack of a developed singing voice — and partly spontaneous, a response to the sympathetic currents flowing towards her from the increasingly enthusiastic audience. It was intensified from time to time — the many contemporary lithographs suggest — by the contrast between the fixity of her gaze and the painful animation of her body. Suppleness of movement was combined with sculptural force of gesture. Delécluze considered her mime "the most remarkable feature of her acting." "She adopts fantastic postures [...] without ever ceasing to be natural." Thirdly, there was the sense of total identification with the character; and finally, with all its emotional impact, a restraint which doubled the effect. The critic of the *Globe* marvelled that she could be so harrowing yet remain graceful: she was "sublime and simple".

It seems that, though Harriet Smithson had worked out her novel conception of the mad scenes in advance (shutting herself in her room for two days to study the part), something in the shared electricity of the moment took possession of her. One account (from a later performance) speaks of her face as "radiant with suffering". When she entered, wearing a long white dress but wreathed in black, with flowers and straws in her hair, and not singing so much as chanting abstractedly in a clear but soft voice the first strains of her song, a hum of surprise spread through the audience.

From that moment everyone was gripped. The songs were sung not as vocal display pieces, as was the English custom, but in snatches. She would break off in mid-phrase and — something that had not been seen before — mime her grief and madness, with a force that transfixed all present. As she knelt before the black veil (which Ophelia imagines to be the shroud covering her father's body) she gave a sudden sob so heartrending that the whole house was struck to the soul. She made her exit, murmuring "Good night, ladies, good night, good night", amid a kind of subdued hubbub; some applauded, more wept. The tide of emotion continued to rise throughout her final scene. One witness speaks of her "passing abruptly from the most agonising grief to a sort of convulsive joy, as she offers flowers to the people round her [...] and sings, unaware that she is singing [...] But such descriptions are far too feeble to give any idea of the painful intensity of Miss Smithson's mime." Another recalled that "the way she let fall the words 'I would give you some violets but they withered all when my father died' made

many who had contained themselves till then break down in tears [...]
By the time she breathed the final words, 'God a' mercy on his soul, and
of all Christian souls, I pray God', the house was in a state not to be
described." Some left the theatre, unable to bear any more.

Berlioz stayed to the end, but like one in a trance, engulfed by the power
and vitality of the play and the ideal, the dreamlike beauty of Ophelia. It
was as though, he later wrote, a clap of thunder and a single flash of
lightning had revealed to him the meaning, the reality of grandeur,
beauty, dramatic truth, Art as it was and ever should be. He felt it was
as much as his nature could stand; one such burning initiation was
enough. But it drew him back like a moth to a lamp.

> As I came out of *Hamlet*, shaken to the core by the experience, I vowed I
> should not expose myself a second time to the flame of Shakespeare's
> genius ... Next day the playbills announced *Romeo and Juliet*. I had my pass
> to the pit.* But to make doubly sure of getting in [...] I rushed round to the
> box office the moment I saw the posters and bought a stall.

The announcement of *Romeo and Juliet* followed inevitably on Harriet
Smithson's triumph in *Hamlet*. At first Kemble had felt unable to offer the
play — his most celebrated rôle — for want of a suitable Juliet, and was
waiting for the arrival of Miss Foote, who was due on the 18th. But there
was now no need to wait; he had the actress he needed. *Hamlet* was given
again on the 13th, to a house once more full to overflowing. (Mlle Mars
came a second time to see the play and study Miss Smithson, and would
attend every subsequent performance of *Hamlet*.) Two nights later *Romeo
and Juliet* opened, in a version that ended with the tomb scene (as Garrick
had revised it), the effect of which was to concentrate attention on the
two central characters. Kemble and Smithson — they were now thought
of as artists of equal stature — repeated their triumph. Reservations
among the classically minded about the excessively realistic depiction of
the lovers' death-agonies were swept aside in the general enthusiasm.

Though fewer detailed accounts have come down to us, it is clear that
Miss Smithson's supremacy was only confirmed by her Juliet, which was
considered as moving as her Ophelia and, being a much larger rôle, gave
greater scope to her newly awakened powers. Her bright star stood at its
zenith.

We have an account of Berlioz at the opening night of *Romeo*. Pontmartin,
who four nights before had watched Hugo and Delacroix and their "holy
battalion" assemble at the Café Voltaire, noticed him in the pit, in the

---

* Thanks to his friendship with Bloc, the Odéon's musical director.

same row as himself; he did not then know who it was, but such an appearance, once seen, was not to be forgotten:

> His dense shock of light brown hair, swept back, overhung the collar of his suitably threadbare coat. The magnificent, marble, almost luminous forehead, a nose that Phidias' chisel might have carved, the thin finely curving lips, the chin curved lightly, not excessively, the lean look of a poet or an ascetic, made an ensemble that would have been a sculptor's delight or despair. But all these details were eclipsed at the sight of his eyes, of a pale, intense grey, and fixed on Juliet with the expression of ecstasy that pre-Renaissance painters gave their saints and angels. Body and soul were entirely absorbed in that gaze.

"La femme attendue se présente", says Tiersot − or, to quote Berlioz himself in the preface to the Fantastic Symphony, "A young musician [. . .] sees for the first time a woman who embodies all the attractions of the ideal being his imagination had dreamed of". "Love at first sight", says Hazlitt, "is only realising an imagination that has always haunted us." There are no doubt good reasons why Harriet Smithson should have fulfilled this supreme rôle in Berlioz's imagination, should in an instant have become the embodiment of the eternal unattainable feminine, the first so far as we know since Estelle Dubeuf initiated him into the mysteries of that fatal, fruitful religion. Just as his passion for Estelle was from the beginning identified with the awakening of his response to nature and landscape, of which she was the presiding deity, so now it was a double coup de foudre; the actress personified the poet whose divine interpreter she was: worship of the artist and worship of the art, as he acknowledged, were deeply interfused, each intensifying the other.

In everything Berlioz writes about it the two passions are inextricably linked; the "flame of Shakespeare's genius" which brands him is held against his heart by the priestess-goddess. "My fate was doubly sealed," he remarks. It is not only the vision of Harriet Smithson's ideal beauty, experienced a second time in *Romeo and Juliet*, that makes him feel by midway through the play that he can barely breathe, as though an iron hand were stifling him: it is the shattering effect of being transported in succession into two totally different, all-consuming poetic worlds. "After the melancholy of *Hamlet*, after the harrowing griefs, the desolate passions, the cruel ironies and black meditations, the heartbreak, the madness [. . .] the slings and arrows of outrageous fortune, after Denmark's dark clouds and icy winds, to be exposed to the fiery sun and balmy nights of Italy, to witness the drama of that immense love [. . .] the raging vendettas, the desperate kisses, the frantic strife of love and death, was more than I could bear."

Like Estelle's beauty, Harriet's − marked by the same serenity of bearing and dominated by magnificent eyes − appeared to him quite naturally as the beauty of a goddess, pure, dreamlike, remote, and literally as well as metaphorically gazed up to from below, beyond the luminous divide of the footlights. "How", asked Stendhal in his treatise on love, *De l'amour*, "can one help projecting feelings of warmth and affection on to the physiognomy of a well-favoured actress whom one watches night after night for the space of a couple of hours expressing the loftiest sentiments, and whom one knows only thus and not in any other way?" The Romantic cult of the Actress is exemplified in the lives of many of Berlioz's fellow-artists — Hugo, Dumas, Vigny; Nerval, all of whom loved actresses they later reincarnated in their works. In Harriet Smithson's case it coincided with another potent contemporary myth, that of La Femme Anglaise. During the years immediately preceding 1827 there was a renewal of the long-established cult in France of the Anglo-Saxon woman, formed partly from life but more from the blonde, blue-eyed heroines encountered in Scott, Cooper (Alice Munro in *The Last of the Mohicans*) and Mrs Radcliffe, the type of pure, warm-hearted, innocent young woman whose "naturalness", Stendhal observed, was of all attributes "the most favourable to the tender passion". Harriet, in short, was for Berlioz the perfect material for the process which *De l'amour* calls "crystallisation", by which the loved one, like a twig immersed in the salt spring of the lover's imagination, comes out sparkling with a thousand jewels.

To explain, however, is nothing. He himself in his moments of analytical self-detachment could have done so as shrewdly as any clear-sighted commentator. The reality was shattering. Not even the secret sorrows of his adoration of Estelle had been like this. He felt possessed by an overmastering sadness, to which was added a state of jangling nervous tension from the still unabated shock of the Shakespearean revelation on his abnormally responsive sensibilities. He did not need to watch her night after night to be stamped body and soul with her image; and he could not have gone back. Two experiences were enough. He dreaded the thought of a third as one dreads extreme physical pain.

But the Odéon was only five minutes' walk, not so much as that, from where he lived in Rue de la Harpe; he could not keep away, but was drawn back obsessively into her ambience. A day or two after *Romeo* he was there, under the arcade of the Odéon, leaning against a pillar, watching her as she alighted from a carriage and went in at the stage door for a rehearsal of *Othello* (which had been announced for the 18th). He took to frequenting the theatre on nights when the English were not playing. Early in October the company moved across the river and took up residence at the Salle Favart; but they came back to the Odéon again for a few weeks at the end of December, and he resumed his haunting, getting up in the middle of the night, feverishly wide awake, and pacing the deserted arcade. At other times he struck aimlessly into the countryside and wandered about the surrounding plains, or stood half way up the hill of Montmartre, looking down on the city, his thoughts beating round her image. Occasionally, exhaustion overtook him and he stretched out and slept wherever he happened to be, among the corn-stooks near Ville-Juif, by the frozen Seine at Neuilly, at a café table — rare sleeps of oblivion when his body revolted and overruled the turmoil of his mind. Mostly, when his bouts of hopeless yearning were at their height, he could not sleep.

Nor could he work. His creative faculties, turned upside down by Shakespeare, seemed stunned, his mind sapped of all vitality; even the pleasure of studying his favourite scores, even his will to succeed in his chosen career, deserted him. "I speak enthusiastically of all this, my dear friend," he writes to Humbert Ferrand, in a letter which describes the successful performance of his Mass at St Eustache on St Cecilia's Day, "but you don't know how little it all means to me. For three months I have been prey to a sorrow from which nothing can distract me, and which has made me utterly weary of life. Even the success I have just had relieved me only momentarily of the heavy burden of grief that weighs upon me, and now it presses more heavily than before." He adds that he does not feel equal to explaining what he is talking about — that must wait till they meet — and the letter ends mysteriously by quoting "the words of the King of Denmark's ghost to his son Hamlet: 'ferwel, ferwel, remember my'."

But there were times too when the pendulum swung back, his energies flared up with furious intensity, and love — as he told his friend Ferdinand Laforest — was "a rage, a madness which takes possession of all our faculties and makes us capable of anything".

He wrote to Harriet Smithson, declaring his love; and he offered the directors of the Opéra-Comique one of his overtures for a benefit evening for the actor Huet at which Miss Smithson was appearing in scenes from *Romeo and Juliet*. Neither offer was accepted. The actress did not reply in person but sent a message, a coldly formal rejection: she was "unable to reciprocate his feelings".

The letter to Laforest, dated 12 October, gives a glimpse of the oscillations of his mood.

I trust you never experience the unendurable sufferings I've been through since your departure. You left Paris just when the explosion was about to happen. I'll tell it all to you when you're back; for the moment I'm not capable of describing the circumstances of my sad drama. Only in the past few days have I been in a state to write at all.

But enough of that. I'm getting all my strength together to prepare the music for the performance of my Mass, which will definitely take place on 22 November. I should love you to be there. Afterwards about thirty of us, special friends, are meeting for a celebratory meal, at which we'll toast St Cecilia. You'd be more than welcome to join us. I shall bring Valentino and M. Lesueur. Do come.

Three days ago there was a performance of *La Vestale*. Adolphe Nourrit

sang Licinius very badly. As the bottom register of his voice is weak he
presumed to alter the recitatives from one end of the score to the other
whenever he found them awkward to sing: e.g. in Act 3 he sang

instead of   *et vi-van-te* de-scend *dans la nuit des tom-beaux*

et vi-van-te de-scend dans la nuit des tom-beaux

Blasphemer, how dare he mutilate such a rôle and lay godless hands on
the palladium of genius!

Unbearable agitation. I'm in a fever, the pulsations of my heart are
irregular; and yet everything must be brought to a conclusion. Here I am
rambling on, saying things you've no means of understanding.

I can't continue. I'd intended to write you a long letter, but must stop.

Oh, I can't say, like Cortez to Amazily, "Every second of your life is a
blessing from the gods." No it's far, very far from being a blessing.

Farewell, give me your news, and tell me you're coming back soon. I'm
not very demonstrative in these matters, but you can't imagine how precious
your friendship is to me. You have one of those open and genuine natures
which are extraordinarily attractive.

H. Berlioz
58 Rue de la Harpe*

On 22 October Berlioz wrote to Quatremère de Quincy, the Permanent
Secretary of the Academy, asking him for payment of the allowance
(50 francs) due to all candidates for the Prix de Rome, successful or not.
"The fact that M. Guiraut has been paid leads me to hope that my
application will not be without effect. I am at present in urgent need of
the money [. . .] without it I cannot proceed with a musical undertaking
of some importance which I am engaged in, and I count on your kindness
to obtain it for me. Please forgive me for troubling you on so trifling a
matter."

It is clear from the letter to Laforest that the performance of the Mass
had already been planned before the coup de foudre of the Odéon (and
therefore, unlike the concert of the following May, was not designed

---

* The letter, which is unpublished, is a reminder of the gaps in our knowledge of this period
of Berlioz's life. Until it came to light a few years ago, nobody knew of the existence of
Ferdinand Laforest, let alone of his close friendship with Berlioz. Laforest, who enrolled at the
Ecole de Médecine a year after Berlioz, lodged at the Hôtel de Nantes, 79 Rue St Jacques, where
Berlioz lived for a year or two in the mid-1820s. On qualifying and sustaining his thesis (on
"Acute inflammation of the uterus"), he returned to his native Beaupréaux (Maine et Loire) to
practise medicine. The letter belongs to Mr and Mrs Robert J. Fitzpatrick, of Valencia,
California (Mrs Fitzpatrick is a descendant of Laforest) and is quoted by their kind permission.

expressly to attract Harriet's attention). No music of his had been heard in public for more than two years, since the first performance of the Mass at St Roch in July 1825; all the various ideas for getting the Scène héroïque performed and the projected production of *Les francs-juges* had proved abortive. There was still no prospect of putting on the opera, and the Scène, which lasted about twenty minutes, could be performed only as part of a composite programme. The most practical course was to revive the Mass, which had been worked over and revised in many details since the original hearing gave Berlioz the chance to test his ideas in performance.

Little is known of the circumstances in which the St Cecilia's Day performance (on the afternoon of 22 November) was put on. Berlioz's letter of the 29th to Ferrand gives some details but is silent about many others. The orchestra was a very large one, including sixty strings (as well as four horns, six trumpets, three trombones and two ophicleides for the fanfare which would be developed in due course to become the Tuba mirum in the Grande Messe des Morts). Clearly the Odéon's forty players, who according to the *Memoirs* provided the orchestral forces for the occasion and gave their services, were augmented with more than twice that number from other sources, including no doubt the Gymnase, the Bouffes and the Conservatoire — three institutions singled out in the letter, together with the Odéon, as places where he has "a real following". Berlioz conducted the performance himself. It was his début, and considering his total inexperience it went rather well. Above all, the Et iterum venturus, revised since 1825 and much better performed than it had been then, made a powerful impression, despite the chorus being too small for a building as big as St Eustache. This time the music sounded exactly as he had imagined it, and in his overwrought nervous condition he became so excited that he had to sit down at the end of the movement and wait for the trembling to subside before going on with the performance.

The concert may have also been intended as compensation for his failure in the Prix de Rome four months earlier and as a riposte to his judges. He sent letters of invitation to "all the members of the Institute", and by implication some at least turned up, since he says afterwards that he is "content they should hear music they say is unperformable performed — for my Mass is thirty times more difficult than my competition cantata, which you know I was obliged to withdraw because M. Rifaut couldn't play it on the piano, and which M. Berton hastened to declare unperformable, even by an orchestra". Their presence made up for the absence of many others, kept away by the rioting — inspired by the liberal gains of the recent elections — which had been going on in the nearby Rues St Denis and St Martin the two previous days, and which had been put down with a good deal of bloodshed. For the same reason the newpapers, preoccupied with politics, had no time for minor musical events. The *Corsaire* and *Pandore* reported the performance favourably but very briefly, and that was all: there was nothing in the *Journal des débats* (though Castil-Blaze had said he would come), nor in the *Observateur*, nor even in the *Revue musicale*.

None the less the concert was of real benefit to him. It gave him a chance — frustratingly rare at this stage of his career — of hearing his own music. It was the first, albeit tentative, step towards becoming one of the great conductors of his time. And it provided fresh and heartening evidence that, whatever the old classicists thought of him, many of the younger musicians were on his side and would willingly perform his music. The knowledge would be a vital factor in his project, the following spring, to give a concert in the Conservatoire Hall devoted to his most recent compositions.

If the convivial supper took place afterwards as planned, it is unlikely that Le Sueur attended it. He had just lost his daughter Adeline-Marguerite, at the age of nineteen. Berlioz reported her death to his mother early in the New Year:

> She was an angel of grace and beauty. She was on the point of getting married. She'd been ill for a few weeks, but had not stayed in bed. Her parents felt no anxiety about her, they never suspected her of having consumption; the doctors, who were under no illusion, kept it from them till the last moment. A week before she died I was having lunch with the family, and she questioned me about the English tragedies, which she hadn't yet seen. I watched her shudder at the account of the awesome cemetery scene in *Hamlet*; I had no idea then that, like Laertes, I should so soon be accompanying Ophelia to her last home.
>
> She was a little like Nancy to look at, and this, joined to the fact of seeing her regularly and the interest she naturally inspired, has made me miss her bitterly. The whole Chapel Royal was present at her funeral procession. M. Plantade [director of the Chapel], with M. Lesueur's leading pupils, was in charge of the musical part of the ceremony. We laid her in the cemetery of Père-Lachaise, between Delille, Grétry and Bernardin de St Pierre. "And like a rose she lived as roses live, a morning's span" [Malherbe]. Her father is showing great fortitude; but I believe a second such loss would kill him.

The tone of the letter as a whole suggests a lessening of tension between Hector and his family. He is still careful to report that he has been keeping up faithfully with their Dauphinois friends who live in Paris — with M. de Prudhomme, who has recently lost his wife, and with whom he and Alphonse Robert had dinner only the other day, and with M. Teisseyre the barrister, whom he sees quite often as they are near neighbours. But there is an unmistakably more relaxed atmosphere than in previous communications with his family.

> Thank you, dear Mama, for the handkerchiefs you sent by Charles [Bert]. But actually they're what I'm in need of least. What I am short of are

stockings. I've not got one whole pair, and every day the number that are wearable diminishes. Please send me some whenever you can.

So Grandfather's made up his mind to come and visit you? Tell my sisters to give him my love.

Farewell, my dear Mama, I embrace you tenderly.
Your loving son
H. Berlioz

I'm not sending Papa's books yet; [Manzoni's] *The Betrothed* won't be out for another week — I went to the publisher's this morning.

The unfortunate effect of his failure in the Prix de Rome the previous summer had been erased by the news of the Mass at St Eustache. Joséphine Berlioz always softened at the thought of her son doing well with a religious work. Perhaps she was gradually growing resigned to his "vocation", and beginning to see things in the same light as her sensible friend Nancy Clappier, who about this time sent her god-daughter Nancy Berlioz a chatty, gossipy letter which included a gentle homily partly intended for Joséphine's eyes: "I confess to you, my dear child, that I felt a certain satisfaction at Hector's success. This career of his could become honourable if he were to distinguish himself in it by exceptional talents. They are the *fine* arts, after all [. . .] One may regret that he has not chosen a more useful skill, in which one can make an honourable existence without the necessity of achieving the highest rank. But who can hope to direct their children's hearts and inclinations as they would like to! It is enough to be thankful for when they do not go more grievously astray." Attention was in any case about to be diverted from Hector to his thirteen-year-old sister Adèle who, on being sent to boarding school in Grenoble, caused such a rumpus, refusing food, crying night and day and making herself sick, and maintained her defiance with such tenacity, that the headmistress eventually had to admit defeat and Adèle was brought home again. Echoes of this seven-week drama which convulsed the whole clan — uncles, aunts, cousins, domestic servants and family friends — must have reached Hector and struck sympathetic chords in him; but it coincides with a gap in the surviving correspondence.

Some items of news were not communicated from Paris to La Côte. He might give his family an edited version of the great Shakespearean revolution; but on the subject of Harriet Smithson he kept discreetly silent. She still possessed him; and, with no outlet for his passion, he felt half suffocated, imprisoned in the stifling circle of his unending dreams and longings. Harriet's star shone more brilliantly every day. She had added to her Shakespearean triumphs the title rôle in *Jane Shore*, achieving by the power of her acting as great a succès de larmes in the part of the starving heroine of Rowe's mediocre play as she had as Ophelia. Macready recalled that her faint "I have not ate these three days" drew an audible "O mon Dieu!" from the entire theatre.

Berlioz still kept away from the English company's performances, but he was morbidly aware of her continued presence — he could hardly not have been, her portrait was in every bookshop window, and "la belle irlandaise" was the rage of Paris. Her fame reached its apogee in the benefit performance given for her at the Théâtre-Italien on 3 March 1828, when Sontag and Mlle Mars joined her — "the three reigning sovereigns of the Paris theatre", the *Quotidienne* called them — for a glittering evening consisting of Act 2 of *The Barber of Seville* performed by the Italian Opera, Andrieux's one-act comedy *Le manteau* by the Théâtre-Français, and three acts of *Romeo and Juliet*. Hundreds were turned away. The Duc d'Orléans and members of his family and entourage were in the audience; the King sent Harriet a purse full of gold, the Duchesse de Berry presented her with a superb Sèvres vase. Abbott, the manager of the English company, was greeted with immense acclamation when, from a stage deep in flowers, he paid tribute to a talent which had "grown under the eyes" of the French public. Miss Smithson's transformation was complete. An English observer (Mrs Baron Wilson), seeing her again at this time, was astonished at the change that success had wrought in her: "Her personal appearance had been so much improved by the judicious selection of a first-rate modist and a fashionable corsetiere, that she was soon converted into one of the most splendid women in Paris, with an air distingué that commanded the admiration and the tears of thousands who gazed upon her at La Favart. I had remembered her in Ireland and in England, but as I now looked upon her, it struck me that not one of Ovid's fabled metamorphoses exceeded Miss Smithson's real Parisian one."

The fresh demonstration of her renown made Berlioz only more despondently aware of his obscurity and the gulf that separated them. It may have been the benefit night that first implanted the naïve idea of using a concert of his music as a means of forcing himself on Miss Smithson's notice. Like Correggio standing in front of Raphael's "St Cecilia" and exclaiming "Anche io son pittore", he would show her that he too was an artist, and the distance between them would be narrowed. He would put on a concert exclusively of his own works, something not attempted in France before.

Such a move had in any case become urgent. None of the music he had written in the past two and a half years had yet been heard in public; the recent performance of the Mass had not diminished that perennial preoccupation. We see a reflection of it in a letter from his teacher, Le Sueur, to the virtuoso violinist Alexandre Boucher, who had recently returned from a tour of Germany and who, having played with great acclaim in Paris, was planning a benefit concert at the Opéra. "Well, then, my friend, to you who are so obliging I shall recommend M. *Berlioz*, a highly talented composer. You may have heard tell of his *masses* for full orchestra, performed with success at St Roch and St Eustache. If you can include one of his strikingly brilliant overtures in your concert, you will do a great service to a pupil of mine whom I am exceedingly fond of. This young athlete, already full of force and warmth, who is going to go far, is as delighted as I am by the justice that Paris, capital of the arts, has just rendered to your renowned talent. What you can do for him you will do for me [...]"

By the time Boucher gave his benefit concert, at the Opéra-Comique on 2 May, Berlioz was deep in the arrangements for his own concert, at which he intended to perform both his overtures as well as a quantity of other music, all of it for the first time. Quite apart from the good it could be expected to do his career, and the vague but potent hope of its having a beneficent influence on Miss Smithson, the project was exactly what he needed. He might be in no state to compose, but he could organise. The concert took him out of himself. He no longer spent days and nights roaming the streets and the surrounding countryside: there was no time. He had too much to see to. He had vocal soloists to find, the chorus to engage (and somehow pay for, by further economies in his daily régime) and a sizeable orchestra to assemble. Bloc's young Odéon band of forty players would take part again and give their services, as they had done for the Mass the previous November, but they would have to be augmented by the same number. That meant drawing up a list of suitable names from among the mass of musicians in the other theatre orchestras (he knew the capabilities of every player, having studied them over a period of several years), getting in touch with each one personally and persuading him to play for nothing. True, he was on friendly terms with a good many of them, especially at the Opéra and at the Nouveautés (his old theatre), and already had quite a following among the younger musicians. He was also living much nearer the centre of musical life than he had been in the Latin Quarter, having lately moved north of the Seine to 96 Rue de Richelieu, at the Boulevard des Italiens end, where most of the main lyric theatres and the Conservatoire were within a few minutes' walk. But it was a formidable undertaking all the same. "Fixing" an orchestra from scratch (I know by experience) is exhausting enough today, with modern means of communication. In 1828, with nothing but one's will-power, one's pen and one's two feet and no helpful precedents for what one was doing, it was a labour of Hercules.

On top of that there was all the performing material to get ready. Except possibly for the overture to *Les francs-juges* and the two excerpts from the opera he planned to give (which may well have been among the numbers he had copied the previous year with a view to a run-through at the Odéon when that theatre still hoped for permission to put on new French operas), orchestra and chorus parts existed for none of the pieces he intended to perform: the *Waverley* overture, a March of the Magi (about which nothing is known for certain), the Prix de Rome cantata

which the Academy had declared unperformable and the Scène héroïque
on the Greek war of independence. Once again he must write them all
out himself.

15

The Revelation of Beethoven

During the second half of March and all through April, while he toiled away at the preparations for his concert, his mind strove to absorb a fresh artistic upheaval — the discovery of Beethoven at the newly inaugurated Conservatoire concerts. Berlioz later described it as "a new world of music" opening before him, in comparison with the "new universe of poetry" that Shakespeare had revealed. But the Beethoven experience, if in the last resort less far-reaching in its implications, was more direct in its influence, more instantly meaningful. It was in his own language, music — but music not remotely like anything he had heard before. With very few exceptions, his education, at the Opéra and at the feet of Le Sueur, had been in the vocal and choral, non-symphonic music of the French school. At this date music for him still meant opera, mass, cantata, as it did for most French musicians of the time. Apart from the two or three concerts spirituels given every year during Lent and the end-of-term student exercises at the Conservatoire, there was practically speaking no public orchestral music in Paris. There had been a quite active tradition of French symphonic composers a quarter of a century earlier but it had died out, partly thanks to lack of official provision for performance and the financial obstacles to putting on unsubsidised concerts (the tax-inspector took a quarter of the box-office receipts); and Le Sueur had in any case never been part of it. From him Berlioz imbibed the common notion that instrumental music was a lesser, limited branch of the art, which Haydn and Mozart had taken as far as it could go; and the occasional routine, under-rehearsed performance of a Haydn or Mozart symphony on the huge bare stage of the Opéra was not calculated to make him think otherwise.*

Very probably he heard some Beethoven at the concerts spirituels. The First and Second symphonies (the latter with the slow movement of

---

* The story of him coming out of the first night of the English company's *Romeo and Juliet* and exclaiming, "I shall write my greatest symphony on the play" — a story that Berlioz himself denied — cannot be true, if only because at that date, six months before the opening of the Conservatoire concerts, it would never have occurred to him to think in those terms.

the Seventh substituted for its own, to help it out) were given from time
to time — the Second figured on the programme in both 1826 and 1827
— but again not in conditions to make much of an impression or overcome the prejudices and assumptions that were part of his artistic
environment. He went through them in full score, and sensed, as he later
put it, that Beethoven was "a sun indeed, but a sun obscured by dense
clouds". Nothing prepared him for the impact of the Eroica and the Fifth
played by a crack orchestra, meticulously rehearsed, in the perfect acoustics
of the Conservatoire Hall.

Like Shakespeare, Beethoven had been in the air for some time before
the full revelation burst on Paris. The year before, in the *Journal des
débats*, Castil-Blaze (who with all his shortcomings was one of the more
serious critics) had declared it was high time some of the other Beethoven
symphonies were performed.

To do so had long been the ambition of one of the leading Parisian
musicians, the violinist-conductor François Habeneck. As early as 1811
he had directed a performance of the Eroica with an orchestra of Conservatoire students. By the mid-1820s he was a powerful and respected
figure, chief conductor at the Opéra and a senior professor at the Conservatoire. None the less Habeneck proceeded with caution. Even if
Schindler's story of a preliminary rehearsal of the Eroica provoking howls
of laughter among the players and having to be abandoned is apocryphal,
there is no doubt that orchestral musicians were prejudiced against
Beethoven, whose symphonies had the reputation of being bizarre, obscure
and horribly difficult to play. The inaugural session of what was to
become the orchestra of the Société des Concerts du Conservatoire —
widely considered in the 1830s and 1840s the finest in Europe — took
place only through a ruse on Habeneck's part. In November 1825 he
invited a nucleus of thirty of the best players to come and dine with him
on St Cecilia's Day and bring their instruments with them for "a little
music". According to one of them, the horn-player Meifred (subsequently
secretary of the Société des Concerts), they found music-stands set out
with the parts of the Eroica and the Seventh on them. In the relaxed
intimacy of Habeneck's home, with no one to witness their reactions, the
rehearsal went quite well. Other rehearsals followed, more players were
added, and little by little, technically and expressively, the orchestra
mastered the music, and in doing so became fired with a sense of mission
and a unique esprit de corps.[*]

The immense impact of the Conservatoire Concerts was based on the
most thorough preparation, as many people testified (among them
Wagner, who cannot be suspected of partiality to the musical mores of

[*] It was the only orchestra in Paris that existed in its own right, independent of the theatre
and emancipated from the mediocrity of so much of the contemporary operatic repertoire.

Paris but who always maintained that the Beethoven performances he heard there were the best in his experience). But the series also owed its success to solid organisation and adequate subsidy. Habeneck used his influence to secure support at the highest level. The Société des Concerts was established, on 15 February 1828, by ministerial decree, which also guaranteed it the use in perpetuity of the Salle des Menus-Plaisirs, as the Conservatoire Hall was once again officially known (having reverted to its ancien régime title). A good deal of patient diplomacy had gone to achieving this end. Cherubini, the Director of the Conservatoire, had agreed to become honorary president of the Society but had been far from enthusiastic; he had serious reservations about Beethoven's music, and he was even more dubious about anything likely to disrupt the disciplined running of the college.

Not altogether without arrière-pensée, operatic and liturgical music by Cherubini figured prominently at the first of the six concerts which made up the opening season, and again at the third. (Some of it, notably the aria "Suspendez à ces murs mes armes" from *Les Abencérages* and the march from the Mass composed for the coronation of Charles X two years before, made a deep impression on Berlioz, who thought the aria as fine as anything in dramatic music since Gluck and the march the equal of the one in *Alceste*.) All six concerts made liberal use of excerpts and were cast in the miscellaneous, mixed vocal and instrumental format popular throughout the nineteenth century, in which a long work, a symphony or a concerto, would be flanked by an air in a much lighter vein or a solo for flute, horn or cello. The fourth programme was devoted entirely to Mozart, featuring three numbers from the second act of *Idomeneo* as well as the E-flat Symphony, the *Magic Flute* overture and an unidentified piano concerto. But it was Beethoven's music that dominated the new enterprise and gave it its raison d'être and its glory. The Eroica opened the first concert, on 9 March, and was repeated a fortnight later at the second (consecrated to the memory of the composer, who had died almost exactly a year before). After an interval of three weeks, perhaps for intensive rehearsals, the third concert began with the C-minor Symphony, the Fifth, which was heard twice more, at the penultimate and at the final concert (11 May). Also heard during the season were the Violin Concerto (twice), extracts from the two masses, the oratorio *The Mount of Olives*, the first movement of the Third Piano Concerto, the canon quartet from *Fidelio*, and the *Egmont* and *Coriolan* overtures (the latter, as was to be the custom for many years, "followed by the final chorus of *The Mount of Olives*"). Musical Paris, the younger part of it at least, was engulfed and uplifted.

To imagine it may not be easy for us, who have perhaps heard these pieces many times, often in jaded or unremarkable performances, so that they have lost their power to startle and delight. But to the Paris audiences of 1828, music of the force, sonority and intensity of expression, the largeness of scale and design and the driving momentum of the Eroica and the Fifth Symphony was a totally new experience. The Conservatoire Hall was quite a small, compact auditorium, seating about a thousand people, with a live, glowing acoustic that earned it the name of "the Stradivarius of concert halls". The effect of such music heard for the first time, in that setting, performed with precision and fervour by an orchestra of eighty players chosen from the élite of one of the capitals of the musical world, was electrifying. The sense of rapt attention and wonder, of hanging on every note, is captured to perfection in the faces of Eugène Lami's picture "The Andante of the Symphony in A" (the Seventh, performed twice during the following season), just as the sheer unbearable physical excitement is immortalised in the story of the Grande Armée veteran who, hearing the double bass pedal and drum-beats of the long dark tunnel that leads to the finale of the Fifth and the sudden lightning transition from a pinpoint of sound to the great blaze of C major, sprang to his feet and cried out, "L'Empereur!"[*]

For Berlioz the experience brought the last and the greatest of the revelations of the power of music as an expressive language, of what it can be made to do, its freedom of action. The dramatist in him leapt out in response. He grasped at once that the symphony, to an extent he had never dreamed of, was a dramatic form. The effect of the Conservatoire concerts was not to shake his allegiance to dramatic music but to widen his whole concept of it to include the symphonic. Beethoven's symphonies were dramas, both in their detailed and in their larger utterance. The disintegration of the main theme at the end of the Eroica's funeral march — like the similar process that concluded *Coriolan* — was supremely dramatic in its use of music to evoke an extra-musical idea, in this case the cessation of life; but so was the total work, and the Fifth too — conceived in response to a single governing thought. Yet music remained "the be-all and the end-all", wholly in command of the poetic idea that the particular work embodied. As with Shakespeare, formal design was not stereotyped but free, exemplifying a dazzling variety of compositional processes and created afresh in accordance with the demands of each work, which achieved unity in obeying only the rules that were proper to it.

Berlioz's music, after an interval for the absorbing of these profound and powerful lessons, will duly reflect the influence of Beethoven, in great and in small (including such matters as the emancipation of the timpani, which Beethoven was the first to treat as an independent instrument; the revelation in the scherzo of the Fifth of the bassoon's capacity for the grotesque and the macabre; the ungrammatical horn dissonances in the

---

[*] Here, as elsewhere in Beethoven's music, the French were hearing their own music of the Revolutionary period transfigured and universalised.

funeral march of the Eroica; the "Berliozian" change of metre from 3/4 to alla breve in the scherzo; and the superimposition of different rhythmic figures in the slow variation of the same symphony's finale). Occasionally it will sound rather like Beethoven; this is particularly true of the slow movement of the Fantastic Symphony, where the use of certain country images and the sense of space and the holy serenity of Nature evoke the Pastoral, while the movement's great central crisis carries echoes of the first movement of the Fifth (successive fortissimo diminished sevenths rising stepwise, separated by silence) and of Florestan's aria in *Fidelio* (the subsiding of an emotional paroxysm depicted by irregularly metred descending chords). But the influence will be more general than specific, affecting not the style or process of composition so much as the principle. Berlioz will never write music in the tradition of Viennese classicism; but the Fantastic Symphony — "in which a long-breathed melodic line, harking back to Gluck and classical opera, is subjected to Beethoven's technique of thematic generation and trans-formation" (Wilfrid Mellers) — will be the first of a series of works which attempt to extend symphonic drama in the direction suggested by Beethoven's Third, Fifth, Sixth and Ninth symphonies.

As Shakespeare had done, Beethoven further polarised the opposing forces of French artistic life and sharpened the conflict between Romanti-cists and Classicists. The enthusiasm of the younger musicians spread to the painters and writers.* It was not shared by the musical establishment. The composition teachers at the Conservatoire and the members of the music section of the Academy were nearly all either covertly or openly hostile. Berton, like Kreutzer (who would have no truck with the violin sonata Beethoven dedicated to him, and was reputed to have rushed out of a rehearsal of the Second Symphony with his hands over his ears), considered all modern German music by definition bad; Paër went round telling stories about Beethoven which showed him in a derogatory light; Catel had quarrelled with music and would have nothing to do with Beethoven's; Boieldieu regarded it with frank bewilderment. Berlioz was constantly having to listen to the most absurd pronouncements on the subject. Only Reicha did not join in the general disparagement. Even Fétis, though a professed admirer, was forever criticising Beethoven for his breach of the hallowed rules of harmony.

During these heady weeks in the early spring of 1828 Beethoven was a topic often raised when Berlioz was at the Rue Ste Anne. To his disap-pointment Le Sueur refused to respond to his enthusiasm; he would

---

* Balzac later confessed, on hearing the Fifth, that "Beethoven is the only man who has made me experience jealousy [. . .] There is in this man a divine force [. . .] What we writers depict is finite, determined; what Beethoven gives us is infinite."

rather not get involved, insisted on holding himself aloof from the whole experience. The old man couldn't conceal his astonishment that symphonic music by anyone should be causing such excitement, but he had given up going to concerts and on the whole didn't see why he had to make an exception for these. But his pupil would keep on preaching at him about one's obligation — when an event of this magnitude occurred in their art, the advent of a new style on an immense scale — to find out about it for oneself, and not just turn one's back and behave as if nothing had happened. So in the end Le Sueur gave in and, one Sunday early in May, let Berlioz take him to the Conservatoire to hear the C-minor Symphony. He stipulated only that they should sit separately — he wanted to be on his own and listen to the piece dispassionately, on its merits, uninfluenced by his young friend — and he stationed himself out of sight at the back of one of the ground-floor boxes. Berlioz had a seat on the next level up. They arranged to meet when the symphony was over.

The experiment was a triumphant success. When Berlioz came down he found Le Sueur pacing the corridor, his face on fire. "Ouf! I'm going outside, I need some air. It's unbelievable, wonderful! It so moved and disturbed me and turned me upside down that when I came out of my box and went to put on my hat, for a moment I didn't know where my head was. Now leave me alone. I'll see you tomorrow."

Tomorrow, alas, turned out to be another story. When Berlioz arrived at the Rue Ste Anne (only a step from where he lived now), he found a very different Le Sueur, one who was curiously reluctant to talk about the previous afternoon's experience and listened to his pupil's ardent words with an air of constraint. Berlioz could hardly even get him to speak of it, let alone acknowledge how deeply the work had moved him. In the end Le Sueur conceded that it had, but then shook his head, gave a strange smile and said, "All the same, that sort of music should not be written."

Le Sueur's confession, in retrospect, marks a divide in the relationship between pupil and master. They remained friends, and Berlioz continued to go to lessons and frequent his house as an unofficial member of the family. Outwardly nothing was changed. Inwardly, he knew that henceforth the issue of Beethoven divided them irrevocably. It would lead Berlioz, not to lose affection for him nor to forget the gratitude he owed him for vital encouragement and countless kindnesses, but to underrate the importance of Le Sueur's influence on the formation of his musical style and ideas, which for the rest of his life would continue to reflect aspects of his teacher's. *The Childhood of Christ* (1850–54) has clear affinities with Le Sueur's music, not only with his Biblical oratorios which Berlioz heard Sunday after Sunday at the Chapel Royal but with the opera *Les Bardes*; and had Le Sueur lived long enough to attend the first performance of Berlioz's Requiem at the Invalides in 1837 — he died a few months before — he would have been justified in feeling that he had an heir.

It was also hardly just or reasonable to demand so radical a reappraisal from a man of nearly seventy, whose musical personality had been formed before the Revolution, and who could scarcely be blamed for shunning "the painful impact of new ideas" and fearing to face their devastating implications. For his young pupil, however, the Beethoven question was paramount and inescapable. It admitted no compromise. If one was not for him one was against him. And Le Sueur had felt the power of the god, had for an instant opened himself to it and been possessed, and had then turned away!

Berlioz dropped the subject, but privately recognised that the time had come to emancipate himself. From now on he would write another kind of music. Le Sueur, he told his mother, belonged musically to the age of Louis XIV. When, two years later, he composed the Fantastic Symphony — the first fruit of the revelation of Beethoven — he did not show his teacher the score.

16

"A début that will lead somewhere"

⬤━━━━◆━━━━⬤

For the moment, there was the music he had written in the past two years and the concert he was planning for it. He had his orchestra, on paper at least, and a small chorus. The tenor Alexis Dupont had agreed to sing *The Death of Orpheus* (he had been soloist in the performance at the Institute, when the pianist broke down) and two other singers, Ferdinand Prévost from the Opéra and the ageing but redoubtable Mme Lebrun — a supporter of his since the first performance of his Mass — had also promised to take part. It remained to secure a hall to give the concert in.

By the time he took Le Sueur to hear the Fifth Symphony he was already in the throes of negotiating for the loan of the Conservatoire Hall. It was by far the best venue for orchestral music, indeed the only suitable one, as had just been resoundingly confirmed. The Society's season was due to finish in the second week of May. He must get it for the first available Sunday after that. But it would not be easy. The director, Cherubini, was known to have been grudging about letting the Société des Concerts perform there. Habeneck himself had had to manœuvre and exploit his considerable influence to achieve it. In addition to all the other obstacles to his putting on a concert, Berlioz would have to play the diplomat.

A few days before the end of April he went to see the director. Cherubini thought little of his student's idea, and merely grunted that no one could use the hall without the special authorisation of the Arts Secretary, the Vicomte Sosthène de La Rochefoucauld. But Berlioz was accustomed to that sort of reaction from the crustier members of the musical establishment, and knew there were ways of getting round it if one played one's cards right. He had had dealings with the Vicomte before: three years earlier, when he had gone to see him about using the Opéra orchestra for the first performance of his Mass, and again shortly after that when La Rochefoucauld had affably agreed to put pressure on Kreutzer — unavailingly, as it turned out — to include the Scène héroïque in one of the concerts spirituels at the Opéra. So Cherubini's reply, whatever the intention behind it, was more than sufficient. Berlioz wrote to La Rochefoucauld, requesting the favour of a short interview.

At the same time he set his influential Dauphinois contacts in action.

One of them, Chenevaz, was a deputy (Isère), the other, the Comte de Chabrillant, was a peer of the realm. Both were good enough to write to the Vicomte asking him to grant Berlioz permission to give a concert in the Conservatoire Hall on 18 May (the last concert of the Society's season was on the 11th). The Comte de Chabrillant added a postcript: "M. Cherubini, from what M. Berlioz tells me, advised him to put this request to you — a mark of interest, you will observe, on the part of the Director of the school in one of his students." Berlioz had got his campaign off to a good start.

There is a strip-cartoon, Tom-and-Jerry air about the way Berlioz presents his relationship with Cherubini in the *Memoirs*, from their original encounter in the Conservatoire Library over the full score of *Alceste* — when Cherubini and the porter chase him round the table because he has not come in by the authorised entrance — to the neat trick by which Cherubini persuades Berlioz not to apply for a vacant professorship of harmony. But the knockabout treatment was only a burlesque presentation of the realities of the case. By the time they first came into close contact Cherubini was getting on for seventy, very set in his ways, reserving his affection for a small circle of friends, and to the rest of the world, including the students under his charge, notoriously morose and prickly. Apart from his love of Gluck he had nothing in common with Berlioz. The young man's disrespect for hierarchy could only strike him as insolent, to be forcibly discouraged. Equally naturally, manœuvres which Cherubini considered impertinent in a student would seem to Berlioz mere common sense. He belonged to that small but vigorous minority of people who are constitutionally incapable of understanding the claims of authority.

Cherubini's attitude to Berlioz was not in fact one of unequivocal disapproval; though his end-of-term reports on him are at best grudging ("his fugue is passable", "he has ideas but is unruly and long-winded") he was one of the very few members of the Academy's music section to vote for Berlioz's cantata *Cléopâtre* in 1829. As we have seen, he objected to the Conservatoire Hall being used even for the Beethoven concerts: they interfered with academic routine. It is possible that his opposition to Berlioz's giving a concert there was not solely negative and curmudgeonly, but was mixed with a genuine concern that, as he said, such a venture would be bound to land its student presenter in debt.

Berlioz, on his side, admired many of Cherubini's compositions (indeed, learned a lot from them) and never minded expressing his admiration. But Cherubini as reactionary and pillar of the establishment was cast inevitably in the rôle of villain, with whom his young Dauphinois adversary would always have scores to settle. The old man was the enemy of free expression. He represented the spirit of obscurantism and the superannuated past, of rules for the sake of rules, of reasons why something should not be done, which the young Romantics were dedicated to overturning or, as in this case, circumventing.

The first fortnight of May saw a flurry of diplomatic activity. La

Rochefoucauld indicated benign interest, and told Chenevaz he could see no objection and would look into the matter the moment the season was over. But that would be leaving it dangerously late to put on a concert on the 18th. The season did not end till the 11th. On the 3rd Berlioz wrote to the Vicomte, tempering his impatience with politely turned apologies for importuning him, but pitching his appeal high and explaining with some force why it was not possible in practical terms to wait in continued uncertainty.

> A concert such as I wish to give requires a great deal of careful and detailed planning. I have to arrange with my singers and with the chorus where to hold their separate rehearsals, and I cannot get my players to commit themselves definitely until I can tell them the day and precise time of the general rehearsal. Not yet having your consent to my using the hall, I can do nothing and settle nothing; and I fear lest I lack the time to overcome the difficulties in my path. This concert, intended as it is to make me known, is of the utmost importance to me; my entire musical existence is bound up with it. If I obtain the hall of the Royal School from you, I will benefit greatly in many respects; if on the other hand you are unable to grant it to me, it is urgent that I take steps to secure another. I therefore venture to beg you, Monsieur le Vicomte, to let me know your decision as soon as you can. The Conservatoire's final concert is fixed definitely for Sunday 11th May. The Society for the Children of Apollo always hold theirs on Ascension Day, the 15th; in consequence, unless there has been an earlier request, the hall should be free on the 18th. If however it is not, but it were possible for you to let me have it on the 25th or 26th, the Whitsun holiday, I would wait till then.
>
> Monsieur le Vicomte, I ask you to take into consideration the difficult position I am in, and to continue to give me the benevolent protection which I have been favoured with whenever I have appealed to you. The career of composer is becoming daily more thorny, and if a powerful authority does not come to my aid, I very much fear I may consume my energy in fruitless efforts and never attain the goal to which I strive with so much fervour.

Three days later a note from La Rochefoucauld asked Cherubini whether there was any obstacle to his granting the hall to the artist in question, "who has been recommended to me in the most pressing manner by several persons whom I am sincerely desirous of obliging". Cherubini replied that though the hall was technically free on the 18th, the success and high artistic standards achieved by the Society's concerts in the same hall made it very inadvisable for M. Berlioz to put on his own, which would surely disappoint the hopes he placed in it and would besides, given that summer was beginning, be unlikely to draw an audience. "I must add that the [Society's] concerts and the rehearsals they have involved have led to a certain laxity in the pupils' studies in a large number of classes, owing to the enforced absence of their teachers, and it is time that I restored the order normal in education; if concerts continue

Gasparo Spontini: portrait by Grevedon, 1830. Spontini was the most important early influence on Berlioz's musical style. He presented the picture to Berlioz shortly before the latter's departure for Italy, inscribing it: "Greet my beloved country for me, my dear Berlioz, speak to her sometimes of her grateful son Spontini".

Above left: *Cherubini, by Ingres. Drawn in about 1833, it was one of several studies for the portrait in the Louvre.*
Above right: *Rossini, caricatured by Mailly, c. 1850.*
Below left: *François-Joseph Fétis, lithograph by J.B. Madou.*
Below right: *Madame Branchu, portrait by Vigneron*

Paris le 31 Août 1824

Mon cher papa

Je n'ai pas besoin de vous dire combien votre lettre m'a surpris et navré, vous n'en doutez certainement pas, et j'ose espérer que votre cœur désavoue les cruelles phrases qu'elle contenoit. Je ne comprends pas encor comment celle que j'avois laissé à Alphonse a pu vous émouvoir a ce point; elle ne contenoit rien que je ne crois vous avoir dit ou fait entendre cent fois; et je ne pense pas qu'il me soit échappé en parlant de mes parens, aucune expression contraire aux sentimens d'un fils tendre et respectueux. Je suis entraîné involontairement vers une carrière magnifique (on ne peut donner d'autre épithète à celle des arts) et non pas vers ma perte; car je crois que je réussirai, oui je le crois, il ne s'agit plus de considérations de modestie; pour vous prouver que je ne donne rien au hasard, je pense, je suis convaincu, que je me distinguerai en musique, tout me l'indique extérieurement; et dans moi-même la voix de la nature est plus

Letter from Berlioz to his father, reaffirming his musical vocation: "I am driven involuntarily towards a magnificent career — no other adjective can be applied to the career of artist — and not towards my doom."

Charles Kemble and Harriet Smithson in the tomb scene of Romeo and Juliet, *lithograph by Francis, 1827.*

to be given at the Royal School, I cannot reestablish discipline in class as promptly as I wish to [...]"

On the following Monday morning, 12 May, Berlioz went to the Conservatoire and had a terse exchange with the Director. Cherubini informed him that he had written to the Vicomte to dissuade him: it was so late in the season that no one would come and costs would not be covered, the orchestra would suffer in comparison with the Society's, all these concerts disturbed classes and wasted the students' time, and what was more, he, Cherubini, wished to get the platform cleared, the risers taken down and the desks removed.*

Berlioz, striving to remain calm, answered each point in turn, then went back to his room in the Rue de Richelieu and sent a long account of the conversation to La Rochefoucauld, using as a pretext for writing to him yet again the suspicion which, he realises, he must be under of having lied to the Vicomte when he claimed that he had been advised to apply to him for permission by this same M. Cherubini who was now suggesting that he shouldn't be allowed to have the hall. "Yet I can assure you that had he not positively said, 'You must ask M. le Vicomte de La Rochefoucauld', I should not have importuned you with letters as I am doing [...] The reasons he gave me this morning are very feeble. [Berlioz proceeds to list them, and his replies.] If my letter reaches you too late and your decision is already taken, this will be the second time your benevolent intentions on my behalf will have been frustrated at the whim of a subordinate ['agent subalterne']." He then reminds the Vicomte of the letter of recommendation he was good enough to write to Kreutzer a couple of years ago, in spite of which Kreutzer refused to have his work performed at the concerts spirituels. He ends by appealing to him against Cherubini's "mauvaise volonté" and begging him, since he cannot now be ready for the 18th (on which day, moreover, everyone will be at the races in the Champ de Mars), to let him have the hall for a week later.

He was by now on desperate tenterhooks; but he must have been confident of the Vicomte's desire of pleasing Chabrillant and Chenevaz (and perhaps also annoying Cherubini) to speak of the Director of the

---

* According to the dramatised account of the interview given in the *Memoirs*, Cherubini took great exception to Berlioz's including his Prix de Rome cantata *Orphée* in the proposed programme of the concert: "No, that I weell not 'ave. Eet is bad, eet — eet is not posseeble to play eet." — "That was how you judged it, sir, and now it is my turn to judge. If a bad pianist couldn't accompany it, that doesn't prove that it's unplayable by a good orchestra." — "So you are planneeng an insult to the Academy?" — "No, simply an experiment. If, as is probable, the Academy was right in declaring my score unplayable, clearly it won't be played. If on the other hand the Academy was mistaken, it will be said that I took its advice and that I have corrected the work since the competition."

Royal School in quite such disrespectful terms. In the meantime La Rochefoucauld had already made up his mind and written a curt reply to Cherubini, informing him that since he had promised M. Berlioz, he proposed to let him have the hall on the 18th, and instructing him to let him know without delay. This necessitated a further letter from Berlioz to the Vicomte, it being by now too late for the 18th. And two days later, on the 16th, the longed-for authorisation was finally his: he could have the hall on Whit Monday the 26th — a day when the Royal School was on holiday and no classes need be disrupted. The Vicomte, taking up the "agent subalterne" of Berlioz's letter, invited him to make all the appropriate arrangements with M. Cherubini, "who has received the necessary orders".

Now that the signal was given, he leapt into action. The orchestra must be alerted, individually, as to the times of the rehearsals, the chorus and soloists confirmed, the press invited and the concert publicised. On the 17th he went to see one of the administrators of the Opéra to get permission for two singers on the payroll, the tenor Alexis Dupont and the bass Ferdinand Prévost, to take part. The day before, he visited the offices of four newspapers and periodicals which specialised in the arts — *Corsaire*, *Pandore*, *Figaro*, and *Revue musicale* — and delivered an open letter to the editor explaining and justifying what he was about to do. The letter is a nice example of the technique of stirring up public interest and controversy by pretending that they already exist. He may also have hoped that it might just catch the eye of Harriet Smithson.

> Permit me to appeal to your goodwill and enlist the aid of your journal so that I may clear myself in the eyes of the public of certain rather serious accusations. Word has spread through the musical world that I was proposing to give a concert made up entirely of my own music, and already disparaging rumours about me are going the rounds. I am charged with presumption and rashness, and the most absurd pretensions are being imputed to me.
>
> To this I reply that all I wish to do is to get myself known, so that if I can I may induce the writers and directors of our lyric theatres to place some confidence in me. Should a young man be blamed for wishing such a thing? I do not believe it. If on the contrary there is nothing reprehensible in it, what is wrong with the means I am employing to accomplish it? Because concerts have been given made up entirely of the works of Mozart and Beethoven, does it follow that in doing likewise I have the ridiculous pretensions that people imagine I have? I repeat that in acting as I am I merely employ the most direct means of getting my attempts at dramatic music known. As for the rashness which makes me risk exposure before a concert public, it is perfectly natural. My justification is that for the past four years I have been knocking at every door, and none has been opened to me. I cannot obtain an opera libretto, nor get the one that was given me [*Les francs-juges*] performed. I have tried without success all the usual means of getting a hearing, except one, and I am now employing that. I think I could

do worse than take as my motto Virgil's line: *Una salus victis nullam sperare salutem.*

Yours etc.,
Hector Berlioz (Pupil of M. Lesueur)*

Another call was on the tax official responsible for levying the poor-tax on takings at all public concerts. This was laid down as a quarter of box-office receipts, but Berlioz succeeded in striking a bargain whereby, in consideration of his student status and the fact that he was paying the chorus, the inspector agreed to accept a lump-sum payment of 150 francs on the eve of the concert. Reporting this to his father, he begged him, with many apologies, to help him out if he possibly could: he had to have the money by Saturday the 24th. In other respects, he said, everything was ready and in train. La Rochefoucauld had let him have the hall; Cherubini was resigned to the fact, and had actually offered him the use of the Conservatoire's choral class — but he could not dispense with the Opéra chorus, though they were having to be paid.† Dr Berlioz promptly sent a money order for 200 francs, payable on the 24th.

The final démarche was a flowery, elegantly penned letter to the Vicomte de La Rochefoucauld, begging him to add one more to his many other kindnesses by attending the concert that would not have been possible but for him. "The final rehearsal, which took place today, has given me the hope of being well performed; but of what value could even a great success be to me unless I obtained it in your presence?"

Two full rehearsals were held, on the 23rd and 24th. Attendance was by no means exemplary. Some players arrived late, others left before the end. But, for the composer, it was a moment of suspense and excitement and satisfaction only equalled by the first experience of hearing his Mass three years before. And compared with his recent music the Mass, even when revised, was a prentice work. He had come a long way since then, he knew. The pieces in this programme represented a far wider range of expression and colour, a surer grasp of means and ends. They might be nothing beside the prodigious orchestral dramas of Beethoven with which the hall was still ringing; but they were his own in a way that the Mass — most of it, at any rate, he could not help recognising — was not. And the response of the musicians was so whole-hearted and so gratifying in its spontaneous enthusiasm that even if the concert were never to take place

---

* "The defeated have one salvation: to hope for none." *Revue musicale*, 16 May; *Figaro, Pandore* and *Corsaire*, 22 May. In addition the *Corsaire* published a news item about the concert in the same issue.

† The Opéra choristers had already been engaged. There was also no time to copy additional chorus parts, nor money to have them copied professionally.

the rehearsals by themselves would have accomplished part of his aim, would have established him in the musical world as a name to be reckoned with.

Compared to that, it was a minor disappointment that Alexis Dupont's sore throat had obliged Berlioz to remove his Prix de Rome cantata from the programme and replace it with the Resurrexit from the Mass (which many of the chorus and orchestra already knew), and had foiled his plan to put a note in the programme: "*The Death of Orpheus*, scena for voice and orchestra, declared unperformable by the Academy of Fine Arts, performed on 26 May 1828". In fact the conductor, Bloc, who was used only to operas with spoken dialogue (the repertory of the Odéon), had shown his inexperience with accompanied recitative by getting certain passages wrong every time they rehearsed them: there was no guarantee he would not have done so at the performance. (The contretemps prompted an ancient music-lover present at the rehearsal to exclaim, "Give me the old Italian cantatas any day — there's music that doesn't confuse the conductor: it plays itself." In his over-excited state Berlioz could not help retorting, "Yes, like an old donkey that finds its own way round the treadmill.")

On the other hand it had been extremely satisfying to hear the orchestra bring off the Bacchanal with such panache; it made amends for the humiliation of the previous summer, when he had been forced to withdraw his cantata after the Institute pianist broke down in that very passage. The final section of the cantata — where the clarinet echoed Orpheus' hymn to love while chromatic harmonies on tremolo strings suggested the moaning of the wind and the harp gave forth fragmentary arpeggios as though the cords of Orpheus' abandoned lyre were vibrating momentarily — had made a profound impression on the orchestra and been greeted with loud bravos at the end. It had been the same with the introduction to the *Francs-juges* overture. At the first run-through, during the passage dominated by the trombone theme in D-flat major, one of the violinists, his friend Turbry, had cried out that it was as though "the rainbow were the bow of his violin, the winds were playing the organ, and the weather beating time", and the whole orchestra had stopped and cheered. An Opéra musician in the orchestra told a colleague later that the trombone passage was "the most extraordinary thing he'd ever heard". — "Except for Beethoven, you mean." — "Except for nothing — I defy anyone to find an idea as tremendous as that."

At the concert itself, even more than the sight of Auber, Hérold, Habeneck, Dérivis, Nourrit, Dupont, the directors of the Opéra and the Odéon, Le Sueur and Reicha applauding him, it was the approval of the performers that pleased him most. At the end of the Resurrexit, which concluded the first half, they threw aside convention and rose to their feet, clapping and cheering and stamping, while cello and double bass bows rebounded like hailstones. The composer, in his corner of the orchestra, was not surprisingly stirred to the depths and, burying his face in the nearby timpani, burst into tears.*

The success of the Resurrexit was some consolation for the failure of the previous item, the Mélodie pastorale from the second act of Les francs-juges, which was hopelessly botched. Of the three soloists, two, Prévost and Mme Lebrun, were past their best, while the third, the young tenor Gilbert Duprez, was a last-minute replacement for the indisposed Dupont. The chorus, singing from single-line manuscript copies in which the solo parts were only briefly indicated, miscounted their bars and, getting no cue from Bloc, failed to come in and uttered no sound. Poor Bloc also nearly ruined the final section of the Scène héroïque, "Des sommets de l'Olympe", by conducting the opening trombone motif at the wrong speed and then causing momentary confusion among the violins when he adjusted the tempo; and the long Spontinian crescendo and whirling choral outburst, "Le monde entier", though every bit as dramatic as he had imagined (even in an inadequate performance he could see that), fell far short of what it should have been because the chorus was much too small. It brought the afternoon to a rather tame conclusion. But the Waverley overture, which opened the concert, was vigorously applauded; so was the Sacred March of the Magi; Duprez did a great deal better by the other excerpt from the opera, Conrad's aria from Act 3, than he and his two colleagues had done by the Trio; and if the Francs-juges overture, which opened the second half, made a less immediate and vivid impression on the audience than on the players themselves, their reaction to it remained a precious boon, the response that counted most of all. The scenes of enthusiasm at the rehearsal were re-enacted at the concert, when the timpanist, unable to restrain himself during the long unison theme for the brass, seized Berlioz by the arm and, gripping it with ferocious intensity, exclaimed at intervals: "It's superb! ... My dear fellow, it's sublime! ... it's terrifying! — enough to make one have a seizure!" — "With my other hand", reported Berlioz to the receptive Ferrand, "I grasped a tuft of my hair and tugged it furiously; I should

---

* An action which would seem more histrionic today than at that time. We may assume that Berlioz played percussion at the concert, as he did at the first performance of the Mass in 1825 (see page 170) and at the concert of 1 November 1829 (when he played the bass-drum solo that he had recently added to the development section of the Francs-juges overture). The tam-tam stroke with which he set St Roch resounding in 1825 had been removed from the Resurrexit during revision, but the cymbal clashes which accompany the piccolos in the introduction to the overture figured in the score by this date. Having failed to get the opera performed at the Odéon, Berlioz and Ferrand were rewriting it for the Opéra, whose orchestra was twice the size of the Odéon's. Berlioz had long remarked the sympathetic resonance set up when cymbals and piccolos are used in combination, as in the Bacchanal in The Danaids (one of his favourite scores in the early 1820s), and had more recently observed the effect in Freischütz.

have liked to be able to cry out, forgetting it was my own piece, 'Yes, tremendous, colossal, prodigious!'"*

Reckoning up the gains afterwards, he could reasonably feel that they outweighed the losses. The losses were, most obviously, financial. There had been only a thin house — plenty of important figures from the musical world, and personal friends, but very few from the general public. That old snake Cherubini had been right: summer had started, and a lot of people who might have come had gone off to the country for the day. (Perhaps the down-payment of 150 francs to the poor-tax inspector had not been such a bargain after all.) Berlioz was obliged to explain in a carefully worded letter to his father that he had "not been quite able to cover his expenses": the hall was not so full as it would have been if he had had time to publicise the concert properly, and the labour of putting it on had also meant that he had not been able to fit in any of his pupils the whole month, so that all in all despite his father's generous money-order of 200 francs he had had to borrow an extra 200 from Charles Bert to meet his obligations.

The artistic losses, on the other hand, could be learned from. Another time he must try to get better soloists, and he must have a larger chorus; thirty-four voices were not enough. He must also find a more decisive conductor than Bloc. As for the gains, the greatest was the renewed and confirmed suffrage of his fellow-musicians. Even the sceptical had been won round, like the violinist Tolbecque, who when he first heard of Berlioz's projected concert had thought it "the height of conceit" and said it would be "utterly boring", but who had played in it all the same and at the first encounter with the *Francs-juges* overture had been stirred to the depths and turned pale as death. There was also the useful discovery of just what one was up against in putting on a concert of one's own music — the two performances of the Mass, both of which took place within the context of the church, had not fully prepared him for it.

Finally, there were the notices in the press — a satisfactory crop, even though nothing had appeared in the *Débats* (Castil-Blaze was away at the time). All the critics who reviewed the concert wrote favourable about it. The day after, *Figaro* published an enthusiastic account, enrolling him in the ranks of the young creative artists who would break the monopoly of the old guard, and praising him for his talent and courage: "M. Berlioz chose as his device *Una salus victis nullam sperare salutem*. He can now replace it with *Audaces fortuna juvat*† [...] His style is full of

---

* The timpanist's feat (assuming that he also fulfilled his role as timpanist) is perfectly feasible, given that the drums play only once during the twenty-five slow bars of the brass theme. The same applies to the cymbals.

† "Fortune favours the bold": another Virgilian tag (misquoted for "Audentes fortuna adjuvat").

energy and originality, but at times there is a wildness about it [. . .] The most striking piece, in our view, is the overture to *Waverley*, which received a triple ovation, and then the second part of the Cantate héroïque. Courage, Monsieur Berlioz! You have all that is needed to succeed. Be always yourself and follow nature; only, be sure to remember that effects in music are powerful only so long as they are used sparingly [. . .]" The review in the *Voleur* (written, he discovered later, by Guillaume Ross-Despréaux, one of his rivals in the Prix de Rome competition) was more complimentary still, and ended by generously predicting that "M. Berlioz is destined to become one of the mainstays of the French school" and urging him to fulfil the expectations he had so brilliantly aroused.

Fétis' article in the *Revue musicale* was more cautious and critical in tone, but its conclusions too were encouraging.

[. . .] M. Berlioz has the happiest disposition. He has ability; he has genius. His style is energetic and sinewy. His ideas are often graceful; but more often the composer, carried along by the fire of his youthful imagination, overextends himself in combinations of an original and passionate effect.

There are a lot of good things in all this; there are also some bad. Often M. Berlioz's originality verges on the bizarre; often his instrumentation is unclear; his melodies are sometimes arid; he is prodigal with large-scale musical effects, and this exaggeration makes him overshoot the mark when by the same means, properly controlled, he would attain it with no difficulty.

His pieces are almost all too long; the *Francs-juges* overture would have had twice the effect if it had been half the length. M. Berlioz is a pupil of M. Lesueur; the advice and even more the example of his master will no doubt succeed in convincing this young composer that simplicity of style and well-marshalled ideas in no way preclude the vigour and vivacity he is so partial to.

These reflections, dictated by good will and fairmindedness, will have answered our intentions if in due course they have some influence on M. Berlioz's work; for the rest, they will dispense us from a detailed examination of each of the pieces that made up his concert. We will say only that the *Waverley* overture, the March of the Magi and a few passages in the Credo deserve applause. In this last piece the tenors' part is written much too high.

Although M. Berlioz's music bristles with almost inextricable difficulties, the orchestra, under M. Bloc, performed it with praiseworthy ensemble and precision. We owe an honourable mention to Mme Lebrun and Ferdinand Prévost, who graciously put their talents at the service of the young composer. Prévost fils was in the audience; we should rather have seen him on the platform; his fine voice would have been very useful in the recitatives of the cantata which concluded the concert.

Fétis was subsequently heard to follow up this measured pronounce-ment by declaring publicly, at a salon: "Now that is a début that will lead somewhere." The remark was repeated and went the rounds. At the Opéra, when Berlioz resumed his sessions in the pit, the great Augustus, emperor of the claque, who had come to the concert with two of his aides-de-camp, "held out his massive hand to me and said (in French of course) 'Tu Marcellus eris' in heartfelt fatherly tones."

The concert continued to be talked of, and led temporarily to discussions with theatre managements about a possible opera. A dramatisation of *Atala* was mooted. Another idea, which interested Laurent, director of the Théâtre-Italien where the English company was at present established, was for an opera based on Knowles's tragedy *Virginius*, which Miss Smithson had appeared in shortly before. Perhaps after all the concert would be the means of making her less remote and unapproachable!

A month after the concert Berlioz wrote to Ferrand giving news of these various projects, but urging him to send the promised revised text of the first and third acts of *Les francs-juges*, since it was quite possible nothing would come of any of them, though he was on the point of going to see Laurent to discuss *Virginius*. He also reported a conversation with Albert Du Boys' old music teacher Pastou, for Ferrand to pass on when he saw Du Boys.

> I ran into him two days ago in the Rue Richelieu, and without giving me time to say "Hello" he launched straight in: "Oh, I'm so glad to see you — I came to hear you. Do you know? — you're the Byron of music, that's what you are. Your *Francs-juges* overture is a *Childe Harold* — and then, what a harmonist you are! By jove, the other day I was out to dinner and they were talking about you, and a young man said he knew you and you were a very good fellow. 'I'm buggered if I care what he's like,' I said; 'when someone can write music like that he could be an absolute devil for all it mattered to me.' I never imagined, when we were applauding Beethoven together and shouting and stamping, that a month later in the same hall and on the same bench it would be you that was making me experience feelings like that. Goodbye, my dear chap, I'm proud to know you." Can you beat it? The man's a madman.

Berlioz's letter, written in reply to heartwarming congratulations from Ferrand, gives a slightly less gloomy picture of his state of mind than the one written after the performance of the Mass the previous November. The concert had galvanised him out of his grief. At least there is music, "music alone", enabling him to bear the "poisoned, disenchanted existence" he has led for the past nine months. And to strengthen his hold on life there is Ferrand's friendship, ever more real and precious to him, even though his friend as yet knows nothing of the torments of his heart.

When it came to the point, he did not go to see Laurent, as a long postscript revealed.

> 28 June, 8 hours later

> I've returned not from M. Laurent's but from Villeneuve St Georges, ten miles outside Paris — I rushed straight off there, alone, from my place. All

my muscles are trembling like a dying man's. Oh my friend, send me something to work on, throw me a bone to gnaw. How beautiful the country is! How rich, how luminous! All the living creatures I saw as I returned had such an air of happiness. The trees shimmered, and I was alone in that wide plain, around me space, distance, oblivion, grief, rage. In spite of all my efforts life eludes me. I clutch only the shreds of it. [. . .]

Sunday morning 29 June 1828

Don't be alarmed at these wretched aberrations of my heart. The crisis is over. I don't want to explain the cause of it in writing, a letter can go astray. I urge you not to mention my state to anyone; a word is so easily repeated, and it might reach my father and lose him his peace of mind.[. . .] Be careful, I beg you: say nothing about it to Du Boys, as he could pass it on to Casimir Faure, and from there my father would hear of it [. . .]

By this time Hector and his father were once again embroiled. His explanation of the financial losses incurred on his concert had been as diplomatic as he could make it, but Dr Berlioz was not amused. He reacted by cutting off his allowance, and a month later was still sticking to his resolve; Nancy was deputed to write to her brother and tell him so. In the meantime Félix Marmion, who had seen reports of the concert and had also been sent a bundle of reviews by his nephew, wrote to Nancy from his garrison at Sarréguemines, taking a studiedly cool view of "our maestro's burdensome quasi-success" but arguing that they should consider it cheap at the price. "This method of getting himself known was a perilous enterprise from which he has emerged victorious, and I don't think that however incomplete it may seem to you, 200 paltry francs is an excessive amount to pay for it. If he gets an opera accepted and a partial success with it, that really will be something. Wait till he falls flat on his face before you withdraw all support. That is my advice, my plea if you like, and I beg my brother-in-law to listen to it. His son is an expense to him in Paris, I agree, but a very small expense. His transgression, if that is what it is, is not a heinous one. One can't help being impressed by his persistence in the face of so many frustrations, such slender means and above all so many obstacles. I've just written to him telling him not to be discouraged but to throw himself into his work and always remember what I've told him a hundred times, that success will alone win him absolution."

Félix Marmion's brother-in-law, however, was unlikely to have welcomed the phrase "200 paltry francs" from a man who owed him more than 12,000, and he remained unmoved. He also turned down Hector's request for the entrance fee for the Prix de Rome. Berlioz might not have been able to compete if Le Sueur had not insisted on paying it for him.

17

Second Prize

———◄◆►———

On 2 July 1828, at the usual unseemly hour of seven in the morning, the Prix de Rome candidates assembled at the Institute for the preliminary exam or concours d'essai and were set the test of the obligatory fugue. The following afternoon the music section of the Academy met to judge the fugues and decide who should go through to the second round. Five had entered: Berlioz; Guillaume Ross-Despréaux, last year's second prize (who had written the friendly review of Berlioz's concert in the *Voleur*); Pierre-Julien Nargeot, another Le Sueur pupil and a second violinist at the Théâtre-Italien who also played viola in the Conservatoire orchestra; Alphonse Gilbert, cellist at the Odéon and a hardy annual of the Prix de Rome (he competed from 1825 to 1830); and one other whose name has not survived. For the past three years four had been admitted to the competition proper; but an unidentified member of the music section is recorded in the minutes as proposing that there should be only three.[*] On deliberation, however, it was decided to admit four – Gilbert, Despréaux, Nargeot and Berlioz. After a day in which to prepare for their weeks of incarceration, the four candidates reassembled at the Institute on 5 July and the chosen poem was dictated to them. They were given an episode from Tasso. The text, by the symbolically named Vieillard, showed Erminia the infidel Queen of Antioch, racked by her tragic unrequited love for the Christian crusader Tancred, resolving to leave Jerusalem and ride out disguised in borrowed armour to the succour of the wounded knight.

It was, like the Orpheus torn by the Bacchantes of the previous year, a dramatic subject whatever the feebleness and hollow rhetoric of the

---

[*] Possibly a move on Berton's part to lessen Berlioz's chances of being admitted. This is not mere conspiracy theory. The documents show Berton repeatedly trying to prevent him from winning the Prix de Rome. It was Berton who in 1827 declared his *Orphée* "unperformable" and who argued most forcefully against him in 1828. In 1830 he was the sole member of the music section not to vote for Berlioz's *Sardanapale*.

actual verse.* And the poetic situation, if not the words, was from Tasso — a fellow-sufferer, another artist driven mad by love and frustrated ambition! But Berlioz had vowed this time to be circumspect: he would curb his instincts and compose a score that mollified his judges and lost little in being reduced to the piano. He was "en loge" from the 5th to the 28th July, on which date he handed in his finished score — an exceptionally neat and handsome piece of calligraphy — to the Institute office.

During these three and a half weeks he renewed acquaintance with his old friend the Institute usher Pingard and had further long conversations with him, in which he heard more about the South Seas and the great French explorers Levaillant and the Comte de Volney ("Oh, that was a fine man, Comte de Volney, so natural — he always wore blue woollen stockings"). It was Pingard who told him — meeting him on the stairs at the Institute on the evening of Judgment Day — that he had just been awarded second prize, and had missed first prize by only two votes; there had been a prolonged argument about him among the musicians on the jury, during which one of them (?Berton) had claimed that he was mad — "Beethoven has turned his brain" ("Who is this Mr Beethoven that everyone's talking about?" asked Pingard; "he's not a member of the Institute"). The discussion had grown so heated that several painters got bored and left without voting. Otherwise he might have won.

Berlioz always argued against the double voting procedure whereby the whole Académie des Beaux-Arts in full session had the power to alter the "jugement préparatif" of a particular section — a power that was sometimes exercised.† In this he was being remarkably if typically dis-passionate, considering that he benefited directly from it; but he could not accept that the prizes for musical composition should be decided by artists working in totally different disciplines and possibly quite ignorant of music. In fact, he himself owed his second prize to the painters, sculptors, engravers and architects, and not to the musicians. On the musicians' preliminary vote he had come nowhere: the first prize went to Despréaux, the second to Nargeot. There was no honourable mention, and no "deuxième second grand prix" (as there quite often was); an unnamed member of the music section, perhaps Le Sueur, made the proposal that one should be awarded, but it was turned down.§

* Fétis in the *Revue musicale*, commenting on the choice of poem, criticised "ces cantates usées et décrépites". It was the fifth time in the twenty-five years of the competition's existence that the subject of Erminia had been set.

† E.g. in the music competition, in 1827, in 1828, and in 1824 when, the composers having decided not to award a first prize at all, the jugement définitif of the full Academy awarded it to a competitor who had not even been placed by the music section.

§ When the full session of the Academy rescinded the musicians' vote and gave Berlioz second prize, a proposal to award a second second prize was accepted, and it went to Nargeot.

All this was highly significant. Berlioz's cantata had qualities that could appeal immediately to unprejudiced listeners, whereas one has the feeling that most of the music section was set on putting him down whatever the piece was like. The section's report on the cantata awarded second prize virtually says as much: "In proposing a second prize for [Nargeot], the section does not disguise the fact that this composition is a little feeble and lacks original ideas; but the section considers that naturalness of vocal writing and simple and unpretentious orchestration are qualities that are becoming rarer every day, and it sees it as its duty to encourage those who do not disdain to follow this path." Berlioz stood for "tendencies" which must be discouraged. Had he not demonstrated, the year before, with *Orphée*, his contempt for tradition and the rules of the competition? Since then, his unashamed admiration for Beethoven had identified him more damningly still with the heresies of Romanticism. (Berlioz was not one to keep his enthusiasms to himself; one can't see him remaining silent when Berton and Boieldieu and the rest carried on about the barbarities of Beethoven's music.) It hardly mattered what sort of piece he had written.

In fact he had kept himself pretty scrupulously in order. Of his three surviving Prix de Rome cantatas (the fourth, *Sardanapale*, exists only in fragmentary form), *Herminie* is by far the most discreet and the least dissident. The subversive Berlioz shows his face only in the long diminuendo to a pianissimo ending, cellos alone left playing, which replaced the expected final cadence for full orchestra. Disconcertingly bizarre modulations are mostly avoided. There are a few grammatical errors, but such were not uncommon among competitors for the Prix de Rome, which was the reward for the most promising student. The vocal writing is energetic but sober and thoroughly "natural", and we may well imagine that Mme Dabadie, one of the leading singers at the Opéra, whom Berlioz had got to sing his cantata, would have given a fair account of it. The orchestration is for conventional forces − classical eighteenth-century orchestra with the occasional addition of cymbals − which are handled with skill and touches of eloquence (the soft glow of the wind in the introduction, the charming woodwind decorations to the reprise of the first aria) but hardly unconventionally and in no way "pretentiously": it would suffer less than most Berlioz scores in being reduced for piano, and the music's strengths − rhythmic impetus and sense of movement in the second and third arias, recitatives enlivened by a few bold contrasts and some vivid word-setting but fundamentally classical in conception − would be correspondingly more evident. The text is treated with a deference not found in Berlioz's *Orphée* of the previous year nor in the *Cléopâtre* of 1829; only at the very end of the final aria is a small adjustment made, where a couple of lines from the preceding recitative are incorporated in the aria's reprise. All in all, while it is perfectly understandable that the music section should have rejected

Orphée and *Cléopâtre*, they should in justice by their own lights have given *Herminie* the prize. But the desire not to do so was too strong.

According to Pingard's account of the full session, one of the academicians (propably Berton) made much of the fact that Berlioz had set some lines in the final and prescribed "air de mouvement" as a slow prayer, and argued that such a breach of the regulations should be made an example of; but the Permanent Secretary of the Academy, Quatremère, defended Berlioz and advised his lay colleagues that the liberty was a very minor one. To that extent Berlioz had yielded to his instincts, feeling — as he later put it — that "the trembling Queen of Antioch could hardly be expected to implore the 'god of the Christians' with melodramatic cries to the accompaniment of a raging orchestra". The prayer, "Dieu des chrétiens", was much admired by Pingard, who said that though he knew nothing about music it "fair churned him up inside"; and Berlioz used the tune for the "Chant sacré" of his *Neuf mélodies*, published in 1830. The most striking thing about this prayer, however, is its recall by flutes, clarinets and horns in the orchestral epilogue of the "air de mouvement", above the rapid beat of strings and bassoons, in a long diminuendo which suggests Erminia galloping away on her desperate errand of mercy — one of the first of the receding vistas which are such a feature of his music. This, in conception at least, is pure Berlioz and perhaps calculated to raise the eyebrows of the stricter classicists, though it is a poetic effect often found in Cherubini's music. The long arcs of melody in the second aria, "Arrête! arrête! cher Tancrède", and the panting accompaniment, with its accented dotted rhythm out of phase between first violins and lower strings, show a clear Spontinian influence (another bad mark with Berton, who assured Berlioz that Spontini did not "enjoy a very high reputation among connoisseurs"; but Berlioz's style remained indebted to Spontini all his life). The aria looks forward, however distantly, to some of the music of the embattled heroines of Berlioz's final years, Cassandra, Dido and Beatrice.

Most interestingly of all, the middle section of the aria — set to the words "In vain I voice my feeble plaint, I entreat him, he hears me not" — contains an early version of the main theme of the Fantastic Symphony, the famous "idée fixe": the 40-bar melody, differently treated, is already present almost in its entirety. It used to be assumed that Berlioz "had recourse" to the cantata when he wrote the symphony, and that a similar process covers all the so-called borrowings of thematic ideas from the Prix de Rome scores (e.g. the *Romeo and Juliet* melodies that first appear in *Sardanapale*). But more likely the opposite was the case, and the opportunism worked the other way: when composing to a given text under competition conditions he tried out ideas already sketched that lent themselves to the particular requirements of the moment. Though it is not impossible that the idée fixe first came to him "en loge" at the Institute, my feeling is that it already existed, associated with Harriet Smithson and his unrequited passion for her and waiting for a time when it might be developed in a full-scale work; meanwhile he used it to express the lover's exalted yearning for a beloved who is both physically distant and unresponsive. The importance of the melody is emphasised by its first two phrases being stated at the outset of the work, in the orchestral introduction; for the whole premise of the poem is the hopelessness of Erminia's love for Tancred and the suffering and havoc it has wrought in her life.

Whatever Berlioz thought of the Prix de Rome and of the bizarre system to which he owed his second prize, it was an undeniable step forward. It gave him a reasonable hope of coming first next year, and in the meantime free entry into every operatic theatre in the capital and a medal which could be sold for a modest but handy sum. Above all, it was a passport to the good graces of his family. He sent them the news and announced that he would come home for the holidays at the beginning of September. His father promptly despatched a money order for 300 francs, and reimbursed Charles Bert the 200, still outstanding, which Hector had borrowed before the May concert. Berlioz could now repay his namesake Auguste Berlioz the 50 francs he owed him, and have the copy made of the full score of the Resurrexit and of the Mélodie pastorale from *Les francs-juges* which he had promised Humbert Ferrand but had not been able to afford before.

He knew from experience, however, that it would be wise not to assume his father had come round for good. Less and less did he relish having to depend on so wayward a benefactor; and he disliked being a financial burden to him almost as much as he disliked living under the constant threat of having his lifeline cut. It was high time he achieved some independence. That, rather than a genuine threat to his allowance at this particular moment, seems to be the explanation of the somewhat fanciful letter he now sent, with Le Sueur's collusion, to the Minister of the Interior, the Comte de Martignac, applying for a government grant. He had, he wrote, just been awarded second prize in the Institute's music competition; but he came from a numerous family and his father, exhausted by great sacrifices, was no longer in a position to support him in Paris, and in consequence his career was about to be brought to a standstill. Several artists, second prizes like himself, had been given state grants to go to Rome to complete their education. He was not asking for anything as grand as that, simply for help towards remaining in Paris and perfecting his musical studies while he aspired to win the first prize in a subsequent competition. With the petition went a glowing covering letter from Le Sueur — "member of the Institute, director of music to the King's Chapel, knight of the royal orders of St Michael and the Legion of Honour, professor of composition at the Royal School of Music" —

testifying that his pupil was a young man of the most brilliant promise who for the glory of France was destined to become a great composer, but who needed help so as to be able to complete his studies, which still required another year or eighteen months. "M. Berlioz was born for music; nature seems to have singled him out among many others to become a composer of exceptional gifts who will be a painter in the art of music; but his genius will be lost if he does not obtain the protection of our French Mæcenas [...] If he does, he will be able to declare with pride all his life, 'It was M. le Comte de Martignac who started me on my career.'" The Minister's reply was in the negative.

In the four weeks between the jugement définitif of 2 August and his departure for La Côte St André on the 30th, it is likely that Berlioz worked on the revised and expanded *Francs-juges*, of which Ferrand had just sent him the first and third acts. More important, he read and re-read Goethe's *Faust* in the new translation by Gérard de Nerval which had come out a few months before. Berlioz had probably seen one of the earlier French versions, the one published in 1822 by the Marquis de Saint Aulaire or Albert Stapfer's which appeared in 1823 (and which was reissued this same summer of 1828 in a large octavo edition illustrated by Delacroix's lithographs). They were tame, uninspired renderings, however, and had made little impact. Nerval's was of a different order, the work of a poet, a true translation which opened the enchanted realm of Goethe's enigmatic drama to the French Romantic imagination. As Jacques Barzun remarks, everything about *Faust* "struck home — the theme, the form, the realistic variety, the Nature philosophy". It purified the fashionable Gothic horrors of the contemporary taste for medieval Germany, raising them to universal heights. Its freedom of design and diversity of forms, moods and textures reinforced the lessons of Shakespeare's plays. *Faust* was the supreme modern expression of the unfettered quest for experience, yet it laid bare the demons of disgust and alienation that lurk within men's souls, the Spirit of Negation waiting to turn the world to dust.[*]

Once Berlioz had his hands on the book he could not put it down but took it with him and read it anywhere and everywhere, in the café, in the street, on his bench seat in the pit before the show began.

For a musician, *Faust* was particularly rich in suggestion. The whole work was full of references to music. But the lyrics which Goethe scattered through it — and which Nerval's mostly prose translation rendered in verse — were the most obvious invitations to musical setting. In the

---

[*] *Faust* at that date meant Part 1 only: there was as yet no hint of the redeemed, enlightened hero of Part 2, a sequel still incomplete and not to be published for another decade. To readers of Gérard de Nerval Faust seemed almost as surely damned as his counterpart in Marlowe and the old versions of the legend. Mme de Staël, in *De l'Allemagne*, concluded that "the author's intention is evidently that Marguerite shall perish but that God shall forgive her, and that Faust's life will be saved but his soul lost".

middle of September, while travelling in a stagecoach through his native Dauphiné, Berlioz thought of a tune for Marguerite's song "The King of Thulé" and jotted it down in his notebook.

Perhaps it was the sight and feel and smell of the country of his boyhood which he had not revisited for three years, that inspired the antique ballad-like air of the melody, with its touchingly angular rise and fall, its rustic "alpine" sharpened fourth followed by the plangent Berliozian-Dauphinois flattened sixth, its shifting drone bass and gently rocking 6/8 metre. He copied out the song with a simple piano accompaniment to give to Humbert Ferrand, along with the promised scores of the Resurrexit and the Mélodie pastorale from *Les francs-juges*. Ferrand had agreed to come and stay for a few days at La Côte. Berlioz wrote to him begging him not to let them down; they were all looking forward to his visit – his sisters and their friends because of the balls and picnics that were being organised in honour of his return and for which "amiable young men are in short supply", he because he was badly in need of his friend's company. "'Horatio, thou art e'en as just a man as e'er my conversation coped withal.' [...] We'll read *Hamlet* and *Faust* together. Shakespeare and Goethe! the silent confidants of my woes, the interpreters of my life. Come, do come! No one here understands their inspired ragings – the sun blinds them; they think it merely odd." He would also be able to tell Ferrand, at long last, about Harriet Smithson.

We have no direct knowledge of how Hector was received by his family; but the absence from Nancy's diary of any word of tensions is eloquent of the changed situation. His second prize in the Prix de Rome and the narrow margin by which he had missed coming first had had their effect.

For Nancy her brother's return lit up her existence. He had travelled to La Côte with Alphonse Robert, and the contrast between the two cousins was promptly noted in her diary: Hector "full of fire, of impetuosity, of life, youth, beauty, the other with that settled middle-aged air which lends little charm to the features and the expression (though always kind and gentle), and looking in the first moment of arrival as bewildered as a fish out of water". Nancy had long ago decided that Alphonse could never "inspire feelings of passion". But Hector's friend Ferrand promised to be rather different. The letter that Hector read out to the whole family revealed a superior mind and a lofty soul; Nancy was particularly impressed by one phrase in it, apropos of the monastery of the Grande Chartreuse: "It is not yet heaven, but it is no longer earth. Religion, my dear Hector, is not an empty word."

Ferrand arrived. Alas, what disenchantment! "I was transfixed by his nose and chin, which have an irresistible attraction one to the other. His voice also struck me as very singular." Altogether, she found him "much inferior to his letter". However, one evening was "not sufficient for judging a young man. So, my conclusions tomorrow."

Nancy's subsequent report provides the only portrait of the man who remained for over forty years Berlioz's closest friend.

M. Ferrand stayed three days. It took me the whole of the first day to digest that *nose* and *chin*. But from the second day his face, his voice, everything about him was quite redeemed in my eyes; he reveals his nature with such directness and lack of calculation, he shows himself as he really is with a frankness which is so much to his advantage, that before long you recognise what a fine spirit he has, you see it reflected in the play of his mobile features. I greatly enjoyed hearing him talk of religion with a respect and enthusiasm which reveal a faith so vital that even to those who share it it seems something fresh and unexpected. Placed between him and M. Casimir [Faure] at dinner, I listened to a most interesting, and for the times we live in unusual, discussion on the subject. A moment of happiness for me to meet, at last, two young men exempt from the universal epidemic! Impossible that the noble frankness with which M. Ferrand expresses his religious sentiments should not subjugate even those who do not at all share his beliefs [...] I could wish that my brother had such a friend constantly at his side; I should hope much for him from such society, but it's impossible, they are destined to live apart. Yet there must be many points of affinity between them, otherwise they would not be such close friends. There is much that is noble in my brother's soul. All that's grand, generous, sublime makes a deep impression on it.

To anything more mundane it was rather less responsive, if we are to judge by the remarks of the Berliozes' friend Nancy Clappier, who had been staying with the family for part of the time that Hector was there. "I am very glad I saw him during his brief visit," she wrote to her god-daughter Nancy. "I have a great interest in him. One can't deny that he is very gifted and that nature has been prodigal with him. Perhaps too much so. Those lofty, exalted sensibilities of his separate him too much from the mass of humanity and make him a stranger to the concerns that are the lot of other mortals but which strike him as too gross to bother with. I can conceive how inconvenient that must be! He lacks something that will act as ballast to such a vivid and suggestible imagination [...] I find him the perfect hero for a novel, except for his not being in love." (The secret of Harriet Smithson had been well kept.)

The truth was that in the three years since he had last been home he had developed rapidly; he had become an artist, and his whole world had expanded almost out of recognition, while the world of La Côte and Grenoble had remained the same. He loved his family, was still closely linked with them despite all the passionate disagreements of the past seven years, but he felt increasingly detached from their milieu. His thoughts, his life were elsewhere. Nevertheless he went through the social round with a reasonably good grace, appeared at receptions, accepted invitations to parties, danced, listened politely while he was congratulated

on his prize, visited his worldly, amiable Uncle Victor and his ravishingly pretty Aunt Laure in Grenoble and chatted with his young cousins
Odile and Jules (with whom he was a great favourite), called on his
grandfather in Meylan and heard that Estelle Dubeuf had lately married
a wealthy Grenoble judge fifteen years older than her, and, when he
could, escaped for long walks in the hot countryside. He saw his old
Côtois friends, most of whom had finished their studies and come back
from Paris, and told the most intimate of them, Edouard Rocher, in
strictest confidence all about Harriet Smithson.

One great gain from his stay was a much closer rapport with his elder
sister Nancy, now a young woman of twenty-two with more of a mind of
her own. Her own difficulties with their parents (who were refusing to
discuss with her the various offers of marriage that came in) had made
her less unsympathetic and more understanding towards her brother's.
In her he discovered, beneath her inhibitions, a nature not after all so
different from his, avid for experience, impatient of the bourgeois values
she was trapped in. He also got to know his brother Prosper, already at
eight showing signs of unusual intelligence, and was made much of by his
adoring fourteen-year-old sister Adèle; he listened with a certain fellow-
feeling as she told him how she had made her parents take her away from
the horrid boarding-school they had sent her to the previous spring.

All in all the three-week visit was a success. For the first time there
were no recriminations from his parents, no tense and tearful scenes. His
father, whatever his private disappointments, seemed resigned to his vocation and no longer bent on opposing it. He gave Hector 600 francs to
spend on clothes, and handed him another five hundred on the day he
left and caught the coach for Paris (27 September 1828). The next time
the family saw him, two years hence, it would be as first-prize winner, en
route for Rome.

18

Scenes from Faust

————◆◆◆————

The King of Thulé, whose tune came to Berlioz during his stay in Dauphiné, proved to be the first of nine settings of lyrics from *Faust* (nine lyrics but eight scenes, because the soldiers' chorus was combined with Marguerite's "D'amour l'ardente flamme" into a single scene). According to his letter to Goethe of the following spring, he had at first resisted writing any music to *Faust* but had finally been unable to prevent himself from doing so. Certainly, once he had begun, it poured out of him. The score was completed within a few months of his return to Paris. By the beginning of 1829 he was having it engraved, at his own expense. The work was issued at the end of March or the beginning of April by Maurice Schlesinger (whose shop was in the Rue de Richelieu next door to where Berlioz lived), and bore the designation "Œuvre 1". It was — if we except some studies for guitar in the form of variations on "Là ci darem la mano" which have not survived — the first music Berlioz had published since the romances with piano accompaniment of 1822 and early 1823.

The fact highlights the immense distance covered in those six years; but even more significant is the distance between the *Eight Scenes from Faust* and the music Berlioz had been writing not so long before — *Waverley*, *Orphée*, *Les franc-juges*. The most characteristic of these scores, the overture to *Les francs-juges*, is without doubt a strikingly original and effective piece, which still holds its place in the concert repertory. Like the haunting epilogue for clarinet and harp and tremolo strings in *Orphée*, it could not be by anyone else; the unmistakable voice of Berlioz speaks through it. But it does not speak with the clarity and unerring certainty of nearly all the *Eight Scenes*.

Herminie, the work immediately preceding *Faust*, is not really a valid point of comparison, since when writing it Berlioz deliberately kept his fancy on a leash in the hope of avoiding offence. But it is noticeable that in the guise in which the cantata presents it the idée fixe, the future main theme of the Fantastic Symphony, is still a long way from its true character, whereas nearly all the *Faust* melodies hit the mark first time; the form they will take sixteen years later in *The Damnation of Faust* is

273

already achieved, a few details apart. Only the Concert de sylphes would need extensive revision to become the fabric of deceitful enchantment familiar from the *Damnation*; and even here, despite the many ways in which Berlioz subsequently refined and strengthened the movement, its most exquisite passage, the dense yet weightless sequence of downward-drifting harmonies near the end, is the work of 1828–29. The Easter Hymn – after the sylphs' scene the movement most altered in harmony and orchestral texture – is recognisably the same piece. The brief peasants' chorus was elaborated in 1846, but without alteration to the original idea.

All the numbers for solo voice remained essentially unchanged. Brander's Rat Song, with its blunt, variably stressed yet headlong vocal line and its grunting, burbling obbligato bassoons cut across irregularly by scrabbling strings (the musical embodiment of the brutal, jeering joviality of the text), is almost identical in both versions. So is Mephistopheles' riposte to it, the debonair but menacing Song of the Flea, a piece which shows Berlioz already master of the art of writing genuinely fast music; the delicate yet graphic string writing would require little modification in 1846, and the introduction to each verse already hinted at what was to be one of the central ideas in the composition of the *Damnation*, the representation of the devil by music which jars against the conventional order of metre and tonality. Mephisto's Serenade, with its devilishly catchy tune and irresistible air of false geniality, would have only the tessitura and key changed (from tenor to baritone and from E major to B) and the accompaniment of single guitar replaced by the dry guitar-like clatter of pizzicato strings. Both Marguerite's songs, "The King of Thulé" and the Romance "D'amour l'ardente flamme", were little different in shape and expressive intensity from what they would become. In each of these last two numbers an obbligato instrument framed and accompanied the plangent utterance of the singer; and as with Brander's grotesque bassoons, Berlioz's ear for instrumental colour led him to the ideal timbre: a solo viola for the remote, imagined sadness of "The King of Thulé", the dark cor anglais for the passionate, inconsolable grief of the Romance.

Ernest Newman called the *Eight Scenes from Faust* "the most outstanding Opus 1 that the world of music had ever known". It is Berlioz's opus 1 both in the literal sense that it is the first major work he published, and in the real sense that it is his first completely characteristic score. All at once, under the inspiration of Goethe, he is able to create sounds that spring straight out of the dramatic idea and translate his thought into the precise musical image. Nothing had done that before – not the words of the Latin Mass, nor Ferrand's texts for the Scène héroïque and *Les francs-juges*, nor the competition cantatas. Shakespeare had given him his crucial artistic initiation and had provided him with a bible, a primer whose teaching he would draw on all his life; but though musical ideas for *Romeo and Juliet* had certainly occurred to him and been noted down by this time, it would be some while yet before the composition of the first works on Shakespearean subjects, the *Tempest* fantasia of 1830 and the *King Lear* overture of 1831. The discovery of Beethoven would not bear fruit in a large-scale symphonic work till after an interval of two years; though the genesis of the Fantastic Symphony probably goes back to 1828, the music was not written till 1830. Berlioz's sudden achievement in the autumn of 1828 of a musical identity and a style entirely his own certainly reflects a new confidence, following his lessons with Reicha and the experience of hearing his own recent compositions at the concert in May, and following the recovery of his creative powers from the virtual paralysis induced by the successive impact of Shakespeare and Beethoven; but *Faust* acted as the catalyst. It gave his imagination the right degree of shock and stimulus, set all his faculties alight without scorching them, and in its songs — compact lyrical or dramatic "scenes" — provided his genius with the scope it was ready for.

Fired by the "marvellous book", his mind reached out towards other, larger projects. The germ of the Fantastic Symphony was a "descriptive symphony on *Faust*", beginning to take shape in his imagination at about this time. For a few months at the end of 1828, while he was composing the *Eight Scenes*, there was talk of his being commissioned to write the music for a *Faust* ballet whose scenario, by the editor of the new *Figaro*, Victor Bohain, had been accepted by the Opéra.

I have no doubt that he was also thinking, however hazily, of the large-scale dramatic work that he would write on the play when he was prepared for it, and that this half-formed idea of what the *Eight Scenes* would one day become was one reason why, having gone to the labour and expense of getting the work published, he changed his mind six months later and withdrew it, destroying all the copies he could lay his hands on (on the face of it a strange decision). The *Eight Scenes* was a series of disconnected, brilliantly illuminated moments, a musician's response to the most obviously "musical" passages in the drama, not a unified whole. In one scene Mephistopheles was a baritone, in another a tenor. The settings, beginning with full orchestra and chorus and ending with a single guitar, were far too diverse to lend themselves to complete performance, as well as impractically demanding on instrumental resources (an ophicleide required for ten notes only in the entire work). And it totally omitted the protagonist of the drama; Faust did not appear.

Berlioz himself gave as one of his reasons for withdrawing it the incompleteness of the work. The other reason was that it was "badly written". He certainly removed some grammatical errors in the harmony when he came to revise the Easter Hymn. But the immediate cause of his second thoughts was hearing the sylphs' scene at the concert he put on later in the year, and acknowledging that the piece did not sound well and needed thorough overhauling. To publish a major work without having first tested it in performance was in fact quite uncharacteristic of him. He had a very fine aural imagination but he was also a practically minded musician who preferred to wait till he had experienced his music in action. Yet you can understand why he rushed into print with the *Eight Scenes*. His haste reflected the excited sense of pride and achievement, the realisation that *Faust* had touched a spring within him and his musical personality had clicked into focus, and he was going to be — in Le Sueur's words — "a painter in the art of music". The published score was a milestone in his progress; it was a grand stock-taking (including a dedication to the Vicomte de La Rochefoucauld in tactful tribute to his helpful acts of high patronage) and a declaration of Romanticism: in addition to the printing of short passages from Nerval's translation, introducing and linking the separate scenes, each number carried an epigraph in English from *Hamlet* or *Romeo and Juliet*. The Concert de sylphes was headed by Mercutio's "I talk of dreams", the Song of the Flea by Hamlet's "Miching mallecho: it means mischief", Mephisto's Serenade by "It is a damned ghost", the Romance by Romeo's "Ah me, sad hours seem long", the Easter Hymn by Ophelia's "Heavenly powers, restore him", and the ballad by her "He is dead and gone; at his head a grass green turf, at his heels a stone".

19

Burning in the Void

————◆◆◆————

"Ophelia" had been a powerful presence behind the composition and whole conception of the work, as the quotation from Moore's *Irish Melodies* on the title page emphasised: "One fatal remembrance, one sorrow that throws / Its bleak shade alike o'er our joys and our woes". He had written the music for Harriet Smithson.

The autumn and winter of 1828—29 saw a new direction in the course of Berlioz's phantom relationship with his starry, remote beloved. In the beginning it had been a classic amour de tête, though of peculiar intensity. Following the coup de foudre of. the Odéon he had tried to make contact with her but had not persisted when, as he must have expected, he received through an intermediary a brusque and summary rejection. Later he had nourished vague but futile hopes that his concert at the Conservatoire would be the means of bringing him to her attention. But, for the rest, he had remained the same "unknown planet, revolving obscurely round its dazzling sun". Now there came a change. Harriet was no longer an irrevocably distant and godlike being but a creature of flesh and blood, who might be approached, even perhaps wooed.

Partly it was that, physically speaking, she was no longer distant. The furnished apartment where she lived with her mother and sister was at the corner of the Rue Neuve St Marc and the Rue de Richelieu, just opposite the house where Berlioz had taken a room the previous spring when he had decided to move north of the river to the centre of Parisian musical life and had settled on no. 96 Rue de Richelieu, not knowing that she lived there, though drawn — he could not but believe — by magnetic attraction. From now on he was acutely and daily aware of her presence. He knew her comings and goings, when she went out in the morning and came back at night, when she left Paris and when she returned; from his window he saw her get into and out of her carriage, he observed the movement of her shadow behind the shutters, saw the light go on in her bedroom, watched for the moment when she put it out.

Imagination leapt ahead of reality. So as to be able to write to her — perhaps speak to her! — in her own tongue, he enrolled in an English language course which held classes three times a week. Only, it was

277

frustrating — he told his sister Nancy — that he could not afford a private teacher, with whom one could learn in fifteen minutes what it took an hour to learn in a class.

He did not tell Nancy his particular reason for taking the course; but in a letter to her two months later, in reply to one in which she raised the general question of marriage, he took the subject up eagerly as a pretext for letting the family know his ideas.

> You speak of marriage. I can assure you we think the same way about it. Don't worry, never shall I marry for money, even supposing I had the chance. It's not that I can't appreciate wealth: indeed, I prize it a thousand times more than the many who seek it only as a means of luxury and ostentation [...] Do you suppose that when my sleep is disrupted by the din of the insolent carriages of the businessmen who inhabit this district, I feel perfectly indifferent, when with a quarter of what they spend I could accomplish many ardently desired but fruitless ambitions? But even if I had a thousand more motives for wanting to be rich, it could never make me forfeit what so many people dismiss as the minor attributes of marriage. Yes, my dear sister, you are absolutely right to look to a husband for a support, a guide, a protector, rather than a banker. For me, I shall look for a woman on whom all my affections can be concentrated, for whom I experience all that passionate love contains of the deepest and tenderest feelings, and who is worthy of such love. I do not ask that she feel for me all that I feel for her, that perhaps would be to ask too much and I might never find it; let her have a less intense feeling for me, but lofty enough to be able to understand me, and I am satisfied. I do not seek beauty and brilliance. I could be presented with a woman as beautiful as the Medici Venus, as brilliant as Mme Malibran and as brainy as Mme de Staël, and yet want none of her. I must love her, from the depths of my heart — that is the one essential condition. And be sure, no external considerations would have any influence on my feelings, no prejudice would weigh with me. The very existence of prejudice against her would only make dearer still the person for whom I defied it. If I once met such a being, you may imagine that neither heaven nor earth could stop me striving to the uttermost to obtain her. [10 January 1829]

The letter — as he told Ferrand a few weeks later — was intended to prepare the ground for asking his parents' consent to his marriage, in case it should come to that. An actress, a foreign actress at that, was prime material for prejudice.

Events had moved fast. Since Harriet Smithson's return to Paris from a tour of the French provinces at the end of November, Berlioz, without actually meeting her, had contrived — so he imagined — to advance his cause. He had made friends with the manager of the house where Harriet had her apartment, M. Tartes, and found in him, if not an ally, a sympathiser; and he had also got to know the Englishman, Turner, who had become her agent and who was therefore constantly in her company.

Somehow, Turner and his wife gave him the notion that there might after all be hope. He was led to believe that Harriet was interested and was only prevented from speaking to him by the presence of her very dominating mother, and that once the English company started a new season (there was at present a lull in their performances) she would be able to do so. As it was, she had already managed to talk about him twice with Turner.

Berlioz was in a fever of alternately mounting and fading hopes. He longed for an end to the torturing uncertainty; "but it seems to recede continually before my passionate pursuit".

Three weeks later, at the end of January, he was almost delirious with joy. Turner had actually quoted her as saying, "If he really loves me, if his love is not of the kind it's my duty to scorn, a few months' waiting will not wear out his constancy." "Oph. is not so distant from me as I thought," he wrote in jubilation to Ferrand. "There is some reason — what it is I may not be told for the moment — which makes it impossible for her just now to declare herself openly." But she was about to go to Holland, where she would have plenty of opportunity to talk freely to Turner — "she wishes to, much and often". Turner, "casting aside his British phlegm, said to me, 'I tell you, I shall succeed, I'm sure of it; if I go with her to Holland, I am sure to send you excellent news in a little while.'" And now he *was* going with her, in a few days' time. "Oh God! if I really love her! [. . .] I shall send her my score [*Eight Scenes from Faust*] to Amsterdam. I have written just her initials in it. What! Shall I succeed in being loved by Oph. or at least will my love flatter her, please her? My heart expands and my imagination struggles to comprehend this intensity of happiness, but cannot. What! What! Am I to live, then, am I to write, and spread my wings?* Oh dear friend, oh my heart, oh life! love! All! All!"

Yet he strove not to let his ideas run away with him. "Does she really want everything in the open?" he wrote to Edouard Rocher. "Maybe I'm being deceived." And to Ferrand: "Don't be alarmed by my joy. It's not as blind as you may fear. Unhappiness has made me wary." Nothing was yet sure.

In the last ten days of February the whole insubstantial edifice collapsed. What had caused it to be dreamed up in the first place? Perhaps for a brief moment Harriet had been flattered by Berlioz's attentions, and made enquiries about him, only to be warned on no account to have anything to do with him (she told him, much later, that she had been assured he was an epileptic). At all events, the dream turned bad. The journey to Amsterdam was postponed several times, and Harriet remained in Paris for a few weeks more. While she was there, Berlioz had no hope of a positive reply — the letter he had written would be handed to her

* The following words in English.

only when they got to Amsterdam; he could then apparently count on a few lines from her in answer. "Oh God, what will she say to me?" For the moment, however, he was in the strange situation, for a lover, of longing for the departure of the beloved.

Abruptly, his patience gave out. Unable to bear any longer the uncertainty, exacerbated by her continued unapproachable presence just across the street, he wrote her a declaration of love. No answer came. He wrote again, in English, imploring her for one word in reply. There was still no answer. He sought out the friendly M. Tartes — and found that the letters had never reached her: her servants had had strict orders not to admit any communication from him!

In the meantime the organisers of a charity performance at the Opéra-Comique in aid of the poor had taken advantage of Miss Smithson's delayed departure to persuade her to appear, with Abbott, in scenes from *Romeo and Juliet*. Berlioz, still pursuing his will o' the wisp, had got the manager of the theatre to add the *Waverley* overture to the programme (which also included a new opéra-comique by Auber with the title of *La fiancée*). By the time the performance took place, on 25 February, his hopes were in ruins. From now on he was like one in a nightmare. When he arrived at the Feydeau for the rehearsal of his overture, the English actors were still on stage, rehearsing the tomb scene; he came straight in from the street to see Juliet lifeless in Romeo's arms, and with a cry fled from the theatre (while Harriet warned her fellow-actors to beware of "that gentleman with the eyes that bode no good"). Returning later for the rehearsal — the theatre was just round the corner from where he lived — he listened in a trance.

On the evening of the performance he left the moment the overture was finished, and went round to the Rue Neuve St Marc to talk to the manager during Harriet's absence. M. Tartes had already tried in vain to get Miss Smithson to reply to his letter; the conversation he reported had confirmed Berlioz's grimmest suspicions: all the hopes he had been fed on were false, and Miss Smithson "did not consider she was obliged to reply". M. Tartes had promised nevertheless that he would try again and beg her to grant Berlioz a few lines, and it was to hear her answer that Berlioz was now calling on him. The answer was decisive and peremptory: she did not wish to hear the subject mentioned again; she had made it perfectly clear two years before that there could never be anything between them. "I cannot understand why he persists." — "Then it's quite impossible?" — "Oh, monsieur, nothing is more impossible." The way she spoke the phrase, according to Tartes, and her expression as she spoke it, said even more than the words themselves. Tartes had the feeling that there was some secret reason which absolutely precluded her from contracting any engagement. The previous year, he said, she had refused in most unceremonious fashion an extremely brilliant offer of marriage. It might well be that she was already engaged to someone in

London or even secretly married.

Berlioz went back across the street to his room and lay down on the bed. The following afternoon he was still lying there. Mechanically he got up and went to the window and looked out. At that moment Harriet was getting into her carriage. He watched her drive off, as he thought, on the first stage of her journey.

In fact, though she had been due to leave on the day after the benefit performance, there was another postponement and she stayed nearly a week longer. Berlioz made no further attempt to communicate with her. "The pangs of despis'd love", which Hamlet counts among the cruel evils of existence, had him in their grasp, making him feel, as he later wrote, as though his heart were being wrenched up by the roots and the blood were running ice-cold through his veins, and over all a sense of total emptiness and isolation.

A few days later he roused himself and wrote to his friend Albert Du Boys to tell him of the shattering of his hopes. Du Boys had been his confidant during a visit to Paris the month before; it had been after a discussion with him that he had written his note in English entreating a reply. But that was in another life. Now all was over. She was leaving tomorrow, for Amsterdam, and then London ... The thought that she was not free, that she was committed to another and because of that determined to avoid the least suspicion of inconstancy, only made her more dear to him. His imagination caressed the idea grievingly. But he no longer wept. Sorrow had numbed him. "Perhaps I shall grow resigned to life. And yet ... It seems to me that I stand in the centre of a circle whose circumference expands continually; the physical and mental world is on the circumference, which all the time is moving further and further away, and I remain alone in ever greater isolation, remembering." Tears came when he read Thomas Moore — her compatriot — and when he listened to Beethoven and heard echoes of a vision of an ideal world that Beethoven too was destined never to see. The day before, at the Conservatoire concert, the Seventh Symphony had burst on the Parisian public. The slow movement — "that inconceivable achievement by the great master of sombre and profound meditation, placed between music of the most intoxicating joy" — had been encored. "What agony. Oh, if tears had not come the second time, I should have gone mad." In the street he saw a torn poster advertising the Opéra-Comique benefit, in which fragments of his name and Harriet Smithson's were bizarrely juxtaposed above the bitterly ironic *La fiancée*.

She has just put out her light; in a moment she will be asleep. The idea of returning to some loved one gently rocks her rest.

Her mother is still busy in the apartment. I hear the noise of Carnival maskers under my window. The carriages rattle her windows and mine at the same time. Tommorrow they will no longer be hers.

I shall go out early. Hiller expects me at ten, and will play me a
Beethoven adagio. My eyes will not still be dry then as they are tonight.
That is all I hope for [. . .]

He was, as Peter Raby remarks, "playing all the parts in this imaginary
scenario".

Little by little, life resumed. On returning from his morning with
Ferdinand Hiller he wrote to La Rochefoucauld asking him to be so good
as to accept the dedication of the *Eight Scenes from Faust* — his first
publication — as a token of gratitude for what he owed the Vicomte. La
Rochefoucauld accepted graciously. It was, as Berlioz said, "not meant
for him" (it was for *her*); but his name and his offices — " Aide de Camp
du Roi, Directeur-général des Beaux-Arts" — figured prominently on the
splendid title page. Below the composer's name were quotations from
Gérard's translation* — "I give myself to the tumult, to the joys that are
most sorrowful, to Love that is akin to hate, to Peace that is akin to
despair" — and (in English) from Thomas Moore: "One fatal remembrance,
one sorrow that throws / Its bleak shade alike o'er our joys and our
woes". At the top, in the magnificent flourish of the title — "Huit Scènes /
de / Faust / Tragédie de Goëthe / Traduites par Gérard" — clusters of
lines radiated outward from the proud name "Faust" like the rays of the
rising sun.

Ferrand lent his friend money to pay the printer; he had offered
unprompted to do so, no doubt knowing that Berlioz would not have
been able to bring himself to ask for a loan. The score was ready at the
beginning of April. A few days later, encouraged by Ferdinand Hiller,
Berlioz sent a copy to Goethe.

Hiller was not the only connection with Goethe. The previous autumn,
while at work on *Eight Scenes from Faust*, Berlioz had become friendly with
another young German musician, Theodore Schloesser, younger brother
of the Louis Schloesser he had met briefly as a fellow-pupil of Le Sueur
five years before. Theodore Schloesser had arrived at Le Sueur's with a
letter of introduction from his brother one day when Berlioz was there.
Meeting again soon after, they had become involved in a long and comic
misunderstanding over Rossini, each imagining the other to be a passionate
Rossinian but prevaricating out of politeness, so that neither of them let
on what he really felt. "What do you think of *Le comte Ory*?" Berlioz asked
eventually, after they had spent a quarter of an hour stalking round the
subject. — "By jove, it's not . . ." answered Schloesser. — "Fabulous,
you mean?" — "On the contrary, it's vile." — "So you're not a Rossinian?"

---

* Gérard (Labrunie) had yet to adopt the pseudonym de Nerval.

— "Me? God forbid! How could an admirer of Weber and Beethoven and Spontini possibly be one? It's your being one that astonishes me, if you'll forgive my saying so." — "Well — if Rossini had to make do with me for a partisan ... What on earth gave you that idea?" — "At that", reported Berlioz to his sister Nancy, "we collapsed in laughter at our wary conversational manœuvrings." After this their talk took wing. Schloesser proved to be an admirer of Shakespeare (whom he could read in the original), and to have known Weber well. Berlioz and he spent several hours at the piano, introducing Le Sueur to music from *Freischütz*, *Oberon* and *Euryanthe*, which they performed by heart, Schloesser accompanying and singing in German, Berlioz singing everything that had been translated into French.

The link with Weber was precious, but more exciting still was the fact that Schloesser knew Goethe. Indeed he had seen him again only the other day, on his way to Paris, and he enthralled Berlioz with his description of the old man's ageless fire and vitality and the charming simplicity and warmth with which he received strangers. The thought emboldened Berlioz, the following spring, to send a copy of his *Eight Scenes* to the poet in Weimar. Hiller wrote to Goethe's friend and secretary Eckermann to announce its coming, and heard from him soon afterwards that the score had arrived and that Goethe was greatly intrigued by it and delighted with Berlioz's letter, to which "he will certainly reply, if he has not already done so". Goethe's letter was awaited with eager impatience.

Berlioz had met Ferdinand Hiller some time in the winter of 1828—29. The precocious young pianist from Frankfurt who had lately arrived in Paris was teaching at Choron's school of church music in the Rue de Vaugirard and they may have first met there — Berlioz had been asked by Choron to write a work for voices and organ (since lost). Soon they were often in each other's company; the Beethoven session at Hiller's referred to in the letter of 3 March to Du Boys was one of many. Berlioz was nearly eight years older than Hiller and sometimes treated him rather bossily (perhaps in compensation for the sense of inferiority he felt at his young friend's greater musical culture). "In comparison with me", writes Hiller, "he was a man matured by harsh experience, though his intensely youthful manner reflected that southern vivacity which never completely left him. I was very much attracted by this overflowing nature of his. What I had to offer in return was of a musical kind. A short while before, he had got to know Beethoven through his symphonies, which had been revealed to Parisian music-lovers by Habeneck at the so-called Conservatoire Concerts. His enthusiasm knew no bounds. We raved together; and it was my privilege to acquaint him with the master's sonatas and to take pleasure in the delight they caused him."

Ferdinand Hiller's friendship must have meant more to Berlioz than the ability, however much prized, to play him Beethoven sonatas. By drawing him out to talk about his childhood, about his medical studies (of which, "with that strange, wild, shrieking laugh of his he would tell me things that made me shudder"), about the conflict with his parents and his first experiences and struggles in Paris, he clearly fulfilled a need. For Hiller on his side, Berlioz was the object of deep if slightly alarmed fascination. He could not get to the bottom of the paradox of the man, the mixture of extreme emotion and fundamental sanity, the bewildering combination of detachment and passionate egoism. Hiller's reminiscences were set down more than forty years later. Like all such impressions they reflect the outlook and bias of the observer — in this case a somewhat prim and puritanical youth of eighteen, brought up in artistic but highly respectable circles, whom his mercurial friend liked to tease by deliberately playing the maverick and blasphemer. Nevertheless the picture rings true and deserves quoting at length. It is the most detailed account we have of the young Berlioz.

Hector Berlioz was a complete human being, who never betrayed his nature. It was made up, however, of many contradictory elements: energetic to the point of heroism, stubborn, vehement; on the other hand pliant, weak even; patient, reflective, tenacious, yet a prey to the impressions of the moment; good-natured, pleasant, affable, grateful, and then again bitter, cutting, even vindictive. He had a generous measure of contempt for the world, and for life in general, but with it an overmastering ambition. Success intoxicated him, yet at the same time he expressed a violent disdain for the public. Devoting himself compulsively to the high artistic tasks he had set himself, not shirking the most tedious drudgery if his purpose required it, he could yet waste his time like a boy and squander it in mad adventures. What dominated him, beyond reason, was the constant contemplation of himself, of his own passionate feelings, his behaviour, everything he did. He was one of those people to whom it is a necessity always to appear interesting to themselves, who need to attribute an exalted significance to the least thing they do, feel, suffer, the good and the bad, whatever happens to them. Yet he didn't give the impression of being vain, which is quite remarkable, since often he talked about himself to the exclusion of almost everything else. Not that he didn't include God and the world, music and poetry, peoples and nations, within the scope of his outpourings; but he remained constantly — to use a very German expression — *subjective* in the highest degree. Of course most people would like to talk about themselves all the time, if only they were allowed to — La Rochefoucauld remarks that we would rather say dreadful things about ourselves than not say anything at all; but I have not met anyone, apart from actors, in whom this condition was so highly developed. Fortunately his personality was so attractive, so unusual, his speech so lively and picturesque, his way of thinking so keen and singular — now incisive and logical, now humorously exaggerated, witty or extreme — and his enthusiasms so ardent, his aversions so definite and decided, that one was not merely happy to let him carry on, one did all one could to provoke him to fresh "expectorations".

He was in the true meaning of the word a man of honour. He may have had a few passionate weaknesses to reproach himself with; but you were no

more allowed to offend his personal dignity than he himself was. All devious-
ness was alien to him. He would rather harm himself, and others, by being
tactlessly outspoken than get what he wanted by underhand methods.

His artistic self-confidence was very strong. If as a critic he was sometimes,
in his later years, perforce less open than it was his nature to be, he carried
this only so far as to praise, when circumstances compelled him to. He
never, from either envy or self-interest, decried men or works whose worth
deep down he recognised. In criticising what he disliked he may from time
to time have gone further than was necessary, through sheer irritation —
for his whole being was of an extreme nervousness, and passionate through
and through.

I do not believe anyone meeting Berlioz could have failed to be struck by
the unusualness of his physiognomy: the high forehead sharply cut away
above deep-set eyes, the arrestingly prominent hawk-like nose, the thin
finely sculpted lips, the rather short chin, all this crowned with an extraordinary abundance of light-brown curls whose fantastic growth was never
curbed and trimmed by the barber's scissors. Once seen, such a head could
not be forgotten. With this went the unusual mobility of his face, his look
now shining, nay blazing, now dull, almost lifeless, the expression of his
mouth varying between energy and the most scathing contempt, a friendly
smile and a sardonic laugh. He was of middle height, slim though not
elegant — his posture was careless. The sound of his speaking voice was
rather soft, though it goes without saying that it varied with his mood. He
had a pleasant singing voice [. . .]

Eight years older than I was, he had spent the last six years in the French
capital and had come face to face with the struggle for existence [. . .] Not
only did he know what it was to economise to the bone in order to keep
alive: he went so far as to work, secretly and for a long period, as chorister in
a vaudeville theatre — not without the fear, incidentally, of being recognised
by one of his friends. That had come to an end by the time I met him, but
he was still supporting himself by giving guitar lessons and reading proofs
for publishers. I can still see him in a café in the Rue Richelieu (where, in
that very human Parisian way, he was allowed to occupy a table for half a
day), correcting the proofs of Halévy's first success, *The Dilettante from
Avignon*. All this didn't particularly cramp his style, though it bored him.
Occasionally he managed to augment his income, as for instance when he
sold the gold medal he got for winning second prize at the Institute (it
fetched 200 francs).

The change that had taken place in Berlioz during the years he had lived
in Paris can hardly be grasped. Not least, the change with regard to his
musical talent. Out of the naïve flautist-guitarist who had attempted to
compile a kind of potpourri based on assorted Italian airs had come the
composer of the Fantastic, out of the solitary student of the Ecole de
Médecine a forceful young man who felt absolutely no requirement to
kowtow to the eminent musical personalities of the day. But above all, the
metamorphosis his whole world of thought and feeling had undergone! In
relation to me he was something of a Mephistopheles (by which I do not at
all mean I see myself in the rôle of Faust — rather that of the poor student).
All trace of his Catholic upbringing had vanished; he was haunted by
doubts of every kind, and his contempt for everything that he labelled
prejudice was devastating. We often met late in the evening in a café and

stayed over a cup of tea till well after midnight. The things I heard then! So far as my religious beliefs were concerned, I had been brought up as a pure deist; and my artistic principles, one might say, were deistic. But Berlioz believed neither in God nor in Bach, neither in absolute beauty in art nor in pure virtue in life. With Shakespeare, Goethe and Beethoven we raised a common hymn of praise; I followed his accounts of his experiences in a state of sympathetic suspense. But when he gave his tongue free rein, destroying everything in his path like a river in spate, sometimes a kind of fear seized my heart. "I would like to trample on every prejudice," he exclaimed one evening. "If it came to it, I should be ready to marry the bastard daughter of a negress and an executioner."

Hiller, like others, was made privy to his friend's infatuation with Harriet Smithson. "During our walks he would fill the neighbouring streets and indifferent boulevards with wailings of love. The greatest sympathy — which his friends willingly gave him — was needed to make them listen patiently and conceal their exhaustion. We were spared nothing — it was all described to us: the sleepless nights, the attacks of nervous weeping, the long roamings in and around Paris, the sudden gleams of hope, the desolate renunciations. 'If it had been anyone else', said Girard, the well-known conductor and a sceptical man of the world, 'I should have sent him packing.' "

Berlioz's letters to Ferrand and Edouard Rocher show that throughout the spring and summer of 1829 Harriet Smithson still tore at his vitals.

9 April It is thirty-six days since she left, each of them twenty-four hours long; and "there is nothing more impossible".

3 June This pain will kill me. I am told constantly that hope alone can sustain love; but I am very much proof of the contrary. Ordinary fire requires air, but fire that is electric burns in the void.

25 June I am alone ... wandering the streets at night with a bitter grief that haunts me: it's like a red-hot iron on my breast [...] Company, society do nothing; I am occupied all day but it is powerless to distract me [...] You speak of my parents. All that I can do for them is to live, and only I know the effort it takes me to do that.
21 August Fresh agitations, "the new pangs of my despised love"* are un-happily the explanation of why I forget everything. Yes, my dear, poor friend, my heart is the furnace of a raging fire. It's a virgin forest that lightning has set ablaze. At times the fire appears to abate, then a gust of wind, a fresh flaring up, the cry of trees engulfed in the flames, reveal its terrible power of devastation.

But though he burned on, she had given him his congé. There was nothing more impossible.

* In English.

H. G. Smithson.
Né à Ennis le 18 Mars 1802.

Harriet Smithson by Achille Devéria, c. 1827. The lithograph is captioned "Born in Ennis 18 March 1802", but her actual year of birth was 1800.

Above: *Bust of Beethoven by Franz Klein, based on the life-mask of 1812.*
Below: *"The Andante of the Symphony in A" by Eugène Lami, 1840, showing rapt
listeners in the Conservatoire Hall. Beethoven's Seventh Symphony was first performed
by the Société des Concerts in 1829.*

Above: *The title page of* Eight Scenes from Faust, *Berlioz's first major work to be published.*
Below: *Autograph bassoon part for "The Tale of a Rat", the fourth of* Eight Scenes. *Berlioz spent many months in the 1820s copying orchestral parts for performance of his music.*

A page from the autograph full score of Berlioz's Cléopâtre, *the third of his four Prix de Rome cantatas.*

20

In the Steps of the Master

———◆———

Not surprisingly the winter's traumas and the gnawing obsessive state of
mind he had been in since then began to tell on his health. In June he
had a minor nervous collapse; there were days when he could hardly
walk or even get dressed in the morning, he was shaking so badly. At
times he was so strung up that the music he loved best became an
affliction scarcely to be endured: the suffering he recognised in it spoke
too agonisingly to his own. Yet it was music that made existence possible;
without it (he told his father in a rare moment of indiscretion) he could
not go on living.

Throughout the winter and the spring of 1829 he had steeped himself
in the study of Beethoven's music. On 21 December a special Conservatoire concert, devoted largely to Beethoven, included the Fifth Symphony and *Coriolan*; and during the second season of the Société des
Concerts, which opened on 15 February 1829, both the Seventh and the
Pastoral were introduced, the former played three times, the latter twice,
and the Eroica and the Fifth, the great revelations of the previous season,
were given again. At the magnificent final concert on 3 May (added to
the original six at the request of the Duchesse de Berry) the afternoon
began with the Seventh Symphony and concluded with the Fifth.

Within two weeks a company from Aachen in Germany opened at the
Théâtre-Italien for a short season which included three performances of
Fidelio, as well as *Freischütz* and *The Magic Flute* (two modern masterpieces
of German opera which Paris till then had heard only in the travestied
form of Castil-Blaze's *Robin des bois* and the grotesquely mutilated *Les
mystères d'Isis*). Despite the low standard of orchestral playing at the
Italien, here were fresh discoveries and joys. Meanwhile Hiller had been
playing him the piano sonatas; and in March a string quartet led by
Baillot gave the Paris première of the C-sharp minor, op. 131. At the
same time he was correcting proofs of a new edition of the symphonies
which the publisher Troupenas was about to issue (starting with the
Fifth). In the Conservatoire Library he read through the Ninth — not yet
performed in Paris — and studied and pondered the Pastoral and its
lessons for the symphony that was taking shape in his imagination. He

had the score open at the Storm, one day, when Castil-Blaze looked over his shoulder. "Ah, I used that in my opera *La forêt de Sénart* — I stuck in trombones, they made the devil of an effect." — "Why stuck in when they're there already?" — "No, they're not." "What's that, then?" (indicating the two staves of trombones). — "Bless my soul — I never noticed them."

The incident, however farcical, was symbolic of the gulf that still separated a genius of Beethoven's greatness and daring, not merely from the mass of the public but also and particularly from most musicians. There *was* no such thing as absolute beauty; the proposition that shocked Hiller was, alas, logical and inescapable. Berlioz gave melancholy expression to his thoughts in a letter to Nancy.

> Ah, but you speak of the beautiful, the great, the sublime — and a host of ideas rise up, all gloomy. The sublime is not sublime for everybody. What transports some people is for others unintelligible, sometimes actually ridiculous. There are the prejudices that come from education, and then there are the totally different ways people are made. The higher the great geniuses soar the further out of reach of those who claim they are created for them. This is especially so in music and dramatic literature. The other day I heard one of Beethoven's last quartets [op. 131]. M. Baillot introduced it at one of his evenings. I was intensely curious to see what effect this extraordinary work would have on the audience. There were nearly three hundred there, and precisely six of us half dead with emotion — we were the only ones who didn't find the work absurd, incomprehensible, barbarous [. . .] He soared into regions where one breathes with difficulty. He was deaf when he wrote this quartet; for him, as for Homer, "the universe was clasped within his mighty soul". It is music for him alone, or for those who have followed the incalculable progress of his genius.*

The immensity of the gulf between Beethoven and Le Sueur was cruelly emphasised at the sixth Conservatoire concert (26 April), at which two movements from Le Sueur's coronation oratorio were performed at his special request in a programme also containing the *Eroica* and Weber's *Oberon* overture, with disastrous results. All the wags, wrote Berlioz to his mother, were having a field day — the more so as Le Sueur had just been created a baron by the King, whereas Cherubini, Le Sueur's fellow-director of the Chapel Royal, whose music had also been heard in the series of concerts and had stood up well to comparison with Beethoven and Weber, had been omitted from the royal benefaction.

---

* The allusion to Homer shows Berlioz assimilating Beethoven to his private pantheon of gods and heroes. Later he will call the funeral march in the Eroica "Homeric". See also the feuilleton in the *Journal des débats* in which he dreams of being rich enough to buy the plain of Troy and transport a large orchestra there for a performance of the Eroica at the foot of Mount Ida (28 January 1841).

Le Sueur's daughters were "cut to the quick; they inveigh incessantly against Beethoven, who can't do much about it, and against Cherubini, who only triumphs the more [. . .] My rôle is limited to concealing from him as best I can what people are saying. He is persuaded that it was due to the singing, which indeed in his music was very bad that day, so bad one might have suspected it was deliberate. But the performance could have been perfect without its making any real difference."

At least Le Sueur's failure to meet the challenge of Beethoven was an honest failure; the old man had in effect admitted that such music was beyond him. His attitude was preferable to the equivocations of pretended admirers, who treated Beethoven with insolent condescension, graciously acknowledging his genius but "marking" his compositions like a student's. Fétis, reviewing the Seventh Symphony after its Paris première at the Conservatoire concerts in 1829, described the first movement and the finale as "protracted improvisations by a gifted composer on an off day". He conceded that "occasionally the great man retrieves himself; more often he loses his way completely. I have no space to list all my criticisms of these two movements; I will cite only the second repeat in the first movement, which contains a series of dissonances that resolve upwards, in a manner excruciating to the ear. A grammatical error may be condoned if the effect is happy; when the effect is as outlandish as this it is inexcusable"; only those blinded by enthusiasm could fail to regret it.

It was partly this kind of attitude that enticed Berlioz, early in 1829, to begin writing criticism — that "millstone", as he was later to see it, that "hazardous grind which has come to play so large and lamentable a part in my existence". He seized on it at first as a weapon for defending and explaining his gods. The principle of the "critique admirative" — the reasoned appreciation of a piece of music for which the critic has a profound (though not necessarily blind) enthusiasm — was worked out and refined by Berlioz during the 1830s, when he began to write regularly, first for the *Rénovateur* and then, in succession to Castil-Blaze, for the *Journal des débats*; but we can see its earliest, crude foreshadowings in the three letters published in the "Polémique musicale" section of the *Corsaire* in the mid-1820s. In the last of these, a defence of Gluck's *Armide* against Castil-Blaze's dismissive remarks in the *Débats*, occurs the prophetic assertion that the critic's true task — in contrast to the classicist doctrine based on preconceived rules and canons of good taste — is to reveal and expound genius.

By the time Berlioz tried his hand at criticism again his powers of expression had matured. "Calamity — I become a critic" is the heading of the chapter of the *Memoirs* which recounts how he came to be embroiled. From his point of view it was a calamity, as it must be for any composer who finds himself forced to rely on it for a living because his music does not pay, and for whom a good deal of the job consists in reviewing ephemeral work for which he feels no sympathy. When on top of that he was told that criticism was actually what he did best (his election to the Institute in 1856 prompted the mot: "they were supposed to elect a composer, not a journalist"), it is no wonder he regarded it with a jaundiced eye. But you have only to read the letters he wrote even as a very young man to see that he was a born writer. His instinct for expressing his convictions and enthusiasms and persuading others to share them, his story-teller's flair, his intelligence, his humour, his sense of words — everything combined to make him so. The "calamity" was inevitable; the disgust he often gave vent to at the métier of critic came from the servitude it symbolised, not from any natural disability.

The first piece of criticism to speak with his unmistakable voice is the "Letter from an Enthusiast on the Current State of Music in Italy", which he wrote in Rome in 1832. By contrast the Berlioz of 1829 is still feeling his way. The writing lacks the later incisive clarity; it is unleavened by the humour which gives his best pieces their irresistible verve and piquancy. Nevertheless the articles he wrote in 1829 show something of the future critic in embryo; they broach some of his central and abiding preoccupations: truth of dramatic expression in religious music, freedom from the tyranny of routine and of rules mechanically applied, the uniqueness of Beethoven.

The review for which they were written was the *Correspondant*, a liberal Catholic weekly launched by Lamennais in March 1829 under the editorship of the young Comte de Carné with the aim of bringing the progressive impulses in French society, with which it sympathised, under the wing of a rejuvenated church and reconciling them with Christianity — a programme that did not appear hopelessly utopian in that brief period of optimism between the Villèle and Polignac ministries, when all society seemed in fruitful ferment and new ideas on politics, philosophy, science and the arts were being freely debated as never before. Carné was on friendly terms with Berlioz's two monarchist friends, Humbert Ferrand and Albert Du Boys, and it was Ferrand who had the idea of recruiting Berlioz as the paper's writer on music. He was not a practising Catholic nor a fervent monarchist, but unlike many musicians he was interested in ideas, he knew how to write — Ferrand could vouch for that — and in any case music was a subject apart, traditionally independent of the particular stance of the journal it appeared in. The paper agreed to give him a trial run. He submitted an article, the editors liked it, and it was printed under the title "Reflections on Religious Music". The article, signed "H", appeared in the Holy Week issue of the paper (21 April 1829). From June onwards he would be paid for what he wrote. That was another argument in its favour.

In addition to providing a means of defending the beautiful, it gave one an opportunity to attack what one regarded as its opposite. "Considérations sur la musique religieuse" is the first outing of that gamely persistent Berliozian hobby-horse, the absurdity of the obligatory fugues which litter the religious works of the masters new and old (and from which Beethoven himself is not immune). The article set out to explore the reasons why church music was in such sad decline and put forward several: the disappearance of cathedral choirs (only that of Nôtre-Dame survived, in a very run-down condition), the lack of material encouragement to composers to produce new works, the paltry scale of most performances, the dead hand of routine which scholastic prejudice laid on the genre.

By far the greater part of the article is taken up with this last point. At times the young Berlioz is driven by the warmth of his feelings into some confusion of thought and is in danger of replacing one prejudice with another. It seems a little illogical, for example, to take specific exception to fugues on Amen or Kyrie elesion, when the dramatic concept they embody is as rich and meaningful as the concept embodied in Hosanna in excelsis. At one moment he appears to equate sacred music in fugal style with sacred music which is inexpressive and does not move the listener — a false assumption, and an odd one in a composer some of whose most moving and beautiful pieces in the religious vein are fugal: for example, the Offertorium (Requiem) or the Convoi funèbre in *Romeo and Juliet*. It gradually emerges, however, that what he is really objecting to is not the fugal style itself, nor the study of fugue in music colleges (on the contrary, he agrees, a most useful training), but the abuse of a tradition, the routine, unthinking convention of fugue-writing in religious music and the anti-expressive aberrations which in his opinion have all too frequently resulted from it.

Berlioz's hostility was sharpened by the insensitive bawling which often passed for religious expression in contemporary performances and to which the writings of other critics bear witness. (He was to parody the manner of singing as well as the style of music in the fugal Amen sung on the death of a rat by the drunken revellers in Auerbach's cellar in *The Damnation of Faust*.) The article concedes that a modified fugal style in slow tempo can be employed with happy effect. It directs its fiercest fire at fast fugues. "Let anyone who has never heard it imagine the religious effect which follows from fifty voices braying furiously at a very rapid tempo and repeating the word 'Amen' four or five hundred times, or vocalising on the syllable 'a' as though imitating loud laughter, and it will give him an idea of vocal fugues not greatly to their advantage. I defy anyone gifted with a feeling for music who listens without prejudice to a fugue on 'Amen' not to take the choir for a legion of incarnate devils, turning the sacrament to ridicule, rather than for a gathering of the faithful met to sing God's praises [...] And they call this the religious style!" Berlioz then considers the claim which is sometimes made, that the fugal style is suited to sacred music by its very lack of expression, and answers it by challenging the assumption on which it is based — that "a Mass is not meant to move people". Why, he asks, should it be forbidden to do so? In what way is propriety offended when fine sacred music well performed moves one to tears? Does the emotion one experiences on listening to Cherubini's sublime Communion March have anything worldly about it? Is not the music's depiction of divine love, is not its sense of passionate yet humble adoration, rather, the highest expression of religious feeling?

> What is the aim of religious music? To move and uplift the soul by the expression of the sentiments embodied in the words of which it is a setting. In what does it differ from dramatic music? In that religious ideas exclude anything potentially of a light character incompatible with them. But that is the only way in which they differ. In fact, the expression of feeling is as much the object of the one as it is of the other. The latter will give rise to the same sense of gravity, grandeur, solemnity, awe as the former whenever it is concerned with ideas of that sort. The style of a well-conceived religious opera is exactly the same as that of an oratorio: the scores of *Adam* and *La mort d'Abel* [operas respectively by Le Sueur and Kreutzer] are there to prove it.

In all this Berlioz is the faithful disciple of his master. Le Sueur had been the first French composer of his generation to treat sacred music as unashamedly dramatic, introducing the element of large-scale orchestral forces into church performance (and thereby causing considerable scandal and controversy). He was a dedicated opponent (in his own words) of "fugues which express nothing and whose only object is to display the composer's vain erudition and the solution of some problem". "They should be banished from our churches." If Le Sueur's direct musical influence on his pupil faded with the advent of Beethoven, many of his ideas left a permanent impression.

In May 1829 Berlioz sent his family an account of his new activity, choosing to write to his mother — a long, gossipy letter — perhaps because he knew she would be pleased that his first article was about religious music. The letter also announced that he was going to be the Paris correspondent of the *Berlin Musical Gazette*. The proprietor, Adolf Marx, who was in Paris, had called on him and asked him to do it. "No one here knows that I'm writing for these two papers — otherwise I shouldn't be able to say the half of what I think, whether good or bad."*

In one of his first reviews for the *Berliner allgemeine musikalische Zeitung*, an account of the German company's season in Paris, he took advantage

---

* Félix Marmion, who had been informed by Nancy of Hector's new métier, wrote to say that he approved of it, though political journalism was more lucrative. "The time is past and gone when Gluck and Piccinni divided France into two bitterly opposed camps. However, if, as looks highly likely, our institutions settle down and opinions continue to merge until there cease to be parties, then for want of anything better for people to argue and get worked up about, their minds will turn to trivial questions."

of his anonymity to make a detailed anatomy, section by section, of the wretchedly feeble Théâtre-Italien orchestra: the violins saved from total incompetence by four young men from the Conservatoire with a working knowledge of the instrument; one adequate viola; one first-rate cello (the young Franchomme) out of a total section of three (the other two given more to nodding off than to playing); seven at best mediocre double basses; good flute and clarinet but appalling oboe and bassoon; one excellent horn, Gallay, the ablest in Paris, but unfortunately playing only the third part; and a timpanist of some force but more devoted to ogling the ladies than to counting his rests.

Despite this, he reported, *Freischütz* was a popular success, thanks to the singing of the tenor, Haitzinger, the charming simplicity of Mme Fischer's acting as Agathe, the effectiveness of the new décor, and the chorus, whose ardour, almost unknown in Paris, made up for their uncertain pitch. But not surprisingly the first act of *Fidelio* left the audience cold. Not till Florestan's aria, superbly sung by Haitzinger, did the house begin to pick up and applaud. Even when the resident conductor, the hapless Grasset, was replaced by the company's own conductor, Telle (who had a grasp of the tempos), the want of ensemble, of precision and force, not to mention expression, was pitiful. The opening of the Act 1 trio was so badly played by the violins that the pit burst into loud laughter. The director, the article concluded, should think seriously of finding a better orchestra — the Odéon's, for example — for the return visit of the company next year.

The review debated the wisdom of having the masterpieces of so new and unfamiliar a genre introduced to Paris by a provincial troupe whose singers, Haitzinger apart, were far below the standard of those usually heard at the Italien. It also described the alarm and outrage among the cavatina-fanciers at the profanation of the sacred precincts by the uncouth din of a Weber, but reported that some of them welcomed the advent of the Germans on the grounds that it must make everyone "recognise that the Italian is the only true music, and the collapse of the German school will follow accordingly". This called for a riposte (the more so as Rossini had been heard in the foyer assuring his entourage that Weber's music "gave him colic"). Berlioz chose it as the theme for his second piece in the *Correspondant*, only to have the article returned with a note from Carné requesting him to write on some other topic. "I'm thought to be 'a little hard' on the Italian school," wrote Berlioz to Ferrand. "So the Prostitute finds lovers even among men of religion."

Instead he wrote a longish biographical piece on Beethoven. The essay, which appeared in three instalments during the summer and autumn of 1829 (4 and 11 August, 6 October), was designed as an answer to a summary of Beethoven's career which had appeared in Fétis' *Revue musicale* a few months before, and in which Fétis attempted to explain Beethoven's defects (as remarkable as his qualities) by reference to the events of his life, in particular his tragic deafness. The first part of Berlioz's essay is occupied with fairly routine anecdotal stuff, stories — some of them perhaps told him by Reicha — about Beethoven's relations with Haydn, about what Mozart said to him, about his prowess and capriciousness as an improviser, and so on. The stories, however, are chosen so as to illustrate Beethoven's determination to make his own rules and not be bound by academic models. Berlioz follows Fétis' division of the œuvre into three distinct periods (one of the earliest occurrences of what was to become the standard formulation), but in the last instalment reaches a diametrically opposite conclusion. Whereas for Fétis the third period saw the decay of Beethoven's once splendid creative powers and his final abandonment of all civilised restraint, when composing degenerated into mere day-dreaming, for Berlioz it is the climax of Beethoven's career: Fétis' "progressive decline" becomes, in a phrase that clearly alludes to it, a "progressive ascent". The Ninth Symphony, which had yet to be performed in France, is singled out for admiration. "As for us, we have read the score attentively, and without flattering ourselves that we understand it in its entirety and in all its aspects we have no hesitation in regarding it as the culmination of its author's genius." Berlioz finds the explanation of the heterodox forms and unprecedented style of Beethoven's final period not in the incapacitating effects of total deafness but in the intensity of his sufferings, of which deafness was only the most extreme: traditional forms were no longer sufficient to contain and express such depth of emotion. Similarly, the essay's account of the performance of the C-sharp minor quartet (touched on in the letter to Nancy quoted above) by implication challenges Fétis' sweeping dismissal of the work, emphasising its difficulty but also its greatness, and dwelling on the totally opposed impressions it made on different sections of the audience: the majority bewildered and indignant, protesting openly at this nonsensical music (even ardent admirers of Beethoven deploring the loss of his reason), a small handful of devotees moved to the depths of their souls.

The contrast between Berlioz's approach to the C-sharp minor quartet in the *Correspondant* piece and Fétis' in the long essay published in the *Revue musicale* the following year could hardly be more profound. It is not simply that Fétis' article treats the music analytically and Berlioz's impressionistically. Berlioz believes in Beethoven, is willing to go where he leads and, as in an Orphic initiation, to follow him into strange and at first forbidding regions of the spirit unexplored till now. It is an act of faith on his part; he trusts the composer whose symphonies have revealed to him a new world of music of unparalleled grandeur, intensity and scope.

Fétis suffers no such disabling humility. His immediate reaction, in his earliest comment on the quartet, is to label the work "the final spasm of a demented imagination" and to question the sincerity of those who profess to admire it; and during the intervening months, between the comment and the essay, his attitude is only superficially modified. That so recent a work by a composer of Beethoven's acknowledged innovatory genius might be expected to present difficulties which required time and patience to overcome doesn't seem to enter his head. There is no question of his giving the composer the benefit of the doubt: it doesn't occur to the supremely self-confident critic to have any.

Fétis' analysis, behind its façade of lofty and sagacious impartiality, is a sustained exercise in nit-picking, in the spirit of his comment on the Seventh Symphony: "grammatical error may be condoned if the effect is happy; when the effect is as outlandish as this, it is inexcusable". Fétis' whole article is a monument to the schoolman's wrong-headed and patronising pedantry. Its burden is that Beethoven, like the genius he unquestionably was, had felt — all honour to him! — more and more impatient with the conventional limits of musical form and expression and had had the worthy object of widening them, but, partly because of his deafness, had been lured into errors from which a more profound knowledge and a more thorough schooling would have saved him. The late quartets, says Fétis, are from the point of view of both musical conception and compositional skill very defective works; and the C-sharp minor, though the least defective as well as the easiest to understand, is itself "full of false harmonic progressions", even at times of mere "school-boy howlers" ("incorrections d'écolier").

He proceeds to demonstrate this with a wealth of musical examples. Again and again, he points out, dissonances are neither prepared nor correctly resolved. There is no longer any settled sense of tonality: though the work begins and ends in C-sharp minor, in between it wanders restlessly from one key to another. Nor is there any regular rhythm, but a constant juxtaposition of three-bar and four-bar and even six-bar phrases. Beethoven never establishes any ordered sequence of thought but is forever throwing in some unexpected idea, sometimes grave and austere in character, more often grotesque and clownish. In the first movement the endless ungrammatically dissonant harmonies are a penance to listen to; the second movement, though full of mistakes, is less fatiguing to the ear; in the long central slow movement, despite its excessive length, one recognises the composer of superior talent to whom the world owes so many admirable things (though here too there are passages of painfully incorrect harmony); and he is also visible in the finale, a movement, however, of exhaustingly extravagant fantasy. As for the scherzo, it is "difficult to figure out what Beethoven is aiming at, unless it is to demonstrate total licence by indulging in buffooneries for which music offers no parallel". In general the quartet shows how the "tendency to diffuseness which is one of the chief characteristics of Beethoven's style even in his most reasonable compositions" is carried to extremes in his last works.*

Fétis had begun his analysis with the judicious observation that "to assess these quartets properly one must guard against both a blind enthusiasm and a contemptuous and overhasty condemnation". He concluded by predicting that "Beethoven's grand idea — emancipation from the restrictions of musical form — will come to fruition only in the hands of someone who combines genius as powerful as his with purer taste".

These were the pronouncements of one of the more enlightened academics. Most of the establishment dismissed the works of Beethoven's third period out of hand as the ravings of a deranged mind. Given such attitudes to musical innovation, what were the prospects for a young French composer who aspired to follow in Beethoven's footsteps and "go beyond the limits of conventional form and expression"? Whereas the poets and dramatists formed a numerous and well-organised force, Berlioz was in effect on his own, carrying on a one-man campaign against a conservatism still entrenched in positions of power. For the writers, the barriers were coming down. Dumas' *Henri III* was performed at the Comédie-Française in February 1829; at about the same time Alfred de Vigny's translation of *Othello, Le maure de Venise*, went into rehearsal; and Hugo's *Hernani* was accepted by the reading panel of the same theatre — against furious opposition — for production the following year. In comparison, Berlioz had nothing to show for his efforts — above all nothing in the opera house, the goal of his instincts and ambitions and the way to prosperity.

---

* As late as 1860 a Parisian musical pamphlet rebuked Hans von Bülow for performing Beethoven's piano sonatas uncut.

21

The Rebel and the Schoolmen

———◆◆———

Throughout this period circumstances conspired to make Berlioz more than ever aware of the unsatisfactoriness of his position. "I work very hard", he writes to Albert Du Boys in April 1829, "but all this restless activity is to no purpose — I'm getting nowhere." The letter goes on to tell of a visit he has just had from George Onslow, one of the most eminent living composers of instrumental music, who called on him at his lodgings to congratulate him on the *Eight Scenes from Faust*, of which he had just seen a copy. The juxtaposition of ideas is significant. The praise of individual musicians was very gratifying. He received it quite often. But it did not gain him access to the institutions which dictated the destinies of musical life in the capital.

The causes of frustration lay partly in the anomalousness of his position. The impatient young genius conscious of what he could do in dramatic music and desperate to get an opera libretto accepted was still officially enrolled at the Conservatoire; the composer of the *Eight Scenes from Faust* and the *Francs-juges* overture was an aspirant to the Prix de Rome; the sophisticated voice that spoke with authority in the public press about the weakness of the Théâtre-Italien orchestra, that proclaimed Beethoven's Ninth Symphony not a monstrous aberration but the summit of modern music, that challenged the sacrosanct rôle of the fugue in musical settings of the Mass, would shortly be set to write a fugal exercise to determine whether or not he was fit to compete for the prize. Berlioz had outgrown his student status; he had ceased to act like a student, in so far as he had ever done. This was inevitable. But it hardened the reputation he had already begun to acquire as an outsider and a subverter of rules — a talent, undeniably, but a fundamentally eccentric and maverick talent. It was a dangerous reputation to have in Paris. His well-advertised romantic passions did nothing to lessen it. People doubted his sanity. Harriet Smithson was reliably informed that he was epileptic, if not actually mad; and she was certainly not the only person to think of him as someone whose "eyes bode no good" and who should not be encouraged. (Even the father of his dear friend Humbert Ferrand suspected him of being a gambler, and was quite sure he had a bad influence on his son.)

Not all the older musicians went as far as Henri Berton, who warned an architect fellow-member of the Academy that "that young man is a hopeless case — Beethoven has turned his brain"; but with the best will in the world most of them had no idea what to make of him. They viewed him with a mixture of half-affectionate puzzlement, disapproval and alarm. This was not the sort of image calculated to help one get on. Getting on in Paris (as Félix Marmion never ceased reminding his nephew) meant having a success in the theatre — and theatre managers preferred safe bets. In so far as he was beginning to make a name for himself in the concert hall he was actually jeopardising his chances, given the Parisian love of categorising artists. Berlioz knew only too well what he was talking about when, years later, he wrote on the subject in the course of an article on prejudices active in the musical world which was later included, aptly, in his collection *Les grotesques de la musique*:

> In Paris, prejudice wills that a musician is qualified to do only what he has done already [...] If his first effort was a fine Mass, they'll say: "Fancy him wanting to write for the theatre! It will be all plainchant. Why doesn't he stay in his cathedral?" [...] If he starts by writing a symphony and that symphony creates a sensation, he is classified or rather pigeon-holed accordingly: He's a symphonist, he should produce only symphonies, he must keep away from the theatre, he's not meant for it, he wouldn't know how to write for the voice, etc. What is more, the prejudice-mongers will call everything he does thereafter "symphony". Words, when they speak of him, lose their normal meaning. What, produced by another, would be called by its correct name of cantata, etc., is named symphony when it's from his pen: an oratorio — symphony; an unaccompanied chorus — symphony; a Mass — symphony. Everything's symphony coming from a symphonist. He would have avoided this inconvenience if his first symphony had passed unnoticed, or if it had been an utter commonplace; he would even have found some theatre directors prejudiced in his favour. "This fellow hasn't succeeded in the concert hall, he's sure to succeed in the theatre. He doesn't know how to write for instruments, so he's bound to know how to write for the voice. He's a poor harmonist, the musicians say, so he must be absolutely bursting with melodies." Contrariwise, they would not fail to say: "He handles the orchestra like a master, so he can't write for the voice. He's a noted harmonist — his melodic invention, if he has any, must be suspect. In fact, he refuses to write like everyone else, he believes in expression in music, he has a system — he's a dangerous man." The advocates ["prôneurs"] of these splendid doctrines have powerful protectors in heaven, whose names resemble those of the patron saints of shoemakers: St Cretin and St Cretinian.

The satire is scarcely exaggerated. When Berlioz tried to get the Opéra to put on *The Trojans* he was informed by the director that he should stick to symphonies — that was his forte.

"A dangerous man who refuses to write like everyone else" — that was already how Paris had begun to think of Berlioz in the late 1820s.

Already the pattern of his career was being laid down: suspicion and distrust among the powers that be, passionate interest and good will among individual musicians and music-lovers. During these years, even before the Fantastic Symphony, he had made a mark; he was building up a sizeable personal following. Only, it was not in the circles that mattered most. The young Odéon orchestra were almost to a man his staunch supporters. They formed, gratis, the nucleus of the orchestra which played both for the St Eustache performance of the Mass and for the concert at the Conservatoire in May 1828; and the following October they gave further evidence of their regard by inviting him to a banquet held in honour of their conductor Nathan Bloc, who had defended their interests during the recent collapse of the Odéon administration and the temporary closure of the theatre. "After the formal toasts", wrote Berlioz to his sister Nancy, "M. Bloc stood up and proposed the following: 'Gentlemen, I drink to the success of an artist who is not on the staff of the Odéon but whom we should all be proud to possess — M. Berlioz.' The motion was received with applause, shouts and hugs, to such a point that I was quite overcome. I was so little expecting, or rather I was so far from expecting, a display of interest and regard of the sort that I was intensely moved by it. A moment later I proposed a toast to the memory of Weber and Beethoven. You can imagine how that was received. And to crown it they took advantage of it to present M. Bloc with the complete edition of Beethoven's works, as a present from the whole orchestra. Loud and prolonged applause!"

It was not only at the Odéon that the players were on his side. He had friends and allies at the Opéra, at the Opéra-Comique, even one or two at the Italien, theatres that he had been frequenting for the past six or seven years and with whose musicians he had been discussing musical and technical matters for almost as long. He was a familiar and respected figure to them. The publication of *Eight Scenes from Faust* caused a stir among the musicians as well as the composers. Many leading players at the Opéra got hold of copies of the score, and every evening he was there he found himself the object of fresh congratulations. Of the composers, Meyerbeer wrote about the work in flattering terms to his friend Schlesinger, its publisher. Even Rossini contrived to say something very complimentary about it when Berlioz was finally introduced to him. As for Onslow, he was "beside himself. He called on me and showered me with the most impassioned praise, to such an extent that I was quite disconcerted, and couldn't find words to reply to him. What flattered me inexpressibly was his obvious sincerity; for, as he said, if he didn't mean such eulogies he wouldn't have come to visit me. 'I've never seen such original music,' he said; 'and though I like my own works a great deal, I confess I feel very far from capable of doing anything like that,' etc., etc. A few days later he sent his servant with a request that I accept a copy of the score of his quintets. Unfortunately he has just left for the Auvergne, where he owns a huge estate (he has an income of 40,000 francs); with his connections he would have been very useful to me in Paris, and would have liked to be, had he stayed a little longer."

In the press, too, highly complimentary things were said about the *Eight Scenes*. Fétis' *Revue musicale* gave it an unusually warm and helpful review, concluding that it was "the work of a man of abundant talent and facility. If M. Berlioz obtains from the directors of our lyric theatres the encouragement he deserves, and if he can calm a little the fever that torments him, we do not hesitate to predict for him the greatest success."[*]
Even more flattering was the interest taken by the great Adolf Marx, who devoted the lead review in the *Berliner allgemeine musikalische Zeitung* to this "new shoot springing out of the positively Chinese stagnation of French art": notwithstanding certain shortcomings, the young composer had earned admiration for the work, which showed a most healthy emancipation from the decadent tastes of the Opéra public and a nobility of artistic ambition and a wealth of poetic imagination rarely seen among his compatriots. Herr Berlioz "mixes the colours of his rich palette so freely, often so boldly that one would have supposed him a pupil of Beethoven rather than of the Conservatoire."

Coming from Germany, this was high praise. But the good opinion Berlioz was most eager to receive never materialised. All through the spring and summer of 1829 he waited in vain for the letter from Goethe which Hiller assured him was on its way. Goethe had indeed been pleased with the "very finely engraved score" which "a Frenchman had sent him", and intrigued by its "evidently most unusual patterns of notes". He had fully intended to reply but had waited first for his old friend Carl Friedrich Zelter, his mentor on musical matters, to send him his expert assessment. When it came it was so damning that there could be no further question of a reply; discreet silence was the only possible course.

> There are people who cannot register their presence and mark their activity, in whatever circumstances, except by spitting noisily, sneezing, hoiking and belching. M. Hector Berlioz appears to be one of these. The smell of sulphur which Mephistopheles gives off attracts him, and makes him sneeze and snort in such a way that all the instruments of the orchestra leap about in a frenzy. Not a hair on Faust's head stirs. All the same, thank you for sending it. I shall find an opportunity, one of these days, in a lesson, to make good use of this excrescence, residue of a miscarriage resulting from a foul incest.

---

* The review (apparently not by Fétis himself) is signed "S." — probably Stephen de la Madelaine, who contributed to the paper during this period.

Berton is left far behind. As Julian Rushton (editor of the modern edition of the *Eight Scenes*) remarks, the very violence of Zelter's denunciation may have "arisen from perception of a genius which the elderly musician [...] could not assimilate".

We do not know whether Berlioz got to hear of it. (If word did reach him via Hiller and Eckermann, that could have been an extra stimulus to withdrawing the score in November 1829.) For the moment, the non-arrival of the letter which he awaited with such impatience was disappointment enough; he had naturally longed to be able to add the approval of the great author of *Faust* himself to the other plaudits the work had won him.

To be praised for a score which he had been able to publish only by borrowing money from his friends did nothing to advance his career in material terms, however; it only underlined his sense of not getting anywhere. In terms of the theatre this whole period is the record of one abortive project after another. The idea for a *Faust* ballet, whose scenario had been accepted by the Opéra and whose music the management had apparently agreed to entrust to Berlioz, was dropped when another *Faust*, at the Porte St Martin (with Frédérick Lemaître and Marie Dorval, and incidental music by the theatre's resident composer Alexandre Piccinni) became the hit of the winter season (1828–29). In May 1829 Ferrand's *Francs-juges* libretto was finally read to the Opéra committee and rejected as being obscure and long-winded. Berlioz told Ferrand that he intended to have it translated into German; he would make it into an opera like *Freischütz*, a mixture of musical numbers, melodrama and spoken dialogue, and take it to Cassel, where Spohr was director of the theatre and was said – unlike so many established composers – to be keen to help the young. "If I win the Institute prize, I shall leave for Cassel a few days later." Berlioz did not win the Institute prize, and that project too was dropped. Nor did anything come of another libretto (by whom and on what subject is not known) which was presented to the Opéra-Comique in August, and of which Berlioz had high hopes.

In France there was a general and serious lack of provision for composers trying to start a career; no one seemed interested in helping the young. This was a constant theme of Fétis' articles in the *Revue musicale*.

The precarious position of young men who take up musical composition is a fact which I have been bringing regularly to the attention of the appropriate authorities ever since I first undertook the publication of the *Revue musicale*; but to do anything positive about it involves so many administrative formalities, so many bureaucratic delays, so many confidential meetings to redress abuses, that my frequent airing of this question of first-rate musical interest has had no result, apart from the setting up of competitive concerts for the students at the Royal School of Music. Financial interests, administrative blunders which have at all costs to be covered up have till now prevented the establishment of a second Opéra-Comique, where young composers would have both the spur of competition and a secure livelihood.*

The possibility of a new opera house where French operas could be put on had long been canvassed — a few years earlier, at the time when Berlioz was writing *Les francs-juges,* there had been a lot of talk of the Odéon's being authorised to do so — and in the summer and autumn of 1829 it was again in the air. But once more it proved to be a mirage. Nothing more was heard, either, of the Société du Gymnase-Lyrique, an ambitious project for a new concert-giving body, offshoot of the Théâtre du Gymnase-Lyrique, which was announced the previous November and of which Berlioz was to have been orchestral manager-cum-librarian, responsible for choice of players, scores and orchestral parts, and hire of instruments.

Quite apart from the artistic frustration, the financial consequence of getting nowhere was a constant drag and worry. He unburdened himself about it to his sister Nancy:

I reflect often about having to depend on my parents. I'm over twenty-five, I work hard, and yet I don't support myself. It's because I'm in a false position. I was not brought up for an artistic career; my parents opposed it and gave way only when I persisted. Not having been trained from an early age, I didn't acquire a performing skill by which I could have earned my living until the time when my compositions brought me enough. All the young composers I know have this advantage. And then, the prolonged opposition I had to face put me back a good three years; I would have had that wretched Institute prize two years ago if I'd been able to prepare for it sooner. But when my father opposed my taking up music he thought that it was only a passing fancy, a hare-brained young man's obstinate fantasy, and that I was not destined to shine at it, in short that in no way was it the right thing for me, and that with patience it would be possible to overcome my ideas and turn them in another direction. Experience proved to him the contrary, but it was very damaging to me. For it is obvious that if instead of trying to stop me and depriving me of the means of getting on fast, my father had done everything in his power to help me along, my lot would be better. But he thought he acted for the best, and indeed was prompted to it by his love for me. I have never doubted that. It's terrible to think that parents' love can have such bad and sometimes disastrous consequences for their children. The reason is that they hardly ever have a really thorough knowledge of their children's character; and children are marked so deeply by the impressions of their upbringing, which prevent them from talking to

* See also Castil-Blaze's article in the *Débats* of 6 November 1829 pointing out the absurdity of the government's training young French composers for the lyric theatre and then denying them access to it.

their parents as one talks to one's intimate friends. But it's the only way you can reveal yourself as you are.

Throughout this period his letters to La Côte St André keep returning to the double preoccupation of the practical handicap of being short of cash and the burden on his parents of maintaining him in Paris.

20 December 1828, to his father, in response to the question, is he short of money: Yes, he is, to pay the rent, to buy firewood, to pay for his English course.

10 January 1829, to Nancy: Having heard nothing further from his father, he was forced to borrow 50 francs; and after paying his rent on the first of the month, he has nothing left.

10 May, to his mother: The money he will get for writing for the *Correspondant* will be very welcome; at the moment his time is squandered copying parts for a concert next winter. Nothing exasperates him so much as using up months on hack-work which he could be rid of for a 100 francs.

His interest in the Prix de Rome was above all financial. It would make him independent of his parents and solve his constant money problems. He wrote, on 29 June 1829, to Humbert Ferrand: "I'm counting on the Institute prize to repay what I owe you." Five days later, on 2 July, he went "en loge" for the third time, armed with another effusion by Vieillard, author of the previous year's *Herminie*; the subject was the last moments of Cleopatra.

The 1829 Prix de Rome brought to a fresh pitch the frustrations of Berlioz's existence. He should have won without question. *Cléopâtre* is the finest of his competition cantatas, a strikingly imaginative piece which, though never sanctioned by him, has been revived in modern times and rightly treated as an unpolished but authentic early product of his genius. The final pages are astonishing and the Meditation a fully realised inspiration, masterly alike in its grand enharmonic progressions and its cavernous sonorities, over a strange, insistent rhythm in slow 12/8 time. But in the real world it never stood a chance. As the *Memoirs* remark, the Meditation by itself was good enough to win him the prize and for that reason did not.

It may be said that this time, with almost suicidal recklessness, he brought his troubles on himself. In the eyes of his judges his score combined in much more extreme form most of the aberrations which had doomed him in 1827 and which would have done so even in 1828 but for the votes of the non-musicians. The relative restraint of *Herminie*, the concessions to convention and the "little bourgeois orchestra in two or three parts" that he had confined himself to, were thrust behind him. Right from the start the orchestral introduction reeled like a thing distraught, undermining all sense of stable tonality in its evocation of the turmoil of Cleopatra's thoughts, and the harmonic audacities continued to the end, where they reached a climax in chromaticisms, crunching dissonances and graphic juxtapositions of key prophetic of the tomb scene in *Romeo and Juliet*. The modulations in the recitatives, and the sweep of the declamation, went far beyond *Orphée*, as did the rhythmic invention. Even the one brief conventional passage, in the second recitative, ended with a bold stroke, as the shadow of a darker D minor fell across the dark C sharp minor cadence at the words "dans l'éternelle nuit". The orchestration was Berlioz at his grandest, with magnificently sombre, sonorous scoring for clarinets, bassoons, brass and lower strings. Long before the offending Meditation which so bemused Boieldieu, the opening aria, reduced to the piano, must have seemed to its listeners quite devoid of sense in its mixture of classical opera and the wildest Romanticism (a mixture which looks forward thirty years to Cassandra's music in *The Trojans*). The depiction of Cleopatra's death agonies — the pulse faltering, the blood seething as the poison coursed through her body — stretched the language of music to its limits. Needless to say the cantata culminated not in a full orchestral flourish, but in a diminuendo, ending — after a last spasm — pianissimo, on cellos and basses only. By this time obligatory aria had long given way to accompanied recitative, by means of a transition which was beautifully managed and precisely motivated but which would not have appealed to the judges even if they had noticed it. The rules of the game could hardly have been more resoundingly flouted.

Only in the liberties taken with the text did *Cléopâtre* yield to *Orphée*. Though several lines of recitative were repeated in the subsequent aria, there was none of the wholesale cutting and rearranging perpetrated in the earlier cantata. To make up for that concession, Berlioz prefaced the Meditation (his own title, not prescribed in the text) with the first line of Juliet's invocation in the vaults of her ancestors, written in English at the top of the page: "What if when I am laid into the tomb ... (Shakesp.)". It was a misquotation for "How if ...", but his examiners were unlikely to have been troubled by that aspect of it.

What possessed him? What was he thinking of? Had he forgotten all the lessons painfully learned in 1827, most of which he had taken to heart and profited by in 1828? Before the competition began a friend in the Opéra orchestra gave him some advice which, as he admitted afterwards, he "ought to have taken": "You should have yourself bled in all four limbs and go on a milk diet for two weeks. Then those gentlemen will be pleased with what you do." Auber, who was now a member of the Institute (having been elected to Gossec's vacant chair), said the same thing after it was over: "You shun the commonplace, but you need never fear that you will commit platitudes. So the best advice I can give you is to try to write tamely, and when you have produced something that seems horribly tame to you it will be exactly what's required."

Berlioz followed this advice in 1830 and won the prize. But in 1829 several things drove him to his own destruction. One was the tradition of awarding the prize to the reigning second-prize winner. It had happened the previous four years: Guillou second in 1824, first in 1825, when Paris came second; Paris first in 1826, and so on to the victory of Despréaux, 1827's second prize, in 1828. The other second prize of 1828, Nargeot, had not entered in 1829, and the opposition was particularly weak; everyone was saying that Berlioz would win. The weight of custom was reinforced by the understanding that this time his examiners wanted him to win (if only to get him off their hands). He had taken the precaution, a few months before, of asking the Isère deputy Champollion, who was keeper of manuscripts at the Bibliothèque Royale and knew Cherubini personally, to go and see the old man and persuade him to overlook his grudge against him. Auber, the new member of the music section, was sympathetic, and of course there was Le Sueur. Their influence could be expected to outweigh Berton's. All in all, he knew that there was a surprising amount of good will towards him in the Académie des Beaux-Arts.

The knowledge was fatal. He thought the prize was as good as his and he could let himself go and write his sort of music. It irked him, it made him feel ashamed, that with *Herminie* the year before he had had to "clip my own wings and not give way in the slightest to inspiration". The Cleopatra scene's Shakespearean echoes alone demanded that it be the real thing: for the subject had affinities with *Romeo and Juliet* — Juliet about to drink the potion in the vaults of the Capulets, face to face with the dark unknown, a scene for which he had already imagined a musical setting. This in turn called up images of Harriet Smithson. Shortly before the competition his passion had flared up again, inexplicably, futilely, and shaking off the nervous prostration of the previous weeks he had struck out into the surrounding countryside, walking at a furious pace and returning with his feelings wrought up to a desperate irritation, ready to pour them out upon the first major composition since the wreck of his hopes the previous winter.*

Even as he copied the text of *Cléopâtre* in the Institute assembly hall on the first afternoon of the competition its possibilities must have flashed out behind the conventional phrases and ignited his imagination. However antique the language, the situations in the poems set for the Prix de Rome were nothing if not dramatic, but none more so than this: Cleopatra

---

* The very appearance of his score, compared with the neat, impeccably regular *Herminie*, suggests the energy and speed of his ideas: the bar lines are not ruled but drawn by hand, the string tremolos incised with rapid strokes of the pen.

abased, insulted, left with no alternative but suicide yet fearful how the great Pharaohs at rest in their pyramids will receive her guilty, cringing soul in the kingdom of the dead, then clasping the asp to her bosom and finding in the moment of death a flicker of her former pride. He could not resist it. He had to have the prize — but above all not by compromise. Surely the judges would see, would not be able to help responding. He must win on his own terms.

He completed his score and handed it in at the Institute office on 23 July, a week before the preliminary judgment by the music section. The time was spent preparing the performance. The redoubtable Mme Dabadie, of the Opéra, who was his Herminie the year before, had agreed to sing for him again; the pianist was his friend Stephen de La Madelaine, a graduate of Choron's school and a good musician. They rehearsed at the soprano's house in the Boulevard des Italiens, round the corner from Berlioz's lodgings. At 9 a.m. on the 30th the four candidates and their artists assembled at the Institute and the cantatas were performed. They then withdrew and the music section deliberated.

Its conclusion was that no first prize should be awarded. Prévost got second prize and Montfort an honourable mention. The report contented itself with stating that "none of the four compositions indicated a talent sufficiently developed, a taste sufficiently formed to satisfy the requirements embodied in the first prize [...] The one by the exaggeration, the other by the feebleness, which is to be observed in their compositions, can only gain from further studies at the School. M. Prévost's composition (no. 1), although devoid of originality and dramatic impulse, has a certain naturalness in the voice part and a not incorrect style [...] M. Montfort's (no. 4) lends itself in almost equal degree to the same criticism and the same approbation."

The judges — who, as Berlioz remarked to Ferrand, were "not the Francs-juges" — were in a genuine quandary. They had wanted to give him the prize but he had made it impossible for them. The absence of Le Sueur was a blow (he was ill), though it was counteracted by the absence of Berton. Catel and Boieldieu could not make head or tail of his score. Even Auber and Cherubini felt that, though it would be a mockery to give any of the other contenders first prize ahead of Berlioz, they could not in all conscience vote for him; it was out of the question to present the full session of the Academy with such a recommendation. The only solution was not to award a first prize. To do so was not unprecedented. It had happened last in music — and in architecture — in 1818, and in painting and sculpture twice since then.

For Berlioz there remained the second round. There was an even more recent precedent for the Academy awarding a first prize after the music section had withheld it; they had done so in 1824. The painters and sculptors and architects would not have forgotten, either, that their vote had given Berlioz the second prize twelve months before.

Perhaps as good committee men they would have considered it a little too disruptive of order to repeat the process only a year later. In any case, all hope of a dramatic reprieve was dashed when Mme Dabadie withdrew at the last moment because of a clash of engagements: she had been summoned to rehearse at the Opéra in the rôle of Jemmy in *William Tell* the same afternoon as the Academy was holding its decisive session.* In her place she sent her sister, Mlle Leroux, a student at the Conservatoire who, with only a few hours in which to learn a totally unfamiliar and formidably demanding score, could make nothing of it. In the circumstances the piece had no chance. Berlioz had to sit by and hear it massacred. The non-musicians were as baffled as the musicians had been; it was, wrote Berlioz to his father, like setting the nine-year-old Prosper to read *Faust*. The Academy converted Montfort's honourable mention into a "deuxième second grand prix", but there was no larger reversal. All that Berlioz had to console himself with was the information, which his friend the usher, Pingard, reported to him and which he made much of in the ticklish letter he had to write to his father, that both Ingres and Pradier, the sculptor, got up after the vote and protested at the frivolous way the Academy brushed aside a candidate as considerable as Berlioz, whose score could not possibly be judged on such an inadequate performance. But by then the decision had been taken.

Next day Berlioz had to listen to a long tragi-comic discourse from Boieldieu, who spotted him on the boulevard and held him in conversation for an hour.

"My dear boy, you had the prize in your hands and you simply threw it away."

"I assure you, sir, I did my best."

"You shouldn't have done. That is exactly what we have against you. We thought you would be more sensible than you were last year and behave better, and instead you behaved a hundred times worse. We could not encourage that sort of thing. I came with the firm intention of giving you the prize — we all did. But when I heard your work!... How do you expect me to award the prize to a piece of music that means absolutely nothing to me? I can only judge what I understand. I don't understand half of Beethoven, and you want to go further than Beethoven! How do you expect me to understand? You take pleasure in difficult harmonies, you're prodigal with your modulations, whereas I — I've not studied harmony much, I have no experience of that side of music. Perhaps it's my fault. I like soothing music ['la musique qui berce']".

"But, sir, if you wish me to write soothing music, you shouldn't give me a subject like Cleopatra: a queen in deepest despair who lets an asp bite her and dies in convulsions."

"Oh, my friend, one can always be graceful in whatever one does. I'm

* The première of *William Tell* took place two nights later, on 3 August.

certainly not saying that your work is bad — I'm simply saying that I need more time to understand it; it should be played by an orchestra, not by a piano."

"Have I any objection?"

"And then, when I saw all those strange forms, that aversion to anything familiar, I could not help saying to my colleagues at the Institute that a young man who has ideas like that must despise us from the bottom of his heart. You're a volcanic person. But not everybody is made of that stamp, and one is not writing just for oneself. Why did you have to go and introduce that unheard-of rhythm in your invocation to the Pharaohs? Mme Dabadie is a first-rate musician, but it was obvious that she needed all her skill and concentration not to go wrong."*

"I didn't realise music was meant to be performed without skill and concentration."

"Oh well, you always have an answer. But take the lesson to heart for next year, and meanwhile come and see me. It would be a real pleasure for me. I want to study you. We'll have a chat. I shall take you on — but like a good old-fashioned French gentleman."

Berlioz went to see him in his rooms nearby in the Boulevard Montmartre; "he shows me", he told Nancy, "a strange respect, mixed with a sort of astonishment". He also had a session with Auber, who told him that these cantatas should be written as one writes a symphony, without concerning oneself with the expression of the words. He added that "if you wrote music only as you conceived it, the public wouldn't understand you and the music dealers wouldn't buy what you wrote". "Once again", cried Berlioz in exasperation to Ferrand, "when I write for bakers and dressmakers I won't choose for my text the passions of the Queen of Egypt and her meditations on death. Oh Ferrand, I wish you could hear the scene where Cleopatra wonders 'how her shade will be received by the shades of the Pharaohs entombed in the pyramids'. It's awesome, tremendous! It's the scene where Juliet meditates on her entombment in the vaults of the Capulets, surrounded alive by the bones of her ancestors and the corpse of Tybalt: the growing dread, the thoughts that culminate in cries of terror, accompanied by cellos and basses plucking this rhythm:

pp Oh! Shakespeare, Shakespeare!' "

The conversations with Boieldieu and Auber merely intensified his antipathy to all the Academy stood for.† They also served to clarify his

---

* Boieldieu is referring to the performance on the 30th.

† In February 1830 when the Athénée Musical chose two of his *Neuf mélodies* for performance at one of its concerts and named him in the programme "Prizewinner of the Institute" (in recognition of his second prize in 1828), he insisted on the offending title being removed.

ideas about the artist and the public. Commercial art such as Auber was in effect advocating drew large audiences. But serious art by definition appealed only to a limited number. The sublime was not sublime to more than a few. To some it was ridiculous, to most uninteresting. Soothing music was what the general public in Paris wanted. For that reason (Berlioz wrote to Ferrand) it was totally unreasonable of Spontini to be furious at the popular success of Rossini. As though the author of *La Vestale* and *Fernand Cortez* should bother courting the people who applauded *The Siege of Corinth*, as though he wrote for the "public" at all!

Boieldieu said a composer didn't write just for himself; but Beethoven did in his last quartets, for himself and those who "followed the incalculable flight of his genius". The rest, the huge fickle majority, flocked to see Goethe's *Faust* debased to a cheap melodrama at the Porte St Martin. Their imaginations were satisfied with Rossini and the circus horses of Franconi. One did not, one could not write for them; rather, one strove to "win what is most precious for an artist, the approval of people capable of appreciating him". At the performance of the C sharp minor quartet only a tiny handful, even in an élite audience, had been willing and able to go with the composer's thought. On them the music had had an extraordinary effect, unlike any normal experience; the rest had been repelled by it. How explain such an immense discrepancy? It was not merely that to understand such a work one's ear had to be thoroughly attuned to modern music and accustomed to its most extreme difficulties: several distinguished composers listened to the quartet with evident impatience. No, one's whole being had to be capable of responding to the author's, one had to have experienced the kind of feelings that the music depicts, to know the ills that Shakespeare speaks of:

> The oppressor's wrong, the proud man's contumely,
> The pangs of despis'd love, the law's delay,
> The insolence of office, and the spurns
> That patient merit of the unworthy takes.

A human being whose experience of life was limited to minor and passing unhappiness was necessarily untouched by such music: it sounded no echoes in his heart. "And [Berlioz adds] one can only say how lucky he is."*

All this, of course, was the mythology of Romanticism. But it corresponded to the facts as he perceived them — the facts of Parisian musical life and of his own nature. Granted his nature, he could not compromise; he could only be true to his ideals and be himself. If that meant that he

---

* The third of his three Beethoven articles, which included this account of the performance of the C sharp minor quartet, appeared in the *Correspondant* on 6 October 1829, but was written in August, just after the Institute competition.

would not win a large following or sell a lot of copies, so be it. All idea of concessions was alien and impossible. A part of him might continue to hope that what he experienced so intensely, the truthfulness of what his music expressed, must communicate itself no matter how great the obstacles in its way. The one positive advantage of writing criticism remained, through all the ennui associated with it, the opportunity to persuade, to cajole and charm and inspire his readers to a grander and loftier conception of music. Berlioz would never abandon his childhood vision of music as a truly popular art, expressed in great festivals whose ancestry derived from the French Revolution and, beyond, from the ceremonies of antiquity. But in his heart he had no illusions. Not only was the Paris public not a serious public. Even among musicians and genuine music-lovers there were precious few — as Boieldieu would say — of his stamp, who felt music as he did. Next time the Institute competition came round he would make one last effort to abide by the rules. But *Cléopâtre* had polarised the issues. The experience marks an important stage in the evolution of his ideas, hardening his determination to write as he felt, to compose only his kind of music whatever the consequences. Nature had made him an outsider in nineteenth-century Paris. "What the devil was the good Lord thinking of ["Où diable le bon Dieu avait-il la tête"] when he had me born in 'this pleasant land of France'?" But since he had been given the rôle, he would do his best — Boieldieu or no Boieldieu — and play it to the top of his bent.

22

A Vital Consolidation

———◆◆———

The Prix de Rome débâcle had the expected result. His father (Berlioz told Ferrand) was growing weary of letting him have an allowance. Unfortunately he could not do without it; so he was going back to La Côte St André to face more awkward scenes. "Never mind, I must go, and *you* must come and see me. Think how seldom we see one another, how fragile my life is, and how near each other we shall be." Joséphine Berlioz wrote to Nancy, who was staying in Bourg with her friend Rosanne Rocher (now Mme Goletty), to give her the news of the Prix de Rome and Hector's impending return. Ten days later she reported to Nancy that Louis Berlioz had notified his son that he would not be supporting him any more in Paris. She added the sage comment: "another passing storm that will soon calm down". Shortly afterwards, in fact, an accommodation was reached between father and son. From now on Hector would receive a reduced allowance of 50 francs a month. The truth was that Dr Berlioz, increasingly shut off by his deafness, was growing weary of many things. There were other worries to preoccupy him — the prolonged drought which threatened the harvest, the difficulty of controlling his other son, the nine-year-old Prosper, Nancy at twenty-four still unmarried, with no suitable husband in sight, and politics again threatening to disturb the peace of the land. At the beginning of August Charles X dismissed Martignac and his ministers and appointed the reactionary Prince de Polignac to head a new government of the extreme right. The royalist party was split, the liberals, till then disunited, rallied and closed ranks, and there were the first rumblings of a new revolution. A few days later the great General La Fayette passed through La Côte St André on his way to Grenoble. The leonine old liberal and white-haired wheeler-dealer was on a triumphal tour of central and southern France; he spent the night in La Côte at the house of the Berliozes' friend M. Chanrond, and was given a royal reception by the townspeople, as Joséphine Berlioz reported to Nancy.

M. Charon [*sic*] didn't spare himself to make it go. Cavalcade, illuminations, cries of Long Live Lafayette! Tumult and uproar! I vow I was quite

311

alarmed, even though I kept out of it and like your father stayed in my corner. In fact I think the political crisis was the reason for all the shindy. A few drunkards, too, thought it the moment to cry Long Live the Emperor as well. I was quite frightened. Happily nothing came of it, and the noble deputy was in Grenoble next day, after having graciously thanked the inhabitants of La Côte for their devotion to him or rather to his party.

Soon afterwards, to her bitter disappointment, Nancy heard from Hector that he would not be coming after all. Nancy still found herself awkwardly placed between her brother and her parents and could manage only by agreeing with each party in turn (in the same letter her mother writes, "As for him, he is as you say madder than ever, thank God his sister is not like him, though he thinks she is"). But brother and sister had grown a lot closer during the past year and prized each other's friendship. She was attracted as well as disturbed by his ideas, while he recognised in her a potentially kindred spirit who should be encouraged to escape from her circumscribed and melancholy existence. Nancy wrote back to beg him to change his mind; but, as he explained, it was impossible.

> Your letter too made me very sad. I had to force myself to resist your entreaties, the more so as, for me, I would give anything to be able to spend a couple of months with you all. I had actually begun getting ready to come. But now it's out of the question. My father writes to say that he agrees to let me have the 50 francs a month I asked for. Please thank him for it; I shall do everything in my power to cost him as little as possible. But as you will understand, I cannot live in Paris on 600 francs a year, so I must find a way out, and that means not letting any opportunity slip. I have just started with two composition pupils, who bring in 54 francs a month — if the lessons are kept to exactly; I cannot give them up. Then the editor of the score of *William Tell** has chosen me to correct the proofs and see it through the press, which will also bring in a little money. If I went away all this would be lost, and then what would I do when I got back at the beginning of winter with my 600 francs? I have a lot of other things in train which I cannot interrupt just at this moment. It is pretty well certain that on All Saints' Day [1 November] I shall have the chance to have a few pieces from *Faust* heard in public. I must prepare for the performance a long way in advance.

So he stayed.

It was at about this time that he found another source of income, teaching guitar at a girls' school in the Marais, a circumstance which was to have profound repercussions in his personal life. For the moment, the

---

* Troupenas, whose shop was near Berlioz's lodgings, round the corner in the Rue St Marc.

All Saints' Day concert was the chief preoccupation. He had been planning it since the spring, originally, it seems, with the intention of giving the *Eight Scenes from Faust* a hearing: in early June he told Ferrand that the programme would consist of "*Faust*, with two overtures, and some Irish melodies" which he was composing to Thomas Gounet's translations of Moore. By September "*Faust*" had become "a few pieces from *Faust*", and by October only one, the Concert de sylphes.

Why this should have been we do not know; orchestral parts survive for two other numbers — Brander's Rat Song and the Song of the Flea — and may well have been copied for others as well, if not for the whole work (there are frequent references in Berlioz's letters at this time to the copying of parts). Perhaps the same growing sense of the incompleteness and miscellaneous character of the work that made him withdraw it soon afterwards decided him against performing it in its entirety. Possibly, too, there were difficulties in finding soloists. For want of the right singers he had to drop three other items which a month before the concert he was intending to include: Conrad's aria from *Les francs-juges*, with Dabadie; Agathe's scena from *Freischütz*, which was to have been sung in German by Mlle Heinefetter, a new star at the Théâtre-Italien (she failed to get the director's permission, owing to a gala performance at the theatre on the same day); and *Cléopâtre*, with Mme Dabadie.

To have brought off a grand orchestral performance of the offending Prix de Rome cantata would have been an excellent coup (though it might not have done any good to his chances for the following year); but Mme Dabadie, having agreed to take part, again had to stand down. *Cléopâtre* was replaced by the Resurrexit (with the addition of a recitative accompanied by four pairs of timpani playing chords, later developed in the Tuba mirum of the Grande Messe des Morts), and the *Freischütz* and *Francs-juges* arias made way for some Italian items. In the end only one new piece of Berlioz's was played, the Concert de sylphes. It did not make a good impression. There was a general feeling, to which the critics gave expression in their reviews, that the music failed to live up to the promise of the programme note, which spoke of the spirits of air, summoned by Mephistopheles, sounding their magic instruments and evoking an enchanted realm of ever-renewed delights. At that stage the piece was not a choral movement, as it became in *The Damnation of Faust*, but a sextet for solo voices.

Altogether the vocal side of the concert was the weakest. The sylphs were six Conservatoire students of varying degrees of inexperience; the main vocal soloists, Rosa and Mlle Marinoni, were of no great brilliance. On the other hand the instrumental side was first-rate. In addition to solos by Urhan (violin) and Dorus (flute) — two of the leading young musicians of the day — Ferdinand Hiller gave the Paris première of Beethoven's Emperor Concerto. The huge orchestra was conducted not by the willing but limited Bloc but by the great Habeneck himself; and the relative familiarity of the Resurrexit and the *Francs-juges* and *Waverley* overtures, combined with the enthusiasm of Berlioz's many partisans in the orchestra, fired the performances with thrilling conviction. "You cannot think what such an orchestra is like," he wrote to his mother. "Beforehand I was feeling so exhausted I could hardly bring myself to get up in the morning and go to my rehearsal — I dragged myself as best I could to the Menus-Plaisirs [Conservatoire Hall]. But once my orchestra was launched a sort of electric force revived me; I was like a man who has taken too much brandy. The applause of the musicians intoxicated me less than the effect of my music." But the musicians' applause too was heady. At the first rehearsal they turned to him after the *Francs-juges* overture — he was playing in the percussion section — with shouts of acclamation. After the rehearsal he scribbled a jubilant note to Ferrand at a table in the Restaurant Lemardeley, two doors up from his lodgings, while he waited for his dessert:

> Ferrand, Ferrand, why aren't you here? In a moment I'm going to the Opéra to find a harmonica [for the Concert de sylphes]; the one they brought this morning is too low [. . .] Yesterday I was ill, I couldn't walk. Today, the fires of hell which dictated the *Francs-juges* have given me incredible energy. This evening I have once again to run errands all over Paris. The Beethoven concerto is a prodigious conception: astonishing, sublime. I can't tell you how I admire it [. . .] And the Last Judgment, which you know, plus a recitative accompanied by four pairs of drums in harmony. Oh Ferrand, Ferrand — three hundred miles apart! [. . .] I've written myself a bass-drum solo, pianissimo, in the *Francs-juges*. *Intonuere cavæ gemitumque dedere cavernæ.*[*]
>
> Yes, it's tremendous. All that my heart contains of rage and tenderness is in that overture.

Exhausting though they were, the arrangements for the concert went much more smoothly this time. Cherubini made few difficulties about lending the hall; and the event was publicised better, with advance notices in *Figaro*, the *Corsaire*, the *Quotidienne* and the *Revue musicale*: the *Corsaire* printed the programme in full, the *Quotidienne* announced that "the reputation of the young composer and the variety of the programme assure the occasion a large gathering of music-lovers", and the *Revue musicale* urged "all who love good orchestral and vocal music to secure their seats in advance".

The concert, in fact, drew a much bigger house than the first had done

---

[*] Virgil, *Æeneid*, II 73: "The great hollow space groaned and rumbled" — Æneas' description of the Wooden Horse reverberating under the impact of Laocoön's spear.

and, despite the many complimentary tickets, made a profit.[*] All in all;
if the occasion lacked the pioneering éclat of his previous concert, at
which nothing but his music was played and most of the works had not
been heard before, it achieved a vital consolidation of that breakthrough;
it added to his reputation as a young composer of great promise; and it
demonstrated that his music could stand up to the toughest
competition — for the overture to *Les francs-juges*, coming immediately
after the Emperor Concerto, held its own and took the house by storm, as
it had not done the previous year, when it had made a much deeper
impression on the orchestra than on the audience.

The immediate reaction to all these excitements and exertions was a
state of deep depression. But two days after the concert he roused himself
to send his father a full report of his success. This time there was no need
to gloss over anything: he had covered his costs and actually made 150
francs. Apart from a few mistakes, due to shortage of rehearsal time, the
large-scale pieces had been performed with great power by the immense
(100-strong) orchestra under Habeneck, though there were too few voices
in the Last Judgment chorus (Resurrexit) and the orchestra overpowered
them. Only the *Faust* sextet had failed to make an impression. "Hiller,
the young German I told you of, played a piano concerto by Beethoven, a
quite marvellous work. Immediately after it came my *Francs-juges* overture.
When my friends saw the effect of the sublime concerto they thought I
was done for, and I confess that for an instant I was terrified. But the
moment the overture began I was aware of the response of the pit and
had no more worries. The effect was prodigious, volcanic; the applause
went on for nearly five minutes, with shouting and stamping. When it
calmed down, I tried to slip between the desks to fetch a pile of music
that was on a bench in the hall (the orchestra is on the stage), but the
audience saw me, and the shouts and bravos began again, and the
players joined in, with a hail of bows on violins and cellos and music
stands [...] If only you had been there. I was the only one of the
family — everyone was hugging me except my father, my mother, my
sisters! [...] When it was all over and I thought everyone had gone, I

___

[*] Berlioz's attempt to get exemption from the ancient tax which the Opéra levied on
box-office receipts of all musical events in Paris was unsuccessful; the director of the Opéra,
Lubbert, though willing to forgo the 65 francs due, failed to obtain permission from La
Rochefoucauld. But La Rochefoucauld sent Berlioz a grant of 100 francs to help defray expenses.

The names of the recipients of complimentary tickets are a cross-section of Berlioz's public
and private life. Politics: La Rochefoucauld, Champollion; musical establishment: Cherubini,
Kreutzer, Habeneck, Chénié, Nourrit, Pleyel, Schlesinger, Castil-Blaze; art and letters: Ingres,
Guérin, Lemoine, Ducis, Latouche, Carné, Jouy (librettist of Rossini's *Moïse* and *William
Tell* and also of *La Vestale* and *Fernand Cortez* and a fellow-worshipper of Spontini); young
musicians: Stephen de La Madelaine, Simon, Prévost, Turbry, Richard, Urhan, Desmarest;
friends from Paris and La Côte and family connections: Gounet, Alphonse Robert, Charbonnel,
Adolphe Bert, Joseph Rocher, Teisseyre. The list, in Berlioz's hand, is in the museum at La
Côte St André.

left the building, but the musicians were waiting for me in the courtyard of the Conservatoire and, seeing me appear, started cheering all over again. Last night at the Opéra,* when I arrived in the pit, the musicians all came and congratulated me."

The critics, while not going into detail, and contenting themselves with the usual generalities, were mostly very complimentary. One even called him "le Victor Hugo de la musique". *Figaro* hailed the *Francs-juges* overture as "the work of a genius", the *Gazette de France* expatiated on the new art of instrumentation, at which M. Berlioz was already an adept, the *Journal des débats* (Castil-Blaze) used the occasion to castigate the government for limiting instead of increasing the opportunities for young composers to have their operas performed, and the *Corsaire* called on the authorities to do something at last for an artist whose ideas impelled him so far off the beaten track and who was "that rare thing in this century of ours, a true creative genius". Only Fétis, in the *Revue musicale*, wrote a hostile notice, criticising Berlioz for his wild style of composition, and castigating the same Concert de sylphes which his journal's review of the score of the *Eight Scenes* a few months before had singled out for special praise.†

For weeks afterwards the concert continued to be talked about. Berlioz found himself an object of interest and curiosity. He received messages of good will (one from a forgotten but once famous name, Rouget de Lisle, composer of the Marseillaise who, present at a musical gathering in the country outside Paris, asked if anyone there knew Berlioz and found that one of them had played in his orchestra). At soirées, when his name was announced, strangers came up and congratulated him on his success; and he dined out frequently. His mother was moved to enquire about the state of his wardrobe; and a few weeks later, in a letter which gives an idea of the more active social life he had begun to lead, he asked Nancy to

tell Mama that I have just ordered a complete set of clothes which is costing me 160 francs. As you can imagine, this is setting me back all right; but I

---

* 2 November. The work was Auber's *La muette de Portici*.

† "The outstanding number in the work" and "an invention which does honour to M. Berlioz's imagination" became music of "weird, twisted shapes, harmonies without resolution, without rhythm or reason", "effects, nothing but effects" and "no trace of tune, not so much as a poor little tune a few bars long". Fétis asserted that the Emperor Concerto might have been put into the programme expressly to give the young composer a lesson in composition – and this despite its not being a particularly good piece: "The first movement, which is the best, is too long, the adagio has nothing remarkable about it, and the rondo is monotonous." The *Gazette de France* too was critical of the Concert de sylphes, but found the slow movement of the Beethoven concerto a ravishing invention and an example of suave, seductive music that the composer of the Concert de sylphes could well have taken as a model. Berlioz himself was dissatisfied with his scene (it was after the performance that he withdrew the whole work from publication) and later, when incorporating it in *The Damnation of Faust*, made many alterations, as well as replacing the sextet of solo voices with a chorus.

couldn't manage without it any longer. My whole wardrobe is worn out. I have to dress up much more often this winter, as I often go out. I have bought some folded cravats and a few dozen detachable collars. M. le baron de Trémont, who is a great lover of music, gives superb musical parties at 2 o'clock every Sunday; a couple of weeks ago, when I was dining at Kalkbrenner [the pianist]'s place, he was there and invited me to come. On Sunday evenings I go to M. Leo's, a rich German music-lover who is very fond of me. Sometimes we have to stomach Blangini's vapid nocturnes, but not often. Usually there is good music and delicious tea; a lot of people come, and everyone is very much at home. On Tuesday I occasionally go and spend the evening at M. Mazel's, another music-lover who also gives enjoyable parties; a lot of artists come, but sometimes, too, little girls who regale us with Pleyel sonatas. Sometimes, in the morning, I go and see Delatouche, the Mephistopheles of modern literature.*

The rest of the time I work, though when I have a moment I read new books – Hoffmann, I liked his *Contes fantastiques* very much, and I was very moved by [Cooper's] *The Puritans*. I'm waiting for the life of Byron by Thomas Moore. Talking of Moore, I'm dedicating my Irish melodies to him.†

A mark of Berlioz's greater sense of worldly confidence is that his letters to the family give a less strictly edited version of his life than they used to. He does not conceal from his father that his concert precipitated a violent reaction afterwards, in which he was constantly on the verge of tears and so depressed that he wished he could die, nor from his sister, some weeks later, that he is in the grip of a furious attack of spleen which makes him want to destroy everything.§

A letter to his father, written on 3 December 1829, speaks both of his poor state of health and of the notoriety his concert has brought him. It is clear that the physical and emotional strains of the past year had left him

---

* Henri de Latouche – novelist, poet, critic, editor of Chénier's poems – had recently caused a scandal by bringing out a novel about a hermaphrodite, *Fragoletta*. Balzac reviewed it enthusiastically but others were not amused.

† Other works that his letters of 1829 show him reading as soon as they are published are Hugo's second collection of verse, *Les Orientales*, and his fictional tract against capital punishment, *Le dernier jour d'un condamné*.

§ "Nine tenths of the time I am fed up with everything. My engravers let me down, my lithographer makes silly mistakes, my boots leak, my teeth ache, my nose too, I rage against everything, I bang my fist down on my piano, I should like to shatter, to exterminate everything [...] I go out, it's cold, I climb the hill to Montmartre and warm up, I see a wide waterless plain, I think of La Côte and of you all, I return, I see Montmartre cemetery, Hamlet, Shakespeare, life, grief, death, activity without purpose leading to nothing, the possibility of a brief but immense happiness, the rarity of it, and then I hate everything with an intense hatred, next I think of philosophy, I burst out laughing, I grind my teeth, I think of music and then I blush and become serious again, I stop, I think, I make plans, I hear my heart beating, I live."

in a very run-down condition. A few years before he would probably have kept quiet about the fact that he had been confined to bed by a bad go of tonsillitis — the second, he admits, in two months. "I don't know how to prevent them nor how to bring them to an end — normally they last a week — and I am enough of a child not to be able to resign myself; the impossibility of my discovering either why I am vulnerable to such attacks or what causes them irritates me to such a point that my muscles are in a constant state of contraction."

While still in bed he was visited by two authors, both strangers, and both hoping to get him to set their work to music. One was an ageing Voltairian poet who came on the recommendation of a mutual friend to offer Berlioz his opera librettos, including a grand opera, *Tancrède*, which Rossini had turned down;* he insisted on reading one of his efforts aloud — tastefully versified stuff but full of worn-out characters and hackneyed situations. "He kept on about his verses. How curious they are, these ancien régime writers, with their verses; it seems that versification is the most important thing in a drama. While I was arguing with the powdered classicist, who should walk in but the young Gérard [de Nerval], author of the most recent translation of *Faust*, who had been at my concert and wished to make my acquaintance — he had called several times without finding me in." A bizarre conversation ensued, observed by Berlioz with wry amusement from his sick-bed, between the representatives of the new and the old in French literature — the former airing his Romantic opinions while the latter gradually realised that the newcomer was there on the same errand as himself, and each making veiled attacks on the other's position. "Gérard in fact had come to ask me to write some music to the Schiller ballads he has just translated. I don't know them, and besides they have recently been set, by a German composer, with too great a talent for me to try my hand at them. In any case, just now I'm completing my collection of Moore's Irish melodies, which I am having published as soon as I can."

The early Romantics' admiration for Thomas Moore is one of those crazes that a later age finds baffling. True, so far as French readers were concerned, in prose translation the verse lost both its soft-centred lyricism and its relentless dactylic rhythm, neither of them qualities conducive to tragic utterance. But what did that leave beyond, with few exceptions, an atmosphere — of drawing-room balladry, nostalgic patriotism, tipsy conviviality tempered by sobering reminders of the Almighty, discreetly

---

* Rossini had composed a *Tancredi* many years before, but had lately been adapting several of his Italian operas to the French stage.

sensuous romance, and fantasies of escape to a better land on the other side of the sunset?

In his defence it can be said that he did not aspire to the rôle that was thrust upon him. He wrote the verse to help preserve the old Irish national airs which had lately been rescued from threat of oblivion by Bunting's published collections; it was designed to go with the music and, to begin with, was not intended to have an independent existence. Without doubt the crypto-erotic vein in his poetry had strong appeal in a period when such matters of deep universal interest could not be described openly. (Byron attributed his obsessive sexuality partly to the effect on a willing adolescent imagination of reading *The Loves of the Angels*, a long narrative poem according to which the chief feature of life on the astral plain, as in a Dennis Wheatley novel, appears to be the unlimited opportunity it affords for copulation.) But in Moore the early nineteenth century saw much more than a titillator and a hawker of daydreams. He was a thinker, an oracle of truths about the human condition. Berlioz called him "mon désolateur"; Moore, says the narrator in *Lélio*, has "completed the work of devastation in my soul begun by Shakespeare". Moore's "one fatal remembrance, one sorrow that throws / its bleak shade alike o'er our joys and our woes", chosen for epigraph to the *Eight Scenes from Faust*, joined Hamlet's "pangs of despis'd love" as the literary embodiment of his unrequited passion for Harriet Smithson.

Soon afterwards Berlioz would confess to finding him incomplete — a little like Lamartine, who "never came down from the clouds". Yet Moore remained for him a great poet. At one of the most grimly exalted moments of his emotional life he invoked his "Believe me, if all these endearing young charms" to incarnate the constancy of his childhood love for Estelle Dubeuf, persisting fresh and undimmed into old age — an idea such as no other great writer, not even Shakespeare or Balzac, had imagined.

Despite his lofty opinion of Moore, Berlioz chose poems mainly of the lighter kind for his *Mélodies*. The songs were mostly composed during the second half of 1829, as and when his friend Thomas Gounet supplied him with verse translations.

Long before they became associated in his mind with Harriet Smithson, Moore's *Irish Melodies*, in Louise Belloc's prose versions, had been a favourite book, first read in the summer of 1826 by the gliding Seine as he ate his dinners of bread and grapes on the terrace of the Pont Neuf at the foot of Henri IV's statue, during the period of the composition of *Les francs-juges*. He had re-read them countless times since then. A brand new copy of the book (which combined *Irish Melodies* and *The Loves of the Angels* in one volume) was one of the luxuries with which he celebrated his new-found financial independence in the autumn of 1827, at the time of his signing on as a chorister at the Nouveautés and setting up house with Antoine Charbonnel in the Rue de la Harpe.

The composition of the *Mélodies*, however, was very much a joint venture with Gounet, an aspiring poet who shared with Berlioz the triste distinction of being hopelessly in love with an unresponsive star of the theatre.* The score was published at their joint expense, and dedicated to Moore. A musician from London who knew Moore agreed to take a copy back with him and present it to the poet.

We do not know if Berlioz had already sketched any Moore songs before this. In any case the texts would have been quite different. Louise Belloc's translations were meticulously literal and in prose. Gounet aimed to recreate the originals in contemporary French verse; at times he treated them very freely, paraphrasing, sometimes even modifying the sense, or conflating several sources: thus at least two separate poems, "War Song" and "Forget not the Field", went to make the text of no. 3 of the *Mélodies*, "Chant guerrier". Gounet's ambitions chimed with those of Berlioz, who wanted some smaller pieces to serve as interludes and diversify the programme of his November concert. For Berlioz Gounet was in some ways a more satisfactory collaborator than the procrastinating Ferrand. If he too sometimes kept him waiting for material, at least he lived in Paris, and only a few streets away, in the Rue Ste Anne.

In the end, though a good many of the songs were in existence by the time of the concert, none of them were performed at it, perhaps for the same reason — lack of the right singers — that other vocal items were dropped. By the beginning of December, when Gérard de Nerval called on Berlioz to ask him to set his translations of Schiller's ballads, Berlioz was "just completing" the work and intending to have it published at the earliest possible moment. A few weeks later it was, as he thought, complete and being engraved: he told Ferrand that he would "receive our collection of *Irish melodies* within three weeks", which presupposes a publication date in about the second week of January 1830. In the event the score, published by Schlesinger, appeared early in February. It was named Berlioz's "Œuvre 2" — a designation which had been given only a month or two before to his *Ballet des ombres*, a setting for chorus and piano of a poem by Herder translated by Berlioz's friend Albert Du Boys, and composed some time in 1829. (For some reason, having gone to the expense of publishing this rather engaging piece of diablerie — an evocation of Hamlet's "witching hour of night, when churchyards yawn and hell itself breathes out contagion to this world" — he withdrew it again almost immediately.)†

---

* The opera singer Jawurek. See Berlioz's letter to Ferrand of 29 June 1829: "I'm writing to you from the Café Richelieu, at a table near the boulevard. Jawurek has just appeared on her balcony, which reminds me that poor Gounet is in none too good a state either."

† Hamlet's words were inscribed, in English, on the impressively sinister black-and-white title page, which showed a churchyard thronged with ghosts.

The *Mélodies* took longer to appear than Berlioz expected, partly because the engravers failed to keep their promised dates, but also because of the unexpected composition of a ninth. The final song of *Neuf mélodies*, the "Elégie", was not one that Gounet had translated. Its text was taken from Louise Belloc's prose translation. Hence the title given it in the score: "Elégie en prose". Some time in January 1830 a sudden flaring up of Berlioz's obsessive passion drove him out into the country on one of his long, desperate treks. Returning hours later and taking up the volume of Moore that lay open on his table at "When he who adores thee" — the tribute to the Irish patriot Tom Emmet executed in 1803 — he wrote a setting of it on the spot. The song was headed by an anonymous epigraph in French: "He died. His lyre was placed on his tomb. On stormy nights the winds drew from it harmonious moans, with which the strains of his last forlorn lament seemed to mingle still"; and it was inscribed "F.H.S." — i.e. "For Harriet Smithson".

"Elégie", with its powerful harmonic tension, grand declamatory vocal line and vividly idiosyncratic piano writing (reflecting the influence of the Beethoven sessions at Hiller's), strikes a dramatic note not heard in the rest of the collection, even in the preceding song, "Adieu Bessy". (It is only in the revised edition of 1849 that "Adieu Bessy" is made to prepare for the passionate intensity of "Elégie" by means of a cumulative force of expression in harmony and accompaniment not present in the original version of 1829.) The predominant tone of the *Mélodies* is gentle. Even the two extravert pieces for men's chorus, "Chant guerrier" and the hearty "Chanson à boire", include reflective solo verses, and the choral refrain of "Chant guerrier" contains whispered pianissimo as well as rousing forte. The third choral number, the six-part "Chant sacré", "Dieu puissant" (whose refrain uses the music of the prayer "Dieu des chrétiens" in the Prix de Rome cantata *Herminie*), is solemn in mood. Of the three other solo songs (apart from "Elégie"), two — "Le coucher du soleil" (subtitled "Rêverie") and "L'origine de la harpe" — are mild, dreamlike pieces, pleasant but a little pallid and, with all their breadth of melody and eccentric touches of harmony, not entirely characteristic in the way that every solo number in the *Eight Scenes from Faust* is stamped with Berlioz's melodic personality. But the third, "La belle voyageuse" ("Rich and rare were the gems she wore"), is a fully realised idea in which the graceful vocal line and lilting 6/8 metre are subtly combined with irregularity of phraselength and unexpected harmonisation to evoke the shining innocence of the poem's theme. Freshest of all is "Hélène", a ballad for two voices in a skittish 2/4 time of irresistible good humour, whose teasing alternation of 3-bar, 4-bar and 5-bar phrases (an effect enhanced by the contrasting directness of the horn-like hunting refrain in 6/8) is so devised that the music sounds at once unpredictable and supremely natural.

The use of Moore's own word, "Melodies", for the title of these songs is little more than a gesture of homage and presumed affinity. Not surprisingly, they show a big advance on the songs Berlioz published seven or eight years before, soon after he arrived in Paris; but he is still a long way from *Les nuits d'été* of a decade later — true melodies in the sense of a French equivalent of the German *Lied* — or from "La mort d'Ophélie's" exquisite shaping of modified strophic song into a single flowing continuum, let alone from the miniature tone poem of the final version of "La captive". Apart from the explosive "Elégie", *Neuf mélodies* — a miscellany, not a cycle — is contained fairly comfortably within the modest tradition of the *romance*; its irregular phraselengths and passing harmonic unorthodoxies only hint at something more ambitious. That, no doubt, was why it was well received. No less a figure than Adolphe Nourrit, reigning tenor at the Opéra, took up some of the songs and sang them at musical soirées. The Athénée Musical, a society formed the previous autumn by Chelard and Bloc with the aim of providing young composers and performers with a platform, gave two of them at one of its concerts in the Salle St Jean of the Hôtel de Ville, on 19 February 1830, as Berlioz reported to his father:

> I must tell you, my dear Papa, that yesterday evening I scored quite a success. Two of my melodies, one for full chorus, the other for single voice with piano only, were performed at the Athénée Musical before a large audience. I had the pleasure of seeing all those people, who had listened rather coolly to the preceding items, listen to mine with the utmost attentiveness. A prolonged "Ssh!" enjoined silence throughout the hall; my name, spoken on all sides, indicated that something special was expected. And in fact the predisposition in my favour had its effect. Although the two pieces performed, "Rêverie" and "Chant sacré", are in a calm and melancholy vein and in consequence not of the kind to rouse an audience, they were greeted with salvoes of applause. The organisers of the Athénée Musical asked me straightaway to let them have some other pieces for their next concert; and many people came up on to the stage to congratulate me, etc. In short, I had the honours of the evening. The newspapers have gone on so much about the originality of my music that it's become received doctrine, I have only to write half a dozen notes for people to find something original in them. The "Chant sacré", which, if it has some merit, has the merit of expressiveness and breadth rather than anything else, was found to be unlike any known music, entirely new, etc. Nothing could be less true; but one has to let this good public have its say! I'm beginning to have all that's required for a notorious reputation — impassioned partisans, and ferocious antagonists whose contention is that I'm half mad and have no self-control, or that I'm an evil genius come to destroy and not to create — my innovations exasperate them. However, I had the pleasure, yesterday evening, of catching a confirmed classicist in the snare of my ruminative phrases: M. Miel, who only likes gentle music, and who does the reviews in the *Universel*, came up to me and expressed his great satisfaction; he asked me for a copy of the *Mélodies*, and I think wants to write about them in his paper.

Two days later the *Universel* reviewed the concert and singled him out for praise: "We hasten to draw a distinction between these imitators [the composers of the previous items] and M. Berlioz, who is certainly not in a rut. This young musician takes wing and soars, and a lofty flight it is. The two melodies of his which we heard, to words from Thomas Moore's *Irish Melodies*, are full of character. One of them in particular, the 'Hymn to the Eternal' with chorus, is notable for a noble and religious style perfectly suited to its subject. While keeping an open mind about a budding talent which is not yet sure of itself and still feeling its way, we must congratulate M. Berlioz on obeying none but his own inclination."

And shortly afterwards, Fétis' *Revue musicale*, in a brief notice of the *Mélodies* in its issue of 6 March 1830, was all smiles: "We can only congratulate M. Berlioz on adopting a much more graceful type of melody in this work than in his other compositions. There is charm in this collection of songs, and it is quite evident that M. Berlioz has but to wish it in order to take a natural direction, the only one which leads to lasting success." Fétis' approval must have struck Berlioz as ironic, coming at the moment when he was about to begin writing the Fantastic Symphony.

A week after the concert at the Hôtel de Ville, on 25 February 1830, Victor Hugo's Spanish melodrama *Hernani*, with Firmin, Michelot, Joanny and Mlle Mars, opened at the Théâtre-Français amid scenes of revelry and riot rarely if ever witnessed at that citadel of tradition. The Classicists, the "perruques", having failed to stop the play being put on, had arranged to hiss it off the stage; but Jeune-France turned out in force to frustrate them. Organised in platoons under designated leaders (Gérard de Nerval commanded one, the eighteen-year-old Théophile Gautier, in outrageous pink waistcoat, another), issued by the playwright with passes coloured red and bearing the Spanish word "Hierro" (iron), beards untrimmed and hair left to grow long as a gesture of contempt for their "baldpate" opponents, they took up their positions hours before the performance and picnicked in the theatre in Rabelaisian style. The old guard fought hard, contesting the play night after night, but they were outfought. Each audacity was challenged and noisily defended. When Don Riccardo announced that it was "nearly midnight", the shouts of protest at the flouting of one of classicism's sacred prohibitions were drowned by counter-cheers.*

---

* The conflict of the generations led to exchanges of famous absurdity, as when Hernani's "Vieillard stupide!" was misheard as "Vieil as de pic!" ("Old ace of spades!") by an indignant academician, who repeated the phrase incredulously, whereupon his young neighbour, who had missed the actual line, exclaimed, "Why not? Cards were invented in the reign of Charles VI. Bravo pour le vieil as de pic!"

The significance of the battle of *Hernani* was above all strategic. It established in the heart of French conservatism the modern dramatist's right to freedom — freedom of language, of theatrical style, of technique. By no means all the artists who came to support it actually liked the play. Balzac thought its dramatic action unconvincingly dependent on contrivance; Stendhal found its long tirades curiously reminiscent of the classical tragedies it claimed to supplant. Berlioz's enthusiasm, too, was decidedly cool: "Some things in it I find sublime — thoughts especially," he wrote to Nancy, "and other things and ideas ridiculous — no great novelty in that. But as for the verse, as I dislike it in the theatre, those lines that run over and those broken half-lines which so upset the Classicists leave me cold; when spoken, it's just like prose — I would rather it had been. But since *Hernani* is written in verse, and Hugo knows very well how to, it would have been better to conform to the taste of the public as a whole, as well as less taxing to the lungpower of the pit. The innovation doesn't lead anywhere. Still, Hugo has destroyed the unities of time and place, and just for that I have an interest in what he's done, as one would in the action of a soldier who braves the bullets to set the match to a mine beneath an old fortification."

Berlioz apparently failed to see an analogy between Hugo's attempt to liberate the rule-bound alexandrine and his own development of a free irregularly stressed melodic line. The analogy was very evident to Théophile Gautier when he wrote, a few years later: "Just as Victor Hugo displaces the cæsura, runs on from one line to the next and varies by all sorts of devices the monotony of the verse period, so Hector Berlioz changes the beat, deludes the ear when it was expecting symmetry, and punctuates the phrase as he pleases."

Perhaps Berlioz was too preoccupied with his own ambitious departure from tradition to be responsive to Hugo's. Within a week or two of the première of *Hernani* he would be embarking on the Fantastic Symphony.

23

The Fantastic Symphony

———◆———

The *Neuf mélodies* may not have been the only composition of this period originally meant to figure in Berlioz's concert of 1 November 1829: the Marche des gardes from *Les francs-juges*, the piece that became the fourth movement of the Fantastic Symphony, was quite possibly another. Some such conclusion is prompted by the title page of the manuscript score. "Marche des Gardes / du Franc comte / Dans l'opéra des Francs juges / musique de / Hector Berlioz": the existence of such a title page, naming the composer and the work from which the music comes, is evidence that the piece in question has been extracted from its context in order to fulfil, however temporarily, a different, independent rôle — most probably performance at a concert.

When it was composed we do not know; there is no reference to it in the correspondence. All we can be sure of is that it does not come from the original *Francs-juges* of 1825–26. Everything about the manuscript and the music proclaims a later date — scoring, for an orchestra much bigger than the forces of the Odéon Theatre for which the opera was intended; layout of the score, with the violins in the modern position beneath the wind and percussion, not at the top of the page (as they are in the manuscript of 1825–26); size and type of paper; handwriting; and style of the music, which has an authority and power not found in the surviving fragments of the opera.

The provenance of the Marche au supplice, the March to the Scaffold, was the subject of an internecine feud among French Berlioz scholars at the beginning of this century, conducted with extraordinary ferocity in the correspondence columns of *Le ménestrel*, a musical journal in which Julien Tiersot was publishing a series of weekly articles entitled "Berlioziana". Tiersot stoutly denied that the Marche des gardes and the Marche au supplice had anything to do with each other. Adolphe Boschot and Charles Malherbe maintained, in increasingly sneering and triumphal tones, that they did; and the argument raged backwards and forwards for several months ("La marche au supplice vient des Francs-juges", "La marche au supplice ne vient pas des Francs-juges", "La marche au supplice continue à venir des Francs-juges", etc.).

As it happens, Boschot and Malherbe were in a strong position, for Malherbe owned the manuscript of the Fantastic Symphony, in which the double title-page of the fourth movement, "Marche des gardes" and "Marche du supplice", is plain to see; and it remains a mystery how Tiersot failed to see it, even during the brief examination of the score which Malherbe allowed him — unless Malherbe actually concealed the first title page. In any case the whole controversy now seems pointless. Modern scholarly work on the fragments of Les francs-juges has confirmed once and for all that there is a musical as well as a documentary connection between the March to the Scaffold and the opera; but in today's more enlightened climate that is no longer a fatal admission. After all, why shouldn't there be? Some of the most sacred, most quintessential passages in Fidelio were borrowed from other works of Beethoven's, and no one thinks the worse of it for that. Though Malherbe and Boschot thought to discredit the Fantastic by proving the connection, and Tiersot, and Barzun after him, to vindicate the work's good name by denying it, it is common enough in the genesis of art for elements of the finished work to have started life in a quite different context. I doubt very much whether, if we knew nothing about the history of the March to the Scaffold, it would ever occur to us to feel that its inclusion in the symphony is arbitrary. The distant, thudding drums and eerie hand-stopped horn chords of its opening bars grow out of the ominous drum-rolls and sustained horn of the slow movement's concluding page; the March fits naturally into the dramatic and musical progression whereby the dreams of the first three movements become the nightmares of the last two.

In the *Memoirs* Berlioz states that he composed the March in a single night (whereas the Scène aux champs, he says, cost him great difficulty and weeks of labour). Strange to say, it is still necessary to point out that the destination of a piece of music and the time taken to compose it are separate matters, and that Berlioz's statement is not disproved by demonstrating that the March was originally written for the opera, not for the symphony. The composition, in short score, of a 164-bar movement of the character and form of the March in the course of one night is a remarkable but not an impossible feat, especially if, as was the case, it involved reworking and developing existing thematic material.

The history of the March is complicated by the fact that the surviving libretto of the opera makes no formal provision for one; the nearest it comes to it is a stage direction in Act 2 which speaks of "innumerable battalions" passing to the strains of "grim music" — "une musique farouche" ("musique farouche" is also how Berlioz described the Marche au supplice in the letter to Ferrand announcing the completion of the symphony). But in Act 3, when the hero falls asleep in the forest, and the orchestra, in a dream sequence, plays reminiscences of music from earlier in the opera, one of the scenes recalled, according to the libretto, is "la marche des gardes d'Olmerik" (the tyrant-villain of the work and the "Franc comte" of the March's title page); and on the torn-off remnants which are all that exist of this part of the manuscript the four notes discernible in the cello and double-bass part are clearly notes 6–9 of the first theme of the March to the Scaffold, though the key signature is G major, not G minor.

The most plausible conclusion is that, making use of thematic material from the earlier, less developed "musique farouche" of 1826, Berlioz wrote the present March for the grand-opera version of *Les francs-juges* which he and Ferrand planned when their hopes of a performance at the Odéon (an opéra-comique theatre) finally collapsed. Exactly when he did so remains an open question. Ferrand, late as always and having to be prodded by his friend, did not send the revised libretto till April 1829; but the decision to compose a more elaborate and extended march is one that Berlioz could have taken without it. One possible date is January or early February 1829, when Berlioz, believing that Harriet Smithson was interested in him after all, felt a surge of confidence in his powers ("Oph.'s love has multiplied my capabilities a hundredfold"); in such an exalted state of mind he could well have sat up all night composing the March in a sustained burst of inspiration. But a later date is equally possible – for instance, September 1829, a month or two before the concert of 1 November, at which Berlioz may have planned to perform the March. An alternative possibility which cannot be ruled out is that the Marche des gardes was composed shortly after the concert of 1 November and was to have been performed at one of the inaugural concerts of the Athénée Musical, the new society at whose soirée on 18 February two of the *Neuf mélodies* were given and whose conductor was Berlioz's friend and champion Bloc. In either case, however, the reason for not performing it was the same: some time between composition and projected performance Berlioz had decided that it belonged to the symphony.

That the March should have yielded to the gravitational pull of the Fantastic Symphony is not really surprising. Whatever the precise date of its composition, it came into being at a time when the symphony was forming itself insistently in Berlioz's mind.

The symphony had a long period of gestation. Its composition was the climax of a process traceable in his correspondence over more than a year; the genesis of the work goes back at least to the beginning of 1829, if not further. It is already hinted at in the letter he wrote to Edouard Rocher on 11 January, when the possibility that his passion for Harriet Smithson might have a happy outcome is broached for the first time:

Oh, if only I did not suffer so much! . . . So many musical ideas are seething within me . . . Now that I have broken the chains of routine, I see an immense territory stretching before me, which academic rules forbade me to enter. Now that I have heard that awe-inspiring giant Beethoven I realise what point the art of music has reached; it's a question of taking it up at that point and carrying it further − no, not further, that's impossible, he attained the limits of art, but as far in another direction. There are new things, many new things to be done, I feel it with an intense energy, and I shall do it, have no doubt, if I live. Oh, must my entire destiny be engulfed by this overpowering passion? . . . If on the other hand it turned out well, everything I've suffered would enhance my musical ideas. I would work non-stop . . . my powers would be tripled, a whole new world of music would spring fully armed from my brain or rather from my heart, to conquer that which is most precious for an artist, the approval of those capable of appreciating him.

Time lies before me, and I am still living; with life and time great events may come to pass.

These are more than prophetic words; they link with the letter written three weeks later to Ferrand − at the high tide of his illusions about Harriet − to make it clear that the work that became the Fantastic Symphony was already active within him. "Listen, Ferrand: if I succeed [*sc.* with Harriet Smithson], I feel certain beyond a shadow of doubt that I shall become a colossus in music. For some time I have had a descriptive symphony on *Faust* at work in my brain. When I have released it, I mean it to stagger the musical world." (That the "Faust symphony" and the Fantastic are fundamentally the same work is confirmed by the statement in the *Memoirs* that the latter was written "under the influence of Goethe's poem".) Early in June 1829 he is still "meditating an immense instrumental composition" which he hopes to perform in London, thus achieving "a brilliant success in *her* presence".

By the beginning of 1830 he is almost ready to begin the actual work of composition. On 2 January he asks Ferrand not to send him his poem "Faust's Last Night": once he had it in his hand he would be unable to resist it. As it is, his plan of work is mapped out for a long while ahead; in particular he has a very large orchestral composition to write for his next concert. Four weeks later, on 30 January, he tells his sister Nancy that he has just arranged to give a concert at the Nouveautés on 23 May, for which he is preparing a lot of new music, among other things an immense instrumental composition in a new genre; he has had the skeleton of the work in his head for a long while, but he fears it may not be ready in time, for to bind together all the different elements and put the whole thing in good order requires long and patient labour. The next paragraph echoes the sense of "great events" impending and unknown territory to be explored expressed in the letter to Edouard Rocher twelve months before:

Ah, my sister, you cannot imagine what pleasure a composer feels who writes freely in response to his own will alone. When I have drawn the first accolade of my score, where my instruments are ranked in battle array, when I think of the virgin lands which academic prejudice has left untouched till now and which since my emancipation I regard as my domain, I rush forward with a kind of fury to cultivate it. Sometimes I address a few words to my troops: "You uncouth fellow who up to now have only been able to swear, come here and let me teach you how to speak properly. You delicate little sprites, who've been confined to the dusty closets of learned theoreticians, come and dance for me and show me you're good for something better than acoustical experiments. Above all (I tell my army), you must forget barrack-room songs and the habits of the parade ground."

Yet a week later he has not yet started:

After a period of calm violently disturbed by the composition of the "Elégie en prose" which concludes my *Mélodies*, I have just been plunged back into the anguish of an endless, uncontrollable passion without motive, without object. She is still in London, and yet I feel her about me; all my memories awake and combine to rend me. I listen to the beating of my heart, its pulsations shake me like the pounding pistons of a steam engine. Each muscle in my body quivers with pain ... Futile! ... Horrible!... [...] I was on the point of beginning my big symphony (Episode in the life of an artist), in which the course of my infernal passion is to be depicted; I have the whole thing in my head, but I can write nothing ... We must wait.
[6 February 1830, to Ferrand]

At about the same time, to another friend, Stephen de la Madelaine, he writes enclosing a copy of his *Mélodies*: "I was going to come and see you today, but the frightful state of nervous exaltation which I have been struggling against for the past few days is worse this morning, and I am incapable of carrying on a conversation of any reasonableness. An obsession ['idée fixe'] is wearing me out, all my muscles twitch like a dying man's. Three years of patient persistence, of efforts of every kind, of almost uninterrupted labour in an art that I worship, have not brought the slightest change to ———."*

The long letter to his father written on 19 February gives a remarkably frank account of his state, of which, though not mentioning Harriet Smithson, he speaks with a candour that shows how much his relationship with his father had changed since the early years in Paris. After describing his efforts to deal with a bad attack of toothache, he passes to more personal matters.

I wish I could also find a specific to calm the feverish excitement which so often torments me; but I shall never find it, it comes from the way I am

* This suggests that Berlioz had made another approach to Harriet Smithson and had been again rebuffed.

made. In addition, the habit I have got into of constantly observing myself means that no sensation escapes me, and reflection doubles it − I see myself in a mirror. Often I experience the most extraordinary impressions, of which nothing can give an idea; nervous exaltation is no doubt the cause, but the effect is like that of opium. What surprises me is that I can remember having experienced exactly the same thing from the age of 12; my memory clearly recalls days spent in a continual emotional state of grief without subject or object. Especially on Sundays I see myself at Vespers, in the days when you were taking me through Virgil's *Æneid*. The effect of the calm, unvarying Vespers chant, combined with that of some of the words such as *In exitu Israel*, spoke to me so powerfully of the past that I was seized with an almost desperate sense of anguish, my imagination called up around me all my heroes of Troy and Latium, the unhappy Turnus especially broke my heart; the good King Latinus, the submissive Lavinia, and then the flashing weapons that I could see through clouds of dust reflecting the sunlight of Italy, and all that way of life so different from ours, all mixed up with biblical impressions, ideas about Egypt, and Moses, wrought me into a state of indefinable suffering: I should have liked to weep far, far more than I did.

Well, this imaginary world ["ce monde fantastique"] is still part of me, and has grown by the addition of all the new impressions that I experience as my life goes on; it's become a real malady. Sometimes I can scarcely endure this mental or physical pain (I can't separate the two), especially on fine summer days when I'm in an open space like the Tuileries Garden, alone. Oh then (as M. Azaïs* rightly says) I could well believe there is a violent "expansive force" within me. I see that wide horizon and the sun, and I suffer so much, so much, that if I did not take a grip of myself I should shout and roll on the ground. I have found only one way of completely satisfying this immense *appetite for emotion*, and that is music. Without it I am certain I could not go on living. First and foremost, the works of the great *free spirits* make me live from time to time with incredible energy − and then, my own music.

Yet the music that was waiting to give form to this "monde fantastique" lay locked within him. Two weeks later, in early March, still seemingly paralysed by the hopelessness of his passion, he poured out his woes in an incoherent letter to Ferdinand Hiller. "Can you tell me what it is, this capacity for emotion, this *force of suffering* that is wearing me out? Ask your angel, the seraph who has opened for you the gates of paradise[†] [...] Wait a moment, my fire's going out ... Oh, my friend, do you know? To light it, I used the manuscript of my 'Elégie en prose'! ... Tears, nothing but tears! I see Ophelia shedding them, I hear her tragic voice, the rays from her glorious eyes burn me up. Oh my friend, I am indeed wretched − inexpressibly! [...] Today it is a year since I saw

---

* Swedenborgian philosopher and social theorist.

† Hiller's girl friend, the pianist Camille Moke.

HER for the last time ... Unhappy woman, how I loved you! I shudder as I write it — how I *love* you!"

It was the final spasm. Soon afterwards he must have set to work; for the next we hear of it, six weeks later, the symphony is complete. On 16 April he reports to Ferrand that he has "sanctioned my resolve with a work that satisfies me completely" and of which he has "just written the last note". The "resolve" is nothing less than his abandonment of his passion for Harriet Smithson, in the face of the "horrible truths" ("affreuses vérités") he discovered about her, which set him on the road to a recovery that "will be as complete as the tenaciousness of my nature allows".

The letter contains the first draft of the famous programme of the Fantastic Symphony. At that stage the Waltz ("Un bal") came after the Scène aux champs, not before it.

Here is the subject [of the work], which will be set forth in a programme and distributed in the hall on the day of the concert:

Episode in the life of an artist (grand fantastic symphony in five parts). *

FIRST MOVEMENT: in two sections, made up of a short adagio, followed without a break by a fully developed allegro (intimations of passion; aimless daydreams; frenzied passion with all its bursts of tenderness, jealousy, rage, alarm, etc., etc.).

2nd MOVEMENT: *Scene in the country* (adagio: thoughts of love and hope, disturbed by dark premonitions).

3rd MOVEMENT: *A ball* (brilliant, stirring music).

4th MOVEMENT: *March to the scaffold* (grim, imposing music).

5th MOVEMENT: *Dream of a witches' sabbath.*

Now, my friend, this is how I have woven my novel, or rather my history, whose hero you will have no difficulty in recognising.

I conceive an artist, gifted with a lively imagination, who, in that state of soul which Chateaubriand so admirably depicted in *René*, sees for the first time a woman who realises the ideal of beauty and fascination that his heart has so long invoked, and falls madly in love with her. By a strange quirk, the image of the loved one never appears before his mind's eye without its corresponding musical idea, in which he finds a quality of grace and nobility similar to that which he attributes to the beloved object. This double obsession ["idée fixe"] pursues him unceasingly. That is the reason for the constant appearance, in every movement of the symphony, of the main melody of the first allegro (no. 1).

After countless agitations he imagines that there is some hope; he believes himself loved. One day, in the country, he hears in the distance two shepherds playing a *ranz des vaches* to one another; their rustic dialogue plunges him

---

* The double title echoes E.T.A. Hoffmann, whose *Contes fantastiques* (including one called "La vie d'artiste") Berlioz had discovered a few months before. The symphony's scenario also has something of the character of a Hoffmann tale in miniature.

into a delightful daydream (no. 2). The melody reappears for a moment across the themes of the adagio.

He goes to a ball. The tumult of the dance fails to distract him; his *idée fixe* haunts him still, and the cherished melody sets his heart beating during a brilliant waltz (no. 3).

In a fit of despair he poisons himself with opium; but instead of killing him the narcotic induces a horrific vision, in which he believes he has murdered the loved one, has been condemned to death, and witnesses his own execution. March to the scaffold; immense procession of headsmen, soldiers and populace. At the end the *melody* reappears once again, like a last reminder of love, interrupted by the death-stroke (no. 4).

The next moment he is surrounded by a hideous throng of demons and sorcerers, gathered to celebrate sabbath night. They summon from far and wide. At last the *melody* arrives. Till then it had appeared only in a graceful guise, but now it has become a vulgar tavern tune, trivial and base; the beloved object has come to the sabbath to take part in her victim's funeral. She is nothing but a courtesan, fit to figure in the orgy. The ceremony begins; the bells toll, the whole hellish cohort prostrates itself; a chorus chants the plainsong sequence of the dead (*Dies iræ*), two other choruses repeat it in a burlesque parody. Finally, the sabbath round-dance whirls. At its violent climax it mingles with the Dies iræ, and the vision ends (no. 5).

So there you have it, dear friend; the plan of my immense symphony has been carried out. I have just written the last note. If I can be ready by Whit Sunday, I shall give a concert at the Nouveautés, with an orchestra of 220 [*sic*]; but I'm afraid of not having the parts copied in time. At the moment I feel like an idiot; the fearful effort of concentration which produced my work has exhausted my imagination and I should like to be able to rest and sleep the whole time. But if the brain slumbers, the heart is awake, and I am very much aware that I miss you. Oh my friend, am I never to see you?

It is often suggested that the "discovery" of Harriet's baseness was what determined the character of the symphony's finale, which might otherwise have been quite different: the movement was an act of revenge, a violent gesture in reaction to the traumatic dethroning of the beloved. To my mind that is to impute far too specific an artistic influence to the immediate events of his personal life. For one thing, it was not his way to put his emotional experiences straight into music (his composition of the Elégie in the uncooled heat of the moment was, he pointed out, quite exceptional). For another thing, though the finale took on in the light of events the character of an act of revenge, it was "not written in that spirit", so Berlioz told Ferrand — a friend to whom he was not given to lying. Above all, the documents all indicate that the "plan of the symphony" had been in existence for some while before the discovery in question, waiting to be given form but frustrated by the too-present, incapacitating intensity of the "infernal passion" it was to depict. The likelihood — to put it no stronger — is that it included a nightmarish finale, the character of which had its origin in Goethe's *Faust* and in particular the Walpurgis night scene, combined with the "Ronde du sabbat" from Hugo's *Odes et ballades*, which Berlioz had certainly read by 1829. The "affreuses vérités" reported to him in March 1830, not long after his letter to Hiller, and purporting to reveal the pure and spotless Harriet as an all too human and imperfect woman, had a general, not a specific effect: the revelation, by freeing Berlioz from his thraldom, released his pent-up energies. Its immediate result was to precipitate the most dramatic of all his marathon treks into the country. But though his "vessel cracked horribly" (he told Ferrand), it "righted itself". And, as he had predicted would happen once his "destiny" was no longer "engulfed by an overpowering and hopeless passion", everything he had suffered served to enhance the force of his musical ideas; "a whole new world of music" sprang fully armed from him. Once cured, he flung himself into the task of working out and setting down on paper the immense orchestral composition that had been forming in his mind for more than a year; and within six intense, concentrated weeks it was done. The one substantial change that was made to the scheme of the work after his change of heart about Harriet — the addition of a fifth movement, the Waltz, to the original four — had nothing to do with her.[*]

The best place to seek the facts about the Fantastic Symphony is the score — the music itself and the autograph manuscript. It is necessary to insist on this point; for few works in the history of music have been subjected to so much idle theorising, and till recently none was so much talked about and so little studied. The notion that the symphony was "largely patched together from previous works"[†] had a remarkably long run, despite the lack of evidence for it; and its consequences linger on, oozing down through unconsidered programme notes and casual critical asides, even after the speculations on which it was based have mostly been refuted, and even though, as Edward Cone observes, "the unity of the symphony speaks out clearly" against such a view.

It may be said that none of this pseudo-musicological finger-wagging has done the work lasting harm; it remained a popular and much-performed piece notwithstanding what certain scholars were saying about it; and its continuing to be controversial is a kind of tribute to its undiminished

---

[*] That Berlioz intended a four-movement symphony when he began composition is shown by the manuscript title pages of the first movement and the March, both of which are headed "Simphonie [*sic*] fantastique en 4̶ 5 parties", while the March is "no. 3̶ 4". Since the added movement cannot plausibly be the Adagio (Scène aux champs) — for that would have meant that in the original scheme there was no slow movement — it must have been the second movement, the Waltz, at first placed third, after the Adagio, but, some time between the letter to Ferrand of 16 April and the draft of the programme written in May, moved to its present position.

[†] *Collins Music Encyclopedia* (1959).

vitality: that people should still be persuaded that it introduced a totally new if not alien and improper element into symphonic composition shows that at least it is in no danger of being taken for granted. But that would be to imply that being controversial is the best that can be hoped for Berlioz. And the controversy about the nature and essence of the Fantastic Symphony involves wider issues than the critical opinion of one particular work: it is central to the ancient and fallacious doctrine of Berlioz the composer unlike any other and, beyond that, to the whole muddled, contentious question or non-question of Programme Music.

The concept — in the exclusive sense of a fundamentally different kind of music — has been so deeply ingrained in the minds of generations of music-historians and amateurs, has set such deep and irresistible torrents of ink flowing, that I suppose it is too late to ask whether after all there is such a thing. But what does it amount to, in any practical and meaningful sense? And what is it based on, except a false distinction: that music which is not programme music is "pure"? As Wilfrid Mellers has pointed out, it would be hard to find a more "imbecile notion" than the concept of pure music, "for the simple reason that although in a sense all music must be programme music, since it is concerned with human emotions, in another sense music, in so far as it *is* music, can never be anything but pure".

The unreality of the distinction becomes disconcertingly evident when, as happens from time to time, a piece of absolute music is revealed to be programmatic after all. Is Berg's Lyric Suite somehow made less purely musical by the discovery, fifty years after its first performance, that it embodies the detailed "programme" of the composer's love affair with Hannah Fuchs-Robettin? For that matter, is Mendelssohn's *Hebrides* overture less than pure because its musical imagery is dictated by Nature, by the multitudinous sea in all its humours? Is Beethoven's Pastoral Symphony experienced differently from the other eight by reason of its movements having titles which unequivocally declare the music's extra-musical associations and point the audience in a specific direction? Is such a work in practice — that is, in its effect on a sensitive listener — different in kind from a Haydn symphony? or even from a Bach partita?

To go further, is one's experience of opera or song — music attached to and motivated by a text — different *in kind* from one's experience of instrumental music?

The change introduced by the Romantics was a change of degree, a development. Music did not abdicate its prerogative. It remained sovereign. What the Romantics did, and what Liszt meant when he coined the term programme music, was to make explicit what had been implicit before. Taking their lead from Beethoven, they brought music's inherent expressivity further, so to speak, into the open (a process already begun in the eighteenth century). At the same time they widened its frame of reference (like Beethoven again, in his Ninth Symphony); and, in keeping with the spirit of an age concerned with the unification of the various arts, they blurred the distinction between "absolute" music and music associated — as most music has been since the beginning of time — with words or an identified situation. Under the inspiration of Beethoven, whose symphonies they perceived as dramas — the Eroica and the Fifth no less than the Pastoral and the Ninth — they brought the theatre into the concert hall. Berlioz's introductory note to the Fantastic Symphony calls it an "instrumental drama", whose "outline, lacking the assistance of speech, needs to be explained in advance". "The following programme", he goes on, "should thus be thought of as like the spoken text of an opera, serving to introduce the musical movements, for whose character and expression it provides the motive." As in an opera, the communica-tiveness of the musical images depends on the listener being made aware of the reference.*

This is not to deny that the Fantastic Symphony was an audaciously innovative work. It was typical of Berlioz's freedom of spirit that he should have chosen, in his first major orchestral work, to override the still accepted categories of musical discourse and attempt a mixture, a "mélange de genres" analogous to what the Romantic dramatists were attempting under the influence of Shakespeare. In fact he never again used the device of a detailed literary programme in a symphony. His second symphony, *Harold in Italy*, like the Pastoral, has movement-titles only ("Harold in the mountains — scenes of melancholy, happiness and joy", "March of the pilgrims chanting the evening hymn", etc.); so has his fourth, the Symphonie funèbre et triomphale; and in the third, *Romeo and Juliet* (which is subtitled "Dramatic Symphony"), the drama is arti-culated by means of a text sung by a chorus, which in one form or another appears in four out of the work's seven movements. Berlioz thus adopted varying solutions to the problem of acquainting the listener with the frame of reference within which the symphonic narrative is to be heard.

One can say that in each case the content of the work dictated its own particular mode of communication; but you could also argue that had Berlioz written the Fantastic Symphony ten years later he might have confined himself to movement-titles, after the example of *Harold* — a practice which indeed he authorised many years later in a note prepared for a joint performance of the symphony and its sequel *Lélio* when he

---

* Cf. Berlioz's article "On Imitation in Music" (*Revue et gazette musicale*, 1 and 8 January 1837), in which he points out that Weber does not actually "depict" moonlight in the second act of *Freischütz* nor Rossini the movement of oars in *William Tell*, as they are often considered to have done; rather, they create sounds which the listener, being apprised verbally of the context, accepts as plausible images of moonlight and the movement of oars. "For the original of such images to be recognised, the listener has to be notified in some indirect way of the composer's intention."

wrote that "if the symphony is performed on its own [i.e. without *Lélio*] [...] the detailed programme may possibly be dispensed with, only the titles of the five movements being retained, since the symphony can (the author trusts) provide its own musical interest independently of any dramatic intention". This is in effect what happens whenever a listener who knows the work hears it again: you respond to it as to any other piece of music; to quote Rudolf Reti, "the music stands its ground, while the programme evaporates into the void". It may even happen when you hear it for the first time. The programme is not necessarily indispensable for an immediate response to the music — just as there are people who happily listen to the music of the *The Ring* without having much idea what is going on.[*]

True; but, rather as understanding the words of an opera or a song adds something essential to our perception of it, the programme of the Fantastic Symphony — even though, once we have absorbed it, we may well forget about it — is at some stage an integral part of the experience. Berlioz, at the time of composing and first presenting the work, was in no doubt of it.

Some writers, seeking to defend it against the damning associations of "programme music", have tried to wriggle out of this awkward fact. They explain it by reference to the climate and conditions of the time. Thus, Berlioz in 1830 was introducing music of startling novelty to a public which had only lately come into contact with Beethoven's symphonies and which was still convulsed and divided in its mind by the encounter. Furthermore, literary exegesis was a natural and important weapon for the French Romantic artist, the composer as well as the writer and painter (and this not merely because, as Schumann said, "to the French, music by itself has no interest"). Artistic manifestoes were both fashionable and necessary; they were propaganda in a war of liberation in which, in an atmosphere of the barricades, the artists of Jeune-France strove to free art from triviality and the life-denying restraints of academicism, and endow it with the beauty of naked unvarnished truth. It was a cause that needed, and wanted, to explain itself publicly; and it was to this fraternity of writers and painters, not to the Parisian composers of the day, that Berlioz naturally belonged. He was also not above exploiting his well-known and fashionably hopeless passion for Harriet Smithson to whip up interest in his symphony. (The mixture of sharp calculation and naïve spontaneity is one of the most disconcerting things about Berlioz. It is not that there aren't thousands of people who experience life and suffer with an equal intensity of emotion. But they don't usually feel free to talk about it, nor do they often combine it with the capacity for detaching themselves from their emotions and observing them with

---

[*] Bruckner asking, after a performance of *Die Walküre*, "Why do they set fire to Brünnhilde at the end?", is only an extreme example of a not uncommon phenomenon.

the objectivity of a scientist examining a specimen under a microscope.) And it is a fact that the programme, publicised in advance in the press, caused a very useful stir and aroused the curiosity of the musical and literary public both because of its known autobiographical connotations and because of the unprecedented degree to which it associated instrumental music with a story.

All this, though undeniable, does not alter the fact that Berlioz himself saw the symphony in autobiographical terms and made no bones about it. "You will have no difficulty in recognising its hero," he told Ferrand, to whom, while he was still planning the work, he had announced that it was to "depict the course of his infernal passion". Even allowing that Berlioz tended to play the role of hyper-Romantic and "artiste maudit" in his relations with Ferrand, that is a statement which, to say the least, is difficult to get round. But why should we wish to get round it? Once we have rid ourselves of the whole concept of programme music as a different (lowlier) form of the art, there is nothing to apologise for. What matters is not what goes into a work but what comes out. The integrity of the Fantastic Symphony, like that of the Lyric Suite, is not to be impugned by demonstrating that the work sprang directly from the turmoil of the composer's emotional life and that a network of personal associations underlies the musical argument. The Fantastic Symphony survives not because it tells the story of a fatal and at times lurid obsession with a particular woman but because it expresses, in a musically coherent form and with a beauty and vividness of imagery and an originality of sonic invention that remain fresh and vital, the agonies and ardours, the dreams and nightmares, of the young imagination. Its power, and its eternal youthfulness, come both from its mastery of large-scale musical narrative and from the undimmed intensity of recollected emotion that the composer poured into it.

For Berlioz himself it represented more than the distillation of his passion for Harriet Smithson. This is shown by the lines from Victor Hugo which he wrote on the title page of the manuscript, some time after the work was completed, especially by those which speak of "My heart's book inscribed on every page", "All I have suffered, all I have attempted", "The loves, the labours, the bereavements of my youth".* The symphony

---

* The complete passage quoted – part of the opening poem of *Feuillets d'automne* (1831) – reads:

> Certes, plus d'un vieillard, sans flamme, sans cheveux,
> Tombé de lassitude au bout de tous ses vœux,
> Pâlirait s'il voyait, comme un gouffre dans l'onde,
> Mon âme où ma pensée habite comme un monde,
> Tout ce que j'ai souffert, tout ce que j'ai tenté,
> Tout ce qui m'a menti comme un fruit avorté,
> Mon plus beau temps passé sans espoir qu'il renaisse,
> Les amours, les travaux, les deuils de ma jeunesse,
> Et quoiqu'encor à l'âge où l'avenir sourit,
> Le livre de mon cœur à toute page écrit.

was the repository of his entire imaginative life up till then; it was the expression of the inner world, the "monde fantastique" of which he spoke to his father shortly before he began to compose the work, and which had been his spiritual home since boyhood.

One of the tutelary spirits of that world was Chateaubriand; his concept of the "vague des passions" — that state of dreamlike melancholy in which the young imagination feeds on its own impossible desires and "one inhabits, with a full heart, an empty world"[*] — is invoked in the introductory note to the symphony.

But the presiding divinity was Estelle. It was her theme — the setting of Florian's "Je vais donc quitter pour jamais / Mon doux pays, ma douce amie", written in his teens, ten years before — that Berlioz chose to open the symphony, scoring it for the muted string quartet with isolated pizzicato phrases for the double basses pulsating like the vibrations of a stone dropped into still water, the whole image like a far-off remembered country still "visible to him across the timeless air", though seen through a veil of tears. He said that the theme recurred to him when he was planning the symphony, and he adopted it "because it seemed to me apt for the expression of that overpowering sadness felt by a young heart first tortured by hopeless love". Beyond that was the kinship that related the theme's intervals and contours to the tonus peregrinus, the Vespers plainsong whose "sad persistent chant" (springing to a plangent minor sixth, then sinking back) set off his Virgilian visions in the church at La Côte St André, and whose influence sounds repeatedly through his music. The Estelle theme was also very apt in its relationship to the main melody of the work, the idée fixe (the melody that had been associated with an ideal, unattainable beloved at least since 1828, when Berlioz used it in *Herminie*). Not only is the theme's first phrase echoed in the second part of the idée fixe, but, when it is repeated in the relative major — with a rippling accompaniment of flutes and clarinets suggestive of the river in which Némorin gazed at the reflection of Estelle's beauty — the phrase becomes identical with the motif of the sighing fourth, followed by the dejected descent to the leading note, which is the idée fixe's most important element. Thus the Berlioz / Chateaubriand concept of "rêverie" — striving towards fulfilment and creating from its unsatisfied desires their ideal object — was mirrored and embodied in the music's melodic evolution. Autobiography was absorbed into art.

The other literary sources of the Fantastic Symphony fed the compositional process in a similar way and were transmuted into the musical images they inspired. We can trace them because of the written programme, as we usually cannot in the case of other works which sprang from

---

[*] See pp. 69–70.

comparable extra-musical ideas and experiences, but of which the composer left no record.* These sources included, in addition to *René* and *Faust*, Victor Hugo's "La ronde du sabbat", from *Odes et ballades*, in which the striking of midnight on a monastery bell precipitates a hideous gathering of witches, demons and grotesque half-human, half-animal creatures who dance a whirling round-dance and perform obscene parodies of church rituals. Hugo's *Le dernier jour d'un condamné*, which Berlioz read in 1829, also contributed ideas and images: not only the general notion of an "idée fixe haunting the mind every hour, every moment" but the picture of the chained convicts in the prison courtyard dancing furiously in a ring, while "the rhythmic clashing of their chains served as orchestra to their raucous song". "If I were looking for an image of a witches' sabbath I could not find a better nor a worse one." In the same passage the convicts catch sight of the condemned man looking down from the window of his cell and give a roar of delight — the same "rugissement de joie" that occurs in the finale of the symphony when the appearance of the murdered beloved, transmuted into a prostitute (the idée fixe trivialised as a vulgar, lewdly cackling tune on the E-flat clarinet), is greeted by a roar from the whole orchestra, complete with violent change of key, metre and orchestral colour.

Chateaubriand, again, may have helped to suggest the piping shepherds' call at the beginning of the Scène aux champs. In the same passage that describes René crying out to the mountains and torrents to give him "the ideal object of his waiting passions", he speaks of "listening to [the shepherd's] melancholy songs, which reminded me that in all lands man's song is naturally sad, even when it is expressing happiness". Another source was de Quincey's *Confessions of an Opium Eater*, in the French version by Alfred de Musset which came out in 1828. In one of the passages which Musset added to the original the hero imagines, under the influence of the drug, that he has committed a frightful crime and, in a darkness lit by flaring torches and the gleam of pikes and halberds, hears the sentence of death pronounced on him. Elsewhere, he

---

* To find musical suggestion in non-musical things was far from peculiar to Berlioz. The capacity to do so is, after all, one of the distinguishing marks of a musician. Extra-musical ideas provided the impulse for many more works of Beethoven than the Pastoral Symphony. Cf. the testimony of the Taylor family, with whom Mendelssohn stayed in Wales in 1829: "We observed how natural objects seemed to suggest music to him. There was in my sister Honora's garden a pretty creeping plant, new at the time, covered with little trumpet-like flowers. He was struck with it, and played for her the music which (he said) the fairies might play on those trumpets. When he wrote out the piece (called a capriccio in E minor) he drew a little branch of that flower all up the margin of the paper. The piece (an Andante and Allegro) which Mr Mendelssohn wrote for me was suggested by the sight of a bunch of carnations and roses. The carnations that year were very fine with us. He liked them best of all the flowers, would have one often in his button-hole. We found he intended the arpeggio-passage in that composition as a reminder of the sweet scent of the flower rising up."

attends a ball one evening when he has not taken opium and catches glimpses of his beloved through the brilliant throng.

These and no doubt other sources went to the making of Berlioz's instrumental drama. Did he also take opium? Even though, as Nicholas Temperley has said, "the industry and achievement of Berlioz's life make it certain that he was not a drug addict", it seems likely that he had experimented with it[*] and, like so many of his contemporaries, knew from personal experience the images — the hags, the Satanic goat-faced deities, the magicians and prostitutes — conjured up by the potency of the poppy seed. Whether the March to the Scaffold and the Witches' Sabbath came from his imagination unaided or were drawn up from its darkest depths by de Quincey's "subtle and mighty opium" is immaterial. They remain classic visions of nightmare; the enormous developments in orchestral colour since 1830 have not dimmed their power.

After the completion of the score in April 1830 the March underwent virtually no change and the finale, though shortened, was not otherwise altered. The first three movements, on the other hand, were extensively revised over a period of several years. The revisions show Berlioz constantly striving to clarify expressive detail and to strengthen the symphony's unity-in-diversity at every level. Some of them were aimed at establishing closer links between one movement and the next, and were in part a consequence of the decision to change the sequence of the movements and make the Waltz the second, not the third; they involved the composing of a new ending to all three movements. Others were concerned with structure, shape and the ordering of events within a movement. Important changes of form and detail were made to the first movement, and both the Waltz and the Scène aux champs were rewritten a year or two later.

This is not surprising, in view of what he was attempting to do. He was engaged in a struggle to achieve, in Kern Holoman's phrase, "formal organisation of his free-flowing melodic ideas" — to find a way of moulding a melodic style founded on French classical opera to the demands of symphonic argument, of making it generate musical continuities and unify the diverse material of sharply contrasting dramatic episodes, on a scale far larger than he had attempted before. Beethoven, with Shakespeare, was the exemplar, but his symphonic dramas were inspirations rather than models. Berlioz had to create coherence by other means. The Fantastic Symphony has been called the most miraculous birth since Athene sprang fully armed from the head of Zeus; but the work's "taut

---

* Cf. the letter to his father, quoted above, in which he says that the sensations he experiences in his own imaginary world resemble the effect of opium.

discipline" which Mellers comments on, the unity that "goes much deeper than the mere recurrence of the *idée fixe*" (Cone), was certainly not attained all at once, in the six-week burst of sustained effort that produced the first version of the score. When Berlioz wrote to Ferrand, on 16 April, that the symphony "satisfied him completely", he was giving expression to a feeling of exhilaration at having just finished a work far surpassing in power and scope anything he had done before, and also to an overwhelming consciousness of release — the sense in which he had spoken to his father, two months earlier, when he wrote of the "monde fantastique" seething within him and of his "prodigious appetite for emotion" which could be "satisfied completely" by only one thing, music: that of the great "free spirits" and his own. The extensive alterations to which the manuscript bears witness are proof that once the excitement of composition had cooled and the postponement of the Whitsun concert had removed the immediate pressure, he was far from being completely satisfied with what he had written.

For the moment, however, he was committed to performing the symphony on Whit Sunday, 30 May. Preparations for the concert, in the Théâtre des Nouveautés, were gathering pace; the orchestral material was being copied, partly by the composer, partly by paid copyists; the 55-strong Nouveautés band under Bloc was being augmented to more than twice that number with players from the Société des Concerts and the greatly improved Théâtre-Italien orchestra; and Haitzinger and Wilhelmine Schroeder-Devrient, the two leading singers from the German troupe (in residence again at the Italien), had agreed to take part, the concert being scheduled for a Sunday evening, when the opera houses were closed. In the event the concert was cancelled.

Berlioz may well have felt relieved when, after all, it did not take place. The whole thing had been rushed into precipitately. A letter to his father, written three weeks before the concert was due to take place, shows him anxious on several points. Dr Berlioz, who had written to him in an unusually positive and solicitous vein, actually talked of coming to Paris to hear the symphony — an unheard-of departure. But what if he came and then the concert for some reason had to be called off?

It was the nearest Dr Berlioz ever got to hearing his son's music.

My excellent father,

How grateful I am for your letter! It has done me so much good. So you are beginning to feel a little confidence in me. May I justify it! It's the first time you have written to me like that, and I can't thank you enough. It is a great happiness to be able to give pleasure and do honour to those one loves. Yes, indeed, I should be delighted if you could hear me. But, for a journey to Paris, something more certain and definite is needed than a concert which can be cancelled at the whim of the authorities. For the past week I've been waiting, with intense impatience, for permission from M. Mangin the chief of police to advertise the concert; I am to go back tomorrow to find out whether I'm to be allowed to do so. You have to go through the heads and assistant heads of division, who solemnly treat a simple formality as if it were an affair of state. For my two previous concerts I didn't have to bother with it, but this time it's an evening concert and in a theatre, and the Nouveautés' directors don't want to make final arrangements with me before they have the official police document in their hands. Then, M. de la Rochefoucauld could if he wished prevent my evening from taking place; musicians are among the slaves in this free country of ours. Then again, the success of my symphony is unsure: the audience at this time of year will be less musical than in the winter, everyone in high society with any sort of musical education is in the country, and I doubt if the unusualness of my instrumental drama will excite sufficient curiosity in those cool-blooded gentry to get them to come back to Paris for it.* And there's another cause for anxiety — the performance itself. My orchestra will be blazing a trail through virgin forest. Quite apart from the many things new to them, the greatest difficulty of all is the expression. In the first movement especially, the music has such fiery impetus and such intensity of feeling that it will require a lot of rehearsal and the patience of a saint on the conductor's part before they take in all my intentions and learn how to convey them. Luckily it's no more difficult than the *Francs-juges* overture (which I'm repeating once again), and that was marvellously played.

I'm already following your instructions as to régime. I normally eat little and have virtually given up tea. For the past few days I've done nothing except correct orchestral parts, keep an eye on my copyists, and copy parts myself. In the evening I go to the German theatre, where the director has been so courteous as to give me a free pass without my having asked for one. I'm counting on the fabulous Haitzinger to sing at my concert and complete the programme.

Three days later (13 May) he reported to Ferrand that agreement had finally been reached with the directors of the Nouveautés, and the copying was complete, at a cost of nearly 400 francs. "It is to be hoped our takings are presentable; it's Whit Sunday, all the theatres will be closed. The fabulous Haitzinger is to sing, and I hope to have Mme Schroeder-Devrient; the two of them are taking the Salle Favart by storm in *Fidelio* and *Freischütz* every other night." Rehearsals for the concert were due to begin on 16 May.

Yet another unresolved subject of anxiety was the question of provision for a large orchestra on the stage of the Nouveautés — the space required, the desks and risers they would want. He tried to make the directors see how vital it was to get such practical details settled in advance; but every

---

* Two years before, when Berlioz gave his first concert, also at the end of May, the upper crust was out of Paris and, as Cherubini had warned, didn't come.

time he raised it with them they told him there was no need to worry — the head scene-shifter was very resourceful and would see to everything.[*]

On the 21st the *Figaro* announced the coming performance of the symphony (adding that Haitzinger and Schroeder-Devrient would sing, and the concert would conclude with the *Francs-juges* overture), and printed the literary programme of the work in full, preceded by an editorial puff:

It often happens that a composer sits down at his piano, torments the keys of the instrument, strikes some chords, and scribbles notes on to staff-paper, without so much as glimpsing, in the entire course of his labour, the least glimmer of what is known in artistic parlance as an idea.

Even more commonly he will, with the liberal aid of invitations and bill-posters, assemble friends, music-lovers, and an orchestra, and have his scribblings performed and his audience will find in it an idea, or will quite misunderstand the nature and drift of the idea, always assuming the composer has had one.

M. Hector Berlioz, a young composer with an original imagination, is determined to play a different game. He does not wish to be misinterpreted, so he has himself analysed his own inspirations. The symphony of which he has written the programme has not yet been performed in public. What effect it will produce one can, in advance, only guess; but the programme of the different movements which compose it already constitutes an act of candour and whimsicality that cannot but impress the reader.

M. Berlioz, moreover, has assembled a splendid array of performers in order to give his enterprise a fair chance of success. The performance of the *Symphonie fantastique* will be in the hands of the orchestra of the Nouveautés (which has won and consolidated its reputation in a very short space of time), reinforced by the élite of the Conservatoire performers. All these musicians, to the number of a hundred, will be disposed on the stage and conducted by M. Bloc.

A grand effect is to be expected from this gathering of artists who have acquitted themselves with such brilliance at the Conservatoire concerts, and who have gained for their orchestra the reputation of the finest in Europe.

---

* In the midst of preparations for the concert he found time to go and see Nancy's friend Rosanne Goletty, Edouard Rocher's cousin, who was in Paris with her husband, staying in the Rue St Jacques with her sister Melanie Thomas. Rosanne reported the visit to Nancy: "I've left it to the end of my letter to tell you that I had the pleasure of seeing your brother, but I assure you it was a very real pleasure. I didn't dare hope for it, as it was just the time when he was arranging his concert.[. . .] He turned up, large as life, with handsome side whiskers — I didn't recognise him, it wasn't the same person I last saw three or four years ago. He's a man now, and a man who is making his mark. I was talking the other day to my compatriot — she too is a great musician — and she said that he is singled out among the young men; when people see him pass they say, '*That's* the man.' In fact, though his concert couldn't take place, from a combination of circumstances that it was easy to foresee, the opinion is that he's made a very good start and will win a big reputation." In her reply Nancy was characteristically sniffy about Hector's prospects: "I should think it *was* time at twenty-six to show what one is. But as for his talent and the career he's embraced, a little celebrity is all it is, nothing suggests that he will soon succeed in obtaining something more positive."

As Berlioz had counted on its doing, the programme caused a stir, and before the concert's cancellation everyone had been trying to get hold of a copy of the *Figaro*. In a letter to his father, written a few days later, he explained why it had been cancelled:

> I'm just back from the country, where I have been since the beginning of the week, staying with a rich Spaniard of my acquaintance whose daughter I gave some composition lessons to last year. Her father and mother have so often invited me to go and see them in the country that I took advantage of *my concert not taking place* and went [...]
>
> This is why the concert is postponed. The German theatre is giving one that evening at the same hour. And the Conservatoire is giving one as well [in the afternoon], in order that the King of Naples can hear Beethoven's symphonies — the Duchesse de Berry has requested it, and it will be a brilliant affair; we shouldn't have had many people at the Nouveautés, even if I'd been able to put on mine, which of course I can't, *without singers*, since Haitzinger and Mme Schroeder, who had promised to take part, have to sing at their theatre, and *without orchestra*, since the one I was counting on bringing to the Nouveautés was partly drawn from the Conservatoire and the German theatre. I cannot perform my symphony with an orchestra as scanty as the Nouveautés' [...] We had already had two rehearsals, very bad ones, but it would have gone all right in the end after five or six more sessions. I had not miscalculated in what I wrote. It is all as I thought it — only the Marche du supplice is far more terrifying than I expected. I cannot give a concert now before November, All Saints' Day. When I do, Habeneck has offered his services, we are going to put on the symphony as one does a grand opera, and the performance will be what it should be, *tremendous*.

Given Berlioz's understandable habit of minimising setbacks and censoring bad news in his letters to the family, we may catch here a discreet echo of the scene described with such gruesome relish in the *Memoirs*, and also in an article in the *Rénovateur* of 15 December 1833 recounting the tribulations involved in putting on his first symphony. In the *Memoirs* in particular Berlioz made much of the "very bad" rehearsal (he mentions only one) and gave it as the sole reason for postponing the concert. The Nouveautés stage, as he had feared, proved too small for so numerous an orchestra, even with the violins placed in the pit, and there were not enough chairs or music stands to go round. He and Bloc strove in vain to get the orchestra set up (on the same stage where three years before he had appeared in the chorus of *The Straw Man* and *Mr Jolly the Singing Bailiff*), while the carpenters noisily knocked together some makeshift desks and the flustered scene-shifter (symbolically named Poulet) flew agitatedly about, trying to protect his flats and struts from the hordes of displaced musicians. In short, chaos reigned: "it was a veritable rout, a musical Passage of the Beresina".[*]

---

[*] The river crossing which was one of the greatest disasters in the Grande Armée's Retreat from Moscow. The allusion occurs in the *Rénovateur* article as well as in the *Memoirs*.

It is a fact, however, that an extra Conservatoire concert was added, three weeks after the end of the season, in honour of visiting Italian royalty, and took place on Whit Sunday afternoon, the day planned for the Nouveautés concert; and Beethoven symphonies (nos 2 and 5) were the main items in the programme.* As Berlioz told his father, this was pretty certain to have deprived him of part of his potential audience that evening (as well as most of his Conservatoire players), even without the concert at the Salle Favart, which left him without another part of his orchestra and without soloists.

It seems likely that, however disastrous the first rehearsal, more than one was held and the second went less badly than the first, since as late as the 21st — the day of the *Figaro*'s announcement, and five days after rehearsals were due to begin — the concert was still scheduled to take place. It was cancelled a day or two later, presumably on the announcement of the rival events; so the ability of the players finally to make a path through "virgin forest" was not, for the time being, put to the test. But they struggled through some at least of the work — enough for the March to arouse their enthusiasm, and perhaps for Berlioz to acknowledge that he had been a little over-optimistic in declaring that the first movement was no more difficult than the *Francs-juges* overture.

One way or another, the experience had given him food for thought and a valuable breathing-space which, between now and the première, he would use to make his first important revision of the score. Besides, there were other pressing affairs to attend to. Some time during April, Hiller's "good angel" had become his. He was in love with Camille Moke, and was loved in return.

---

* Nos 1, 2 and 4 were all introduced during this, the third season of Conservatoire concerts. The *Corsaire* reported that the Whit Sunday concert began very late, owing to the delayed arrival of the royal party, and "the entry of their Sicilian Majesties was greeted with some catcalls". Elwart, while deploring the "lack of deference", sees it, with hindsight, as a "precursor of the storm that burst in July".

24

Camille

————◄◆►————

Marie ("Camille") Moke — the daughter of a Belgian father and a German mother, but born and brought up a Parisian — was eighteen when Berlioz first met her, and according to general report bewitchingly attractive. The lithograph by Alophe, drawn at about this time, pictures a young woman with large eyes, dreamy yet purposeful, set wide apart in a pale oval face, black hair parted in the centre above a flawless brow, a perfect nose, straight but with a hint of retroussé and small, exquisitely shaped nostrils, a rosebud mouth saved from too much sweetness by the puckish upward slant at the corners, and an air of only half concealed sensuality that is intensified by the teasing demureness of the hands folded chastely in her lap. None of the portraits of Harriet Smithson can hold a candle to it. You can see how Berlioz, confronted with a real woman after more than two years' enslavement to an image, should have found her irresistible — a girl of vivacious personality and intense charm who, far from being distant and dismissive, was unashamedly attracted to him and herself took the initiative, placing herself in his way.[*]

Camille taught the piano at the school where Berlioz, towards the end of 1829 or early in 1830, was appointed to take a class in guitar; but there were many other ways they could have met — through Camille's teacher Kalkbrenner or the Baron de Trémont, to whose houses Berlioz was invited after the success of his Conservatoire concert in November 1829, through Fétis, who was a friend of the Mokes, or through Hiller himself.

Hiller had been welcomed into Parisian pianistic circles when he arrived from Frankfurt the year before; and though Camille was already ahead of him[†] and would far outstrip him to become one of the most famous virtuosos of the mid-nineteenth century, it was natural that the

---

[*] This is reflected in Berlioz's sketch for one of the monologues in *The Return to Life* (later called *Lélio*), the sequel to the Fantastic Symphony conceived in celebration of his recovery from the "infernal passion" depicted in the symphony: "[. . .] the day you spoke the magic words I love you, the spell was broken [. . .]"

[†] Fétis' *Biographie universelle des musiciens* says that by the age of fifteen she was "reckoned among the leading pianists of the age".

two young people should make friends. They were the same age and had both been child prodigies. Hiller became a regular caller at the Mokes' apartment, where, as he later wrote,

> music was made, under the eyes of Frau Mama, in such a lively and intimate way that the desire naturally suggested itself to meet without Mama or piano. Nothing was easier to arrange. The young pianist was not only amiable and beautiful, she possessed an exceptional talent and was one of the most sought after teachers; accompanied rather than surveyed by a very easy-going duenna, she went to the furthest quarters of the city to give lessons to society ladies and young girls at boarding school. One met as far from the house as possible, and did not hurry back.

The whole treatment of this episode in Hiller's *Künstlerleben* is oblique and full of sly hints, representing it as happening not to him at all but to a friend and compatriot of his. Whether or not Hiller and Camille were lovers is impossible to say with certainty. He would obviously like the reader to infer that they were, which, when taken together with the rather virginal impression he makes in his account of his friendship with Berlioz, inclines one to think they weren't. In the *Memoirs* Berlioz described Hiller's adoration of Camille as "platonic" (he had an interest in doing so). For a teenage girl living at home and not setting foot outside without a chaperone, even though an easy-going one, the opportunities for making love were few if any. On the other hand Camille, to judge by her subsequent form, was not one to waste time and let an affair drag its heels; and the reference to her in Berlioz's letter to Hiller (cited above) as "the seraph who has opened for you the gates of paradise" sounds like Thomas Moore poetic diction for sexual love.

At any rate, when Berlioz first met her she was very much Hiller's friend, while he was dedicated body and soul to his great Shakespearean passion. Hiller spoke often to him about Camille, and Berlioz listened — he could hardly not do so, considering how patiently Hiller had listened to him — and no doubt offered him sage advice.

It may have been in January 1830 that Berlioz began giving guitar lessons at Mme d'Aubrée's school in the Marais where Camille Moke taught the piano. In a letter to Ferrand written on 2 January he described himself as "poorer than a painter": he was down to his last twenty francs, even though he had just had his allowance. Ever since he had begun publishing his own music (*Huit scènes de Faust*, *Le ballet des ombres*, and now *Neuf mélodies*, had all been engraved at his expense in the past year), his finances had got hopelessly behind. He was about to be paid 200 francs by Troupenas for correcting the proofs of *William Tell*, but his only regular income was the forty-four francs a month that he got from his two pupils. "My father sends me money from time to time; then, when I have got everything straight and look forward to being a little more comfortably off, his commissions come, which nearly always have to be paid and upset my entire economy. I owe you money, I still owe Gounet more than a hundred francs; this constant state of financial embarrassment, the whole idea of being in debt, even though it is to close friends, is a continual torment to me." At least his wardrobe was no longer a problem; a case of clothes arrived from his mother in early January, crossing with his letter announcing that he had just had a complete set of clothes made for 160 francs.* But he was in dire need of a regular source of income; and perhaps it was at this point — quite possibly at Hiller's suggestion and through the good offices of Camille, who taught there — that he secured the post of guitar teacher at Mme d' Aubrée's. The school, in the Rue Harlay-Marais, was a pension for girls with orthopædic disabilities, and had a good reputation; the pupils were given treatment — massage, exercises, baths — and an all-round education. Berlioz was let loose on the younger inmates.

Three times a week I would emerge from my attic in the Rue de Richelieu and wend my melancholy way along the endless boulevard nearly as far as the Place de la Bastille, to teach Carulli's *Divertissements*. [The boulevards of that epoch were confined to the northern half of Paris and ran in a single continuous arc — Madeleine, Capucines, Italiens, Montmartre, Poissonnière, Bonne Nouvelle, St Denis, St Martin, Temple, Filles du Calvaire, St Antoine — from near the Place Louis XV (the present Place de la Concorde) to the Place de la Bastille.] My pupils were scarcely more than infants, almost all of them as timid as lambs and as intelligent as guinea-fowls. It was sending me into a decline, and would have finished me off altogether if two or three "big girls" hadn't had the bold idea one day of joining my "class" and begging me to drop the guitar lessons and replace them, not with bright and lively conversation but with a little music. Sing us something, they said. Had they known Latin they could have said, "Canta canticum novum"! I needed no begging. From that moment the guitar lessons turned into music lessons and became quite bearable, and my pupils began to progress. I even remember one day, after I had sung Orpheus' romance "Objet de mon amour, / Je te demande au jour, / Avant l'aurore", one of the young ladies exclaimed, "Sir, who's that by?" — "It's by Gluck." — "Oh — don't know him. All the same, it's awfully pretty. Even prettier than Romagnési's latest romance. Have they done an Orpheus quadrille?" — "No, not yet." — "Do let me know when it comes out, I want to buy it. Oh, it's so nice. Please sing it again … 'Avant l'aurore!'" Young and old thus acquired a rather less vague idea of the art of music than they would have got from arpeggios on the guitar.

The innocent Hiller had no qualms about his beloved's being thrown into contact with Berlioz; on the contrary, he was a convenient go-between

---

* "You must have felt vexed at not telling me of your intention, when you read my letter to Nanci. But it all fits perfectly; the coat fits even better than the one I had made for me here."

for transmitting messages and billets-doux, away from the sharp eye of Frau Mama. Hiller often talked to Camille about his friend's amazing infatuation for a woman he had not even met, and naïvely declared that one person he could not feel jealous of was Berlioz, since it was certain he of all people would never fall in love with her. "The effect of this rash avowal on a true Parisian may be imagined. She became possessed with the desire to prove her too trusting and platonic worshipper wrong." Thus Berlioz in the *Memoirs*, reliving the bitterness of the affair's culmination. Hiller's version too is understandably cynical: "The volatile pianist, on hearing of the love-messenger's grand Shakespearean passion, thought it would be amusing to divert it in her direction."

Camille's side of the case has tended to be overlooked. We cannot tell how deeply she felt about Hiller; but there is no reason to doubt that she fell in love with Berlioz. It was not her fault that Hiller, who was somewhat under the spell of his remarkable friend, spent so much time telling her about him; and it is perfectly plausible that she should have been roused first to curiosity and then to sympathy by the romantic story of his long, hopeless attachment to Miss Smithson, just as it is plausible that when she met him, and found herself quite frequently in his company, she should feel increasingly drawn by the force of a personality made more interesting still by the poor man's withdrawn and melancholy manner, and that being herself, though so young, a person of spirit and determination, she should set about breaking down his reserve and getting him to respond. His very unresponsiveness — for this was the period when he was "plunged back once more into all the anguish of an endless, uncontrollable passion without motive, without object" — would unwittingly serve to fan the flame.

That Camille simply invented the "horrible truths" which she reported about Harriet Smithson is in the highest degree improbable. Even if Berlioz was, subconsciously, ready to be given a pretext for ridding himself of his burden, he would hardly have swallowed them so easily. Camille must have repeated — with the cunning of the lover seeking to advance her cause, but in good faith — some gossip that was going round about Harriet, of the sort that the theatre is never short of. The gossip "linked" Harriet with her manager Turner — the same who a year before had raised Berlioz's hopes that the actress might not be so distant after all and who claimed to be doing everything he could to promote his happiness.

The illusion of the fair Ophelia was shattered. Berlioz disappeared for thirty-six hours, striking out blindly south-east of Paris and walking till he dropped from exhaustion and lay, dazed but sleepless, listening to the night noises of the countryside, the farm dogs barking, the jangle of cowbells, the whirring partridges, the voices of waggoners passing on a nearby road, then at first light walking on, still without food or drink, until at the edge of a field somewhere near Sceaux he collapsed into a ditch and slept the sleep of the dead.

The purge was drastic but effective. Released from his paralysing obsession, he was free to write the symphony that had been gathering force within his "teeming brain"; the act of composing, the process of expelling his idée fixe and objectifying it into art, completed his recovery. Cured, he looked about him, and gradually became conscious of Camille and aware for the first time of her very palpable charms.

Camille, who had been in love with him for some time, needed no further encouragement. "Since my recovery", wrote Berlioz to Edouard Rocher two months later, "I loved her, but she had loved me long before the hydra left my heart — she loved me even when she was thought to be involved with someone else. She was the first one of us to declare it."

For a woman to take the initiative was a bold step under the rules of the time, but that Camille did so is confirmed by Hiller's account. She wrote to Berlioz asking him to meet her — she needed to talk to him about Hiller, she said; but Berlioz, absorbed in the composition of the Fantastic Symphony, forgot to turn up. Unabashed, she confronted him at Mme d'Aubrée's and told him to his face that she loved him. It was the first time anyone had said that to him. A few days later he told her he loved her in return.*

It is possible that Berlioz and Camille became lovers quite early in their relationship — neither of them was lacking in the ingenuity and determination required to foil the less than foolproof system of surveillance under which Camille lived. On at least one occasion she contrived to visit him in his attic room at 96 Rue de Richelieu. But nothing is known for certain of the beginning of their love affair, except that it dates back at least to April 1830. Berlioz talked a lot about Camille to Edouard Rocher when the latter was in Paris on a visit from La Côte St André during the first half of the month. They passed her in the street one day. Edouard was surprised to see his friend give a start. Following his gaze he saw an uncommonly handsome and lively looking girl with dark hair and ravishing blue eyes. Berlioz told him who she was and said that it was to her that he owed the revelations about Harriet Smithson which had finally freed him from his monomania. But he did not confide fully in Edouard, lest his family get to hear of it prematurely.

At the end of May events accelerated rapidly. Camille told her mother

---

* Even the slanted account given in the *Memoirs* — an account whose studied flippancy cloaks feelings still raw and unforgiving — does not conceal the enthusiasm of his response, though seeking to pass the whole thing off as a brief if violent interlude: "After somewhat brutally playing Joseph to her Potiphar's wife for a few days, I yielded and let myself find consolation for all my sorrows in a new passion [...]" He also tries rather awkwardly to laugh off any suggestion of treachery to Hiller (thinly disguised as H—), but only makes it worse by the Biblical comparison. Hiller, however, shows no rancour towards him for stealing his girl; on the contrary, it is a providential deliverance: his "inexperience" (in using his friend as go-between) "brought him luck, in as much as it led to his being disabused".

that she loved Berlioz and wanted to marry him, and he wrote to his father asking for his consent and begging him to come to Paris and lend support to his cause. On the same day he sent Edouard Rocher the news.

I have written to my father, giving him all the preliminary details about her family, her education, her talent, her financial resources, which are far more brilliant than mine, since she earns ten or twelve thousand francs a year by her lessons and her private recitals. Her mother, who intended a brilliant match for her, was furious; she wanted to part us, but in the end consented to admit me to the house, so as not to reduce us to despair. I was there yesterday evening. [Camille] is anxious and unhappy, and I can hardly keep going, I will know no peace till my father replies or comes here himself. I have implored him to come. If he talks to you, urge him to make the journey; there are so many reasons in favour of it from my point of view. Tell him that you have heard of Mlle Moke's prodigious talent as a pianist; tell him that I pointed her out to you one day, but without taking you into my confidence, and that that is all you know. But don't let him know anything of my cruel obsession with H. Smithson. There's no point [...] [Mme Moke] is convinced that my father won't give me anything, and she doesn't wish to acknowledge her daughter's passion for me.

The day after, 6 June, there was a dramatic new development. Apparently deciding on a coup d'état to force the issue, and perhaps exasperated by the constraints they were living under, Camille and Berlioz eloped. The episode is obscure; the lovers got no further than Vincennes on the outskirts of Paris before turning back. But it was a day, or night, that remained graven on Berlioz's memory. Curiously enough the escapade does not seem to have ruined their cause. In the artistic world that the Mokes inhabited, virginity and sexual irreproachability were not the precious counters they were in the marriage stakes of the bourgeoisie. Berlioz continued to be received in the Faubourg Montmartre. But from now on Camille was under heavy surveillance.*

Hector's letter, which arrived on the 10th, caused a flurry of excitement in the Berlioz household. Nancy was deputed to answer at once, conveying his parents' consent, while Dr Berlioz pondered a more detailed reply. She also wrote to Rosanne Goletty asking her to find two rooms in a quiet hotel near her sister Melanie's apartment in the Rue St Jacques, as she and her father might be coming: "Hector wants to get married and has written to his father to come at once to Paris so that he can judge for himself whether he has chosen honourably. My father is in delicate health and is alarmed at the thought of making the journey alone."

While her brother waited on tenterhooks, Nancy confided to her diary

---

* "Henceforth the daughter was closely watched, though the tempestuous suitor could not be denied entry to the house" (Hiller).

an interesting tête-à-tête with Edouard Rocher over a week-end game of boules in the Rochers' garden at La Côte:

A snatched conversation

M. Edouard. "I have news of Hector to give you, Mademoiselle, I received it two days ago."

"Oh" — quickly working out the dates— "you did, did you? And he told you nothing special?"

"Well . . . er, not exactly."

While speaking to him I looked him straight in the face and saw from the way his ears turned red that he knew *everything*. The game of boules started up under the arbour, and I looked for a way of resuming the conversation without attracting more attention than we had already aroused by the funny expression on our faces at the moment when he accosted me.

"It appears that Hector has confided in you."

"Oh yes."

"Was it on Thursday that you got his letter?"

"Yes, Mademoiselle."

"Did he speak of this when you were in Paris?"

"No, but he often talked about the young person."

"Did you see her?"

(Now who am I partnering? How are we to arrange the play?)

"Yes, I saw her."

"Where?"

"In the street."

"Is she handsome?"

"Yes, exceedingly — charming."

"Dark?"

"Yes, dark."

"Tall?"

"Not quite as tall as Rosanne."

The game gets going. By chance I make two or three good scores, crack a few jokes without knowing what I am saying, and laugh very convincingly. I assume a mask of careless gaiety as I edge towards M. Edouard, and find a way of securing a further six minutes' tête-à-tête on a bench a little removed from the players. He in turn asks me a few questions to which I reply with the air of one saying, "I fear it may rain this evening." We arrange things so well that at supper he places himself between me and my sister, and the conversation flows more easily. He tells me pretty well all he knows, without any attempt at disguise — I was afraid my other neighbour, M. Charles [Bert], would pick up the thread.

"She's extremely beautiful — superb! When we met her I was —"

"And you've had news of Delphine?"

"Yes, I've had news of her. I was with Hector, I saw him give a jump" (and he imitates it). "I didn't know why."

"Oh, you didn't know his electric nature. How old is she? Twenty?"

"No, eighteen."

I shoot him a withering look to make him speak more quietly.

But, bah! these imbecile men never understand the language of glances, they've as much perception and tact as a goose. I again hastily interrupt a particularly interesting report he is giving me, in the hope of putting my silent neighbour off the scent; he assures me — with, I suspect, deliberate malice — that he is deaf in his right ear. In short, to learn what I learned, on a subject so dear to my heart, without attracting indiscreet eyes and ears, is devilish hard work. I have no doubt people imagined we were courting on the sly. No matter! I found out what I wanted.

In the end, though Rosanne Goletty provisionally booked them two rooms at a nearby hotel on the east side of the Luxembourg Gardens, Nancy and her father did not come to Paris. Dr Berlioz's natural reluctance to make the journey (he had always hated leaving La Côte, even to go to Grenoble) found ready support in Mme Moke's obvious doubts about the suitability of Hector as a son-in-law. He talked of coming, hesitated, then thought better of it. Instead he wrote to Joseph Rocher, Edouard's cousin, who was a judge at the Appeals Court in Paris, and asked him to make enquiries about the young person and her family. The letter he sent his son informed him that unfortunately he could expect only a very small allowance on marrying.

This was a blow. Mme Moke's attitude was severely practical. She depended on her daughter's marrying well. Camille's husband must have a good income. If Berlioz was to be considered seriously as a suitor, his situation would have to improve significantly. He must win the Prix de Rome, but more important still, he should have an opera accepted and performed with success.

Thus the most urgent and passionate personal motives reinforced his natural ambitions.

He was deeply in love with Camille, and she with him. Of that there is no question. He did not delude himself when he poured out his heart to Edouard: "Do you realise? She loves me — I who have never been loved by anyone. And by such an angel, and a talent perhaps without equal in Europe. If you knew how this love began! You'd be amazed [. . .] Oh my Camille, despite all the pain our love has already brought me, despite the terrors and the tensions I am so often prey to, I bless the moment when it began." His letters over the following six months are touching testimony to the depth of his feelings and hers, and to the persistence with which he fought to make her his wife. And Camille, though under constant pressure to give him up, for the moment stood firm.

The issues at stake, and his feelings about them, are set out in the long letter, the first of the series to have survived, that he wrote to Nancy in reply to hers conveying his parents' consent.

Paris, Wednesday [?16] June 1830

Dear Nanci,

My good, my excellent sister. How grateful I am for your sweet affectionate letter. I hadn't hoped for so prompt a consent on the part of my parents, and I was almost mad with joy when I read it. I hurried to show it to Mme Moke. She hadn't thought the reply would be so favourable (for she is always quite unwilling to hold out any hope for us), but when she saw her daughter's joy and mine she couldn't help sharing it. It was a day of happiness for me — a happiness strangely disturbed the following day by the letter from my father. But I mustn't anticipate. I told you in my first letter that I had no *positive promise* from Mme Moke, and it was that that made me so anxious for a reply saying that my father was coming. Since then an incident has occurred which upset us both terribly. Out of the blue someone with a large fortune, very high up in artistic circles in Paris, asked for her hand in marriage.* He thought that with his position and the friendly regard Mme Moke had always shown him, he would be favourably received. But he was wrong. He was refused — first of all, in writing. He persisted and came in person to plead his cause with her mother, who finally told him the true reason why he had been turned down. However, since it was a match that suited her very well, she promised him she would put pressure on her daughter and see if she couldn't sway her. She represented to her the brilliant future she was being offered, pointing out that she would not have to go on being a performer and wearing herself out giving lessons as she does, that her talent would benefit, and that, though she didn't want to go against her wishes, I on my side had practically nothing to offer her, and that if she were to consent to our marriage it could only be much later, and Camille would run the risk of multiplying her difficulties and worsening her circumstances. None the less Camille declared and repeated in front of me that she would never be anyone's but mine, whatever happened.

Mme Moke's answer was, "All right, I agree, it's done, let's hear no more of what I said to you, but you are absolutely not to think of marrying M. Berlioz until his situation changes. In any case, let us await the reply of his parents." The rest of the evening passed more cheerfuly than it had begun. Two or three days later your letter arrived; but Mme Moke, while sympathising with our joy, said again that she absolutely insisted on our waiting a year, two years if necessary, until I had a more acceptable position. "In any case," she said, "if you love each other so much, you have no reason to fear such a trial of your constancy. I don't want to have everybody blame me. At the same time I am happy to get to know M. Berlioz better, and to test both of you." What you said about "our fortune being founded only on our talents" worried her a lot.

After that, Papa's letter arrived and confirmed that not only did he consent but he expected everything to be settled during your stay in Paris. Then I read on and discovered that, so far as money was concerned, I couldn't hope for more than a thousand francs a year on marrying. I cannot tell you what it made me feel, to find that I had his consent but not the means of making use of it. I didn't know what to do or think. In the evening I went to Mme Moke's, much less cheerful than usual; and without telling her that I had had my father's letter I hinted adroitly at the possibility that he might only let me have the income from twenty thousand francs. "Well,"

---

* Very probably Pleyel, the piano manufacturer.

she said, "and what are you going to do with a thousand francs a year? Even supposing that you earn something yourself, it won't be enough. Either my daughter will have to change her way of life and give up the comforts she's accustomed to, or she will have to work for two, and I don't think you would accept that idea. She has only been working for two years; her father sacrificed all his remaining fortune to enable her to continue her studies in Paris; she in turn wished to help him, which was very natural, but it means that she has not yet put anything by. Wait till she has accumulated something. In the meantime you will do the same, your situation will improve, and you will have got on sufficiently to be able to marry. Imagine, if she fell ill or injured her hand and lost her skill entirely or even partly, what would become of you, without the means of supporting her? No, no, for the time being I cannot consent to it."

At this I objected that my chance of winning the Institute prize was very great, and that if I got it the grant of a thousand crowns [3,000 francs] a year plus my father's would give me time to turn my compositions to account. She saw the force of it; and I really think that if I win the prize our period of trial will be shortened, whether I get permission to stay in France or whether I am forced to spend a few months in exile in Italy.

Mme Moke is a most intelligent and methodical woman. Her house is not luxurious but it is maintained with unusual comfort and good taste. It has to be, because of her daughter's position. Her relations with high society and the Parisian aristocracy oblige her to keep a comfortable ménage. She has two domestics, Camille's chambermaid, and a cook. Yet nothing could be simpler and more economical than the way they live. They rarely have people to the house, and very few, because of the enormous amount of time Camille has to devote to her instrument. She never works less than four or five hours a day, not counting the time spent giving lessons. Her mother, who loves her dearly, cannot bear the thought of her daughter having to go on wearing herself out, and would like nothing so much as an establishment which would raise her above such necessities. However, she is not without sympathy for what we are going through; she said to me again yesterday that I could "set my mind at rest, she wouldn't try to marry her daughter to another, and I should not torment myself with uneasiness on that score". Mme Moke is sure of her husband's consent to whatever she does for her daughter.

But whatever she may say, I am racked with uneasiness. I cannot conceal it: if I wrote so calmly to my father the first time, it's because I thought it essential on such an occasion. But I love her intensely, passionately, and if I didn't count on her promises, on her assurance so often repeated that I "have got to be sure of her", that "nothing will separate her from me", really I should die of anxiety and alarm. Must we, for a few thousand francs more or less, see happiness, future, existence, everything endangered? I don't know if Papa will want to make the journey now. I won't urge it, if he thinks it could affect his health; but if it wasn't for that, I should give ten years of my life to have him here, with you.

The Institute competition will probably open in the first fortnight of next month. There are two prizes to be awarded, the chance is double, and the general opinion is so loudly in my favour that I must believe I shall have one of them. I shan't fail to give them academic music, whatever the subject is. I've no objection to writing a poor score now. To have money, I don't know what I wouldn't do.

But to be shut up for three weeks, three weeks with boors, three weeks without seeing her! ... You will be able to see me, however, every day between 6 and 8.* Good Nancy, tell Adèle that I was very touched by the interest she takes in my situation, I am only sorry that her fondness for me should grow like this, I should like to kill off the feelings of affection you all have for me, they will serve only to cause you bitter pain; I am someone predestined to misfortune. Damnation! Still, I shall try to look on the bright side. Mme Moke said to me yesterday: "Why get so worried in advance? After all, nothing is lost, you will wait a little while, you will have the prize, a theatre will open its doors to you; she will save some money, you will have given proof of constancy and faithfulness; I am letting you see each other from time to time, in my presence, she assures you that you can count on her, I will not try to marry her behind your back; your parents, who give their consent now, will have all the more reason for giving it then. So there — everything is sure to be all right."

It's true, but ... who can say what will happen in the meantime?

A week or two later he wrote again to Nancy, who had asked for a description of Camille:

Nothing is so absurd as lovers' pen-portraits. All the same I should like you to be able to picture her. She is nearly as tall as me, with a slim and graceful figure, she has magnificent black hair, and large blue eyes which can shine like stars, but at other times become opaque like the eyes of a dying person, when the spell of music takes possession of her. She has a playful disposition, and a mind that can be caustic and biting, but a fundamentally kindly nature. Something of a child, even more timid than you, yet strong when she has to be; capricious in small things. When her mother was pointing out this fault to me, she stopped her and said, "Yes, I am changeable, but as a silk dress is: the shade varies but the colour stays the same." At her piano she is a Corinne [heroine of Mme de Staël's novel]. No more childishness or hilarity then. In the long paragraphs of the adagios she holds her breath till the end of a phrase, pales, turns red, grows animated, subsides, accelerates, pauses, following the inner thought of the composer or her own. It is almost painful to listen to her, and to watch her play is positively so. Her talent has something miraculous about it, but she doesn't like hearing me praise it — she wants it to play no part in my love for her. No, though I admire her, this is not what attracts me. Nor has pride at being loved by such an angel anything to do with it, much as my self-esteem is flattered.

As for him, he had days of indescribable rapture followed by days of black presentiments which persisted until the moment when he saw her

* At that stage Nancy's visit was still on the cards.

again. "Her smile is like the sun that disperses the mist. Yet I don't know whether her bursts of high spirits delight or distress me; her faith in the future is stronger than mine. I almost prefer her little fits of jealousy, which she doesn't try to hide. The other day we were discussing the last performance of *Fidelio*, in which Mme Devrient had been sublime. As I was talking about the German tragedienne and using that epithet, which applies to so few artists, Camille interrupted me and said with a slightly cross air: 'I don't wish you to speak of that woman in this way, I forbid you, *sir*, to find any other woman sublime except a certain person that I know.'"

The vein of archness in Camille does not seem to have irritated him in the least. He was charmed and fascinated by her. Considering how young she was, she was a remarkably complete person, and marvellously unspoiled by the pampered yet exacting upbringing she had had as a child prodigy. Her slight bossiness, far from being oppressive, delighted him. It was the first time in his life that a young woman had cared for him wholeheartedly, without reserve. He could hardly believe his luck, as he told his mother: "I wonder daily, all the time, if it's really possible that I am loved by this enchanting Corinne: I feel it must be a dream, a fiction. But then I see her, and hear her; slim and graceful like a spirit of the air she flies to meet me, and then I have proof that my dream is reality, my fiction fact." "You have wished so much, my dear Mama" (he goes on, a little naïvely) "that I would be tidier in my appearance. Well, you will be more content when you see me. Camille is taking great pride in improving it. She's putting things right one by one. But I have to take particular trouble with my hair, for which she has a special affection."

He was by now tolerated in the Moke household. His visits, however, were rationed (as well as strictly chaperoned). When Camille fell ill and, fearing it was the first onset of consumption, insisted on his being sent for immediately, her mother would not hear of it, and he did not see her till next day, the time appointed for him to come. They met only at her house, or if away from it, in a public place. During the two weeks that he was shut up in the Institute it was Camille's maid who came to visit him, without Camille. The escapade to Vincennes had not been forgotten.

His stock rose, however, after an encounter at the German theatre between Camille's mother and Pixis, the German composer and pianist, who was a friend of the Mokes. Berlioz, who had been given a box by the director, took Camille and Mme Moke (and had the satisfaction of observing that they were an object of interest to the artists in the audience: when they got up to go before the end of the evening people opened the doors of their boxes to watch them pass along the corridor). As they were leaving, they met Pixis, who engaged Mme Moke in a long conversation in German. "Camille, who understands it, told me afterwards that it was all about us, and that Pixis told her mother he had perceived what my feelings were, but had no hesitation in talking to her, as he thought that she couldn't be opposed to it. Thereupon he lavished all sorts of praise on me, while I listened without the slightest embarrassment, not understanding a word. I don't know if a lot of people have spoken of me in the same vein, but for the past few days she seems to have taken a liking to me. We've both noticed it. However, she still insists on regarding our marriage as a long way off. The Institute competition is getting near. Oh, if I don't win the prize!"

A fortnight later, on 14 July, he sat the preliminary exam, the concours d'essai, with nine other candidates, and next day was chosen as one of six young composers to enter the competition proper; on the 17th he went en loge. It was the fourth time. He vowed that, whatever happened, it should be the last.

The chosen text — by the Hellenist scholar and amateur poet Jean-François Gail — treated the last night of Sardanapalus, the hedonistic king of Assyria whose death was on the scale and of the reckless splendour of the debaucheries which brought his downfall. It began with a sunset instead of a dawn ("Déjà la nuit a voilé la nature"), but in other respects conformed to type in expressing a violent situation in language of exemplary stiltedness. The opening recitative and aria showed the great voluptuary, though already beset by enemies, preparing with his concubines for another night of pleasure. In the second, having learned that his power was overthrown and Nineveh had surrendered to his foes, he rejected their terms — life and liberty in return for abdication — preferring to die as King of Kings. In the third he resolved to enjoy one final feast, ordered the funeral pyre to be made ready, gathered his slaves round him, and called on Mithra, goddess of fire, to send his fame blazing down to posterity.

Here was a subject that cried out for dramatic treatment on the grandest scale, that positively invited an act of Romantic defiance — a subject hallowed by Byron and treated by Delacroix in his most notorious canvas, "The Death of Sardanapalus", exhibited two years earlier amid general obloquy. But this time Berlioz knew better. He resisted its enticements and played safe. The idea of concluding with a big orchestral set-piece depicting the burning of the palace and all within it was very tempting, but it would be suicidal self-indulgence to yield to it. Reduced to the piano, it could only ruin his chances. Better to repress his instincts and forget about it until he had won the prize. There was no need to remind himself how much depended on it.

Camille was constantly in his thoughts. From his candidate's cell he wrote to Ferrand to tell him about his "entrancing sylph", his "Ariel". "We've been separated for several days now; I'm shut up in the Institute, *for the last time*. I must have the prize, a large part of our happiness hinges on it. Like Don Carlos in *Hernani* I tell myself, 'I shall have it.'" Every other day, as she had promised, Mme Moke sent Camille's chambermaid to bring him their news and take back his. As in previous years, the candidates held evening reception in the Institute courtyard and had their friends to dinner; but, for Berlioz, one sad difference was that his old friend Pingard, usher to the Institute and authority on the East Indies and the Cape of Good Hope, was no more. It was another reason for having done with the place. He composed his score rapidly and confidently, and was finished in less than a fortnight. The fair copy of the cantata was written out to the boom of cannon and the rattle of musketry from the fighting on the opposite side of the river. The long-threatened revolution had come.

25

Revolution and the Prix de Rome

The July Revolution might conceivably have been avoided, but not by a king of the outlook and temperament of Charles X. Alfred de Vigny summed it up in the diary he was keeping at the time.

> The only way of reconciling the Restoration and the Revolution, those eternal enemies, was to govern with the two centre blocs and use their united weight to crush the extremists on either side [...] From his accession I predicted that Charles X would attempt to achieve absolute government. He hates the Charter and doesn't understand it. His favourites and the old women at court govern him. Having succeeded in making M. de Polignac prime minister, he is determined to keep him there come what may. He regards the return of the two hundred and twenty-one [liberal deputies] to the Chamber as a personal insult; he thinks he can play Bonaparte. But Bonaparte was there standing behind the cannon at St Roch. Charles X is at Compiègne. He said, "My brother fell because he yielded. I shall resist and shall not fall." He is wrong. Louis XVI fell to the left, Charles X to the right. That's the only difference.

The alliance that brought down the last of the Bourbons was a loose and impermanent coalition of interests which sought freedom for different and often incompatible reasons and were united only by the King's ineptitude. The liberal politicians wanted power; the journalists wanted liberty of the press; the bankers wanted unimpeded wealth; the young artists wanted an end to censorship and to antiquated restrictions of every kind and a true Napoleonic "career open to the talents"; the students, roused by the republican ballads which Béranger fired off from his prison, wanted a juster society; and the poor wanted bread.

Charles X understood none of this. At heart an ancien régime monarch, conscientious but blinkered, high-minded, feeble, yet obstinate and uncompromising, he had charm and was capable of imaginative and popular gestures (as when he personally overruled an attempt by the Academy to exclude Victor Hugo from the Comédie-Française), but had no idea how to govern in post-Revolutionary France. Scandalised by his brother Louis XVIII's culpably liberal measures, on becoming King he set vaguely about re-establishing the authority of the throne in the image of divine right. One by one he marshalled the most powerful elements in society against him, until even traditionalists like Chateaubriand felt alienated and began to make common cause with the liberals.

Charles X's moves against the independent newspapers, the focus of his indignation, brought the diverse opposition to a head. The year before, the prosecution of the moderate, centrist *Journal des débats* succeeded only in concentrating hostility to the régime; and it was a wholesale attack on the press that precipitated the revolution of July 1830. Believing that his successful military campaign in North Africa — Algiers had just been captured — would distract attention from discontent at home, the King moved to curb its freedom drastically: the "July Ordinances", a package of anti-liberal measures drafted by Polignac, were promulgated in the *Moniteur* on Monday 26 July. Their effect was instantaneous. The leaders of the liberals met in the editorial office of the banned *Précurseur* and formed a committee of vigilance which proceeded to distribute arms to all sympathisers. Within two days the forces of revolution had fused and caught fire. While the King stayed aloof in St Cloud, fighting broke out in the Faubourg St Antoine and spread westwards along the river. The National Guard, students, army veterans led by officers on half pay, workers armed with sticks and iron bars — the "sainte canaille" or holy scum of Auguste Barbier's famous poem — fought alongside one another in a spirit of intoxicated comradeship. Tales of reckless bravery passed along their ranks like fire along a powder-train, inflaming them to fresh feats. There was no opposing them. They stormed the barracks in the Rue Pépinière in twenty minutes; and the weapons and ammunition they found there were seized and apportioned to those without them. Yet there was no rioting and virtually no looting. A common sincerity and purity of purpose seemed to animate and exalt them all.*

A determined dictator would have made short work of them; but faced only by a leaderless and indecisive power (whole regiments refused to fire on the mob), they swept on irresistibly.

On the second day, the 28th, they were at the Hôtel de Ville; the sound of gunfire along the quais, mixed with the roars of the crowd and the drums of the National Guard, carried clearly down the river; Berlioz heard it in his attic room at the Institute. On the 29th the insurgents

---

* The defenders showed the same spirit of quixotic bravery. Vigny noted the case of a lieutenant of the Sixth Regiment of Guards who, ordered to fire, refused because the street was full of women and children. When the colonel threatened to arrest him, he snatched up a pistol and blew his own brains out. "Le Motteux, a captain in the First Regiment, had sent in his resignation on the day of M. de Polignac's absurd ordinances. On the evening when fighting began he went to see his colonel and begged him to treat his resignation as null and void. His company was surrounded at the Madeleine, among the columns of the church that is being built. He was called on to surrender, but refused and was killed. These two examples may serve as perfect symbols of the Royal Guard's attitude and feelings. It did its duty nobly, but its heart was not in it."

reached the Palais du Louvre, on the other side of the river opposite the Institute, and under heavy fire from the Royal Guard began the assault. The defenders, from behind the pillars of the colonnade and the windows of the palace, kept up a continuous fusillade but the attackers pressed on. By mid-afternoon the Louvre was theirs and the fighting was effectively over. It had taken three days.

To his chagrin Berlioz had missed almost all of it. "Only the desperate importance of the competition", he wrote to his father, "could have kept me immured in our fortress while people were getting killed under our eyes [...] The thought that so many brave men have paid with their blood for the conquest of our liberties, while I was one of those who did nothing, gives me not a moment's peace." He was putting the finishing touches to his cantata as the final assault began just across the Seine, while stray bullets whined over the roof and pattered on the wall beside his window, and a cannon ball from the battery trained on the Pont des Arts smashed a hole in the façade of the Institute (conferring a momentary lustre on that citadel of reaction). By the time he handed in his score at the Institute office and was free to slip out into the streets it was 5 o'clock on the afternoon of the third day and the Louvre had fallen. His first thought was for Camille, and he ran through the smoking streets to her house to reassure himself of her safety. Then out again in quest of arms and any action there might still be left. After a long search he found a pair of pistols without ammunition; and eventually, after an abortive visit to the Hôtel de Ville where he was sent by some National Guardsmen, only to discover they had run out of cartridges, he succeeded in arming his weapons by stopping passers-by and getting bullets from one, powder from another, and a knife to cut the lead from a third. But that was as far as it went. It was too late to find a use for them. He "had not fired a single shot".

Next evening, at the report that Charles X was organising counter-revolution, he joined a large crowd converging on the Etoile, but the rumour proved false; the guards posted in the Bois de Boulogne were withdrawn and everyone dispersed. The uprising had achieved its immediate object; the régime was no more. "All is quiet," Berlioz told his father on 2 August; "the admirable order which reigned throughout this three-day revolution is being maintained and confirmed: no stealing, not an offence of any kind. The people are sublime."

Three days later, on the 5th, he gave a fuller account in a long letter to Nancy.

Paris is so calm you would think nothing had happened. The barricades have been taken down, the roads are being repaired and the street lamps replaced by torches. Only the poor trees on the boulevard can't be revived. If you could only see the poor women weeping for a son or husband or father or brother by the black cross set up in front of the Louvre to mark the grave of the National Guardsmen — it's a heartbreaking sight. But the spirit of the people is so fine! The day before yesterday [the 3rd] a rumour went round that good King Charles was up to his tricks and was planning to stay on at Rambouillet with the handful of men left to him. Lafayette gave orders for ten thousand Parisians to march on Rambouillet and take him. But the crowd grew and grew until by the time it reached the Etoile barrier it already numbered more than thirty thousand armed men, some on foot, some on horseback, some in carriages. They stopped all the cabs, coaches and omnibuses and made the occupants get out and make way for the National Guard. Today the dethroned King is on his way to Cherbourg, where he'll embark for London.

Last night at the Opéra the Marseillaise was called for. Ad. [Adolphe] Nourrit sang it, his tricolour in hand, backed by the full chorus and orchestra. You can't imagine the effect. Immediately afterwards a note was thrown on to the stage and, on being read out, informed the audience that the author of this sublime hymn, Rouget de Lisle, was living in poverty; it proposed that a collection be taken for him. At that everyone streamed into the foyer and a large sum was raised for the modern Tyrtæus.* Luckily none of my friends was killed or wounded, though almost all acquitted themselves with honour. One only was shot at, by a Swiss, who fired from so close that the pocket of his coat caught fire. Beside him was a little metalworker, aged fourteen, armed only with a hammer, who kept saying, "Heh, general, bring one of the bastards down so I can take his gun." In fact Richard (that's his name — he's the translator of Hoffmann's *Tales*) brought down a Swiss, and the second the little rogue saw him fall he threw himself on the body, seized the still-loaded gun and discharged it into the fleeing remnant of the troop. There have been thousands of extraordinary deeds, each more so than the last.† At present, instead of despairing, as you do, one should hope on the contrary for the most brilliant future for our country [...]

I think the great flag must be floating now on top of the church tower at La Côte, as it is all over France. They are going to put the bust [statue] of Napoleon back on the column in the Place Vendôme, too long bereft of it.

---

* 4 August. The Opéra, closed since 28 July, re-opened that evening with a benefit performance in aid of widows, orphans and wounded of the Three Glorious Days. The programme consisted of a shortened version of Auber's *La muette de Portici*, the Opéra's biggest hit of this period, and the première of a new patriotic cantata, *La Parisienne*, Auber's adaptation of a popular song to words by Germain Delavigne. It transpired that Rouget, the author of the Marseillaise, had been granted a pension of 1,500 francs; he donated the collection to the wounded.

† Mendelssohn's father, Abraham, in Paris at the time, reported to his family a similar incident which he heard from a cab-driver. "A cabman who drove me the other day told me that on the dreadful Wednesday [28th], when he and some of his fellow-citizens fought in the Rue St Honoré, several children from twelve to fourteen years of age joined the crowd. He asked their leader, 'What are you doing here, you poor thing? You haven't even any weapons.' — 'I'm waiting till you're killed so I can take yours', was the retort, which could not be the invention of a cab-driver. It made me shudder, and I know nothing like it." Delacroix commemorated the legendary bravery of the Parisian working-class children with the pistol-brandishing gamin in his picture "Liberty leading the people".

All the Englishmen in Paris are overcome with admiration for the French people. Several of them fought at the siege of the Tuileries; so did three Germans of my acquaintance. Farewell, write to me at once and tell me what happened in Grenoble and with you. Farewell.

Meanwhile, however, the wheels of politics had begun to turn. The Duke of Orléans was presented to the assembled people by La Fayette, unimpeachable symbol and defender of revolutionary liberties, from a balcony of the Hôtel de Ville on the afternoon of 3 August and accepted with acclamation: he was to be a different kind of ruler, a republican monarch, Louis-Philippe, King not of France but of "the French". His partisans had distributed posters claiming that, though a cousin of the deposed king, he was actually a Valois, not a member of the despised and discredited Capets-Bourbons. Behind the scenes he rejected La Fayette's suggestion that the National Guard should be opened to all ranks of society. The foundations of the bourgeois monarchy were being laid. Abraham Mendelssohn, still in Paris, observed gloomily that nothing had changed in France. "One thing is clear: with Charles X only a small part of the corruptness, baseness, avarice and intrigue of the upper classes has been banished." Yet he too foresaw "a prosperous time for the young generation. They can and will make their way, and will find an immense sphere of action opening before them." The new monarch was the focus of general optimism; he was felt to embody the dawning of a new age. Alfred de Vigny, at first sceptical of a king whose throne was based neither on legitimacy nor on popular demand, was impressed in spite of himself when Louis-Philippe reviewed the National Guard in the Champ de Mars and, reining in his horse in front of the battalion which Vigny commanded, "took off his hat and said, 'M. de Vigny, I am very pleased to see you, and to see you here. Your battalion is very fine, kindly say so on my behalf to all these gentlemen, since I cannot say it to all of them myself.' I found him handsome, and with a resemblance to Louis XIV – rather as Mme de Sévigné found Louis XIV the greatest king in the world after having danced with him."

Before very long disillusionment would replace these fond expectations. For some people it was a prosperous time, but not for many. "What is a revolution?" Théophile Gautier would ask, in the preface to his collection of stories, *Les Jeunes-France:*

It is people firing at each other in the street. A number of window-panes get broken, and the glaziers do well. The smoke blows away. Those who come out on top put the others down. The grass grows more luxuriantly next spring; a hero makes excellent petits pois. The bits of rag known as flags are changed on the town-hall flagstaffs. The guillotine, the great harlot, puts her scarlet arms around the necks of those the bullets have spared and the executioner, if need be, takes over where the soldier left off. Alternatively, the first rogue on the scene climbs furtively on to the throne and sits in the place left vacant. And one continues to catch the pox, pay one's debts and go to the latest opéra-comique, under this one just as one did under the other. It hardly seems worth disturbing so many harmless paving-stones.

For the moment everyone rode the crest of the wave; the chivalry and ardour of "Les Trois Glorieuses" left a thrilling afterglow. A letter from Maria Malibran to a friend, sent from Norwich where she was on tour, sums up the mood of the time:

I am pleased, proud, conceited, vain in the highest degree to belong to the French [Malibran was born in Paris]. You shed tears at not having been there? Not a day passes when I am not heartbroken, I, a woman, that I did not have a leg smashed fighting for the cause of the golden age . . . I tell you that when I think of Paris my soul takes wing. Do you imagine that soldiers armed with rifles could have stopped me crying "Long live liberty!"? It's said things haven't yet calmed down in France. Write and tell me, and I'll come. I wish to share the fate of my brothers!

"Now", exclaimed Horace Vernet, "I can paint anything without fear of censorship!" Above all, the young artists promised themselves an end at last to antediluvian rules and restrictions. Victor Hugo hailed their supreme hour in a ringing ode to "La Jeune-France" which appeared in the *Globe* with an editorial note declaring that "poetry has not been slow to celebrate the greatness of the late events; they were made to inspire all endowed with heart and voice". There was a spate of patriotic publications, in poetry and music. Many of the latter featured the new hit, the *Parisienne*. The streets shook with song, and the Marseillaise, banned before the July Revolution (and banned many times subsequently), was struck up at all hours of the day and night. Choron performed it between excerpts from *Samson* and *Judas Maccabæus* at an oratorio concert at his School of Church Music. Louis-Philippe had to keep appearing at his window in the Tuileries to beat time for the crowds bellowing it in the courtyard below.*

Berlioz shared to the full in the heady emotions and confident hopes of the moment. Long afterwards, when the hopes had been utterly confounded and he felt only a profound cynicism about revolutions and the good that

---

* Nancy Berlioz, staying in Valence with her friend Elise Julhiet, was stirred to the depths as she watched a steamboat passing down the Rhone with a detachment of troops on board, the soldiers in their brilliant uniforms grouped on the bridge, and heard "a military band playing the *Marseillaise* (don't be alarmed, Mama!) as they arrived and departed, the sound dwindling into the distance − a scene I shall remember for a long time".

was supposed to come of them, the emotions of the time remained fresh and unsullied:

> Never shall I forget how Paris looked during those famous days: the fantastic bravery of the guttersnipes, the enthusiasm of the men, the wild excitement of the whores, the grim resignation of the Swiss and the Royal Guard, the strange pride of the working class in being, as they said, masters of Paris and stealing nothing; and the fantastic bragging of some of the young men, based on feats of genuine courage but so embellished in the telling as to sound preposterous. Thus, having taken the cavalry barracks in the Rue de Babylone, with heavy losses, they felt obliged to announce, with a gravity worthy of Alexander's veterans, "We were at the capture of Babylon." The full title was too long for convenience; and the phrase was repeated so often that the abbreviation became indispensable. Then, the portentous way they delivered the word "Babylon", with a prodigious lengthening of the "o"! Parisians! Charlatans — charlatans of genius if you like, but charlatans!
>
> And the music, the songs, the harsh voices resounding through the streets — no one who did not hear them can have any idea what they were like.

Fired by the gala evening at the Opéra at which Nourrit had sung the Marseillaise, but noting, amidst his emotions, that something more could be done with the piece, Berlioz composed his own arrangement of all six verses of the hymn, scoring it for double choir and an orchestra without oboes but with six trumpets, and with a large force of drums used to formidable effect at "Marchons, marchons" to suggest the tramp of multitudes. Above the choir's first-entry ("Allons enfants") he wrote: "Everyone with a voice, a soul, and blood in his veins".[*]

He was reminded of it soon afterwards. Crossing the courtyard of the Palais Royal, at the far end of the street where he lived, he was agreeably surprised to hear a group of young men singing one of his *Irish Melodies*, "Chant guerrier" (the one based partly on Moore's "Forget not our wounded

---

[*] Cf. Mahler's inscription in his copy of Bruckner's Te Deum, in which he crossed out "for solo voices, chorus, orchestra, organ ad libitum" and wrote instead, "For the tongues of angels, heaven-blest, chastened hearts, and souls purified in the fire!" Berlioz's version of the Marseillaise was published soon afterwards by Schlesinger, with a dedication to Rouget de Lisle. Other characteristic features include the rapidly rising scale for cellos and double basses, followed by a proud descending phrase in dotted rhythm, at "Contre nous de la tyrannie l'étendard sanglant est levé", the prominent flattened sixth (G flat in the key of B♭ flat major), the distant, Spontinian effect of trumpet triplets piercing the sombre texture to suggest the approach of the "farouches soldats", the exalted tenor descant two bars from the end, and the dramatic contrast between the unaccompanied sixth verse and the great uprush of the orchestra re-entering for the refrain. At about the same time Berlioz arranged another Rouget hymn, the "Chant du Neuf Thermidor", a celebration of the downfall of Robespierre. The existence of this arrangement was unknown until the score turned up a few years ago in the library of the Geneva Conservatoire, among the papers of Berlioz's friend the conductor Nathan Bloc, who moved to Geneva early in 1831 and to whom Berlioz had presumably given it as a parting present.

companions"). They were singing it at the wrong speed, however, and without revealing his identity he had an altercation about it with their leader. Tension was resolved by his joining the choir and singing a firm bass in the next piece, a setting of Béranger's "Vieux drapeau" by the conductor. Meanwhile a crowd had gathered, and a few National Guardsmen who were keeping a space clear round the performers took off their shakos and made an impromptu collection for the wounded. The scene appealed to the Parisian sense of the bizarre and the audience grew larger and larger until the singers had scarcely room to breathe and took refuge in the glass-covered Galerie Colbert. The crowd poured after them and invited them to continue. From the first-floor window of a haberdashery store whose owner asked them in they started the Marseillaise. The seething mass below grew still, and it remained so even at the refrain, "Aux armes, citoyens, formons nos bataillons!"

> After the fourth verse, unable to contain myself longer, I yelled, "Confound it all − sing!" The great crowd launched into its "Aux armes, citoyens!" with the energy and precision of a trained choir. Picture it − the arcade leading to the Rue Vivienne full of people, as were the arcade that gives on to the Rue Neuve-des-Petits-Champs and the central area beneath the dome, and these four or five thousand voices crammed into a reverberant space bounded to right and left by the clapboards of the shops' shutters, overhead by the glass roof and beneath by the paving-stones, and most of them moreover, men, women and children, still hot from the struggle − and then imagine the effect of that stupendous refrain. I literally sank to the floor; and our little band, aghast at the explosion, was struck dumb, silent as birds after a thunderclap.

It seemed in every sense a "harmonious revolution". There was a general belief that the overthrow of the Bourbon régime would inaugurate the new era for the arts which so many, Berlioz among them, had long and impatiently looked forward to. "We are on the brink of the emancipation of the theatre," he wrote to Nancy on 5 September; "the revolution was intended specifically to achieve freedom for the arts; I shall succeed ten times quicker than I should have done without it."

His interest in the abolition of privilege was not exclusively personal and artistic, however: he also looked forward to "the betterment of the largest and poorest class in society". The phrase appears in a letter that Berlioz wrote from Rome a year later, in July 1831, to Charles Duveyrier, a lawyer who was a leading member of the utopian reformist group known as the Saint-Simonians; but it is clear that by the latter part of 1830, though not yet converted to Saint-Simonism (and fundamentally resistant to the mystical side of its teachings), Berlioz had begun to be attracted to ideas of radical social reform. After a lull following the death of Saint-Simon himself in 1825, the movement was again active. From April 1830 it held regular meetings in the Rue Monsigny (where it rented a whole floor, and subsequently two floors, of the Hôtel de Gesvres), and in November it bought a newspaper, the *Globe*, to propagate its views. We do not know whether Berlioz attended any of the meetings, but he had met and talked to Duveyrier by the time he left Paris for Rome at the end of December. One of several Saint-Simonian friends could have introduced them — Ferdinand Hiller, Adolphe Nourrit, the cellist Dominique Tajan-Rogé, or Franz Liszt, whom Berlioz met at the beginning of December. It was Saint-Simonian policy to recruit artists of note or promise, who would help to spread the movement's ideas. The artist was to be the priest of the new social order.

Before long these grand notions of a more enlightened and just society would evaporate; but for the moment, in the immediate aftermath of July, it seemed a possible dream.

Three weeks after the Revolution Berlioz cleared the first of the obstacles that stood between him and marriage to Camille Moke. The music section of the Academy met on the morning of Thursday 19 August, heard the competing cantatas, and by six votes to two awarded the first prize to Berlioz's. Berton attempted a last stand, voting "no" to the question, "Should a first prize be awarded", and then trying to convince his colleagues that "an academy neither should nor could encourage music of that sort". But Berlioz's self-restraint had done the trick. Cherubini told Le Sueur that his pupil "must have worked devilishly hard since last year". "And God knows," wrote Berlioz, reporting the news to his family, "there's nothing non-academic in my score. But Berton has got it into his head that I am a sort of Attila come to lay waste the musical world — a revolutionary who should be locked up in solitary confinement and if necessary guillotined. Old creep, who was constantly kow-towing under the Bourbons and now sports two tricolour ribbons in his button hole and a cockade as big as the rising sun in his hatband".[*]

Berlioz had promised to call at 2 o'clock at the Mokes with news of the result, but Le Sueur, who was to give it to him, was delayed and did not get home till 6, by which time Berlioz was already late for dinner in the Chaussée d'Antin. It was 8.30 by the time he was free. He found Camille, who had not eaten all day, stretched out on her mother's sofa half dead with anxiety.

There was no danger that the full session of the Academy would reverse the musicians' verdict this time. Twenty-three of the twenty-five members present voted for him. Pradier the sculptor, who had championed his cause the year before when *Cléopâtre* was in question, came out of the conference hall to look for him and, finding him waiting in the library, shook him warmly by the hand and said, "You have got it". Berlioz had also to accept the compliments of Berton, who had the nerve to accost

---

[*] In the same letter he calls Berton "ce Polignac de la routine".

him and offer his congratulations with every indication of the most sincere affection. No matter: he had got it. As Camille had said to him, "The *world* believes it is a sure sign of talent; you must stop its mouth."

Whatever he thought of the Prix de Rome, it was gratifying to be able at last to write a letter to La Côte beginning, "My dear Mama, I am pleased to announce that I have won that precious prize: it is mine". And the joy his success gave Camille was one he understood and shared; even her mother had been moved by it. But it would be nothing to the pride and delight he would feel when she could hear some real music of his, at the concert in November at which he planned to give his Fantastic Symphony: she would see that he could make an orchestra speak as she did her piano. "God, how I love her! It's indescribable. Nothing can convey what I feel — there is only music, no other language has the strength or the depth." "M. Moke will be here soon" (he goes on); "his wife showed me a letter of his, in which he says some nice things about us. But I shall not obtain Camille until I have had a success in the theatre — that is the condition her parents insist on. Very well, I shall have it; but, for that, it is necessary to stay in Paris. I am going to apply to be let off this ridiculous journey to Rome. But instead of going to the Minister of the Interior I shall speak directly to the King; he is so accessible and so unassuming that I trust he'll listen to me and understand."

Hector's news had a mixed reception from the family. It did not noticeably improve relations with his parents. His sisters were in ecstasies, but Dr Berlioz waited ten days before writing. The letter crossed with one from his son saying that, though Adèle's joy delighted him (she had written at once), he would have been very happy if he could have heard from his father or his mother, and asking if his father could possibly advance him the 200 francs due in November for the last two months of the year, since the government grant didn't begin till January, all his pupils were still away in the country, he had two concerts coming up in November and he had just had to buy a new set of clothes (a Prix de Rome received many invitations, and "my black suit was the only decent one left and I can't wear it all the time").*

Joséphine Berlioz sent the 200 francs, together with a whole series of voluble reproaches: he had said nothing about coming to see them, which showed that he loved Camille more than his family; he never called on their Dauphinois friends in Paris; he should be more careful not to air his horrid political opinions so openly. It drew a firm retort: "I do not deserve these reproaches; and, while holding very decided political opinions, I can assure you that I rarely give expression to them, since I

---

* By the same post he wrote to Edouard Rocher asking for a six-months' loan of 500 francs with interest on the security of his grant, to help pay for his concerts.

find all conversations on such subjects excessively boring. I have not neglected M. Rocher nor M. Teisseyre, and I saw M. Prudhomme three days ago. The picture I gave you of the various activities which keep me in Paris surely made it clear that I cannot come and see you yet. And why grudge me the affections which attach me here? Oh, Mama, how wrong you are if you think they can weaken the feelings I have for you."

The Berlioz household gives a rather melancholy impression during this period: the doctor fearing that he is beginning to lose his sight as well as his hearing, and hiding in his study when unwelcome visitors call; Mme Berlioz agitated by the Revolution and indignant at the loss of position by her royalist friends (though her brother Félix Marmion has confounded their worst fears by surviving the mutiny at Metz and being promoted, not before time, to the rank of Lieutenant-Colonel); Prosper still a handful; Nancy still without a husband — she has just refused the hand of an old recluse with a fortune of five hundred thousand francs, and fears that if the fact gets known her reputation will be done for and she will be set down forever as romantic, if not mad. Only Adèle, aged sixteen, writing to her sister in Valence, seems in calm and cheerful spirits:

As you can imagine, my dear, we spend our time very quietly. We work a lot, and read. As my father's sight is still a little weak we read aloud. Mme Bert lent us a work of M. Moke's [brother of Camille], The Sea Beggars, or Belgium under the Duke of Alba. We find it most interesting, the more so as most of the events in it are historical. And my father has lent me Le génie du Christianisme; I find it very very interesting. I'm mad about this M. de Chateaubriand. No doubt you'll laugh, but I don't care. Thanks to him I'm not bored, so see if I don't owe him a debt of gratitude, and besides, my dear, it helps me bear your absence patiently.

For Dr Berlioz, Hector's Prix de Rome was the end of a struggle that had lasted nearly ten years. It gave the final quietus to his hopes of seeing his son follow a different career. Perhaps that was why he waited more than a week before writing to him. Adèle's enthusiasm for Génie du Christianisme was a poignant reminder of Hector's at a similar age, in the days when he was educating him to be his successor.

While he waited, a long and florid letter arrived from Le Sueur.

My dear Monsieur Berlioz,
   Your son has won, unanimously, the first prize for musical composition awarded by the Institut de France.* He has a government grant for five years. The path of glory, and perhaps of fortune, is now open to him. *Handel* died a very rich man; *Gluck* left fifty thousand francs; *Grétry* thirty thousand; I knew *Paisiello* intimately when he enjoyed an income of forty thousand

---

* Actually, as we have seen, by 23 votes to 2.

francs, thanks to the numerous grants that he received from all the courts of Europe and the interest they brought him; *Rossini* possesses a very large fortune; *Méhul*, amply pensioned, lived in great comfort; *Haydn*, it is true, had no more than a decent competency, but like many other great composers he made a European name for himself.

Your son will do likewise, and if I may trust the genius which already is developing so surely and powerfully, he will render illustrious the name of Berlioz, and I shall have been right not to deflect him from the impulse which urged him irresistibly towards the higher study of an art that has honoured and enriched so many famous composers.

Moreover, he appears on the scene just at a time when the vain protection of influence and of humiliating patronage will no longer serve to support mediocrity. His great talent will progress of its own accord, for he possesses at once facility of workmanship and great diligence in having his works performed — works which are well thought out, bold in conception, always new, sound in direction, and off the beaten track.

I venture to predict that his reputation will rise to the highest rank which a great composer can achieve, and that honour, consideration and fair repute will not be withheld from him.[*] With that, one cannot but attain, if not to a very large fortune (often a chancy matter), at least to a respectable livelihood.

I congratulate you and his dear family; he is worthy of you sir, of you who are yourself a man of talent, of honour, of high qualities, and who are so keenly sensible of what is great, natural, and appertaining to lofty ideas: in a word, he is worthy of your honoured family.

I am not telling him that I have the honour to write to you; I wish simply to justify him in your eyes for having renounced other professions or callings. He has nevertheless turned his time to good account, and at twenty-six years of age has arrived at the point that other artists, artists of unquestionable talent, reach only at thirty-five or thirty-six. For that, it is necessary to have *l'estro divino*, the inspiration, the inner ardour, the pure genius for the fine arts; and this, art or nature, loving him well, has richly endowed him with.

It is now for a father's authority, which he loves unreservedly, as he does his mother's, to pour into this soul, devoured by admiration for the Beautiful in human thought and creation, all the weighty counsel he needs in the great career which opens before him, and which he purposes to follow for his glory and the glory of his kith and kin. I consider him a fine and rare character: complete your task, plant in this fertile soil the moral and philosophical seed which has already borne such admirable fruit. You will have made of your son a true man, and strong enough in himself to achieve not only his own happiness but the happiness of all who belong to him.

Fortunate parents! . . . It is not the effect of his success on the city of Paris and the sensation it has caused that delights him most, it is making sure it is

[*] Did Le Sueur remember Berlioz's Aunt Laure, "Racine's enemy", who said, "A good name, Hector, matters more than anything"?

known to the father and mother he loves. That is his keenest pleasure, that alone. At the thought of it, his heart overflows with joy.

In his conduct, he already understands the golden rule, to be strict with himself and indulgent to others; already he knows all the intricacies of men's hearts, and can draw from them what is good, already he knows how one must behave with them; he will render only service to the artists of his profession, and out of gratitude his very rivals will become his supporters, it is they who will carry him to glory.

This way of doing good in his particular sphere will be the image of Napoleon's in his immense sphere.

Who knows? He may one day be the Napoleon of musical science, by reason of the giant steps he will cause it to take, given the other accomplishments that he brings to the fine arts and especially to music, that art which is so potent with the hearts and imaginations of men when it is composed with genius. Nothing can prevent his being, in religious as in dramatic music, a musician-poet such as *Terpander* and *Olympe*, a musician-philosopher such as *Gluck*.

I have the honour to be, my dear Monsieur Berlioz, your most devoted, attentive and obedient servant

Le Sueur

25 August 1830

Prolix, trusting, quixotic, with all its Napoleonic euphoria and its unworldly attempt at worldliness, the letter is noble testimony to the old man's eight years of conscientious, generous-hearted guardianship.

Only a fragment of Dr Berlioz's reply is known:* "My son is already on the threshold of Fame and Fortune. It is to your affectionate counsels, it is to your learned teachings, it is to you, his master and his friend, that he owes it." Whatever his thoughts, he answered in kind.

Apart from a reference in a letter from Mme Berlioz to Nancy ("a letter of congratulation from M. Lesueur which will amuse you when you see it") there is nothing more about Le Sueur's eulogy in the extant correspondence. It is possible that the doctor never mentioned it to his son.

Berlioz was chagrined that his prize elicited so lukewarm a response from his parents. He never grasped the root cause of his father's resistance to his becoming a musician, never understood that his constant efforts to impress and convince him were in a profound sense irrelevant, that it was not a question of success; and Dr Berlioz, loving him deeply, but withdrawn, unable to communicate directly with any of his children, never explained it to him.

Even after the healing of the breach caused by Berlioz's marriage to Harriet Smithson, Dr Berlioz seems to have regarded him as a son who had been taken from him, one that was lost and has not been found. In all the surviving letters that Louis Berlioz wrote to his two daughters

* From a sale catalogue quoted by Boschot.

during the last dozen years of his life — the years of the Requiem, *Romeo and Juliet*, the Symphonie funèbre, *The Damnation of Faust*, the prestigious tours of Austro-Germany and Russia — Hector's name appears only three times, in passing.

26

Prospero and Ariel

——————◆◆——————

Now that the Prix de Rome was won, Berlioz had a busy autumn ahead of him. There was the performance of the Fantastic Symphony to organise — the concert was scheduled for 21 November — and the score to revise in the light of the rehearsals at the Nouveautés in May. There was a piece to write for a concert on 1 November at the Théâtre-Italien, the conductor of whose much improved orchestra, his friend Emile Girard, had offered to perform something new of his as a consolation for that abortive enterprise. There was a long article to write for the *Correspondant* summing up the present state of music following the Beethoven revolution and the new genre of dramatic, expressive instrumental music it had created.[*]

Above all there was the campaign for the two things on which his future happiness depended: a contract for an opera and authorisation to remain in Paris during the first period of his Prix de Rome and forgo the journey to Italy. Within days of winning the prize he was mobilising his influential contacts, and was talking freely of his intentions — as Abraham Mendelssohn reported to his wife Leah on 27 August.

> The day before yesterday [Hiller] introduced me to Hector Berlioz, the author or composer of "Faust", who struck me as agreeable and interesting and a great deal more sensible than his music [Zelter, Felix Mendelssohn's teacher, must have shown them the score or told them about it]. You cannot imagine how all the young people look forward to Felix. Berlioz has just obtained the *grand prix de composition* and for five years will receive a

* The article, which appeared on 22 October under the title "Aperçu sur la musique classique et la musique romantique", drew a fundamental distinction between music which was free to follow its own bent and make its own rules (Romantic music) and Classicist, academic art. (See pp. 221–22) It also took issue, tacitly, with Fétis' recent educational pamphlet "La musique mise à la portée de tout le monde" (the very title of which, as Katherine Reeve observes, was heresy to Berlioz, as well as deeply if unintentionally ironic, given that Beethoven's greatest music was not "à la portée" of Fétis himself). Fétis' definition of music — "the art of moving us by combinations of sounds" — became, in Berlioz's formulation, "the art of moving [...] those with sensibility, intelligence, knowledge and imagination"; music truly spoke only to them, and that was precisely why it was not for "tout le monde".

scholarship of 3,000 francs for a sojourn in Italy. He does not, however, wish to go there, but intends to apply for permission to remain here. (This is grist to your mill, Leah!) In all classes and trades here young people's brains are in a state of ferment: they scent regeneration, liberty, novelty, and want to have their share in it.

But first of all Berlioz had unfinished business at the Institute. Now that the prize was his and he could look forward to performance by an orchestra, he could take up the idea set aside out of prudence in July and write his grand conflagration scene. It would be one in the eye for the Academy, and it would make some atonement for the compromise that had secured him the prize.

The score of Berlioz's *Sardanapale* survives in fragmentary form: we have only the grand finale — or a draft of it — preceded by part of the last stanza of the third and final aria. This is enough to show that Berlioz concluded the official part of his cantata with the fortissimo full close and obligatory orchestral flourish which he had failed to write in previous years. But what we know about the rest of the cantata proper — the bulk of it — has to be deduced, from letters, reviews, concert leaflets and the manuscript of the subsequently written orchestral dénouement.*

How poor it was we cannot tell. Berlioz himself professed a very low opinion of it. Only the conflagration, he said, was the real thing. Obviously this was, with him, an article of faith, given his views on the Academy and the Prix de Rome competition. He had written, perforce, their kind of music; and the same Academy that had given the thumbs down to *Cléopâtre* — very much his kind of music — had awarded *Sardanapale* the prize. By definition it was mediocre. Typical that Cherubini should see it as proof of his having made substantial progress since the previous year, when in fact he had "reduced himself by half" in order to write it!

It is possible, as Peter Bloom argues, that Berlioz "exaggerated the stale academic qualities of his score out of a kind of embarrassment at having been rewarded by some of the old fogies whose judgment he had made it a principle to detest". But by his own lights he was justified in doing so. The worthlessness of that judgment as he saw it was exposed not only

---

* In a letter to his father written the day after the ceremony he states: "Since being awarded the prize, I had added a big piece of descriptive music for the burning of the palace of Sardanapalus: I had nothing more to fear from the academicians, and I let my imagination go. In the midst of the tumult of the blaze I recall all the motifs of the cantata, compressed together: on the one hand the dancing-girls' song from the first number, changed (with the melody modified) into cries of terror, on the other the piece [aria no. 2] in which Sardanapalus proudly refuses to give up his crown." On the final page of the conflagration scene the words "fin Camille" have been scribbled, evidently in great haste. For further discussion, including a conjectural reconstruction of the complete cantata and a detailed account of the competition of that year, see Peter Bloom's "Berlioz and the Prix de Rome of 1830" in *Journal of the American Musicological Society*, vol. XXXIV, no. 2 (1981), and the same author's "Sardanapale and the Symphonie Fantastique" in the *Berlioz Society Bulletin*, no. 128, Summer 1986.

by their rejection of *Cléopâtre* (and even of *Herminie*, which the music section would have none of), but also by their glowing report on the score which, in conformity with the regulations, he sent back from Rome in 1831 and which was none other than the Resurrexit from the Mass first heard in 1825: the Academy reported that the work offered most heartening proof that M. Berlioz had learned to profit from wise criticism, and urged him to continue in the same way and not to stray from the path of soundness and good sense on which he had so happily set his feet. While the Academy were perfectly entitled to prefer the kind of music he had been writing five years earlier, he could hardly be expected to agree with them.

On the other hand, what survives of the final aria is not unimpressive. In fact it includes two motifs which in different form we have learned to admire and be stirred by − the poignant, surging melodic line to which Cassandra sings "et voir s'évanouir du bonheur le plus pur la séduisante image" in the first act of *The Trojans*, and the rising chromatic phrase in Dido's "Adieu, fière cité". Two other thematic fragments that are recalled by the orchestra during the conflagration scene were used subsequently in the second movement of *Romeo and Juliet* (or more probably were borrowed for *Sardanapale* from themes already sketched for *Romeo*), and a third was adapted for the cantata of 1855, *L'impériale*. Furthermore, Berlioz did not think so badly of his score that he was not prepared to include it twice in programmes of concerts that he gave after getting back from Italy, in 1833 and 1834 − though that may have been chiefly in order to attract the public by exploiting the notoriety which still clung to the work by reason of its spectacular climax.

What Berlioz objected to in his cantata, I believe, was its refusal to respond to the challenge of the dramatic situation, its studious neglect of the bold " contrastes et oppositions" which were to him an essential and integral part of dramatic music, and its safely conventional use of the orchestra, the medium which "since my emancipation I regard as my domain". It could contain strong themes worth using again and yet, without these elements, be of little value in his eyes.

Certainly, he is emphatic in his dismissal of it at the time both in letters to his family and in one to the composer Adolphe Adam, who had asked him for a ticket for the Institute performance: "I must warn you that it is an extremely mediocre work, not at all representative of my innermost musical thought; there is very little in it that I acknowledge. The score is well below the level of the present state of music. It is full of commonplaces and hackneyed orchestration that I was forced to write in order to win the prize. If you are so good as to take an interest in my compositions, I would rather you came to the Opéra on Sunday 7 November, when they are to perform an overture for *chorus, orchestra, harmonica* and two *pianos*, four hands, that I have composed on

Shakespeare's drama *The Tempest*. It is likely to be well performed. At least, there I speak my own language and am not gagged."[*]

As ill luck would have it his calculated gesture to the academicians misfired; owing to a mistake in the orchestra the grand set-piece, which had caused a great stir at the final rehearsal the day before, failed to ignite on the day itself. The prize-giving ceremony was held four weeks later than usual that year, partly because of the bureaucratic disruption consequent on the July Revolution and the change of régime (the Department of Fine Arts had a new staff, and Sosthène de La Rochefoucauld had gone). On the afternoon of Friday 29 October all had gone well. The rehearsal in the Institute Hall had, unusually, attracted a full house, and Berlioz's cantata, sung by Alexis Dupont and complete with conflagration scene, was loudly applauded and the composer surrounded by admirers, including some of the older members of the orchestra — normally impervious to what they were playing — and one or two academician composers, who took his little trick in good part. At the Opéra that evening, fresh congratulations. Next afternoon the hall was crammed. The Academy's "séance annuelle" was a prestigious event in the artistic life of Paris and received wide coverage in the press (the 1830 prize-giving was reported by at least ten newspapers). This time the usual crowd that came every year — administrators, academics, critics, relatives and friends of the prize-winners — was augmented by artists attracted by rumours of the previous day's rehearsal. Two members of the Institute who were present and very likely came out of personal interest in Berlioz — they are not recorded as having attended in previous years — were Andrieux and Gay-Lussac, whose lectures, in literature and experimental physics, respectively, he had followed in his first years in Paris. So great was the crush that Malibran herself (back from her tour of England) could not find a seat and had to perch on a stool between two double-basses.

Berlioz's *Memoirs* include a positively Dickensian account of a typical Institute prize-giving, with the Academy's Permanent Secretary, the venerable archæologist Quatremère de Quincy, making the same interminable speech as in all other years and the prizewinners, crowned with their wreaths of artificial laurels and clutching the gold medal "which will pay their rent until they leave for Rome", scrambling up and down the tiered benches to loud and prolonged laughter and applause, tearing

---

[*] Mendelssohn agreed with Berlioz's estimate of his Prix de Rome score. See the account in the *Memoirs*: "At our first meeting [in Rome] he mentioned my *Sardanapalus* cantata [...] parts of which my fellow-laureate Montfort had played to him. On my revealing a positive dislike for the opening allegro, he exclaimed delightedly, "Thank heaven for that! I congratulate you ... on your taste. I was afraid you might be pleased with it. Frankly, it's pretty awful." Of course, Mendelssohn felt the same about the works in which Berlioz did speak his own language. As for Adolphe Adam, *Sardanapale* was one of the rare Berlioz scores that he might be expected to have approved of.

one spectator's dress, trampling another's hat, sending a third flying, in a desperate attempt to reach and embrace parents, sisters, cousins, aunts, girl friends, etc.

This time, however, there were variations, The cantata began with a sunset instead of the traditional dawn; and Quatremère was indisposed, though the architect Lebas did his best to make up for it by reading the report on the pensionnaires at the French Academy in Rome in a hurried mumble that rendered it inaudible. And for Berlioz it was not a festive or amusing occasion. He had no relatives present, Le Sueur was ill in bed, and Mme Moke, having promised to bring Camille, had changed her mind — people, she said, would notice them and say they were only there because of him.

In the circumstances it was perhaps as well they did not come. Berlioz's letter to his father, after describing the triumph of the general rehearsal (and adding, "Oh my father, if only you had been there!"), continues:

> Well, yesterday at the distribution of the prizes, where I also had a great success — both when the names were read out and after and during the performance of my scene (for they interrupted the orchestra in the middle to applaud) — would you believe it, by mischance the whole grand effect of my conflagration was lost! The end, the collapse of the palace, the climax of my fireworks display, an immense thing, quite new, and mine alone, failed completely. The instruments which should produce the effect have to count their rests and then go off like a thunderclap. But from lack of concentration and then sheer panic, they didn't.

Being less than completely confident in the conductor Grasset (under whose feeble direction the Théâtre-Italien orchestra had sunk to an exceptionally low state the previous year), Berlioz had stationed himself near him, score in hand, and now signalled to the players to start. But they did nothing. "The violins and cellos went on with their futile tremolo — no explosion: the fire went out without so much as a pop." In a fury he hurled his score into the orchestra and sent the nearest desk crashing to the ground ("Mme Malibran sprang back as if a mine had gone off at her feet"). He got three rounds of applause at the end, none the less (the orchestra had continued playing). But what comfort was that? On the way out, the smooth Joseph Rocher assured him that everything had been felt and appreciated. "But, by God, you can't feel and appreciate something that you don't hear."

> Imagine, all those people roused to a high state of expectancy, as I heard, by those who had been there the day before and who kept saying, "Just wait, you'll hear something extraordinary, quite amazing, you'd think you were watching the Kremlin go up" [...] And Spontini was there, he had come on purpose to hear it — God — and I was offering him something grand and new, it was the first time he had heard my music. And this morning the

Journal du commerce has fun describing my fury, and says it didn't understand my work, "no doubt through our own fault", the reviewer says. I like the reticence [...] All my admirers from the previous day came up afterwards, not to embrace me this time but to inveigh with me against the blunder of the performers [...] Mme Lesueur and her daughters are convinced that it was a plot by Berton to prevent me from completely crushing his pupils. [Montfort, the other prizewinner, whose cantata was played first, to rather tepid applause, was a Berton pupil.] They have an extraordinary mania for seeing conspiracies everywhere. The players responsible — only four in number — are firm friends of mine, and are in despair at their mistake. I had not intended to give *Sardanapale* at my concert, but now I must; it will draw the crowds. Besides, I shall have my own, huge orchestra, and the effect of the conflagration will be quite different.

According to the *Journal du commerce*, which, together with the *Courrier français*, reported the composer flinging down his score in a rage ("it appears that the orchestra, normally so obedient to M. Grasset's bow, on this occasion lacked precision and accuracy of ensemble"), Berlioz was with difficulty persuaded to go up and receive his crown.

Despite the failure of the conflagration the notices on the whole were favourable. The *Journal des débats* thought that Berlioz's cantata "at times bristled with bizarre melodies neither pleasing to the ear nor remotely moving to the soul"; but the *National* was full of praise of his vigour and originality, and was particularly impressed with the breadth and nobility of the final aria, which alternated dramatic and lyrical passages in a masterly way and "showed profound knowledge of all the resources of the art"; and the unpredictable Fétis, in the *Temps*, chose the occasion to deliver his most positive report to date on the composer's development:

M. Berlioz is a man apart: his bold imagination rejects familiar methods and takes a new path. Sometimes he goes astray, but his rapid progress makes it clear that he will finally attain his goal. His mind is now entirely absorbed with the quest for novel forms and undiscovered effects; in consequence his melody is occasionally null and his harmony not without harshness; but he finds what he is looking for and does what he wishes to do. With a few more years of the unremitting hard work and the commitment to art which distinguish M. Berlioz's productions, his place among the artists who have enlarged the domain of music will be established.

Ironically, of all Berlioz's early works, not excluding the Fantastic Symphony, *Sardanapale* received by far the largest attention in the press.

Fétis also paid the most flattering attention to Berlioz's *Tempest* overture, giving space in the *Revue musicale* for a detailed advance announcement and analysis of the work (the same article, written presumably by Berlioz, appeared in the *Courrier des théâtres*), attending the final rehearsal — at which he was heard talking in warmly approving terms of the work and the composer — and writing a highly commendatory review.

Composition of the overture occupied Berlioz in September and part of October. He owed the idea of the work, he told Ferrand, to his adored Camille, in whose "slender figure, soaring flights of fancy, intoxicating charm and genius for music I recognised Shakespeare's Ariel". Ariel is the presiding spirit of the opening sequence, which returns at intervals during the work, and whose delicate, flashing piano trills and arpeggios are a tribute to Camille and the luminous brilliance of her playing when in skittish and fanciful mood. The piece, as we have seen, was written at the request of Girard, the new conductor at the Théâtre-Italien who had done so much in a short time to raise the standard of the orchestra after the slovenliness of Grasset's régime. But when the score was completed both he and Berlioz agreed that it demanded larger forces — a more numerous orchestra and a less tentative chorus (Girard had not yet had time to get to work on them). It needed the Opéra, in fact. To Berlioz's surprise Lubbert, the Opéra's director, agreed at once, when he went to see him, to add the overture to the programme of a special Sunday performance in aid of the theatre's pension fund, and then, when Berlioz pointed out that the date proposed by Lubbert, 23 October, would leave too little time for rehearsing an unfamiliar modern score, postponed the whole event to the Sunday two weeks later (the intervening Sunday, 30 October, being taken up with one of the periodic public reviews of the National Guard). *La tempête* was given at the Opéra, Habeneck conducting, on 7 November, between the first act of *The Siege of Corinth* and *La sonnambula*.

Whether, this time, Camille was allowed to attend and hear the music she had inspired we do not know; no letters from Berlioz to his family are known from the four weeks between the concert at the Opéra and the première of the Fantastic Symphony on 5 December. Berlioz expected her to be there: the performance (he wrote to Adèle on 21 October) "will be a gala event for Camille, who has never heard my music". But her mother was quite capable of changing her mind and withholding permission. They had agreed to keep it a secret from her till the last moment; for "if something occurred to prevent its taking place, she would not fail to say, 'There, you see, you're always deluding yourself; you will never come to anything.' " Nothing of that sort did occur. But just before the performance a freak storm, a tempest of the most inopportune kind, burst over Paris, turning the streets and pavements into impassable torrents, and the theatre was almost empty for the first part of the evening; the performers outnumbered the audience. The débâcle at the Institute had not used up his allowance of bad luck. It was also very hard on the theatre's pension fund (though more people turned up for the second half), and another evening was designated for it, three weeks later, on the 28th, at which the overture was apparently given again.

In the meantime the *Corsaire* hailed it as "a large composition in a totally original genre, full of charming and picturesque effects", in which "the Storm, the Farewell to Miranda sung by the chorus with accompaniment of two pianos and harmonica, and the brilliant march which concludes the overture, are in the happiest contrast and prove that the composer is master of more than one style"; and Fétis published his laudatory review.

A truly remarkable piece was performed last Sunday at the Opéra [. . .] the overture to Shakespeare's drama *The Tempest* by M. Hector Berlioz. I have already had occasion to remark on the happy gifts for musical effect and inventive instrumentation with which nature has endowed this young musician. These powers are energetically developed in the piece in question.

The writing for orchestra and chorus is marked by great originality; most of the means employed are new, the combination of sounds being quite unusual and the voices treated with uncommon intelligence in an absolutely individual method. It may be remembered that four years ago, in an article on "The orchestral revolution" which figured in the first volume of the *Revue musicale*, I spoke about the necessity of discovering, within a much richer system of sonic modification, a greater source of variety of effect, and about the means of realising such richness of sonority. Well — what I said then M. Berlioz is realising and putting into practice. Prompted by his make-up to respond to music in this way, he was destined to lead it into new paths [. . .]

Two sections of his overture are particularly worthy of the closest attention of connoisseurs. One is the "tempest", which is quite unlike anything done before and full of novel effects; the other is the "chorus of aerial spirits".

It must be said that Fétis had a knack of putting his money on the lesser works of Berlioz and slating those which have lasted, like the Fantastic Symphony, the Sylphs' scene and the *Francs-juges* overture. He was, in theory, all for innovation in the art of music — the need to expand the frontiers of musical form and expression is a constant refrain of his articles — but the conservative and pedagogue in him tended to recoil from the reality of it. Yet, to be fair to him, he was consistent where Berlioz was concerned. Like many critics he categorised him as a colourist, an orchestral inventor of genius, who lacked the stability of purpose to construct symphonic music on a large scale. And the best pages of the *Tempest* overture are remarkable. The brief storm is a vividly original marine landscape in sound, a thing of pure colour handled with exhilarating freshness, the orchestra treated as a series of distinct timbres, contrasting registers, and separate planes juxtaposed and tilted at startling angles to one another to suggest the exuberant upheaval of sky and sea, the whole a miniature tour de force apt to Prospero, the virtuoso magician who calls it to life. The work loses direction after that and becomes something of a hodge-podge; the melody adapted from Cleopatra's "Du destin qui m'accable" is much less expressive in its jauntier extended form than it is in the cantata; the concluding fanfares are brash and empty. Even so, the latter part of the score includes some fresh and pleasing touches, like the lumbering figure on lower strings, clarinets, horns and bassoons, in five-beat phrases, for the dancing Caliban, and the ardent, angular theme, alternately eager and timid, by which the composer (as his analysis shows) meant to suggest the young Ferdinand's "shy passion". Above all, the opening chorus of the spirits of the air, evoking Ariel's magic and the island's "noises, sounds and sweet airs which give delight and hurt not", is an exquisite and for its date remarkable trouvaille, all air and rippling light, the handful of instruments — piccolo, flute, clarinet, two groups each of four solo violins, muted, and piano duet — all playing in the upper register, the soft insistent summons of the voices ("Miranda! Miranda! tu conoscerai l'amore") scored for five-part chorus without basses, the whole glinting, diaphanous texture hovering seemingly weightless above the earth, and the harmony circling in and out of F major as though in response to some benign natural force. The work marks the first appearance of the piano as an orchestral instrument. Berlioz, who rarely repeated himself, never made use of it again. The next to do so in non-operatic orchestral composition was Saint-Saëns in his Third Symphony (and after that Ives, Mahler in "Um Mitternacht" and the Eighth Symphony, and Stravinsky in *Petrushka*). The piano as a regular member of the orchestra is a twentieth-century phenomenon.[*]

Performance at the Opéra, even if it was only performance of a fifteen-minute concert work, had for Berlioz symbolic importance. It was a foot — a toe at least — in the door of the theatre where he had discovered his vocation eight years before, and to which every interest, artistic, amorous, financial, drew him. It could — he wrote to his mother a few weeks before the performance — have very advantageous results. "Sooner or later that splendid orchestra will have to belong to me, and I will give all those great musical forces a new direction."

But a new direction was just what the Opéra administration feared to take. It recognised that something had to be done — the old repertoire no longer appealed to the public, and most new works were equally unsuccessful — but it hesitated to branch out. Berlioz was much too controversial to gamble with. Besides, was he not a composer of music for the concert hall, a symphonist, and therefore not meant to write operas?

---

[*] Originally, like the Sylphs' scene in its first form (in the *Eight Scenes from Faust*), the *Tempest* overture had a part for harmonica (a kind of glockenspiel) and there were two pianos à quatre mains, not one. Who wrote the Italian text is not known. Italian, as Berlioz's press hand-out remarks, is "une langue sonore et harmonieuse" (it is also the native tongue of the country from which the characters in the play derive); but it was presumably chosen in the first place as being the language in which music was sung at the Théâtre-Italien, the original destination of the work.

For all aspiring French opera composers, and not only for him, the situation had long been absurdly obstructive. He summed it up, a few months before the July Revolution, in a letter to his father, explaining why he stood more chance of getting an opera put on in Germany than in Paris:

I have a grand opera libretto on *Atala* which the Opéra jury accepted *unanimously, without condition or modification*, two months ago. The other day Onslow, who had just read the score of the *Francs-juges* overture which I lent him, went hurrying off with that young man's enthusiasm of his (though he is 49) to see Lubbert, the director of the Opéra, to talk to him about me. Knowing *Atala* had been accepted and was intended for me, he urged Lubbert to get me put on; he said it was quite ridiculous the way obstacles were put in my path, and that it was in Lubbert's own interests to remove them. To all that he merely replied that many people had spoken to him about me, some with admiration, others saying I was mad, others that I was not a dependable investment; but that, be that as it might, it was his intention to write to me and advise me not to compose the music for *Atala* since, despite its being accepted, he did not *wish* to put on that libretto, it was a genre that he did not *wish* to introduce at the Opéra. "Besides", he added, "I must repeat what I have said so many times already. I have to make money. Nothing does as well as Auber, because the public like him. Auber and Rossini: they are what I need. If Beethoven and Weber returned to life and brought me an opera, I'd turn them away."

The Feydeau [the Opéra-Comique] is in the last stages of musical collapse. They couldn't perform me. The director is about to go bankrupt. There has to be a new theatre with the right to perform new music, the odious privilege has got to be done away with. And it will be, if the Chamber of Deputies demands it. Benjamin Constant and two others were going to introduce a measure, but the prorogation intervened. Can you imagine it — the Germans, the Italians, in fact any foreigners, can set up an opera house in Paris for part of the year, while the French alone are obliged to be massacred at the Feydeau or else keep their scores to themselves.

The Nouveautés has a superb orchestra and a passable chorus, which are employed on vaudevilles or pieces taken from foreign scores [...] I say, for God's sake let them all be free to perform what they like, grand opera or little, give them no subsidies, and let them ruin themselves. It will cost the taxpayer less, and some of them will find a way of making a profit.

Berlioz was by no means the only one to advocate an end to subsidies as part of a comprehensive programme of operatic reform. The whole question of the freedom of the theatres — in fact, of a return to the state of affairs which had obtained under the French Revolution and the Consulate and the first few years of the Empire — had been in the air for some time before the fall of Charles X. In particular there had been much talk of authorising another opera house — at first the Odéon, and then a company established specially for the purpose — to perform new French works; but there had been no action. The July Revolution was confidently expected to remedy this situation. Liberty for the arts was one of the grand causes for which it had been fought; it was part of the "brilliant future for our country" — as Berlioz wrote to Nancy in the first euphoric aftermath of the Three Glorious Days — to which they all looked forward. A month later he could still feel that the "emancipation of the theatre" was "imminent", and that it could not be long now before an opera house admitted him.

Unfortunately, in this as in other respects, the new régime proved to be essentially no different from the old. Some of the individual functionaries had changed; but the same interests, the same privileges, the same resistance to new ideas barred the way. With commendable promptitude a government commission was appointed early in August to look into the state of the theatre — and, observed Fétis two and a half months later in the *Revue musicale*, all it had yet done was to meet to decide where its meetings should be held, and having determined that, meet to decide how often it should meet, which after further deliberations was agreed should be once a week except where something occurred to prevent it. Like most commissions this one was composed of the wrong people.

> Its brief is to go into the question of freedom in all its aspects, so they choose two men of letters who signed a grotesque petition to the King "against the activities of Romanticism". It involves the fortunes of theatrical impresarios, so not a single one is included on it. It is concerned with the progress of French music and the lot of young artists, so instead of nominating eminent and capable composers they fill it with barristers (no fewer than five), deputies, privy councillors and appeals judges, on the pretext that the first task is to examine the legislation governing the theatre — as if all the necessary legislation [. . .] were not already in existence.

Fétis took the opportunity of the publication of a pamphlet by Etienne Gosse on "The Abolition of Privileges and the Emancipation of the Theatre" to argue the case for freedom. The assertion was often made (said Fétis) that unlimited freedom was against the interest of the theatres themselves. But, as M. Gosse showed, to refute it one need only refer to the sixteen years, from 1791 to 1807, when it was in force. They were years of unexampled prosperity for the Paris stage, when the number of theatres was never fewer than seventeen and rose at times to twenty-three. Among them as many as eleven performed opera and opéra-comique. It was precisely in that period — no one denied it — that French music attained its highest point, French composers established a vigorous genre, since imitated by musicians of other nations, and Méhul, Cherubini, Le Sueur, Berton, Boieldieu, Kreutzer and others became European names. There was also an extraordinary abundance of first-rate singers. At the same time none of it, except the Opéra, cost the state a penny; and there were no government commissars, no inspectors, no controllers, no censors. That was what happened when the theatre was given its freedom.

As for subsidies, as M. Gosse demonstrated, they were not actually of benefit to the opera houses, except to the Opéra, whose grant, bigger than the rest put together, existed to support the lavish spectacle for which the Opéra was unique. The others had little to lose by the abolition of subsidies and much to gain. For example, the Opéra-Comique's annual grant of 180,000 was immediately reduced to 70,000 by the automatic deduction at source of 110,000 in pensions for former members and employees; and that 70,000 itself was turned into a minus quantity by the poor-tax, which levied ten per cent of box-office receipts, or as much as 90,000 in a good year. To give money with one hand and take it away with the other was on the face of it the height of bureaucratic absurdity. In fact, subsidy was a means by which government maintained a hold on the theatre. That was why it would not be abolished and why the much more rational and productive system proposed by M. Gosse, under which the government would cease to have anything to do with theatre admin- istration and the minister would no more have the right to appoint a stage-doorkeeper than he had to appoint the caretaker at a factory, stood no chance of being adopted. Ministers were frightened of freedom. Besides, those whose interest it was to prevent it were in high favour. M. Gosse had proved conclusively the necessity of reforming the régime under which the drama languished (one could not say, under which it lived); but nothing would change. In a little while all the talk of emancipation and abolition of privilege would be heard no more.

The prospects for the young composer, in short, were no better than they had been before the July Revolution. But at least Berlioz had a libretto (*Atala*) accepted by the Opéra; and Lubbert, the director who did not want to stage it and who would have shown Beethoven and Weber the door, was himself on the way out. The new administration might be more enterprising and sympathetic. There was still hope for the success in the theatre on which Mme Moke's consent to the marriage was conditional. He could not possibly achieve it, however, if he was not there to push his claims. All through the autumn he campaigned for a dispensation that would allow him to draw his Prix de Rome grant in Paris.

It would not have been a totally unprecedented exception to the rule. Only the year before, he discovered, it had been granted on compassionate grounds to a painter called Vauchelet. Berlioz's surviving letters make no further mention of appealing to the King. Most probably he did, though to no avail (a couple of months later we find him writing to Louis- Philippe to invite him to his concert). He pulled every other string that by influence and ingenuity he could lay his hands on. The aid of the powerful Dauphinois family of Périer, very prominent under the new régime, was enlisted; and his uncle Victor Berlioz the lawyer wrote him a letter of introduction to the Comte d'Argout, a peer of the realm and another Dauphinois, who had won the approval of the liberals by attempting to persuade Charles X to abandon the July Ordinances, and who was soon to become a minister in Laffitte's government.

At the same time he got his doctor, Jules Guérin, to write a certificate stating that "for the past five years he had treated M. Hector Berlioz for nervous disorders accompanied by symptoms of cerebral congestion, and had observed that this state of ill health was particularly marked during the summer and was augmented under the immediate influence of the sun's action [...] In consequence", he concluded, "I believe that it would be dangerous for M. Berlioz to live in a hot climate such as that of Rome where he would be exposed to factors liable to renew and intensify his morbid tendencies." The certificate was put on one side until needed.

A month later, writing to his mother, he remained fairly optimistic: though there was still no positive reply, he had been told when he went to the Ministry of the Interior that there were going to be several important changes in the regulations governing the Academy of Fine Arts; he should wait till that happened, and then they would see if they could allow him to stay in France. "I am more than ever anxious not to leave; every possible reason is against my going. The other day Rossini, speaking of me to someone I know, urged him to persuade me not to go to Italy, if I was meaning to do so. 'Tell him there's nothing to do in that country, he'd waste his time there and not get anything out of it.' I must go and see him and ask him to sign my petition, his name will do more with the directors of Fine Arts than all the rest. The academicians refused to support my application, claiming that if I got it that might lead to the Prix de Rome being abolished. But I'm counting on the support of Spontini, who is in Paris."

Yet only a day later, in a letter to Adèle, his chances seem much less rosy: there is "no progress at the Ministry of the Interior with regard to the arts. The Minister has many other interests to occupy his mind. There is so much unrest everywhere that politics is all they think about." The new men were too busy to have time for the ideas of freedom in whose name the revolution had been fought.

A week later, on 28 October, he formally petitioned the Minister, Guizot, for "authorisation to enjoy in Paris the pension which the government in its munificence grants to the laureates of the Academy".

Permit me, Minister, to beg you to make an exception in my favour. I am contracted with two theatre directors in Paris to stage works of mine during next year; several of my orchestral compositions, which demand large forces, are due to be performed in France and Germany next summer. An enforced absence would do fundamental harm to my interests and would be a considerable setback to the progress of my musical career.

There is also the fact that the sustained hard work to which I have

devoted myself has seriously impaired my health, inducing a nervous irrita-
bility which too hot a temperature only intensifies. I have experienced it
many times, as the certificate which I have the honour to enclose with my
application attests.

In addition, four testimonials were appended to Berlioz's letter. Rossini's
name was not among them, but Spontini's and Meyerbeer's were. Le
Sueur wrote that "the state of the numerous enterprises which M. Berlioz
has in hand justifies an exception being made, this once, to the rules",
and Fétis confirmed that the motives advanced by M. Berlioz for wishing
to enjoy his grant in Paris "are, to my knowledge, genuine. This young
artist merits your benevolence by reason of the boldness of the work on
which he is engaged for the advancement of his art, and I take the liberty
of begging you to make an exception in his favour and exempt him from
the regulation which obliges the government's prizewinners to spend a
more or less lengthy time in Italy, which he will be able to employ more
usefully in France."

It was a brave effort; but it was to no avail. In the margin of Berlioz's
application someone pencilled the single word "impossible". The Minister's
reply, regretting his inability to set aside the regulations even on grounds
as strong as those put forward, was sent only after a delay of nearly seven
weeks, on 14 December; but by then Berlioz already knew the worst.

Whether or not his operatic projects had got as far as a definite
agreement with the theatres concerned (as he claimed, and as Fétis
appears to corroborate), it was a heavy blow. Such projects required
vigilant attention and continued presence on the scene. In his absence,
inevitably, they languished and were forgotten, as was the spoken promise
he had had from the Société des Concerts to perform the *Francs-juges*
overture during the coming season.

Berlioz could not have been forced to leave Paris at a worse moment in
his career — nor a worse moment in his personal life: for he was leaving
Camille to the mercy of her mother's schemes and going away without
the assurance of the one thing that might have secured Mme Moke's
blessing, performance in the opera house. He was in a cleft stick. He
could stay only at the cost of renouncing the other thing that Mme Moke
had made a condition, the Prix de Rome.

The letters from the autumn of 1830 trace a worsening in Berlioz's
relations with Camille's mother ("l'hippopotame", as he called her). Early
in September, in the aftermath of his victory at the Institute, they still
seem quite cordial; he tells Edouard Rocher that she "is opposed only in
the short term to our getting married". But two weeks later (to Edouard
again), Mme Moke is "tormenting us and driving us mad; she'll push us
to the limit!" This is probably a reference to their never being left alone
together for more than a moment — though it may also refer to some
fresh scheme for marrying Camille off to a wealthy suitor.

A month after that, he enlarged on their tribulations in a letter to Nancy:

> Mme Moke has changed her tone and manner towards me. She still receives me as often as before [i.e. about three times a week], but no longer with cordiality and affection. She is doing all she can to separate Camille from me. She's a calculating woman who would rather her daughter didn't marry at all if she doesn't make a rich marriage that will enable *her* to live comfortably. She is only too happy to have the poor child at her disposal and to do as she wants with all the money Camille earns, be introduced by her into the most brilliant circles and depend on her for all the pleasures of her existence. Imagine, Nancy, what a torment it is for me. We are reduced to waiting till Camille comes of age and can make submissions to her mother. (Her father's attitude is not the same as Mme Moke's; at least, the letters of his that speak of me and that I have seen are not at all discouraging.) You think I'm very happy. And yet I hardly ever see her alone for two minutes. Her mother never leaves the room when I'm there. We have to talk of trivial things. The constraint breaks my heart. It's true that one word from Camille, a secret sign, reassures me; but when there is so much to say, it's torture. Her mother said to us a few weeks ago, "I've made no promises whatever." — "But I have," put in Camille, "and I shall keep them."
>
> She has no fears; she knows that I won't change, that my existence is bound to hers and nothing can make me give her up, and she also knows that her mother is more dependent on her than she is on her mother, and that her talent is her fortune. But I with my diabolical imagination have not a moment's respite, the future terrifies me. To have to wait two years! — She was 19 in September. That is what we are reduced to. Camille said to me the other day, "Well, if you don't get your scholarship in Paris and have to spend a year in Italy, I shan't be able to see you; but it will still be a year gained; and really it's too painful to have these continual scenes with Mama when you come, and to spend such gloomy evenings."[...] She said to me one day, "I want everyone to know about us, so that they stop plaguing us with demands and proposals of marriage." She had just refused two. I think of the way she said goodbye to me yesterday evening when her mother couldn't see us. I can still feel her hand in mine, and it makes me less unhappy.

M. Moke, though under his wife's thumb, might have been a help if he had been there; but his arrival, and that of his eldest son, was constantly put off and in the end he didn't come. The college at Alost of which he was head was in turmoil following the revolution that broke out in Belgium at the end of August (inspired by the example of France and sparked off by a performance of Auber's *La muette de Portici* at the Brussels Opera); and in addition to the failure of his business enterprises he was in danger of losing his position. His son, who had been a leading journalist on the staff of the Brussels *National*, had lost his. Camille's earnings were thus all the more indispensable. "All this makes Mme Moke even less inclined to give her consent to our marriage. Camille has resigned herself bravely to it and is encouraging me to endure a long and painful period of waiting."

Meanwhile Mme Moke, having originally agreed to bring Camille to the Institute prize-giving, had decided against it after all, and cold-shouldered the ceremony which Berlioz had thought of as a celebration for him and Camille. And as we have seen, there is no certainty that Camille heard the *Tempest* overture, the work she had called into being.

There remained the première of the Fantastic Symphony. Ever since the collapse of the projected Nouveautés performance, in May, he had planned to give a concert, with Habeneck's help, in November at the Conservatoire. By mid-August it had been fixed provisionally for 14 November, but a few weeks later that had become the 21st. Eventually they settled on Sunday 5 December.

The orchestra which Berlioz collected was over a hundred strong, drawn, as before, mainly from the Nouveautés, the Théâtre-Italien and the Société des Concerts. Rehearsals, some of them sectional and taken by Berlioz himself, began a fortnight before the concert. Familiar though the players were with the composer's style, these sessions were very tough going. The enormous length of the work; the virtuoso demands made on each section (especially in the first, fourth and fifth movements); the tendency to treat the orchestra in separate planes rather than homogeneously; the unprecedented freedom and complexity of the rhythms and the vital part played by rhythm in the shaping and stressing of the long melodic lines; the equally novel intricacy of the dynamic markings, veining the music with a network of constantly varying expressive nuances – at first all this seemed an impassable obstacle not merely to idiomatic performance but to performance of any kind. He had to summon all his patience and persuasiveness to reason and cajole the disheartened musicians into going on. Then, just when a little light was dawning, the ranks would begin to thin, as invariably happened when the players were giving their services: two trombones and an ophicleide would have to go to fulfil their National Guard duty, the first horn was suddenly not in his place – he had an important lesson that he couldn't miss – and half a dozen young Conservatoire violinists packed up and left to attend Baillot's class, not having been able to get exemption. Gradually, however, the outlines of the music emerged and at the final rehearsal under Habeneck the work took shape.

What the audience heard that Sunday afternoon in the Conservatoire Hall was in a number of respects different from the work that was finally published fifteen years and several revisions later. The March to the Scaffold and the Witches' Sabbath were pretty much as they are now, and though the second movement, the Ball, would be altered sufficiently for Berlioz to feel it necessary to copy it out afresh, in Rome, the changes may not have been major ones. But the opening movement, Rêveries-Passions, was to undergo important modifications in the next few years; and the Adagio (Scene in the Country) was completely rewritten.

Berlioz had worked on both movements between the Nouveautés rehearsals in May and the première in December, and the revisions made during those months were concerned with the same questions of formal balance within movements and musical and dramatic continuity from one to another which would keep him working on the symphony for some time to come. Thus as a result of a long cut, the first movement had already acquired its present keystoned-arch form, and the famous concluding section of the Adagio, for solitary cor anglais and four pairs of timpani, had been added, framing the movement by making the end recall the beginning and providing, by sonority and mood, a link with the ominous distant drumming that begins the March to the Scaffold. Yet the movement as a whole, in the composer's words, "bore little resemblance to what it later became". And in the main (allegro) part of the first movement, if we could hear the version performed at the première in December 1830 we would be struck not merely by many differences of detail in articulation and orchestral texture but even more by the complete absence of the long oboe solo that leads to the final forte statement of the idée fixe by full orchestra, and by the end of the movement, which closed not, as in the definitive version, with the idée fixe pensive and pianissimo, followed by solemn hymnlike cadences, but with a couple of brusque chords — a disconcertingly and unconvincingly abrupt conclusion, for all that the contrast of orchestral tutti and pizzicato strings balanced, on paper, the final bars of the introduction.

None the less the concert of 5 December 1830 is rightly seen as a landmark both in Berlioz's career and in the evolution of the orchestra. Even in this incomplete form the Fantastic Symphony was a huge advance on anything he had written till then. It was the final emancipation of his musical personality and the vindication of the belief which he had nurtured within him since boyhood and had struggled to keep alight and justify against opposition that would have quenched a less determined spirit. From an untutored country boy, practically ignorant of music, he had in nine years developed a new language, derived from study of the composers of his predilection — Gluck, Spontini, Beethoven and Weber — but unique to him, and had become the master of a new medium, the modern orchestra. It was not just the addition of instruments, sonorities and textures not associated with the symphony orchestra — cor anglais, E-flat clarinet, cornet, harp, ophicleide, large percussion battery, trombone "pedal-notes", multiple string-divisions: it was the demonstration of what the orchestra might do, of how subtle and potent a poetic vehicle it could become. A gulf separates the music of Berlioz from that of Liszt and

Wagner — a gulf of style, method, organisation, as well as a fundamental difference between their sound, which is piano-suffused, and his which, with all its innovations, is classically based, from the eighteenth century. Yet the presence of the young Liszt in the audience at the Conservatoire is none the less one of the great symbolic facts of nineteenth-century music — most obviously for what stemmed from it: not only the rise of cyclic form (which Liszt developed from Schubert's Wanderer Fantasy as well as from the recurring idée fixe of Berlioz's symphony) but even more the revelation of the boundless expressive potential of the orchestra. That Liszt and, even more, Wagner, who submitted to the same profound influence a decade later when he heard Berlioz's *Romeo and Juliet*, would turn the discovery to quite other ends does not make it any less crucial an encounter.

Liszt called on Berlioz on the day before the concert. It was the beginning of twenty-five years of close friendship which would be for Berlioz of immense benefit and encouragement. Liszt was one of his most effective and generous champions. He brought out at his own expense the piano transcription of the Fantastic Symphony, which for eleven years was the only published score and which prompted Schumann to write his famous essay on the work in the *Neue Zeitschrift für Musik* (a riposte to a scathing review by Fétis). He also transcribed *Harold in Italy* (for viola and piano) and the *Francs-juges* overture, and wrote numerous articles in defence of his friend, whom he regarded, until Wagner appeared on the scene, as the leading composer of the day; and when he became music director at Weimar in the 1850s he staged *Benvenuto Cellini* and put on three festivals of Berlioz's works.

Considering how small the Paris artistic world was and how large Berlioz's circle of acquaintance in it, it is curious that they had not met before. Liszt and his parents moved to Paris in 1823, when he was twelve, and he quickly became a celebrity, performing at public concerts and private recitals (at one of which the phrenologist Franz-Joseph Gall took a plaster cast of his cranium). He had appeared on the same platform as artists whom Berlioz knew personally, like Baillot and Tulou the flautist, and was a friend of Berlioz's friend the violinist and violist Chrétien Urhan.

They soon made up for lost time. Of their first meeting, at 96 Rue de Richelieu, we know only that Berlioz brought up the subject of *Faust*, which Liszt had not yet read, and that they felt drawn to one another instantly. At the performance of the symphony the following afternoon Liszt took a leading part in the demonstrations of enthusiasm provoked by the new work, and afterwards insisted on the composer's coming to dine with him. It was not till later in the evening that Berlioz called at the Mokes' apartment and saw Camille.

The concert is less well documented than those of 1828 and 1829 — on the surviving ticket plans most of the seats are simply reserved in Berlioz's name; and because of the newspapers' preoccupation with political events there were fewer reviews than usual. Brief, laudatory notices appeared in the *National* and *Figaro*, and the event received a couple of paragraphs in Fétis' *Revue musicale*, which announced that two movements of the symphony, the Ball and the March to the Scaffold, "proclaim a large imagination" and that the work as a whole was evidence of the composer's remarkable powers and (when compared with the *Francs-juges* overture) of the progress he had made, though Fétis added that it inspired more astonishment than pleasure, as well as a regret that he did not employ his abilities in a manner more consistent with the proper aims of art. But there was nothing in the *Moniteur*, nothing in the *Courrier universel*, nothing even in the *Journal des débats*, though the name of Bertin, the editor and a future patron of Berlioz, figures in the seating plans. The *Débats* was largely taken up with the "procès Polignac", the trial for treason of Charles X's senior ministers, and published no "chronique musicale" for almost the whole of December. It was a foretaste of the difficulties Berlioz would experience in his struggle to impose his music on the Paris of Louis-Philippe.[*]

Within the artistic community it was a different matter. Already he had vehement partisans as well as passionate detractors. The hall was full and the reception noisily appreciative, even though for every one who like Liszt or d'Ortigues or Bloc really felt the symphony there were fifty who only applauded it for its novelty.

No independent account exists of the first half of the concert: *Francs-juges* overture, "Chant sacré" and "Chant guerrier" from the *Neuf mélodies*, *Sardanapale* (in which the "incendie" caught fire this time and was a great success), and an unspecified piece for solo violin by Mayseder, played by Chrétien Urhan. The symphony monopolised attention. The movements which made the strongest impression were the second, the fourth and the fifth. The third, the evocative Scene in the Country, made little if any impact (Berlioz, recognising that it came nowhere near fulfilling his idea, took the decision then and there to rewrite it). The first movement also must have passed the audience by, for there is no mention of it in any of the accounts of the première. Even in its incomplete form, without the revisions that altered it subsequently, it is magnificently eloquent and incisive music; but its rapidity of rhythmic and dynamic change and the long, asymmetrical rising and falling melodic lines which, constantly

---

[*] The *Journal des débats* published a news item beforehand (as did *Figaro*, the *Corsaire* and the *Revue musicale*, the latter printing the symphony's programme in full), but it did not get into the paper until the day of the concert: "Sunday next [*sic*], 5 December at 2 o'clock at the Conservatoire of Music, M. Berlioz will give a grand concert in aid of the July wounded. The programme is calculated to arouse the liveliest curiosity of the dilettanti. Among the compositions of M. Berlioz one remarks a fantastic symphony in five movements whose programme is most singular. The orchestra, of more than a hundred musicians, will be under M. Habeneck."

varying in expressive character, embody the formal organisation of the movement, make it the hardest of the five for the listener to come to terms with, the most demanding on the players' skill, responsiveness and familiarity and on the conductor's fire and grasp of phrasing and accentuation, and the one most likely to suffer from shortage of rehearsal. The Ball, on the other hand, and the Witches' Sabbath were well enough performed to have an immediate effect. And the March to the Scaffold brought the house down. At its conclusion the composer — who, though he does not say so, was presumably playing in the percussion section as was his wont — had to come forward and acknowledge the tumultuous applause, in which he noticed Pixis, Spontini, Meyerbeer, Liszt and even Fétis, among others, joining with the utmost enthusiasm. Better still, standing at the front of the platform he was near the box occupied by Camille and her mother and saw Mme Moke signal her approval and heard Camille cry "Superb, superb, prodigious!"

The audience demanded the March again. It being already late, however, with the last movement still to come, the performance continued. But at the end the hall went wild with shouting and stamping. Dozens of people queued up to embrace him or shake his hand. On all sides there was a demand for a repeat performance. "I am being pressed to give a second concert next Sunday, including the overture and the symphony," he wrote to his father next day, giving news of his success. "I'm going to see if Cherubini is willing to lend me the hall again, and if Mme Malibran will sing and Beriot play a violin solo, and I shall conduct the orchestra myself; I think we'll make a profit. This time it won't be in aid of the wounded." The following Sunday proved too soon to organise everything, or else the hall was not available; but on the 7th he wrote to tell Ferrand that the concert had been fixed provisionally for the 26th. In the end, out of prudence, he decided against it: it could be an expensive venture. The players had given their services the first time, but this time, he realised, many of them would have to be paid. 26 December was perilously near the New Year; the Polignac trial was still dragging on; and Malibran was not free.

It did not matter. The repercussions of the concert of 5 December continued to have benign influences on his life. One was the interest and warm approval of Spontini. His presence at the concert had more than compensated for the absence of Le Sueur (who was still ill and had again to be represented by his wife and daughters). Spontini had been heard to exclaim, after the March, that only Beethoven could have equalled it; and when Berlioz called on him two mornings later, the great man's words of praise, uttered face to face, made his head swim. Who could have imagined, when he first became a devotee of *Cortez* and *La vestale* and sang them in the dissecting-room at the Hospice de la Pitié, that their author would one day be saying complimentary things about his music, would be asking to see his scores, giving him his advice and predicting a great career for him? That the man whose music had played the largest part in the formation of his musical style should, as it were, preside over his coming of age as a composer conferred a magical imprimatur on the event. The letter to Spontini which Berlioz enclosed with the scores of the Fantastic Symphony and the *Francs-juges* overture acknowledged the debt by citing one of those extended, undulating Spontinian melodic phrases which left so deep a mark on his music — a quotation from the great orchestral passage where Julia the vestal priestess opens the temple doors to let in her lover, waiting in the warm darkness outside. Berlioz underlined the affinity by slightly misquoting it, rendering a downward scale of quavers as triplet crotchets, as though assimilating it to the final phrase of the idée fixe in the Fantastic Symphony. Spontini replied by sending him a copy of the full score of *Olympie*, "costing", Berlioz told Nancy, "120 francs, and inscribed on the title page, in his own hand, 'When you glance at this score, my dear Berlioz, remember from time to time your affectionate Spontini'".

The whole experience, wrote Berlioz to Spontini, was the realisation of a dream. "May the most cherished of all become reality in its turn," he added, with understandable fervour. "May I one day prove that I was not unworthy of the friendly welcome that SPONTINI granted me; may I make others feel a hundredth part of the enthusiasm with which he has filled my heart, and I shall be happy."

Though Malibran was not available on the date of Berlioz's projected second concert, she sang at an event which took place on the evening of the première of the Fantastic Symphony: a benefit performance at the Opéra organised by Harriet Smithson in an attempt to restore her shattered fortunes. While Berlioz's star was rising hers was in decline. A few hours after the performance of the symphony whose "heroine" she was, she was playing the deaf-mute Fenella in Auber's opera *La muette de Portici*, a part she had first appeared in the previous month. She had been offered it when the closure of the bankrupt Opéra-Comique, where she had been playing another dumb rôle in a tragic melodrama, deprived her of her livelihood and most of her savings. Harriet had had a success in the piece, *L'auberge d'Auray*, the previous summer; the press, with a few exceptions, acclaimed her performance. But what a falling-off from her Shakespearean triumphs! Berlioz brooded morbidly on her misfortunes. The woman herself, maybe, was debauched and unworthy: she was "that wretched Smithson", she was "the Smithson wench", who was "cheapening herself more and more" and whom he "despised and pitied" as at best "an ordinary woman, with an instinctive genius for expressing agonies of the soul which she herself has never experienced, and incapable of understanding a grand and lofty feeling such as I honoured her with". Ophelia was dead. But her idea, smirched and sullied, continued to haunt him. He had actually been introduced to the all too human embodiment of it, as he told Ferrand, writing to him at a table in a street tavern on the Champs-Elysées one sunny October evening:

[...] Farewell. The marble I'm writing on is freezing my arm. I think of the wretched Ophelia: ice, chill, damp earth, Polonius dead, *Hamlet living* ... Oh, she's wretched indeed. She lost more than six thousand francs through the bankruptcy of the Opéra-Comique. She is still here. I met her the other day. She acknowledged me with the utmost sang-froid.* I was upset the whole evening. But then I went and told my *enchanting Ariel* about it, and she smiled at me and said: "Well, you didn't feel faint? you didn't fall in a heap?" No, no, no, my angel, my genius, my art, my thought, my soul, my poetic existence! I suffered in silence − I thought of you; I worshipped your strength; I gave thanks for my recovery [...] Ariel, Ariel, Camille, I adore you, I bless you, in a word I love you, more than the poor French language can express. Give me an orchestra of a hundred musicians and a chorus of a hundred and fifty and I will tell you.

Ferrand, my friend, farewell. The sun has set and I can't see any more − farewell. No more ideas − farewell. Far too much feeling − farewell. It's six o'clock. It takes me an hour to get to Camille's. Farewell!

Though the coincidence of Harriet Smithson's holding a benefit performance on the same day as the première of the Fantastic Symphony must have struck his sense of irony, he did not go to the Opéra that evening. After dining with Liszt he went to the Mokes', where Camille's mother received him with a warmth that was quite new. Spontini's patronage was matched by another immeasurable boon that the concert had brought him. It altered his status in the Faubourg Montmartre at a stroke.

At first Mme Moke had refused to hear of Camille's attending the concert. (Berlioz's original idea, that she should play a solo, was of course out of the question.) Mme Moke herself absolutely declined to go, having been prejudiced against his music, he told Nancy, by her friend M. de Noailles, an aged amateur who detested Weber and Spontini. She told Berlioz to his face that nothing would induce her to listen to his music: the symphony was certain to be booed, and she was convinced it was just a "tissue of extravagance". Eventually he had persuaded her to let Camille attend in the company of Mme Pleyel (mother of Camille's suitor). Then Mme Pleyel fell ill; and Mme Moke had overcome her prejudice and agreed to come and bring Camille, and had been impressed. "That evening," wrote Berlioz to Nancy, "oh, that evening − when I arrived, Mme Moke said, very feelingly, 'I am so sorry about all the disagreeable things I said to you before I had heard your music, I had no idea your talent was so great. Truly, it was irresistible, never in

---

* This was presumably their first contact since the brief and traumatic encounter at the rehearsal for the benefit evening in February the previous year.

my life have I had such emotions from music.' And Camille — God! the things she said to me — I feel I'm dreaming still." Now that she had heard his Witches' Sabbath he was "her dear Lucifer, her lovely Satan". Since his success (he continues), everything has changed. "So it's my music I have to thank; to it I shall owe Camille! Think of it, Nanci — Mme Moke has given her consent. I am to marry Camille in fifteen months, on my return from Italy. I have to go — Mme Moke insists, and if I didn't I should lose my grant." Meanwhile he saw Camille every day, instead of only three times a week. Her mother no longer complained about him and had stopped making their lives a misery. She promised they should marry at Easter 1832. And M. Moke wrote from Belgium to say that he would not oppose his daughter's marrying "in due course". "Since we know that he will leave all authority in the matter to his wife, 'in due course' will happen. But, oh Nanci, to be separated, to have to leave — it is heartbreaking."

Several times Camille begged him to stay (fearing what might happen in his absence?). But she did not persist; and in their calmer moments they agreed that he had no choice but to go. They exchanged engagement rings and vows of eternal constancy.

The rest of the last two weeks was a round of leave-takings. He had convivial farewell meetings with his friends — Gounet, Pixis, Richard, Desmarest, Hiller, Liszt — and discussed the Adagio of his symphony with Hiller, who offered suggestions, which he noted, for the radical revision he planned to carry out in Rome. He again saw Spontini, who presented him with a lithograph portrait inscribed, "Greet from me my beloved fatherland, my dear Berlioz! speak to it a little of its grateful son Spontini", and promised to write on his behalf to his brother, who was a monk in Rome. Less gratifyingly, Spontini also voiced doubts as to the wisdom of his marrying Camille. Towards the end of December he received a fan letter from Rouget de Lisle, who had heard of his arrangement of the Marseillaise and wrote suggesting a meeting and perhaps a fresh collaboration: "Your mind seems a veritable volcano in continual eruption. Mine never produced more than a flash in the pan; the fire's going out now, though there's still some smoke. But the richness of your volcano and the remains of my little fire combined might do something . . . Come to Choisy and have lunch with me or dinner. It will not be much, but you are a poet and won't mind, and the country air will season it." Berlioz wrote back on the 29th to explain that the pleasure of meeting Rouget must await his return. On the same day he sent a diplomatic note to Fétis: "I wish I could have had the honour of seeing you before my *enforced* departure for Italy. You were out when I called. I should like to thank you most sincerely for all your kindnesses towards me."

In the small hours of the 30th, shortly before the coach left for Lyons, he scribbled a letter to Stephen de La Madelaine.

My dear Stephen,

I haven't been able to find a moment to say goodbye to you. All my evenings were taken up (you can guess by whom), so it was impossible to come to the Opéra; I must say my farewell to you in writing. I am leaving — but, happily, without fear. My Ariel, my angel, can no longer be torn from me. We are so closely bound that only our own wills could separate us. I still had one sorrow to experience, the sorrow of such a parting ... Oh bestial routine — how much longer must its reign continue! ... I belabour it to no avail, it keeps raising its silly stupid head. One day I trust I can make it bend enough for me to tread it underfoot and crush it.

During my exile I shall attempt to write something big; I will try to realise a large-scale project that I have in mind, and on my return we'll stir up the musical world in an unusual fashion. Meanwhile try to knock down what's left of the academic redoubt — you will be giving fresh proof of friendship to your devoted

Hector Berlioz

Paris, 30 December (2 in the morning)

P.S. I leave in six hours. ALONE. Farewell.

27

Tempests

Berlioz's arrival in La Côte on 3 January took his family by surprise: they had not been expecting him for another week. Though he was already very late in leaving — all the other Rome prizewinners had been gone some while — his original intention had been to remain in Paris until the first week in January. (Laureates were normally expected to be in Rome by the beginning of the new year, leaving Paris in December, when the Alps were still passable, and travelling down together through France and Italy in a coach hired for the purpose; however, it was not unknown to get there quite a lot later: it simply meant that you did not start drawing your grant until the month in question.) Berlioz may have put forward the date of his leaving Paris on the principle that the sooner he reached Rome the sooner his exile would be done with and he could come back to Camille and resume his interrupted career. Yet having reached La Côte he was in no hurry to proceed. He wrote to his fellow-prizewinner Montfort on 10 January asking him to tell Horace Vernet, director of the French Academy, to expect him in Rome during the first two weeks of February; but he lingered in Dauphiné for more than a month and did not finally set out till 8 February — a delay not fully explained by the fact that, part of the time, he was ill in bed. Nancy's diary reported him as being generally morose, taciturn, in a state of gnawing gloom.

Although he told Stephen de La Madelaine that he was parting from Camille "without fear", it looks as if he hesitated to leave France in case some new development demanded his instant return to Paris — as if, though he felt sure of Camille, he was still deeply distrustful of her mother. A remark in a letter written to Ferrand from Lyons at the outset of his long-delayed journey to Italy suggests he may come back quite soon: "I shall return like a red-hot cannon ball. So try to be in Lyons — I will merely pass through La Côte."

In the event it would be worse than he had imagined in his darkest fits of foreboding. What he was unprepared for was that Camille should not only fail to warn him of her mother's fresh schemes but should connive in them.

Hiller, recalling it all as an old man fifty years later, wrote to Berlioz's biographer Edmond Hippeau that, though he did not know it for a fact, he was convinced that Camille's marriage to Pleyel "was already settled by the time Berlioz left for Rome". ("Mme Moke", he adds, "certainly went 'ouf' when she knew that her son-in-law (?) was safely out of France, and I don't think her daughter shed any tears.") Yet it is hard to believe that Berlioz would not have perceived the truth, had that been so. Passionately in love but, as his letters make clear, far from euphoric, he could hardly have been so deceived, or have so deceived himself, as to fail to detect that her promises, her insistence that nothing and nobody could separate her from him, her words of love, the tress of her hair she wove for him as a parting gift, their exchange of rings, their stolen caresses, their whole intimacy, were nothing more than an elaborate game on her part.

Several considerations could have made Camille decide in due course against marrying him. There are hints of them in his letters. "I shall see her today [. . .] I can hear her mocking me for my melancholy air and, at the sight of the tears in my eyes, exclaiming, 'Now, now, what's this I see, come along, sir, no childishness I beg you, or I shall be cross. I don't wish you to be weak like that; I order you to be as impervious as a rock.' 'But it's not love,' she says to me sometimes, 'it's frenzy.' Yes, it is love — but love as felt by a ravenous soul, a brain consumed by music, and a heart that beats a hundred times more strongly than do many other hearts. Certainly it is not possible she should conceive the full grandeur and intensity of the feeling that I have for her." Nancy Berlioz, in an outburst in her diary against the egoism of men, expresses a similar sentiment from a feminist point of view: "Poor Camille! how I pity her. She loves him with all her woman's heart! Yet it's still not enough for him, for *him* who in return gives her only the passion of a man, and who in overturning her entire existence and shackling it for ever to his makes her share in a life in every sense tormented, devoured by a thousand inconstant desires [. . .]"

Camille could easily, at times, have felt oppressed by the violence of Berlioz's feeling for her; oppressed too by the intensity with which his imagination fed on dark anxieties about the future (thus helping to precipitate the very crisis it dreaded). She was always expected to be the strong one, the rock. She herself might well have been apprehensive about what would happen to her talent in competition with his. After hearing what he could make an orchestra do, all she could feel was contempt for her piano: it was "mean and paltry". Yet it was her piano that her life was dedicated to. After her marriage, as Marie Pleyel "the celestial pianofortist" (in de Quincey's phrase), she lived only for her art — "my one true friend", she told Jules Janin. Perhaps Spontini saw this, and that was why he tried to dissuade Berlioz from marrying her. She was not available for the rôle Berlioz had cast her in; she had a different part to play. None of her many lovers even possessed her. Berlioz aptly named her Ariel. Even Prospero has to renounce his hold over that elusive spirit and release him into the elements that are his home. "[Pleyel's] net is made of gold but its mesh is too wide," wrote Berlioz after the débâcle, "and the bird he took from me will escape." She did, despite the extremely liberal and unburdensome terms her middle-aged husband granted her. "He has been good enough to agree to my continuing with my lessons," she wrote to the Baron de Trémont a few months after her marriage; "you know I'm attached to my independence, and as I'm always with my mother I feel as if I were still Mlle Moke, and as if my husband were a good angel who watches over me." At nineteen she knew what she wanted and was determined to have it; and, though this particular arrangement did not last very long, the independence it gave her remained the watchword and guiding principle of her life. Marriage to Berlioz would not have been at all the same thing.

Yet however true, these considerations are not enough by themselves to explain the rapid and drastic turn of events which followed Berlioz's departure from Paris. Had they married, she might indeed have quickly discovered the unwisdom of doing so. Before they did, mature reflection might have persuaded her to break off the engagement. But there was scarcely time for mature reflection. Within a few weeks of his leaving, with her ring on his finger and fortified by her solemn vows, she had thrown him over. Unless we are to believe her a consummate hypocrite and a sadist to boot, or else a brittle and shallow flirt (and no one seems to have thought her that except Berlioz who, still smarting under the pain of an unhealed wound, portrayed her in those terms in the two short stories in which she figured, "Suicide through Enthusiasm" and "Euphonia"), there must have been some reason. Something happened to loosen the knot which bound her to him, something which made her feel sufficiently unsure and disenchanted for her mother to be able to return to the attack and this time to prevail — to persuade her that Berlioz was not the right person for her and would only bring her trouble, and that marriage to kind, understanding, rich M. Pleyel would give them all their heart's desire.

The clue — a dim, enigmatic clue — may lie in two letters that Berlioz wrote to Ferdinand Hiller while he was at home with his family, waiting to set out for Italy. Hiller had written hinting broadly that a certain person in Paris was taking his absence with remarkable unconcern, and informing him that the people he was so worried about would hardly thank him for it. In the course of an angry reply, Berlioz wrote:

First of all, I am not worried about people. Then, I have to tell you that if you have your reasons for judging severely the person I am worried about, I have mine for assuring you that I now know her character *better than anyone does*. I am well aware that she is not worried. The proof of that is that I am where I am — had she persisted in begging me not to go, as she did several times, I should have stayed. What should she be so worried about? She knows perfectly well where she stands with me, she now knows all that my heart contains of devotion (not all, though — there is one more sacrifice, the greatest of all, that she doesn't know about, which I shall make for her). She knows that if her mother were so treacherous as still to try to alienate her from me, it is simply up to her to resist! You do not know what it is that torments me, no one in the world knows but *her*; till recently she too knew nothing of it.

A week later, he repeated what he had said, while still keeping Hiller — and us — in the dark as to what it referred to:

Yes, my friend, I must keep secret from you a frightful sorrow ["chagrin affreux"] which I shall suffer perhaps for a long time to come. It is connected with circumstances of my life that are completely unknown to anyone (C. excepted). At least I have the consolation of having told her about it without — but enough.

Without upsetting her? Without making (as he thought) any difference to their love? Did he have the naïvety and egoistic insensitivity to confide in her some earlier and hopeless but persistent passion (for Estelle? for someone we know nothing of?), and if so was it a blow to her trust in him and her sense of the completeness, the uniqueness of their relationship? Or was it something quite different? It is frustrating to have to acknowledge that we have no idea what he is talking about, nor what is the "sacrifice, the greatest of all" that he intends to make for her. But I believe that there, if we could only penetrate the secret, we would find the explanation of Camille's behaviour. She felt herself, in some way, let down, and the ties that united them were weakened. On his side, the fact that she knew, she alone, the secret of his "chagrin affreux" would be an extra twist to the bitterness of the betrayal.

For the moment, though cast down by the sadness of their separation, and distrusting her mother, he still felt confident of Camille. On 22 January, on his return from a week of visits and party-going in Grenoble with his mother and sisters and his brother Prosper, he found a letter waiting. Immediately on arrival his mother had hurried in to tell his father of Hector's very low state; and Dr Berlioz, coming smilingly towards his son, embraced him and said there was a letter for him from Paris. The packet contained two letters, one from Mme Moke and one from his fiancée. Their contents apparently reassured him. "I was as delighted as it is possible for me to be in my hateful exile," he told Hiller. Next day Hiller's letter came, with its hint that Berlioz was luxuriating in feelings of grief that were not shared by the other party. He replied at once (part of his letter has already been quoted):

> So don't talk to me about those who are dear to me and how much if at all my sorrows are theirs, for you know nothing about it. How could you? You don't know what she is feeling, what she is thinking. Just because you saw her at a concert, looking happy and cheerful, it doesn't mean you can draw from it an inference fatal to me. If that were the case, what would you have concluded from my behaviour in Grenoble if you had seen me one day at a large family dinner with my two charming cousins of seventeen and eighteen on either side of me*, laughing and fooling with them in the most extravagant manner? What would she, my fiancée, have thought if she had seen me kiss my cousin Odile's hand and try my engagement ring on her finger, where Odile wanted to keep it? My letter is brusque, my friend, but you have offended me horribly. I shall be staying here at least another nine days. Ferrand arrives tomorrow. If you would write back by return of post you would please me greatly — it would get here in time.

Ferrand's visit would have done him good, but it never materialised. After days of waiting he received a letter which said simply that he was prevented from coming to La Côte; he suggested Berlioz come to Bellay instead.

Though Hector's family continued to surround him with loving concern and bore patiently with his gloom and extreme taciturnity — sometimes he hardly spoke a word all day — nothing could lift the cloud from his spirits. When he felt well enough he saw his old friends — Edouard Rocher, Charles Bert, Charbonnel. But much of the time he spent in bed. Sometimes he unburdened himself to Nancy. Being able to talk about Camille was a solace. The weather was bitterly cold. Dr Berlioz would not hear of his leaving until he was better. His grandfather Nicolas Marmion came over from Meylan to stay.† At the end of January Hiller's second letter arrived. Berlioz again replied immediately. The first half of his letter was a lecture to Hiller on the need to be more canny in the execution of his musical projects: Hiller had been planning a concert.

> Since you have already, at your age, discovered a vein of gold in this poor mine where we're all digging, try to follow it all the way; but remember that you're beneath a vault which you yourself burrow out as you advance and which may collapse behind you. The blunder you made in asking Cherubini for the Conservatoire Hall before the end of the Concert Society's season was inexcusable. You should have known those gentlemen would never consent; and it's highly disagreeable to be crossed by some will that one's

---

* Odile and Pauline Berlioz, daughters of Hector's uncles Victor and Auguste respectively.

† The old man took a lively, slightly prurient interest in his grandson's love-affair; in a verse-letter written after his return to Meylan he imagines dandling Camille on his knee.

own is powerless to oppose. I have to tell you that sometimes you do things too precipitately. I believe one should reflect a great deal about what one intends to do and then, when every measure has been taken, strike a decisive blow so that all the barriers are thrown down. Prudence and force — they're the only way of getting where you want to in this world. I'm afraid I won't be allowed to leave before Saturday or even next Monday [7 February]. I'm still ill, I don't get up every day, and the cold is frightful. And all this time is being wasted ... I have still so many months to eat up! ... If I spoke to Seghers* about many things that I should have kept silent about, it was in a moment of rage at not having taken the journey to Vincennes further — I wanted at least to make use of it to force Mme M. to consent. As you may imagine, I very soon gave up trying to use that method.

Berlioz then refers to the "chagrin affreux", whose nature he must keep secret from Hiller, and continues:

Although I am forced to make a mystery of this matter, I don't think you have any cause to do the same where other matters are concerned. I implore you therefore to tell me what you mean by the phrase, "You wish to make a sacrifice. There is one which I have long feared, and have every reason to believe, that you will have to make one day." What sacrifice are you talking about? I urge you, in your letters, never speak in hints, especially where it concerns her. It's torture for me. Don't forget, explain it frankly. Write to me in Rome, poste restante, and be sure to frank the letter as far as the frontier, otherwise it won't reach me.

On the same day that Berlioz wrote to Hiller, Nancy wrote to Camille, a carefully penned letter of sisterly affection which she copied into her diary. The prompt reply, which arrived only a week later, was a grievous disappointment. It was brief, formal, and distantly cordial — "nothing in it seems felt", confided Nancy to her diary; "it has none of the charm, none of that feminine delicacy which can confer value even on everyday expressions: in a word, nothing addressed to the heart or that seems to come from it!" Whether she disclosed her feelings to Hector, or showed him the letter, she does not say. He also must have heard from Camille, and the letter must have satisfied him, for next day, 8 February, he set out at last on his journey. From Lyons, on the 9th, he wrote to Thomas Gounet, settling accounts with him over the *Neuf mélodies* (which they had published at their joint expense) and sending him a 20-franc note for the printer of the programmes of the Fantastic Symphony: the remaining 42 francs that he owed he would send from Italy. "I'm leaving this evening. At least I shall know in 10 days the duration of my infernal exile. Oh! my dear Gounet, I am so unhappy, nothing I can say can give you an idea of what I suffer. And you — how are things with you? Are you cured yet? I

---

* Belgian violinist in the Conservatoire, Odéon and Nouveautés orchestras.

think of you often, and imagine that you are sad.* Write to me sometimes — Rome, Villa Medici.''

He had intended to visit Ferrand, needing his company badly, and booked his seat on the coach to Bellay, thirty miles north of Lyons. But he hesitated, knowing that Ferrand's parents would be less than delighted to see him (they regarded him as a bad influence on their son), and also feeling that each day he lingered only lengthened the time of his absence; and he finally left for Marseilles that same evening, not by the Rhone steamboat as he had planned — it was making overnight stops at Valence and Avignon — but by the diligence. On about 12 February he was in Marseilles. It was the first time he had seen the sea. The sight filled him with gratifying exaltation. ''What a sublime monster it is,'' he wrote to Adèle. ''I was delighted to see it come and lick my feet and cover them with its foam, roaring like an enraged beast.'' He took a small boat out into the harbour, and longed for the moment when he would be on the open sea; the thought roused him in spite of himself. As for the town, ''Marseilles is superb. But for the frightful tumult of my thoughts I should have been thrilled by it.''

In the harbour he wandered along the quay, enquiring about ships crossing to Italy, but could find nothing except some ill-favoured little cargo-boats with nowhere to berth but on deck with the crew of three or four villainous-looking sailors and among the bales of wool or the oil-casks or the mounds of animal bones exported to Italy for the manufacture of blacking. Soon afterwards he got into conversation with some young Italians in the main street of Marseilles, the Cannebière. They told him of a Sardinian brig that was leaving shortly for Leghorn and was taking passengers; they were sailing on her and suggested that he come too and mess with them: it was necessary to supply one's own food and drink, as it would not be provided on board. They were to sail on the 14th on the evening tide.

In fact the captain delayed departure for two days. Luckily Berlioz had found some acquaintances in Marseilles, Paris Conservatoire students some of whom had played in his concert of 5 December. They made much of him and secured him entry to the opera house. He saw *Le tableau parlant*, and thought it as feeble and threadbare as the other Grétry operas, *Le caravane du Caire* and *Panurge*, which had tried his patience and that of his fellow-Gluckists in the days of their missionary fervour at the Opéra. Within a few years Grétry would have gone up in his estimation and joined Dalayrac and Monsigny, exponents of the late eighteenth-century Classical school of opéra-comique for which his affection remained constant for the rest of his life. But now it was just a product of ''the

* Gounet had been hopelessly in love with a singer at the Opéra.

ancient French provincial muse, whose bespectacled nose smells of snuff at ten paces".

During the daytime he discovered the supreme pleasure of exploring a sea-shore and spent many hours among the rocks below the cliffs from which the church of Notre-Dame de la Garde keeps watch over land and sea. On the 16th, with his new companions, he set sail for Italy.

The weather was lovely, so mild that they dined on deck, the wide blue sky overhead and on the port side a glowing panorama of wooded coastal hills dotted with villages and, floating high above, the Alps, spread out in the afternoon sun. It was a sight that grew unexpectedly familiar as day followed day and the vessel made barely perceptible progress along the coast. The crossing to Leghorn was said normally to take well inside a week; but after a good start the wind had dropped and for three days they remained becalmed off Nice. At evening a light breeze got up, only for the prevailing current to carry them back during the night. Each morning, coming on deck, he asked the sailors the name of the town just visible to the north and each morning got the same answer: "E Nizza, signore. Ancora Nizza. E sempre Nizza."

To kill time he and his fellow-passengers practised pistol-shooting on deck, firing at a ship's biscuit tacked to a pole attached to the stern of the ship, whose rolling added to the sport. As the days went by he found out more about the young men he was travelling with, all of whom spoke French. They were Italian officers in exile, members of the Carbonari, the secret society of Italian patriots based in France; they had been waiting to return and join the insurrectionary movement which aspired to free the Italian states from Austrian domination and unite them in a single nation. That moment, they believed, was at hand. The July Revolution had set Italy alight. Modena, inspired by the great liberal leader Menotti, was rising against the Duke, and they were on their way to take part in a revolt which had already spread to Tuscany and was beginning to engulf the Papal States.

The officers found a French artist who had been in Paris during the Three Glorious Days and had seen it at first hand the ideal person to talk to. Berlioz heard many fascinating tales. One of them had fought in Greece under Canaris, whom he claimed to know well; and the others questioned him eagerly about the heroic incendiarist whose fire-ships had caught the imagination of liberal Europe. Another, a Venetian corsair called Jermann, boasted that he had commanded the corvette that Byron fitted out for his travels down the Adriatic coast and through the Greek islands. Byron, he said, had provided him with a brilliant uniform covered in gold lace and enrolled him as companion in his orgies — the Venetian described them in meticulous detail — and had paid personal tribute to the man's courage one day during a storm, when the poet invited him below for a game of écarté: the ship, lurching violently, had sent table and players flying. "Pick up the cards — we continue," cried Byron. — "With pleasure, my lord." — "Captain, you're a brave fellow." The Venetian was a distinctly dubious-looking character, and spoke appalling French, but his stories sounded too good to be invented — the uniform and the episode of the card-game had the Byronic touch — and Berlioz was only too happy to believe that he was talking to someone who had been with Childe Harold on his pilgrimage. His Italian tour had begun under the best possible auspices.

The man showed his mettle soon afterwards when, after a week of windless calm, the weather changed dramatically in the Gulf of Genoa, and they struck a freezing tramontana, a ferocious north wind straight off the Alps. The ship's captain, anxious to make up lost time, left all the sails set, and the brig heeled violently to starboard; waves broke over the deck and water poured down the hatches. Still the captain refused to take in sail and held the ship on course towards the Gulf of Spezia. That night the gale worsened. Berlioz, who did not suffer from sea-sickness, was lying in his bunk trying to sleep and watching the convulsions of his fellow-passengers colliding with each other as they made for the gangway, when he heard the Venetian cry out to the sailors, "Corraggio, corpo di dio, è niente", and realising that it must be something, and something serious, got up and went on deck, followed by four of the Italians. It was a horrendous sight.

> For all that I did not then set much store by my life, my heart began to beat wildly. Imagine the wind howling with an intensity such as you have no idea of on land, the waves towering up from the surface of the sea and crashing down in spray, the ship so steeply inclined that its right side was under water, and with all that, fourteen huge sails spread, catching the full fury of the gale.

It was impossible to stand upright. They clung on as best they could, wedging themselves in tight. The wind continued to rise, and they heard the Venetian exclaim, "Stupid bugger, with all that canvas — he'll have us drowned."

> I saw then that there was nothing for it, and my heart resumed its normal beating [...] I had wrapped myself in my coat in such a way as to pinion my arms; I thought to forestall a long agony by preventing myself from swimming, and hoped to go to the bottom like a cannon [...] I am pleased now to have undergone this trial and seen for myself that death is uglier at a distance than close to. The truth is that at the outset of the night's storm I could not have stopped myself shaking with fear, but once I believed it was all up with us, when I saw the raging sea whiten us with its spume, like the American boa constrictor which covers its victim with slaver before devouring it, I surveyed it all with nothing but a strange indifference; I thought of the morrow, and of how those white valleys I could see foaming before me would rock me and put me to sleep with no pain.

Meanwhile some of the crew had begun to call on the Madonna, when the Venetian yelled out, "Forget the Madonna, for God's sake get those sails in or we'll sink!" The other Italian officers now found voice: "Captain Jermann, take command, you can see that old fool is out of his mind. Quick, quick, all hands to the yards!" In an instant the masts swarmed with sailors. At that moment an even stronger gust drove the brig almost flat on its side, and with a crash audible above the storm every loose object on board, barrels, tables, chairs, cupboards, kitchen pots and pans went over, the captain with them. It proved their salvation. The wheel relinquished, the rudder swung free and the ship turned end on to the wind just as the sailors succeeded in furling the biggest of the sails. The vessel righted herself. Now it was all hands to the pumps. Soon afterwards smoke was seen drifting up from below decks. The lamp in the cabin had fallen over and, on breaking, set fire to some bales of wool. When that was put out, the tumult gradually subsided. Under a single sail they drove before the gale; the ship was still heeled over, but he heard the sailor next to him say, "Oh! adesso mi futto del vento", and knew that the crisis was passed. Now it was "a concert of another kind, the wind, whistling in the bare rigging and shrouds, grinding and sniggering like an orchestra of piccolos [...] What a night! and the moon, as it raced through the clouds, looking down on us with a face all distorted — it seemed in a hurry to get somewhere, and annoyed at finding us on its route."

That same morning they reached Leghorn and, putting up at the Aquila Nera, slept off the effects of the journey. Next morning the whole crew of the brig called on them at the hotel to wish them bon voyage and, after much pressing, agreed to stay and share in an improvised meal and drink to their joint escape from the perils of the sea; but they absolutely refused to accept any money, not wishing their hosts to think they had come out of any ulterior motive. "Poor wretched human creatures! To work for your living like that, to spend your life in a floating prison, climb the mast at night with the elements raging round you, cling to the rigging above the abyss like a spider suspended from its web, and all for a ration of biscuit hard as a board, seasoned with raw cod and a drop of wine. When I talked to them about it (for they all speak French), they said, 'What would you have us do? At least it's better than being a brigand in Calabria or dying of starvation.'"

From Leghorn he and his Italian companions struck north for Pisa, and from there east to Florence, where Berlioz hoped to find letters for him, for he had asked for them to be forwarded from Rome.

From the moment it set foot on Italian soil the whole party, Frenchman and Italians, found itself an object of interest to police and customs authorities. To stay overnight in a town required numerous formalities, and their baggage was searched constantly. Two of the Italians were arrested by the Tuscan police and gaoled before they got to Florence.

The rest managed to allay suspicion and continued on their way to Modena to join Menotti's forces. Berlioz parted from them in Florence.

There to his frustration he was forced to stay nearly a week. Though Rome remained loyal to the Pope, much of the Papal States was in the hands of the insurgents, and Rome itself had been shaken by an outbreak of mob violence in the Piazza Colonna, of which French students, eternal exporters of revolution, were believed to have been the instigators. The liberals in France were speaking out openly in favour of the revolt, and both sides expected France to intervene. Any Frenchman, especially one bound for the Villa Medici in Rome, was suspect. When Berlioz presented himself with his passport at the office of Cardinal Bernetti, the papal nuncio in Florence, he was refused a visa.

Meanwhile there was disappointment of a deeper sort: at the poste restante in the main post office on the Piazza del Gran Duca (the modern Piazza della Signoria) no letters were waiting for him. He went there every day, but none came, except one from Horace Vernet, director of the French Academy in Rome, announcing that he had taken the necessary steps to secure his entry, and enclosing a voucher for 175 francs, his February grant (so he had not lost all of it by his late arrival), and confirming that no mail had arrived for him. At least there was none at all, not only none from Camille but none from his family either, nor from any of his friends. Perhaps there was some problem with the posts from France, and all would be satisfactorily resolved. It was a crumb of hope.

While he waited for the papal bureaucracy to disgorge the visa, he tried to distract his tormenting thoughts with sight-seeing, and paced the monuments of what was to become his favourite Italian city, musing on Dante and Michelangelo and the great spirits who had once been the glory of Italian art. In the evening it was the turn of their latter-day descendants. His first encounters with modern Italian music on its native soil were not reassuring. Bellini's new opera *I Montecchi ed i Capuleti* was opening at the Pergola Theatre. Some fellow-guests at Berlioz's hotel, who had seen it in Venice, recommended it strongly to him as a work of remarkable freshness and expressivity in a new genre, quite different from the usual imitations of Rossini, with a first-rate libretto into the bargain. Was he about to hear a true operatic *Romeo*, worthy of Shakespeare at last, after the feeble travesties of the last thirty or forty years?

It was not to be. The overture, or as much of it as the puny orchestra, placed in a kind of deep trench, was able to project above the noise of the spectators, seemed a mere string of commonplaces; and though the chorus — including a dozen or so boys of fourteen or fifteen of whom the altos were excellent — sang quite well, the soloists were all out of tune with the exception of two women. One of them, who was tall and powerfully built, played Juliet, and the other, short and spindly, Romeo. So that was it! Bellini the great innovator had bowed to Italian tradition and simply copied Zingarelli, copied the vacuous Vaccai whose *Giulietta e Romeo*, with

Romeo played by a woman, he had experienced in Paris at the Théâtre-Italien a few years before. This was how the composer saw the man who pierces the fiery Tybalt to the heart, who forces the gates of Juliet's tomb and, provoked by County Paris, lays him lifeless — as a beardless boy — and the passions which consume him as the attributes of a eunuch!

The work itself exemplified the same craven, prosaic spirit:

> ... in the libretto, no ball at the Capulets', no trace of Mercutio, no garrulous nurse, no grave and tranquil hermit, no balcony scene, no sublime soliloquy for Juliet as she takes the hermit's phial, no duet in the cell between the banished Romeo and the disconsolate friar, no Shakespeare, nothing — a botched piece of work, mangled, disfigured, *arranged*. And in the music, where was the double chorus of Montagues and Capulets, where the passion of the two lovers, the great orchestral outbursts, the vivid instrumental patterns, the new and searching melodies, the bold progressions lending colour to the scene, the unexpected modulations? Where was the musical drama, the dramatic music, that such poetry should give birth to?

Only once had the composer risen to the occasion and found a phrase worthy of the dramatic situation, at the point (not in Shakespeare's play) where the lovers, dragged apart by their infuriated parents, broke free for an instant and rushed into one another's arms, crying in unison, "We shall meet again in heaven", to a melody of admirable élan and intensity. He was startled into applauding enthusiastically. But, for the rest — did Bellini not fear that Shakespeare's ghost would come to vex his sleep?

The experience set him thinking again of the dramatic symphony that he had first begun to discuss a couple of years before with the poet Emile Deschamps, translator of Shakespeare's play, and of the elements for which such a work must find musical expression and form:

> To begin with, the dazzling ball at the Capulets', where amid a whirling cloud of beauties young Montague first sets eyes on "sweet Juliet" whose constant love will cost her her life; then the furious battles in the streets of Verona, the "fiery Tybald" presiding like the very spirit of anger and revenge; the indescribable night scene on Juliet's balcony, the lovers' voices, "like softest music to attending ears", uttering a love as pure and radiant as the smiling moon that shines its benediction upon them; the dazzling Mercutio and his sharp-tongued, fantastical humour; the naïve old cackling nurse; the stately hermit, striving in vain to calm the storm of love and hate whose tumult has carried even to his lowly cell; and then the catastrophe, extremes of ecstasy and despair contending for mastery, passion's sighs turned to choking death and, at the last, the solemn oath sworn by the warring houses, too late, on the bodies of their star-crossed children, to abjure the hatred through which so much blood, so many tears were shed.

The second novelty he tried, Paccini's *La Vestale*, was worse still — Licinius played, naturally, by a woman, and not a glimmer of the grandeur of *La vestale* as he knew it. It reminded him that he owed a letter to Spontini, who had made him promise to send him his news. But Spontini had also advised him against marrying Camille. Berlioz put off writing to him.

A happier encounter was his running into the Danish architect Benjamin Schlick whom he had got to know in Paris when Schlick was in charge of redecorating the Odéon. But this too had sombre associations. "A Dane — it evokes Shakespearean thoughts," he told his father. "We spoke of Elsinore, and Hamlet's castle. A Roman Hamlet! For all that I am in Italy, my skies are dark and brooding. My existence is in Paris; there is not a moment, not an instant, day or night, when I can put my hand on my heart and give thanks that it still beats. I regret the salt water. Three more days before I can leave for Rome: I am impatient to find out how long Vernet means me to be away [in Italy]. And no letter from Camille! Had there been any in Rome they would have been sent on to me."

On about 5 March he left Florence and began the slow 175-mile journey to Rome. There were no other passengers; he had the old four-wheel sedan to himself. Conversation with the driver was not possible — the man spoke no French, and the most his Italian would run to was "It's hot", "it's raining", "when's dinner?" In no mood to admire the scenery, he tried to bury himself in some memoirs of the Empress Joséphine that he had picked up at a bookstall on their way through Siena. The rest of the time was spent inwardly cursing Italy and all its works, the Institute for insisting on his being there, and the total lack of comfort in the towns and villages where they stopped for a bed or a meal.

On the fourth morning, as they were passing through a small cluster of houses called La Storta, the driver brought the horses to a halt and, having poured himself a glass of wine, said, "Ecco Roma, signore." Looking up, Berlioz saw the man gesturing with his thumb towards something that gleamed far off to the left in the midst of a dark and desolate plain. It was the cross on the dome of St Peter's. The coachman's casual announcement had a magical effect. Instantly he forgot his ill-humour; his spirits lifted; everything at once became clothed with an aura of the poetic and the sublime; and as the Eternal City gradually defined itself before him he gazed at it in a mood of intent contemplation which no longer measured the tedious slowness of their progress. The grandeur of the Piazza del Popolo through which the main road from the north enters Rome induced in him a still deeper sense of awe. Shortly afterwards, to the sound of the church bells ringing the Ave Maria, they ascended the western slope of the Pincian Hill and stopped in front of the imposing Renaissance palace which had been since the seventeenth century the home of the French Academy in Rome.

It was dinner time, the porter told him, and he was shown to the refectory, where his new comrades gave him a taste of life in the Villa Medici.

The moment I appeared in the doorway of the large hall, where some twenty diners were seated noisily around a table groaning with food, a roar went up sufficient to have shattered the windows had there been any.

"Look who's here! The great Berlioz in person! Gad, sir, what a head! What hair! My dear, the nose! Admit it, Jalay, your nose has lost face."

"What about your hair? He makes you look bald."

"Ye gods, what a mop!"

"Hey, Berlioz — don't you recognise me? Remember? The ceremony at the Institute — *Sardanapalus* — those damned drums of yours that wouldn't start the conflagration? Was he mad! By jove, he had a right to be. Now don't you recognise me?"

"Yes, I do recognise you, but your name — "

"I say, listen to this — he addresses me as 'vous'. We're getting affected in our old age. Everybody's 'tu' here straightaway."

"All right — what is your name?"

"His name's Signol."

"Rossignol, you mean."

"That's a vile pun. Rossignol is a vile pun."

"Beneath contempt."

"Let the poor thing be."

"What, the pun?"

"Ass, no — Berlioz."

"Not puns but punch, I say. Hey, Fleury, bring some of your best. We need it to take away the taste."

"So our music section is complete at last."

"Here, Montfort, allow me to present your esteemed colleague."

"Montfort!"

"Montforte!"

"Montfortissimo!"

"Shake hands."

"Let's shake hands."

"They shall not shake hands."

"Shake hands they shall."

"Shake hands they shall not."

"Here, you idiots, while you're carrying on like this he's hogging all the macaroni. Would you be so good as to leave me a little?"

"Well, let's all shake hands with him and then call a truce."

"Truce be damned. Let battle commence. Here comes the punch. Don't bother with your wine, Berlioz."

"No more wine!"

"Down with wine!"

"Come on, who'll break a bottle with me? Look out, Fleury!"

Crash!

"Gentlemen, gentlemen! At least you might spare the glasses — unless you would rather drink it in small glasses?"

"Perish the thought!"

"Good man, Fleury. Well stopped. The whole lot nearly went that time."

Fleury is the resident factotum, an admirable fellow who fully deserves the trust which successive directors have placed in him. He has waited on the inmates for as long as anyone can remember and has witnessed so many scenes of the sort that he has learned to take no notice of them; and the contrast between his impassive demeanour and the tumult around him adds to the fun. When I had recovered from the shock of my reception I looked round the hall. It was a curious sight. Down the length of one wall hung framed portraits of about fifty former laureates. The opposite wall was covered with a kind of fresco consisting of a series of indescribably grotesque life-size caricatures, the originals of which had all been residents of the Academy. Unluckily the space had run out and the great work had had to be discontinued; newcomers whose appearance lent itself to treatment no longer had the honour of being exhibited there.

After dinner he paid his respects to the director Horace Vernet, settled his effects in one of the small, sparsely furnished rooms allocated to the pensionnaires (of which Ingres' drawing gives a suitably austere impression), and was then taken on a tour of the premises, culminating in the obligatory visit to the Café Greco, just below the Academy, in the Piazza di Spagna, at the foot of the broad marble staircase known as the Spanish Steps. The Café Greco was a fearful hole, dark, dirty and, in winter at least, always uncomfortably crowded, and the coffee served there, on minute wooden tables encrusted with grease and in a steamy atmosphere thick with the smoke of cheap cigars, left much to be desired; but the place had long established itself as the headquarters and meeting-place of expatriate artistic life in Rome. Though the English, the Germans and the French had each their own room, it was the French — the most numerous and the noisiest — who dominated. Amid the deafening din Berlioz's new companions brought him up to date on the political situation. The rumours he had heard in Florence proved to have been exaggerated but not unfounded: the Academy was not under siege, but there had been threats to its safety; it was the focus of popular hostility among the trasteverini, the denizens of the poor quarter south of the river, for whom all Frenchmen were by definition against the Pope and on the side of the revolt. They boasted that they would burn down the Villa Medici and slit the throats of its inhabitants. Several suspicious-looking men had been seen hanging round the back of the palace, and Horace Vernet had come across one in the garden, in one of the alleys: the fellow had drawn a long knife from under his cloak and brandished it at him before making off. Vernet protested to the Vatican, then, getting no satisfaction, retorted by arming everybody with muskets and pistols. There being no French ambassador in Rome at the moment, the director was having to take all such decisions himself. But they all had complete confidence in him. Vernet was one of them. He was equal to any emergency, as well as being a first-class swordsman and a crack shot.

Berlioz listened to their talk, while trying to remember what they were called (for several days he was in the odd position of "tutoying" people whose names he hadn't grasped — he had to keep asking, "Comment t'appelles-tu donc, toi?"). But his thoughts were elsewhere. On arriving he had enquired about letters. There were none. He wrote at once to Camille saying that if he did not hear from her very soon he would come straight back to Paris. True, he had no letters from anyone; bleak as that was, it was a kind of comfort. Yet the other inmates received letters from France, from Paris. Each post-day brought fresh heartbreak, when at the midday meal the servant came in with the bundle of mail and there was some for everyone but him. The silence, and the horrible imaginings it prompted, tortured him. In the seclusion of his room he wept inconsolably. What had happened — to Camille, to them, to their pledges of steadfast, unchangeable love?

He spoke to Horace Vernet, not telling him outright but hinting at it, and begging his permission to return to France. Vernet was sympathetic but sought to restrain him: if he went he would lose his grant. Even so, within a week of his arrival he had made plans to go. (Mendelssohn, who was in Rome, told his mother, in a letter dated 15 March, that Berlioz was leaving two days later.) Then he hesitated. "What is the point", he wrote to Nancy, "of relapsing once more into tears and cries of love, of speaking a language no one understands, devoting myself fruitlessly to someone who, after perturbing my whole existence, now shows me nothing but indifference, and feigning respect and affection for her two-faced mother whose detestable egoism would disgust the devil himself! ... Two months without a letter! ... No one ..." He would stay and wait for an answer to his ultimatum.

28

Return to Life

He stayed, but could settle to nothing. Nothing distracted him from his heartache or impinged on his restlessness and constant, fearful preoccupation — not the friendliness and compulsive high spirits of his fellow-inmates; nor the exquisite spring weather; nor the soirées in the director's sumptuous apartments, at which the whole Vernet family treated him with kindly consideration and Carle Vernet, M. Horace's old father, thrilled to discover that Berlioz loved Gluck, buttonholed him continually ("You see, it's just that M. Despréaux [Berlioz's predecessor] said it was all rococo and Gluck was just old hat"); nor the continued threats of the trasteverini, who came at night and sang songs under their windows prophesying the imminent death of all Frenchmen.[*]

Only Mendelssohn's company had the power to take him out of himself. Berlioz was introduced to him by Montfort the day after his arrival in Rome (no doubt their mutual friend Hiller, too, had told Berlioz to be sure to look him up). Mendelssohn was a frequent visitor at the Vernets', but Berlioz took to calling on him most mornings in his room nearby, at 5 Piazza di Spagna. Mendelssohn would play a Beethoven sonata or some of his own music, or passages from Gluck's *Armide* while they both sang. Then he would take Berlioz on a tour of the ruins of ancient Rome, which he knew well, having been there since the previous November, or they would hire horses and go riding in the Campagna. Mendelssohn formed the lowest opinion of Berlioz as a composer — he wrote in horrified terms to his mother of the Fantastic Symphony, of which he had seen the score — but liked him personally; they were at one on many musical matters and found each other's company agreeable. They swapped experiences of the ignorance and parochialism of Italian musical culture. Mendelssohn knew a priest of the Sistine Chapel, a cultivated man, who told him he had heard tell of "a young composer of promise called

---

[*] "As Horace Vernet had armed us all, they would have had a fine reception if they had attacked us," wrote Berlioz to Ferrand. "But the fools did not so much as try to set fire to our old academic barracks. Who knows, I might have helped them."

414

Camille Moke: lithograph by Alophe, c. 1831, after her marriage.

The opening of the first movement of the Fantastic Symphony, from the autograph full score.

Above left: *Detail of a self-portrait of Horace Vernet, director of the French Academy in Rome.*

Above right: *Mendelssohn, by an unknown artist, c. 1835 (photograph Boissonnat).*

Below: *The garden façade of the Villa Medici, home of the French Academy. The portico with the fountain, where Berlioz played his guitar on summer evenings, is visible in the centre of the picture.*

"Goethe at the window of his lodgings in Rome", by Tischbein, 1787 (photograph, Ursula Edelmann).

Mozart". Berlioz, trying to buy a piece by Weber in a Roman music shop, had been met with blank incomprehension: "Weber, che cosa è? Non conosco. Maestro italiano, francese, ossia tedesco?" — "Tedesco." — "Niente di Weber, niente di questa musica, caro signore. Ma ecco Il Pirata, La Straniera, I Montecchi e Capuleti dal celeberrimo maestro signore Vincenzo Bellini, ecco La Vestale, I Arabi del maestro Paccini." Berlioz claimed that he cut the man short by saying, in Italian, "That will do. Have you no shame?"

It was to Mendelssohn, he told his friends in Paris, that he owed the only bearable moments he spent during those first weeks in Rome. "He is one of those utterly candid souls such as one finds so rarely", while "his skill as a performer is as remarkable as his musical genius, which is saying a great deal. Everything of his that I heard delighted me. I truly believe he is one of the supreme musical talents of the age."

When Berlioz announced again, during Holy Week, that he was returning to Paris, Mendelssohn didn't take him seriously this time, and bet him the cost of a dinner for three that he wouldn't go. But he had finally made up his mind. The mood of bitter stoicism in which he had written to Nancy had not lasted. His morale had worsened under the strain of uncertainty; his soul was in turmoil. He could stand the mystery and suspense, the agonising sense of abandonment, no longer. Horace Vernet, seeing that he was in earnest, advanced him money for travel from his grant, while making it clear that the moment he left Italian soil he forfeited his Prix de Rome automatically. On Wednesday 30 March Mendelssohn paid his wager, and the two of them, with Montfort, had dinner together. Two days later, on Good Friday, 1 April, Berlioz retraced his steps to Florence on the first stage of his return to France.

Even now he vacillated. Should he go straight to Paris, or should he wait a little longer in case word came? In Viterbo, on the second day of the journey, he wrote to the architect Constant Dufeu and asked him to forward any letters that arrived for him to Florence until further notice. In Florence he put up at the Hôtel des Quatre Nations. From there he wrote to Pixis for news of what was going on in the Faubourg Montmartre, saying he would await reply in Florence. At this point one of his violent sore throats, such as often attacked him in periods of extreme nervous tension, laid him low and he spent several days in bed. When he felt a little better he worked on the second movement (the Ball) of the Fantastic Symphony, which he had brought with him; he began writing out the movement afresh on manuscript paper bought in Rome. On about 9 April he was well enough to go out and went to the poste restante in the Piazza del Gran Duca. There were no letters for him.

Still he waited. The weather was lovely and he walked a mile or two out of Florence along the north bank of the Arno, taking a volume of Shakespeare with him, and amid the spring green of the woods read *King*

Lear for the first time. The experience filled him with an appalled exultation which acted as a safety-valve, banishing for the moment the furies of his own tormented thoughts. Back in his hotel room he inscribed some lines from the fourth act of the play on the title page of the score of his symphony: "As flies to wanton boys are we to the gods: They kill us for their sport". He also sketched the plan of an oratorio on "The world's last day", a lurid scenario of a corrupt civilisation, governed despotically by a sort of Antichrist, who is interrupted in the middle of a mass orgy by the arrival of the Day of Judgment.

On the evening of the 11th, still hungry for distracting sensations, he went to a funeral. As he sat in the darkening nave of the Duomo a long line of priests, choristers and penitents in white, carrying torches and a cross, left the sacristy and processed towards the west door. He got up and followed them out of the cathedral to a splendid mansion nearby, the property of a rich Florentine whose young wife had died that morning. A large crowd was gathered outside to watch the removal of the catafalque. Candles were distributed, which lit the dark streets with a sinister clarity as the convoy made its way to the church where the funeral service was being celebrated. There, the service performed, the pall-bearers opened the catafalque and, taking a new-born child from its minuscule coffin, placed it with the mother. So the woman had died in childbirth and was going to be buried with her baby. By now many of the bystanders had gone. Berlioz, his morbid fascination rising, followed the procession to the outskirts of the town where the coffin was placed in a sort of morgue, awaiting removal to the cemetery.

One of the choristers came up to me and said, in French, "Want to go in?" — "Yes." For a *paolo* (12 sous) he took me with him and went and whispered to the guardian of the morgue, and I was allowed in. The poor *sposina* had been lifted from the coffin and laid on one of the wooden tables which furnished the cave-like interior. "You see these tables?" my chorister said with a cheerful air; "well, there are days when all are full, every one, and then, two in the morning, the cart comes, and all gone! But have a look at the lady." So saying he uncovered her. God! she was charming. Twenty-two years old, she wore a fine cambric dress fastened below her feet; her hair was not yet too dishevelled. Apparently she had died of an abscess on the brain; a yellowish liquid trickled from her mouth and nostrils. I wiped her face for her. The brute then let go of her head and it fell back with a thud which shook all the tables. I took hold of her hand — she had an enchanting hand, small and delicate, white; I could not let it go. Her child was ugly, it made me sick to look at it. For a *paolo* I touched that beautiful creature's hand, while her husband mourned her. Had I been alone I should have embraced her; I thought of Ophelia. For a *paolo*! And, no question, when the cart-driver comes at two in the morning to collect his prey, the Charon of Florence makes the dead pay for their passage — he will not have let her keep her fine dress, he'll have stripped her of it. I thought of this while I held her hand for a *paolo*.

Next morning, in the church of Santo Spirito across the river near the Palazzo Pitti, he attended a funeral of another sort — the burial service of Napoleon-Louis, son of the Emperor's brother Louis Bonaparte, who had died at Forlì in the Papal States while fighting for the Italian patriots against Austrian forces. Though he had had a price on his head, and his mother, Queen Hortense, and his surviving brother (subsequently the Emperor Napoleon III) had had to flee the country, the Napoleonic glamour and influence could still secure a first-class service, with a torchlit church draped in black, a massive catafalque and an imposing funerary array of black-robed priests. Berlioz's imagination brooded on the mighty resonances of the dead man's name, and — remembering the book he had been reading about the Empress Joséphine — on the strange reversals that forty years had wrought in the fortunes of Napoleon-Louis' mother, the young creole child, dancing and chanting Caribbean songs on the deck of the ship that brought her and her mother Joséphine de Beauharnais to the Old World, who became adopted daughter of the master of Europe and then Queen of Holland — and now forced to return to the New World bereaved, exiled, stateless, a fugitive. It was the cue for inspired music. But this was Italy; and the great organ of the church — he told Ferrand, in a letter written just after the service — was in the hands of "two workmen, one of whom filled the bellows with air and the other channelled it into the pipes by placing his fingers on the keys. The latter, under the inspiration of the occasion, had pulled out all the piccolo stops and was playing *happy little tunes* which resembled the twittering of wrens. You asked for some music; well, I'm sending you some. It's not much like birdsong, though I'm as blithe as a lark." He then quotes the Dies iræ and its parody from the Witches' Sabbath, concluding with an Amen set to the final cadence of the popular song "J'ai du bon tabac", and adds, borrowing from Boileau, "mix the grave and the gay, the witty and the austere". "I shall wait a few more days for a letter which should come for me, and then I'll leave."

The letter came two days later. He found it at the poste restante and tore it open on the spot. It was from Mme Moke and it announced that Camille was marrying Pleyel. Mme Moke, far from apologising, insisted that she had never consented to his request for the hand of her daughter, accused him of having caused them nothing but trouble, and advised him not to kill himself.

Though he had often imagined the worst, the shock when it came was shattering. The brutal effrontery of the letter's tone gave an added violence to the blow. Some central barrier within him gave way. A cauldron of rage, half hate, half love, seethed up and boiled over. Then, in a moment of sudden clarity, he knew what he must do. Yes, he would kill himself — but not before he had killed Camille and her mother and the wretched M. Pleyel. He saw it all. He would go to Paris, and present himself at the house — but disguised, so as not to be refused admittance: they would be half expecting him to come, they would be on the look-out.

He went straight to see his friend Schlick the Danish architect and showed him the letter. Realising that to reveal his plan would hamper his freedom of action he told him that he was still going back to France, but to his father's house, not to Paris — only, he must leave at once: he "couldn't answer for himself tomorrow". Reassured, Schlick undertook to use his influence to have his passport stamped without delay and to arrange for him to be given a seat in the mail-coach which left the Piazza della Signoria at 6 that evening.

By the time Berlioz came to describe the events of the next few days, twelve years had passed and it had become an "épisode bouffon", a passage of burlesque comedy. He was intent on playing down its importance. At the same time, obedient to his powerful sense of the absurd and unable to resist the impulse to send up his younger self, he highlighted its comical elements. In the context of the *Memoirs*, where the account in *Voyage musical* recurs virtually unchanged, it was part of a systematic attempt to minimise the seriousness of his relationship with Camille Moke.

The attempt, in the nature of things, could hardly be successful: the drastic nature of his actions and the agony of mind that dictated them strike through the veil of farce by which Berlioz sought to hide his wounded feelings from his readers and from himself.

Love betrayed and spurned, bitter despair, rage, are no less so for being recalled with conscious detachment and irony. Only, that degree of irony, so liberal an admixture of levity with such extremes of passion, is a disconcerting trait. It is a trait that Berlioz shares with the author of *Don Juan*. The journey from Florence to Nice is a passage from Byron. Byron, not Picard, is the presiding genius of the game — Byron, under whose auspices Berlioz began his Italian journey, and whose spirit will guide and inform so many aspects of it. The complete lady's maid's outfit — dress, hat with green veil, etc. — for which Berlioz had himself measured regardless of expense at a milliner's shop on the left bank of the Arno is an authentic Byronic touch. Actually it was a not unsensible precaution, given the necessity of gaining entry to the Pleyel household. As himself, he would not have been admitted. Strung almost to breaking point as he was, and with the "restless, sickly air of a mad dog", his mind was working with a feverish lucidity.

The afternoon was spent preparing for departure. In his room at the Quatre Nations he loaded a pair of double-barrelled pistols he had brought with him, checked that his phials of strychnine and laudanum were full and securely stoppered (he would need them for himself if one of the barrels misfired) and replaced them in his pocket, threw a few clothes into a suitcase; scribbled a note on the first page of the revised Ball scene ("I don't have time to finish it myself. Finish it as in my other copy. Because of the changes, all the parts will have to be recopied"), parcelled up the whole score, addressed it to Habeneck and put it with the other music and most of his effects in the trunk which he was leaving in the hotel (there was no room for it in the mail-coach), and instructed the head porter to send it on to La Côte St André at the first reliable opportunity. At 5 he returned to the milliner's. His lady's maid's outfit was ready and fitted exactly. As he paid for it the proprietress bowed with a theatrical gesture and predicted "a great success for his little comedy". At 6 he said goodbye to Schlick, boarded the coach, stowed his female apparel in a side-pocket, and set off.

This time the coach was an express and they devoured the miles. Three mornings later they were in Genoa. Throughout the two and a half days and nights he had sat in silence, with dry, constricted throat, exchanging no word with the driver — except once, when the latter asked him to uncap his pistols and conceal them under the cushions in case they met brigands (who would be liable to kill them if they saw they were armed) — and taking no food, swallowing nothing but a little orange juice. On arrival in Genoa he discovered that he no longer had his disguise; it had been left in the side-pocket when they changed coaches at the seaside village of Pietra Santa two nights before. But he was not going to be deflected. Grimly he set about replacing it, and after several failures found a milliner willing to recruit enough labour to have a fresh set of clothes made before the coach left again in the evening. He was now weak from lack of food, kept going only by the insistence of his will-power. That afternoon as he stood on the ramparts where the cliff goes down sheer into the water, a wave of giddiness swept over him and with it the despair of a child; he felt himself slipping; and, suddenly without will to resist, fell into the sea. Someone fished him out with a boat-hook after he had gone down twice, and hauled him to safety. He lay for a long time stretched out in the sun, vomiting up brine and bile and air. The salt water had nearly claimed him.

The experience had only dented his resolve, however; still his fury drove him on. When he had recovered he collected his new lady's maid's outfit and went to reclaim his passport from the police — to be told that, as a Frenchman, a potential revolutionary, he could not have a visa to travel via Turin but must take the longer, slower coastal route to France via Nice.

On the road west from Genoa his rage began to cool. He had been going through the plan of his arrival in Paris — the lady's maid calling at the house with an urgent letter from the Countess X and, on being admitted to the drawing-room, shooting two guilty women and one innocent man and, having done so, presenting the fourth barrel to his own head — when, abruptly, he realised that he did not want to die. To persist in carrying out his plan involved cutting short his music along with his life. It meant not only leaving behind the reputation of a savage who did not know how to live: it meant leaving his first symphony uncompleted and the other, greater works taking shape in his brain unwritten, unharvested − like Chénier, who just before his execution struck his forehead and exclaimed, "To die − when I feel so much here!" It meant causing unspeakable sorrow and shame to his family.

Then his "almost blunted purpose" reasserted itself, and he repeated obstinately, like a litany, "No, no, no, no, they must die, all of them, I must destroy them, I must blow their brains out − I must and I shall." And the horses trotted on, bearing him towards France. It was night. Somewhere on the Riviera road high above the sea his feelings came to their crisis. At the top of a steep descent the driver stopped to attach the drag to the wheels, and in the silence that followed Berlioz heard the thump and rattle of the waves crunching the pebbled shore at the foot of the precipice, where the cliff "beatled o'er its base into the sea". The sound awoke a fresh storm of grief and rage within him. He gave a shout of anguish and, his hands thrust against the seat, a convulsive start that might have cast him headlong from the cliff top had he not been inside the carriage. But in that moment the fever had passed its height. As they descended the slope, the internal debate swung from death towards life. He began to acknowledge that it was so and, with detachment, to reason that if he could find something secure to hold on to he would be able to weather the next crisis when it came. By now they had come down to sea level. The coach stopped at a small village right by the sea. While the horses were being changed he went into a café and wrote a hurried note to Horace Vernet:

Diano Marina, 18 April 1831[*]

Sir,

I write in great haste, snatching a brief moment of calm. I have been the victim of an atrocious crime, a *breach of trust*, and in a frenzy of rage which lasted from Florence as far as here was flying back to France to exact a just and terrible revenge. In Genoa, in a moment of dizziness [Berlioz then describes his fall from the cliff and his rescue]. But, finally, I live, I *must* live, for my two sisters, whose deaths I would have caused by my own, and for my art.

Though I'm still trembling like the between-decks of a ship firing to port and starboard, I pledge myself to you on my honour not to leave Italy. This is the only way of preventing myself from carrying out my plan. I hope you have not yet written to France, and that I will be able to keep my grant. Please write to me in Nice − I am on my way there.[†] Because of the absolute necessity of rapid communications with my family I shall stay there, a fortnight at the most, and will then come back. Farewell. The

---

[*] The letter is postmarked 19 April.

[†] Nice, or Nizza, belonged to the Kingdom of Sardinia, and was therefore in Italy.

struggle between life and death is not over, but I shall stand firm, I have sworn it on my honour.

Yours faithfully,
H. Berlioz

P.S. Please send me just one word to Nice to let me know the fate of my grant.

He wrote "urgent" on the envelope and, having posted the letter, got back into the carriage feeling easier in his mind — and for the first time realised that he was ravenously hungry. He had eaten nothing since leaving Florence.

Berlioz stayed in Nice for a month. At first he put up at a hotel for a day or two, then he rented a room in a house at the top of the Ponchettes rocks, directly above the water. By then he knew there was no further risk of his throwing himself into the sea. Yet to begin with he was still subject to fits of despair, and grief for the loss of the love he thought had been his. Gradually they became less intense. While waiting for Vernet's reply he made enquiries about coaches to Lyons; but he stayed put. Letters from his family were his lifeline.

He broke the news to them soon after his arrival.

Nice, 21 April

Well — was I wrong to be worried? Camille is marrying Pleyel. The mother wrote to tell me, and had the unbelievable impudence to speak as if she had never consented to have me as her son-in-law. The perfidy, the shamelessness of it! I should tell you that Mlle Moke, whom I had *never thought of*, came to *me* and told me that she loved me, begged me on her knees to love her, ran away with me, and I abducted her, all in June last year — and her mother knew all about it, and now gives her to another!

Don't ask me what I did, or what I wanted to do when I learned of this infamy. Let's talk no more of it. I'm alive: that's enough. I shall live for you and for my art. I'm beginning to eat a little more than just oranges. Till now I have not shed a tear, my eyes are dry as craters. Her father and her brother have lost their positions in Belgium and are ruined. Pleyel is very rich and is adopting the whole family. That's what decided her to accept him when he asked a second time — last year she refused him because of me. She's a child, a coquette with no heart and no soul. She has not even written me a word, no attempt to soften the blow. Her mother is an odious blackguard who had been planning her stratagem for more than five months: she showered me with compliments, called me her son-in-law, to make sure I left for Italy. She knew she could rely on Pleyel's infatuation, and she fed him on hopes that have been fully realised. She felt it would be easy, once I was out of the way, to destroy her daughter's slight feeling for me. It all worked. In none of her letters did she mention the promise she had made me — she wrote to me as though I had been a cousin or a nephew.

There is no justice in heaven or on earth when such crimes go unpunished. They wouldn't have done, had it not been for you. But now I'm saved. I shall live. Write to me quickly, lots of letters, every other day — I'm very close to you. *Nice, poste restante.*

H. Berlioz

As the post didn't go yesterday, I'm writing again.

At the moment I'm quite all right. After my letter yesterday my convulsive trembling started up again, worse than ever; it was the final struggle between life and death, between forgiveness and revenge. I shall stand firm. I am proud of my strength and strong in my pride. And yet it's horrible: I feel as if my bones and my skull were disarticulated and were shaking like the rest of me. It is essential that I occupy myself with something positive; don't send me vague consolations, but suggest a future that my mind and my heart especially can take hold of.

I had never been loved before; it's the loss of that affection (frail though it may have been) that harrows me most. You must marry me off, Father; perhaps you'll be more successful at it than I. Find someone I can love, and to whom I can become dear, recommend someone, anyone, rich or not, that I know.

I could love Odile [his cousin] a lot, and I bet she could love me, but my uncle [Victor] won't be willing — I'm not solid enough for him. Let me know what you think.

I am going to embark on a really big work. I must not just sit back and daydream; what I dread most is the revival of tenderness, the memory of happiness. Show me the future and I shall forget the past. Odile is very young, but no matter, we can wait. I shall write to her; she'll be very surprised to find I'm anything more than a cousin. In two years she'll be charming. Let's see.

I have rented a delightful room, from an old lady, at the top of a little fortified hill, my windows overlook the sea. I have two young men from Arles for fellow-lodgers, the good lady introduced me to them this morning. The address is H.B., care of the Widow Pical, Maison Clerici, Neapolitan Consul, aux Ponchettes, Nice Maritime.

I beg Adèle and Nanci not to cry but to be strong like me. Nice is a lovely town, fresh, glowing, sea, mountains, everything verdant. I'm so close to you that it costs only 62 francs to Lyons. Everybody speaks French. Oh my sublime young orchestra — so we shall see one another again! We have great things to do together. There is a new world of music; Beethoven was its Columbus, I will be Pizarro or Cortez.

I must write to Spontini, when he said goodbye he made me promise to, and I've not yet done so.

I expect a letter from Pixis; he will be dismayed by what has happened. Our marriage delighted him — he loved us both. He's a German of great purity of soul, straight, artless.

What vileness! It will make a big stir in Paris, unhappily for Pleyel. His net is made of gold but the mesh is too wide and the bird he took from me will escape.

Well — but art, life are mine; as for political upheavals, I don't give a damn, and I wish people bothered less about them.

Farewell, dear Mother, I embrace you tenderly.
                    H. Berlioz

   Little by little his system unwound and the shock-waves subsided. He
decided to remain where he was; it would be best to be on his own for a
while and work out his salvation by himself. The French consul, when he
went to see him, agreed to apply to the governor of Nice on his behalf for
permission to stay in the town for a few weeks, and it was granted. The
consul seems to have believed that his protégé was a painter, or else to
have thought it advisable to pass him off as one. As for his declared
reasons for being in Nice, Berlioz, with or without the collusion of the
consul, decided it would be better to invent them than to give the true
ones.

                                             Nice, 26 April 1831
My dear Commandant,
   A young Frenchman called Berrioz [*sic*], pupil at the Royal Academy of
Fine Arts in Rome, on learning that his father was dangerously ill, did not
hesitate to sacrifice his grant in order to be present at his deathbed. At Nice
he found a letter assuring him that his father was out of danger and indeed
convalescing, whereupon he resolved to go back to Rome; for if he returned
to France he would forfeit all right to the grant which is his for 5 years. He
has written to Rome to announce that he will come back after spending two
or three weeks in Nice, resting and taking a few very picturesque views
which have impressed him. I have questioned the young man. Like me you
will decide, when you see him for yourself and hear his explanations, that
you may without the slightest inconvenience grant him the visitor's permit
that he asks for.
   I request it on his behalf and will be most obliged for the welcome you
accord to his demand and to mine. The young man is lodging at the house
of the Neapolitan consul.
                    Yours etc.,
                    Chevalier Masclet

   Berlioz also wrote to the hotel in Florence, instructing them not to
send his trunk to France if they had not already done so, as he would be
back shortly to collect it himself, and meanwhile to forward any mail
that came for him. He sent long letters to his friends, the thought of
whom was a continual source of consolation.
   Every other day a letter arrived from one or other of his sisters,
sometimes from both. None of these has survived, but Nancy's diary
gives a glimpse of the family's reaction to Hector's first dramatic letter
from Nice and to a second one, written a week later in answer to their
frantic questions, which revealed that he had intended to kill Camille and
her mother. That Camille (Nancy wrote) had allowed herself to "forget
the dignity of her sex and expose her honour" to the point of *giving* herself
to a man was dreadful enough; but granted that she was "swept away in

a moment of madness, then there can be no question, she must face everything for the man to whom she gave such proofs of love!" And then the horrifying thought of what would have happened if Hector had persisted with his plan! It would have been like *Le dernier jour d'un condamné*, only real. If he had been two hundred miles nearer Paris! But he was well rid of such a woman.

Perhaps the last word on the Camille Moke affair should be left to Nancy's godmother, the shrewd, sympathetic Nancy Clappier, a woman for whom Berlioz had a warm regard and who had watched him during the difficult years of his apprenticeship to music and life with a clearer, more understanding eye than his own family.

Uriage, 29 April

[...] I am deeply upset about poor Hector; I fear lest, after this show of courage and pride, he relapse into extreme dejection and have no strength to combat his grief. I fear a reaction − it would be grievous both for him and for you. However cruel the experience has been, what inestimable good fortune that the blindfold was removed before the indissoluble tie was formed. I cannot form a clear notion of this Camille. Her seductive portrait, of course, came from Hector himself. Was she just a vulgar, commonplace person − or one of those people with a lively intelligence but no warmth of heart, who get carried away but have no steadfastness? Or did she simply yield to her mother's authority and sacrifice herself for her family? That would extenuate, but not justify her. One may sacrifice one's own happiness, but not another's. To play with that unfortunate young man's existence! It's an appalling thought. I cannot find justification for it. Yet perhaps if we knew what was going on within her, and around her, we might feel sorry for her. For the mother, her part is shameful, vile − disgusting duplicity. Why did she not openly and honestly invoke her rights as a mother and send Hector packing, keep her daughter from him? To give him every hope, in order to induce him to go, is an act of shameful duplicity such as made her unworthy to be allied with a family like yours. And what cruelty to treat the hopes and griefs of that poor young man as a plaything. It's normal for the maternal instinct to be somewhat selfish, but that goes beyond anything. All the same, my child, you must forgive them. It's probably for the happiness of all concerned. It is lucky Hector has so much love for his art. That will give continued interest to his life; the other will gradually dwindle. His returning in your direction, his needing the proximity of his family, is as auspicious as it is touching. Poor Hector!

At the beginning of May came Horace Vernet's reply, a friendly, paternal letter which set his mind at rest: his name had not been removed from the register of the Academy, the Minister should never hear of the escapade, he could return to Rome where he would be received with open arms; in the meantime, the two sovereign remedies for an afflicted mind were work and love of one's art.

Berlioz looked back on these few weeks in Nice as the happiest of his life. "Life and joy came running, music embraced me." He proved the validity of Horace Vernet's advice. In a fortnight of concentrated work he composed a concert overture on *King Lear* (which he had first read in Florence a few weeks before); then, having completed it, he began another, based on Scott's *Rob Roy*. Thanks to this creative activity, grief was kept at bay; there was no relapse into dejection, and the tensions of the past months were released into music.

The *King Lear* overture has closer connections with the recent events of Berlioz's life, and for that matter with the play, than were apparent to Tovey when he said of it that it was simply a "magnificent piece of orchestral rhetoric in tragic style" which we should be content to call "the Tragedy of the Speaking Basses, of the Plea of the Oboe, and of the Fury of the Orchestra". The "noble and indignant" phrases for the lower strings, beginning in proud strength but dwindling to an abstracted mutter, are clearly inspired by the stubborn, once masterful old king (as well as by the example of the instrumental recitatives in the finale of Beethoven's Ninth Symphony). So is the angry, obsessive first theme of the allegro — just as the pure, artless oboe melody of the introduction has its origin in the character of Cordelia. The reflections of Berlioz's life consist not in any direct allusion but rather in the extreme tautness and dry, electric sonority of the string writing and in certain textures and colours reminiscent of the Fantasy on *The Tempest*, the work written the previous autumn to celebrate his "Ariel". The long-drawn, lyrical second theme, too, breathes regret, conscious or not, for lost happiness; the theme runs for more than fifty bars, and even then Berlioz cannot let it go: it refuses to die, keeps putting forth fresh, more poignantly expressive tendrils of melody; a short way into the development section its second strain is heard again, in the minor; and in the coda it is the subject of a sustained and violent conflict in which the opening phrase of the theme is whirled round and round and finally sucked into the fiery orchestral vortex. This can stand for the tragic destruction of Cordelia; but it is also surely an echo of something more personal and painfully real: the loss of Camille Moke and the annihilation of her love.

The balm of work was combined with body-restoring holiday. He ate normally and slept long hours; strolled about the town, listened to the Austrian military band in the public gardens, played billiards with a couple of Piedmontese officers he met at the café where he took his meals, and surrendered to the pleasures of sun and sea and the sheer exhilaration of being alive in the midst of nature at its most rich and enchanting. From his window, on getting up, he drank in the sight and sound of the eternal sea, the white-maned ranks charging shoreward, the continual harsh, sweet thunder that wove itself into his waking consciousness. At night he went to sleep to the crash of the waves battering at the base of the rock on which the house stood. When it grew calmer he went swimming, and felt a glow of well-being he had never thought to experience again. He renewed the delight, discovered in Marseilles, of exploring the sea-shore, finding enticing inlets and bays hidden among the cliffs, where the rocks were carpeted with bright green seaweed and the water was perfect for bathing. On the shore one night he sealed his convalescence by puting an end to an abstinence which (he told friends in Paris) had lasted since the previous June: "As I didn't want to bring my *lover* back home, I took her to a cave I knew on the edge of the sea. But on our entering, a growl came from the back — it was some sailor asleep — or perhaps it was Caliban himself. We left the field to him, and our union was celebrated without ceremony, some way off, on the beach. The sea was raging, its waves broke at our feet, the night wind blew fiercely, and I cried, with Chactas, 'Majestical nuptial rites, worthy of the grandeur of our untamed loves!'* You see that I am cured." By day he wandered through the abundant orange groves, or from the hills above Villefranche, to the east of the town, watched the tiny fishing boats move over the wrinkled sea and, farther out, the silent forms of ships slowly define themselves and melt into invisibility again.

"What a sunset," he writes, one evening (9 May), to his sister Nancy; "it's pure Claude Lorrain! The sea is covered with those little 'golden paths of rays' that Moore speaks of, which seem as if they must 'lead to some bright isle of rest'. 'It sinks and fades, the day declines, but elsewhere will bring in another life. Oh! had I wings to soar and follow it into a brightness without end!' The quotation reminds me that I gave my *Faust* to a painter at the Academy — he began my portrait but didn't have time to complete it."

The Academy! His idyllic existence was drawing to an end. He had thought of staying much longer and having his allowance paid to him there, but Horace Vernet was not being cooperative. The police, too, were beginning to think he had been in Nice long enough: this mysterious young Frenchman who wandered about with a notebook in his hand and spent days at a time on the shore (drawing plans?) and, when not doing that, was seen engaging officers of the garrison in conversation. His original application had been for a permit for two or three weeks. That period was over. It was time he left.

His departure was fixed for 19 May. In the event he stayed two days longer. On the 20th he wrote to his friend Edouard Rocher in La Côte to congratulate him on getting engaged and to offer some advice, in which the normal (male-dominated) morality of the age is interpreted in an unexpectedly severe spirit of provincial pudeur, modified by a dash of

---

* From Chateaubriand's *Atala*.

idealism. Perhaps he still regretted not having blown Camille Moke's brains out.

Nice, 20 May 1831

Dear Edouard,

So you are getting married!

That's good news. You'll be happy — not as happy as I would wish you to be, but as happy (I trust) as our depressing civilised society can permit. From what I have heard you have made an excellent choice. Use it, don't abuse it. Marriage is a *strong* tie, since it cannot be broken; it involves the happiness or unhappiness of a lifetime; and which of those it will be often depends, in a way, on us ourselves. If you want to know what I think, here it is (though you may say I don't have a great deal of experience): Once the first moments of ecstasy have passed nothing in the world can bring them back; and yet you can, if you love your wife and she has a disposition at all responsive, clip pleasure's wings and make it stay with you much longer than it is reckoned to. In the first place, she whom you have chosen must be convinced that you are devoted to her body and soul, that you will never deceive her and that you have total confidence in her. If she deceives you, kill her without hesitation; but if ever you are unfaithful to her, never look me in the face again (you could not do so without shame). I know these precepts are not those of the smart world, but I am only too glad they aren't, and I think too well of you to suppose that you have ever shared the notions of that world called smart, which I find so tawdry.

For the physical side, I advise you always to show the greatest delicacy in conjugal relations. *Try to have separate rooms from those of your wife*, never get dressed in front of her, and never treat her familiarly. You may be sure that much depends on these apparently trivial matters. Never be weak — it is for the elm to support the vine; but don't be lacking in consideration either; marriage, like government, requires that iron hand in the velvet glove that Napoleon employed. Keep your wife as much as you can away from those people without mind or heart who infest society; you can easily do so, and it's vitally important.

Now to speak of me! No doubt you know that Camille is married — to Pleyel. From what you know and *what you do not*, you can gauge the extent of the crime and the black depths of her heartlessness. But her mother is a thousand times viler than her. It's because of all that that I'm in Nice. Good luck decreed that we should be separated by nine hundred miles. You know me well enough to guess what I did and what I intended to do. I was supposed to leave for Rome yesterday, but am not going till tomorrow. It'll be the third time I have travelled across Italy *entirely on my own*. But this time I belong to my art and my friends — restored to life, to friendship, to music. It will be a joy to see you again; I'll reveal then what I daren't write. Write to me in *Rome, French Academy*, and tell me all about yourself. I'll deal with money in my next letter.

Farewell. Your devoted friend,

H. Berlioz

Don't forget to remember me warmly to Charles [Bert]. He's an excellent
fellow, and I'm very attached to him. I shall write to him from Rome. Please
answer at once and tell me when your wedding is.

Well, Charles, when are you going to follow Edouard's example? Shall I
bring you back a Roman girl? I shouldn't dream of doing so! They're
nothing but bitches, all of them. A curse on all bitches — I was about to say
women. Farewell. H.B.

Will you do me a favour? Go and drink a punch on my behalf, with
Antoine [Charbonnel] — just the three of you. I'd love you to.

Next day he set out, in superb weather, back along the Route du
Corniche, Napoleon's feat of engineering carved into the cliff face high
above the sea. On the 23rd he was in Genoa, where he went to the opera
and saw a once-famous piece from the dark ages before the dawn of
Rossini, *Agnese di Fitz-Henry* by Paër, naturalised Frenchman and member
of the Institute, purveyor of malicious gossip about Beethoven, Spontini
and Rossini, whom Auber had caricatured as Signor Astucio in his one-
act opera *Le concert à la cour*. Berlioz was agreeably surprised by Paër's
opera. It was cast in the comfortable mould and bland style of Cimarosa
but was rich in expressive melody (though some superior person had
"improved" its modest orchestration by adding a bass-drum). The orchestra, he noted, was much better than the one at the Pergola in
Florence: the violins played in tune and the wind instruments kept more
or less in time. But Genoa as a whole was sunk in commerce. The
Genoese showed no interest in their fellow-citizen Paganini: no one could
point out the house where the violinist was born. Berlioz also looked in
vain for any memorial to Christopher Columbus.

From Genoa to Florence he was again the only passenger. This time he
had an extremely talkative driver, and as the young man spoke no
French he gave Berlioz in effect a concentrated three-day course in
Italian; by the time they reached Florence, on about 26 May, he could
get along quite passably in the language. At the Quatre Nations he found
his trunk waiting for him, with the rest of his effects and the score of the
Fantastic Symphony, and was given the room he had had before. It was
his third visit to Florence in three months. The city delighted him more
each time he saw it. In weather that continued glorious he renewed
happy acquaintance with its churches, palaces and gardens; but he
avoided the Pergola Theatre. A few days later he set out for Rome in the
company of three very friendly and courteous Italian monks who were
going up for the Feast of Corpus Christi. Two of them spoke excellent
French; and all three could talk of nothing but the splendours of the
coming ceremony. The procession, they said, was something quite indescribable, a miracle of golden vestments and incense and gem-encrusted
crosses. When Berlioz questioned them on the subject of the music that
would accompany the procession they were rather less forthcoming; but

he gathered that at any rate there was going to be an "immense chorus".
Was Italy about to confound his prejudices?

On the last full day of the journey, early in the morning, he left his
baggage and his coat in the carriage at San Lorenzo and went on ahead,
walking all day, along the shore of Lake Bolsena and into the mountains
north of Viterbo. It was the first of many such days during the next
twelve months.

As on his later treks through the Roman Campagna and the foothills of
the Abruzzi, and as hardly ever happened in Rome, ideas came to him.
While he strode along, his mind was busy with a project he had been
meditating for some time, a dramatic sequel to the Fantastic Symphony
in the form of a "mélologue" for speaker, solo singers, chorus and
orchestra. He stopped from time to time to draft the spoken monologues
in his pocket-book. For the music, he intended to use existing compositions
worth preserving and perpetuating in a larger context — songs or genre
pieces that lacked an occasion, plus the better things from the two Prix
de Rome cantatas *Orphée* and *Cléopâtre*, unheard till now. They would be
introduced and given a pretext by the monologues, which would take up
the "Episode in an Artist's Life" at the point where the symphony had
left it (at the climax of the opium-induced nightmare) and at the same
time touch on some of the æsthetic questions of the day. The whole work,
entitled *The Return to Life*, would be at once an experiment in music-
drama, a slice of autobiography, and an artistic manifesto, a broadside in
the battle for freedom of expression. It and the revised symphony would
together form the programme of a concert. By the time he rejoined the
coach the work was essentially complete.

Lélio — to borrow the title that Berlioz later gave the work and its
artist-hero — is usually assumed to have been conceived in Nice, during
his recovery from the Camille Moke débâcle; but the evidence points to
the scheme of the work having been already formulated before he left
Paris: it was the large-scale project he told Stephen de La Madelaine he
hoped to realise in Italy. The "return to life" it celebrated was his
recovery from the Harriet Smithson obsession, a recovery intimately
associated with Camille. It was Camille's "beloved hand" that pushed
back the gates of hell after the horrors of the opium-dream, and her love
that encouraged him to live again, in the fragment of text referred to
above,* just as it was Camille who inspired the enchanted Ariel music in
the Fantasy on *The Tempest*, the work with which the Artist re-dedicates
himself to Art at the conclusion of the drama. (The allusions to the

* See p. 346n.

Harriet-inspired idée fixe in the published version of *Lélio* belong to Berlioz's much later revision: they are not in the original score.) Two other passages in the spoken text — the Byronic evocation of the delights of the brigand's life and the daydream of swooning to death in the arms of the beloved — were written down before the rupture with Camille; and the second of them, in the form in which it first appears (in a letter to Ferrand), was concerned specifically with her. It is also significant that though on leaving Paris Berlioz deposited most of his manuscripts for safe keeping in the Conservatoire Library, he took with him all but one of the musical numbers that are incorporated in the melologue. The conception of the work and the drafting of its scenario and perhaps of some of the monologues date from the time immediately before his departure from Paris — the aftermath of the Fantastic Symphony, to which it was the sequel, and the high tide of his love affair with Camille Moke.

To continue with it after the traumatic collapse of that affair argues not opportunism so much as a high degree of detachment. Given that the idea seemed to him a good one, it was worth pursuing no matter how drastically the circumstances of his life which helped to inspire it had changed. If he needed a personal rationale, the second "return to life" he had just experienced provided it. The writing of *Lélio* sanctioned the resolve made in Nice to give up both his dreams of love and his suicidal designs and live for his art. We hear an echo of this in the final monologue (which we may imagine Berlioz scribbling in his pocket-book as he walked along Lake Bolsena): the Artist, having previously imagined himself sleeping his last sleep in the arms of the beloved, acknowledges that it is not by abandoning himself to such poetic illusions that he can be reconciled to life. "Another Faust, only more unbelieving, as disgusted as he with vulgar sensations and as hungry for happiness, unlike him I cannot call on magic to realise my dreams. Death will have none of me — I flung myself into his arms and he repulsed me with indifference. Let us live, then, and may the heavenly art to which I owe the rare flashes of happiness that have lit up my dark existence solace and guide me in the wilderness which it remains for me to traverse. Oh music, pure and faithful mistress [...] I abandon myself to thee!"

The doubts about *Lélio* concern, rather, the quality of the work.

True, the idea is understandable enough, in the artistic climate of the time: a continuation of the Fantastic Symphony which, combining music and theatre, brought the symphony's drama into the open.* Such a work

---

* Though the Melologue was given in the Conservatoire Hall, Berlioz envisaged performance in a theatre, with the orchestra and chorus invisible behind the curtain, so that until the curtain rises on the final number, the *Tempest* fantasy, the music is imagined as taking place in the mind of the protagonist — an externalisation of the "singular faculty" of which he speaks in the final monologue, that of "thinking music so intensely that I have so to say at my command imaginary performers, who move me just as though I heard them in reality".

could be expected to "stir up the musical world in an unusual fashion" (as Berlioz said to Stephen) and to re-establish him decisively before the public after his two-year absence from the scene. It is understandable too that he should want to salvage interesting music from the wreck of his Prix de Rome cantatas *Cléopâtre* and *Orphée*, neither of which had been performed in public or was ever likely to be. (He could not have foreseen that *Cléopâtre*, which he never published, would one day become a popular work.) The *Chanson des pirates*, a swashbuckling setting of Victor Hugo written in 1829 in immediate response to *Les Orientales*, also merited hearing for its rhythmic verve and jovially ferocious orchestration: it could without impropriety be transferred from piracy to brigandage, supplied with a new text extolling the pleasures of the brigand's way of life (among them drinking one's mistress's health from the skull of her lover) and introduced by a tirade on the topical Romantic theme of the brigand as free man. And though the *Tempest* fantasy might reasonably look forward to a future of its own as an independent concert piece, its glittering new sounds — from which, as the Artist-Narrator states, "sombre colours are excluded" — made an ideal conclusion for a work dedicated to the magic power of music to banish the dark night of the soul. The six musical numbers, richly varied in character, tempo and sonority, could be arranged so as to make a well-contrasted dramatic sequence.

Nor was the genre of the work so outlandish. Neither the notion of a "melologue" nor the word was new: they came from Thomas Moore. Moore had written a "Melologue upon National Airs" for performance at the Dublin Theatre, and in a note to the published text (included in the French edition of *Irish Melodies* that Berlioz was so familiar with) had defined the term as the "mixture of recitation and music which is frequently adopted in the performance of Collins' Ode on the Passions", and of which the "most striking example" was to be found in Racine's *Athalie*. The second half of the eighteenth century saw many experiments in the combining of speech and music.* More recently, there was Beethoven's *Egmont*, and there was the example of Weber. Berlioz almost certainly did not know his cantata *Der erste Ton*, for reciter, chorus and orchestra, a celebration of the coming of music into the world, but he knew the Wolf's Glen scene in *Freischütz*. In offering his audience his own mélange he was doing nothing at all eccentric.

On the contrary, no work of his made so immediate an impact. The mixed, quasi-theatrical genre caused no problems; and the monologues on Shakespeare and Beethoven and the ungodly who continued to blaspheme them, the attacks on the philistinism of Paris society, on the "worshippers in the temple of routine" and those who tamper with works

---

* A tradition which, as Barzun observes, is as old as drama. See his survey in *Berlioz and the Romantic Century*, I 224—7.

of art (this last in clear reference to Fétis and his "improvements" to Beethoven's symphonies), the vision of the New World of music discovered by Columbus-Beethoven now lying open to "free and adventurous spirits" and awaiting its Cortez and Pizarro — all this was meat and drink to the public which filled the Conservatoire Hall when Berlioz presented the work, together with the Fantastic Symphony, in December of the following year. The allusions to the composer's private life only added spice to his treatment of these topical themes, while the Romantic rhetoric of the prose style and the histrionic displays of personal feeling, the sighs and the shouts of rage or derision or enthusiasm, were thoroughly attuned to the times.

Precisely because they were à la mode such things have dated the work irretrievably. The idea is valid and logically devised but the execution no longer sustains it: the style of the monologues, so effective in its day, has become over-rhetorical and contrived, betraying the thinness of intellectual content; the expression of sentiments, however sincere and deeply felt they are, now seems like posturing. With the help of historical imagination and in a good performance, declaimed and acted with humour and relish, *Lélio* can still be rich, eventful entertainment — but enjoyed as a period piece, not taken wholly seriously: an act of pardonable folly. Whereas in the Fantastic Symphony autobiography is objectified into art, and the artist's griefs and longings become independent, eternal statements, in *Lélio* it remains autobiography — not art but journalism. Berlioz never returned to its mixed genre. It represents an aberration in the development of the large-scale concert work on a dramatic theme which forms one of the central preoccupations of his career.

Whatever one thinks of *Lélio*, it is symptomatic of Berlioz's Italian journey that the one major work to be completed in the course of it should involve practically no new composition. On the face of it there will be very little to show for the next twelve months. The time is not lost; but what is gained will be for later.

29

Fruitful Idleness

------◄━◆━►------

"The weather today is detestable; the sirocco's blowing and the air's thick like smoke. You feel quite *avili*, as the Romans say, and incapable of doing anything. Oh my lovely little Nice, and the sea, the verdant rocks, and the fresh breeze!"

The refrain runs through the whole of Berlioz's sojourn in Italy. For Nice and its sea and rocks, read Castelgondolfo, Frascati, Tivoli, the blue lakes, the foothills of the Abruzzi. But Rome is impossible. The atmosphere of the Holy City lies on him like a pall, stifling his faculties, most of all his creative invention. In Rome he can do nothing. The environment is to him fundamentally and fatally anti-artistic; and not all the distractions of life at the Villa Medici and the dedicated high spirits of his fellow-pensionnaires can alter the fact. Each time he comes back from the country — which he does usually because his allowance has run out — he is returning to "barracks".

While he is there he takes part in the convivial activities of the community: games in the garden; parties; "drinking deep" and chain-smoking cheap cigars at the Café Greco; Sunday expeditions into the country outside Rome to see the sights; attending the regular Thursday parties or fancy-dress balls in the director's residence or the occasional receptions at the French embassy; holding impromptu "English concerts", a kind of infernal round in which each participant chooses a different tune and, setting off one after the other, bawls it in whatever key he likes, to the accompaniment of all the dogs in the district, while the barbers in the Piazza di Spagna come out on to their doorsteps and winking knowingly at one another say, "Musica francese". But his humour is frequently melancholic; the spleen devours him, and much of the time he is "surly as a chained hound". The nickname invented by his fellow-students in Paris — "Père la Joie", "Old Father Jollity" — follows him to Rome. He spends many hours in morose seclusion; his companions, with a few exceptions, are "vulgar creatures, without the soul of artists". After an evening of cavatinas in the Vernets' drawing-room or a ball at the ambassador's — where the cognoscenti gravely compare Beethoven and Vaccai and ask whether he doesn't think *Faust* charming — unable to sleep he goes down into the garden and sits till dawn, wrapped in a hooded cloak, listening to the hooting of the owls in the Villa Borghese garden and pursuing the misanthropic current of his thoughts. In the dog days of summer he repairs to St Peter's and, settling himself in a confessional with a volume of Byron, remains there for hours, "absorbed in that ardent verse, following the corsair across the sea on his audacious journeys, adoring the extraordinary nature of the man, at once ruthless and of great tenderness, generous-hearted and without pity, a strange amalgam of two feelings seemingly opposed — love of a woman, hatred of his kind". He imagines the poet in that very spot, treading that marble floor, contemplating those figures of Canova's, breathing in the grand harmonious solemnity of the place whose stillness still seems to echo to his words — words of love, perhaps, to Teresa Guiccioli (Berlioz had seen her, with her long golden hair and sad face, at one of Vernet's soirées): "Yes, beloved — a poet — free — rich — he was all those things, while I . . .", and in the silence of the confessional he grinds his teeth "till the damned must have heard it and trembled". He envies the undemanding ignorance of the peasant whom he watches going up to the statue of St Peter and kissing its big toe: "You believe, you have hope. The statue you adore was formerly Jupiter Tonans; its right hand held thunderbolts, not the keys of paradise. You don't know this and are not disillusioned. What will you be looking for when you go out of here? A patch of shade to sleep in. The wayside shrines are yours, you will find it there. What are your dreams of wealth? The handful of piastres necessary to buy a donkey or get married; three years' savings will achieve it. What is a wife for you? Someone of a different sex. What do you look for in art? A means of giving tangible form to the objects of your worship, making you laugh or providing something to dance to. For you, painting means the Virgin coloured in red and green, drama means puppets and Punch and Judy, music means the bagpipe and the tambourine — but for me hatred and despair, since I lack everything I seek and have given up hope of finding it."

In Rome his thoughts luxuriate in the macabre and the apocalyptic. After a ball at the French ambassador's he imagines an enormous meteorite falling on the embassy and crushing the place and everyone in it. In the same lurid vein he develops the scenario of "The World on the Last Day", the oratorio conceived in Florence which is to depict mankind in the final stages of corruption, surprised in the midst of a blasphemous orgy by the trumpets of the Last Judgment.

In all this it is not hard to see a liberal dash of attitudinising, of willed and wilful resentment. (Actually, reading between the lines you have the impression that he was on much friendlier terms with his fellow-pensionnaires than he likes to make out; his sense of otherness leads him to exaggerate his unsociability.) When Ernest Legouvé arrived at the Villa Medici, not long after Berlioz had returned to France, he heard him talked of as "a witty and intelligent man, but queer and taking pleasure in being so"; he had the reputation of a poseur.[*]

Boschot, imagining what fun it would have been to be a pensionnaire at the French Academy under a blessedly unceremonious character like Horace Vernet, thought that "one would have to be indeed dedicated to gloom ['ténébreux']" to see in that "delightful Abbaye de Thélème an 'academic barracks'!"

For Berlioz, however, it could not be fun: not because he was determined to be "ténébreux" but because Rome denied him the necessities of his existence. "I count the days I still have to spend in this idiotic barracks," he writes to his mother not long before leaving. "I shall be delighted to see Rome again, for its sublime plains and enchanting mountains; but then I shall be free, and now I am not; then, enforced absence will not make me ill for lack of music, on the contrary I shall have come here to refresh myself, as in a beautiful garden, and will appreciate it much more." In the present circumstances he was simply not in a position to appreciate it.

Not that he was untouched by the physical beauty of Rome and the power of its associations. The Colosseum stirred him profoundly. So did St Peter's. The setting of the Villa Medici — Rome spread out below it on one side, its own superb grounds on the other — was "truly regal"; the garden above all was a continual source of pleasure, with its noble ilexes and ancient-scented box hedges and its shady alleys culminating in bursts of sunlit sculpture. But none of this could compensate for the nourishment he craved. The modern city was a rather run-down provincial town, sparsely inhabited, culturally impoverished, living without much conviction on its past greatness, and crawling with priests. It had almost nothing directly to offer a musician. Being there against his will could only seem an incarceration. Rome cut him off not only from active pursuit of his career just at the point where he had begun to achieve a break-through, but from the "jouissances musicales" he had come to depend on. Rome made him "ill for lack of music" — the musical life that he was accustomed to in Paris and that was going on there during his enforced absence: the first performances in France of Beethoven's Ninth Symphony (the work he had recognised from his reading of the score to be the beginning of a new era), Paganini's recitals, and the advent — in Meyerbeer's *Robert le diable* — of a novel kind of opera, said to combine lyric drama, modern staging and scenic effects and the post-Beethovenian orchestra into a grand synthesis of the arts which heralded the end of the

---

[*] Not, however, with Mme Vernet and her daughter Louise, both of whom defended him staunchly — and Legouvé adds, "women are more perspicacious at divining exceptional men than men are". Later, on getting to know him, Legouvé found him anything but a poseur: "to pose is to calculate, to be master of oneself" — whereas Berlioz "lived at the mercy of himself and was the slave of his impressions".

hegemony of the Italian school. His place was there, sharing in all that activity. Instead, he was exiled from it. It is hardly remarkable that the Academy should be for Berlioz the symbol and focus of his frustrations — the more so as the reason for being there, his engagement to Camille, no longer applied.

The lack of music in the sense in which he understood it was made more frustrating still by the parody that passed for it most of the time in Rome. The Corpus Christi procession of 2 June 1831 was only the first of a series of experiences that caused his already low opinion of Italian culture to sink to new depths. From what the Florentine monks had said, he had been led to expect something splendid on the visual side at least, a modern equivalent of the Panathenea of the Greeks; but "never had he seen anything so squalid, so cheap, so devoid of dignity". It was the most abject procession imaginable: pitiful soldiers who wore their shakos and carried their rifles like raw recruits, standard-bearers in down-at-heel shoes covered with mud and stockings with holes next to cardinals dripping with gold, rascally little abbés joking loudly among themselves when they were not simpering up at the ladies on their balconies. As for the music, the monks' "enormous chorus" resolved itself into a handful of out-of-tune castrati, sounding like an ensemble of rusty gate-hinges, while the band with its croaking clarinets and circus trumpets and bass-drum would have been apter to Silenus and his satyrs than to statues of the Blessed Virgin; it reminded him of the din set up by the band outside the Lottery Office in the Rue St Honoré when a big win is announced. "That is how religious festivals are regarded in the capital of the Christian world, the city we are sent to 'to admire the masterpieces of the art of music'. [...] How much better it is, the Corpus Christi procession, in France. I could never watch it even at La Côte without being moved — and here I felt only disgust."

Secular music, he soon discovers, is just as bad. In the salons you are lucky if you hear any Rossini: it is mostly music by the imitators of his imitators. The opera choruses are worse even than the Opéra-Comique in Paris (a byword for rottenness) and the orchestras are in the last stages of feebleness and incompetence. The only theatres worth fre-quenting are the antique theatres at Pompeii, San Germano, Tusculum, among whose ruins the wind makes a sweeter music than anything heard at the Fondo or the Pergola.

If we think Berlioz is exaggerating we should read the comments on Italian artistic life in the letters Mendelssohn was writing to his family in exactly the same period. He expresses himself in more sober and temperate fashion, but the observations are identical.

> The Papal singers [...] are almost all unmusical and do not execute even the most familiar pieces in tune [...] Any performance [of my compositions] is quite out of the question. The orchestras are worse than one can believe

[...] The two or three violinists play in quite different styles and come in when they please; the wind instruments are tuned either too high or too low; and they execute flourishes in the subordinate parts like those we are accustomed to hearing in the streets, but hardly so good. In short, the whole thing forms an absolute caterwauling, and this applies even to compositions with which they are familiar [...] Everyone seems so indifferent that there is not the slightest prospect [of improvement]. I heard a flute solo in which the flute was more than a quarter of a tone sharp; it set my teeth on edge, but no one noticed, and when it ended with a trill they applauded automatically. If the singing were even a shade better! [...] Just as a *cicisbeo* will for ever be odious and repulsive to my feelings, so also will Italian music [...] Recently, at the Philharmonic [in Rome], after the music of Pacini and Bellini, when the Cavaliere Ricci begged me to accompany him in "Non più andrai" [Figaro's aria from Act 1 of Mozart's opera], the very first notes were so utterly different and so infinitely remote from all that had gone before that the whole thing became crystal clear to me [...]

I long to hear an orchestra or a full chorus where there is at least some sound; here there is nothing of the sort. This is our domain, and to be so long deprived of such an element leaves a sad void. The orchestra and chorus here [Naples] are like those in our second-rate provincial towns, only more ragged and incorrect. The first violinist, all through the opera, beats the four quarters of each bar on a tin candlestick, which is often more distinctly heard than the voices [...] and yet in spite of this the instruments and voices are never together [...] The days when every Italian was a born musician, if indeed they ever existed, are long gone by [...] It is no worse with regard to music, however [...] than with their attitude to every other branch of art. For when some of Raphael's *loggie* are wantonly and barbarically defaced by pencilled scrawls, when the lower part of the arabesques is totally destroyed by Italians with knives and heaven knows what else besides, inscribing their wretched names there [...] and when cattle are driven through the splendid salons of the Villa Madama, the walls of which were painted by Giulio Romano, and fodder stored in them – all this is certainly much worse than a bad orchestra, and painters must be even more distressed by such things than I am by their music. The fact is that the people are mentally enervated and apathetic. They have a religion which they do not believe in, a Pope and a government which they ridicule, and a brilliant and heroic past which they ignore. It is thus no marvel that they do not delight in Art, for they are indifferent to all that is serious [...] Why should Italy still insist on being the Land of Art, when it is in reality the Land of Nature, delighting every heart! [...] Nature, and the genial December air, and the outlines of the Alban hills, stretching as far as the sea, all remain unchanged. There they can scribble no names and compose no inscriptions. These every individual can enjoy in all their freshness, and to these I cling.

This is in exactly the same spirit as the cry that ends Berlioz's pæan, in *Voyage musical*, to the beauties of the Italian landscape: "Oh great, strong, wild Italy, heedless of your sister, the Italy of Art, 'the lovely Juliet stretched upon her bier'!"

So deadening did Berlioz find the atmosphere of Rome that he felt devoid of creative ideas and virtually unable to compose. The sole work of real importance that he did there — towards the end of his time at the Villa Medici, with the early prospect of escape — was the rewriting of the slow movement of the Fantastic Symphony. The work on *Lélio* which occupied him on his return to Rome from Nice was largely concerned with revising and editing.* *Quartetto e coro dei Maggi*, the short Christmas piece dating from early 1832, is pleasant but of no great consequence (and may in any case be related to the *Marche des Mages* of 1828). The two most important new pieces of this period, the *King Lear* overture and the song *La captive*, were both written while Berlioz was away from Rome — the one in Nice and the other in Subiaco. As for the *Rob Roy* overture, begun in Nice and completed in the mountains, it can hardly count as one of his Roman compositions, though it is significant that Berlioz included it among them in the list given in *Voyage musical* and the *Memoirs* — as though to say, it was bad enough to have been written in Rome.† The theme for the refrain of *Le cinq mai* (a setting of Béranger's poem on the death of Napoleon, begun in Paris a year or two earlier) came to him in Rome one day as he was scrambling out of the Tiber, having fallen in when the ground gave way while he was walking on the edge of an escarpment of the Pincian Hill; but he made no further headway with the work, and it was not completed till 1835. Only with *Méditation religieuse*, a setting of Moore ("This world is all a fleeting show") for chorus and wind instruments written "one day when the spleen was killing me", does he succeed in turning the ennui of Rome to positive account and, in the melancholy downward curve of the phrases and the haunting alternation of major and minor sixth, make music out of his desolation.

Deprived of active enjoyment of his art, which alone could "satisfy my immense appetite for emotion", he found himself increasingly prey to fits of spleen whose intensity recalled his first experience of the disease, when as a boy of sixteen, listening to the plaintive Rogation chant fade slowly out of earshot, he had been overwhelmed by a terrifying feeling of total isolation. Although certain pieces of music could bring on an attack, in general it was music, the music of the "great free spirits" and his own, that kept it at bay. Music and love: for a contributory cause of the

---

* Only the "Chant de bonheur", an insubstantial fantasy on the main melody from *La mort d'Orphée*, is unquestionably new. It came to him as he lay on the flat top of one of the broad box-hedges in the Academy garden on a day of sirocco and, it must be said, sounds rather like that.

† *Roy Roy*, as Berlioz recognised after its one and only performance (1833), is long-winded and diffuse, though containing the germ of the later *Harold in Italy*. He destroyed the score, and the work survives in the scribal copy which he submitted to the Académie des Beaux-Arts, together with the *Quartetto*, as his envoi from Rome for the year 1832.

frequency of the attacks he suffered in Rome must have been the emotional void left by the ending of his affair with Camille Moke. As Tiersot points out, the "mal d'isolement", the spleen, returned in full force precisely then, in the period of his greatest "inaction sentimentale", after several years of intense romantic involvement, first with the remote but starry Miss Smithson, then with Camille.

The virulence of the disease is a dominant motif of his life in Rome, far-reaching in its effect. It intensifies in him the sense of otherness and the conviction of the inescapable solitariness of the artist's calling. Exile from music and society becomes symbol of a deeper isolation. These months in Italy make of him, in a sense, a permanent exile.

When the fit fell he had only one remedy: to leave Rome and strike into the wide-open countryside, to do what he had learned to love as a boy and walk thirty miles a day or more, driving his body to the limit, to forget what artistic Italy could not provide and take the other, "wild Italy", to his heart. When he could afford to he shook off the dust of the Academy and made for the mountains, two or three days on foot to the east. When he could not he explored the country nearer at hand: Castelgondolfo, Frascati, the Alban Hills, Cicero's villa at Tusculum, Tivoli, the wandering Anio, river beloved of Horace which the ancients called Aniene, and the inexhaustible Campagna.

Such experiences did much more than alleviate, for a while, his stifling ennui: they gave his nervous system respite, freed him from the shocks and sustained tensions of his Paris existence. His doctor had warned against sending someone in his overstrung state to Rome and he had tried hard to get out of going. In fact it was what he needed − a prolonged holiday, a time of fruitful idleness. For the first time since he had come to Paris ten years before, he was at liberty to do nothing, simply to collect himself and absorb.

In this respect, for all its frustrations the year in Italy was a blessing for Berlioz, and a blessing only partly in disguise, as he acknowledged in the articles he wrote immediately after his return to France. Their emphasis is different from that of the account in *Voyage musical* and the *Memoirs*; they are more explicit about the benefits of the experience. Strictly speaking it may be an absurdity to send young composers to Rome to study music; but " 'one is none the less a man for being a musician', and I do not regret the two years I lost there".* Though the musical life is the equivalent of the wasted, spectre-thin dancers one sees in sea-ports, wriggling their hips at the sailors for a few sous, "it is in this regard alone that I find the Italian journey a nonsense for a musician. In every other it is bound to have a powerful influence on lively and poetic imaginations."

---

* Berlioz was away from Paris for the best part of two years, but spent just under fifteen months in Italy. The quotation adopts Tartufe's line in Molière's play: "Ah! pour être dévot je n'en suis pas moins homme."

Its influence on Berlioz was profound and permanent. His Italian journey is second only to his childhood and adolescence in the richness of remembered suggestion it stored within him. Out of its sensual and imaginative impressions comes the atmosphere of half a dozen major works. Some of them, planted earlier, ripen in the warm south. We see *The Trojans'* "shadow ere itself", like Thisbe's lion in Jessica's "In such a night"; the work conceived in the young Hector's encounter with Virgil is a felt presence throughout these months, called to prophetic life by the Virgilian associations of the land he walks over and the sea he looks down on from the coastal hills. *Romeo and Juliet* begins to take shape and colour "under the starlit Italian sky" (as the contralto sings in the introduction to the work) in that heat-saturated air pierced by the sweetness of the nightingale's song. And though the relating of a composer's music to his life is a chancy business, it is plausible to regard Italy both directly and indirectly — the positive effect of its harmonious landscapes, the holiday from the Parisian vortex — as a factor in the fuller resonance and greater roundness of sonority, as well as in the conscious preoccupation with beauty of sound, that begin to mark his orchestral writing from now on. (Only compare the Fantastic Symphony of 1830 with *Romeo and Juliet* of 1839.)

Again, while the sense of space and luminous landscape evoked by the slow movement of the Fantastic Symphony may or may not be the consequence of his Italian experiences (the original version not having survived, we cannot tell what is new in the revision drafted in Rome), the presence of comparable qualities in *Harold in Italy* is surely attributable to them. So, of course, are the elements of Italian folk-music in *Harold* and *Benvenuto Cellini* and the scenes of Italian popular life commemorated in both works.

Even the negative aspects of those experiences contribute, by reaction, to the genesis of certain works. The Berliozian concept of monumental church music as the "soul" of the building it is performed in, which finds expression in the Grande Messe des Morts and the Te Deum — a concept, inherited from the composers of the French Revolution and, beyond, from the early Italian baroque, in which space and mass are an integral part of the composition and the music is designed and executed on a scale commensurate with its surroundings — receives fresh impetus from the discovery that the majestic interior of St Peter's is served by a small organ on wheels and a choir of eighteen voices augmented to thirty-two on special occasions. Similarly, against the decadence and lassitude of modern Rome *Benvenuto Cellini* places the imagined vitality of its Renaissance counterpart; the vivacity and complexity of rhythm, the variety and vividness of colour and the lyrical breadth of melodic style all aspire to re-create an ideal Italy where Art is once again the equal of Nature. Twenty-five years later, though cast in a much smaller mould, *Beatrice and Benedict* celebrates the same vision.

It is hardly an exaggeration to say that by the time Berlioz crossed the Alps into France at the end of May 1832 the work of the remaining thirty years of his career lay mapped out before him. As Boschot remarks succinctly in his summing up of the Italian journey, "very few immediate results, but a most fertile inner working."

30

"To feel that we exist . . ."

———————◄◆►———————

The trip to Nice cost Berlioz 1,050 francs — an inconveniently large slice of his allowance. For the moment he was stuck in Rome, and he settled back into the routine of life at the Academy which he had become familiar with in March. His fellow-inmates, who had given him a hearty welcome on his return, tactfully refrained from alluding to the reason for his departure (though everyone knew about it). But he was conscious of being watched, and talked about behind his back. "So as not to appear what they call 'affected' I have to school myself in their way of looking at things and speaking, enjoy what they consider fun, and not show enthusiasm for anything they don't know about." In time he discovered that some of them were not such philistines after all, and he made friends with several of the architects and painters among the inhabitants of the Villa and among the "lower orders", as they called the French artists in Rome who were not part of the Academy, whom they saw at the Café Greco down the hill; but in his current mood the atmosphere of institutionalised good humour grated and oppressed, after the freedom of Nice and the open road, and he felt ill at ease.

Life at the Villa Medici could not have been more undemanding. There were no obligations beyond sending back a sample of your work to the Institute at the end of the year, and no irksome restrictions except those imposed by shortage of cash. You could come and go virtually as you pleased, work undisturbed or not work, browse in the library which, though devoid of modern literature, had quite a good collection of standard classics, and go into meals in whatever you were wearing when the bell rang (a servant went round the palace and the gardens ringing it before lunch and dinner). For recreation there was tennis or quoits, or pistol-shooting, or playing with the director's puppies and training them to be gun-dogs; there was plenty of game to shoot in the Campagna, and there was riding. On Sundays there was usually an expedition to one of the sites of interest near Rome — San Lorenzo Fuori-le-Mure, the Villa Pamphili with its splendid garden designed like the Villa Medici's by Le Nôtre, or Ponte Molle, where one drank the syrupy, medicinal Orvieto wine, or the magnificent tomb of Cecilia Metella on the Appian Way, whose famous echo was a source of endless amusement. On Thursday evenings the Vernets held open house in their sumptuous apartments; the students were invited as well as the élite of Roman society (including representatives of the many foreigners, the English prominent among them, who came each year to Rome). There was no compulsion to go, but the whole family was so easy and welcoming that it was no hardship. Horace Vernet was in firm control of the Academy but rode his charges on the lightest of reins. He behaved more like their boon companion than their director. Vernet was a child of the Napoleonic era, with its ethos of freedom from irrelevant restrictions and careers open to talent. At the age of twenty he had given up his chance of the Prix de Rome in order to get married but had made his mark as an artist without it, had been personally decorated by Napoleon, had fought for the Emperor's return, alongside Géricault, on the barricades in 1814, and was now one of the most sought-after painters of the day. With all his nonchalance and carefree gaiety and his love of dancing and dressing up, "M. Horace" was a model of industry, delighting in the exercise of his craft and working with extraordinary zest and facility, though needing the stimulus of company and noise to do so: his studio, a pavilion set among the alleys and shrubberies of the garden, was always in cheerful uproar, with resident monkey and parrots, several dogs, and a constant stream of visitors.*

It was as well for Berlioz that he had so liberal and unselfimportant a man to deal with; a more conventional, disciplinarian director would not have taken his Nice escapade so lightly. His appraising sketch of Vernet, in a letter to Nancy written in Nice, says as much: "a short, lean man with an elegant figure, urbane but warm-hearted; an attentive son, loves his daughter like a brother and his wife like an uncle; makes twenty thousand francs in a week; a swordsman and a pistol-shot in the Saint-Georges class; plays the drum and dances the tarantella with his daughter with a verve that brings the house down; tough, spare, friendly, outspoken; likes Gluck and Mozart, detests the Academy; a great deal of good in him."

Berlioz soon decided that unlike his father, Carle Vernet, whose love of Gluck was unfeigned and deep, "M. Horace" did not really have much feeling for music, though he claimed to be mad about it. ("I notice that those who talk about their great love of music are precisely those with the least sense of it.") He was simply "the happiest man you have ever seen. At forty-two he still has the tastes of someone of eighteen. The other day

---

* As you approached, wrote Mendelssohn, who sat for his portrait in the spring of 1831, an amazing din issued from it: dogs barking, voices raised in argument, someone playing the trumpet; and inside, "the most picturesque disorder: guns, a hunting horn, a monkey, palettes everywhere, a brace of dead hares, the walls thick with finished and unfinished paintings". During his first sitting more than twenty people dropped in, while Vernet "rushed at the canvas like a hungry man at a plate of food".

he carried off the honours at a masked ball at the Princess Volkonsky's. His daughter was in Neapolitan costume and he in the uniform of a captain of Hussars, they danced the Tarantella and the Mazurka together with staggering success [...] This evening it's his birthday party and there's to be a great ball; old Carle Vernet will come looking for me again to talk of Gluck. He's so pleased I'm not like my predecessor, who said it was 'all mere rococo'! He's a curious man, who spends half the day on horseback (he doesn't paint any more) and the rest of the time making puns and fretting about the health of his son, whom he loves as old men rarely love. Anyway, it will while away the evening, with the aid of half a dozen cups of tea, always supposing Mlle Horace [Louise Vernet] doesn't regale us with some fashionable air."

As before, it was to Mendelssohn that he owed most of the rewarding moments of these first few weeks after his return to Rome. Mendelssohn, who had been on a trip to Naples, reappeared on 6 June, a few days after Berlioz arrived back from Nice, and remained in Rome till the 19th. Berlioz took to spending part of the morning in his sunny room overlooking the Piazza di Spagna. When the spleen was bad he would lie on his friend's sofa listening to him play music by composers they both admired, or singing, while Mendelssohn accompanied, the exquisite G-minor aria from the third act of Gluck's *Iphigénie en Tauride* — after which Mendelssohn would exclaim that he could hear it all day and never grow tired of it. He played through, from the manuscript score, his just-completed *Hebrides* overture, which became for Berlioz a favourite work.[*]

Despite the many admirations they had in common, however, theirs was not an easy relationship. Looking back on it twelve years later Berlioz remarks that Mendelssohn was "as prickly as a porcupine when the talk was of music; you never knew where to take hold of him without getting hurt". (He adds that "on any other subject — being very good-natured and of a sweet and charming disposition — he never minded being contradicted, and I on my side used to impose on his forbearance during the religious and philosophical arguments we sometimes engaged in".) The truth is that it could hardly have been otherwise between them. Mendelssohn found Berlioz deeply disconcerting; he was nonplussed that a man who wrote such awful music should yet reveal such an acute feeling for the art and express such sensible and discerning opinions on so many important musical topics.

The comments on Berlioz contained in Mendelssohn's letters to his family show him veering between recognising his undoubted qualities as a musician and patronising this curious Frenchman who presumes to regard himself as his equal. At one moment he complains of his "merely

---

[*] See the "critique admirative" he devoted to it in the *Revue et gazette musicale* of 27 February 1842 on the occasion of its first performance by the Société des Concerts.

external enthusiasm", "his originality in italics", his "groping in the dark without a spark of talent while fancying himself the creator of a new world, writing the most frightful things yet dreaming of nothing but Beethoven, Schiller and Goethe", so that Mendelssohn feels he "would like to throttle him — until he chances to eulogise Gluck, and then I quite agree with him"; and he concludes that "were he not a Frenchman (and it is always pleasant to associate with them, as they have invariably something interesting to say) it would be beyond endurance". Another time, without any less vehemently dismissing his music, he writes more in sorrow than in anger, for Berlioz "makes me sad, because he is really a cultured, agreeable man, and yet composes so badly". Mendelssohn, who has been looking at the score of the Fantastic Symphony, then gives a résumé of its programme, and continues:

> How utterly loathsome all this is to me I don't have to tell you. To see one's most cherished ideas debased and expressed in perverted caricatures would enrage anyone. And yet this is only the programme. The execution is still more miserable: nowhere a spark, no warmth, utter foolishness, contrived passion represented through every possible exaggerated orchestral means: four timpani, two pianos for four hands, which are supposed to imitate bells, two harps, many big drums, violins divided into eight parts, two parts for the double basses which play solo passages, and all these means (to which I would not object if they were properly employed) used to express nothing but indifferent drivel, mere grunting, shouting, screaming back and forth. And when you see the composer himself, that friendly, quiet, thoughtful person, calmly and confidently going his way, never for a moment in doubt of his vocation, unable to listen to any outside voice since he wishes to follow only his inner inspiration, when you see how keenly and correctly he evaluates and recognises everything, yet is in utter darkness about himself — it is unspeakably dreadful, and I cannot tell you how deeply the sight of him depresses me. I have not been able to work for two days.

As with Zelter's explosion of anger at the *Eight Scenes from Faust*, there may be more here than meets the eye — an alarmed half-awareness of a musical style and personality not dreamed of in Mendelssohn's philosophy. To a genius of his character and upbringing the Fantastic Symphony was necessarily incomprehensible; it was simply too heterodox to be borne. He seems never to have wavered in his adverse view of Berlioz's music. Schumann, Liszt, Wagner, Verdi would all take it seriously and be responsive to its power; alone among Berlioz's peers, Mendelssohn continued to regard it as "drivel".

Fortunately he concealed his true opinion, merely admitting that "he could not understand it", and often asking him to hum one of his Moore songs, which he said he liked, and of which Berlioz presented him with his last remaining spare copy. (In 1843, when the two men met again in Leipzig, Mendelssohn would find it possible to praise a double-bass entry in another Berlioz song, "Absence" — rather in the spirit in which he complimented Wagner, after a performance of *Tannhäuser*, on a canonic passage in the finale of the second act.) But Berlioz sensed a constraint, finding Mendelssohn, as he told Hiller, "a little cold in his dealings" with him, and feeling nettled by the condescending manner he sometimes fell into.[*] His admiration for Mendelssohn's genius did not make him any less confident of his own worth. He might not greatly object to Mendelssohn's telling him, at their first meeting, that the opening aria in *Sardanapale* (which Montfort played him) was "frankly pretty awful", since he felt the same about it himself. But when next day his new friend raised an eyebrow at his praise of Gluck and exclaimed "Oh — you like Gluck?", as though what he really meant was, "How can a musician of your sort possibly have the loftiness of ideas and the feeling for grandeur of style and truth of expression required to like Gluck?", it stung. Berlioz nurtured the slight and took his revenge soon afterwards, placing a manuscript copy, with the composer's name omitted, of a beautiful but little known piece by Gluck (Asteria's "Ah 'ho presente ognor" from *Telemaco*) on Montfort's piano one day when Mendelssohn was due to call. Mendelssohn sat down at once and, assuming it to be Bellini, gave it an extravagant reading in the manner of Rubini singing at the Théâtre-Italien. Berlioz had the satisfaction of interrupting him with, "Oh, don't you like Gluck, then?".

Mendelssohn on his side was annoyed by Berlioz's prejudice against Bach (whose St Matthew Passion he had been instrumental in rescuing, two years before, from its century-long neglect); it was too silly and ignorant to bother about, but it offended against an article of faith as deep as the Lutheran piety which Berlioz sometimes shocked by his irreverent attitude towards the Bible. Whenever Mendelssohn spoke of Bach he would add, ironically, "your pupil". They also argued about the usefulness of the metronome, which Berlioz considered indispensable — as did Verdi and Tchaikovsky (and as have most twentieth-century composers) — but which Mendelssohn, like Wagner, Brahms, Bruckner, Mahler and the German Romantics generally (though not Schumann or Spohr), was only too happy to dispense with. On Berlioz's referring to it Mendelssohn squashed him by asking what possible point there could be in so futile a device: "Any musician who cannot tell the tempo of a piece of music by looking at it is a duffer." Berlioz thought there were more than enough duffers in the musical world to justify its use. He didn't say so; but he quoted Mendelssohn's words back at him one day when his friend, glancing at the score of the uncompleted *Rob Roy* overture preparatory to playing it through on the piano, asked him for the tempo. (Mendelssohn of course might have retorted that he didn't regard it as music.)

---

[*] In a letter to Hiller the following year he confesses to having "mixed feelings" about Mendelssohn.

Above: *The Roman Campagna, with the Claudian aqueduct, 1826—28, by Corot.*
Below: *View of Rome from Castelgondolfo, 1830, by J.D. Harding.*

From a letter dated "Roma, 4 or 5 March 1832" to Albert Du Boys. Berlioz describes the delights of his vagabond existence in the hills of Italy, and what it meant for him.

Berlioz in the early 1830s. The drawing is thought to be by Ingres.

GRANDE SALLE DU CONSERVATOIRE DE MUSIQUE.

Dimanche 9 Décembre 1832, à une heure précise,

GRAND

CONCERT DRAMATIQUE,

Donné par M. Hector Berlioz.

PROGRAMME.

ÉPISODE DE LA VIE D'UN ARTISTE,
Symphonie fantastique, en cinq parties (1),
de M. *H. Berlioz.*

1re. *RÊVERIES. — PASSIONS.*

2me. *UN BAL.*

3me. *SCÈNE AUX CHAMPS.*

4me. *MARCHE DU SUPPLICE.*

5me. { *SONGE D'UNE NUIT DU SABBAT.*
Messe funèbre burlesque.
Ronde du Sabbat.
Dies iræ et ronde du Sabbat réunis.

(1) Un programme détaillé de la Symphonie sera distribué dans la salle.

LE RETOUR A LA VIE.
MÉLOLOGUE, (mélange de musique et de discours) EN SIX PARTIES, faisant suite à la Symphonie fantastique; paroles et musique de M. *H. Berlioz.*
Le rôle parlé de l'artiste sera lu par M. BOCCAGE.

1re. { MONOLOGUE DE L'ARTISTE.
LE PÊCHEUR, Ballade imitée de *Goëthe*, chantée, avec Piano seul, par M. A. DUPONT.

2me. { MONOLOGUE DE L'ARTISTE.
CHOEUR D'OMBRES (avec Orchestre).

3me. { MONOLOGUE DE L'ARTISTE.
SCÈNE DE LA VIE DE BRIGAND. Chant, Chœur et Orchestre; le capitaine, chanté par M. HÉBERT.

4me. { MONOLOGUE DE L'ARTISTE.
CHANT DE BONHEUR (avec Orchestre et Harpe), chanté par M. A. DUPONT.

5me. { MONOLOGUE DE L'ARTISTE.
LES DERNIERS SOUPIRS DE LA HARPE. Souvenirs (Orchestre seul).

6me. { MONOLOGUE DE L'ARTISTE.
FANTAISIE SUR LA TEMPÊTE, (Drame de *Shakespeare*) pour Chœur et Orchestre.

L'Orchestre, composé de plus de **100** MUSICIENS, sera dirigé par
M. HABENECK.

Le Piano sera tenu par M. **FESSY.**

PRIX DES PLACES : Balcon, Stalles et Premières, 6 fr. —Secondes et Rez-de-Chaussée, 5 fr.—
Parterre, 3 fr. — Amphithéâtre, 2 fr.

On trouve des Billets chez M. Réty, *au Conservatoire*; M. Schlesinger, *rue le Richelieu, no.* 97;
M. Pleyel, *boulevart Montmartre*; MM. Lemoine, *rue de l'Échelle*; M. Messounier, *rue Dauphine*; M. Frey, *place des Victoires.*

LA SALLE SERA ÉCLAIRÉE.

VINCHON, fils et successeur de Mme. Ve. BALLARD
Imprimeur, rue J.-J.-Rousseau, No. 8.

Leaflet for the concert given on 9 December 1832 in the Conservatoire Hall, at which the complete "Episode in an Artist's Life" — the Fantastic Symphony and The Return to Life *— was performed for the first time.*

Yet with all their differences, each found amusement and stimulus in the other's company. They explored the ruins together, visited Tasso's tomb at Sant'Onofrio, and went on riding excursions in the Campagna (during one of which Berlioz, still meditating a large-scale symphonic work on *Romeo and Juliet*, said he thought it surprising that no one had written a scherzo on Mercutio's Queen Mab speech — and then, until he had written his own, lived in fear of hearing that Mendelssohn had done so). Mendelssohn was a frequent visitor at the Villa Medici, and Berlioz often dropped in at his lodgings in the Piazza di Spagna. It was a keen disappointment to him to discover, on getting back from an expedition to Tivoli on 19 June, that Mendelssohn had left Rome that morning. They would not meet again for another twelve years.

The expedition to Tivoli, fifteen miles across the Campagna, was Berlioz's first sortie into the hilly country east of Rome which became his spiritual home. He and the sculptor Antoine Etex (one of the "lower orders", an unsuccessful candidate for the Prix de Rome, later celebrated for his bas-reliefs on the Arc de Triomphe) set out at 2 in the afternoon across the dusty plain and covered a dozen miles before the heat overcame them and a passing carriage gave them a lift for the last few miles. In Tivoli they ordered dinner at the Albergo della Sibylla and then strolled by the lake. The sight of the clear water was so tempting (Etex recalled) that they went in for a swim, singing the lakeside duet "O Mathilde, idole de mon âme" from *William Tell*; but "it was so icy that in an instant we turned blue, out teeth chattered and we had had enough; without a word we made for the shore. We were more than happy to eat our dinner by a blazing brushwood fire lit for us in the fireplace of the room where they served our meal. An hour later we were fast asleep." Next morning they got up at dawn and saw the sights. "I've never seen anything so ravishingly beautiful," wrote Berlioz to his family.

The waterfalls, the clouds of spray fine as powder, the smoking whirlpools, the fresh cool river, the caves, the innumerable rainbows, the olive-groves, the mountains, the country houses, the village, it's all novel and enchanting. The people are strikingly handsome, but even more beggarly than in Rome. Only their begging does not have the unpleasant degraded character of the Romans. As they beg so openly, it becomes rather droll. They indicate to us the sum they want, and laugh as if it was a joke. Some young men and women of twenty or thirty, who were at work on the harvest, saw us passing and called out: "Hey, sirs, give us half a *paolo* (five sous), give us a *baioco* (a sou), what's it to you?"

I also saw Hadrian's villa. Its superb ruins filled me with such thoughts and sensations, they seemed to be determined to compensate for the non-impression all those of Rome made on me. Imagine a country house three or four miles in circumference, within which the Emperor Hadrian realised the stuff of dreams. Just inside there was a Greek theatre; all that remains of it are two columns and a few amphitheatre arcades, the middle is a patch of cabbages. But, to do the owner justice, it's the only part that is cultivated: all the rest is in the most splendid state of abandonment. The imperial palace, the baths, the library, the rest-houses, the courtyards are quite well preserved for ruins. In the emperor's guardrooms sparrow-hawks and kites build their nests. The "Vale of Tempe" (imitated from the one in Greece) is today a forest of reeds; I didn't see Tartarus nor the Elysian Fields nor many other things whose names I forget, there's so much it's bewildering; walls six feet thick of extraordinary height, covered in stucco, painted with frescoes; towers; vaults; columns everywhere; no statues, because some pope, I don't know which, had them removed to make into lime. On entering the place I found myself for the first time in the presence of the greatness of Rome: I was aghast, overwhelmed. If only I had been on my own! But it can wait. It's only half an hour from Tivoli, and when I'm settled here I shall let myself spend the day there from time to time.

Back in Rome he hastened to finish the Mélologue. When it was done he would decamp. Luckily nearly all the necessary work was complete, on paper or in his head, before he returned from Nice, for in Rome "I have no ideas, no sensations; ennui has set up its domain". There were a couple of movements to put in order. One of them, the sepulchral invocation to the spirits of the Pharaohs in *Cléopâtre*, was being altered to become a Chorus of Angry Shades, placed now in the context of a discussion of *Hamlet* and the "undiscovered country from whose bourne no traveller returns"; the solo vocal line was adapted for mixed chorus and given a new text in an "unknown tongue" (an idea taken from Swedenborg's "language of the damned"), and the orchestration augmented to balance the chorus: the wind parts enriched, bass-drum and tam-tam added, and the violins divided into four parts and given a more elaborate, spectral figuration.* That left only the Aeolian Harp, the orchestral epilogue to his *Orphée* cantata; he intended to put it in unchanged, but he had not brought the score with him to Italy — it was with the music he had deposited in the Conservatoire Library when he left Paris. Ferrand had a copy — Berlioz had had it made for him in 1828. Just before he left for the mountains he wrote to him, asking him to copy out the page in question and send it.

One evening at the Villa Medici near the end of June an almost forgotten pleasure lifted his spirits, so that he felt "some real emotion for the first time in this monastery of ours":

There were four or five of us, sitting in the moonlight round the little fountain above the steps that lead down to the garden. We drew lots for who

---

* Skilfully though it is done, the adaptation sacrifices something of the immediacy of the original.

should go and fetch my guitar; and as the audience was composed of the small number of inmates whom I can stand I needed no urging to sing. As I was beginning an aria from *Iphigénie en Tauride*, Carle Vernet appeared. Within a minute or two he started weeping, sobbing out loud, then, unable to bear any more, took refuge in his son's drawing-room, crying in a choking voice, "Horace, Horace! come here!" — "What is it, what is it?" — "We're all in tears." — "Why, why — what's happened?" — "It's M. Berlioz, he's singing us some Gluck. Yes (turning to me), as you say, sir, it makes you want to go on your knees. Believe me, I know you, you're a melancholic character, there are some people who . . . " He couldn't finish; and yet no one laughed. The fact is, we were all moved. I felt in the mood, it was night, there was nothing to inhibit me beneath that echoing portico, and I let myself go as if I had been on my own.

These ritual communings with his household gods became an occasional feature of Berlioz's life at the Academy. As he had done at the Opéra six or seven years before, he gathered round him a small band of fellow-worshippers. According to Legouvé he had an uncanny knack of suggesting the entire sound of an operatic score by the combination of guitar and a virtuoso technique of humming. The portico with the marble fountain — a cool corner of the Villa on hot nights — must have resounded to some weird and wonderful sounds as he took his acolytes through favourite numbers from *Freischütz*, *Oberon* and *Euryanthe* and sometimes whole acts of *Iphigénie*, *La Vestale* and *Don Giovanni*.

Soon after the first of these nocturnal music-makings the Berlioz guitar found another employment: playing for the peasants of the Abruzzi to dance to, and earning for its owner the local name of "the gentleman who plays the French guitar" — "questo signore chi suona la chitarra francese". On about the 3rd July he took the coach to Tivoli with luggage for a longish stay and a few possessions — modest enough, he told Mme Le Sueur, not to tempt any brigands he might run into: a cheap guitar, his double-barrelled gun, sketchbooks for making notes and a few books. By the 9th he was installed at Subiaco.

Letters to His Family

Tivoli, 8 July 1831

I'm here, by the great falls, writing to you in a little temple of Vesta, three quarters of which is preserved. It's next to the inn; there's a table in the middle, no doubt on the very spot where they used to maintain the sacred flame. It's right on the edge of the precipice down which the water plunges. I have just had some tea brought to me and my guitar. I am more distressed than I can say. On going this morning to Hadrian's Villa, which I told you about the other day, I asked some small boys I met for news of Antonio, a child of 14 who had acted as my guide the first time I came here — I had taken a great fancy to him and had attached myself to him immediately without quite knowing why. They told me he'd been very ill for the past ten days. When I got back from my tour of the ruins I was shown little Antonio's house. I climbed the stairs to a wretched dilapidated room; his mother and little sisters were round the bed. He was sleeping, pale and drawn yet still beautiful with that Raphael-like beauty that I have seen only in Italy. His mother told me he had gone fishing in the Anio and got his head wet and had sat in the sun, and since then had been in the condition I saw him in now. I went and fetched some money. When I returned he was awake. He recognised me but could not speak. I gave the mother what I could spare. She tried to get Antonio to make an effort to thank *lo signore francese*, but he could say nothing intelligible, I could understand only his great lustreless eyes turned towards me. The poor mother began to weep; she said she didn't know what to do, they had tried leeches on his head but he cried every time, she was desperate, yet she couldn't believe the Madonna wouldn't preserve her son for her. I told her he would be in bed for some time but for sure the Madonna would save him. I could not say another word, I was choking. I slipped away and climbed the hill behind Tivoli. Right at the top there is a rough wooden cross; I sat down at the foot of it. In the distance I could see the stupid city of Rome and, all around, the immense plain and the winding Anio, and the far-off lakes reflecting the sun. I stayed there a long time … It began to rain heavily. There was no shelter to be found except under some rock so I stayed out in it and picked some heather and wild myrtle (the first I have seen); I came back with my bunches of myrtle, I got changed, and tried to think of a little music by working myself up with my guitar, but am without ideas: my mind keeps returning to that poor woman with her "Madonna", and all the time I see before me poor Antonio who a few days ago was so merry and now is dying.

I'm writing to you this evening because tomorrow I have a seat booked for Subiaco, a little market town in the mountains another twenty-five miles on from Tivoli − I don't know how long I shall stay there and it's not certain a letter from there would reach you [. . .] Is Mama now recovered from the fatigues of the silk-worm crop? There are mulberry trees here that would make her deeply envious if she could see them. Papa must be very pleased with Alphonse [Robert]'s recent success [. . .] The other night I had a strange dream: three brigands had come into the dining-room at La Côte and were trying to drag my father away by force. I cried out, and Claude Ferlet [the blacksmith] rushed in. He felled one of them with his hammer and I severed the forearms of the other two with a large curved dagger. In fact I had handled an Arab dagger of M. Horace's not long before, which is why it came back into my mind. How bizarre! …

Our director has gone to France in the steamship *Sphinx*; he's taken his carriage with him on board, and reckons to spend only a fortnight on the journey: ten days there and back and five days' stay in Paris. That's what's known as a flying visit.

I wasn't able to take advantage of the invitation from the officers of the *Sphinx* that I told you of in my last letter;* my passport wouldn't allow me to

---

* The letter has not survived.

travel with them, nor was I tempted to go to Cività Vecchia on my own.

Farewell, night's coming on. "The shrine of Vesta's temple is profaned/The sacred flame is out,* and . . ." I can't see any more.

Subiaco, 10 July 1831

It's raining at last! I see clouds! Blessed be the sky of Subiaco and cursed the eternal blazing metallic sky of Rome where there is never either thunder or lightning. This is the most picturesque place I've seen in my life. It hasn't got Tivoli's waterfalls but there's a raging torrent almost as big as the Anio which cataracts down in two or three places with as loud a roar if not with the grandeur of the large falls at Tivoli.

And then there are the mountains — ah! I came back from them an hour ago. This morning I climbed a large eminence that the landscape-painters call the Whale, and which is just like an enormous whale coming up for air. At one in the afternoon I reached the summit and built a little pyramid out of bits of rock, with a flat stone at the top, like a druid altar. Oh how I breathed, how I gazed, how alive I felt. Not a cloud. I scrambled up with hands and feet for half an hour, then lay down on some tufts of box, lulled by a caressing breeze. Before reaching the high peaks I came upon a little deserted house; I crossed a garden full of vines and maize and, jumping over the boundary hedge, found myself in a delightful levelled meadow planted with olive trees. At once I thought of Mama, fifteen years ago, singing

> Oh for a cottage thatched above
> And all around an orchard's shade,
> And the springtime to spend on love,
> With my muse and my fair maid.

Higher up, at the point where the vegetation ends, I saw some peasants, reaping a little sparse corn. They seemed alarmed to see me climbing all alone and without apparent purpose (I'd left my gun in Subiaco). There's a superstition here about *jettatori* (people who cast spells), and I think they took me for one. They asked me in surly tones where I was going and what I proposed doing up there. Luckily I had an inspiration, and replied that I had made a vow to the Madonna and was on my way up to fulfil it. At that they stopped worrying and went back to their harvesting. From the top I saw below me the monastery of St Benedict where I had been the day before. The monastery reminded me of our old curé Durand who often used to tell us of St Benedict hiding under a thorn bush to escape the temptations of the Evil One. I've seen the cave where St Benedict fought with the devil. The chapel is constructed in such a way that the cave is just behind the altar. Beside it there's a little plantation of rose-bushes, and in one corner a pile of rose-leaves which the Benedictine monks give to sick people who see visions; the leaves make them go away. In the church the remains of two muskets have been hung up, as proof positive of two important miracles: some sportsmen who had overloaded their weapons called on St Benedict while they were going off, and were quite unharmed. These Benedictine

* *La Vestale.*

gentry are not like the Carthusians, they didn't offer me so much as a glass
of water, though I was in need of one. Subiaco is a dirty village, dedicated to
St André (second point of resemblance to La Côte) and built round a sugar-
loaf hill crowned with a fortress. At the bottom flows the roaring torrent,
which would make the fortune of another people but here serves only for
washing their rags in [. . .]

Where I am there are several French painters, come to Subiaco to copy
the beauties of nature. We dine together; one of them is a friend of mine
from the Academy. The other inn is full of Swedish, Irish and French
landscape painters; we've all got to know each other already.

Yesterday evening the children of the house danced the saltarello to the
sound of a tambourine played by a young girl, a neighbour of theirs. I went
and watched them. Then the eldest girl, who is 12, putting on a coaxing air,
said, "*Signore, oh! signore, pigliate la chitarra francese.*" I took the *chitarra francese*,
and the *ballo* started again fast and furious. Their lordships the painters
heard our *ballo* and came and joined in. All the little peasant girls were
beside themselves with delight and danced with the most charming abandon,
while their neighbour flourished her tambourine and I flayed my fingers
improvising saltarellos on the *chitarra francese*.

The whole place knows already that there's a *maestro dell'Academia di
Francia* here. I'm beginning to be got at, through my friend the painter who
is well-known in smart Subiaco society, to take part in the musical reunions
of the town. Yesterday, while we were having lunch, the choirmaster arrived
with one of the local swells to sound me, but Gibert (that's the name of my
academician) gave them to understand that I was a thoroughly unsociable
fellow and would be very difficult to tame, and they didn't venture to make
a direct approach. I trust they'll steer clear of me. There are some fine
women in the choir, but I've seen them on the promenade and it wouldn't
be sufficient to compensate for the ill their music would do me, and I'd be of
no use to them.

17 July

Oh how Nanci would adore this place, and how Adèle would shine at
climbing the hills! (I remember our expedition to St Eynard, Adèle thirty
yards ahead of us all the way.) Now that I'm busy working,[*] I defy ennui,
which sometimes plagues me so. We often have rain; and when it gets too
hot in Subiaco I can always go down to the torrent and find a bend
sheltered from the burning sun, where you can sleep on some hollowed-out
rock, not so much lulled as deafened by the din of the water. Yesterday the
landscape painters who are working by the torrent took me with them. I
brought my guitar (it will soon be like Mme de Genlis' famous harp, which
she lugged everywhere and never stopped talking about), and we sang to our
hearts' content "Sur les Alpes, ah! quel délice", and the great hunt from *Les*

---

[*] Presumably on his *Rob Roy* overture which was "completed and instrumented in the
mountains of Subiaco".

Bardes, and my ballad "Hélène", which they make me give them regularly twice a day, and *Orphée*, and lots of other things. It was lovely, though the noise of the torrent was a bit too close for hearing properly. The good M. Lesueur will hardly have imagined his music being admired in Subiaco. His "Bardic Hunt", which we sang as we trudged across the mountain, delighted our listeners; some little peasants who were following us showed their pleasure vividly by the way they moved in time to the music. I got a letter from him just as I was leaving Rome — I had written to him from Nice. M. Horace took him a second letter from me, in which I gave him details of my work.

Today is the great festival of the Madonna del Carmino; last night there were illuminations and the firing of mortars. Tomorrow we're going to the wedding of a young brigand called Crispino, who has not been in the mountains for three months, and who's invited us all. I made him a present of a silk neckerchief that I bought in Nice. He told me he would give it to his *ragazza* as it was too pretty for him. All night we hear him serenading his *ragazza*, who lives near us. Sometimes he sings to the bagpipe, sometimes to mandolin, guitar and triangle. The tune is a kind of loud, doleful cry, ten bars long at most, on which he improvises the words. There are many barbarous customs in this part of the country. The wives work like beasts of burden while the husbands rest. When they're going to kill one of their cattle, before taking it to the slaughter they chase it through the streets, pelting it with mud and sticks and stones, shoving it into the ditch and tormenting it in endless different ways, exactly like the Hurons when they sacrifice a prisoner. There is extreme poverty, and the greatest possible filth. Some of the women are of remarkable beauty — almost all of them blonde, which is very surprising in Italy. They think a colony of Saxons once settled in Subiaco and peopled it with fair-haired progeny. [. . .]

"In the mountains, ah! what bliss." Berlioz had enthused about "Sur les alpes, ah! quel délice" in his letter of 2 July to Mme Le Sueur, written just before he left Rome. "Is there an Italian musician anywhere who could have thought of this *ranz des vaches*, the work of a Swiss peasant of the Geneva region?" Then, having transcribed the tune and the words, "There's colour for you! I see the great hob-nailed boots of the chamois-hunter, his long-barrelled gun, his loaf of black bread and hunk of cheese, his big jovial face, his stentorian voice making the echoes rebound. To me it's admirable, admirable, admirable!" Something of the tune's melodic shape as well as its character of open-heartedness touched with melancholy and its G-major tonality went into the melody of the *Rob Roy* overture and thence into the motto theme of *Harold in Italy*. The song's sentiments became a leitmotiv of his Italian journey. Like the chamois-hunter he could not "thrive in the plains" but must be "drawn to the hills"; there, his "heart unburdened and void of care", he could rove freely under the span of heaven, "o'erleaping boulder and torrent".

During the two weeks of this first visit to Subiaco he began to explore

the whole district, striking out into the unknown and covering wide tracts
of country. On one of his longer forays he got as far as Isola di Sora, forty
miles to the south-east (where the owner of one of the local paper-mills
turned out to be a fellow-countryman, from Voiron on the road between
La Côte St André and Grenoble — Berlioz identified him by the villainous
twang of his Dauphinois accent). He was without ties, at liberty to do
anything and go anywhere. If there was no lodging where he happened to
be when darkness came on there was always some cave in the rocks to
spend the night in. Few villages possessed an inn. They were too poor,
sparsely populated and remote for that. Most of them were built on and
around the top of a hill, the houses plastered like swallows' nests against
its precipitous sides: from a distance picturesque, from close to squalid
and tumbledown. Olevano, Vico-var, Genesano, Arcinasso: there was
little to tell one from another. Civitella (the modern Bellegra), though as
filthy as the rest, boasted an inn, run by the rich man of the neighbourhood,
Signor Vincenzo, a man with a commendable partiality for the French,
though inclined to pester them with questions about the political situation
in France, of which he was a keen if distant student. French artists often
came to Civitella, and Il signor Vincenzo would sit by the hearth in his
ancient frock-coat waiting for them, and start asking about Louis-Philippe
and La Fayette and the National Guard the moment they crossed the
threshold; however desperate for a drink you might be there was no hope
of one until you had satisfied him. Civitella was altogether exceptional.
The huge slabs of rock heaped one on another on which one flank of the
village rested were like fortifications from the age of the Titans, they
seemed too massive for men to have moved them. And the view was
superb — on one side hill upon hill, on the other vast blue distances,
wood-encircled lakes and the far-off sparkling sea.

Sometimes his way lay through pine forests or great woods of Spanish
chestnut, where on the higher ground he would come suddenly on the
remains of some castle or tower, among which at dusk the figure of a man
might loom up for an instant and as silently vanish. It might be a
herdsman, or perhaps a brigand: often the still-smoking ashes of a fire
told that they were not far away. Sometimes he took his gun and went in
pursuit of game in the valleys. When it became unbearably hot he cooled
off by plunging fully dressed into the Anio. Everything about his solitary
excursions delighted him, even the periodic hunger, exhaustion and physical danger. He was sweating from his system more than just the ennui of
Rome; and in the solitude of his communing with nature he was brought
in touch with his innermost self.

When he felt the need of conviviality and familiar company, and a
change of clothes, there was Subiaco to come back to: his friends the
painters — Jean-Baptiste Gibert, who was working on a landscape nearby
for his "envoi" to the Academy in Paris, and Isidore Flacheron, who was
courting and would later marry a local girl — and the heart-warming

welcome of the taverna, whose dances had taken on a new dimension since the arrival of the maestro dell'accademia di Francia and his guitar.

Not only the hills and valleys of wild Italy refreshed and renewed the man and the artist, but also the people who lived there, whose very simplicity and lack of pretensions acted on him like a tonic. They grew used to the sight of the wiry, angular figure with the forest of red-gold hair and the expensive-looking gun, whose first appearance in their villages they had greeted with sullen disbelief and whose gun they coveted; suspicion gave way to tolerant approval of his eccentric humours and independent ways. With one of them, the young Crispino, he struck up a closer relationship. Crispino was probably the nearest he got to meeting a real brigand; for the young man claimed it was for brigandage and not mere thieving that he had done a couple of years in the galleys at Città Vecchia, though Berlioz was inclined to doubt it ("he had probably not killed so much as a monk"). Their mutual respect and affection dated from the night Berlioz helped Crispino serenade his ragazza, coaching him in a duet which they sang to a different tune that he had picked up in Tivoli. In return Crispino took to supplying him with gunpowder and tobacco, cigars and scented pipe-stems. He also gave him the benefit of his encyclopædic knowledge of all the girls within a radius of twenty-five miles and their varying degrees of accessibility. They became firm friends. Crispino always burst into song when Berlioz reappeared in Subiaco, yelling out, "Bon giorno, bon giorno, bon giorno, signore, come state?" to a variant of the original serenade Berlioz had heard him sing to his ragazza. The melodic phrase, with its repetition of the dominant, culminating in a rapid flourish followed by a descent to the leading note (emphasised by the singer with a powerful glottal stop), seemed to be common to the whole Abruzzi region. Berlioz heard it many times during his wanderings, sung at varying speeds, articulations and gradations of loud and soft, usually in the night-time. When he wrote his opera *Benvenuto Cellini* a few years later he made use of it for the foundry-workers' song "Bienheureux les matelots", sung as darkness falls in the last act, replacing Crispino's mandolin with guitars and his stimbalo, an iron triangle-like instrument, with the tap of the goldsmiths' hammers on their anvils. No other Italian folk-tune has been identified that found direct echo in Berlioz's music. But the beat of the saltarello is prominent in *Benvenuto Cellini* (which sometimes gives the impression of being practically written in compound time); and the whole exhilarating, liberating Abruzzian experience lies behind the pungent colours and rhythmic exuberance of both *Benvenuto* and *Harold in Italy*, the two works most closely indebted to his Italian journey. We can hear them as we read his pæan to the pleasures he tasted and the sights and sounds he drank in in the mountains:

[...] the rows of shrines to the Madonna along the tops of the high hills where at evening, returning late from the plain, the reapers pass, chanting their litanies, while from somewhere comes the sad jangle of a monastery bell — pine forests resounding to the rustic tunes of the *pifferari* — great girls with raven hair and swarthy skin and raucous laughs whose passion for dancing so often taxed the patience and the fingers *di questo signore che suona la chitarra francese* — the traditional tambourine beating time to my improvised saltarellos — the *carabinieri*'s insistence on forcing their way in and joining our tavern ball — indignation of the dancers, French and Abruzzian — Flacheron's prodigious fists flailing — humiliating expulsion of the soldiers of the Pope — dark threats of ambuscades and long knives — Flacheron, without a word to any of us, slipping off to his midnight tryst armed only with a stick — total absence of *carabinieri* — wild delight of Crispino.

In the third week of July his money ran out and he returned to Rome: by donkey along a narrow switchback mountain path as far as Tivoli, and thence by coach. For the next two months he was at the Villa Medici. After the mountains Rome was deader, its lack of nourishment for a musician more oppressive, than ever. To his grandfather Nicolas Marmion in his rustic retreat at Meylan he wrote contrasting the freedom of the vagabond existence he had been leading with the constraints of Rome, which offered no compensating advantage — for "the god I serve is unknown here". In Rome there was no mountain to climb, no torrent, no refreshing shade, but streets and squares hot as the floor of a furnace, a yellow muddy trickle of a river, inhabitants who were always half asleep, and abbés and monks wherever you turned, even in the Academy gardens and Vernet's studio. The endless uniformity of cloudless skies weighed heavily on someone who "likes wind, rain, thunder, tempest, which set off the beauty and tranquillity of the days when the sun shines". In his frustration he felt himself becoming surly and misanthropic. To his family he enlarged on the now familiar theme:

> Since my return here ennui has had me in its grip as never before. Used to an extremely active mental life, I am pinned down in a place where there are no books, no music, no theatre. If I compose I cannot find so much as a pianist capable of decently accompanying a romance. It's more than I can cope with to attend Mme Horace's soirées very often. Always the same old story: dancing; talking about nothing; looking at engravings; reading old newspapers; drinking weak tea; moving over to the window that overlooks Rome to mouth in the moonlight a few utterly stupid, academic and thread-bare reflections; holding forth about the cholera epidemic, the riots in Paris, the collapse of the Poles, the French defeat at Algiers, the fireworks and the illumination of St Peter's, the way Mlle Horace dances, her father's un-quenchable high spirits, the intrigues of some cardinal, the Tiber baths — and I come away more solitary, more bored than before [. . .]

There were only two things the "Roman people" got really animated about: what they called love, and their Madonna. Wherever you went outside the walls of Rome you came across little wooden crosses set in a mound of pebbles, marking the place where someone was murdered: "A woman did in her lover", the coachman would say with a shrug, or "A Frenchman insulted the Madonna and was shot." The Romans were always assumed to have a keen feeling for the arts — "as if such a feeling can exist in people devoid of all the others, and for whom life consists only in the satisfaction of their external senses. The other day I spoke to a model about Raphael. He said he didn't know such a painter, he's never posed for him. As for music! And I have to live here! There's nowhere but Paris, for everything."

His thoughts were often there. More than the doings of the musical world absorbed him. Since returning from Nice he had met François-Alexandre Cendrier, an architect (one of the "lower orders", not a Prix de Rome, though later celebrated as the designer of two famous railway stations, Lyon-Perrache and the Gare de Lyon in Paris). Cendrier was a follower of Saint-Simon, and they talked long and earnestly about the doctrine which had aroused the interest of Berlioz (as of many other artists) during his final months in Paris.[*] Someone, perhaps Cendrier himself, lent him some back numbers of the *Globe*, the journal of the movement. On 28 July, a day or two after his return from Subiaco, he wrote to Charles Duveyrier, a lawyer on the staff of the *Globe* and one of the high priests of the hierarchy, to announce his conversion:

My dear friend — rather, my dear father: you words were not lost on me. The warmth, the passion with which you preached me the doctrine to begin with took me aback more than it moved me, but in this as in every other case time has to do its work. Since I left, fresh storms have broken over my head. Shameless deceit plotted my downfall. As you may have heard, Camille has married Pleyel, in despite of the strongest, most sacred ties, in despite of her honour and reputation. No more of that. Since getting back to Rome I have got to know one of *ours*, Cendrier the architect, and we've often talked of you and Saint-Simon. His cool, calm conviction has given me a lot to think about. I've been going eagerly through a bundle of issues of the *Globe* which I was lent recently, and my last doubts have been completely removed. In all that concerns the *political reorganisation of society* I am now convinced that Saint-Simon's plan is the sole right and complete one; but I have to tell you that my ideas on all that concerns the extra-human, God, the soul and the afterlife, etc., have not changed in the slightest. I don't think that need be an obstacle to my working whole-heartedly with you for the betterment of the largest and poorest class, for the natural ordering of talents and for the abolition of all those privileges of every sort which, hidden like vermin in the recesses of the body social, have till now paralysed every attempt to cure it.

[*] See pp. 367—68.

Write to me about it, and I'll answer at once and give you my ideas on
how I might be used musically to further the Great Work when I am back in
Paris. I can assure you that while waiting for that moment, which I long for,
I shall do everything in my power to spread these deep convictions of mine
among the artists I frequent. Farewell — I wait and hope.

The letter was intercepted on its way through Verona by the Austrian
censor, who had a copy sent to Metternich in Vienna. Metternich
promptly alerted the Austrian embassy in Rome to the presence of a
dangerous revolutionary in their midst and instructed it to inform the
papal authorities and warn "young artists in Rome who are subjects of
the Emperor" to avoid contact with him. Thanks partly to this copy —
the original having disappeared in the 1930s — it has been possible for
the editors of Berlioz's *Correspondence générale* to reconstruct his letter to
Duveyrier in full.

Standing on its own, without antecedent or successor, the letter is a
curiosity. When Berlioz met the Austrian Chancellor fifteen years later in
Vienna, it was as a revolutionary whose subversive activities were confined
to music. Metternich had no objection to the Musikverein's making
Berlioz an honorary member. He merely asked him if he was the fellow
that "wrote for an orchestra of five hundred?"; to which Berlioz replied
that he "sometimes used only four hundred and fifty". What happened to
the fervent convictions the letter bears witness to? Berlioz remained on
friendly terms with Duveyrier at least into the 1840s; but we hear nothing
more of any involvement with the movement after his time in Italy. The
scenario of *Le dernier jour du monde*, the project for an oratorio/opera which
was much on his mind during these months and which crops up several
times in his letters to Humbert Ferrand (Berlioz was trying to interest
Ferrand in writing the text), has a strong Saint-Simonian flavour to it: an
unjust society stewed in corruption, opposed by a small band of the
faithful. But after that there is no trace. The ironic tone with which, in
the account of his missionary "Evenings at the Opéra" that appeared in the
Journal des débats in 1835, he recalls rallying his more faint-hearted Gluckist
companions "with sermons worthy of the disciples of Saint-Simon" shows
him well distanced from the convictions of four years earlier. Already by
January 1832, less than six months after the letter to Duveyrier, he can
refer caustically to a concert review in the Saint-Simonian *Globe* as
written in a "mezzo-philanthropico-mystical" vein.

The phrase is significant. A month or two before, a crucial change had
taken place in Saint-Simonism. Under the dominant influence of le Père
Enfantin it was moving towards a quasi-religious mysticism and away
from schemes of social amelioration (alienating its socially radical ad-
herents in the process). This would be enough by itself to explain why
Berlioz's enthusiasms cooled so rapidly; the aspects of the doctrine which

appealed to him were eclipsed by those calculated to excite the demons of dissent.

Add to this a natural scepticism (shared with his father) as to the possibility, however devoutly to be wished, of achieving generally beneficial change by revolutionary upheaval. The beneficiaries of the July Revolution, it was becoming abundantly clear, were the bankers, the industrialists and of course the politicians; it had done nothing for the workers, nor for the artists. We can follow his thoughts on the subject in the comments he makes in his letters on the contemporary riots in Paris and Lyons. They veer between, on the one hand, a lively sympathy with the plight of the "largest and poorest class" and a desire for the "abolition of privileges of every sort", and on the other a revulsion from the violence and physical destruction that serious revolution seems to entail; and they culminate in a profound and total disenchantment with politics and political action.

Scepticism too as to the reality of the dream of the Parisian populace responding to high art, and as to the feasibility of putting on popular performances of the sort of work he is interested in writing. Some of his minor choral works will carry echoes of Saint-Simonian ideas, most notably the *Chant des chemins de fer* (the movement was a keen advocate of railways as a means of furthering the unity and brotherhood of mankind). And in three of his major compositions — the Requiem (1837), the Symphonie funèbre (1840) and the Te Deum (1849) — he will address the nation at large, the ideal community, in the populist tradition of the composers of the French Revolution; but the first two will be, exceptionally, the result of a government commission, while the third, for want of one, will take six years to put on. By that time, as a composer, a worker in the art most dependent on practical circumstances for its realisation, he will have come to see despotism as the best hope for a musician: it pays you as much for your work as republicanism or constitutional monarchy makes you spend on it. In that sense the conversation with Metternich helps to explain the transformation in the dangerous revolutionary of 1831. He is an artist whose ideas often require large forces for their expression and whose nature rejects compromise, and his art comes first. The brief dream of a society remade in the interests of the people is submerged in the struggle to make his way.

For the moment, in the stifling limbo of Rome, he had nothing to do but dream and project himself elsewhere.

Since I can't be in Paris, I should like to travel, roam the world, see something quite new, cover the largest possible segment of life's constricted circle, try two, three, ten, thirty different kinds of living, take gambles: perhaps a week or two of complete satisfaction might emerge from the combination of possible chances. There would always be the amusement of the game and, even if one lost, of seeing the full extent of the hoax that ninety-nine per cent of all feeling and intelligent beings are victims of. It's not that I would wish to imitate Byron, that would be pitiful; but I should like to see America, the South Sea islands, the great natural catastrophes, young nations, towns newly sprung from the earth. I should like to try everything, become planter in the Antilles, philanthropist in the United States, patriot in Peru, quaker in Otaiti, pioneer in New Holland, and then come back to Europe to see whether the old crone is still drivelling, whether her raging fever has passed and she has found out what she wants. At least, if at the end of it life had eluded me, it would not be for want of having vigorously pursued it. And I have to rot here! ... I would walk a hundred miles in the blazing sun to get my hands on my sort of books — *Notre-Dame de Paris*, *Les intimes*, and others.[*]

At least there was the Campagna on his doorstep, the endless plain of Rome that Keats, when he first caught sight of it, likened to an inland sea. Practically nothing of the wide bare landscapes and numinous places that Turner and Corot painted has survived the onslaught of post-war industrial Italy, and you would search in vain among the belching refineries for the "splendid sadness" of Henry James's "mighty plain" which is "still so full of all that has passed from it". But in the time of Berlioz it belonged unchallengeably to the ancient world. The treeless earth almost untouched by modern cultivation seemed, in Chateaubriand's phrase, to be made of the very dust of the antique dead, to have remained as old as the ruins which were its indigenous plants and forests.

It was a scene whose melancholy mirrored his own state of mind too closely to provide a real escape. Like Isabel Archer he saw it through the veil of his personal sadness. But to a determined walker it offered a rich field. A landscape that at first sight looked uniformly arid and desolate disclosed unexpected variety of forms and moods: deep ravines, shady groves along the margin of secret watercourses, small sulphurous lakes hidden in folds of ground. The light, especially in late afternoon, had a Claude-like roundness and luminosity which softened the bleakness, warming the bones of temples and towers and the aqueducts vanishing towards the vaporous horizon. He ranged far and wide over it in his old grey shooting-jacket and straw hat, walking fast and devouring the miles, or taking his time and stopping to examine a tomb, or to look back from

---

[*] *Notre-Dame de Paris*, Victor Hugo's novel of medieval Paris, had appeared in March, and *Les intimes*, by Michel Raymond, at about the same time. The nearest proper reading-room (belonging to a Frenchman, Vieusseux) was in Florence. In the Papal States the Index was in energetic operation, to the dismay and frustration of foreign travellers. Sir Edward Bulwer Lytton, who arrived the following year to work on *Rienzi*, was astonished to discover that it was "impossible to buy a Gibbon anywhere in Rome"; and special permission had to be sought from a friendly cardinal before Joseph Severn (the artist who had come to Rome with the dying Keats and stayed on) was allowed to lend him his copy.

a low hill-top towards Rome and the gleam of the cross on the dome of St Peter's and in the surrounding stillness catch the distant boom of its great bell, whose tolling he would echo in the horns' recurring C natural in the slow movement of *Harold in Italy*.

Both the act of walking and the associations of the Classical past stimulated musical ideas; he would halt and lay down his gun to note them in his sketchbook. Virgilian memories were alive in him; this was the country of the later books of the *Æneid*: the death of Pallas son of Evander the Arcadian, the young prince's funeral cortège and his war-horse Æthon weeping great tears, the siege of Latium, Amata hanging herself from a beam of the palace, Æneas invoking for his son Ascanius on the eve of battle Hector's immortal fame, the final confrontation with Turnus, and the shade of the Rutulian king fleeing angrily to the gloom below. They were the familiar spirits of his world. Sometimes, when he had his guitar with him and not his gun, he would improvise on these epic conflicts like some bard of the ancient days, chanting "a strange recitative to still stranger harmonies", and with the aid of drink work himself up into a state of wild exaltation and nostalgia in which his own personal griefs mingled. Then tears began to flow, and uttering snatches of Dante, Shakespeare and Virgil − "Nessun maggior dolore . . . Good night, sweet ladies . . . Fugit indignata sub umbras" − he sank to the ground and fell asleep. During these bouts he was, as always, the keen observer of his own emotional and bodily experiences.

After the city, long days in the open made him alive again. He could have exclaimed with Byron, "The great object of life is sensation − to feel that we exist, even though in pain". In Rome he did not exist. What he called "the intense consciousness of being alive" that Nature and physical freedom endowed him with drained away and he was without sensation. He must be on the move. Three nights running that August he and a companion, the sculptor Debay, set out late from the Porto del Popolo with their guns and two of Vernet's dogs and walked through the night so as to reach their chosen hunting-ground at daybreak for a few hours' shooting in the cool of the morning, before repairing to a tavern to drink Orvieto wine and then sleep in a haybarn in the hottest part of the day.* The three-day shoot, he told Ferdinand Hiller, had exhausted him, but had kept ennui at bay.

Correspondence with his friends was a frail lifeline. He had much

---

* The third of these expeditions, to the country north of Rome round Isola Farnese (the Veii of the ancients and scene of Coriolanus' fateful encounter with his mother), during which it poured with rain and the two sportsmen became "caked with mud, as Marius must have been when he emerged from the Minturnan marshes", is described in diary form in *Voyage musical* and *Memoirs*, chapter 42.

greater need of it than they and much more time to write and then wait for an answer; the long silences that succeeded his letters intensified his sense of exile. Only Thomas Gounet was a prompt and punctilious correspondent. Ferrand was capable of letting half a year pass without writing back. Hiller answered very irregularly. His latest reported a visit to the Mokes, who had returned to him for safekeeping the jewellery Berlioz had given Camille, together with his Prix de Rome medal. "The whole lot is worth more than two hundred francs," Berlioz commented in reply; "so if I die of cholera before I get back to Paris my little debt to you will be paid." As for Camille's things still in his possession, "an architect from the Academy who has just left for Paris has undertaken to deliver to our Holy Virgin a parcel containing her presents, her 'love'-letters, her ring etc.".

The architect, Joseph-Louis Duc, was one of the more sympathetic spirits among the inmates of the Villa Medici and his departure left a gap. (They would remain friends, and Duc would play a part in two of Berlioz's works, the Symphonie funèbre and *The Flight into Egypt*.) Berlioz had talked music with him and made him keen to hear Beethoven's symphonies, and before he left gave him a letter to take to François Réty, the Conservatoire accountant, in which he asked Réty if he would help Duc get into the Society's concerts, in case of its being still as difficult as it was to procure tickets. At the same time — Ferrand having failed to respond to his request for a copy of the page he needed from his *Orphée* — he asked Réty to extract the cantata from his bundle of scores in the Conservatoire Library and give it to the new Prix de Rome, Prévost, to bring with him if he came to Rome — Prévost was apparently undecided whether to take up his prize.[*]

The rest of the letter is a cri de cœur on the violence of the spleen that has him in its grip. It is at this point in the narrative of his Italian journey in *Voyage musical* and the *Memoirs* that he places his discussion of the disease. For an outsider it is difficult to have any conception of what it was like. Berlioz himself calls it "inexprimable", unutterable — appalling but also impossible to describe. His account of it is clinical. It borrows an analogy from physics (as befits the one-time student of Gay-Lussac): the reaction that occurs when a cup of water and another containing sulphuric acid are placed side by side under the glass jar of an air-pump and a vacuum is created, resulting in the water's boiling and then evaporating and the temperature's falling until a small lump of ice forms at the bottom.

Something comparable occurs when this sense of isolation, this feeling of absence takes possession of me. A vacuum forms round my panting breast,

---

[*] Prévost delayed nearly two years (eventually turning up in October 1833). Berlioz instead got Hiller to go to the Library and copy the page for him.

and it is as if my heart, subject to an irresistible force of suction, were evaporating and about to dissolve by expansion. My skin smarts and burns all over my body; I flush from head to foot. I have an impulse to cry out, to call my friends or even strangers to comfort and protect me, defend me, save me from destruction, catch hold of my life which is fleeing from me to the four points of the compass.

During these crises one has no thought of death; the very notion of suicide is intolerable. Far from desiring death you yearn for life: you long to live it with a thousand times as much energy. It is a prodigious capacity for happiness, which is exasperated for want of use, and which can be satisfied only by immense, all-consuming delights, equal to the superabundance of sensibility you feel endowed with.

This state is not spleen, though it precipitates it; it is the boiling and evaporation of heart, senses, brain and nervous system. Spleen is the process of congealing, the lump of ice.

Even in a calm state I am always conscious of a little of this "isolation" on Sundays in summer, because the city is inactive, because everyone has gone to the country — because they are joyful a long way away, because they are absent. The adagios of Beethoven's symphonies, certain scenes in Gluck's *Alceste* and *Armide*, an aria in his Italian opera *Telemaco*, and the scene in the Elysian Fields in *Orphée* also produce quite strong attacks of the disease, but these masterpieces carry their own antidote: they stimulate tears, and tears bring relief. The adagios of one or two Beethoven sonatas and Gluck's *Iphigénie en Tauride*, on the other hand, are provokers of spleen and irrevocably associated with it; it's cold in these works, the air dark, the sky overcast, the north wind moaning.

There are moreover two kinds of spleen: one active, mocking, passionate, malignant*, the other morose and wholly passive, when your one desire is to be left alone in silence to do nothing except sleep. For anyone possessed by this latter kind, nothing has any meaning left, the destruction of a world would scarcely stir him. At such times I could wish the earth were a shell filled with gunpowder; I should put a match to it for my amusement.

One day in late September, prostrated by the passive variety, he was dozing just inside the laurel wood at the Academy, rolled up on a heap of dead leaves like a hedgehog and watching out of one jaundiced eye the lizards darting about in the sun, when he felt feet prodding him awake. It was Constant Dufeu the architect and the elder of the two Dantans (a sculptor like his younger brother). "Hey, old Father Jollity, do you want to come to Naples? We're just going." — "Go to hell! You know I've no money left." — "Fool — we have, we'll lend you some. Here, Dantan, help me up with this great baby or we'll never get anywhere. There! Now brush yourself down and go and ask Vernet for a month's leave, and when you've packed your bag we'll be off. All right?"

---

* Berlioz used his first-hand experience of it to portray Mephistopheles in *The Damnation of Faust*.

They made a party of five with the addition of one Russian and one Prussian. The coach took them via Ceprano, Monte Cassino, Capua and Caserta. By the time they reached Naples, on 1 October, Berlioz's spirits were restored.

Letters to His Family

Naples, 2 October 1831 (Mount Posilippo)

I arrived in Naples yesterday evening, I'm writing to you from Mount Posilippo, on the tomb of Virgil. It's the first thing I've visited. An old woman took me to the house of the proprietor in the middle of whose vineyard the grave is located, and here I am. While I eat some golden grapes my eyes wander over the gently swelling sea and through the layers of mist make out the island of Capri, where I'm shortly going to stay, and I think back to those first poetic impressions that I owed in my childhood to the *Æneid* and its author. The journey here was fascinating. I saw the ruins of the famous city of Capua, so fatal to Hannibal's soldiers; I made the climb up to Monte Cassino and admired the renowned Benedictine abbey. It's bigger than the Grande Chartreuse and more richly decorated than any other religious monument. The church where the remains of St Benedict and St Scolastica rest in the same grave surpasses St Peter's in magnificence; the floors are made of agate and porphyry, rare and priceless marbles, gold, alabaster and brass; the frescoes, and all that concentration of wealth piled up on the top of a barren mountain, bear witness to the devotion of the Italians to the twin saints and the immense influence of the Catholic religion in the middle ages. I'd already visited, in the mountains of Subiaco, the two monasteries where brother and sister founded their orders, and was very pleased to run into them again, sleeping on their garnered wealth. I also saw the King of Naples' palace at Caserta; it's immense, magnificent. But nothing eclipses or even equals the great bay that unfurls before me, Vesuvius smoking, the sea covered with boats (in the midst of which I can make out the coastguard vessel crossing back and forth on the look-out for cholera), all this motley, strident people thronging the streets, the crowds of soldiers in their red and gold uniform, on one side the blare of military bands, on another the clatter of musket practice, on the hillside splendid poplars laden with luxuriant vines, which would break beneath the weight of their cascading grapes but for the stout trees that support them, groves of acacia, pomegranate, fig and orange, the peasant women of the islands in their green bodices with brass stripes, a red kerchief on their heads, the armies of fishermen pulling up their nets, the naked children who leap from the cockleshell craft and hare through the water along the sand. What life! what animation! what dazzling bustle! How different it all is from Rome and its sleepy inhabitants and untilled, desolate, denuded soil! The austerely melancholy Roman countryside is to the plain of Naples as the past is to the present, death to life, silence to vivid, harmonious noise.

5 October

"Eh! eh! Eccellenza! Eccellenza! *quatro* carlini. No, *tre* carlini, e un bono somaro, vedete, bianco e polito — No, no — Oh! celenza, *due* carlini, lo mio somaro è più forte — No, ancora una volta, andaro a piede — Alora celenza, per *uno* carlino — Per niente, corpo di Bacco, andate al diavolo — Buon viaggio, celenza."* So I went to Vesuvius on foot, despite the shouts of the peasants of Resina who absolutely insisted on his "Excellency" taking a donkey. I came back tonight aching in every limb but don't regret my trouble. I was with two Frenchmen, a Prussian and a Russian, who were on the journey from Rome with me. When we reached the hermit's we drank some delicious water and a vigorous Lacryma Christi which revived us a little, the Russian and me; the others were on donkeys and didn't feel in the least tired. From there we launched on to the sea of lava which surrounds the base of the cone. It's fearful — the pavements of hell could not be more hideous. As we were plodding our way up — turning round occasionally to watch the sun setting — we heard the yelp of female voices echoing in one of the valleys; it was some French women singing the Marseillaise. The notions of politics and patriotism have something so ludicrous in such a context that I experienced a kind of vertigo caused by the jangling of a thousand disagreeable thoughts. Finally, by now in profound darkness, we reached the great crater, today filled with lava almost to its brim — two months ago the level was five hundred feet down. You walk on a glowing crust, bestriding crevasses in which you can see the red-hot lava, motionless, six inches from your feet. We came right up to quite a large stream of lava, which gave off so powerful a stench of sulphur that one could hardly breathe. However, we managed to stay there for a while and, with our faces averted because of the heat, extracted a few blobs of the burning liquid on the ends of our sticks. From time to time an eruption from the centre of the crater lit up the darkness and revealed the whole magnificent scene. There's nothing finer than the rain of molten rocks falling from an immense height after the explosion and rolling back down the outside of the cone where they remain fixed without going out, like a fiery necklace round the giant throat of the volcano. To our right, as we emerged from the main crater we saw the fishermen's lights, a countless host of them illuminating the sea, like a gathering of glow-worms in a meadow. In the midst of the mountainside an abscess had formed in the past few days, and a river of lava was issuing from it in four divergent streams, all these fiery torrents making in the direction of Pompeii. Vesuvius seems to be waiting for the ancient town to be entirely cleared before engulfing it a second time. I tell you, it was the Blocksberg scene in *Faust* exactly: a ballet of sparks, snakelike flames, death rattles from the abyss, sudden gleams and flashes alongside total darkness, cries from the

---

* "Hey! hey! Excellency! Excellency! *Four* carlini. No, *three* carlini and a fine donkey, look, white and well-behaved — No, no — Here, 'xcellency, *two* carlini, and my donkey is stronger — Once again, no, I'm going on foot — 'xcellency, for *one* carlino, then — For nothing, corpo di Bacco, go to the devil — Pleasant journey, 'xcellency."

heights and the depths, in the valleys below, on the mountain tops, "far and close at hand", the flickering torches, the starry sky, fire on the water, fire on the earth, fire in the air. Even the witches were not lacking; our French females with their shrill conversation and screeching laughter and their shopgirl style (to go no further) could have filled the part to perfection.

As soon as I've recovered from the fatigue of the excursion I shall go to Pompeii, where I expect to find some French artists of my acquaintance.

At the café this morning they were saying that the *new volcano* which came up off the coast of Sicily not far from Stromboli two or three months ago has just been engulfed and extinguished by the sea from which it came. What a fearsome encounter that must have been! A volcano and the sea in combat.

The animation of Naples and the effrontery of its inhabitants exhilarated him. He loved the brilliance of the light on clear days, when the oranges on Capri looked near enough to pick, the incorrigible optimism of the lazzaroni and their deep instinct for the main chance, the way the fishermen stopped everyone they met, even if he was dressed for a ball, in the expectation of making a sale and the fruit vendors, the moment they had disposed of all their produce, threw their baskets down and curled up on the spot like dogs and slept in the street till evening.

At last, too, there was an opera house, the San Carlo, where a lover of music need not abandon all hope on entering. For the first time since coming to Italy he breathed a recognisably musical atmosphere. True, the chorus was feeble and the conductor, in order to ensure strict time, struck the desk with his bow rather too zealously, and the work that was playing, Mercadante's *Zaira*, left something to be desired. But the orchestra was a real orchestra: the wind instruments could be listened to in perfect safety, the violins knew their job, and the cellos, though too few (fewer than the double basses, in the bad Italian tradition), played with a fine singing tone. And in Tamburini the San Carlo had a tenor of rare talent and accomplishment, whose voice and artistry were a pleasure to hear. At the opera buffa theatre too, the Fondo, the standards of performance were far above those usually obtaining in such houses. He saw Donizetti's farce *Le convenienze ed inconvenienze teatrali,* and while noting the score's heavy indebtedness to Rossini had to admit that the thing was skilfully done and performed with great brio. In a few days Naples provided greater musical stimulus than all the other towns he had been to in Italy put together. At the museum he examined the ancient instruments discovered beneath the volcanic dust at Herculaneum. The wind instruments were too incomplete to play, but he tried two pairs of antique cymbals and conceived the idea of incorporating their delicate, penetrating tones into the modern orchestra, as he would do both in his Queen Mab scherzo (a composition perhaps already beginning to take shape in his mind, as his conversation with Mendelssohn a few months before suggests) and in the fourth act of *The Trojans.*

"What a town Naples is," he wrote to Mme Le Sueur after his return to Rome. "Noise, brilliance, movement, abundance, action, theatres — everything we don't have here and more." Naples might lack the sense of the prodigious past which gave Rome and its encircling plains their desolate grandeur; but it had Vesuvius and the splendid sea with its enchanted islands and the bay of Baiæ, whose thronging Virgilian memories "suit me at least as well as crumbling tumuluses and the dust of emperors". In Naples he felt whole and at one with his environment. The resonant past and the vibrant, living present were held in balance; he need not bury himself in the one to escape from the inadequacies and frustrations of the other.

After a week of company it was time to spend a day by himself and experience its sensations on his own, undistracted. He would visit the little island of Nisida in the Bay of Pozzuoli, the Baiæ of the ancients. The weather was perfect and he was in a susceptible state, having woken that morning in a mood of romantic tristesse "such as one experiences at the age of fourteen, when you still believe in happiness and look at life through a poetic prism and weep over the novels of Florian, and an old tower on a dark rock sets your fancy flying". (Was he thinking of Estelle, when he associated Florian and the old tower and his feelings at fourteen?) His mood deepened gratifyingly when, in the garden of the Villa Reale, a soldier on guard told him to take off his straw hat and pointed to a little pavilion, where in the centre stood a statue of Tasso. By the time he neared the bay his mind, having gone through all the appropriate sentiments about the woes of love-lorn poets, had passed from Tasso to Cervantes and from Cervantes to his *Galatea* and the delicious creature who shone even in the company of the nymph of that enchanting pastoral (which he had read and re-read in the days of his adoration of Estelle) and whose name was the same as the island he was about to visit, Nisida. In his excitement he ran the last part of the way and arrived on the shore panting. There was the bay where Æneas landed with his battered fleet and Nero arranged a little water-sport for his mother Agrippina, and there was a small fishing craft waiting to ferry him over to the island.

I ask for four rowers. Six present themselves. I offer them a reasonable sum, pointing out that I don't need six men to get me over to Nisida in a cockleshell. They smilingly insist and name the equivalent of about thirty francs for a trip worth five at the most. Meanwhile two boys are standing a little way off, saying nothing but watching with wistful eyes. I feel in a good humour and am tickled by my oarsmen's impudent demands; so (indicating the two *lazzaronetti*), "All right then, yes, but all eight of you come, and row your hardest!" Yells of delight; young and old leap for joy. We pile into the boat and in a few minutes are at Nisida.

Leaving his crew he climbed past vineyards, through groves of orange, fig and olive. A soldier who spoke French volunteered to act as guide and showed him round, and at the end startled Berlioz by waving aside the proffered money and asking him instead to pray for him. Despite the discovery that the summit of the island, which from a distance recalled Moore's "I long to tread that golden path of rays/And think 'twould lead to some bright isle of rest", was occupied by a convict settlement, he would have stayed longer, but one of his oarsmen hurried up with the news that the wind was freshening and they had better re-embark at once. The return journey was an alarmingly different affair from the voyage out, with the frail craft tossing like a leaf and the lazzaroni feeling for their rosaries. "But the sea-god relented and, deciding the sport had gone far enough, suffered us to land safely." Instead of separating after Berlioz had paid his thirty francs, they all went off to a shack in the woods a mile or so from the sea and dined together off a mountain of macaroni and several large jars of Posilippo wine, from which each drank in turn, beginning with the senior lazzarone, a toothless old man who needed little encouragement to launch into an impassioned account of King Joachim of Naples, to whose memory he was devoted, and then of his own hazardous journey in a small boat to the island of Elba, where it was said Napoleon was later exiled. To the delight of his companions Berlioz listened to the old man's story with the gravest attention and at the end congratulated him warmly on his epic adventure. As he rose to leave, one of the young lazzaroni, as a token of eternal friendship, handed him an enormous shallot, which he carried like a banner while they escorted him to the top of Posilippo.

When they had left he stayed there and, alone in boundless space, watched the sun go down behind Cape Misenum. The associations that had been accumulating all day flooded over him; and in a sudden access of exaltation he gave himself to the sovereign beauty of the scene and worshipped the power of genius, undiminished across the centuries and no less potent than in the days of his boyhood, though destined in the end to fade and go down like everything else into the dark. A whirlwind of memories streamed round him, and as he gazed out over the fabled coast he seemed to see the glittering panoply of his Virgilian heroes rise up before him.

He was brought back to earth soon afterwards when, as he hobbled footsore home along the darkening road, a carriage passed and seeing the chance of a free ride to Naples (there was no footman on the box) he jumped up — only for the pretty Parisian inside to call out in a shrill voice to her driver, "Louis, there's someone behind!" The next moment he received a sharp cut of the whip across his face. The last few miles were completed on foot, while he indulged in sexual fantasies about what he would do to her if he had Crispino with him to keep the coachman quiet (a day which began with Estelle had ended with Camille), and from there to the brigand's life and the attractive career it offered an honest man, if only they would wash occasionally.

His thoughts turned to Subiaco and his beloved mountains. After the excitements of Naples and its surroundings, it would be too much of an anticlimax to return to Rome by prosaic coach — so why not do the journey on foot, across the mountains, taking in Subiaco on the way? He was ready to part from his fellow-travellers, whose company was wearing thin; he had felt cramped by their presence and talk during the tour of Pompeii: it intruded on his own private ancient world.

That is not how one should experience Pompeii. Inwardly, I inveighed against the circumstances which prevented me from wandering by myself, with only the moon to observe me, past columns and the ghosts of columns, free to give myself up to every caprice of my impressionability (not to be always saying "imagination"). How fine it must be to be able to let your thoughts roam in the silence, walking on the large polished flag-stones, down the long echoing streets, through the temples and palaces; to sit in the theatre where tragedies were performed and think of Sophocles and Euripides; to see behind the veil of the past to the fearful combats of gladiators, lions and tigers in the immense amphitheatre, and more terrifying still the yelling populace possessed by blood and watching avidly for the moment when the victim's heart is torn open by the sword or the claws of some frantic beast. How I should have liked to sleep in one of the handsome apartments, paved with mosaics, that one's fancy peoples with fine women in Greek drapery, proud and imperious of eye, around them ravishing slave-girls playing the lyre and singing of voluptuous delights. But all that is out of the question. There are custodians everywhere who keep a careful eye on you; I could not so much as steal my father the tiniest fragment of fresco or mosaic.

A day or two later he went with his companions to Castellamare on the far side of the bay. At breakfast on the 13th Munier the marine painter who was staying there suggested to Berlioz a trip to Sicily; but it turned out to be beyond their means and the idea was abandoned. For the same reason Berlioz would have to forgo Salerno, Amalfi and Pæstum and return to Rome. His money was running out. He said goodbye to Constant, Dantan and the two foreigners and took the dusty road back to Naples.

That evening, in Naples, he got talking to two Swedish officers of his acquaintance, Bennet and Klinksporn, and discovered that they too intended walking to Rome. Both spoke excellent French and seemed likely to be congenial travelling companions; one of them knew Subiaco and was as fond of it as he was. It was agreed they should make the journey together, striking through the mountains and emulating the chamois-hunter "o'erleaping boulder and torrent". Their luggage was deposited at the coach-station for sending on after them, leaving them to travel light, with purse (very light in Berlioz's case), sketchbook and walking-stick. They set out on the morning of 14 October in ideal conditions and covered the twenty-five miles to Capua, where they spent the first night.

It was the perfect season to be at large in Italy. The sun no longer beat fiercely down, there was a gentle breeze, the fruit had ripened and the harvest was in progress, and for the first few days they practically lived on grapes, pears and figs. When the owners weren't there to sell them their produce they helped themselves. Once, this led to a tense situation, when the owner, who had heard them knocking down pears in his orchard, appeared shouting and gesticulating as Berlioz was peacefully filling his hat with fruit; but with an effrontery that the Neapolitans would have approved the culprit turned indignantly on his attacker and accused him of keeping them hanging about for half an hour trying to buy his wretched pears. Having presented him with a small sum of money he was helped back over the fence by one of his companions and made off, leaving the man staring at the copper coin in his hand.

On the 17th they were at San Germano where they stopped for a day, beguiled by the beauty of the country. Next day they were in the mountains. Here the arduous part began. The terrain was much more difficult, and inns hard to find and fearfully primitive when there were any. On the evening of the 18th, after walking a good thirty miles, they arrived in Isola di Sora with blistered feet and raging thirsts to find no trace of an inn of any sort and a discouraging indifference on the part of the inhabitants. Fortunately Berlioz remembered the name of the French mill-owner from Voiron whom he had met there in the summer, and asked to be directed to the house of Signor Courrier. Someone pointed out his brother among a group of bystanders. Berlioz explained their predicament and after a moment's reflection the man answered in his powerful Dauphinois twang, "Pardi, on vous couchera ben" ("We'll surely give you a bed"). M. Courrier and his wife received them very cordially, produced a good supper and put them up in one vast bed where they slept soundly. Berlioz gave one of the children a watch-chain of jet pearls he had brought with him from Naples; Bennet, who was a keen amateur artist, presented the family with a drawing of Mme Courrier braiding her little girl's hair which was pronounced an admirable likeness, and the whole visit passed off very well. Their host encouraged them by assuring them that two days' strenuous walking would bring them to Subiaco.

Because of the paucity of inns and the desolateness of the country directly ahead, they now turned west towards Veroli and Alatri, dining after a fashion at the first of these hill-top villages and pushing on another eight miles to the second, which they entered just before nightfall, followed by an inquisitive crowd of women and children. Their lodging proved to be a frightful hole; and between the fleas, the rock-hard beds and the youth of Alatri serenading their ragazze to the accompaniment of guitar and squawking clarinet, they slept little. By the morning Berlioz had a high temperature and was shaking with ague. However, as there was no staying in such a place, a special effort was required. Having conferred with the friendly villagers in the main square and settled on their route, they set out in the direction of Arcino, and within a couple of hours' rapid walking the fever had begun to abate. This was by far the hardest part of the journey. There were no paths. They made their way over large boulders along a tortuous mountain stream to Arcino, where they fortified themselves with eggs and maize roasted on the cob over an open fire. Here they took a guide, who led them to within eight miles of Subiaco. The last part of their trek lay over high ground, across the turf of broad plateaux amid the immemorial stillness of pastoral Italy. They passed no one except an old shepherd with his flock, and walked for several hours in silence. It was dark by the time they reached the hills above Subiaco and saw the lights of the town below them.

Their arrival caused equal excitement and incredulity. "Eh! lo signor Stefano . . . lo signor maestro! benvenuti, signori! . . . Come? di Napoli? . . . a piede! . . . d'avvero! non è possibile!"* Gibert lent Berlioz some clean clothes while his own were being washed. They stayed two or three days to ease their limbs, then resumed their march and took the road to Tivoli. There Berlioz showed his friends the sights: the Temple of Vesta, the falls, Neptune's grotto and the huge stalactite that stood above the site of Horace's villa, the villa of Mæcenas where Virgil recited his *Georgics* and Horace his *Epicurean Odes* and which now rang with the clangour of an iron foundry powered by a branch of the Anio that flowed through the vaulted hall; then further down, the Villa d'Este (Tasso again!) and Hadrian's Villa, and so back, still on foot, to Rome, which they reached some time in the final week of October 1831. It had been, he wrote to his father, the most fascinating journey he had ever made.

---

* Stefano: one of the Swedish officers, presumably. Of the two it seems more likely to have been Bennet who, as the artist, was the habitué of Subiaco. Despite a walk of nearly forty miles there was no going straight to bed; "Flacheron came running, with his beautiful Mariucia clutching a tambourine, and willy nilly it was dancing and the saltarello till midnight."

31

"Si je n'étais captive"

<hr/>

In the same letter to his father Berlioz remarks that the friendship of the Swedish officers, besides being very agreeable in itself, could well prove useful during his year in Germany (the obligatory third year of the Prix de Rome) if he decides to visit Stockholm: they have excellent connections there, being members of King Bernadotte's personal bodyguard. From now on increasingly in Berlioz's letters to family and friends the question of his departure becomes dominant. In theory he has a further year to do. But pensionnaires are only required to spend it in Italy, not in Rome. Though Vernet will not bend the rules in his favour it may be possible to circumvent them by moving to Milan — a plausible move for a composer, given that it is the capital of Italian musical life — and having his allowance paid into a bank there, and then making clandestine arrangements to draw the money in Chambéry, at that date part of the Kingdom of Sardinia yet only a day's journey from La Côte St André. At first his return to France is to be effected without the knowledge of M. Horace, who will believe him still in Milan. Later, everything is above board and Vernet agrees to his leaving Italy six months before the official expiry of his time, on condition that he stays in La Côte and does not show his face in Paris till the end of the year.

By early January his departure from Rome is fixed for the beginning of May. His thoughts turn more and more towards Paris and the performance of the double "Episode in an Artist's Life" that he plans to give there before "launching into the musical ocean that is Germany"; much of his time is spent copying orchestral parts. He has the Melologue translated into German, so that he can give it in Berlin and elsewhere, and the chorus parts copied professionally: the "unknown language" of the Chorus of Shades excites the suspicions of the papal censor, who — perhaps in consequence of Metternich's warnings — searches it for hidden evidence of subversion.

These remaining six months in Rome (November to April) repeat the earlier pattern. There is the same alternation between spleen in Rome and the exhilarations of "la vie sauvage". Since the excursion to Naples he is more broke than ever (his finances have never fully recovered from the escapade to Nice), so long trips are rare. But within a few weeks of getting back from Naples he is off briefly to the mountains again, walking all day in pouring rain from Tivoli to Subiaco and arriving drenched to the skin but with a bag full of game for the pot. He manages to spend the whole of the first half of February in the Abruzzi, using Subiaco as his base. In March he explores the country immediately to the south-west of Rome — Frascati, Albano, Castelgondolfo — and in April revisits for the last time Tivoli, Subiaco, Palestrina and Albano.

In Rome there are some variations in the routine of life at the Villa Medici. He receives a visit from Crispino, who arrives in his room early one morning in the hope of borrowing money ("turning over in bed I find myself staring at a great sun-bronzed rapscallion with pointed hat and twisted leggings, waiting politely for me to wake"). At one of Vernet's soirées he meets the Russian composer Glinka, en route for Naples from Milan, and hears some of his songs, sung by the St Petersburg tenor Ivanov, Glinka's travelling companion; their unusual melodic idiom makes a vivid impression on him. He manages at last to get hold of a copy of Victor Hugo's *Notre-Dame de Paris* and for a few days is transported out of his surroundings. He acts as pander-cum-waiter for his friend Gibert the painter and his inamorata, a peasant girl from Albano who sometimes poses as a model at the Academy. Gibert, unable to have the girl to stay in his room at night, gets her to come there in the afternoon and then, so that she won't go hungry while he is at dinner, persuades Berlioz to feign illness so that he can have his dinner brought to his room and take it down the passage to share with the Italian girl while Gibert is in the refectory with the lads, fortifying himself with punch. In November and December a severe influenza epidemic rages through Rome; the poor die in hundreds. Berlioz, wearing his hooded greatcoat, accompanies the death-carts to the Trasteverine Church and, thinking Hamlet-like thoughts, watches the bodies being lowered on iron hooks into a communal grave below the inner courtyard, while Garrez the architect does a drawing of the scene.

Another morbid task occupies him about this time. At the end of November a letter from de Carné, proprietor of the *Correspondant* to which he contributed in 1829 and 1830, asks him to write a piece on Italian musical life for the *Revue européenne*, the successor to the *Correspondant*. "I shall do my best to satisfy him, though I don't find much pleasure in studying a corpse in so advanced a state of decomposition." Music in Italy, he tells Maurice Schlesinger, must have "suffered the fate of Carthage: 'The traveller, standing on the shore, / Searches but finds it there no more' ". But it will give him a chance to assemble and sum up his scattered impressions, work off some of his anger at the Institute's folly in insisting on sending young composers to Rome, and earn a little much-needed money.

His "Letter from an Enthusiast on the Present Condition of Music in

Italy" is a 5,000-word survey of all he has encountered till then: Bellini's *Montecchi e Capuletti*, Paccini's *La Vestale* and the funeral of Napoleon-Louis in Florence, Paër's *Agnese* in Genoa, the Fête-Dieu in Rome, the abject condition of the Roman opera houses and churches, peasant music in the Papal States, the San Carlo and the Teatro del Fondo in Naples. Much of the material will be used later, in revised and expanded form, for the Italian chapters in *Voyage musical* and the *Memoirs* (some of it has already been drawn on in the preceding chapters of this account). The essay shows a striking advance on the pieces written a year or two before. He has learned to write. The style is altogether more assured and more vivid, the irony less forced, the accumulation of personal impressions to build up an indictment skilfully done. Berlioz presents his case in the form of a series of cruel disillusionments which overtake him one by one as the hopes he cherished for something better (dutifully forswearing prejudice) are shattered: the authentic *Romeo and Juliet* opera which everyone tells him Bellini has written, the imposing obsequies that the death of a Bonaparte could be expected to inspire, the splendours of the Corpus Domini procession as vaunted by the Florentine monks, the standard of musical performance in the theatres of Rome, which cannot possibly be worse than in the churches but is.

The music during Holy Week is not included, since he was, he says, away at the time; from which he concludes that "the musical riches of the church in Rome must be saved up for it all year". The rest of the year, operatic arias performed during divine service, with all the attendant train of roulades, pedal points, cabalettas and final cadences, and the overtures to *La Cenerentola* and *The Barber of Seville* arranged for organ, indicate the degree of artistic seriousness and religious dedication. Not to make it a catalogue of unrelieved doom, the good points are also insisted on: the incorruptibility and fashion-defying beauty of Allegri's Miserere, the fine quality of the solo voices and the natural facility of vocalisation characteristic of the Italians, the singers who stand out from the mediocrity of their colleagues by virtue of being genuine artists, such as Caroline Ungher (solo alto at the première of Beethoven's Ninth Symphony), Mme Marini and Salvator Cartoni. But they are powerless against the general slovenliness and anti-artistic atmosphere. The choruses in the leading opera houses in Rome are on the level of the Nouveautés and Vaudeville in Paris, the orchestras rival the army of the Prince of Monaco in discipline and force. At the Teatro della Valle (a theatre where several Rossini and Donizetti operas had their première) the cello section numbers precisely one player, a man who earns his living as a goldsmith, in which respect he is better off than a colleague in the same orchestra who earns his repairing cane-bottomed chairs. The Apollo is no better appointed, except that it boasts two bass-drums — he heard them in Vaccai's *Zadig e Astartea*, one in the pit and one on the stage (but as they hardly ever played in time with each other, the effect was like "being present at a siege, the cannon from the ramparts replying to the artillery of the besieging army"). None of this is surprising when you consider that the musicians' pay does not exceed three paoli (thirty-three sous) for a session.

This state of decay is contrasted with the vigour of the typical Abruzzian serenade, which though very primitive is at least fresh and uninhibited. More remarkable (Berlioz had just encountered it for the first time and liked to think it a relic of antiquity) is the music of the pifferari, the small groups of strolling musicians who towards Christmas come down from the hills armed with bagpipes and oboe-like "pifferi" and dressed in long woollen coats and the pointed hats brigands sport — their whole appearance instinct with a sort of mystic savagery — to play in pious homage before the statues of the Madonna:

> I have spent hours at a time watching them in Rome as they stand, heads bent slightly to one side, bright eyes fixed adoringly on the holy mother, almost as still as the image they worship. The bagpipe, supported by a large *piffero* blowing the bass, sustains a harmony of two or three notes, over which a double *piffero* of medium size gives out the melody, and above that two very short tremulous little *pifferi* play trills and rhythmic figures, drenching the rustic tune in a shower of the weirdest ornamentation. After a lot of lively, cheerful refrains repeated over and over again, the concert concludes with a slow, grave piece like a prayer, deeply felt and full of solemn patriarchal dignity. Close to, the sound is overpoweringly loud, but at a certain distance this strange ensemble produces a most charming and poetic effect, and even people not normally susceptible to that kind of impression are moved.*

At this point the imaginary recipient of the Letter intervenes.

> "Are you seriously telling me that bagpipes, mandolins and *pifferari* are all you can find of interest in the way of music in the ancient capital of the world?" Alas, my friend, it's only too true. "Rome is no longer in Rome"† — it's moved to Paris, Berlin, Vienna, London even. [...] "And

---

* Subsequently he came across the pifferari in their native habitat, in the Abruzzi, and was even more struck by them. "Volcanic rocks and dark pine forests are the natural setting and complement of such primordial music. When the scene also included some great Cyclopean mass of masonry, monument of a vanished age, and a few shepherds dressed in rough sheepskins with the fleece worn outside (the garment of the Sabine herdsmen), I could believe myself back in the time of the ancient peoples among whom Evander the Arcadian settled, the liberal host of Æneas." Berlioz also conjectures that the double piffero may be the direct descendant of the Phrygian instrument mentioned by Virgil in *Æneid*, IX 617. Represented by oboes, it makes an appearance in the opening scene of *The Trojans*.

† Corneille, *Sertorius*, III 2.

it's there that the French Institute annually despatches its prize-winning composers!" As you say. What exile better calculated to waste their time and dampen their spirits, delay their careers, clip their wings (if they have any) and generally make life difficult for them – which one must conclude to be the objective of those responsible for the regulation, since they stick to it in defiance of common sense and the repeated warnings of impartial witnesses who have gone to see for themselves, and in doing so make themselves the laughing-stock of Europe. By all means send painters, sculptors and architects to Rome – but composers! No one laughs more than the Romans.

Search among the capitals of Lombardy, the Kingdom of Naples, the Kingdom of Sardinia, France, Austria, England, Bavaria, Prussia, the grand duchies of Hesse and Saxe-Weimar, Sweden, Denmark, for the most anti-musical, the most backward and the most devoid of great artists, and you will be forced to award the palm to the Papal States. The Institute has chosen wisely. The Institute is admirably consistent. It has adopted the device of Molière's doctors: "Even though the patient should die, we would not depart one jot from the hallowed prescriptions", and it follows it to the letter.

Berlioz now turns to Naples and (as we have seen) finds there at last a genuinely musical atmosphere. Yet even at the San Carlo corners are cut and the shoddy exerts its influence. The chorus has resisted all efforts to get it to sing accurately in four parts; the sopranos, being unable to hold a line independently of the tenors, double them at the octave. This kind of thing makes plausible the otherwise incredible reports he received of a performance of Mozart's Requiem in which, in default of women, boys or castrati, the soprano and alto parts were taken by tenors and basses singing an octave lower, with shattering results for the harmonic syntax of the work. "If in reading this letter, my friend, you have been tempted to borrow the favourite expression of Dominie Sampson in Scott's *Guy Mannering*, I fancy that this time 'prodigious' will not suffice, and like the good pedagogue when he learns of the crimes of the smugglers you will exclaim 'Enormous'!"

In conclusion, he says, one could write volumes on the reasons why the art of music stagnates in Italy while making giant strides in the rest of Europe, but he has been asked only for his personal impressions. "I give them to you, incomplete as they are. I have, admittedly, seen neither Milan nor Venice. As it is only fair in such cases to allow the benefit of the doubt and impute the highest qualities to what is unknown to us, we shall assume these two capitals to be richly endowed with original composers, inspired organists, singers with a keen sense of drama, lively and forceful choruses, vigorous orchestras full of zest, intelligence and agility, and dilettanti sufficiently devoted to art to enable the artists to live without repairing cane-bottomed chairs."

The article was finished in the second week of January 1832 and despatched to the journal's office in the Rue des St Pères. It appeared in three instalments in the March, April and May issues of the *Revue européenne*, and was later reprinted in the *Revue musicale*.

Meanwhile the news from France was making him restless and increasing his impatience to be there. Meyerbeer's *Robert le diable* had taken Paris by storm. The reports in the newspapers suggested that a new genre of dramatic art had arisen; perhaps it would transform the operatic scene and remove the old obstacles, opening the future to a bold and innovative spirit. Berlioz passed a sleepless night after reading them. To be immured in Rome (he wrote to Hiller) when great things were afoot in Paris which he could be part of! And in Lyons! "I could have been there too — I should have joined in." On the same day as the première of *Robert*, 21 November 1831, the silk-weavers of Lyons took to the streets to back up their demand for higher pay. For a week or two they were effectively in control of the town. As in Paris in July 1830, there was no looting. "Would you really be capable of marching against those poor devils whose turn to enjoy life has come at last?" His only worry was for his friend Auguste Berlioz, who was a member of the Lyons National Guard. For Ferrand too he would normally have been anxious: the man was quite capable of involving himself in some lunatic right-wing plot. Fortunately he had just got married.

Everyone was getting married. He and Thomas Gounet were almost the only ones to escape the contagion sweeping through the ranks of their friends. "Do you understand this universal matrimoniomania?" he wrote to Gounet on 17 February 1832. "My sister too has just got married, to a Grenoble judge. Albert Du Boys, whose 'Cantata for the Duchesse de Berry' you will recall and the curious letter he sent with it, is marrying a rich beauty from the département of Drôme. Auguste, Ferrand, Edouard Rocher, de Carné — all wedded in the past year. Be careful! 'Birds, preserve, preserve your precious liberty.'"*

Nancy's marrying Camille Pal (to the despair of her local admirers) was the event of the winter at La Côte. He was sixteen years older than her, at forty-one an important Grenoble judge, related on his mother's side to the Teisseyres, a clan long on friendly terms with the Berliozes. Camille Pal's late father had been rector of the university. Nancy was marrying into a very respectable and distinguished Grenoble family. Hector took the news of the engagement rather coolly, writing to his mother with a studiedly quizzical detachment which suggests he regarded his former ally and confidante as having settled for a *mariage de convenance*. "So

---

* From Béranger's "The Coronation of Charles the Simple".

that business is concluded — Nanci's getting married. From what she tells me and from Adèle's indiscretions I gather my future brother-in-law is being very attentive. As for Nanci I can see her now — at a loss what to do or what to say, crying at everything, getting upset without knowing why, frightened of her own shadow yet after all gradually becoming attached to her fiancé, so that if any harm of any kind were to come to him she would lose her indifference and feel quite despairing." As though relenting, he hopes they will be able to delay their planned visit to Paris until he is back, so that they can all three be there together.

A month after the wedding he writes to his sister in the same vein.

I was about to take up my pen and write to you, my dear Nanci, when Mama's letter arrived. The address is in your hand — but why no more than that? You could well have favoured me with a few lines. However, as Mama is always saying, "after all, we're only in this world to", etc., etc.

So here you are, married, and your husband the best of men, amiable, loving, utterly charming — at least, that's what Adèle means me to believe, and until you tell me the contrary I shall have to hold to that opinion. I send you both my Benediction. So be it.

And then there's the ball: "The glittering ball, the ball of rich delight, / She thought of it all day, she dreamed of it at night".* You dance, you whirl, you're fêted, you're showered with invitations. Well, dash it all, why not enjoy ourselves just for once. Does your husband dance? I gather you're living en famille at your mother-in-law's. The parting when Mama went back to La Côte must have been a little. ... I presume Grandfather let fly with the obligatory epithalamium. He is quite capable of having used for *your* Camille the one he had intended for *mine*.[†]

Nancy's departure did not improve the atmosphere in the Berlioz household. She and her mother were close; and now there was one fewer to deal with Prosper. The eleven-year-old boy had become a problem child. His parents did not know how to deal with him. In the light of the talent for mathematics and music that he later revealed, before his death at the age of nineteen, he may well have been an exceptionally gifted child. But he seemed irredeemable. He would not stay at any of the schools they tried; and Dr Berlioz's attempts to teach him Latin himself, as he had taught Hector fifteen years before, were fruitless. Prosper

* Hugo, *Les Orientales*, "Fantômes".

† In fact, Nicolas Marmion turned in an orginal work. His verse-letter, "Epithalame de Nancy ma petite-fille" is chiefly remarkable for the salaciousness with which the old man licks his lips at the thought of the marital rites shortly to be performed behind closed doors, far from prying eyes, and, while pretending not to, pictures the moment when his granddaughter unveils her chaste treasure before the gaze of her enraptured spouse.

refused to learn. He had taken to running away from home and being picked up on the road. They talked desperately of sending him to sea. A teacher from the local seminary was called in. The man came to the house twice a day, and at first appeared to make progress. Then, as Joséphine Berlioz reported to Nancy:

> Master Prosper went on strike. Last week your father unwisely decided the teacher should not discipline him too severely, for fear of turning him against him completely, and the little monkey must have divined it, for he wouldn't do anything he was told. I said to your father that he must give the man complete authority, which he did. That was too much for Prosper, who gave us the slip and ran off down the Champier road. When we discovered it Monique and Durand set off after him but before they could catch him up he had come back by himself by the Béal road. Your father took it very badly and gave him a few strokes with the horsewhip [...] Today he ran off again, along the Marcilloles road; M. Pion the doctor saw him but he took to his heels. When he came back your father horsewhipped him again. [...] Your father is in such a state as I cannot describe. [16 March 1832]

In the meantime Dr Berlioz's difficulties with Prosper had prompted a long letter from his elder son, in which he unburdened himself frankly to his father on a number of topics, including education, money and marriage.

Rome, 18 February 1832

I was on the point of writing to you, dear Father, when your letter arrived. It aroused in me a mass of disturbing and painful thoughts. I see you so sad, so unhappy, from a thousand causes that you had no reason to expect. My sister's marriage itself, by separating her from you, must have made your solitude more grievous and profound. Nanci was not the one of the family who understood you least well, and I fear that though you don't mention it such a separation has cost you a great deal.

I can imagine even more all that Prosper's follies must be making you feel. If I'm not mistaken, it's less from "unsociability" that he so stubbornly refuses to accept the educational establishments you've tried to send him to than from an amour-propre uncommon in a child of his age, which makes him try to attract attention. He wants to make an impression; he's found a way of doing so and he exploits it. All the same I don't imagine that by the time you receive this letter you will still be in favour of the drastic method for bringing him to heel that you tell me of. If Prosper had been born in a port, it might have worked — used to the maritime world from childhood, the idea would not strike him as at all extraordinary. But as it is, if you insisted it would certainly be for him an appalling humiliation which he would never forgive as long as he lived, and the danger would be that finding himself treated on the level of a galley-slave sent to the hulks, the effect on his character and conduct would be the exact opposite of what you intended. Only if he desired it himself — and why should such an idea enter his head?

My ideas on education are very different from yours, I think I can say so openly without fear of displeasing you. I consider French provincial education, for many children, totally absurd. Parents have only two careers in view, law and medicine; but even when they have no clear, decided objective for their sons they persist just the same in making them waste — I use the word deliberately — the ten best years of their life in the mire of a college learning a dead language which they will never master. What is the use of even knowing Latin very well — except to qualify for one of the two faculties? A young man who has English and German, who from an early age is involved in what's going on around him, without troubling himself what the Greeks and Romans did, a young man who has been in a position to observe, from an early age, the world with which he will have to deal, not an extinct world which is of no interest to him, is a thousand times better placed to get on and find his natural level. For politics, diplomacy, travel, the navy, the arts, literature, business, even the exact sciences, it's clear that nowadays we have to begin by being able to communicate freely with the great centres of civilisation which adjoin ours. The rest comes later and is learned much better. It's true that with my brother it would have been equally difficult to follow such a plan. In that case I think a radical step was called for — to send him right away, to Paris for example; he would not have come back without having gained a great deal in many ways. By spending two years at an English boarding-school he would have learned to speak the language of his schoolmates fluently, without noticing, he would have got to know a completely different world, different ideas would have developed in him, he would have begun to stand on his own feet instead of stumbling at every step despite the leading-strings which exasperate him but which he can't yet do without. All this is very confused and ill-considered, I've not thought it out. I speak only from my memory of what I remarked in myself at various stages. Children reason little; but they feel the inopportuneness of certain things. I remember clearly that from the first I was convinced I should never be a doctor. If instead of struggling so long I had been free to set my own course and deploy all my faculties as later I was to do, I should be not five but ten years further on. To finish my ramblings on the subject, I should tell you that in any case I know only one seafaring man, the captain of the *Sphinx*, a large steamship which plies regularly between Toulon and Algiers or Naples. He came to Rome a few months ago and I saw him daily. He's an excellent man, of great gentleness. M. Horace knows him well. His name is M. Salzat.

Now, to turn to me. After my last letter had gone I feared that what I replied to Mama on the subject of money might have upset you and I regretted having let it slip. But since you broach it it's better I should speak frankly. I genuinely believed that the income of a thousand francs which you promised me at the time when it was a question of my getting married would still be mine on my remaining a bachelor, especially since you never said anything to the contrary. I made arrangements accordingly, never imagining for a moment that you needed the money. When Mama, in sending it to me, chided me a little — very gently and indulgently, I must say — I felt I was back under the old system which I always found so tormenting, when I was *kept on a leash*, and I admit it came as a shock to me. It's better I should say so and be quite open about it. Every compulsory restraint, every obvious bridle, everything that threatens my freedom in the least degree, is unendurable to me. I have suffered terribly the past eight years, the most recent period of my life is a sad story of which you know only a few minor episodes, and which has formed my character as it is today. I am like someone who has been flayed. Every part of me has become excruciatingly sensitive so that I howl at the slightest touch. As a result, I should infinitely rather be short of money than have it at that cost. Five hundred francs agreed and settled would I swear be worth more to me than five thousand that I had to obtain by degrees, irregularly, complete with criticisms etc. Besides, now that I know for a fact that you would be going short on my account, I don't wish to hear any more about it. I shall manage in other ways. My personal expenses are not great, and with my grant I should not have needed anything, but for the trip to Naples that I had just made. The sole privations I experience for lack of money are to do with my art; it is only for that that I should like to be rich, so as to be able to exert my musical powers sooner and on a larger scale.

You talk of marriage, I have ideas on the subject that would take us far, too far for me to express them freely here. It's enough to tell you that at present I'm not in the least inclined to it. I'm only too well aware that an ordinary marriage, what is called a sensible marriage, a placid, *reasonable* marriage, would be the death` − .

The letter breaks off there; the rest has disappeared. It is unlikely it said much else on the subject; the drift is clear. Soon afterwards his mother reported the contents to Nancy:

[...] Received a letter from your brother, I have not sent it to you as I think it's enough for you to know that he's the same as he always is, never having in a letter but one dominant idea, he's replying to one your father wrote to him after Prosper's little pranks, his letter gives his opinion on the education of children in the provinces, and he argues even more seriously than usual, he then goes on to talk in veiled terms of the sorrows of every sort that he's been having for the last ten years and of his antipathy now to marriage which he says would be harmful to his art even if he was lucky enough to find a wife of the right sort for him, ah! poor boy, I answered yesterday with a long epistle which will prove to him that I share his ideas and that with his mind ["tête"] he is not made for domestic bliss, never will the poor child be happy except in expectation, and his parents never − if at least our second son too didn't have a mind and a character a hundred times worse, my child I didn't want to speak to you about it but my thoughts have carried me away [...]

What Berlioz writes to his father about marriage is echoed a couple of weeks later in a letter to Albert Du Boys. "I was never further from tying myself down; there's no commitment that seems to me more incompatible with my temperament than marriage."

Such remarks reflect the disillusionment that followed the rupture of his engagement to Camille Moke. The blow it gave his confidence was heavy; the wound cut very deep. She was, as he said, the one woman that had loved him. In a natural reaction of injured pride and self-protectiveness he seeks to minimise the affair: it is only a minor episode among the sad events of his recent life which have formed his character as it is today, leaving him like someone who has been flayed.

The stage is set for the reappearance of Miss Smithson. But not in a revival of the old play. The Camille Moke débâcle hardens his sense of the impossibility of a relationship of the intensity he dreams of, given his exalted notions of love and the unlikeliness of his ever being loved by a woman who shares them. Anything less — a "sensible marriage" — is unthinkable, as well as fatal to the artist in him. It is all or nothing; and since "all" is unattainable, it must be nothing. Not only the trauma of his jilting but the whole Italian experience serves to convince Berlioz of his essential solitariness.

Certainly Harriet Smithson was often in his mind during his time in Italy. When Mme Vernet mentioned her, during a conversation about Shakespeare some time in the winter of 1831–32, the nervous trembling her name provoked would have reminded him, if he had needed reminding, that she had not lost her hold over him. Tiersot maintains that the moment the new flame went out the old one was rekindled. Berlioz, who was "enamoured of love rather than of a particular woman [...] could never bear loneliness of heart": that was the main motive force of his emotional and psychological being. "The truth is that from the day when all was over with Camille he fell irresistibly once more under the power of Harriet Smithson."

Perhaps; but not, I am sure, in the same way as before. Even if her once-tarnished image was restored to its former purity, and he ceased to believe the "horrible truths" about her which he had willingly accepted in the first flush of his love for Camille (they had come, after all, from Camille!), it was not as it had been. He no longer thought of her as someone to pursue, a prize to aspire to, however far beyond his reach. "If I could but find the Juliet, the Ophelia my soul yearns for," cries the narrator in *Lélio*. But only the longing remains, not the hope. His adoration has become passive. He expects nothing from it. During his stay in La Côte in the second half of 1832 he will break his long silence and tell his father something of the five-year infatuation that gave him so much unhappiness, thus putting the "minor episode" of Camille Moke in perspective. But the dethronement of Camille does not reinstate Harriet to primacy in the old dynamic sense. If all or nothing means in effect Miss Smithson or nothing, that is as much as to say nothing, since it cannot be Miss Smithson, who is now truly unattainable; she has receded and become like Estelle an irrevocably distant beloved. Till the final months of 1832 Berlioz has no idea of seeing her again, let alone of what fate has in store for him.

Letters to Family and Friends

To Ferdinand Hiller

1 January 1832

Ah, so you didn't write "because you were busy setting up house". That's a priceless reason. It would have been better to say, "because I am in Paris, and in Paris one forgets the rest of the world". Anyway, we'll say no more about it. I presume that you received the note I sent you via Schlesinger and that you won't keep me waiting for the little piece that I asked you to let me have [the epilogue to *Orphée*]. I saw something about your concert in the *Globe*, which gave you quite a good review, mezzo-philanthropico-mystical, and claimed that you are an ex-student of the Paris Conservatoire. I've not seen anything in the other papers; M. — [Fétis] was presumably too busy describing Mme Malibran's latest roulade, or explaining a second and third horn chord in *Robert le diable*, to bother with a trifle like your concert ...

We should have felt most flattered by the judgment which that greasy meathead let fall from his high succulence on your latest efforts. He has so fine an understanding of the poetry of art, has our Falstaff. But patience: I've given him a kick up the crupper (as we say in Dauphiné) in a certain melologue which I *beg you to say nothing about*, and in which I've opened the sluice-gates a little and released some of my pent up bitterness. When it's performed it's going to have the effect of a grenade in an ambassador's drawing-room* [...]

Remember me to Mendelssohn, whom we often talk of at M. Horace's. At Mme Fould's the other day I heard the symphony he performed in London [no. 1] and which he "deranged" for violin, cello and piano duet. The first movement is superb, the adagio I don't have a very clear memory of, the intermezzo is fresh and piquant, the finale, complete with fugue, I detest. I can't understand how such a talent can turn note-spinner as he sometimes

---

* Berlioz's low opinion of Fétis as critic and improver of Beethoven might just suffice to explain the public attack on him in *Lélio* (where he and his kind are likened to birds that perch on statues of the Olympian gods in public gardens and bespatter them with their droppings); but the animosity revealed by his remarks to Hiller springs from a deeper source. The whole passage speaks of revenge for what is felt to be a personal wrong. Given Fétis' close friendship with the Mokes, it is probable that Berlioz had reason to believe, or at any rate believed, that Fétis had played a part in the break-up of his relationship with Camille. He could have heard of it from several of his Paris correspondents − Pixis, Gounet, Hiller himself − or conceivably from his fellow-pensionnaire Montfort (a pupil of Fétis) or from Mendelssohn, who knew Fétis and disliked and despised him. There were rumours that Fétis was one of Camille's lovers. See the discussion in Peter Bloom's *François-Joseph Fétis and the Revue Musicale*, 231−4.

does. He understands, however. It's always the same story: there's no such thing as absolute beauty [...]

Give my regards to Gounet, but without impiety, because it upsets him and that is the last thing I want to do. My New Year's wish for him is an increase in salary, grade and status and a radical indifference towards politics. For *all the others*, since they've not given me a sign of life, I wish them a well-cut pen and a little less laziness in using it.

To Humbert Ferrand

Rome, 1832, 9 in the evening, 8 January

[...] You waste your breath proving what is obvious already. Certainly there is no absolute good or bad in politics; certainly, today's heroes are tomorrow's traitors. I have known for some time that two and two make four. All I needed to be told was that Auguste was safe and sound, and Germain too. I regret that Lyons took up so much of your letter. When we are in the sanctuary at last, what do we care about the clamour from outside? I can't understand how you can be so fanatical on the subject. You ask me what difference there is between the barricades of Paris and those of Lyons? The difference that separates a large force from a lesser one, the head from the feet. Lyons cannot resist Paris, therefore it is wrong to annoy Paris. Paris drags the rest of France in its wake, therefore it can go in whatever direction it likes. That's all.

Your *Fairies' Wedding* is ravishing in its grace and freshness and light. I'm keeping it for later, this isn't the moment to write music for it — orchestration is not advanced enough — wait till we've immaterialised it a little, then we'll make Oberon's attendants speak. At present I'd compete unsuccessfully with Weber [...]

To Thomas Gounet

Rome, 17 February 1832

[...] If you write one of your charming little poems, would you reserve it for me and send it to me? On my return to France I mean to publish another collection, in the style of the *Mélodies*, to words by various authors. The other day I wrote a little air on Victor Hugo's *La captive* which I'm sure you will like. I've just come back from the mountains, where I spent the whole of the first part of the month, roaming around, my gun on my shoulder, despite the biting cold, the snow and the ice, sleeping now in one village, now in another,* happy to satisfy my "restlessness and desire to see things",† free at any rate of the trammels of academe. I'm leaving here at the beginning of May and will make for Grenoble, playing a trick on M. Horace, who will think me in Milan. From there I shall go briefly to Paris,

---

* Those visited included Civitella, Olevano, Genesano and Palestrina.

† La Fontaine, "The Two Pigeons".

and I "leave you to imagine what joy it will be"* to find you again, and
music, and our teas at the Café de la Bourse and our elegant dinners at
Lemardeley's, and the talk and the gossip: for we can allow ourselves such
things, we who are not married [. . .]

To Nancy Pal

Rome, 23 February [1832]

[. . .] I'm just back from the mountains, as the brigands say; I went to see
the snow. I roamed from village to village, my gun on my shoulder, eating at
night what I'd shot by day, stopping where I pleased, never giving ennui
time to catch up with me, and singing a hymn to liberty through all the
pores of my body. There's nothing to touch it! To wander like a chamois, at
every step to come on some new and glorious scene! For the first time since I
came to Italy I heard the cracking of ice. I've been back here only four days;
Mme Horace was intrigued by the motive of my long excursion; she imagines
I've got some mountain lover, which is far from true. Some of them look
magnificent, with flashing eyes, but all these pearls shine out of a squalor
whose smell is enough to make me keep my distance. People in high society
do not have the remotest conception of the pleasure I've been having, they
imagine it's only to be found in their noisy and tedious salons. It's true I
enjoy myself there from time to time, but I do so by laughing at them.

Next Monday we're to have a big fancy dress ball at the ambassador's;
M. Horace is lending me his Scottish costume. I'm going as Allan, the
officer of fortune in Walter Scott. My hair will be the sensation of the
season. All I'll be missing will be a bloodstained head in my left hand. I'd
have no trouble finding one, but it would not be "appropriate" — it would
give Mme de Marcell the screaming horrors — she is the reigning beauty in
Rome this winter† [. . .]

To Ferdinand Hiller

Rome, 16 March 1832

[. . .] By an extraordinary delay in the post I've just this moment received
your letter dated 17 February. It's taken a month to reach me. I'm ill — as
always — with that precious sore throat of mine, which will kill me if I give it
time. I've just read your letter and have got straight out of bed to answer
it [. . .]

Now, money: I think I can pay you back this summer, unless M. Horace

---

* La Fontaine, "The Town Rat and the Country Rat".

† Possibly Mme de Marcellus, wife of the celebrated diplomat, traveller and writer. As Pierre
Citron remarks, Berlioz certainly chose his disguise with more than a passing glance at his
murderous project of the previous April. Allan, a character in Scott's *A Legend of Montrose*, kills
his rival to prevent him from marrying the girl they both love.

In the event, the ball did not take place; the ambassador cancelled it as a gesture of sympathy
with the Pope and in protest at the French liberal government's occupation of Ancona.

objects to my drawing my whole allowance when I leave Rome. But here is a better idea: you have the packet that female gave you; open it, I give you permission — privately, on your own, or as you wish, I don't give a damn, and take my medal, which must be in it, and sell it at the exchange in the Passage des Panoramas. It's worth 200 francs, maybe more. [...]

I brought back [from the mountains] among other things a little *orientale* of Hugo's for single voice and piano. This little piece is having an incredible success. Everyone's taking a copy of it, at M. Horace's, at Mme Fould's, at the ambassador's, at the houses of all the French people they know. All the inmates of the Academy whistle the wretched thing incessantly, at meals, in the corridors, in the garden. They're beginning to make me wish I'd never written it. M. Horace himself is singing it now.* [...]

I shall be in Paris in November and December, we'll see each other then. But Mendelssohn will have gone. Then I shall see him in Berlin, or I shan't see him. As usual I heard by a letter more recent than yours that his enchanting *Midsummer Night's Dream* overture has been given at the Conservatoire. It's being spoken of very admiringly. There's no fugue in it. Adieu, adieu, adieu ... Remember me (Shakespeare, *Hamlet*). It's perishingly cold and I'm going back to bed.

To Humbert Ferrand

Rome, 26 March 1832

I've received your letter, my dear Humbert, and your sublime confession of laziness. Will you never cure yourself of it? If you knew what torment it is to be an exile and how "sad hours seem long"[†] in this dull barracks of mine, I don't believe you would make me wait so long for your replies.

You've written me a fine homily; but I assure you it's beside the point, and there's no need to be alarmed at the Callot-like tendency you imagine

---

* Cf. *Memoirs*, chapter 39: "In the inn where we used to stay [in Subiaco] I was watching my friend Lefebvre the architect drawing at a table, when a sudden movement of his elbow knocked a book on to the floor. I picked it up: it was a copy of Hugo's *Orientales*; it had fallen open at that enchanting poem 'La captive'. I read the poem, then said to Lefebvre, 'If I had some manuscript paper, I would set this to music — I can *hear* it.' — 'Don't let that deter you — I'll make you some'; and taking a pen and a ruler he rapidly drew a few staves, on which I jotted down the tune and the bass [...] A fortnight later, in Rome, during some music at the director's, I remembered 'La captive'. 'I must show you a song I thought up in Subiaco,' I said to Mlle Vernet. 'I'm curious to know if it's any good — I have no idea.' I scribbled the piano accompaniment and we performed it there and then; and so well did it catch on that a month later the desperate Vernet admonished me: 'Look here, Berlioz, next time you go up to the mountains please don't bring back any more songs. That "Captive" of yours is beginning to make the Villa uninhabitable. It's everywhere. [...] One can't move a yard without hearing someone bawling or grunting "Le long du mur sombre ... le sabre du Spahis ... je ne suis pas Tartare ... l'eunuque noir" and the rest of it. It's driving me mad. Tomorrow I'm getting rid of one of my servants, and I shall engage another on the strict understanding that he does not sing "La captive".' "

† *Romeo and Juliet*, I i, quoted in English by Berlioz.

me falling into.* Don't worry, never shall I be an admirer of the ugly. What I said about rhyme was intended simply to put you at your ease: I don't like seeing you spend time and talent overcoming quite unnecessary difficulties. You know as well as I do there are any number of examples of verse set to music in such a way that the rhyme and even the hemistich disappear altogether. What purpose has versification then? Rhyme and metre have their place in music in which there is no, or very little, repetition of the words, but it's only in such cases that versification can be perceived; otherwise it ceases to exist.

There is all the difference between verse *spoken* and verse *sung*. As for rhyme from a literary point of view, it's not for me to raise the question with you. But I do firmly believe that your horror of blank verse comes from habit and education. Remember that three quarters of Shakespeare is in blank verse, that Byron employed it and that Klopstock's *Messiade*, the epic masterpiece of the German language, is in blank verse. I've just read a French translation of Shakespeare's *Julius Caesar* which is in blank verse; it didn't shock me in the least, though from what you say I ought to have been revolted by it. All this kind of thing is so much a matter of habit that the same people who are shocked by *unrhymed French verse* find the *rhymed Latin* verse of the middle ages barbarous [...] I've been on the move again, to Albano, Frascati, Castelgondolfo, etc., etc.: lakes, plains, mountains, ancient tombs, chapels, monasteries, smiling villages, clusters of houses suspended from crags, the sea on the horizon, sun, silence, a balmy breeze, the infancy of the springtime — like a dream, an enchantment [...]

To Adèle Berlioz

Rome, 7 April 1832

My dear, good, excellent, a trifle mad but never capricious (for me, a transcendent virtue), little Adèle (when I say little . . . but never mind that), I was about to write to you when your second letter came. Congratulate Odile for me. Well, so there's another one happy ever after. We can all be, God be praised. Were you present at the most wonderful day of her life? It must have been fun. From what you tell me, my poor cousin would have married an Æsop (minus the intelligence if necessary) if her parents had told her to. The monastic education she received has succeeded in crushing what little spirit she was born with; she will lead the life of a cabbage, or not much better.

You ask me for details of what I'm doing and what I did at the ambassador's masked ball. That won't take long. The ball never took place. When the French occupied Ancona, M. de St Aulaire, who had very much taken the Pope's side, felt bound to demonstrate his disapproval publicly by not giving

* In a previous letter Berlioz had discussed the libretto of his apocalyptic opera *Le dernier jour du monde* and had advised Ferrand, if he could bring himself to, not to be bound by strict rules of versification and to abandon rhyme altogether when it served no precise purpose. Presumably Ferrand reacted by defending traditional values and compared the freedom Berlioz advocated with the ideas of the painter and engraver Callot, seventeenth-century master of the grotesque who rejected classical practice.

the much-heralded ball. You should have seen the plots and wagers, the pouting vexation and frustrated vanity that ensued. Some had had costumes made for a hundred francs, others for four or five hundred, and all to no purpose. I nearly died laughing. And as the Pope also banned part of the Carnival festivities, all their expectations of pleasure were blighted. It was a double joy for me to see all that high society rabble trailing drearily up and down the Corso, totally deprived of the vain delights they had promised themselves. Perfect!*

My trip to the mountains? I go there so often I'm not sure which one you mean. Most recently I went to Albano, Frascati and other enchanting places. Lake Albano on one side, the sea and the plain on the other — it's beyond description; and besides, I have to tell you that I've decided the descriptive mode is played out — it's too boring. We'll *talk* about it, which is much better. I've still another twenty-seven days here. As it's all quite official and I'm in accord with the Academy, I could leave even earlier if my portrait was finished; but the painter who's begun it won't be free to complete it for another two weeks. I shall be obliged to go by Milan, which will lengthen my route. Many young men of my acquaintance have just left for Sicily; I was extremely tempted to go, but resisted their pressing invitation, thinking of all of you [. . .]

Instead, he made one final visit to Subiaco, to "say goodbye to my dear mountains" and the friends who lived there, and to play one last time for the regulars at the inn. He was there in mid-April, and heard the organist perform the overture to *La Cenerentola* at mass in the local church on Palm Sunday, the 15th. Soon afterwards he was back in Rome; on Easter Day he stood among the hushed multitudes in St Peter's Square and watched the Pope give the pontifical blessing "urbi et orbi".

With the agreement of the director he was paid a lump sum of 1,050 francs in lieu of board and lodging for the remaining six months of 1832, and a further 600 francs' travelling allowance, plus 9 piastres and 15 baiocchi for the cost of copying the score he had sent back to the Académie des Beaux-Arts in Paris as a sample of his work. He also signed, in advance, the monthly receipts for May and June, postdating his signature. Plainly, he was in accord with the Academy.

M. Horace held a farewell dinner in his honour. Most of his evenings were now spent at the Vernets'; they talked, reminisced, made music, sang the trio from *Don Giovanni* for the last time. He wrote in Louise Vernet's album, paying tribute to the charms which had helped to make

---

* Berlioz's outburst of spleen in the *Memoirs* against the mass hysteria and cruelty of the Carnival conflates two separate examples of popular sport under a single heading: the Shrovetide public execution of a condemned criminal and the summer water festival in the Piazza Navona, which he had attended the previous year.

the ennui of Rome bearable for him.[*] With the end of his exile in sight, he no longer felt oppressed by Rome, and was at his most agreeable and entertaining. (This was the impression of him that remained with Mme Vernet and her daughter when, soon afterwards, Legouvé questioned them about him and they praised him as a charming conversationalist, defending him against the charge of being a poseur.) Perhaps he was conscious of needing to atone for his black humour during the previous year, and set out to be agreeable to make amends for it. But he seems also to have become genuinely fond of them and to have been warmed by discovering, to his surprise, how fond they were of him. It was a mutual liking. Whether there was anything more than that between him and Louise Vernet we don't know. She may for a moment have been on the verge of turning into an object of his mythopœic imagination. A year earlier he found the prospect of hearing her perform some fashionable air at a soirée as inviting as the squeak of a bat or the voices of the Le Sueur daughters. Now he sits at her feet while she plays him Beethoven adagios on the piano. In a letter to her mother, a month or two later, he will call her "the graceful Ariel" — the magical spirit invoked not so long before to characterise Camille Moke. And his memory of her singing La captive, or of the singer herself, will be pleasant enough for him to dedicate the song to her. If there was a tendresse on either side (was it she who cut the missing avowal from her album?), it did not develop. Three years later she married the painter Paul Delaroche; and apart from an appearance at the première of the Grande Messe des Morts, which prompts her to send Berlioz a brief, affectionate note, we hear no more of her in his life.

By the end of April Signol had finished his portrait; according to custom, it was hung in the refectory. (Today it is in the director's office, together with Debussy's.) One of the three surviving early pictures of Berlioz — roughly contemporary with Ingres' drawing and Vernet's pen-and-ink sketch — it shows him in the handsome garb of the Jeune-France: dark-brown velvet-collared coat and plum-coloured waistcoat, white shirt with deep, starched neck-band, black silk stock and florid cardinal-red silk scarf fixed with a tie-pin. Something of what attracted the Vernets comes out in the painter's treatment: not merely the halo of hair, brushed forward and falling in soft curls over the pale brow, and the fine aquiline nose, but the trusting candour with which one deep-set blue eye looks out on the world while the other gazes beyond and within, lost in thought.

The last few days were a round of parties, goodbyes and packing up. He drank Orvieto wine with the "lower orders" at the Café Greco and a farewell punch with his comrades at the Academy, dined with the Vernets,

---

[*] 30 April. Part of the page in question was cut out at some later date; but the general tenor of the missing portion is clear from the context.

wrote in various albums, sold his gun, spent a long time stroking Vernet's two dogs, the regular companions of his shooting expeditions, and felt a pang at the thought that he was leaving Italy — his Italy, "wild Italy" — perhaps never to see it again.

The other Italy provided, on the day before his departure, one final reminder of what he would be missing, in the shape of a high mass celebrated with orchestra and chorus in the church of San Luigi de' Francesi on the feast of St Philippe, patron saint of the King, before a congregation of cardinals, distinguished foreign visitors and artists. The French ambassador had engaged the best musicians in Rome, and they proceeded to put on a show that confirmed Berlioz in all his dearest prejudices. The organ was a quarter of a tone flat but the organist played on regardless, the instrumentalists kept tuning desperately while the priests chanted their plainsong, the music was an atrocious medley of cavatinas culled from Vaccai, Paccini and Gallenberg, and the solos in this holy and apostolic farrago were delivered in a soprano voice by a vigorous-looking gentleman with florid complexion and enormous black side-whiskers.

Next day, 2 May, his friends accompanied him to Ponte Molle and saw him and his baggage into a decrepit wagon, and he set off on the return journey to France.

32

Homecoming

———————•◆•◆———————

As though reluctant to leave Italy after all, Berlioz did not take the direct route north but instead made a wide eastward arc, via Narni, Terni, Spoleto and Perugia, not arriving in Florence till ten days after his departure from Rome. The stages of his journey were noted, together with items of expenditure and comments (mostly in Italian) on what he saw, in a pocket-book ruled with music staves which he had bought before leaving Rome: Baccano ("lunch 18 baiochi"), Monterosi, Città Castellana, Vigne, Narni ("delicious Poussin-like landscape"), Terni, Papigno, Lago di Piediluco and its falls ("stupendous, extraordinary, far finer than the falls at Tivoli and Isola di Sora"), Montagna di Somma ("young girls bringing you almonds"), Spoleto, Foligno, Santa Maria degli Angeli ("superb church, heavily damaged in the earthquake"), Perugia ("splendid hill-top town, disagreeable people"), and then across the Umbrian plain into Tuscany and to Florence, where he arrived on the 12th.*

It was his fourth visit to Florence; falling in love with the place all over again, he lingered for several days. But it was disturbing too. Being on his own there, going to the post office to enquire for letters (and finding one from Ferdinand Hiller), brought back the terrible time a little over a year before when he had waited and waited for a letter from Camille. It gave him — he told Hiller in his reply — a bizarre sense of split personality. "When I'm in Florence I feel as if it's no longer me walking along the splendid embankment of the Arno but some foreigner, a Russian or an Englishman, and Berlioz is somewhere else and I'm merely an acquaintance of his. I act the dandy, spend money, strike foppish attitudes. I don't understand it." To Horace Vernet he wrote of the vague sensation of sadness that clouded his spirits.

* The pocket-book was used during the next couple of years for sketches for *Harold in Italy* and *Benvenuto Cellini*. See the article by D. Kern Holoman, "The Berlioz Sketchbook Recovered", in *Nineteenth-Century Music*, VII/3 (3 April 1984, "Essays for Joseph Kerman") and the complete facsimile included with it.

On the first evening he went to the Pergola and saw Bellini's *La sonnambula*. He liked it as little as he had his *Montecchi e Capuleti* in the same theatre the previous year; but his old acquaintance Gilbert Duprez was singing the rôle of Elvino and Berlioz went round to see him in one of the intervals. Duprez, who had been in Italy for the last few years, was the reigning star of Florence. They had not met since the summer of 1828, when Duprez, a recent graduate of Choron's school, sang at Berlioz's first concert. "We rather enjoyed recalling those days. Since then we've both advanced a few steps — I six or seven, he thirty or forty." Duprez was now earning fifteen thousand francs a year. "What is more, he is really talented, has a very attractive, well-tuned voice, and understands music. Unlike Nourrit he is no actor but he sings better; and the timbre of his voice has a more natural, more original quality [...] In a few years he will be the rage of Paris, I'm quite sure."*

On the 15th, having had his boots repaired and, at his mother's request, bought straw hats for his sisters, he left Florence. Instead of making another detour to Elba and Corsica as he had thought of doing, he took the direct route home, across the Apennines to Bologna, then via Modena, Parma and Piacenza to Milan, which he reached on 20 May. Donizetti's *L'elisir d'amore* at the Teatro della Cannobiana was no more to his taste than *La sonnambula*, from what he could hear of it: the din of feet and canes and parasols beating time on the parquet and the buzz of conversation in the boxes, where supper parties were in full swing, was so loud that though the orchestra, for Italy, played with unusual vigour only the bass-drum could be heard clearly.

As the coach moved slowly north-west in glorious spring weather and the white rampart of the Alps defined itself more sharply day by day, France drew him back into its orbit. The entries in his pocket-book changed from Italian to French, and the terrain's rich and poignant Napoleonic associations — the bridge at Lodi, the plains of Lombardy where the young French army's feats of arms first startled Europe and the Bonaparte legend was born — crowded upon him, inspiring thoughts of a composition for wind band which eight years later would become the

---

* Berlioz's prediction was fulfilled. When Duprez returned to Paris in the mid-1830s the exciting Italianate quality of his voice took the Opéra by storm. Nourrit was eclipsed — though Rossini always preferred Nourrit's singing in *William Tell* and compared Duprez's chest-voice top C in Arnold's Act 4 aria to "the squawk of a capon having its throat cut". (See the entry under Duprez in Appendix II of my edition of the *Memoirs*, 539–40.)

Another old friend whom Berlioz may have met again in Florence was his fellow-Gluckist, the aristocratic Augustin de Pons, who in the meantime had become, like his wife, an opera singer, adopting her maiden name of Saint-Ange and — according to the *Memoirs* — "trailing after her from one French and Italian opera house to another". The Florentine address of a Saint-Ange figures in the pocket-book just above Duprez's.

Symphonie funèbre et triomphale. In the pocket-book he noted: "Le retour de l'armée d'Italie — Simphonie militaire en 2 parties: 1? Adieux des hauts des Alpes aux braves tombés dans les champs d'Italie, 2? Entrée triomphale des vainqueurs à Paris", and added: "the idea came to me in Turin on 25 May 1832, on seeing the Alps again, my heart full of the Napoleonic memories aroused by the country I had just passed through."[*]

In Turin he bought a new collar and a pair of boots, and had his hair cut and his beard trimmed. The next two pages of the pocket-book record the final leg of the journey, including the crossing of the Alps into France by the Mont Cenis pass:

From Turin to Grenoble:	2 fr. 50 c.
St Ambroise [San Ambrogio di Tor]	3 fr. supper and bed
Suze [Susa]	3 fr.
Mont Cenis	0
Lanslebourg	3 fr. 50 c.
Modane	8 francs for the coachman
St Jean de Maurienne	3 fr.
Chaparillan	24 sous lunch
	56 sous customs duty on the hats

By the time he reached the last-named staging-post he was in the valley of the Isère, his native river, only thirty-five miles from Grenoble. On the afternoon of 31 May he descended the vale of the Grésivaudan and felt a rush of delight at the dear familiar landscape, the great stream gliding between lines of shimmering poplars, the jagged peaks of the Vercors, the guardian rock of St Eynard and below it Meylan, his grandfather's home and the white house where Estelle stayed and the green enchanted hillsides, all bright and welcoming in the glow of a summer's day.

In Grenoble he deposited his trunks and packages and called on his friend Casimir Faure, and the two of them went to his sister Nancy's, at 10 Grande Rue Neuve. She was not there (it was a public holiday). They called back later but she was still out. The letter announcing his arrival

---

* Hazlitt was moved to similar thoughts when he crossed the Alps in the opposite direction a few years earlier. "It gives one a vast idea of Buonaparte to think of him in these situations. He alone (the Rob Roy of the scene) seemed a match for the elements, and able to master 'this fortress built by nature for herself'. Neither impeded nor turned aside by immoveable barriers, he smote the mountains with his iron glaive, and made them malleable; cut roads through them; transported armies over their ridgy steeps; and the rocks 'nodded to him, and did him courtesies!' "

had gone astray and he was not expected. Nancy returned soon afterwards, as her letter of next day describes:

Grenoble, Friday [1 June 1832]

Do me the favour not to go quite out of your mind, my dear Adèle, when
you admit the bearer of this letter, and please try to read it through to the
end even though he is *there*, right next to you. I am also so exacting as to beg
you to write to me as soon as possible giving full details of his arrival.
Yesterday evening I went with my uncle [Victor] to Gière to see Odile.
When I got back my husband was in bed. I went in to Mme Teisseyre, and
my mother-in-law said, "A gentleman came with Casimir and asked for
you — he's been twice." — "Didn't he leave his name?" — "No." — "Silly
man — how stupid of him." A moment later there was a ring. "Perhaps
that's him." Sure enough, M. Casimir was presented. "Madam, I've brought
someone to see you who has news of your brother." At that I feel a stab of
anxiety, knowing it is a long time since he has written, and hurry forward to
meet the man who is to give me news of him — and find you know who. No
one was ever more flabbergasted. It takes a few moments like that to make
up for so many others in one's life! I wouldn't let him see Camille, I was
most anxious that the first impression should be good, and the appearance
of a man who has just woken up and is yawning and rubbing his eyes was
very much not the one I wished to present him with. He didn't see him till
this afternoon, on his return from court. He'll tell you what he thought of
him, but I thought he seemed pleased. This first encounter had worried
me — you understand. [. . .] If Hector hadn't insisted on leaving this
evening we would have taken him to Meylan tomorrow, but he is in a
hurry to see you all again, especially when he discovered that you were
anxious about him. I'm in hopes that as soon as you are done with your silk-
worms he will make you come and spend at least three weeks here. Mama
must arrange to sell her cocoons or have the silk spun without her. I want
you all to come here soon. If Uncle Victor had not been so cussed as to go
off to St Etienne with his Corsican pony I should have come on a spree and
spent a couple of days with you. As it is, I'm letting you have Hector [. . .]

It was his happiest homecoming. For the first time for many years he
was at ease with his family. Eighteen months before, on his way to Italy,
grief and growing anxiety at parting from Camille had cast a gloom over
the visit; and before that to a greater or lesser degree there had always
been the unresolved conflict over his career. Now he was welcomed
unreservedly. The five months between his arrival from Italy and his
departure for Paris mark the only period of relatively unclouded relations
between them in the whole of his adult life.

His coming brightened the atmosphere of the household and raised
everyone's spirits. He took his brother Prosper on hunting expeditions,
and spent time getting to know him; the twelve-year-old boy thrived in
his company, became more amenable and agreed to go back to school.
He had long talks with his father; he opened his heart to him about many

things, including his unhappy passion for Harriet Smithson, which till then had been kept secret from his family.

With his mother, though he was on better terms than before, there was nothing like the same sense of intimacy (complicity, almost); their minds inhabited different worlds. Yet the trick she played on him soon after his arrival showed that, if on a rational level he was incomprehensible to her, intuitively she understood him perhaps better than his father did. She had been given a letter to deliver to a Mme Fornier who was passing through La Côte in the Grenoble–Vienne diligence, and asked him to go to the coach office in the Place St André and hand it to her. He went quite unsuspectingly and found himself face to face with Estelle, whom he had last seen fifteen years before. Practically no words were exchanged between them; but the shock of the encounter was still visible when he returned to the house. "So — I see that Némorin has not forgotten his Estelle", was Mme Berlioz's malicious but perceptive comment.

Above all, these months confirmed and deepened his tendresse for his sister Adèle, just turned eighteen. The potential affinity with Nancy had been greater. But Nancy, always ambivalent about him, had in his eyes finally given up the struggle and joined the ranks of the bourgeoisie. Adèle was less intelligent but more warm-hearted and sympathetic. He could relax in her company and she was content in his. Of the family she was the one who accepted him as he was with all his moods, asperities and extravagances, who never cast doubt on his vocation, who loved him without conditions. To her alone he did not have to keep justifying himself.*

Ten days after his arrival Adèle sent a report to her sister in Grenoble:

He's really merry, this lovely brother of ours, what a difference from the last time he was here — it's not the same man. I was very curious to know what he feels about the treacherous Camille; I was afraid to bring up the subject, but I needn't have worried, he brought it up himself and talked to me at great length about it. He despises her, so much so that he doesn't even think her worth hating. I can tell you, I breathed more easily after he had said that. We actually joke about it quite often — and about many other things. Yesterday he told us about some of the pranks he witnessed during his time in Rome — we nearly died laughing. He saw so many people and so many things that every day we hear something new. Since he's been here I've been spending my time very happily. He's working hard, and while he works I keep him company, mending his shirts, which may surprise you; but what is more extraordinary, it doesn't bore me in the least — working for *him* is delightful. I can see you laughing, you beast — but I asked for it by the naïve way I've been carrying on.

---

* Twenty-five years later, while composing *The Trojans*, he writes to her of "the extra link that has been forged between us thanks to the interest you are taking in this thing that torments and exalts me, that devours and destroys me, that makes me live".

Berlioz's main occupation during the five months he spent in Dauphiné was to get ready for the concerts he planned to give in Paris before his departure for Germany. There was a lot of work still to do. An orchestra of the size that had played for his last concert and such as he hoped to reassemble this time meant eight or nine desks of first violins, as many seconds and so on; and each separate part had to be written out afresh. Much of the material for *Lélio* remained to be copied, together with the orchestral parts for the revised Scène aux champs, the slow movement of the Fantastic Symphony: it had been drafted in Rome but the fair copy was made in Dauphiné (the score is on French manuscript paper). Writing to Hiller on 7 August he reckoned it would be another sixty-two days before he finished.

For the rest he went out with his old Côtois friends Edouard Rocher, Charles Bert, Just and Laurent Pion, Alexandre Figuet, caught up with the latest novels (Balzac, Saintine, Raymond), attended weddings, bathing parties, parties of boule, visited relatives, and walked whole days on end over the scorching countryside.

He could not feel merry for long. The craving for movement grew. On 3 July, after a month in La Côte, he set out for Grenoble on foot, arriving at his sister Nancy's house thirty-five miles away at 9 in the evening. The next fortnight was a round of visits. He dined with his Uncle Victor and Aunt Laure and his cousin Odile, called on his other uncle and aunt, Auguste and Félicie Berlioz, and went to La Combe, nine miles up the Isère valley, the country house of Albert Du Boys and his new wife ("perfectly all right but nothing more", he reported to Ferrand). His brother-in-law Camille Pal took the day off from the bench and they all went to Meylan for the day to see Grandpère Marmion. A week later the old man returned the visit, emulating his grandson and walking down to Grenoble in the blazing sun.

A very little of Grenoble, as Berlioz again discovered, went a long way. The heat was stifling, but not more so than the almost undiluted company of lawyers. Camille Pal proved to be relentlessly loquacious; but all of them, not only Camille but his brother Henri and their whole circle, were prone to hold forth. "Despite all my efforts to change the subject, they insist on addressing me on art and music and great poetry. And God knows how they speak of such matters in the provinces — such weird ideas, judgments calculated to curdle an artist's blood in his veins, and withal a dreadful casualness and complacency. To hear them talk of Byron or Goethe or Beethoven you would think it were some tailor or bootmaker of slightly more than common ability. Nothing is good enough for them — never any enthusiasm, any respect." It was more than he could bear when they belittled his idols — "my incomparable gods whom I 'wear in my heart of hearts'". "I emerge from these encounters all scratched and jangled." He took refuge in silence. Alone in the midst of bourgeois Grenoble and a heat as oppressive as in the dog days in

Rome, he felt his old enemy the spleen reassert its grip. Only the massed regimental drummers beating through the town excited his spirits, and he would follow them as he had done as a boy.

The brunt of his gloomy taciturnity fell on his unfortunate sister Nancy, who took it ill. Their old intimacy had gone. She could no longer respond to him and he could no longer confide in her. On Hector's return to La Côte in mid-July she wrote to Adèle that she was sending her dear brother back "with all his amiability intact, for he's not spent a farthing of it here. At my mother-in-law's he's been consistently sullen, and you will have to pardon them if they take him for a savage and a misanthrope, for honestly there is no reason why they should think otherwise. Not once did he come in without a dismal, scowling expression on his face. If Grenoble has this effect on him I can't conceive why he stayed here so long. It was really upsetting for me to see him always show himself in such an unflattering light. Sometimes his chilling silence almost choked me physically. It would be impossible to make less of an effort to be agreeable. Perhaps I shouldn't write this to his faithful panegyrist, but I needed to unburden myself to someone and not wishing to do so to Mama it could only be to you."

Back in La Côte Berlioz wrote a long letter to Mme Vernet in Rome, describing his experiences (already quoted) in the "judgmental world" of Grenoble where so many of his acquaintances were attached to the bench or the bar and he felt totally alienated from them all. "And then, I'm suffocating for lack of music. I no longer have the prospect of Mlle Louise's piano in the evenings and the sublime adagios she had the kindness to play me without letting my insistence on her repeating them exhaust her patience or spoil her performance. I see you laugh, Madam; I imagine you saying, he doesn't know what he wants or where he would like to be, he's half mad. To which I answer that I know quite well what I want, but that as to my *mezza pazzia*, since people are generally agreed that that's what I am and since there's often an advantage in being thought so, I let them think it."

Where he wanted to be was Paris. But that, for the moment, was impossible. He must bide his time in the provinces, cut off from the longed-for excitements of the capital, alone with his thoughts which in whatever direction they turned (he told Hiller) dug into him as painfully as a porcupine's quills.

The other day [his letter to Mme Vernet continues] my father thought up the strangest method of restoring me to sanity. He wanted to marry me off. Presuming rightly or wrongly from what he had found out that my suit would be well received by the lady — a relative of ours who is very rich but whose fortune is more or less her only recommendation — he urged me in the strongest manner to present myself, for the irrefutable reason that a young man whose inheritance will never amount to more than a hundred thousand francs cannot possibly pass up the chance to marry an inheritance of three hundred thousand cash down, with the prospect of as much again. At first I laughed, thinking my father was joking. But when he became more insistent I was obliged to declare quite categorically that I felt incapable of loving the person in question and was not for sale at any price. That terminated the discussion. But it left me with a disagreeable impression. I thought my father knew me better.

Did Dr Berlioz feel guilty at not bequeathing his heir a larger inheritance, at having let the family fortune dwindle through his agricultural pursuits and the endless unpaid loans to his brother-in-law Félix Marmion? Did he see the match, cynically, as the ideal worldly solution to the needs of the struggling artist? Or did he, from foreboding, snatch at a straw, divining Miss Smithson's continuing hold over his son's fatal imagination?

The incident did not make Berlioz feel any less of a stranger in his native home. La Côte was nearer to Paris than Rome was, but it was exile just the same. And the household, galvanised at first by his coming, settled back into the daily round. His father, though only fifty-six years of age, was in bed by 9 on most evenings; his mother fretted about her husband's health and her own. Adèle still kept him company while he worked, and he loved her presence. But his mind was elsewhere. Soon she went off to Grenoble to stay with Nancy and he was alone. When not copying parts (which he did "till his thumb ached") he read the materialist philosophers and physiologists whose works were in his father's library – Locke, Cabanis, Gall – and found confirmation for his own disbelief in a personal God, though the authors "can't bring themselves to follow their principles through to the end, for fear of *opinion*".

In the second half of August, after a further month at La Côte, he went to visit Ferrand at his home in Belley. They had not seen each other for four years. "Extremes meet, as you see," he wrote to Hiller. "He is more religious, more fanatical than ever." Once again Berlioz walked the thirty-five miles from La Côte to Grenoble. From there he took the Lyons coach as far as Les Abrets, twenty-five miles south of Belley, having written to ask Ferrand if he could come and collect him there the next morning, 23 August; if not, he would do the last part of the journey on foot. He stayed four days. At first Ferrand's wife Aimée was away, taking the waters at Aix-les-Bains (a few weeks earlier Nancy had done the same at Uriage, in the hope of removing some obstacle to her conceiving a child). The two friends went to Aix to fetch her, and Berlioz met Ferrand's childhood sweetheart whom he had married the previous year. Domesticity had not made Ferrand a more galvanic collaborator. Though they discussed *Le dernier jour du monde* and Ferrand promised to send him something soon, Berlioz was not sanguine about it. (As always, it was he who took the initiative in their relationship. That their friendship lasted all their lives and they continued to take pleasure in each other's company

and correspondence was due largely to his persistence.) Ferrand's projected return visit to La Côte St André did not materialise. Another six
years would pass before they met again.

Berlioz was back at La Côte in the last few days of August and
apparently was there throughout the remaining two months of his stay in
Dauphiné. The summer declined slowly into glowing autumn, Nancy
came on a visit, Prosper went docilely off to school, the time of the wine
harvest came round, the October rains arrived. He would remember all
his life the pouring wet morning when he and Adèle set out together
down to the plain — scoffed at by the rest of the family — and walked for
a couple of hours pressed close together under a large umbrella without
speaking a word.

Berlioz's intention had been to stay till the middle of November, in
obedience to Horace Vernet's vague stipulation that he should not show
his face in Paris "before the end of the year". But the thought that by
waiting so late he risked missing the chance to organize a concert before
he left for Berlin prompted a more liberal interpretation of their agreement.
He must allow himself time to assemble an orchestra and set the whole
affair in train. He wrote to Paris and made plans to give a concert at the
beginning of December. On 28 October he had his passport made, and
four days later took the diligence to Lyons. There he lingered for a day
with the idea of seeing Ferrand; but nothing came of it. On the evening of
the 2nd he went to the Grand Théâtre and had the "deeply unpleasant"
experience of hearing the last movement of the Pastoral Symphony mis-
erably played as the accompaniment to a ballet. "It was like seeing in a
brothel the portrait of some adored angel of one's dreams." But soon he
would hear real music again — after two years without it! "I think I shall
lose my sanity [. . .] I'm entirely alone in this great city. Auguste [Berlioz]
has his own sad preoccupations: he lost his wife's young brother the day
before yesterday, dead of consumption. Oh how alone I feel, how I suffer
within myself! How wretchedly constituted I am — a true barometer,
now up, now down, subject to the variations in the atmosphere, brilliant
or sombre, of my consuming thoughts."

On the journey to Paris his spirits rose. Among his fellow-passengers
were several Paris acquaintances; already he could feel himself coming
into the magnetic field of the capital. He was returning home. The
moment he arrived, on the morning of 7 November, the old intoxication
took hold: he was alive again. The threads of his existence were waiting
to be picked up where he had put them down. It was as though he had
never been away.

Berlioz's first move was to rent a room in the same quarter as before,
near the Conservatoire, the main opera houses and his publisher
Schlesinger. His old room at 96 Rue de Richelieu was, he found, occupied,

so he crossed the street and tried the nearest lodging-house to it, the one
just opposite on the corner of Richelieu and Neuve St Marc. He knew the
landlord, M. Tartes, from the time of his forlorn courtship of Harriet
Smithson four years before; it was the house where she had lived. A room
was vacant in the actual apartment she had had, overlooking the Rue de
Richelieu from the windows he had stared across at in the winter of 1829.
He moved in. It was a characteristic act of mingled bravado and detachment. Like Hamlet he defied augury. The notion might appeal to his
sense of irony and romance; but for the moment he brushed it aside. It
was the obvious convenient and practical step to take, so why not take it?
What was there to fear?

That afternoon he dined with the Le Sueurs, and after dinner met
Gounet round the corner at the Café Feydeau. All his old haunts were
welcoming him with open arms. The concert was already gathering
momentum; his career was resuming where it had left off. The young
guard, Seghers, Urhan, Desmarest, were eager to join it, as was Habeneck
to conduct. Even Cherubini was proving cooperative; the old man seemed
actually pleased to see him back and readily agreed to his using the
Conservatoire Hall. Paris the fickle had not forgotten him in the two
years he had been away. The artistic journals had kept his name alive
during his absence, and his return was hailed as an event.

Even in establishment circles his stock seemed mysteriously to have
risen. At the Institute prize-giving two months before, the Secretary,
reading out the report of the music section of the Académie des Beaux-
Arts, had paid eloquent tribute to his envoi from Rome: M. Berlioz, a
young composer known for an ardour and an originality which bordered
on the bizarre if not on the Teutonic, had earned the warmest praise for a
work written throughout in a large and sober manner, at once original
and natural, everything in its rightful place, thus proving that he had
learned to profit from sound criticism. The validity of the tribute was
somewhat undermined by the fact that the favoured work was none other
than the old Resurrexit, which even in its revised form dated from at
least four years back, before he had had a chance to profit from the
Academy's criticism; but it was useful none the less. He found himself
being treated as something of a celebrity. There was renewed talk of an
opera. Eugène Sue was apparently keen to write a libretto for him.
Berlioz was introduced to the popular novelist through the good offices of
Ernest Legouvé, a rich young littérateur (son of Legouvé the Classical
playwright, author of *André Chénier*) who had been at the Villa Medici
just after Berlioz and had lost no time in writing to request the honour of
meeting him. Alexandre Dumas, author of the prodigiously successful
Antony, was also said to be interested in a collaboration; several people
independently assured Berlioz that the playwright had just finished a
libretto intended for him. The director of the Opéra, Véron, received him
with positively honeyed flattery and, though refusing to release Adolphe

Nourrit (for the tenor numbers in *Lélio*), was letting him have Alexis Dupont and was coming to the concert himself. If Véron liked it and if the concert was a success, an opera commission might result. Creating a public for your music could influence the impresarios in your favour.

Meanwhile the posters for the concert were causing a stir; everyone was talking about it. To play the rôle of the artist-narrator in the Melologue he had engaged Bocage, whose sensational success in *Antony* had made him one of the most sought-after actors in Paris and who was at present starring in another Dumas play, *La tour de Nesle*. The chance of a second hearing of the Fantastic Symphony and the idea of following that extraordinary work with a "sequel" entitled "The Return to Life" — and in the form of a mixture of spoken monologues and musical numbers with titles such as "Scene from a Brigand's Life", "Chorus of Angry Shades", "The Harp's Last Echoing Sigh" — appealed to Parisian curiosity. It suggested one of those grand artistic happenings that periodically enliven the life of the capital. The concert was much canvassed in the press; there was hope of an excellent house.

With twelve days still to go Berlioz wrote to Nancy to report that things were working out almost alarmingly well — never had he been prepared for a concert so far in advance. He was also at pains to allay other misgivings. "My father is anxious at the presence of Mrs Smithson. Tell him to set his mind at rest; she is so changed in every respect, she'll not get me to make a fool of myself again."

Harriet Smithson had reappeared in Paris shortly before Berlioz. After a disappointing season at the Theatre Royal, Haymarket she had decided to try her luck abroad and had naturally looked to Paris, scene of her triumphs in 1827 and 1828. With the vague idea of setting up a permanent English company under her direction she travelled to Paris in late October, taking with her her crippled sister. She went first to the old apartment at 1 Rue Neuve St Marc, then, after a week or two, left it, establishing herself at the Hôtel du Congrès in the Rue de Rivoli opposite the Louvre. A day later Berlioz presented himself at his old lodgings and, finding them taken, crossed the street and moved in in her place.

Berlioz had returned to Paris without any active thought of Harriet. Her star had sunk below his horizon: she had left France not long after he had; there had been no reason why their paths should ever cross again. The newspapers were slow to mention her (it was an item in mid-November in one of the papers read at La Côte that roused Dr Berlioz's alarm). Not till the day after his arrival did Berlioz discover, from the housekeeper at 1 Rue Neuve St Marc, that she was in Paris and had been staying in the house until only two days before.

The coincidence of her appearing at exactly the same moment as he, after they had been at opposite ends of Europe for the past two years, could only impress him deeply. He resisted it, however. He was in no mood for emotional entanglements. He needed to be free. After two years' enforced interruption of his career the concert was all that mattered. There was much too much to do for him to risk falling into the old paralysing languor. Besides, he was enjoying his freedom, or the idea of it. This he made clear in a letter to Nancy, reporting rather boastfully the conversation a friend of his had had with Mme Pleyel née Camille Moke: Camille "put many questions about me yesterday to a musician who was dining with her. Her husband twice tried to change the subject, unsuccessfully. How queer. We'll see. She'll find a Don Juan, not the Werther she is hoping for." In any case Harriet — he had accepted — was an impossible dream. And was she not "so changed" that she had lost the power to make a fool of him?

Yet, like Purcell's lover who "attempts from love-sickness to fly", he was "himself his own fever". He had thought it safely consigned to the past — and the past was rising up to reclaim him. The memories he braved when he chose to move in to the house were, after all, too insistent to be denied. The fact of occupying the apartment she had just left began itself to take on the force of coincidence, heightening the sense of converging destinies. Perhaps, once the concert was over, he would see her. For the moment he avoided doing so. But he followed the progress of her fortunes.

They were waning fast. She lacked the qualities necessary for a theatrical manager and had plunged into the venture fatally unprepared. With weak supporting players, without a single leading actor — she had failed to get either Macready or Kean — and without any striking novelty to offer the public, her company made a feeble impact. In *Jane Shore*, which opened the season at the Théâtre-Italien on 21 November, Harriet was found to be as moving as ever, but the show drew thin houses. Four days before Berlioz's concert, on 5 December, after several postponements, the company presented Southerne's *Isabella or the Fatal Marriage* to an unenthusiastic audience. Receipts were poor and reviews discouraging: once again Miss Smithson constituted the sole attraction and the play was judged to be without interest. The actress-manager was left to rue her rashness and count her debts.

Harriet's misfortunes did not make her any less interesting to Berlioz. He brooded over the irony of their reversed positions: she in decline, he in the ascendant, about to stamp his name on the epoch in a concert of his own innovatory works — the symphony which had sprung from his hopeless passion, conceived when he was obscure and she the goddess of the Paris stage, and the monodrama which celebrated the poet whose supreme interpreter she had been acknowledged, with idolatry, only a few years before.

Berlioz had often imagined forcing himself to Harriet Smithson's attention by winning a brilliant success under her eyes, and had more than once made plans, fruitlessly, to do so. Now, when it happened, he took no active part: he was, he later felt, only one link in the chain of chance circumstances that drew Miss Smithson to the Conservatoire Hall.

Two days before the concert he was in Schlesinger's music shop, when a man looked in briefly and went out again. Moved by a curiosity he could not account for, he asked Schlesinger the man's name. An English journalist, Schlesinger said — Schutter of *Galignani's Messenger*; then, struck by a sudden thought and scenting some useful publicity, he added that Schutter, who knew Miss Smithson, really ought to have a box for the concert, and waving aside Berlioz's hesitations ran out into the street, overtook Schutter, pressed the tickets on him and made him promise to bring the actress if he possibly could.

Two mornings later Schutter found Harriet in the deepest despondency: she would not hear of going to a concert at such a moment. But her sister took Schutter's side — it was just the distraction she needed — and an English actor who was present, and who was keen to take advantage of the tickets, added his voice to theirs. A cab was summoned; Schutter, with the English actor, almost forced the still uncertain Harriet into it; then "The Conservatoire!" and they were off. Only then, on glancing at the handbill which Schutter passed her, did she discover whose music she was going to hear.

Shortly before two o'clock Harriet Smithson took her seat in the stage box, dazed by the sea of musicians at her feet, in a hall packed with the "cohorts of Romanticism" — among them Liszt, Paganini, Chopin, Victor Hugo, Dumas, Alfred de Vigny, Heine, Emile Deschamps, George Sand, Théophile Gautier, Janin, d'Ortigues, and the director of the Opéra Louis Véron. Though neither Harriet in her box, nor Berlioz on stage in the orchestra, was yet aware of it, at that moment their relationship moved out of the world of imagination into the world of fact.

The afternoon of 9 December 1832 is a watershed in Berlioz's existence. It marks the beginning of his sustained attempt to establish himself as a composer and to realise the half-acknowledged dream of great deeds that he brought with him eleven years before when he travelled to Paris from the provinces, a boy of seventeen who had never heard an orchestra. His apprenticeship is at an end. His life's work is already mapped out before him; the germ of nearly all his major compositions is in being. Most of the ideas and issues that are to dominate his energies and influence the course of his career are present that afternoon, explicitly or by implication: Shakespeare the exemplar, the legacy of Beethoven, the development of the dramatic symphony, the expressive orchestra, the necessity of creating a public, of teaching people how to listen to the new music, the war against the philistines, the hostility of conservative critics, the quest for an opera commission. The battle lines are drawn up. Ahead lie thirty years of struggle to seize hold of reality and bend it to his ideals.

A NOTE ON THE SPELLING OF NAMES

Some explanation of the apparently haphazard practice of this book is called for. Generally speaking, when myself referring to individuals I spell their names as they did: for example, "Le Sueur" and "Nancy" Berlioz; but where a letter or other document uses an alternative spelling it has been left unchanged. Many people, and not only her brother, wrote "Nanci". Almost everyone except Le Sueur himself, including the writers of newspaper reports and official citations, and even his wife, wrote "Lesueur". It was an age which, to an extent we find hard to realise, was still not greatly bothered about "correct" orthography. The process whereby the spread of literacy led to the normalisation of spelling was slow. (It also took a long time for the way words were pronounced to be changed by the way they looked: thus "Berlioz" only gradually replaced "Berlle".) When Stendhal's editor worries over his "highly capricious spelling with regard to proper names as well as common nouns" ("he will write by turns Lafon, Lafont or Lafond"), or when Berlioz's editor makes much of his "characteristically erratic" spelling, they are reading significance into something that doesn't have any. The young Berlioz's spelling is actually quite good by the standards of the time, reflecting the quality of his education, as does his sister's. Nancy's spelling is as much an advance on her mother's as her mother's is on that of her Aunt Marie-Antoinette, who writes to her to sympathise with "la painne que vous aviez du gout dessider cas [i.e. qu'a] votre fils ectors pour la cariere qu'il veut suivre". But I doubt if Nancy thought much about it when she was addressed as Nanci, any more than Le Sueur noticed when he was addressed as Lesueur. Consequently, this is how they appear here in Berlioz's letters and in any other documents that happen to spell them that way.

BIBLIOGRAPHY, REFERENCES, ABBREVIATIONS

Académie des Beaux-Arts, Paris, Archives of — BA

Almanach des Spectacles, Paris, 1822— — SPECT

Archives de la Faculté de Médecine, Paris — AMED

Archives de l'Isère, Bibliothèque Municipale, Grenoble — AIS

Archives Nationales, Paris — AN

Banks, Paul, "Coherence and Diversity in the Symphonie Fantastique", in *19th Century Music* VIII no. 1 (Summer 1984), 37—43 — BANKS

Barzun, Jacques, *Berlioz and the Romantic Century*, 2 vols, Boston 1950, rev. New York 1969 — BARZUN

Berlioz, Hector, "Lettre d'un enthousiaste sur l'état actuel de la musique en Italie", in *Revue européenne* March-May 1832, 47—64 — LE

Autobiographical Sketch (BN, Berlioz Papiers Divers no. 38a) — AS

"Voyage musical" and "Académie de France à Rome" in *L'Italie pittoresque*, Paris 1834 — IP

Grand traité d'instrumentation et d'orchestration modernes, Paris 1843 — TRAITE

Voyage musical en Allemagne et en Italie, 2 vols, Paris 1844 — VM

Les soirées de l'orchestre, ed. Léon Guichard, Paris 1968 — SO

Les grotesques de la musique, ed. Léon Guichard, Paris 1969 — GROT

A travers chants, ed. Léon Guichard, Paris 1971 — ATC

Mémoires de Hector Berlioz, Paris 1870 (Roman numerals refer to chapter numbers) — MEM

The Memoirs of Hector Berlioz, tr. & ed. David Cairns, London 1977 — MEMC

Les musiciens et la musique, ed. André Hallays, Paris [1903] (articles from the *Journal des débats*) — MM

Hector Berlioz, Cauchemars et Passions, ed. Gérard Condé, Paris 1981 (articles from various journals) — CONDE

Correspondance inédite de Hector Berlioz, 1819—1868, ed. Daniel Bernard, Paris 1870 — CI

Lettres intimes, Paris 1882 (serialised earlier in *La nouvelle revue*, Paris 1880, which in one or two cases published a fuller text. The recent discovery of the original letters — LI

from Berlioz to Humbert Ferrand, for more than forty
years believed lost, has revealed many editorial cuts,
incorrect datings, etc, in the published texts)

Briefe von Hector Berlioz an die Fürstin Carolyne Sayn-Wittgenstein,   SW
ed. La Mara, Leipzig 1903

Hector Berlioz, Les années romantiques, 1819–1842, ed. Julien   AR
Tiersot, Paris 1904

Correspondance générale d'Hector Berlioz, ed. Pierre Citron,   CG
7 vols, Paris 1972– (NB. CG references are to page
numbers, not to letter numbers)

Berlioz, Louis, *Livre de raison de Louis Joseph Berlioz, Docteur*   LR
médecin résidant à La Côte St André, Reboul-Berlioz Collection, Paris

Mémoires sur les maladies chroniques, les évacuations sanguines et   LBMAL
l'acupuncture, Paris 1816

Berlioz, Nancy, Diary, Reboul-Berlioz Collection, Paris (kept   NANCY
on and off between 1822 and 1831)

Berlioz and the Romantic Imagination: catalogue of the   VACAT
Berlioz Centenary Exhibition at the Victoria and Albert
Museum, London, Arts Council 1969

Berlioz Society (London), Bulletin, 1952–   BSOC
Bibliothèque Nationale (Musique), Paris   BN
Bibliothèque Municipale, Grenoble   BGREN
Bibliothèque de l'Opéra, Paris   BOP
Bloom, Peter, *François-Joseph Fétis and the Revue Musicale* (Ph.   BLOOM
D. University of Pennsylvania), University Microfilms,
Ann Arbor, Michigan 1973

"Berlioz and the *Prix de Rome* of 1830", in *Journal of the*   BLOOMPRIX
American Musicological Society XXXIV no. 2 (1981), [281]
–304.

"Berlioz pendant l'année de la *Symphonie fantastique*" in   BLOOMFAN
Musique et société (Hommages à Robert Wangermée),
Brussels 1988

Music in Paris in the Eighteen-Thirties, ed. P. Bloom (vol. IV   MUSPAR
of *Musical Life in 19th-century France*), Stuyvesant, NY
1987

Boschot, Adolphe, *La jeunesse d'un romantique: Hector Berlioz,*   JR
1803–1831, Paris 1906

Un romantique sous Louis-Philippe: Hector Berlioz, 1831–1842,   RLP
Paris 1908

Celle, Jean, "La vocation musicale d'Hector Berlioz", in *La*   CELLE
vie musicale, 28 May 1903

Charlton, David, *Grétry and the growth of Opéra-Comique*,   CHARLTON
Cambridge 1986

Chateaubriand, Francois-René de, *Génie du Christianisme*,   GENIE
5 vols, Paris 1802

Clerc-Jacquier, l'Abbé L, *La Côte Saint-André ancienne et moderne*,   JACQUIER
La Côte St André [1868]

Comboroure-Thompson, Cosette, *La carrière dramatique en France de Harriet Smithson*, thèse doctoral, 3ᵉ cycle (La Sorbonne) 1973   COSETTE

Cone, Edward T., ed. *Berlioz, Fantastic Symphony* (Norton Critical Scores), New York 1971   CONE

"Inside the Saint's Head", in *Musical Newsletter* I (1971) 3–12, 16–20, II (1972) 19–22   CONEST

Crabbe, John, *Hector Berlioz, Rational Romantic*, London 1980   CRABBE

Dean, Winton, "French Opera" in *The Age of Beethoven (New Oxford History of Music*, VIII, ed. Gerald Abraham), London 1982   WINTON

Delacroix, Eugène, *Correspondance générale d'Eugène Delacroix*, ed. André Joubin, vol. 1, Paris 1935   DELCOR

Journal, ed. André Joubin, vol. 1, Paris 1932   DELJOUR

Delécluze, Etienne-Jean, *Journal*, ed. Robert Baschet, Paris 1948   DELEC

Donnet, V., "Hector Berlioz et la médecine", in *Lettres et Médecine*, Paris 1969, 1ᵉʳ semestre   DONNET

Donnet, V. and Moureaux, C., "Le baccalauréat-ès-sciences d'Hector Berlioz", in *Marseille Médical*, 106ᵉ année no. 3 (1969)   D & M

Dumas, Alexandre, *Mes mémoires*, Paris 1863, vols I–VI   DM

"Comment je deviens auteur dramatique": introduction to *Théâtre complet de Alex. Dumas*, Paris 1863, vol. 1   DTH

Elwart, Antoine, *Histoire de la Société des Concerts du Conservatoire Impérial de Musique*, Paris 1860   ELWART

Etex, Antoine, *Les souvenirs d'un artiste*, Paris [1877]   ETEX

Fouque, Octave, *Les révolutionnaires de la musique: Lesueur, Berlioz, Beethoven, Richard Wagner, La musique Russe*, Paris 1882   FOUQUE

Goethe, Johann Wolfgang von *Briefwechsel zwischen Goethe und Zelter in den Jahren 1796 bis 1832*, Berlin 1833–4, vol. V   GOETHE

Hazlitt, William, *Notes of a Journey through France and Italy*, London [1932] (vol. 10 of the centenary edition); originally written as articles for the *Morning Chronicle*, 1824–5   HAZLITT

Hensel, Sebastian, *The Mendelssohn Family*, tr. C. Klingemann, 2 vols, London 1881   HENSEL

Hiller, Ferdinand, *Künstlerleben*, Cologne 1880   HILLER

Hills, Joan, "Ariel in Vienna", in Bulletin of the Berlioz Society XLIX (January 1965), 2–9   HILLS

Hippeau, Edmond, *Berlioz intime*, Paris 1883   BI

Berlioz et son temps, Paris 1890   BT

Holoman, D. Kern, *The Creative Process in the Autograph Musical Documents of Hector Berlioz, c. 1818–1840*, Ann Arbor, Michigan 1980   HOLOMAN

Catalogue of the Works of Hector Berlioz (New Berlioz Edition vol. 25), Kassel 1987   CAT

"Berlioz au Conservatoire: notes biographiques", in *Revue de musicologie* LXII (1976), 289–92   BCONS

"The Berlioz Sketchbook Recovered", in *19th Century Music* VII no. 3 (Spring 1984, "Essays for Joseph Kerman")   BSK

Hopkinson, Cecil, *A Bibliography of the Musical and Literary Works of Hector Berlioz, 1803–1869*, 2nd ed. rev. & ed. Richard Macnutt, Tunbridge Wells 1980   HOPK

[Hugo, Adèle], *Victor Hugo raconté par un témoin de sa vie*, 2 vols, Brussels 1863   VHR

Imbert, Jean, *Histoire de La Côte St André*, La Côte St André 1944   IMBERT

Jullien, Adolphe, *Hector Berlioz: sa vie et ses oeuvres*, Paris 1888   JULLIEN

Legouvé, Ernest, *Soixante ans de souvenirs*, 2 vols, Paris 1886   LEG

Locke, Ralph P., *Music, Musicians and the Saint-Simonians*, Chicago 1986   LOCKE

Macdonald, Hugh, *Berlioz*, London 1982   MACB

Berlioz Orchestral Music, London 1969   MACO

Maréchal, Henri, *Rome: Souvenirs d'un musicien*, Paris 1904   MARECHAL

Mathieu de Monter, Emile, "Etudes biographiques et critiques: Hector Berlioz", in *Revue et gazette musicale* nos. 24 (1869)–27 (1870)   MATHIEU

Mellers, Wilfrid, *Man and his Music*, London 1962 (Berlioz chapter), 759–73   MELLERS

Mendelssohn-Bartholdy, Felix, *Briefe einer Reise durch Deutschland, Italien und die Schweiz*, Zurich 1958   MBRIEFE

Letters from Italy and Switzerland, tr. Lady Wallace, London 1862   MLET

Mongrédien, Jean, *Jean-François Le Sueur*, 2 vols, Berne 1980   MONGR

Musée Hector Berlioz, La Côte St André   MUSEE

New Berlioz Edition (gen. ed. Hugh Macdonald), Kassel 1967–   NBE

Newman, Ernest, *Berlioz, Romantic and Classic*, ed. Peter Heyworth, London 1972   NEWMAN

The Life of Richard Wagner, vol. I 1813–1848. London 1933   NEWW

Newspapers & Periodicals cited most frequently:

Correspondant   CORR

Corsaire   CORS

Figaro   FIG

Gazette musicale   GM

Journal des débats   DEBATS

Nouvelle revue   NR

Pandore   PAND

Rénovateur   REN

Revue et gazette musicale   RGM

Revue musicale   RM

d'Ortigues, Joseph, *Le balcon de l'Opéra*, Paris 1833   D'ORT

Prod'homme, J.–G., *Hector Berlioz: sa vie et ses oeuvres*, Paris 1905   PROD

"Beethoven en France", in *Mercure de France* no. 690 (15 March 1927), 590–626.   PRODB

Raby, Peter, *Fair Ophelia: a life of Harriet Smithson Berlioz*,   RABY
    Cambridge 1982
Reboul-Berlioz Collection, Paris   RC
Reeve, Katherine, *The Poetics of the Orchestra in the Writings of*   REEVE
    Hector Berlioz (Ph. D., University of Yale), University
    Microfilms International, Ann Arbor, Michigan 1978
Richard Macnutt Collection, Withyham, Sussex   MACC
Stendhal (Beyle, H.), *Oeuvres intimes de Stendhal*, ed. Henri
    Martineau, Paris 1966 including
    Vie de Henri Brulard   VHB
    Journal   STJ
    Correspondance, ed. H. Martineau & V. del Litto, 3 vols,   STCORR
        Paris 1962−8
Temperley, Nicholas, "The Symphonie Fantastique and its   TEMP
    Program", in *Musical Quarterly* LVII no. 4 (October
    1971), 593−608
Tiersot, Julien, *Hector Berlioz et la société de son temps*, Paris   TIERSOC
    1904
    Berlioziana: series of weekly articles in the *Ménestrel* 70−2   MEN
        (1904−6) & 75−7 (1909−11)
    "Berlioz a l'aube du romantisme" in *Musique* nos. 2, 3 & 4   TIERMUS
        (1927−28)
Vigny, Alfred de, *Journal d'un poète*, ed. Louis Ratisbonne,   AV
    Paris 1882
Weber, Carl Maria von, *Writings on Music*, tr. Martin Cooper,   WARRACK
    ed. John Warrack, Cambridge 1981
Wotton, T. S., *Hector Berlioz*, London 1935   WOTTON
Wright, Michael G. H., *A Berlioz Bibliography:* critical writing   WRIGHT
    on Hector Berlioz from 1825 to 1986, Farnborough 1988

NOTES

PREFACE

10   ...he dreamed he was defending his father...: CG I 470–1.

PROLOGUE

14   "If I could only live...": MEM LIX (Postface), 481.
         ...Robert Collet in *The Score*: 20 (June 1957), 66.

15   Henri Barraud has declared...: during an address to the Colloque
         Berlioz, Bibliothèque Nationale, Paris, Oct. 1975.

15   ...Blaze de Bury...: *Musiciens du passé et du présent et de l'avenir*, 1880,
         357. The writer also complains of "cette horrible grimace qui
         balafre comme un signe de malédiction l'altière beauté de son
         oeuvre."

16   ...Heine...: In *Lutezia, Vermischte Schriften*, Hamburg 1854, III 272.

16   [Berlioz] "spent his life...": letter of 20 June [1859] to Carolyne
         Sayn-Wittgenstein, CG V 694.

16   "What the devil was the Good Lord...": MEM XXV 95 ("Où diable
         le bon Dieu avait-il la tête...?").

16   ...the Conservatoire was barred to him: B never succeeded in obtaining
         one of its lucrative and influential professorships. All he did
         obtain was the minor post of Librarian.

16   ...the Société des Concerts...only two occasions: 14 April 1833
         (Overture *Rob Roy*) and 15 April 1849 (Sylphs' scene and Hun-
         garian March from *The Damnation of Faust*).

16n   ...Victor Gollancz...: *Journey towards Music*, London 1964, 38–9.

17   "the work he actually did...": NEWMAN 65.

CHAPTER 1

19   The young genius from the provinces...: cf. Stendhal (quoted by
         Boschot, JR 86): "Remarquez que tout ce qui a un peu d'énergie
         à Paris est né en province", and in VHB 396: "Le souffle de
         Paris, affaiblissant, corrodant la faculté de vouloir [...] Napoléon,
         Fieschi, avaient la faculté de *vouloir* qui manque à M. Villemain,
         à M. Casimir Delavigne [...] élevés à Paris."

19   ...noble and knightly Berliozes in crusader rolls: Jean Berlioz or
         Berlion, of La Terrasse, accompanied the Dauphin Humbert II

on his crusade against the Turks in 1346 (cited in Admiral
Reboul Berlioz's unpublished papers in RC). Noble knights
named Berlioz or Berlion are identified in de Rivoire's *Nobiliaire
de Dauphiné* (Grenoble 1867) and in de Gallier's "Essai historique
sur la baronie de Clerieu" (*Bulletin de la Société Départmentale
d'Archéologie et de Statistique de la Drome*, Valence 1870, vol.
5) as living in Grésivaudan, the canton to which Meylan belongs, in
the 13th and 14th centuries. See also BI 93.

19   ...the termination oz...: see *Dictionnaire étymologique des noms de famille
et prénoms de France*, Paris 1951, and BI 93. The Savoyard influence
suggested by such a termination is not surprising in a region
which was a fief of Savoy for nearly two hundred years.

19   ...a Neapolitan colony...bands of Italian mercenaries...: see
JACQUIER 58.

19   ...a line of Austrian counts...: B's maternal grandmother Victoire-
Blanche-Elizabeth Marmion (née Desroches de Lisle) descended
from counts and barons von Waldner von Freudstein, distinguished in the Austrian army.

19   ...even the ancient world and the Greek inheritance...: see NEW-
MAN 89—96 ("A Man of the South"). B as reincarnation of the
Irish patriot Tom Emmett is discussed in CRABBE, Appendix
113—28.

20   ...the brief family history written by Dr Berlioz...: in LR (see
below).

21   ..."repugnance to glosses and commentaries...": this and subsequent
remarks of Dr B's are from LR unless otherwise stated.

22   ...the main documentary source...: Tiersot included extracts from
the opening section of LR in AR xxxi—xl, but in altered and
truncated form, with paragraph-order rearranged and all references to B's grandfather's anti-republican sentiments expunged.

22   "I feel as if my life...": CG III 572.

23   ...Rousseau's ideal of the "negative educator": Boschot (JR 49) was
the first to make the point.

23   "Give my love to Hector the musician": unsigned letter, "Grenoble le
24 mars" (RC). References to Félix Marmion's attempts to
secure a post in the new Bourbon army (the subject of several
letters in RC) show the year to be 1816.

24   "...a letter is always valued at La Côte": Nancy Clappier to Joséphine
B, 20 May [1819] (RC).

25   ...a term at the...School of Medicine in Paris: Louis B's signature is
in the register for the first term of 1801. He lodged at 4 Rue du
Four St Hilaire with his brother Auguste (also studying medicine)
and took courses in Anatomy and Physiology, Chemistry and
Pharmacy, and Operative Medicine.

25   ...sustaining his thesis...: AMED, *Table générale des thèses soutenues à
la Faculté de Médecine de Paris* (1816), no. 163.

25   Broussais...systematist of the old school: earlier, however, he had
been a follower of the empirical Bichat.

26   ...balanced, meticulous, reasonable: There is, however, a hint of

neurotic obsessiveness in Hippeau's account (BI 100) of Dr B in his later years weighing his food before each meal.

26   "Papa thinks he is completely objective": CG I 83.

26   ...revealing annotation in the doctor's hand: CG I 88n ("du délire", not "de" as transcribed in CG).

26n   ...the entry in *Dictionnaire encyclopédique*...: Vol. 1 (A — ADE). The article (by Debout) also notes Dr B's addition of a sealing-wax head to the needle, an innovation allowing it to be inserted deep without risk of disappearing into the tissue. JACQUIER 293ff, in its account of Dr B's career (which purports to follow Dr Robin's funeral address of 1848), states that Dr B subsequently published a separate study of acupuncture.

27   "2 Floréal": Dr B seems to have been one of the few citizens of La Côte who (like Stendhal) observed the Revolutionary Calendar. Nearly everyone else whose letters are preserved in RC went on using the Gregorian.

29   ...the wrong year for his own marriage: 1802 instead of 1803.

29   ...the date of his son's marriage: October 1833, but given as July.

29   "spoke of his mother with love...": HILLER 67.

29n   ...a letter of Nancy Berlioz's: RC, quoted CG I 99n.

30   An anonymous tribute...: MUSEE. The writer, a woman, may have been one of the Rocher cousins, Elise Julhiet or Rosanne Goletty, both of whom lived till 1886; but the document is a copy, so no indentification by handwriting is possible.

30   ...was popular...as a hostess: see BI 89.

30   [Joséphine Berlioz's] perceptiveness...: MEM III 12.

31   Various accounts [of Joséphine Berlioz]: see BI 88, and the Abbé Angles' verse/prose-letter to Nicolas Marmion, inscribed in one of the latter's verse-books (see below, note to p. 32): "sa touchante mine [...] ses grands yeux [...] cette douce ingenuité/ qui connait bien mieux l'art de plaire/que la vaine frivolité/des élégantes de l'ishere [sic]". Her slimness is also attested by her nickname, Finette.

32   The marriage contract...: RC.

32   ...the marriage was celebrated...: the act of marriage is in AIS (copy supplied by Denise Dumoulin).

32   ...duly signalised the event in verse: Nicolas Marmion was an inveterate versifier. Five books of verse-letters, together with similar effusions on loose sheets, are in RC. Cf. Pauline Beyle (sister of Stendhal) to her brother, describing a visit made with her grandfather Dr Gagnon to Meylan, where "le père Marmion avait fait des vers à mon g[rand]-p[ère] (depuis Hesculape jusqu' aux Grâces et Vénus, tout cela y brillait et lui était comparé). Jusqu'à ce jour, le g[rand]-p[ère] méprisait M. Mar[mion] comme étant une bêtte; à present il l'admire" (STC I 1119).

33   In his *Memoirs*...: I 5.

33   ...Monsieur Berlle...: cf. Hippeau, BI 93: "En Graisivaudan, autour de Grenoble, même à Valence, on élide la finale et l'on dit

Berl' ''. See also a letter of 28 February 1803 from Nancy Clappier addressed to "Madame Berlle née Marmion", and another of a week earlier in which she says, "Je ne m'accoutume point à penser que tu es mariée que tu es M^d Berlle[. . .] Si je connaissais un peu Mr Berlle je lui en ferai une querelle". The next letter from Nancy Clappier, eight months later, is addressed to "Madame Berlloz" (RC).

33 . . . reintroduction of Catholic worship (etc.): JACQUIER 191−9, including Mayor Buffevent's address.

34 . . . La Côte . . . under the Revolution: JACQUIER 67−8, 71, 76−83, IMBERT 171ff. See also Aimé-Louis Chapollion-Figeac, *Chroniques dauphinoises*, etc., 3 vols, Vienne 1880−7, III 424, 462−3, and VHB 133, 171.

36 . . . the baby was baptised . . . : see baptismal certificate in MUSEE.

36 . . . Nancy Clappier . . . wrote: RC. The letter carries no indication of year, but it is clear from the context that the child is Joséphine B's first.

36 Lucille Marquis . . . : Letter dated Rives, 22 February 1804 (RC). Her brother ("le gros Marquis") was a schoolmate of Stendhal's at the Ecole Centrale in Grenoble.

36n . . . diploma [of] "doctor of medicine": RC. Tiersot's statement (AR xxxix n. 2) that Louis B never qualified is thus wrong.

37 . . . about 3500 inhabitants: IMBERT 163, 201, 250, TIERSOC 3.

38 . . . its library . . . as Stendhal remarked . . . : VHB 333. Dr B's library, valued at 6,000 francs in the LR entry made in 1815, was constantly added to in the following years.

39 . . . a tradition reported by Tiersot: TIERSOC 5.

39n [Tiersot, Boschot quotations]: respectively TIERSOC 3 and JR 4. Jacquier, writing in the mid-19th century, speaks of La Côte "couchée entre ses pampres verdoyants et ses moissons dorées" (JACQUIER 2−3). B's description is in MEM I 5.

40 . . . Hannibal . . . encamped: JACQUIER 8.

40 . . . six specialist fairs: JACQUIER 118.

40 A large-scale map of La Côte . . . : this plan cadastre, together with a register of proprietors, is in the mairie at La Côte.

40n . . . Maître Jacques de St Georges: his creation of the great market at La Côte is attested by the Count of Savoy's accounts, quoted by A. J. Taylor in "Master James of St George", *English Historical Review* LXV no. CCLVII (Oct. 1950). Taylor also argues cogently for the Count of Savoy's architect and Edward I's being the same person.

41 The Ferme du Nand . . . : the buildings are largely unchanged. The two-storied pavilion at the western angle of the Chuzeau garden, popularly known as "le pavillon de la malédiction" from being the supposed place where Joséphine B cursed her son, was not in fact built till after that event (see LR for 1827).

41 . . . Grandfather Marmion's farm at Murianette: both it and the Meylan property had been in the Marmion family since the 17th century.

41	...crowned by...Mont Blanc: owing to modern pollution, visible much less often than it used to be.

41   Paris, as Stendhal remarked...: VHB 64.

42   Nancy...all but died...: LBMAL 312.

42   ...great-grandmother Sophie...: her death, and the deaths of Joseph B and Benjamin B, recorded in LR.

43   ...Côtois serving in the Grande Armée: IMBERT 195–6.

43   ...it marked the Emperor's birthday: IMBERT 196.

43   ...a flurry of excitement...: see documents in the mairie at La Côte and IMBERT 197n (where the event is ascribed to 1805).

44   ...fête des époux: JACQUIER 86–7, IMBERT 196.

44   [Félix Marmion's war record]: see RC, also Archives de Guerre, Château de Vincennes (information kindly supplied by Pierre Citron).

44   ...pursue to the gates of the town: see letter of 7 July 1839 from Félix M to General Dernancourt, former commander of the First Dragoons, describing the engagement and recalling that the captain of his squadron claimed the right to the horse (RC). For FM and for the general, clearly, nothing in their subsequent lives equalled the excitements of the war years.

44   "still hot from...the cannon's mouth...": MEM III 10.

45   The great surgeon Larrey...: quoted Robert G. Richardson, *Larrey: Surgeon to Napoleon's Imperial Guard*, London 1944, 53.

46   The [Napoleonic] spell...: B will describe the reports sent back from his German tour of 1842–3 as "bulletins from the Grande Armée".

46   The scars that his uncle showed...: RC and Archives de Guerre. A Nicolas Marmion verse-letter contains the couplet (referring to Félix), "Il montrera les cicatrices/qui sont empreintes sur son front".

46   The departure of recruits...: IMBERT 196–7.

47   ...an associate member [of the Paris Medical Society]: 16 Aug 1816 (RC). Dr B's monograph won the Bordeaux society's prize in 1809.

49   ...quotation from Horace: *Odes* III 3. Louis XVIII (as Dumas describes in *The Count of Monte Cristo*) kept his spirits up in the same way, greeting each new report of Napoleon's progress with a Horatian tag.

49   In 1816 a disastrously bad spring and summer...: the consequence of climatic disturbance due to the eruption of Mt Tambora in the East Indies.

50   ...hussars and the Cossacks...: JACQUIER 86, IMBERT 197–8.

50   Two young Piedmontese officers: Count Rine and M. de St Etienne. The former's thank-you letter of 22 Feb. 1816 is in RC.

50   [deaths of Louise and Louis-Joseph B]: the diagnoses given here were kindly suggested to me by Professor Michael Langman. LR gives a detailed account of the progress of Louis-Joseph B's illness and the various treatments attempted.

50   ...fresh rumours of Napoleon's return: Mayor Buffevent's proclamation

was posted on 2 Jan. 1816. On 25 April a "festival of loyalty" to Louis XVIII was held at La Côte, with solemn mass, concert, lottery and illuminations (IMBERT 205–6).

50n   . . . a letter . . . from Félix Marmion: 1816, c. Feb.

CHAPTER 2

52   In the spring of 1815 . . . : 1816, the date usually preferred, conflicts with indirect evidence in LR, as well as being a year with an exceptionally wet and cold spring. Although Nancy, aged nine, would have been young for her first communion – B (MEM I 6) says they took it at the same time – LR points to 1815. In the family history written at the beginning of 1815, B – baptised Louis Hector – appears as Louis Nicolas Hector, Nicolas being the extra name given at confirmation.

52   . . . the convent of the Visitation: as Tiersot correctly states (TIERSOC 4) B mistakenly locates the episode in the Ursuline convent. The latter was closed down in 1793 and did not reopen. The Visitandines had also been forced to leave, but returned in 1803 and opened an educational establishment which lasted for the next hundred years. NANCY makes clear that both she and Adèle were boarders there. See also JACQUIER 245–7.

53   . . . recounts an incident of his boyhood: CG V 694.

53   " . . . a line from Victor Hugo": *Ruy Blas* III 4 (which B slightly misquotes).

53   . . . describing the first time . . . the classic malaise . . . : MEM XL 157ff.

57   One further episode . . . again concerns the *Aeneid*: MEM II 9–10.

CHAPTER 3

59   . . . the petit séminaire . . . remained in ecclesiastical hands: see JACQUIER 217ff.

59   . . . challenged by . . . Edmond Hippeau: BI 152.

59   . . . accused of trying to blow the place up: BI 147.

60   . . . a letter . . . from his sister Nancy: transcribed in NANCY, Jan. 1826.

60   . . . certificate . . . baccalauréat . . . surviving . . . certificates . . . :   AIS, *Registres des certificats d'aptitude au baccalauréat-ès-lettres*, 1820–24.

60   Looking back on his upbringing . . . : MEM II 8.

60   "the *horde of felt emotions* . . . ": STJ 584.

61   "My whole life", he told Pauline Viardot . . . : quoted by Viardot in a letter of 22 Sept. [1859]. See "Pauline Viardot-Garcia to Julius Rietz (Letters of Friendship)", ed. O.G.Sonneck, in *Musical Quarterly* II no. 1 (Jan. 1916), 43.

61   "Accursed faculty . . . ": MEM XXXV 131.

61   " . . . a man dominated by the imagination": CG I 367.

61   . . . a further list . . . cited by Hippeau: BI 180.

62   . . . the Latin authors the *Memoirs* say . . . : II 8.

62   Again, we read in the *Memoirs* . . . his fascination for Asia . . . : II 8–9.

63   . . . his *espagnolisme*, to borrow Stendhal's word: cf. VHB 215: "cet espagnolisme [. . .] me fait passer, même à mon age, pour un enfant privé d'expérience, pour un fou *de plus en plus incapable d'aucune affaire sérieuse*, aux yeux de mon cousin Colomb [...], vrai bourgeois."

63 John Cowper Powys: in the Cervantes essay in his *The Pleasures of Literature*, London [1938].

64 "read and re-read it secretly...": MEM III 11.

65 ...his expeditions above Meylan...: CG I 473 shows that B had been to the monastery of La Chartreuse — a natural port of call for a walker based at Meylan. Richard Gandy has pointed out (in conversation with the author) what a superb setting the adjoining Gorges du Guiers mort suggest for the scene evoked in Faust's "Nature immense" in the *Damnation*.

65 [Quotations from *La nouvelle Héloïse*]: Part I, Letters XLVIII and XXVI. The book was a favourite in the Berlioz family (see NANCY).

66 The intimate knowledge of all twelve books...: see "Les Troyens and the Aeneid" in my *Responses*, London 1973, 88–110.

66 ...Virgil...a real and keen regret: "I should have loved him" — MEM LIX (Voyage en Dauphiné), 504.

67 "...set in a ring of gold": B knew his Homer as well as his Virgil: the gold rings on the spears come from the *Iliad*.

68 ...he copied out a passage about...Chénier: see MEN 70 no. 7 (1904), 51.

68 [*Génie*] praised the hymns...of the Catholic Church: Chateaubriand's emphasis on the aesthetic power of the Christian religion was an answer to the Enlightenment's claim that Christianity was barbarous and inimical to the arts.

69 ...the earliest reference to the completed symphony: CG I 319.

71 "My whole life...": see above, note to p. 61.

71 His description of the mal d'isolement...: MEM XL 159.

71 ...as Adolphe Boschot suggests...: JR 77.

CHAPTER 4

72 Estelle Dubeuf...: for much of the information about Estelle's family given in this chapter I am indebted to the researches of the late Mme Denise Dumoulin of Grenoble, a direct descendant of Estelle's aunt Emilie Clappier-Delisle. Despite *Littré*, *Petit Robert* and other authorities Mme Dumoulin was adamant that Estelle's pink "brodequins" which fascinated the young B were evening shoes (such as are illustrated in R. W. Chapman's editions of Jane Austen), not the half-boots with which I rendered the word in my translation of the *Memoirs*. In support of her opinion she cited Mme de Duras' novel *Edouard* (1822): "...un pied charmant, à peine pressé dans une petite chaussure en brodequin, en soie aussi, lacée d'or ...."; and I have bowed to her conviction.

72 ...the long drawing-room: B (MEM LVIII 436) describes it as decorated with fantastic birds, in coloured paper, stuck on the walls. According to Tiersot (TIERSOC 32) it had a lofty white-

washed ceiling supported by two large beams, and a tall fireplace at one end.

72   ...he danced with both the Dubeuf sisters: see Félix M's letter of c.Feb. 1816 to Dr B (RC).

73   "...seeing his radiant *stella montis* again": MEM IV 13. Mme Gautier died in 1818 and though the house remained in the family till 1827 it is possible that the Dubeuf grand-daughters, by now living in Vif, stopped coming to Meylan in the late summer and were therefore not there in 1819, 1820 or 1821 when the Berliozes made their annual visit. If so, that would account for B's sense of the brevity of their relationship and perhaps also for the dream described below.

73   By then he was fourteen...: the details in this paragraph and the next are collated from MEM III, XLVI, LVIII and LIX.

75   ...Virgil..."find the way to his heart": MEM II 9.

75   "the overpowering sadness of a young heart...": MEM IV 16.

CHAPTER 5

76   Ferdinand Hiller...concluded...: HILLER 68.

76   ...the lack of a piano...which Hiller...deplored: the accepted view: cf. Tiersot in MEN 70 no. 9 (1904), 68: "The piano would have served him much better when he tried to discover on his own the principles of harmony. By contrast the guitar, an incomplete instrument, could not but give him bad harmonic habits"; and MARECHAL 109: to deny oneself the piano is "to expose oneself to dangers of which clumsiness of workmanship is the least".

77   ...his mother singing "Que je voudrais avoir une chaumière": CG I 472. See below, note to p. 451.

77   Félix Marmion, whose voice was much in demand...: see, for example, a letter from Nancy Clappier to Joséphine Berlioz: "Mr Félix doit être encore occupé de vous. Si n [ous le] retrouvons à notre retour à Grenoble nous espérons le voir et *l'entendre*. Nos musiciennes sont enchantées de son bon gout, de sa méthode et cetera et moi quoique indigne je trouve qu'il chante à merveille." ([28 Feb. 1816], RC)

77   A string quartet by Ignaz Pleyel...: see AS (where, however, the work is attributed to Haydn) and MEM IV 14.

77   ...a couple of pieces from Gluck's *Orphée*: MEM V 21, GM 9 Nov. 1834 (CONDE 186).

77   ...the band of the National Guard: the documents (MUSEE) cited in this section (some of which are referred to in CELLE) were kindly shown to me by Mlle Henriette Boschot, till recently curator of the Museum.

80   ...Imbert paid for the music himself: inferable from an inventory of April 1821, which refers to his successor Dorant as having "touttes les parties de musique d'harmonie achetés de M. Himbert [sic]".

81	...the version given in...*Memoirs*: IV 13.
81	...in one article: RGM 11 March 1849.
81	In another article...: DEBATS 8 Nov. 1858 (GROT 197).
81	In the *Treatise*...: TRAITE 138.
82	...he found an old flageolet...: MEM IV 13.
82n	...ousted by the recorder: however, the flageolet survived sufficiently for Scott to give it a role in the plot of *Guy Mannering*.
83	A letter...to Joseph Faure, written on 4 April...: RC; dated 8 April in CG I 29, which contains several other errors of transcription.
83	...passages for solo flute in Berlioz's works...: to those cited one might add the first statement of the main melody of the Scène aux champs, in which the tone-colour of the flute, though combined with first violins, predominates when the work is played on instruments of the period.
84	...concertos of Drouet...: MEM IV 13. Perhaps they figured among the music recorded in LR as having been bought in Paris in spring 1818.
84	According to the *Memoirs* [Imbert left]...: IV 14 (source for much of this section).
86−7	[Letters to Janet & Cotelle and Pleyel]: CG I 30, 31.
88	It was a fiasco: the fullest account is in AS.
89	Michaud's...dictionary...to which Dr Berlioz subscribed: *Biographie universelle ancienne et moderne, ou histoire, par ordre alphabétique, de la vie publique et privée de tous les hommes qui se sont faits remarquer par leurs écrits, leurs actions, leurs talents, leurs vertus ou leurs crimes. [...] Rédigé par une société de gens de lettre et de savants.* "On doit des égards aux vivants; on ne doit aux morts que la vérité: (Volt.) The encyclopedia does not figure in the inventory of Dr B's library given in LR, nor in Hippeau's list in BI, but an unpublished letter of 6 March 1846 (RC) shows him enquiring if the supplement, vol. 78, to which his subscription entitles him, has come out.
90	...a collection of twenty-five romances: the ms is in MUSEE. See CAT 6−15.
90n	...Berlioz was about to destroy the manuscript...: the story is told by Tiersot in MEN 70 no. 2 (1904), 12.
91	...as has been pointed out, Florian's lines...: by Tiersot in "Un pélerinage au pays de Berlioz" in MEN 51 no. 45 (1885), 355 and TIERSOC 25. See also NBE 16 194, where however the first bar is transcribed incorrectly.
91	Tiersot remarks, not without justice...: TIERSOC 26.
91	...he described the rigidly disapproving attitude...: MEM X 36−7.
92	...an exchange of letters between Nancy...and...Elise Rocher: RC; the episode belongs to the winter of 1823−4.
92	The young Dumas...: DM II 172.
93	...deep impression...of a Cherubini mass...: letters of 29 Jan. and 3 Feb. 1822 from Mme Husson to Félix Marmion (RC).
93	Mendelssohn's uncle Jacob Bartholdy...: letter quoted in HENSEL I 85.

93	...he sent to Paris for a framed engraving...: LR, April 1818.
94	...manuscript notebooks in [Dorant's] hand: MUSEE.
95	...baccalauréat records...in Grenoble: AIS, série T., *Inspection académique: correspondence générale*, 1820–22. Reg. no. 67, Lettre 619.
95	"spent at the bedsides of the sick...": MEM IV 17.
95	"Children reason little": CG I 531.
95	Using as a bribe...the new flute: MEM IV 17.
96	...successful in the case of..."Le dépit de la bergère": assigned by both HOPK (3) and CAT (6) to 1819; but the circumstances of its publication (by Le Duc) remain obscure. The letter of 14 Aug. 1819 to a music publisher (CG I 32–3, François Lang Collection, Abbaye de Royaumont) is a poor forgery — though it could be a copy of a genuine letter (this despite rendering B's invariable "La Côte St André" as "La Côte-Saint-André").
96	[Mme Husson] wrote to him: one of a series of letters from her to Félix Marmion in RC.
97	[Félix Marmion] was put in command of the local National Guard: see his letter of 7 May 1816 (RC).
97	...the Gazette commended Captain Marmion...: 1 July 1816 (RC).
97–8	[Dr B's period as mayor]: "Le 15 août 1817 j'ai été nommé maire de la Côte. J'ai accepté malgré mon extrême répugnance en cédant aux désirs de mes concitoyens et vaincu par les nombreux témoignages de bienveillance qu'ils m'ont donné" (LR). Actes Civiles are signed by him from 4 Sept. See also JR 52–6. Some of the documents on which Boschot based his account have apparently disappeared. He assigns a key role to Joséphine B in inflaming her "docile, ailing" husband to action against Charbonnel; but his style of writing leaves it unclear whether this is fact or mere speculation.
98	...compromise candidate...Adolphe de Monts: his letter of appointment from the Prefect speaks of the accounts of La Côte "not always showing the clarity desirable in a good administration", and looks to the new mayor to observe the legally prescribed forms, best safeguard of the public purse (Mairie, La Côte).
98	...to sign [an] agreement...: LR, 1 March 1818.
98	"a figure out of Plutarch": LEG I 20.
99	Nicolas Marmion would actually describe him...: in a verse-letter (RC). In another he speaks of never intending to see his eldest grandson again. It was probably in the same period (1833) that Hector's confirmation name, Nicolas, was crossed out in LR.
100	...[Berlioz's] passport...: formerly in the Maignien Collection (M was librarian of the Grenoble muncipal library), present whereabouts unknown, but transcribed by Tiersot in MEN 70 no. 1 (1904), 4. Internal passports, brought in formally in 1793, were not abolished till the Second Empire.
100	...a contemporary...passion for dancing...: Antoine Charbonnel; told by his grandson to Jacques Barzun, who told the author.
101	He played boules...: TIERMUS 56, MEN 70 no. 1 (1904), 4.

101   ...when Berlioz and...Charbonnel...disguised themselves...: see
             MEN 70 no. 1 (1904), 4.
101n   ...letter...from Berlioz to Favre...: see AR 2−3, MEN 70 no. 2
             (1904), 12.
102   ...the ability...to be most cool...: CG V 353.
102   To evoke the mal d'isolement...: MEM XL 159.
102   He uses an analogy from engineering...: MEM XLVII 208.
102   A harp chord... "hisses like...molten lead...": MEM LIII (Deuxième
             voyage en Allemagne, Lettre 6ᵉ), 394.
102   ...the sight of the huge waves...: CG I 417.
102n   ...the image of the "mighty bird of Chimborazo...": MEM LI
             (Premier voyage en Allemagne, Lettre 10ᵉ), 322.
103   "I am driven involuntarily...": CG I 64.
103n   ...Delacroix in his Journal...: DELJOUR I 217 (26 April 1847).
104   ...Berlioz, writing to...Hiller...: cf. STJ 448: "Réfléchissons saine-
             ment avant de prendre un parti; une fois décidé, ne changez
             jamais. Avec l'opiniâtré, l'on vient à bout de tout."
104   ...Stendhal's identification of the type dauphinois: variously in VHB
             (64, 276 etc.) and STJ passim.
105   ...see the great Gluck in all his glory: cf. GM 9 Nov. 1834 (CONDE
             187).

CHAPTER 6

106   The public stagecoach...: see Jean Paquet, *Au temps des diligences*,
             Grenoble 1969; H. Cavailles, *La route française, son histoire, sa
             fonction*, Paris 1946; Bertier de Sauvigny, *La restauration*, Paris
             1955, 271ff; and B's review of Adam's *Le postillon de Longjumeau*,
             DEBATS 10 Nov. 1852 (GROT 217−18).
106n   Hazlitt...: HAZLITT 158.
107   [Stendhal's]...immediate impressions: VHB 345, 375.
107   ...signed...the school register: B and Robert are respectively no. 821
             and no. 829 in the *Registre des aspirations au doctorat*, 1821 4ᵉ
             trimestre. (In all, 931 signed.) Drouault, who vouched for them, is
             described as "maître d'hôtel Rue St Jacques no 104". Inscription
             began on 3 Nov. The fact that B (and Robert) registered on the
             last day, 16 Nov., may or may not be significant. We do not
             know when they arrived in Paris. Whenever it was, it was not
             earlier than the 2nd, the date of the last performance of *Iphigénie
             en Tauride* before the one that B saw on the 26th, or later than the
             14th, when they went to the Opéra (see below).
108   We can also imagine what a shock...: cf. WOTTON 13: "...the
             sudden change from the uneventful life of his village to the
             turmoil of Paris must have had an enormous effect on one so
             highly strung."
108   He himself...described the scene: this and the two following quotations:
             MEM V 20−1.
108   "Thou giv'st the little birds...": Racine, *Athalie* II 7.
108   ...he went to hear [*The Danaids*] on the 14th: previous performances of

this revival were on 5th and 9th. The 14th seems the most likely. (Any later would have been after the benefit evening of 18th which B says he attended after seeing *The Danaids*.) The cast included Mme Branchu, Nourrit fils and Dérivis.

109   ...enliven the dissecting room with excerpts...: cf. AS: "While he opened a skull he would accompany the rhythm of the saw or the hammer with the rich melodies of *La Vestale* or *Cortez*."

109   Ferdinand Hiller..."...a spark in a powder-keg": HILLER 68–9.

109   ...six further performances of *The Danaids*...: 19, 25, 30 Nov., 5. 14, 26 Dec.

109n   The Conservatoire Concert Society...: see ELWART 101–3 and SPECT for 1828 (1829), 48–51.

110   ...a capacity of 1,937: details of the Opéra in this and the previous paragraph from SPECT. A pit seat still cost 3.60 ten years later.

110   ...benefit performance for...Dufresne: details in SPECT of 1822, 260.

110   "Imagine, to begin with...": CG I 36–7.

110n   The work had just been revived...: 10 Sept. In all it received ten performances between late Nov. 1821 and early 1826, when it was dropped from the repertory.

111   "...La Fontaine": "Les deux pigeons".

111   ...a couple of romances published...: by Mme Cuchet, 10 Rue Bétisy. See CAT 16, 19.

112   The Teisseyres...in the Rue Chanoinesse: see *Almanach des 25000 adresses*, Paris 1822.

112   "Perhaps you think...": CG I 38.

112   Félix Marmion was...seeing Talma (etc.): cf. letter of 19 March 1822 from his friend Mme Husson (RC): "Je voudrais bien être près de vous quand vous entendez Baillot et que vous voyez jouer Talma, Mlle Mars etc."

113n   In a letter of a few weeks earlier...Félix Marmion...: 18 December, to Nancy. The year must surely be 1821 (not 1822 or 1823, as suggested in CG I 85 n. 2); the context shows that Hector has recently left home for the first time.

114   ...*Iphigénie en Aulide*...: performances on 26 April, 15 May and 9 Dec. 1822. There were seven more up to the end of 1824, after which the work was dropped.

114   The statement in the *Memoirs*..."...like countless others": V 21.

114   ...treated with amused incredulity: e.g. by Tiersot in MEN 77 no. 29 (1911), 226 n.l.: "The truth is [...] that the student did not go through a long period of hesitation before sacrificing medicine to music: the sacrifice was accomplished, or at least decided in his mind, almost as soon as he reached Paris"; and Daniel Bernard in CI 12–13: "When one has already at a tender age [...] hit on the melody which will become the theme of the Largo of the Fantastic Symphony, one doesn't wait for *The Danaids* before discovering that one is a musician to the last fibre of one's being. [...] Knowing with what passionate intensity Berlioz loved his art, I decline to admit any backsliding."

114   Attendance at courses...: see DONNET 8.

114   ...attended Gay-Lussac's physics lectures: MEM V 20–1.

115   ...legal restrictions on dissection...in Britain: not till 1832 did Parliament allow corpses (of the poor) to be dissected.

115   ...students from other countries: among them a Jacques (James) Cairns from Jedburgh. Genealogical research has not yet succeeded in establishing a family connection with the author of this book.

115   ...Lacretelle's lectures: see CG I 35.

115   Andrieux...a famous lecturer: see LEG I 108ff.

116   ...Thénard's chemistry lectures: MEM V 20–1.

116   ...the passage in the *Memoirs*...Gay-Lussac...: V 22.

116   "Once admitted to the sanctuary...": MEM V 22.

116   ...the swelteringly hot summer...: candidates for the Prix de Rome in painting petitioned for an extension on the grounds of the extreme heat.

117   A 120-page manuscript...the two *Iphigénies*: MACC.

117n   In an article in the *Gazette musicale*: 9 Nov. 1834 (CONDE 187–8).

117–18   He was there for a month or six weeks: the date of B's arrival in La Côte has to be inferred from the fact that the payment of 240 francs (? two months' allowance) recorded in LR on 26 July is the last before the 500 given to him on his departure for Paris on 22 Oct.

118   ...he signed on at the Ecole de Médecine: 5 Nov. 1822, the second day of inscription.

118   ...the two cousins had separated: they may have done so earlier, though if so not very far: in the July inscription B's address is still 104 Rue St Jacques, but Robert's is now Hôtel St Benoit, which is named in *Almanach parisien* for 1828 as 102 Rue St Jacques.

119   Nor is it found in the petition of loyalty...: see DONNET 9.

CHAPTER 7

120   Gerono...had published a Theme and Variations...: registered, by H. Gerono, with Dépots légaux in Feb. 1819 (AN F 18* VIII). The fullest account of Gerono is Holoman's in BCONS.

121   The arrival of Le Sueur in Berlioz's life: autumn or early winter 1822, though usually assigned to 1823. B's "Canon libre à la quinte", which names the composer as "Elève de Mr Lesueur", was published by 16 Dec. 1822, on which date it was noticed in the *Réveil*. For the most recent summary of B and Le Sueur see MONGR 977–1022.

121   Looking back on it years later...: MEM VI 24.

121   [Le Sueur's] unpublished pamphlets: discussed by Boschot in JR ch. IV. The pamphlets have since disappeared. On Le Sueur's published treatises see MONGR 100–56 and 157–204.

121   [influence of] Le Sueur's practical aesthetic ideas: see FOUQUE passim.

123	...three songs...recently published: "Amitié, reprends ton empire", "Toi qui l'aimas, verse des pleurs" and "Canon libre à la quinte". See CAT 18, 23, 20–1.
123	...a fourth song: "Le montagnard exilé". See CAT 21–2.
123	Félix Marmion...in pursuit of a wealthy married woman: see letters from Mme Husson to FM, 3 Feb. and 3 March 1823 (RC).
123	His [Félix Marmion's] replies: RC. Shorter extracts quoted in CG I 47–8 n. 1.
124	Hector returned to Paris: see LR: "le 11 mai remis à Hector à son départ pour Paris 400." By that time he had missed signing on at the Ecole de Médecine; the closing date was 9 May.
124	...Joséphine Berlioz wrote to...Félix: the letter is referred to in Félix's letter to Dr B, quoted on p. 125.
124n	It was...then that the dramatic scenes recounted in the *Memoirs*...: MEM X. Some of the arguments for this dating are discussed on p. 173. It is also likely that Joséphine B's opposition to her son's musical career would be most violent the first time it arose as a definite possibility — i.e. in 1823. (In 1822 he was still, officially, a medical student.) If that is right, the "unhappy and useless reproaches" which B recalled in his letter to Le Sueur the following year (CG I 60) refer to the confrontation described in MEM X. The undated letter to Victor Berlioz in which B defends careers in the arts probably belongs to 1824, as Pierre Citron places it (CG I 66–7), but could conceivably have been written after the 1823 visit.
125	Berlioz...bachelier ès-sciences physiques: a further curiosity, noted by Donnet and Moureaux (D & M 2–3, where, however, the illustrations have been printed in reverse order), is that the name written opposite "signature du candidat" on the form of receipt for the 62-franc entrance fee is not in B's hand. Even more curiously, the writing resembles the examples of Alphonse Robert's hand in RC. (The address filled in on the document, and subsequently crossed out, is Rue St Jacques 79 — Robert's address but not, at that time, B's.) Could Robert also have sat the exam in B's place?
126	A letter from Nicolas Marmion...: RC.
128	In his *Life of Richard Wagner* Newman...: NEWW I 68.
128	...as Adolphe Jullien suggests...: JUL 14–15.
129	...obituary tribute to Le Sueur: DEBATS and RGM 15 Oct. 1837 (MM 78, CONDE 161).
129	...Berlioz became almost one of the family: for the following paragraphs see MEM VI, CG I passim and Stephen de La Madelaine's pamphlet *J.–F. Lesueur*, Paris 1841 (copy in BN, VMc. 1126).
129	...he had once seen Gluck: the anecdote is quoted in B's obituary of Le Sueur.
129n	Le Sueur...pleading his cause with [B's] father: see MEM X 34.
131	...what R. W. Southern has called...: in an address at the funeral of V. H. Galbraith, Oxford Regius Professor of History, in 1976.

131 ...the pupil's opinions reflected his master's: Boschot (JR 181 etc.) points out how closely B's writings on works like *Alceste* and the two *Iphigénies* resemble comments of Le Sueur's.

132 ...planting a mine under the Théâtre-Italien: see MEM XIV 49, GM 9 Nov. 1834 (CONDE 188).

133 In its survey of...1823 the *Almanach des spectacles*...: SPECT 1824, 98.

134 ...singers...disfigure the vocal line in French operas: see for example *Annales de la littérature* etc. 1828, 244: "...ces agrémens que le goût italien a mis tellement à la mode qu'ils sont presque devenus indispensables même dans l'exécution des opéras français."

134 ...Gluck's horn parts...the dénouement of *Alceste*...: respectively TRAITE 183 and ATC 212−13.

136 ..."swearing like marauding soldiers...": MEM XV 51.

136 Du Boys held weekly reunions: see JUL 19.

136 ...a short young man with...nutcracker physiognomy: see NANCY Sept. 1828 and CG I 219.

136 When they wavered he harangued them...: see MEM XV (50), the source for most of this and the succeeding paragraph. (MEM XV originally appeared, in book form, in VM I [385]−399, which itself originated in DEBATS 13 Sept. 1835.)

136n ..."mixture of platitudes...from every pore": RGM 10 Sept. 1837 (VM I 249, ATC 26−7).

137 They would get there early...: *Galignani's New Paris Guide* for 1825 gives 6 p.m. as doors-open time at the Opéra; performances began at 7.

137 Ernest Legouvé...a vivid picture...: LEG I 290.

138n ...Augustus: he seems to have been benevolently disposed towards B, but the latter fell foul of him on at least one occasion when he unwittingly seated himself in the middle of Augustus' line of battle (SO 111−12).

139 ..."tragédie lyrique incarnate": ATC 229 (originally DEBATS 24 Oct. 1861).

139 ...combining "minutely studied effect...": MEM LIII (Deuxième voyage en Allemagne, 1ᵉ Lettre), 352.

139 She was accused of forcing. But what he remembered...: see REN 14 Sept. 1834.

139n Hazlitt...: HAZLITT 171. Cf. B's later judgment on Dérivis in SO 213, where he speaks of "l'inflexibilité de sa rude voix".

140 ...the stubbornness of his loyalties: cf. Hazlitt: "I have never given the lie to my own soul. If I have felt an impression once, I feel it more strongly a second time."

140 Le Sueur adored Mozart: see B's obituary of Le Sueur, cited above.

140 ...he heard Sontag as Susanna...: see GROT 256.

141 Andrieux, whose lectures...he still sometimes attended: conjecture based on the evidence of B's friendly relations with Andrieux throughout this period (see p. 377 on Andrieux's attendance at the 1830 Institute prize-giving).

141   Andrieux's...refusal is quoted in the *Memoirs*: VII 26.

141n   Legouvé describes...a performance of...*Otello*...: LEG I 298—9.

142n   ...recounted...by Daniel Bernard: CI 11—12.

142n   ...he reported to...Edouard Rocher: CG I 68.

143   ...making friends with [Mme Branchu]: B may have been introduced
           to her by Le Sueur at the Tuileries Chapel, whose choir she
           sang in (MONGR 982). The song "Toi qui l'aimas" (early 1823)
           was dedicated to her. He knew her well enough to be invited to
           her daughter Pamela's wedding in July 1825.

143   [Berlioz's] letter to Kreutzer: CG I 70—1. Barzun's assigning the letter
           to spring 1823 (BARZUN I 56) is wrong, for the reasons given.
           B was at La Côte throughout the period of the first seven
           performances of *La mort d'Abel*. His letter of 4 [Sept.] 1824 (CG
           I 68) to Edouard Rocher, recalling Cain's aria "Abel seul est
           aimable" and the effect it had on them, must refer to one (or
           more) of the next five performances (23 May to 26 Jan.); after
           that *Abel* was not given till October 1825. On the other hand
           Citron's conjectural dating of Oct. 1824 (CG I 70) seems to me
           too late. I prefer summer 1823. The letter sounds like one written
           immediately after the experience of encountering the work. B
           would have seized the first chance of doing so after his return
           from La Côte — the performance of 23 May 1823 — especially
           as Mme Branchu was in it.

145   ...music "in the grand style, dramatic or sacred": CG I 85.

145   ...the opera *Estelle et Némorin*: see MEM VII 27.

146   Berlioz showed Le Sueur the score: see CG I 60.

146n   ...the catalogue of...the Tuileries Chapel...: information kindly
           given me by David Charlton.

147   As he remarks in the *Memoirs*, "every composer...": VIII 30.

147   ...*The Gamester*: Moore's and Garrick's play was one of the works
           considered for performance at Mansfield Park.

147   The likeliest passage...: see R. H. Hyatt, "Le cheval arabe, Beverley
           and Estelle" in BSOC 60 (July 1968), 11.

147   Dérivis had sung a new cantata by Schneitzhoeffer: 20 Dec. 1823
           (SPECT 1825, 126).

147   ..."a semi-civilised young enthusiast": MEM VII 27.

148   ...Masson...Perhaps Le Sueur had a word...: or Gerono: the
           score of a Jubilate by Gerono which Tiersot found in the Con-
           servatoire Library had the name Masson written on it (MEN
           77 no. 29 (1911), 227). B kept in touch with Masson; Tiersot
           refers to a letter from Masson offering him two basses from the
           St Roch choir for his concerts at the 1855 Exhibition (MEN 76
           no. 12 (1910), 91n.

148n   the young...Dumas...: recounted in DM III 47—8.

CHAPTER 8

149   ...copying...*Iphigénie en Tauride*: the manuscript, inscribed "Copié
           pour études en Avril 1824 H. B.", is in the Pierpont Morgan
           Library, New York (see J. Rigbie Turner, *Four centuries of opera*,

New York 1983, 46–7). On the title page, above "Donné à Mr Ferrand Par Mr Berlioz", is written "Il ment; Il a tué sa mère" (heavily underlined), followed by a note explaining the circumstances in which Gluck made his famous remark. B's words echo the account in *Michaud*. After Ferrand's death the ms was owned by the organist of Belley, Boetz. (See MEN 77 no. 29 (1911), 227.)

150   ...as he reported to Humbert Ferrand: CG I 55–6. This appears to be the earliest surviving letter from B to Ferrand; but NR, where the Ferrand letters were first published before being issued in book form in LI, implies that there were earlier ones. See Preface (1880, IV 808), where this letter is described as "la première lettre un peu importante que nous possédions de cette correspondence".

151   ...he wrote to Le Sueur: CG I 60.

151   ...he told Le Sueur...: CG I 59–61.

152   His letter...to...Edouard Rocher: CG I 57–8.

152n   ...a passage omitted...: sc. from LI 4: it is given in NR (1880) IV 810.

152n   ...*Journal de Paris*: see also SPECT 1825, 463: "Le diapason de l'Opéra, sous lequel tant de voix ont succombé depuis quarante ans, va être baissé d'un demi-ton".

153   ...tipped him and Nancy...: NANCY 26 June: "Il nous a glissé fort adroitement (à mon frere [et] à moi) un louis dans la main".

156   Félix Marmion, writing to Nancy...: CG I 62–3.

156   "My dear Papa...": CG I 63–5.

157   "...Marcello...was son of the Doge of Venice" etc.: where B got this idea I don't know. It is not in *Michaud*, which records merely that Marcello's father was a Venetian nobleman, and that he *supported* his son's vocation.

CHAPTER 9

159   As Dumas...remarked: DM III 193. 18 Oct. 1824; the police diverted the funeral procession to Père-Lachaise (SPECT 1825, 478–9). See also SPECT 1831, 10: "Un artiste du théâtre des Variétés s'étant présenté a l'église de Saint-Vincent-de-Paule pour s'y marier, a éprouvé un refus obstiné de la part du curé de cette paroisse".

159   Cherubini's...Requiem...Berlioz...observed...: see his article in REN 13 July 1834.

160   ...the one surviving copy of the invitation: see CG I 72–3.

161   ...including the redoubtable de Pons: see MEM VIII 30.

161   ...a notice...posted on the door of the church: this is an assumption, but a reasonable one, given that none of the papers carried an announcement.

161   "Thus ended my long cherished dream...": MEM VII 28.

161–2   [Chateaubriand's letter]: Quoted MEM VII 29.

162   ...Nancy Clappier..."I am quite of your opinion...": letter dated 5 April (RC). 1825, from references to Prosper B's serious illness.

162   Hector was "quite mistaken . . .": c. early Feb. 1825, in a letter referred
         to in B's letter to his Uncle Victor, CG I 83.

163   . . . an angry letter . . . the second half of March: CG I 87–9, where it
         is dated c. 2 March. But the letter is not mentioned in NANCY;
         the diary's last entry is for 15 March.

164   . . . Nancy . . . echoed her father's vocabulary: in an undated draft of
         the opening (RC) the words "folie" and "délire" both occur.

164   In his reply, addressed to his father . . .: CG I 89–92.

164   " . . . 50 fr . . . for manuscript paper and copying . . .": possibly for the
         copy of the score of the Mass used by Valentino.

165   . . . a letter to his uncle Victor Berlioz: CG I 82–6.

165   " . . . *Silvain*": in DEBATS 24 Oct. 1861 (ATC 229) B mentions being
         at the Opéra-Comique when Mme Branchu received an ovation
         as Sylvain's wife in a benefit performance of Grétry's opera
         (which was in the O–C's repertoire 1821–5).

167   . . . a letter . . . to . . . Letexier: CG I 80–2.

167   His subsequent account . . . Evenings at the Opera . . .: DEBATS 13
         Sept. 1835 (VM I 397–9, MEM XVI 55–6).

167   "I had taken along a friend . . .": B identifies him as Léon de Boissieux,
         "fellow-pupil at the petit-séminaire at La Côte"; but there is no
         trace of him in the local Actes Civiles.

168   . . . as he reported to Du Boys: CG I 95. "He is indeed the most
         notable horse the royal household has ever had in its service".
         The Vicomte was a favourite butt of the satirical journals. But
         his reign at the Arts is notable not only for the new regulations
         extending the length of ballerinas' skirts and attaching fig-leaves
         to the naked statues in the Louvre but also for the founding of
         the Société des Concerts.

169   . . . Piccinni's *Didon* . . .: 12 June 1825. The encounter with de Pons is
         described in MEM VIII 30.

169   . . . a fastidious dislike of owing money: cf. BI 136 and CG I 300.

169   . . . moving . . . to the Ile de la Cité: there is no certainty when B moved
         to 27 Rue de Harlay. (The evidence of his correspondence is
         inconclusive. There is a gap of four months (July–Dec. 1825).
         The first surviving letter to bear the new address is 14 Dec.
         1825. However, the fact that the letter to Nancy of two days
         earlier gives no address suggests that B had not just moved
         there. But B remembered the "Pont Neuf dining-room", which
         he first began to frequent when it was still summer, as having
         become too cold for him to go on using it (MEM XII 40). That
         can only mean 1825; by the late autumn of 1826 he was already
         installed at 58 Rue de la Harpe: see CG I 135. The household
         account-book which Boschot describes (JR 237) begins on 6
         Sept. 1826.

169n   "while I tried to keep my mind off the poule au pot . . .": MEM XI 38.

170   The dramatic movements, as he reported to . . . Du Boys: CG I 95.

170   . . . *Quotidienne* . . . *Corsaire* . . . *Journal des débats*: respectively 15, 13 and
         14 July 1825.

170n   "F and B..." etc.: DEBATS 24 Oct. 1857 (GROT 215—16). She was the wife of the composer Louis-Sébastien Lebrun, whose *Rossignol* B considered one of the feeblest works in the Opéra's repertoire.

171   ...Augustus...at the Opéra a few nights later: see DEBATS 6 Dec. 1854 (SO 110). More likely on the 15th (*The Danaids*) than on the 13th, when the opera was *Pharamond*, a composite work by Boieldieu, Berton and Kreutzer.

171   ...the wedding of Mme Branchu's daughter...: see CG I 97 and CORS 12 July 1825. She married the young Opéra dancer Lefebvre.

172   ...*Moniteur*...*Drapeau blanc*...*Journal de Paris*...*Aristarque français*: respectively 11, 13, 11, 11 July 1825.

172   ...he wrote to his mother...: CG I 94.

172   ...as Nancy observed: undated draft (RC), reproduced CG I 99n—100n.

172   ...letter of congratulation from...Joseph Faure: 16 July 1825 (RC).

173   Nancy, writing to a friend...: CG I 99n—100n.

173   ...write and warn her brother: 24 July [1825], CG I 99—100, where it is described as "incomplete letter, not sent". But Nancy habitually drafts only the beginnings of her letters.

173   ...letter of Nancy's...: 17 Aug. 1825 (RC).

173   ...the account in the *Memoirs*: MEM X.

173   ...the "glacial reception"...the *Memoirs* speak of: X 34—5.

173   ...letter [from] Nancy...to ...Elise Julhiet: 17 Aug. 1825 (RC). Though the addressee is not named, references to her baby son and to her cousin Mme Thomas (née Rocher) identify her.

174   Hector was one of the party...would recall...Adèle...: CG I 474. The reminiscence must refer to this visit. On his summer visits of 1824 and 1828 he left before the family went to Meylan. In 1823 he was at La Côte in the spring, and in 1822, when he was there at the right season, Adèle was only eight.

174   [Hector's] admission of the truth: CG I 102.

CHAPTER 10

176   Berlioz wrote to...Edouard Rocher: CG I 103—4.

177   ...describes...his...visits to the confessional: MEM I 6.

177   ...Charbonnel..."out chasing grisettes": MEM XIV 47.

177   Scène heroïque..."bore...the stamp of Spontini's...influence": MEM XI 39.

178   The boorish Kreutzer...: the interview is described in MEM XI 39.

178   Berlioz reported to Edouard Rocher: CG I 126.

179   ...letter [to le Normant] reaffirming his position: CG I 110—11.

180   ...letter from La Rochefoucauld: see CG I 181.

180   ...Ferrand published...the text: announced in *Bibliographie de la France* on 29 March 1826.

180   ...Tulou the eminent flautist: see CG I 127.

180   ...letter to his sister Nancy: CG I 101.

180n   ...as Pierre Citron suggests...: CG I 111 n. 1.

183   ..."Polémique musicale" [in] the *Corsaire*: 19 Dec. 1825 (CONDE
         11–13. The two earlier letters to the *Corsaire* quoted on pp.
         131–2 are given in CONDE 7–10).
183n   Castil-Blaze's claim...: see WARRACK 308.
184   Weber's visit to Le Sueur...: this and the other near-encounters are
         narrated in MEM XVI 57–8.
184n   ...Berlioz later recalled...: RGM 3 Dec. 1843 (SO 80–1). In B's
         comic-macabre account the skull of the grocer's assistant, who
         died soon afterwards, figures in the Wolf's Glen scene in the
         production at the Opéra sixteen years later.
185   "And a sailor gets fifty lashes...": MEM XVI 60.
185   Berlioz reported to Edouard Rocher that [Mme Branchu]...: CG I
         128–9.
185n   It was said of [Mlle Quiney]....: *Petite biographie dramatique*, Paris 1826.
186   ...a note to...Thomas Gounet: CG I 112, which interprets the half
         legible postmark as 16 [March] 1826. But B's anathema *Le
         rossignol* was playing. The 10th (*Olympie*) seems to me much
         more likely.
186   ...the death of Hercules which Du Boys had written: see CG I
         119–20. B does not name the author, but among his known
         friends Du Boys fits the description best. CAT 422 suggests
         Stephen de La Madelaine, but there is no history of any literary
         collaboration between him and B, who would hardly have
         described him, even to Compaignon, as having "une grande
         habitude de la poésie lyrique".
186   ...the growing vogue for Scott: see SPECT passim. An *Ivanhoe*, with
         music assembled (by Pacini) from *Semiramide, Moise, Tancredi*
         and *La gazza ladra* opened at the Odéon on 15 Sept. 1826 while
         B was wrestling with Compaignon's adaptation of *The Talisman*.
         The libretto of the most successful opera of the period, Auber's
         La muette de Portici, is derived from Scott's *Peveril of the Peak*.
187   ...cool off...in the nearby Seine: CG I 123.
187   ...with five other candidates...: MATTHIEU (8 Aug. 1869) names
         them as Paris, Simon, Guiraud, Gilbert and Bienaimé.
187   ...enrol at the Conservatoire: 1826, not 1825. For long there was
         confusion about the year of B's first attempt at the Prix de
         Rome – a confusion due to an error in MEM X 34, where his
         failure in the concours d'essai is cited as the reason for his
         return to La Côte (August 1825 – in 1826, *pace* Boschot and
         Barzun, he didn't go there). But in 1825 at the time of the
         competition he was occupied with the performance of his Mass.
         B's first competition fugue has been preserved (BN W 33, 10),
         along with four others on the same subject, signed by their
         authors, who – the BA records show – were all candidates in
         1826. See CAT 34.
188   ...the official report of 1825...: BA 5 E 16.
188   Berlioz reported...to Edouard Rocher: CG I 127.
188   "...please send me [a copy of my birth certificate]: the copy is in RC.
189   ...enclosing a money order for 600 francs...: LR ("sent on 8 July").

189   ...his allowance...cut to 50 francs a month: see CG I 132, 138.

189   ...on 14 August...: see CG I 132.

190   The account in the *Memoirs*: XII 41−2.

190n   ...*Gazette musicale*...: MATHIEU (27 June 1869). The context
        suggests late 1826: "Il fallait du bois, des habits plus chauds. Ce
        n'étaient ni le beau concerto de flûte exécuté un soir sur la scène
        du théâtre de Belleville, ni les leçons de guitare et de solfège à 1
        franc le cachet, qui pouvaient produire l'argent nécessaire à ces
        dépenses."

191   He told Edouard Rocher in early September...: CG I 133−4.

192   ...his mother...sent him 100 francs: see CG I 138.

192   ...carrying their purchases back from the market...: MEM XII 42.
        The two nearest markets (almost exactly equidistant) were the
        Marchés St Germain and Maubert.

192   ...the housekeeping book...: described CI 17−18, JUL 22, PROD
        52−3, JR 237−8, 254−6, MATHIEU 27 June 1869, and men-
        tioned in BARZUN I 72 n. 57 as being in MUSEE; but I found
        no trace of it there.

193   ...immunity from family pressure...: see his firm reply of 28 Sept.
        1826 to Nancy, rejecting her reproaches and reiterating his
        refusal to come to La Côte that autumn (CG I 137−8).

193   "When I want to know if a thing of mine is good...": CG I 101.

193n   ...he took it to show one of the trombonists: see MEM XIII 44.

194   His opera, he told Edouard Rocher...: CG I 128.

194   ...petition to...La Rochefoucauld...: see CG I 139. BLOOMFAN
        102 gives the text of another petition sent two years later to the
        Minister of the Interior.

194   ...a letter to Nancy...: CG I 148−50.

195   ...a brief note to Léon Compaignon...: CG I 150−1.

196   Hector's letter of 4 June: CG I 154−6.

197   ...the tradition handed down...: see JUL 24.

197n   ...letter to a friend in 1848: CG III 546−7, Louis-Joseph Duc.

197n   ...note to Mendelssohn...: MEM LI (Premier voyage an Allemagne,
        4ᵉ lettre), 264−5.

198   ...Fétis' account in the *Revue musicale*: II 326−7 (1827).

199   The reluctant chorister...later declared...: MEM XIV 48.

199   ...anonymous description...in the *Musical World*: 15 Dec. 1837, quoted
        by F. G. E. in "Berlioz in England", *Musical Times* 1 July 1903.

199   "...unpopular with his comrades": he did, however, form a close
        association with one of them, if the Roquemont listed in SPECT
        among the tenors at the Nouveautés is the same as the Rocque-
        mont who in the 1830s became B's copyist and librarian. B's
        Rocquemont is named as a tenor in the chorus for the first
        performance of the Requiem (BN Berlioz Papiers Divers no.
        12).

200   ...*Waverley*...first half of...1827: see MEM XIII 44 and Le Sueur's
        letter of 11 Feb. 1828 to Alexandre Boucher (LM I 535−6),
        which speaks of his overtures in the plural — *Francs-juges* and
        Waverley.

200   . . . autograph manuscript [*of Waverley*]: BN ms 1507.

CHAPTER 11

202   "I learned a lot from [Reicha]": MEM XIII 45.

202   . . . article written in 1835: REN 7 June.

202   Reicha's influence is evident . . . : see MACB 9, 160, 187.

203   Cherubini's laconic reports . . . : see BCONS.

203   . . . he told Nancy . . . before he left his lodgings . . . : CG I 157–8.

204   ". . . my two opponents": Alphonse Gilbert and Guillaume Ross-
           Despréaux. D was a fellow-pupil of B's in Le Sueur's and
           Reicha's classes; G, a Berton pupil, was a cellist in the Odéon
           orchestra and organist at Notre-Dame de Lorette.

204   Life at the Institute . . . : described in MEM XXII, XXIII, CG I
           passim.

204   In his subsequent articles [on the Prix de Rome]: e.g. *L'Europe littéraire*
           12 June 1833, REN 9 July 1833, GM 2 Feb. 1834, 19 June 1836.

206   . . . later remarked in a classic understatement: MEM XIX 71.

208   . . . written record of the proceedings: BA 5 E 17.

208   Berton rubbed in the lesson . . . : see CG I 161.

208   . . . the piano . . . was a guillotine . . . : MEM XXII 83.

208   . . . stuck a penknife down his throat . . . : MEM XIV 48.

209   . . . complaint from the director of the Opéra-Comique . . . : AN F21
           1441.

210   . . . Mme Branchu . . . warned him . . . : see ATC 229–30.

210   Two versions of the . . . libretto . . . : see Pierre Citron's detailed notes to
           the Compaignon correspondence in CG I 113ff. B's letters to
           Compaignon (twelve between May 1826 and Feb. 1827) grow
           less and less frequent as he becomes convinced of his collaborator's
           limitations.

211   ". . . M. Saint Ange": see CG I 150 n. 1.

CHAPTER 12

213   He remarks in the *Memoirs* (apropos of his . . . hesitations . . .): XXI 77.

214   . . . one of the first French composers . . . Hoffmann's . . . example: David
           Charlton tells me of having come across only two cases in the
           18th century, apart from Rousseau's, of French operas written
           to a libretto by the composer: Framery's *La sorcière par hasard*,
           1768 (see CHARLTON 328 n. 17) and Berton's *Ponce de Léon*,
           1797.

215   . . . the five complete numbers . . . that survive: BN Rés. Vm^2 177. For
           the fullest discussion of the autograph material see HOLOMAN
           [215]–36.

216   . . . Méhul's *Euphrosine et Coradin*: B had a high regard for the work
           (1790, later revised). He went so far as to call the duet "Gardez-
           vous de la jalousie" a "most tremendous example of what music
           can do in conjunction with the dramatic action to express passion",
           and recalled being moved to shout out loud in his excitement at
           the culminating phrase, one evening at the Opéra-Comique in
           the mid-1820s (SO 439–41).

216   He described it as... "écumant de rage": CG I 132.
217   ...letter...to Letexier: CG I 80—2.
218   ...the "wild sweetness" of *Freischütz*...: MEM XVI 57.
218n The bass drum solo...was added in 1829: see CG I 279.

CHAPTER 13

220   As Winton Dean points out...: WINTON 87.
220   ...a review of a new work by "Citizen Méhul"...: *Le jeune sage et le vieux fou* in *Chronique de Paris*, 1 April 1793, 4.
221   ...he felt himself to be...Gluck's "son": CG V 551.
221   ...Delacroix, who could...say...: see DELACROIX XXI.
221   "A Survey of Classical Music and Romantic Music": CORR 22 Oct. 1830.
222   Andrieux...striding up and down...: see LEG I 110.
222   Delécluze...: see DELEC 68. See also his attack on "la règne du laid et de la triste réalité dans les arts", quoted by Boschot in JR 136.
222   The *Corsaire* defined Romanticism...: quoted in JR 120.
222   ...the *Quotidienne* and the *Oriflamme*...: see Hugo, *Les misérables*, Book 7, ch. 9.
223   Talma caused a frisson...: described in LEG I 190.
223   ...in Casimir Delavigne's *L'école des vieillards*...: LEG I 25.
224   ...Berton's remark to Berlioz: CG I 161.
224n Antoine Elwart's...conversation with Berton: see his letter to Fétis in LM II 237.
225   ...Scott...preferring Dryden's version of *Antony and Cleopatra*...: see *The Works of John Dryden*, ed. Walter Scott, London 1808, V 287—8.

CHAPTER 14

227   ...in Berlioz's words, "see Shakespeare darkly...": MEM XVIII 67.
227   "an instrument of war...", as Sainte-Beuve said: quoted RABY 72.
228   "It's an invasion!", wrote Delacroix...: DELCOR 198. A slightly different version is given in VHR II 144 — "oreiller" for "poignard".
228   "I saw — I felt — I understood": MEM XVIII 65.
228   "Imagine a man", wrote Dumas...: DTH 14—15.
228   ..."the interpreter of my life": CG I 208. On what the Romantics identified with in Hamlet, (and, by extension, the kind of qualities in him in which B found an echo of himself) see Granville Barker's *Preface to Hamlet*, 310ff.
228   ...the voice out of the burning bush: MEM LIX 448.
228   ...the *Corsaire* questioning...: 18 Sept. 1827.
229   ...*Pandore*...a eulogistic notice...of Ducis: 11 Sept. 1827.
229   ...things English were à la mode: see RABY 50.
229n ...*Pandore* reported...: 29 Nov. 1827.
230   Dumas...arranged to leave his office...early: DM IV 280.
230   ...Armand de Pontmartin...: "Les acteurs anglais à l'Odéon" in *Souvenirs d'un vieux critique*, l^e série, Paris 1881, 268—9.

230	...that rapt and concentrated attentiveness: cf. Lady Morgan (quoted RABY 59): "The theatres of other countries assemble *spectators*; but an *audience* is only to be found in the French theatre."
230	Dumas..."far surpassing all my expectations": DM IV 280.
230	The Classicists, in the entr'actes...: cf. a letter in CORS, 4 Oct. 1827: "A la dernière représentation d'*Hamlet*, je vis au foyer un homme qui s'agitait, pérorait et s'indignait des succès de Shakespeare. Il tenait à la main la traduction de la tragédie[...]."
230	...in whom... boulevard tragedy discovered its Talma...: DM IV 279.
231	Delécluze, in his journal...: DELEC 455-6.
231	*Pandore* voiced the general reaction..."that English candour...": 19 Sept. 1827.
231	Dumas recognised...flesh-and-blood men and women...: DM IV 280. Several accounts mention the naturalness of Harriet Smithson in particular. One, paying tribute to her "incomparable talent" in *Richard III*, went on: "But is it just talent? Is it not nature herself that speaks in every word, every sob, every gesture of the mother who fights for her children's lives against their murderers?" (*Gazette de France*, 28 May 1828).
232	..."what I was searching for...": DTH 15.
232	...Jules Janin's...epigram: DEBATS 1 April 1833, quoted COSETTE 169.
232	...Lady Granville, reported...: RABY 69.
232	On the opening night...played Lydia Languish: if the date given in CG II 83 is correct, B was there and saw Harriet in *The Rivals*.
232	...anonymous account...in the *Gazette musicale*: 7 Dec. 1834.
233	...her diction (which for Janin...): DEBATS 1 April 1833, quoted COSETTE 169.
233	Delécluze considered her mime...: DELEC 458.
233	The critic of the *Globe*...: 18 Sept. 1827.
233	One account..."radiant with suffering": Charles Jarrin in his *Mémoires*, quoted TIERSOC 52-3.
233	...a hum of surprise: *Globe* 18 Sept. 1827.
233	One witness speaks of her "passing abruptly...": see RABY 66.
233-4	Another recalled...: GM 7 Dec. 1834.
234	It was as though...a clap of thunder...: this and subsequent remarks of B's, unless otherwise stated, from MEM XVIII.
234	Mlle Mars...would attend every...performance...: COSETTE 176, RABY 68.
234	...the general enthusiasm: the final scene in particular, the death of the lovers (Garrick's version of the play was used), caused a sensation. "Never have we seen emotion in an audience to equal it, never heard such sobbing. [...] When one considers the difference in theatrical conventions from ours, the difficulty of the idiom for most of the spectators [...], what a triumph!" (*Pandore* 18 Sept. 1827).
234-5	Pontmartin..."His dense shock of...hair...": *Nouveaux samedis*, 18ᵉ série, Paris 1880, 101-2.

235   "La femme attendue se présente"...: TIERSOC 49.
236   ...he was there, under the arcade of the Odéon...: MEM LIX 445.
237   "I speak enthusiastically...", he writes to...Ferrand: CG I 161−2.
237   "'ferwel, ferwel, remember my'": i.e. as a Frenchman would pronounce
          "my", = "me". Though B recalls the line phonetically, he
          certainly owned or had access to a copy of the French translation of
          Hamlet on sale at the Odéon. See CG I 208, where the quotation
          "Horatio, tu es bien l'homme dont la société m'a le plus
          convenu" (Horatio, thou art e'en as just a man", etc.) conforms
          to it and not to the standard French translation by Le Tourneur
          ("Horatio, tu es l'homme dont le caractère sympathise le plus
          avec le mien").
237   He wrote to Harriet Smithson...: see MEM XXIV 90 and CG I 237.
237   ...he offered...the Opéra-Comique one of his overtures for a benefit...
          for...Huet: though there is no direct evidence for this, it would
          explain why B remembered the benefit at which an overture of
          his was performed fourteen months later, at the same theatre, as
          having been for Huet and not − as it was − in aid of the poor.
          Huet's benefit was on 5 Dec. 1827.
238   Berlioz wrote to Quatremère de Quincy: BA 5 E 17. Peter Bloom, in
          "Berlioz à l'Institut Revisited" (*Acta Musicologica* LIII fasc. II),
          gives the text of another unpublished letter in BA (5 E 19), of
          Feb. 1829, from B to the Minister of the Interior, passing on a
          request from the Prix de Rome Claude-Joseph Paris who was
          still in Italy and wished to draw some of his third-year grant
          there. There is no other direct evidence of B's friendship with
          Paris.
239   Berlioz's letter of the 29th to Ferrand: CG I 159−61.
239   ...the Odéon's...players who, according to the *Memoirs*...: VII 30.
239   It was his début [as a conductor]: the only other occasion before the
          mid-1830s was a session with some amateurs who invited him to
          be their conductor and, as a start, to rehearse them in a symphony
          by Gyrowetz. After a contretemps with the clarinettists, who
          persisted in playing their parts, written for clarinets in A, on
          clarinets in C, without making the necessary transposition, he
          abandoned the experiment (DEBATS 7 Oct. 1846, repr. as "Le
          droit de jouer en fa dans une symphonie en ré" in GROT
          35−6).
239   ...he says afterwards that he is "content they should hear...": CG I
          161.
239   The *Corsaire* and *Pandore*...: respectively 24 and 25 Nov. 1827.
240   Berlioz reported her death...: CG I 173−4.
241   ...Nancy Clappier...gossipy letter...: 7 Jan. [1828 (postmark)] (RC).
241   Macready recalled...: *Macready's Reminiscences*, ed. Sir Frederick Pol-
          lock, London 1875, II 443. Macready's quotation conflates two
          separate utterances of the dying heroine.
242   ...the *Quotidienne*: 5 March 1828.
242   An English observer (Mrs Baron Wilson)...: in *Our Actresses*, London
          1844, I 255−6.

242   "Anche io son pittore": quoted MEM XVIII 68.

242   ...a letter from...Le Sueur to...Boucher: LM I 535–6.

243   ...he knew the capabilities of every player...: see REN 15 Dec. 1833 and CG I passim.

243   ...having lately moved...to 96 Rue de Richelieu...: some time between Jan. and April 1828. The first letter to bear the new address is dated 27 April (CG I 175); but before that there is a gap of three months in the correspondence. In a letter of 11 Jan. 1828 (CG I 174) B speaks of M. Teisseire as being almost his neighbour. The *Almanach des 25000 adresses* for 1827 and for 1828, and the *Almanach parisien ou liste de 55000 principaux habitans* of 1828, give the address of "Teisseire, avocat aux conseils du roi à la cour de cassation" as 5 Rue des Grands Augustins. Therefore B was still living at 58 Rue de la Harpe at that date.

CHAPTER 15

245   Berlioz later described it as "A new world of music": MEM XX 74.

245n   The story of...the first night of...*Romeo and Juliet*...: *Illustrated London News* 12 Feb. 1848, quoted in MEM XVIII 67–8.

246   ...in the *Journal des débats*, Castil-Blaze: 1 June 1827. See PRODB for details of Beethoven performances in Paris before the founding of the Société des Concerts.

246   ...Schindler's story...: *Beethoven in Paris*, Munster 1842, 4.

246   According to...the horn-player Meifred...: reported by d'Ortigues, DEBATS 9 Nov. 1856, "Les inventeurs de Beethoven". See also ELWART 61–2.

246–7   ...Wagner maintained that the Beethoven performances...: NEWW I 214.

247   ...the aria...and the march...made a deep impression on Berlioz: see DEBATS 20 March 1842 (MM 33, 35–6).

247   Also heard during the season...: ELWART 130–6.

248   ..."the Stradivarius of concert halls": ELWART 5, 112.

248   ...music remained "the be-all and the end-all": CORR 22 Oct. 1830, 112.

249   Berlioz will never write...Viennese classicism: the restatement of the idée fixe two thirds of the way through the opening allegro of the Fantastic Symphony represents not a sonata-form recapitulation but a stage in the music's evolution, the progress of the melody from monody to harmonisation and integration with the full orchestra.

249   ...Wilfrid Mellers...: MELLERS 762.

249   Le Sueur refused to respond...: his encounter with the Fifth Symphony is told in MEM XX 74–5.

249n   Balzac...on hearing the Fifth...: *Oeuvres posthumes: lettres à l'etrangère*, Paris 1899, I 443.

251   Le Sueur, he told his mother...: CG I 252.

CHAPTER 16

252 By the time he took Le Sueur to hear the Fifth...: performed on 13 April and 4 and 11 May. One of the latter two provides the most likely occasion.

252 Berlioz wrote to La Rochefoucauld...: the correspondence about B's use of the Conservatoire Hall is in CG I 175ff.

253 ...the way Berlioz presents his relationship with Cherubini...: principally MEM IX, XVIII, XXXI, XLVI. See also CHERUBINI entry in MEMC 534—5.

253 [Cherubini's] end-of-term reports...: See BCONS.

253 Berlioz...learned a lot from [Cherubini's compositions]: the art of the long descrescendo which B praises in Cherubini is a characteristic of his own music.

255n ...the dramatised account...in the *Memoirs*: imitations of Cherubini's strong Italian accent were not confined to B. See FOUQUE 134.

256 "Permit me to appeal...": RM III 405—6 (1828), FIG, PAND, CORS 22 May. In addition CORS published a news item about the concert in the same issue.

257 "...Virgil's line...": *Aeneid* II 354.

257 Reporting this to his father, he begged him...: CG I 186—7.

258 "...performed on 26 May 1828": MEM XIX 72. The scribal copy which B gave Ferrand bears, in B's hand, a similar statement but dated 22 July 1828. This date Ferrand then transferred to his copies of two other works performed at the same concert (Resurrexit and Scène héroïque). 22 July 1828 was the date inscribed by B on the score of his *Herminie*. It is possible that B had the copy of *Orphée* with him en loge at the Institute and wrote the wrong date on it at about the same time that he began to write out the fair copy of *Herminie*.

258 ...an ancient music-lover [exclaimed]: MEM XIX 72.

258 ...the trombone theme in D flat...: "In order to depict the terrifying power of the Francs-juges and their grim fanaticism, I hit upon the idea of a theme of sombre and ferocious character played by the brass instruments together in octaves. Normally, composers employ these instruments only to reinforce the ensemble; but by giving the trombones a highly distinctive melody played by them alone while the rest of the orchestra shudders in the background, the formidable effect was obtained which so astonished the players" (CG I 191). The inconsistency between "the brass instruments together in octaves" and "the trombones alone" probably reflects different stages of the score. In the original (Odéon) version the theme would have been scored for trombones only; but in revising the overture for the larger forces assembled for his concert, and perhaps also with the Opéra in mind, B rescored it for all the brass, which is how it appears in the published version.

258	...his friend Turbry...cried out...: CG I 195 and 199. CG I 191, which also quotes the remark, describes it as a "quotation from an old tragedy", but this has not been identified.
259	...the timpanist...seized Berlioz by the arm...: CG I 195. On the sympathetic resonance of cymbals and piccolo see TRAITE 164.
259n	...the cymbal clashes...figured in the score by this date: see the note "Cimbales et timbales Coup de poignard" in the musical quotation in B's letter to Ferrand, CG I 198−9. (The editor of LI misplaced the note: B wrote it under the ff chord in bar 17 of the example.)
260	...in a carefully worded letter to his father...: CG I 192.
260	...the violinist Tolbeque...: CG I 200. There were three Tolbeques, all members of the orchestra of the Société des Concerts in 1828: Auguste (Odéon, leader), Baptiste (Odéon, leader of the violas) and Charles (Opéra, 1st violin). On the assumption that the two Odéon players would have already been supporters of B, it is Charles who is in question here.
260	All the critics...: in addition to the papers named, the *Courrier des théâtres* of 1 June.
261	The review in the *Voleur*...: 31 May 1828.
261	Fétis' article in the *Revue musicale*: III 422−4 (1828).
261	Fétis...declaring...at a salon...: quoted CI 20. See also MEM XIX 73.
261−2	...the great Augustus...: the encounter is described in SO 111.
262	...Berlioz wrote to Ferrand...: CG I 198−202.
263	...Félix Marmion...wrote to Nancy...: 18 June [1828] (RC).
263	Félix Marmion...owed [Dr Berlioz]...12,000 francs: see LR, where the sum, with interest, has reached 12,127 fr. by April 1828. By 1833 (the last entry) it is over 16,000.
263	...turned down Hector's request...Le Sueur...: CG I 203. The letter is undated − "15 juillet" in LI 43 is conjecture by the editor, who also got the year wrong. B says, "Je sors dans 4 jours" (phrase omitted in LI). The ms of his cantata bears the annotation "reçu le 28 juillet". The letter can be dated 25 July 1828 from its reference to a performance of *La Vestale* that evening − "the first for seven months", B adds. BOP and *Journal de Paris* record a *Vestale* on 25 July 1828 (the first since Jan.). In 1829 there was no performance of the work in July, and there had been one in April.

CHAPTER 17

264	On 2 July 1828...: details in this section from BA 5 E 18.
265	...to the 28th July...: see annotation on ms referred to above.
265	...his finished score...: BN ms 1185.
265	It was Pingard who told him...: VM II 21 (MEM XXIII 86); 2 Aug. 1828.
265n	Fétis in the *Revue musicale*...: IV 251 (1828).
265n	...the fifth time...Erminia had been set: JR 298.

267   ... "the trembling Queen of Antioch...": VM II 21 (MEM XXIII 86).

267   ... Berton... assured Berlioz that Spontini...: see CG I 161.

268   ... repay... Auguste Berlioz... a copy of the Resurrexit...: see CG I 203.

268   ... letter... to the Minister of the Interior: CG I 204—5.

269   ... new translation by Gérard de Nerval...: Gérard's *Faust* was announced in FIG on 30 Nov. 1827 but bears the publication date 1828.

269   Berlioz... one of the earlier French versions: inferable from CG I 247 — unless his claim that *Faust* has been his regular reading for several years is a piece of blague to impress Goethe.

269   As Jacques Barzun remarks...: BARZUN I 87.

269   ... took [*Faust*] with him everywhere...: MEM XXVI 95.

269n   Mme de Staël, in *De l'Allemagne*...: Part 2, XXIII (*Faust*).

270   ... travelling in a stagecoach through... Dauphiné...: CG I 208.

270   ... rustic "alpine" sharpened fourth: in a letter to Nancy six weeks later (CG I 211) B explains that the sharpened fourth in the Weber waltz he is sending her is there for "local colour — on the instruments Swiss shepherds use, the fourth is too high, and Weber has rendered it by a sharp."

270   He copied out the song... [for] Ferrand: this is almost certainly the autographs ms in the Pierpont Morgan Library, New York. See CAT 63—4.

270   Berlioz wrote to [Ferrand]: CG I 208.

271   [Nancy Clappier's] remarks... to... Nancy: Uriage, 21 Oct [1828] (RC).

272   Estelle Dubeuf had lately married...: 18 June 1828 (information supplied by Mme Denise Dumoulin). See also Nancy Clappier's letter of 22 July [1828] to Nancy (RC): "Dans sa position ce mariage est une fortune, une grande fortune; et quand on pense que M. Fornier y joint toutes les qualités solides qui assurent le bonheur d'une femme je regarde cela comme le coup de baguette d'une fée qui crée en un moment une nouvelle destinée."

272   ... told... Edouard Rocher... about Harriet Smithson: inferable from the fact that B's next letter to Rocher (CG I 214) speaks openly of her.

CHAPTER 18

273   ... variations [for guitar] on Là ci darem...": the existence of this composition and its publication, by Aulagnier, are known from Whistling's *Handbuch der Musikliteratur*, 1828, but no copy, apparently, has survived. See CAT 56.

274   Ernest Newman called the *Eight Scenes*...: NEWMAN 187.

275   ... the "marvellous book": MEM XXVI 95.

275   ... a "descriptive symphony on *Faust*": see CG I 232.

275   Berlioz['s]... reasons for withdrawing it: MEM XXVI 96.

CHAPTER 19

277 ...remained the same "unknown planet...": MEM XXIV 90.

277–8 Only, it was frustrating – he told...Nancy...: CG I 213.

278 ...letter to [Nancy] two months later: CG I 169–70, where it is wrongly placed: the letter belongs to Jan. 1829, not Jan. 1828. B made the mistake, common early in the year, of putting the previous year's date.

278 ...he told Ferrand a few weeks later...: CG I 232.

279 "but it seems to recede continually...": CG I 228.

279 "Oph. is not so distant...": CG I 231–3. B's "Oph." was changed throughout to "Ophélie" by the editor of LI.

279 "Oh dear friend...": the whole phrase is correctly spelled; B's English has progressed since the "ferwel remember my" of fourteen months earlier.

279 "Does she really...": CG I 228.

279 "Don't be alarmed...": CG I 232.

280 ...the programme (which also included...La fiancée): see FIG 25 Feb. 1829 and SPECT 1830 101.

280 ...Harriet warned her fellow-actors to beware...: MEM XXIV 91.

280 ...went...to talk to the manager...: details from CG I 236–9.

281 The following afternoon...: see MEM XXIV 91.

281 ...making him feel, as he later wrote...: MEM XXIV 92.

281 ...wrote to...Albert Du Boys...: CG I 236–9.

282 ...Peter Raby remarks, "playing all the parts...": RABY 104.

282 ...he wrote to La Rochefoucauld: CG I 240.

282 It was, as Berlioz said, "not meant for him": CG I 245.

282 Ferrand lent his friend money...: B's letter of 2 Feb. 1829 to Ferrand (CG I 231–3) includes an IOU omitted by the editor of LI: "Je reconnais devoir à Mr Humbert Ferrand la somme de *trois cent cinquante francs* qu'il m'a prété".

282 ...Theodore Schloesser...Louis Schloesser: CG I 43 n. 4, following Riemann, confuses the two brothers. It was Louis who studied with Le Sueur in 1823 (MACC has letters of that period written to him by Mme Le Sueur). B's meeting with Theodore is described in CG I 212–13.

283 Goethe was greatly intrigued by it...: see HILLER 118 and *Goethe Jahrbuch* 1890, 99–100, quoted PROD 71.

283 ...Berlioz...asked by Choron to write a work...: see CG I 220. Perhaps through the good offices of B's friend Stephen de La Madelaine, a Choron graduate.

283 "In comparison with me", writes Hiller...: HILLER 68.

284 "...that strange wild, shrieking laugh...": HILLER 68.

284 "Hector Berlioz was a complete human being...": HILLER 63ff.

286 Berlioz's letters to Ferrand and Edouard Rocher: CG I 245–6, 257–8, 261–2, 269.

CHAPTER 20

287 In June he had a minor nervous collapse: see CG I 258, 260.

287 ...without it (he told his father...): CG I 311.

288 ...Castil-Blaze looked over his shoulder...: the incident is recounted in GROT 59.

288 ...letter to Nancy: "Ah, but you speak...": CG I 244, 29 March 1829.

288 "...curious to see what effect this extraordinary work...": this suggests B had read the score (published in 1827).

288 "...'the universe was clasped within his mighty soul'...": unidentified quotation.

288 All the wags, wrote Berlioz to his mother...: CG I 252–3.

289 Fétis, reviewing the Seventh Symphony...: RM V 236–7 (1829). This was his second comment on the work, following its second performance on 29 March 1829.

289 ...that "millstone"...that "hazardous grind...": MEM XXI 76, 78.

289 The principle of the critique admirative...: see REEVE 194 etc.; also the same writer's "Berlioz critique, ou les embarras de l'analyse", paper delivered at the Colloque Berlioz in Grenoble/La Côte St André, Sept. 1980.

289 ...three letters...in...the Corsaire: according to MEM XXI (which doesn't mention the Corsaire letters) B began by writing an article for the Quotidienne defending Gluck and Spontini and attacking the Rossini-inspired cult of music as a purely sensual art, but it was so violent that the editor rejected it. This may be true; but it could represent a garbled memory of the article on the modern Italian school which B wrote for the Correspondant and the editor rejected (see p. 293).

289 "Calamity – I become a critic": MEM XXI.

291 ...the insensitive bawling...: e.g. Fétis in Curiosités historiques de la musique, Paris 1830, 407–8.

292 Le Sueur..."fugues which express nothing...": see FOUQUE 178, MONGR 118ff.

292 ...Berlioz sent...an account of his new activity: CG I 253–4.

292 In one of his first reviews for the Berliner...: 27 June 1829. It was preceded by pieces on Auber's La fiancée and Boieldieu's Les deux nuits (CAT 435).

292n Félix Marmion...wrote to say...: 31 May [1829] (RC).

293 ...Rossini had been heard in the foyer...: see CG I 257.

293 "...on the Italian school", wrote Berlioz to Ferrand: CG I 257.

293 ...summary of Beethoven's career...in...Revue musicale: V 129–31 (1829); discussed REEVE 66ff.

294 The stories [about Beethoven] are chosen...to illustrate...: see REEVE 70.

294 Fétis'...essay [on op. 131]...in the Revue musicale: VII 279–86, 345–51 (1830).

294 "the final spasm of a demented imagination": RM V 129 (1829).

296n ...a Parisian musical pamphlet: Ernest Filloneau, Les concerts de Paris, revue de la saison musicale de 1860, Paris 1860, quoted Raymond Bouyer, "Critiques musicaux de jadis ou de naguère", MEN 76 no. 7 (1910), 50.

CHAPTER 21

297   ...writes to Albert Du Boys in April 1829: CG I 249–50.

297   Ferrand's father suspected him of being a gambler: see CG I 255, 300, 411.

298   "...Beethoven has turned his brain": MEM XXIII 88.

298   ...an article, on prejudices...in the musical world: DEBATS 22 Jan. 1858 (GROT 242–3).

299   "After the...toasts", wrote Berlioz to...Nancy: CG I 211.

299   ...Meyerbeer wrote...to...Schlesinger: see CG I 255, 276.

299   Even Rossini...complimentary about it: see CG I 268.

299   ...Onslow...was "beside himself"...: CG I 250.

300   Fétis' *Revue musicale*...warm...review: V 375–6 (1829).

300   ...Marx...in the *Berliner allgemeine*: Nr. 39, [305]–6, 26 Sept. 1829.

300   Goethe...the "very finely engraved score": GOETHE v letter 650.

300   ...Zelter['s]...assessment: ibid. letter 662.

300n   ...Stephen de La Madelaine: see BLOOM 73.

301   As Julian Rushton...remarks...: NBE 5 VIII.

301   ...the letter...awaited with such impatience: see CG I 260. Eckermann had told Hiller that Goethe would "certainly be writing" to B.

301   The idea for a *Faust* ballet...: see CG I 217, 221, 229. The scenario was by Victor Bohain, one-legged editor and proprietor of *Figaro*, who bought the newspaper in 1827 "to campaign for constitutional liberties against Charles X, and to support the new literature" (BARZUN I 94 n. 26).

301   ...*Francs-juges* libretto...rejected...Berlioz told Ferrand: CG I 256.

301   ...a constant theme of Fétis'...in the *Revue musicale*: the article quoted appeared in Dec. 1829 (VI 451–2), not long after B's concert.

302   ...the Société du Gymnase-Lyrique: see CG I 215–16 and BLOOM-FAN 100–1, which quotes unpublished documents that cast light on this hitherto obscure corner of Berlioz biography.

302   He unburdened himself...to...Nancy: CG I 171 (10 Jan. [1829]).

303   ...his letters to La Côte St André...: respectively CG I 221, 167, 254.

303   He wrote, on 29 June 1829, to...Ferrand: CG I 263.

303   As the *Memoirs* remark, the Meditation...: XXV 93.

304   ...a friend in the Opéra orchestra gave him some advice: see CG I 268.

304   Auber...said the same thing: see CG I 270.

305   ...asking the Isère deputy Champollion...: see CG I 253.

305   ...he had had to "clip my wings"..." CG I 268.

305   ...his passion had flared up again...: see CG I 261–2.

306   ...handed it in...on 23 July: "reçu le 23 juillet" is written on the title page of B's score (BN ms 1505).

306   ...Mme Dabadie...Stephen de La Madelaine...: see CG I 264.

306   The report...stating that "none of the four compositions...": BA.

306   The judges...as Berlioz remarked to Ferrand...: CG I 269.

307   ...like setting the nine-year-old Prosper to read *Faust*: CG I 266.

307   ...Boieldieu...held him in conversation...: the dialogue given here is a conflation of MEM XXV 93–4 and CG I 265–70.

308	"he shows me", he told Nancy...: CG I 268.
308	...Auber...told him...: see CG I 270.
308	"Once again", cried Berlioz...to Ferrand...: CG I 270.
308n	...he insisted on the offending title being removed: see CG I 312–13.
309	...serious art...appealed only to a limited number: cf. Alfred de Vigny, writing in his diary the same year: "Tout Français, ou à peu près, naît vaudevilliste et ne conçoit pas plus haut que le vaudeville. Ecrire pour un tel public, quelle dérision! quelle pitié! quel métier! Les Français n'aiment ni la lecture, ni la musique, ni la poésie. Mais la *Société*, les salons, l'esprit, la prose" (AV 43).
309	...to "win what is most precious for an artist...": CG I 229.
310	"What the devil was the good Lord thinking of...": MEM XXV 95.

CHAPTER 22

311	His father (Berlioz told Ferrand)...: CG I 271.
311	Joséphine Berlioz wrote to Nancy...: 7 Aug. 1829 (RC).
311	Ten days later she reported...: Lundy soir [17 Aug. 1829] (RC).
311	...La Fayette...as Joséphine Berlioz reported to Nancy...: ibid.
312	Nancy wrote...to beg him...but, as he explained...: CG I 272–3.
313	...in early June he told Ferrand that the programme...: CG I 256.
313	By September..."a few pieces from *Faust*": CG I 273.
313	...orchestral parts survive for two other numbers...: BN ms 17466 (see CAT 61–2).
313	...Conrad's aria...with Dabadie: CG I 276: "C'est J. Dabadie qui m'a promis hier de me le chanter". The editor of LI for some reason changed this to "C'est madame J. Dabadie...", causing puzzlement to several generations of Berlioz's scholars, given that Conrad's aria is written for baritone.
313	...*Cléopâtre*, with Mme Dabadie: this is clear from CG I 277, to P.–A. Vieillard, author of the text of the cantata.
313	The huge orchestra...: according to Fétis' review in RM VI 352 (1829), it had many Conservatoire students in its ranks.
314	"...what such an orchestra is like": CG I 285.
314	...a jubilant note to Ferrand...: CG I 278–9.
314	...advance notices in *Figaro*, the *Corsaire*, the *Quotidienne* and the *Revue musicale*: respectively 31 Oct., 28 Oct., 31 Oct., VI 309 (1829).
315	...sent his father a full report...: CG I 279–82.
315n	...attempt to get exemption...La Rochefoucauld sent...a grant...: see CG I 288.
316	..."le Victor Hugo de la musique": reported by Nancy B in a letter of 5 Dec. [1829] to Rosanne Goletty (RC). I have not discovered which paper she read it in. Nancy continues: "Malgré le cas que je fais de certains ouvrages de Mr *Hugo* je ne voix pas qu'en cheminant de compagnie il arrive à la posterité, je doute que ce bagage *Romantique* l'y fasse aller bien sûrement. Au reste c'est

beaucoup que de faire parler de soi tant qu'on vit; que nous importe, après tout, ce que diront nos arrières neveux?"

316   *Figaro* ... *Gazette de France* ... *Journal des débats* ... *Corsaire* ... *Revue musicale*: respectively 3 Nov., 4 Nov., 6 Nov., 7 Nov., VI 348–52 (1829).

316   ... messages of good will ... from ... Rouget de Lisle: see CG I 288.

316   ... he asked Nancy to "tell Mama ...": CG I 291–4.

317   ... in the grip of a furious attack of spleen ...: CG I 293.

317   A letter to his father ... 3 December 1829: CG I 286–9.

318   "He kept on about his verses ...": CG I 287–8.

319   Berlioz called [Moore] "mon désolateur": CG I 167.

319   ... Berlioz would confess to finding him incomplete: CG I 485 (15 Sept. 1831).

319   ... Moore's "Believe me, if all these ...": MEM LIX (Voyage en Dauphiné), 490. Ferrand's copy of *La mort d'Orphée* was inscribed by B with the last four lines (in French): "No, the heart that has truly loved ...".

320   ... he told Ferrand ... he would receive " ... *Irish melodies* ...": CG I 291.

320n   ... Berlioz's letter to Ferrand: CG I 263.

320n   ... the impressively sinister ... title page: reproduced JUL 41.

321   Some time in January 1830 ...: the composition of "Elégie" is usually assigned to Dec. 1829 (see CAT 87); but Jan. 1830 would explain the delay in publication more satisfactorily. "Elégie" was clearly an afterthought.

321   ... one of his long, desperate treks: MEM XVIII 66 does not (*pace* CAT 87 and NBE 13 VIII) imply that "Elégie" was composed in 1827. The "long period of affliction" it talks about, during which the incident took place, is not presented as specifically relating to the immediate aftermath of the Shakespearean revelation of Sept. 1827. The expedition to Sceaux took place in 1830.

321   ... he wrote ... it on the spot: the only time, according to MEM XVIII 66, that he was able to express his deepest feelings directly in music while still under their immediate influence.

321   ... a fully realised idea ...: "La belle voyageuse" is a finely worked piece; but B was surely pulling Hiller's leg when he told him that he composed it very slowly over a span of two weeks, "writing a few bars every day like a counterpoint lesson" (HILLER 105). Hiller may have told B that he composed too quickly.

322   No less a figure than Adolphe Nourrit ...: see CG I 306.

322   ... as Berlioz reported to his father ...: CG I 311–12.

323   ... the *Universel* ...: 21 Feb. 1830.

323   ... Fétis' *Revue musicale* ...: VII 160 (1830).

323n   ... Hernani's "Vieillard stupide" ...: the anecdote is given in DM VI 17.

324   Balzac ... Stendhal ...: their views on *Hernani* are quoted in BARZUN I 129 n. 28.

324   "Some things...", he wrote to Nancy: CG I 321–2. B may or may not have been at the first night. VHR II 267 says he was. Boschot doubts it (JR 376n), but his grounds — that B would have boasted of it — are flimsy, in view of B's reservations about the play. In one sense the question is academic, since given the organised opposition to *Hernani* each performance was like a first night. See also CG I 508 n. 2.

324   ...Théophile Gautier...: *La presse*, 17 Sept. 1838, quoted REEVE 270.

CHAPTER 23

325   ...the manuscript score [of the March]: BN ms 1188.

325   ...the argument raged...for several months: MEN 72 (1906), 153–288.

326   In the *Memoirs*...in a single night: XXVI 96.

326   ...the surviving libretto of [*Francs-juges*]: BN Berlioz Papiers Divers no. 45.

327   The most plausible conclusion...: first put forward in HOLOMAN 225–6. See also David Cairns, "Reflections on the Symphonie Fantastique of 1830" in MUSPAR 82–6.

327   ...the letter he wrote to Edouard Rocher on 11 January: CG I 229.

328   ...prophetic words: cf. MACB 16.

328   ...the letter...three weeks later to Ferrand: CG I 232.

328   ..."written under the influence of Goethe's poem": MEM XXVI 96.

328   ..."meditating an immense instrumental composition": CG I 258.

328   On 2 January he asks Ferrand...: CG I 300–1.

328   ...on 30 January, he tells...Nancy...: CG I 303–4.

329   "...(I tell my army)...forget barrack-room songs...: see Katherine Reeve's interesting analysis of this letter in REEVE 35–6.

329   "After a period of calm...": CG I 306.

329   ...to Stephen de La Madelaine...: CG I 307.

329–30 ...letter to his father...19 February...: CG I 309–13.

330   ...an incoherent letter to Ferdinand Hiller: CG I 313–15.

331   On 16 April he reports to Ferrand...: CG I 318–20.

331n   The double title echoes...Hoffmann: see REEVE 252.

332   "...an orchestra of 220": this was altered to "a hundred and twenty" by the editor of LI (a reading following by CG I, which was published at a time when B's letters to Ferrand were still believed lost), but the figure, whether or not a slip of the pen, is quite clear.

332   ...the finale...was "not written in that spirit": CG I 328.

332   ...Odes et ballades...certainly read by 1829: published 1826. CG I 233 shows B read Hugo's *Orientales* on publication. The full text of B's appraisal (bowdlerised in LI) reads: "Il y a quelques passages ridicules il est vrai, mais il y a des milliers de sublimités".

333   ...his "vessel cracked horribly": CG I 318. "Mon vaisseau a craqué horriblement". Cf. Gérard's translation of *Faust* (Night Scene): "des craquements de mon vaisseau".

333   ...Cone observes, "the unity of the symphony...": CONE 10.

334	..."pure" [music]? As...Mellers has pointed out...: *Scrutiny*, March 1939, 480.
336	...to quote Rudolf Reti, "the music...": *The Thematic Process in Music*, London 1961, 294.
336	...as Schumann said, "to the French...": from the final section of his famous essay on the Fantastic Symphony in the *Neue Zeitschrift für Musik*, July-Aug. 1835. CONE 222–48 gives the first complete English translation.
337	"...recognising its hero", he told Ferrand: CG I 319.
337	...to "depict...his infernal passion": CG I 306.
337	The complete passage [from Hugo's poem]: also quoted on the second title page of the printed libretto of *The Return to Life*.
338	He said that the theme recurred to him...: MEM IV 16.
339	...*Le dernier jour d'un condamné*...read in 1829: see CG I 244.
339	Chateaubriand...the piping shepherds' call: first suggested in TEMP 605.
339n	...the testimony of the Taylor family...: quoted in HENSEL I 226–7.
340	...as Nicholas Temperley has said...: NBE 16 XI.
340	The revisions show Berlioz...striving...: see HOLOMAN 267–75 and BANKS.
340	...in...Holoman's phrase, "formal organisation...": HOLOMAN 275.
340	...the most miraculous birth since Athene...: attributed to Bernard van Dieren by William Mann, in a programme note on the Fantastic Symphony.
340–1	..."taut discipline" which Mellers comments on: MELLERS 763.
341	...the unity that "goes much deeper...": CONE 10.
341	A letter to his father...three weeks before the concert: CG I 323–6.
342	Three days later (13 May) he reported to Ferrand...: CG I 328.
343n	Rosanne reported the visit to Nancy: letter of 1 June 1830 (RC).
343n	In her reply Nancy...: 7 June (RC).
344	...the programme caused a stir: it did not go down well in Dauphiné. Nancy Clappier "agreed entirely" with Nancy B's opinion "about the daydreams which serve as text for your brother's music. Our romantics are wrong when they imagine that to be natural and forceful one must say everything" (letter of 26 June [1830], RC).
344	...to his father...explained why it had been cancelled: CG I 330–1.
344	...the scene described...in the *Memoirs*: XXVI 97: "The extreme care I take over the practical details of concert-giving dates from then".
345n	The *Corsaire* reported...concert began very late...: 1 June 1830, quoted PROD 86.
345n	Elwart...sees it...as a "precursor...": ELWART 149.

CHAPTER 24

346n	...Berlioz's sketch for one of the monologues...: the two-page autograph is in the Bibliothèque Municipale in Grenoble (N 3275).

347	"music was made, under the eyes of Frau Mama...": HILLER 76ff.
347	...Berlioz described Hiller's adoration...: MEM XXVIII 99.
347	...no doubt offered him sage advice: B may also have helped in planning the concert which Hiller gave at the Conservatoire on 10 Jan. 1830, a concert similar in pattern and character to B's concert of the previous Nov. The programme included a prayer to words by Chateaubriand and (until it was withdrawn for lack of rehearsal) an overture on *The Tempest* — the same subject as B would choose for the overture he wrote the following summer. The parallels are piquant but not really surprising, given the two friends' common literary enthusiasms.
347	In a letter to Ferrand [of] 2 January...: CG I 300.
348	...his letter announcing...a complete set of clothes...: CG I 292.
348	"Three times a week I would emerge from my attic...": DEBATS 8 June 1855.
349	"The effect of this rash avowal...": MEM XXVIII 99.
349	..."plunged back once more into all the anguish...": CG I 306.
349	Berlioz disappeared for thirty-six hours...: AS.
350	"Since my recovery", wrote Berlioz to...Rocher...: CG I 333.
350	They passed her in the street...: see CG I 332.
350	At the end of May events accelerated...: at first Camille and B had apparently kept their love quiet. Hiller was still on the scene — he didn't leave Paris till the beginning of June — and still on easy terms with B, up to mid-May at least, to judge from CG I 329, in which B speaks of getting Nourrit to come and sing his "Elégie": "Hiller will accompany, it will be just the three of us". The date of Hiller's departure is shown by a letter of 3 June 1830 from Mme Le Sueur to Louis Schloesser in Darmstadt (MACC): "Nous profitons de l'occasion de M. Hiller, pour vous donner de nos nouvelles".
351	[Berlioz] wrote to his father...: see the letter to Rocher, CG I 332.
351	Camille and Berlioz eloped. The episode is obscure: the story has to be pieced together from the hints in CG I 409, 431 and 445.
351	[Nancy] also wrote to Rosanne Goletty: 10 June [1830] (RC).
351n	"Henceforth the daughter was closely watched...": HILLER 77.
353	...Rosanne Goletty...booked them two rooms: letter of 16 June 1830 (RC).
353	[Dr Berlioz] wrote to Joseph Rocher...: see CG I 354, 370.
353	...he poured out his heart to Edouard: CG I 354.
353	...set out in the long letter...to Nancy: CG I 334–8.
355	"'...she in turn wished to help him...'": cf. CG I 358: "the family is still dependent on [Camille]. She will have to go on helping her father for some time longer — he was, I believe, left with some business debts, and it's she who's paying them".
356	...to Nancy...a description of Camille: CG I 339.
357	...told his mother: "I wonder daily...": CG I 341–2.
357	When Camille fell ill...: see CG I 344.
357	"Camille, who understands [German]...": CG I 340. Her mother was from Germany.
358	From his candidate's cell he wrote to Ferrand...: CG I 343.

CHAPTER 25

360   Alfred de Vigny...in [his] diary...: AV 45ff.

362   "...importance of the competition", he wrote to his father...: CG I
          345–6.

362   ...on the 5th...to Nancy: CG I 346–8. B dates it the 4th, but the
          Opéra did not reopen till that evening.

363n   Mendelssohn's father...to his family...: quoted HENSEL I 256–7.

364   Abraham Mendelssohn...observed...: HENSEL I 255, 259.

365   A letter from Maria Malibran...: quoted LEG I 276.

365   "Now", exclaimed Horace Vernet, "I can paint...": quoted BARZUN
          I 202.

365   Victor Hugo...a ringing ode...in the *Globe*: quoted VHR II 294.

365   Choron performed [the Marseillaise] at a...concert...: JR 448.

365n   Nancy..."a military band...the Marseillaise...: letter of 5 Sept.
          1830 (RC).

366   Crossing the...Palais Royal...: the incident is described in MEM
          XXIX 102.

366n   ...Mahler's inscription...: see Alma Mahler, *Gustav Mahler: Memories
          and Letters*, London 1968 (rev.), 108.

366n   ...Berlioz arranged...*Chant du neuf Thermidor*: see Jacques Tcham-
          kerten, "Un autographe inédit de Berlioz: Le Chant du neuf
          Thermidor", *Revue musicale de Suisse romande* 37 (1984), 22–39,
          and CAT 100–1.

367   ...a "harmonious revolution": MEM XXIX 102.

367   ...he wrote to Nancy on 5 September...: CG I 358.

368   ...Saint-Simonian policy to recruit artists...: for the fullest account
          of the role of music in the movement, see LOCKE.

368   Berton...voting "no"...: in the light of CG I 349 the solitary vote
          recorded in the report of the jugement préparatoire (BA 1 H2
          63) must be his.

368   ..."an academy neither could nor should...": see CG I 349.

368   "And God knows", wrote Berlioz...: CG I 349–51.

368   Pradier...came out of the conference hall...: MEM XXIX 104.

369   As Camille had said..."The *world* believes...": see CG I 352.

369   "My dear Mama, I am pleased to announce...": CG I 349.

369   [a letter] from his son saying that, though Adèle's joy...: CG I 355.

369   ...a firm retort: "I do not deserve...": CG I 362–3.

369n   ...he wrote to Edouard Rocher...: CG I 354–5.

370   [Nancy] has just refused...an old recluse...: see NANCY and CG I
          365, 368.

370   Adèle...writing to her sister...: 23 [Aug.] 1830 (RC).

370   "...The Sea Beggars...": *Le gueux de mer, ou la Belgique sous le duc
          d'Albe*, Brussels 1827.

370   ...long and florid letter from Le Sueur: 25 Aug. 1830, *Revue de musico-
          logie* LVIII (1972) no. 2, 274–6.

372   ...the surviving letters [of] Louis Berlioz...: there are more than a
          hundred in RC.

372n   ...sale catalogue quoted by Boschot: JR 444.

CHAPTER 26

374 ...as Abraham Mendelssohn reported...on 27 August: HENSEL I 257.

374n ...as Katherine Reeve observes...: REEVE 113.

375 The score of...*Sardanapale*: BN Rés. Vm² 178.

375 ...he had "reduced himself by half"...: CG I 350.

375n In a letter to his father...: CG I 379.

375n On the final pages..."fin Camille"...: this raises the possibility that B sketched the conflagration scene while *en loge* and then worked over it later, and what we have is a draft. The music differs from B's account of it in MEM XXX 108–9.

376 ...[letter] to...Adolphe Adam: CG I 374–5.

377 ...Malibran...had to perch on a stool...: MEM XXX 108.

377 ...Dickensian account of...prizegiving: XXX 105–7 (originally VM II [33]–41, based on GM 2 Feb. 1834).

377n ...account in the *Memoirs*: "At our first meeting...": LI (Premier voyage en Allemagne, 4ᵉ Lettre), 261.

378 ...Mme Moke...had changed her mind: see CG I 352, 354, 370.

378 Berlioz's letter to his father...: CG I 380–2.

378 "The violins and cellos went on...": MEM XXX 109.

379 ...*Journal du commerce*...*Courrier français*...: both 31 Oct. 1830.

379 The *Journal des débats*...*National*...: both 1 Nov. 1830.

379 Fétis, in the *Temps*...: 4 Nov. 1830.

379 ...advance announcement [of *Tempest* overture]: RM IX 367–9 (1830).

379 ...*Courrier des théâtres*...: 6 Nov. 1830.

380 He owed the idea...he told Ferrand, to...Camille: CG I 366. See also CG I 372.

380 ...(wrote to Adèle on 21 October)...: CG 373–4.

380 ...on the 28th...the overture was given again: see CG I 383 and SPECT 1831, 32. Though neither SPECT nor DEBATS (in its announcement of the evening) mentions *La tempête* (which SPECT refers to a few lines above, under 7 Nov.), it is a reasonable assumption that it was performed, as B's letter said. SPECT simply states "Représentation au bénéfice de la caisse des pensions" and gives no details.

380 ...the *Corsaire* hailed it...: 9 Nov. 1830.

381 ...Fétis published his laudatory review: RM X 25–6 (1830).

382 ...first appearance of the piano as an orchestral instrument: Boschot (JR 458–9) is at curious pains to deny this, citing Beethoven's Choral Fantasy — a work in which the piano's role is soloistic, not orchestral.

382 ...wrote to his mother...before the performance: CG I 372.

383 He summed it up...in a letter to his father: CG I 324–6.

384 ...observed Fétis...in the *Revue musicale*: IX 330–8 (1830).

385 ...to Louis-Philippe to invite him to his concert: unpublished letter of c. Nov. 1830 first brought to light by Peter Bloom in BSOC 128 (summer 1986), 2–9.

385 ...Victor Berlioz...a letter of introduction...: See CG I 356, 363.

386	...he got his doctor...to write a certificate...: CG I 377 (8 Sept. 1830). G was a contemporary of HB at medical school.
386	A month later, writing to his mother...: CG I 371−2.
386	...a day later, in a letter to Adèle: CG I 373.
386	...on 28 October, he...petitioned the Minister...: CG I 367−8. The Comte de Carné, editor of the *Correspondant*, also wrote on B's behalf, making much of his "deplorable health" and nervous excitability, which the journey to Rome could only exacerbate. See BLOOMFAN 105.
387	The Minister's...inability to set aside the regulations: B was not alone in feeling their rigour. When the sculptor Desprez returned from Rome for reasons of health, the Minister turned down Horace Vernet's request that he be allowed to receive his grant in France (letter of 30 April 1831, Villa Medici archives). On the other hand, when Frederick-Henri Schopin, another sculptor, broke the regulations a year later by going to Paris to see his family, the "special circumstances" were taken into account, and he did not lose his grant.
387	...spoken promise...from the Société des Concerts: see CG I 353.
387	...tells Edouard Rocher that she "is opposed...": CG I 354.
387	But two weeks later (to Edouard again)...: CG I 354.
388	A month after that...in a letter to Nancy...: CG I 369−70.
388	"...I have...and I shall keep them": according to NANCY, Camille called B "le fiancé de mon coeur".
389	Rehearsals, some of them sectional and taken by Berlioz himself: see REN 15 Dec. 1833. B was one of the first conductors to hold sectional rehearsals. See D. Kern Holoman, "The emergence of the orchestral conductor in Paris in the 1830s", MUSPAR 418.
390	...the [slow] movement..."bore little resemblance...": MEM XXI 110.
391	...first meeting [between Berlioz and Liszt]: described in MEM XXXI 110, also CG I 385.
391	...the surviving ticket plans...: in MUSEE.
392	...notices...in the *National* and *Figaro*: respectively 6 and 7 Dec. 1830.
392	...a couple of paragraphs in...*Revue musicale*: X 151 (1830).
392	the "incendie" caught fire this time...MEM XXI 110.
392n	...*Figaro*...*Corsaire*...*Revue musicale*: respectively 4 Dec., 3 Dec. and X 89−92 (1830).
393	..."Superb, superb, prodigious!": CG I 390.
393	...wrote to his father...giving news of his success: CG I 385.
393	...on the 7th he wrote to tell Ferrand...: CG I 387−8.
393	Spontini had been heard to exclaim...: see CG I 385.
394	The letter...Berlioz enclosed with the scores...: CG I 386−7.
394	...*Olympie*, "costing", Berlioz told Nancy...: CG I 390.
394	..."that wretched Smithson"..."the Smithson wench"...: CG I 353, 354, 328.
395	...introduced to [Harriet], as he told Ferrand...: CG I 367.
395	(Berlioz's...idea that she should play a solo...): see CG I 342.

395   Mme Moke...declined to go...he told Nancy...: CG I 389.
395   "That evening", wrote Berlioz to Nancy...: CG I 390.
396   ...discussed the Adagio...with Hiller: MEM XXXI 110.
396   He again saw Spontini...: see CG I 390.
396   ...received a fan letter from Rouget de Lisle: MEM XXIX 103−4.
396   Berlioz wrote back on the 29th: CG I 394.
396   ...sent a diplomatic note to Fétis...: CG I 395.
396−7   ...a letter to Stephen de La Madelaine: CG I 396.
397   "...leave in six hours. ALONE...": could this mean there had been
           some wild scheme for B to take Camille with him − hinted at by
           the remark to Edouard Rocher (CG I 361) that Mme Moke was
           "pushing them to the limit" and that he would "stop at nothing"
           to make her his?

CHAPTER 27

398   Berlioz's arrival...took his family by surprise: see CG I 388 ("Je serai
           à la Côte vers le 15 janvier") and NANCY ("L'arrivée inatendue
           de mon frère...").
398   He wrote to...Montfort on 10 January...: CG I 405.
398   ...a letter written to Ferrand from Lyons: CG I 411.
399   Hiller...to...Edmond Hippeau...: LM II 204.
399   ...the tress of her hair she wove for him: see NANCY (quoted CG I
           433 n. 2).
399   "I shall see her today...": CG 358−9.
399   ...her piano: it was "mean and paltry": CG I 384.
399   ..."the celestial pianofortist"...: quoted BARZUN II 109 n. 15.
399   ..."my one true friend", she told Jules Janin: letter of 14 May 1840,
           quoted HILLS 7.
400   ...she wrote to the Baron de Trémont: LM II 203.
400−1   ...two letters...to Ferdinand Hiller: CG I 403−4, 406−8.
401   On 22 January...he found a letter waiting: see CG I 407.
402   ...he unburdened himself to Nancy: see NANCY c. mid-Jan. 1831.
403   ...on the 9th, he wrote to Thomas Gounet: CG I 412−13.
404   "...What a sublime monster...", he wrote to Adèle: CG I 414.
404   In the harbour...: this account of B's journey to Rome is based on
           CG I 414, 415−18, 425−6, 438−40, IP 17−20, VM II [47]−55,
           MEM XXXII and XXXV.
404−5 * ...a product of "the ancient French provincial muse...": GM 2 Feb.
           1834. See also IP 17.
406   ...under the best possible auspices: the subsequent storm also recalls
           Byron. See his letter of 12 Nov. 1809 recounting a near-shipwreck
           on a Turkish ship off Greece: "The Greeks called on all the
           saints, the Mussulmans on Alla.[...] [I] wrapped myself up in
           my Albanian capote (an immense cloak), and lay down on deck
           to wait the worst".
409   "in the libretto, no ball at the Capulets'...": LE 50.
409   "To begin with, the dazzling ball...": LE 48.
411−12   "The moment I appeared in the doorway...": IP 21, reprinted VM
           II [61]−4 and MEM XXXIII 118−20.

412	...small, sparsely furnished rooms...: cf. MARECHAL 87−8.
412	...the English, the Germans and the French had each...: see IP 21−2. On the Café Greco and nearby Restaurant Lepri see also ETEX 116, 117, 119 and MLET 77−8.
413	..."Comment t'appelles-tu donc, toi?" CG I 441.
413	Mendelssohn...told his mother...: MBRIEFE 119.
413	"What is the point", he wrote to Nancy...: CG I 420.

CHAPTER 28

414	...the exquisite spring weather: see MLET passim.
414	...Carle Vernet...thrilled...that Berlioz loved Gluck: see CG I 441.
414n	"As Horace Vernet had armed us all...": CG I 425.
414−15	..."a young composer of promise called Mozart": MEM XXXIX 154.
415	Berlioz, trying to buy a piece by Weber...: CG I 426.
415	...to Mendelssohn, he told his friends...: CG I 441. Also CG I 450.
415	...Mendelssohn...cost of a dinner: CGI 441.
415	...Berlioz retraced his steps to Florence...: this account of B's journey from Rome to Nice is based on CG I 422−30, 436−7, 441−4, 452, VM II 70−80 and 212−15 (MEM XXXIV and XLIII).
415	...second movement...on manuscript paper bought in Rome: see HOLOMAN 264, 265.
416	...an oratorio on "The world's last day"...: see CG I 467.
417	...died...fighting for the Italian patriots: Napoleon Louis succumbed to a combination of measles and pneumonia, but was popularly supposed to have died of wounds.
418	...an "épisode bouffon": VM II [67].
421	He broke the news to [his family]: CG I 431−4.
421	"...all in June last year": in fact the love affair began in March.
422	"I could love Odile...": there are some signs of an incipient tendresse on her side too: see letter of 7 Dec. 1828 from Nancy to B (longer than the version quoted CG I 219−20) in RC: "Je trouve toujours plus interressante cette petite cousine et je ne conçois pas que son esprit puisse se développer autant avec l'éducation *anti-libérale* qu'elle a reçue, elle est enchantée de la musique que tu lui as envoyée et elle m'a chargée spécialement de t'en remercier, elle l'aurait fait elle même si elle l'eût osé, elle ne se console pas de t'avoir vu si peu ces fériés, mais elle veut s'arranger de manière à ce qu'on l'amène l'année prochaine quand tu seras ici". The letter of 2 April 1830 from Odile to Nancy referred to in CG 432 n. 2 suggests more than the "indifference" attributed to Odile by Pierre Citron: "Mon père a vu Hector qui à ce qu'il nous dit se porte à merveille, et compte venir vous voir cette automne; je pense bien qu'il ne vous donnera pas tout à fait tout son temps, et qu'il nous en réservera une petite partie...". But Victor B would have put a stop to so unsuitable a match for his daughter, had there been any danger of it.
422	"There is a New World of music...Columbus...Pizarro or Cortez": cf. the final monologue in *Lélio* (1831−2 version): "Nouveau

Colomb, Beethoven a découvert une autre Amérique, à laquelle il manque un Cortez et un Pizarro a l'explorer".

422   "I must write to Spontini...": but it would be nearly a year before he did so (CG I 545–6). Spontini had advised him against marrying Camille.

423   "My dear Commandant...": published in Jean Gavot, "Berlioz à Nice", *Cahiers de l'Alpe* no. 46 (1969), 122–4.

423   Berlioz...wrote to the hotel in Florence...: inferable from the fact that his baggage was still there when he returned in late May, occupying the same room as before – see CG I 466.

423   He sent long letters to his friends: the one addressed jointly to Gounet, Girard, Hiller, Desmarest, Richard and Sichel (CG I 438–46) is, as Hiller observes (HILLER 78), the size of a small pamphlet.

424   "...*Le dernier jour d'un condamné*...": Nancy evidently confused it with another novel, for she goes on: "As in the book, a young man with lofty mind, an artist, driven to murder by an extravagant passion such as natures of the sort are prone to – and even the name of the young person, Camille, the same!" – details that do not correspond with those in Hugo's story.

424   [Nancy Clappier's letter]: RC.

424   At the beginning of May came Horace Vernet's letter...: see CG I 445 and MEM XXXIV 125.

425   "Life and joy...": MEM XXXIV 126 – with XXXV and CG I 432–3, 444–6, 447, 450–1 and 454 the source for this account of B's stay in Nice and his return to Rome.

425   ...an overture based on Scott's *Rob Roy*: *Intrata di Rob-Roy Macgregor*. See CAT 107–8, and RLP 8–9, where Boschot suggests that B may have heard, through his friend Victor Bohain (now director of the theatre), that the Nouveautés was putting on a dramatisation of the novel, for which an overture might be apropos. However, the work in question, *Diane de Vernon*, besides opening (on 4 April 1831) before Berlioz had begun on the score, was an opera, with music already supplied for it by another composer, Louis Blanchard. The Nouveautés project, if B heard of it, can at most have given him the idea of writing a work of his own on *Rob Roy*.

425   Tovey..."a magnificent piece of orchestral rhetoric...": *Essays in Musical Analysis*, London 1936, IV 84.

426   ...an abstinence...(he told his friends in Paris)...: CG I 445.

426   "What a sunset"...: CG I 447.

426   "'It sinks and fades...'": *Faust* Part I, sc. 5.

426   On the 20th he wrote to...Edouard Rocher: CG I 451–3.

428   ...*Agnese di Fitz-Henry* by Paër: LE 53–4 (slightly shortened for IP, VM and MEM).

428   ...the room he had had before: see CGI 466.

430   Two other passages in the spoken text...: both first appear in letters – CG I 421 (and 424) and 402–3 respectively. B may have been in the habit of drafting his letters and keeping the drafts, like Nancy, in which case he could have taken the sentences in

question from his correspondence for use in *Lélio*. But the opposite process is at least as likely: when writing letters he made use of passages already written with the melologue in mind. (See CG I 421 n. 1.)

430   "Another Faust...to realise my dreams": this was one of the passages B cut when revising the melologue in 1855.

430n   ...Berlioz envisaged performance in a theatre: see the introductory note on p. 2 of the printed libretto (1832).

431   ...they came from Thomas Moore: cf. CG I 457 ("C'est Moore. qui m'en a donné l'idée") and 459.

CHAPTER 29

433   "The weather today...": CG I 455.

433   While he is there he takes part...: this résumé of B's life in Rome is based on MEM XXXVI (originally VM II [101] ff and IP) and CG I 457, 459–60. 462.

433   ..."drinking deep"...: cf. IP 24 n. 2: "Le lecteur fera sans doute l'observation qu'adresse Hamlet à Horatio: 'Vous n'apprenez donc qu'à bien boire, à Rome, puisque vous en parlez si souvent?' "

434   ..."The World on the Last Day": *Le dernier jour du monde*, as an idea for an oratorio, later an opera, recurs in B's letters during the next two years (CG I 467–8, 520–1, 543–4, II 31, 33, 105–6, 113). Nothing came of it, but some aspects were absorbed into the Requiem. See also CAT 128, Note, and CG I 462 ("un autre grand ouvrage que je rumine") and 521, where the score which B thanks Mme Le Sueur for sending him may well have been the Resurrexit, whose apocalyptic fanfares he intended for use in *Le dernier jour*.

434–5   [Legouvé] heard him talked of...: see LEG I 289–90, 296.

435   Boschot...thought that "one would have to be...": JR 491.

435   "I count the days...": CG I 542.

435   The setting of the Villa Medici...was "truly regal": VM II 57 (MEM XXXII 57).

436   "never had he seen anything so squalid...": CG I 454. See also LE 55–6, IP 3–4 (VM II 96–7, MEM XXXV 131–2).

436   ...you are lucky if you hear any Rossini...: LE 57.

436   The only theatres worth frequenting...: DEBATS 27 Sept. 1835 (MM 131–2). Cf. MLET 98, on the Alban hills: "No lack of music *there*; it echoes and vibrates *there* on every side – not in the vapid, tasteless theatres".

436–7   ...the comments...Mendelssohn was writing...: see MLET passim.

437   "...'the lovely Juliet...'": from Barbier's "L'Adieu" in his collection *Il pianto*. (Cf. CG I 463: "This land is an unjust and partial mother who has given everything to her eldest sons", etc.) Barbier, in his *Souvenirs personnels et silhouettes contemporaines*, says he met B in Rome, but CG II seems to indicate that B did not know him till after his return to Paris.

438   ...virtually unable to compose: unlike Mendelssohn, B required the stimulus of a musical environment. The needs of creative artists

vary. As John Deathridge has remarked apropos of Wagner's dependence on silk underwear, we cannot lay down the law.

438 ...the list given in *Voyage musical* and the *Memoirs*: I 167–8 and XXXIX 155–6.

438 The theme for the refrain of *Le cinq mai*...: see CG III 740 (text in II 258–9) and ATC 343–4.

438 ..."one day when the spleen was killing me": CG I 516.

438 "satisfy my immense appetite for emotion": CG I 311.

439 As Tiersot points out, the mal d'isolement...: TIERSOC 71. However, it is clear from CG I 310–11 and 482 ("le Spleen auquel je suis si sujet, comme vous savez") that B was already afflicted before he came to Rome.

439 ..."'one is none the less a man...'": REN 12 July 1835.

439n ...Tartufe's line...: *Tartufe* III 3.

440 ...the atmosphere of half a dozen major works...: cf. BARZUN I 228.

440 *Romeo and Juliet* begins to take shape [in Italy]: in addition to the other traces left during these months, MEM LVI 418 names "the blue Italian sky" as one of the "sources" of the work.

440 ...the sense of space...consequence of his Italian experiences: as Joseph-Marc Bailbé argues in "Le sens d'espace dans les textes littéraires de Berlioz" in *Romantisme* XII (1976), 37.

440 The Berliozian concept of monumental church music...: MEM XXXIX 149–50 and LIX (Postface) 461–3.

441 As Boschot remarks succinctly...: RLP (rev. 1948) 43.

CHAPTER 30

442 The trip...cost...1,050 francs: see CG I 457.

442 "So as not to appear...'affected'...": CG I 463.

442 Life at the Villa Medici...: see MEM XXXVI and CG I passim.

442 ...Villa Pamphili with its splendid garden...: cf. the description in Goethe's *Italian Journey*.

443 Horace Vernet...: see Amédée Durande, *Joseph, Carle et Horace Vernet: correspondence et biographies*, Paris [1863], 62–3 and 78ff, and MLET passim.

443 His appraising sketch of Vernet: CG I 447.

443 Berlioz soon decided that unlike his father Carle...: see CG I 460.

444 Looking back on it twelve years later...: DEBATS 3 Sept. 1843, repr. MEM LI (Premier voyage en Allemagne, 4e Lettre), 262.

444 his "merely external enthusiasm", etc.: MBRIEFE 124.

445 Another time...writes more in sorrow...: MBRIEFE 119–20 (15 March 1831) and *Composers on Music*, ed. Sam Morgenstern, London 1958, 141–2, quoted CONE 281–2.

446 ...finding Mendelssohn, as he told Hiller...: CG I 487.

446n In a letter to Hiller the following year...: CG I 458.

447 ...excursions in the Campagna...Mercutio's Queen Mab...: MEM XXXVI 137 and n.

447 The expedition to Tivoli...: see CG I 458 and ETEX 120–1.

448 ...in Rome "I have no ideas...": CG I 459.

448	...he wrote to [Ferrand], asking him to copy out the page...: CG I 466−7.
448	...felt "some real emotion...": CG I 460.
449	According to Legouvé he had an uncanny knack...: LEG I 295.
449	...modest enough, he told Mme Le Sueur, not to tempt...brigands: CG I 463.
449ff	Letters to his family: CG I 469−75.
451	"Oh for a cottage...": B (or his mother) misquotes the opening line of Charles-Albert Demoustier's chanson as "Que je voudrais avoir une chaumière" instead of "Je veux un jour avoir...".
452n	..."completed...in the mountains of Subiaco": CG I 516.
453	...his letter of 2 July to Mme Le Sueur: CG I 463−5.
454	...Isola di Sora...the owner...from Voiron...: see CG I 497.
454	...Civitella...Il signor Vincenzo...: IP 10−11 (VM II 145−6, MEM XXXVIII 146−7).
454	...a brigand: often the still-smoking ashes...: according to Etex (op. cit. 121) he and B tried to make contact with some brigands but, each time, arrived just after they had moved on.
454	Jean-Baptiste Gibert: 1829 Prix de Rome who stayed on for the rest of his life − see MARECHAL 90ff.
455	...the young Crispino...: see CG I 475, MEM XXXVII, XXXVIII, XLI.
455−6	...his paean to the pleasures...in the mountains: VM II 134−5 (MEM XXXVII 142).
456	To his grandfather Nicolas Marmion...he wrote...: CG I 483−4.
456	To his family he enlarged on the...theme: CG I 478−9.
457	On 28 July...wrote to Charles Duveyrier: CG I 476−7. B's interest in Saint-Simonism may have been stimulated by conversations with Etex as well as with Cendrier. See ETEX 119−20.
458	When Berlioz met the Austrian chancellor...: see MEM LIX (Post-Scriptum) 464−5, also LIII (Deuxième voyage en Allemagne, 3ᵉ Lettre), 363.
458	Berlioz remained on friendly terms with Duveyrier: see CG III 209−10.
458	...account of his missionary Evenings at the Opera: DEBATS 13 Sept. 1835 (VM I 386, MEM XV 50).
458	Already by January 1832...he can refer...: CG I 515.
459−60	"Since I can't be in Paris...": CG I 479−80.
460	The treeless earth...seemed, in Chateaubriand's phrase...: B, as Citron remarks (CG I 486 n. 2), certainly knew Chateaubriand's *Voyage en Italie.*
460	...a scene whose melancholy mirrored his own...: see CG I 522.
460	The light...had a Claude-like roundness...: CG I 486. Cf. Chateaubriand op. cit.
461	...improvise...and with the aid of drink...: IP 8. By the time this passage was reprinted in VM (II 130−1) "drink" had been removed. See MEMC 589−90.
461	"the intense consciousness of being alive": VM II 132 (MEM XXXVII 141).
461	The three-day shoot, he told...Hiller...: CG I 486. See also CG I 480 and MEM XLII 173−4.

462   ...Berlioz commented..."so if I die...": CG I 486.

462   ...gave [Duc] a letter to take to...Réty: CG I 481−2.

462−3   "Something comparable occurs when this sense of isolation...": VM
         II 173−5 (MEM XL 159−60).

463   One day in late September: this paragraph is based on MEM XL 160,
         CG I 522 and LE 61.

464   By the time they reached Naples...: events on the journey, in addition
         to those mentioned in CG I 488, included "an amusing but
         unprintable scandal that we caused in the little town of Ceprano"
         (MEM XL 160) and the composition of a short chorus, during
         a period of dense mist, as an incantation to make the sun come
         out (CG I 516).

464−6   To his family: CG I 488−91.

466   ...the fishermen stopped everyone they met...: see IP 11.

466   At last...an opera house: see LE 62−3, IP 11, MEM 164−5.

466   Mercadante's Zaira...: see GM 2 Feb. 1834.

466   At the museum he examined the ancient instruments...: see CG I
         493.

467   "What a town Naples is", he wrote to Mme Le Sueur: CG I 522.

467   ...visit the little island of Nisida...: see CG I 492, 523, VM II
         181−6 (MEM XLI 161−4).

468   ...his Virgilian heroes...: three months later he writes to Mme le
         Sueur: "No words can describe the intoxicating effect of that
         combined magnetism of memory, poetry, light, clear air, sunset
         and the creatures of the imagination" (CG I 523).

469   "That is not how one should experience Pompeii...": CG I 494−5.

469   ...took the dusty road back to Naples: in an article in DEBATS
         4 July 1854 (GROT 267) B remarks that vaudevilles and opéras-
         comiques set in Italy invariably feature an orange grove, and
         that one such work located an orange grove on the road between
         Naples and Castellamare. He adds that he would have been
         only too glad of it when walking the same road twenty years
         ago.

470   They set out on...14 October...: for B's journey from Naples to
         Subiaco and Rome see MEM XLI 166−72, CG I 494−8.

CHAPTER 31

472   In the same letter to his father...: CG I 498.

472   "launching into the musical ocean that is Germany": CG I 524.

473   "turning over in bed...a great sun-bronzed rapscallion...": MEM
         XXXVIII 148.

473   ...meets the Russian composer Glinka: see DEBATS 16 April 1845
         (MM 211). If Glinka's memory is correct and he left Rome
         "near the end of October" after a stay of only two weeks, the
         meeting must have taken place immediately after B's return
         from Naples. (See Mikhail Ivanovich Glinka, Memoirs, tr. Richard
         B. Mudge, Norman, Oklahoma 1963, 67 & 68.

473   Victor Hugo's Notre-Dame de Paris...: frustration at not being able to
         read the book is a recurring motif in B's letters from Rome. For
         his subsequent fan letter to Hugo see CG I 507−9.

473   He acts as pander-cum-waiter to...Gibert...: the episode is described in a letter of 1848 to the cellist Tajan-Rogé (CG III 497). The love-affair inspired B's short story "Vicenza" (*L'europe littéraire* 8 May 1833, VM II 119–25, SO 47–51).

473   ...a severe influenza epidemic...: see MEM XLII 172–3, also *The Life and Letters of Joseph Severn*, ed. William Sharp, London 1892, 180–2.

473   ...Italian musical life..."I shall do my best to satisfy him...": CG I 501.

473   Music in Italy, he tells Schlesinger...'The traveller...': CG I 505. Quotation not identified.

475n   "Volcanic rocks and dark pine forests...": IP 7 (VM II 166–7, MEM XXXIX 155).

477   ...reprinted in the *Revue musicale*: XII 65–8, 73–5 (1832) — a shortened version.

477   To be immured in Rome (he wrote to Hiller)...: CG I 504.

477   ...wrote to Gounet on 17 February 1832: CG I 528.

477–8 "So that business is concluded...": CG I 501.

478   ...after the wedding he writes to his sister...: CG I 532–3.

479   ..."Master Prosper...": [16 March 1832] (RC).

479–81 "I was on the point of writing to you...": CG I 529–32.

481   ...his mother reported the contents to Nancy: 2 March 1832 (RC).

481   ...echoed...in a letter to Albert Du Boys: CG I 536.

482   When Mme Vernet mentioned [Harriet Smithson]...: see CG II 84.

482   Tiersot maintains that the moment the new flame...: TIERSOC 70–2.

483ff Extracts from letters...: CG I, respectively 515–18, 518–20, 528, 534, 537–9, 542–4, 546–8.

483n   ...statues of the Olympian gods in public gardens...: the gods referred to — Jupiter, Venus, Hercules — are precisely those represented in the Jardin de Ville in Grenoble.

484   "On my return...publish another collection [of Melodies]": cf. CG I 492. Nothing came of the idea. *La captive* appears to have been the sole "Italian" composition in this form that B published.

485n   As Pierre Citron remarks...: CG I 534 n. 2.

488   ...on Easter Day he stood...in St Peter's Square...: see REN 12 July 1835: "ces magnifiques cérémonies de la fête de pâques [...] et cette indescriptible bénédiction *urbi et orbi* accueillie par les cris d'enthousiasme de cent peuples diverses réunis sous le balcon pontifical et proclamée au loin par les canons du fort St Ange; tout cela vaut bien un opéra-comique...". See also MEM XXIX 102.

488   ...he was paid a lump sum...: the transactions mentioned in this paragraph are recorded in a folder inscribed "Chapitre 1er, Recettes" under the heading "une quittance de M. Berlioz pour 6 mois".

488   Louise Vernet's album...: coll. Mme Henraux, Paris, See also VACAT no. 202.

489 ...prospect of hearing her...inviting as the squeak of a bat: see CG I 461.

489 In a letter to her mother... "the graceful Ariel": CG II 22.

489 ...a brief, affectionate note...: CG II 380.

490 The other Italy...one final reminder...: MEM XXXIX 152–3.

CHAPTER 32

491 ...he told Hiller...a bizarre sense...: CG I 551.

491 To Horace Vernet he wrote...: private coll., sold Hôtel Drouot 20 June 1977.

492 "We rather enjoyed recalling those days...": CG I 550.

492n Donizetti's *L'elisir d'amore*...: see CG I 554 and letter to Vernet cited above. *L'elisir* had had its première shortly before.

492n ...according to the *Memoirs* – "trailing after her...": VIII 30. See SPECT *passim* – e.g. SPECT 1831, 189, which lists, among the company at the Grand Theatre, Marseilles in 1830, "Mme Pons Saint-Ange, première chanteuse" and "Saint-Ange, première basse-taille".

493 ...he descended the vale of the Grésivaudan...: see MEM XLIII 182 (where the date is incorrectly given as 12 May) and III 11–12.

493n Hazlitt... "It gives one a vast idea...": HAZLITT 191.

494 Nancy['s]...letter of next day... "Friday": 1 June, not 8. A letter of 12 June (postmark) from Adèle is a reply to a subsequent letter of Nancy's of the 6th (RC). CG II 13 should therefore be dated 9, not 16, June.

495 ...Adèle sent a report to her sister...: Lundi [11 June 1832 – postmark] (RC).

495n ...he writes of "the extra link...": CG V 378, 26 Oct. 1856. The two undated letters to Adèle which CG I assigns to 1822–3 and 1825 (43–4, 79–80) in my view belong to the late 1820s – CG I 80 in particular, with its reference to Hamlet's "undiscovered country" and to Nancy's having to rely exclusively on Louise Veyron for company, which happened only after the marriage of Rosanne Rocher in June 1827.

496 Writing to Hiller on 7 August...: CG II 26.

496 On 3 July...set out for Grenoble on foot...: see Nancy's letter of 6 July to Adèle (RC).

496 "...all right but nothing more": CG II 18.

496 "Despite all my efforts to change the subject...": CG II 21.

496 "...all scratched and jangled": CG II 25.

497 On Hector's return...she wrote to Adèle...: undated letter (RC).

497 ...a long letter to Mme Vernet: CG II 20–3.

497 ...alone with his thoughts...(he told Hiller)...: CG II 25.

498 ...copying parts (... "till his thumb ached"): CG II 27.

498 ...he read the materialist philosophers...: see CG II 25–6.

498 "Extremes meet...", he wrote to Hiller: CG II 26.

498 ...Ferrand promised...[but] Berlioz was not sanguine...: see CG II 31.

499   He would remember...the pouring wet morning...: see MEM LIX
         (Voyage en Dauphiné), 484 and SW 149—50.
499   He wrote to Paris...: no letters survive, but their existence may be
         inferred: he would not have waited till he arrived before setting
         things in train.
499   On 28 October...his passport...: see CG II 32 n. 1.
499   "It was like seeing in a brothel...": CG II 32—3.
500   ...he dined with the Le Sueurs: see CG II 35. The Le Sueurs now
         lived at 2 Rue Méhul, near their old address in the Rue Ste
         Anne (*Almanach des 25000 adresses*, 1831).
500   The artistic journals had kept his name alive...: chief among them
         Fétis' *Revue musicale* — XI 224 (1831). See BLOOM 227—8.
500   ...report of the music section of the Académie...: BA pièces annexes
         1832 5 E 22.
500   Eugene Sue...Legouvé...Dumas...: See CG II 38.
500   ...Véron received him...: see CG II 37—8.
501   ...Berlioz wrote to Nancy to report...: CG II 37—8.
503   Two days before...he was in Schlesinger's music shop...: MEM
         XLIV 184—5.
503   ...the "cohorts of Romanticism": BARZUN I 232.
503   ...among them Liszt, Paganini...: see seating plans in MACC, also
         CG II 40.

ACKNOWLEDGMENTS

My first thanks — after the three special debts of gratitude recorded in the Preface — must go to the Leverhulme Foundation and to St Antony's College, Oxford, for the Leverhulme Fellowship that I was awarded in 1973, which gave me three years of comparative freedom to travel and get started on the research for this book.

In the course of journeys to Paris and Dauphiné I made many friends. Guy and Yvette Baartmans had me to stay in their apartment in the Rue Férou, Paris 6ᵉ, more times than I can remember; their enthusiasm for Berlioz and their insight into the man and his music were a vital stimulus. So were the long and absorbing conversations that I had with Catherine Reboul-Berlioz during which she talked about her great-great-great-uncle. The late Pierre Moulin, one-time deputy mayor of La Côte St André, among several kindly acts put me in touch with Denise Dumoulin of Grenoble, a descendant of Estelle Dubeuf's family, who generously communicated everything she had discovered about her forbear, and thereafter wrote to me regularly until her death. Her husband Charles Dumoulin took me round the Isère countryside, introducing me to many places associated with Berlioz and his family. Through M. and Mme Dumoulin I met their daughter Chantal Chaveyriat-Dumoulin, to whom, both as librarian at the Bibliothèque Municipale in Lyons and as friend, I am indebted for many kindnesses. Professor Léon Guichard (editor of the modern editions of *Les soirées de l'orchestre*, *Les grotesques de la musique* and *A travers chants*) and his wife Marie-José received me very hospitably in Grenoble and later at their house in Lépin-le-lac, as did their daughter Claire Guichard on many occasions in Paris. Catherine Moureaux, archivist of the Faculté de Médecine in Paris, was tireless in her help and responded to each fresh request for information with the greatest alacrity and good humour. Pierre Citron, general editor of the *Correspondance générale* and editor of most of the letters from the period covered by this book, repeatedly gave me the benefit of his knowledge. Thérèse Husson, general secretary and pillar of the Association Nationale Hector Berlioz, answered my endless questions with unfailing charm and promptitude.

All the above have placed me permanently in their debt. In addition, many others gave me help for which I am most grateful. In La Côte St André: Henriette Boschot, conservateur of the Musée Berlioz, who welcomed me on countless occasions; René Bergeret, former mayor of the town, and his friendly and helpful staff (I shall never forget the banquet over which M. Bergeret presided late one evening after a performance of *L'enfance du Christ* conducted by

John Eliot Gardiner in the great medieval covered market-place of La Côte); Francisque Bottinelli, vice-president of the Association; Joséane Boulard; Jean Carraz-Billat; Lucien Casper; Lucien Charmard-Bois; Monique Clavaud-Knutsson; Geneviève Cuzin; Arlette Gillet; the late Estelle Prud'homme, acting conservateur at the Musée in the early 1960s when I first went to La Côte St André; the late Aimé Suzet-Charbonnel; and Jacqueline Werly and her husband Georges, friends and passionate and perceptive Berliozians whom I first met at the Berlioz Festival which Serge Baudo created in 1979.

In Paris: Anne-Marie Laffitte-Larnaudie, the courteous and helpful conservateur of the archives at the Institute; l'Abbé Robert Chapot, direct descendant of Adèle Berlioz, and his sisters Mme Berlencourt and Mme Rousselon; Dr Bruno Fons, conservateur of the Musée de l'Histoire de la Médecine; Martine Kahane, librarian of the Bibliothèque de l'Opéra; Elisabeth Hermann, of the French branch of Phonogram; Arnaud Laster and his wife Danièle; Madeleine Lavollé; François Lesure, till recently head of the music department of the Bibliothèque Nationale; his successor, Catherine Massip; Charles Pitt, who entertained me at a splendid dinner in his apartment in the Rue de Lévis; Guy Reboul-Berlioz; and Claude Richebé, librarian of the Institute. Elsewhere in France: Serge Baudo, Philippe Berthier, Robert and Joëlle Caillol, Sylvain Cambreling, Vincent Donnet, and Soeur Thérèse-Marguerite Fontaine.

In Italy: the director and library staff of the Villa Medici; Michael and Susan Rose; Ian Taylor, who showed me Rome.

In England, many people contributed to this book. I owe an especially large debt of kindness to John Taylor, Bishop of Winchester, and his wife Peggy, who lent me a room in Wolvesey Palace where all my Berlioz books and papers were housed for several years and where the early chapters were written. Elizabeth Davison, chief organiser of the Victoria and Albert Exhibition and editor of its catalogue, was a staunch friend and a continual source of ideas and encouragement. Richard Bowes generously put at my disposal his profound knowledge of the Berlioz literature. David Charlton was a mine of information on all aspects of eighteenth- and nineteenth-century opera and never grudged his time when I needed to consult him. Richard Macnutt gave me much invaluable help, particularly with the illustrations.

For information, help, encouragement, useful suggestions or the stimulus of their conversation I should also like to thank the following: Dr Paul Banks, Christine Banks, Clive Bennett, Sir Isaiah Berlin, Anita Brookner, Penelope Byrde, Patrick Chorley, John Crabbe, Sir Colin Davis, the late F. V. Emery, Sarah Fenderson, Richard Gandy, John Eliot Gardiner, Barry Gibson, Alph Gore, Barbara Hauber, Thomas Hemsley, Peter Heyworth, my cousin Edward Hodgkin (who first kindled my interest in Berlioz's music), Raymond Hyatt, Michael Kauffman, Francesca Kemp, Peter Longhurst, Hugh Macdonald, Louise Meredith, Roger Norrington, Jack Pole, Stephen Preston, Peter Raby, Julian Rushton, Catherine Smith, Sir Michael Tippett, Michael Wright and Jack Yekutiel. John Whitley, Review Editor of the *Sunday Times*, was a most understanding boss and friend, arranging for me to have leave of absence from my duties as music critic so that I could spend six months at the University of California, Davis.

American scholars have played a leading part in the modern Berlioz revival. I am indebted particularly to Kern Holoman (already thanked on p. 9) and Peter

Bloom for help and advice on numerous matters of detail. Katherine Reeve was a constant guide through most of the stages of this book, making available her exceptionally wide knowledge of Berlioz whenever I wanted. Cosette Thompson, in addition to letting me use her richly informative doctoral thesis on Harriet Smithson, gave me advice on points of French usage. Ralph Locke was an important source of information. And to all the members, staff and students of the music department at Davis, my heartfelt thanks for making my stay in California so pleasant and productive.

Parts of the manuscript were read by Ian Kemp, by the late Sonia Orwell, by my sisters Margaret Yekutiel and Elizabeth Nussbaum and my brother John Cairns, and by my wife Rosemary who, throughout, gave me vital support and encouragement.

The whole manuscript was read by Katherine Reeve, by my son Dan Cairns, by Howard Davies and by Diana Athill, my editor at André Deutsch, and was improved in factual accuracy and presentation of material as a result of their criticisms. To all of them warmest gratitude, but above all to Diana, whose sharp intelligence, feeling for style and sheer good sense were of inestimable value. The shortcomings that remain, of whatever sort, are my own.

Thanks are due to the following for permission to reproduce the above-named illustrations: The Association Nationale Hector Berlioz (1, 3, 9), Madame Yvonne Reboul-Berlioz (2, 23), Pleyel and co (4), The Royal College of Music (6a), Richard Macnutt (6b, 10b, 10d, 13, 17, 24). The Musée Ingres, Montauban (10a), The Bibliothèque Royale, Brussels (10c), Guy Reboul-Berlioz (11), The Theatre Museum (12), The Beethovenhaus, Bonn (14a), The Bibliothèque Nationale (15b, 16, 18, 22). The Conservatoire de Musique, Geneva (19b), The Ente Provinciale per il Turismo di Roma (19c), The Freies Deutsches Hochstift, Frankfurt am Main (20)

INDEX
by Professor G.D. West

Note: "Paris" is omitted from the
Index. HB=Hector Berlioz